DATE DUE

NOV 1 9 1993	
DEC 7 1993	
MAR 2 1 1994	
APR 7 1994	
OCT - 4 1994	
DEC 4 '94	
DEC 1 0 1994	
APR 1 0 1995	
NOV 2 9 1995	
NOV 1 9 1996	
DEC - 3 1996	
OCT 2 0 1998	
OCT 2 3 1998	
OCT 2 5 2000	
OCT - 7 2001	
NOV 22	

Alcoholism

Biomedical
and Genetic Aspects

Pergamon Titles of Related Interest

Knott ALCOHOL PROBLEMS: Diagnosis and Treatment
Clark/Saunders ALCOHOLISM AND PROBLEM DRINKING

Related Journals
(Free sample copies available upon request)

ALCOHOL AND ALCOHOLISM
ALCOHOL
ADDICTIVE BEHAVIORS
JOURNAL OF SUBSTANCE ABUSE TREATMENT

Alcoholism

Biomedical and Genetic Aspects

edited by
H. Werner Goedde, Ph.D.
Dharam P. Agarwal, Ph.D.
Institute of Human Genetics, Hamburg, FRG

PERGAMON PRESS
New York • Oxford • Beijing • Frankfurt
São Paulo • Sydney • Tokyo • Toronto

Pergamon Press Offices:

U.S.A.	Pergamon Press, Inc., Maxwell House, Fairview Park, Elmsford, New York 10523, U.S.A.
U.K.	Pergamon Press plc, Headington Hill Hall, Oxford OX3 0BW, England
PEOPLE'S REPUBLIC OF CHINA	Pergamon Press, Qianmen Hotel, Beijing, People's Republic of China
FEDERAL REPUBLIC OF GERMANY	Pergamon Press GmbH, Hammerweg 6, D-6242 Kronberg, Federal Republic of Germany
BRAZIL	Pergamon Editora Ltda, Rua Eça de Queiros, 346, CEP 04011, São Paulo, Brazil
AUSTRALIA	Pergamon Press Australia Pty Ltd., P.O. Box 544, Potts Point, NSW 2011, Australia
JAPAN	Pergamon Press, 8th Floor, Matsuoka Central Building, 1-7-1 Nishishinjuku, Shinjuku-ku, Tokyo 160, Japan
CANADA	Pergamon Press Canada Ltd., Suite 271, 253 College Street, Toronto, Ontario M5T 1R5, Canada

First edition 1989

Library of Congress Cataloging in Publication Data

Alcoholism : biomedical and genetic aspects.

Includes bibliographies and index.
1. Alcoholism. I. Goedde, H. W. (H. Werner)
II. Agarwal, Dharam P. [DNLM: 1. Alcoholism--
complications. 2. Alcoholism--familial & genetic.
3. Alcoholism--metabolism. 4. Alcohol, Ethyl--
pharmacology.   WM 274   A35555]
RC565.A44514   1989   616.86'1   88-31257
ISBN 0-08-035763-6

Printed in the United States of America

$\underset{\infty}{\odot}{}^{TM}$

The paper used in this publication meets the minumum requirements of American National Standard for Information Sciences -- Permanence of Paper for Printed Library Materials, ANSI Z39.48-1984

Contents

PREFACE

The understanding of various aspects of the disease alcoholism has made significant advances in the last three decades. In the past several years, especially, a fairly continuous progress has been made in the understanding of alcohol metabolism, alcoholism, and various alcohol-associated disorders.

Most of the books and monographs currently available on alcoholism are highly specialized and a great need was felt for a comprehensive and up-to-date overview covering interdisciplinary aspects of alcohol metabolism and alcoholism. Particularly, very few authoritative reviews have been written so far in regard to the rapidly changing concepts concerning gene–environment interactions and ecogenetic factors as related to alcoholism.

In the present volume, recent trends and advances in various areas of alcoholism including biochemistry, pharmacology, pathophysiology, psychiatry, genetics, as well as environmental and sociocultural aspects have been written by authors who themselves have contributed significantly to these developments. Some of the major advances in the recent past and the current as well as future research strategies are reviewed here. A wide range of research and clinical issues have found integration to give an updated, well-referenced collection of interdisciplinary overviews.

The chapter contributors were asked to write general overviews of their themes rather than giving a narrow treatise of their own findings. To avoid unnecessary repetition of major findings, the authors were asked to write their chapters within the scope of the outlines drawn by us for each chapter. Nevertheless, the authors were free to include any particular aspect they considered relevant to the topic and omit any other that they regarded as irrelevant in that particular context. The authors were encouraged to communicate with the other contributors to avoid any overlap.

The book has been compiled into five main sections. Section 1 contains recent advances in the knowledge of alcohol and acetaldehyde metabolism including genetic enzyme polymorphisms, alcohol sensitivity in different populations, as well as metabolic changes and toxic reactions induced by alcohol. In Section 2, neuropharmacological effects of alcohol drinking including adaptive responses, membrane alterations, and alcohol-related behavioral alterations are included. Papers on clinical aspects of alcohol drinking—pathophysiology, alterations in cardiovascular functions, treatment and prevention strategies, alcohol effects in pregnancy, as well as biochemical markers of alcoholism—are grouped in Section 3. Section 4 covers genetic aspects including recent advances in family, adoption, and twin studies of alcoholism and biological markers of alcoholism used for studies of populations at high risk for future development of alcoholism. Cultural, social, ethnic, and epidemiological factors as they relate to alcoholism, as well as gene/environment interactions concerning alcoholism make up Section 5. Finally, current issues and future directions in biomedical and genetic aspects of alcoholism research are critically summed up as "Editoral Remarks."

This volume provides valuable insights toward understanding biomedical and genetic aspects of alcoholism and would present a comprehensive bibliography for scientists, clinicians, and health professionals as well as students interested in alcoholism and related problems. The reader will find in a single volume the state of the art knowledge about various research advances made in the field of alcohol metabolism and alcoholism. We strongly believe that this well-rounded comprehensive work will become the standard reference source in the field of alcoholism.

We thank Dr. Rolf Eckey and Mrs. Madlen Maehder for their help.

H. Werner Goedde
Dharam P. Agarwal

Institute of Human Genetics
University of Hamburg
Hamburg, F.R. Germany

Section 1

Metabolism and Metabolic Changes

CHAPTER 1

Enzymology of Alcohol Degradation

Dharam P. Agarwal and H. Werner Goedde

Institute of Human Genetics, University of Hamburg,
Hamburg, F.R. Germany

INTRODUCTION

Alcohol directly affects major psycoactive functions through a set of complex physiochemical metabolic processes. The fate and effects of ethanol (alcohol, ethyl alcohol) in the human body have been extensively studied in the past decades and vast literature is available concerning the pathways of ethanol metabolism in humans (von Wartburg, 1971; Li, 1977; Rognstad and Grunnet, 1979; Li, 1983). In this chapter, major biochemical findings regarding the degradation of ethanol and acetaldehyde are reviewed emphasizing inter- and intraindividual differences in alcohol metabolism and their implications in acute and chronic effects of alcohol drinking.

ABSORPTION, DISTRIBUTION AND ELIMINATION OF ETHANOL

Absorption

There are many complicating factors in the study of ethanol absorption. The route of administration of ethanol in the body is determinantal to the rate of its tissue distribution and metabolism. After oral administration, absorption of ethanol through the gastrointestinal tract depends on many factors. Ethanol is readily absorbed from the gastrointestinal tract and diffuses rapidly and uniformly throughout the body water (Fig. 1.1).

Because of its fat-soluble nonelectrolyte characteristics, ethanol is absorbed into the circulation by diffusion across the duodenum and jejunum, and to a lesser extent from the stomach and large intestine (Kalant, 1971). The absorption process is normally over in 2 hours and overlaps with the diffusion phase. When it is taken at concentrations above 30 mg/100 ml, ethanol can cause superficial erosions, hemorrhages, and paralysis of the smooth muscular system of the stomach, leading to a decrease in the rate of absorption of ethanol. The rate of ingestion of ethanol also affects its absorption since peak blood alcohol levels develop more slowly if a beverage is ingested rapidly (Payne et al, 1966; Dundee et al, 1971; Moskowitz and Burns, 1976). However, peak blood ethanol levels are higher if ethanol is ingested in a single dose rather than in small doses, presumably because the ethanol concentration gradient is higher in the former case than in the latter (Kricka and Clark, 1979).

Great intraindividual variation in the percentage dose of ethanol absorbed has been observed (Wagner and Patel, 1972). Variation in hormonal status (e.g., stage of the menstrual cycle) affects ethanol absorption (Jones and Jones, 1975). Moreover, ethanol absorption

3

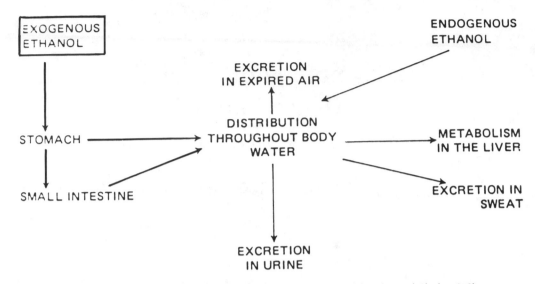

FIGURE 1.1. Absorption, excretion and metabolism of ethanol (Kricka and Clark, 1979).

seems also to be under genetic control (Fenna et al, 1971; Reed, 1978). Various factors that influence the absorption of ethanol in the human body are listed in Table 1.1 (Kricka and Clark, 1979).

Ethanol in distilled spirits is absorbed much more rapidly than is the ethanol contained in wines and beers. The presence of food in the stomach delays gastric emptying and thus reduces the rate and efficiency of ethanol absorption. Ingestion of food either accompanied or preceded by ethanol drinking decreases peak blood ethanol concentration and also increases the time taken to reach the peak concentrations (Lin et al, 1976; Wilkinson et al, 1977). Higher protein, fat, and carbohydrate contents of food increasingly inhibit ethanol absorption.

Other factors also affect ethanol absorption by altering the gastrointestinal motility and circulation. Decreased absorption occurs with decreasing body temperature and physical exercise.

Distribution

The rate of distribution of ethanol in body tissues is variable and depends on factors like blood flow, permeability, and tissue mass. Ethanol quickly reaches peak concentrations in the blood and tissues with high blood flow. Organs such as brain, lungs, kidneys, and liver

Table 1.1. Factors affecting ethanol absorption

Concentration of ethanol
Blood flow at site of absorption
Irritant properties of ethanol
Rate of ingestion
Type of beverage
Food
Emptying of the stomach
Protein deficiency
Body temperature
Physical exercise
Menstrual cycle

From Kricka and Clark, 1979.

reach equilibrium rapidly, whereas the skeletal muscle—which has a poorer blood supply—reaches the equilibrium slowly. The equilibrium concentration of ethanol in tissues depends on the relative water content of tissues and closely follows the absolute water content of the fluid or tissue (Kalant, 1971).

During the initial phase, alcohol diffuses rapidly into the tissues from arterial blood, and from the tissues into the venous blood. Levels in peripheral venous blood then remain higher than those in arterial blood because of lower rates of metabolism and excretion. Peak urine levels of ethanol are usually reached within 30 to 90 min after drinking, depending on whether the ethanol was taken in a single dose or in a series of doses (Erickson, 1979).

Elimination

Traditionally, it has been assumed that elimination kinetics of ethanol follows a zero order (i.e., independent of blood concentration (Widmark, 1932; Goldberg, 1950; Shumate et al, 1967; Mullen, 1977)). However, various alcohol pharmacokinetic studies reported in recent years indicate that a nonlinear course of ethanol elimination may best explain the observed differences in the metabolic rate of alcohol in humans (Wagner et al, 1976; Feinman et al, 1978; Salaspuro and Lieber, 1978; Wilkinson, 1980; Keiding et al, 1983; von Wartburg and Bühler, 1984; Martin et al, 1984).

Less than 2% of the ingested ethanol is excreted unchanged in urine, expired air, and sweat. At elevated temperatures and higher blood ethanol levels, the percent ethanol excreted may exceed this value. Urinary excretion of ethanol is a passive process and clearance rates between 0.9 to 12.7 ml/min have been reported (Blackmore and Mason, 1968). Approximately 90% of the ingested ethanol is eliminated by oxidation to carbon dioxide and water independent of the ingested quantity or the given blood ethanol concentration. The rate of ethanol oxidation is approximately 120 to 150 mg/h/kg body weight. High glucose, fructose, and galactose concentration in the blood can reduce the blood ethanol concentration, perhaps through increased oxidation of ethanol.

Chronopharmacokinetic variation in ethanol elimination has also been observed in humans. Sturtevant et al (1976) reported circadian rhythmicity in the rate of the linear blood level decline following ethanol administration in male subjects. Ethanol elimination was found to be greater in the afternoon than in the evening (Jones, 1974).

GENETIC CONTROL OF ALCOHOL METABOLISM RATE

The alcohol metabolism rate varies between individuals. Both environmental and genetic factors influence the rate of alcohol degradation. Twin studies indicate that interindividual variability in the rate of ethanol metabolism is under genetic control (Vesell et al, 1971; Vesell, 1972; Bennion and Li, 1976; Kopun and Propping, 1977). A striking similarity in ethanol metabolic rate was observed in identical twins whereas a greater variability was noted between fraternal twins (Martin et al, 1985; Martin, 1987).

Ethnic differences in alcohol metabolism have also been known for years. A higher rate of alcohol metabolism in the Chinese, some native Americans, and Japanese as compared to Caucasians has been reported. Interracial comparisons of ethanol metabolism are shown in Table 1.2.

The three racial groups differ markedly in the rate of metabolism based on the rate of disappearance of ethanol from the blood. Native American Indians and Eskimos metabolize alcohol at a significantly slower rate than whites. However, due to significant differences in body mass and dietary habits of the subjects examined, results of such studies are ambiguous (Reed and Kalant, 1977). Genetic and racial determinants of alcohol metabolic rate might be related to the genetic differences in the enzymes involved in the metabolism of alcohol among these groups. Indeed, individuals with different profiles of alcohol metabolizing enzymes also display different ethanol elimination rates (Bosron et al, 1983a; Mizoi et al, 1985; Lehmann et al, 1986).

Table 1.2. Comparative rate of ethanol metabolism in different ethnic and racial groups

ETHNIC GROUP	N	METABOLIC RATE (mg/kg/h)	REFERENCE
Caucasians			
Europeans	16	108.0	Goldberg, 1943
Europeans	23	108	Edwards and Evans, 1967
Europeans	6	103	Nuutinen et al, 1985
North Americans	30	93.2	Bennion and Li, 1976
North Americans	37	103.6	Reed et al, 1976
Canadians	68	108.0	Hanna, 1978
North Americans	17	112.0	Farris and Jones, 1978
North Americans	17	144.9	Fenna et al, 1971
Hindu Reddis	35	122.9	Schaefer, 1978
Mongoloids			
Chinese	15	136.6	Reed et al, 1976
Chinese	39	127.0	Hanna, 1978
Mongoloids (mixed)	24	146.0	Ewing et al, 1974
Japanese	47	133.6	Hanna, 1978
Japanese	68	119-138	Mizoi et al, 1985
Native Americans			
Canadian Indians	26	101.3	Fenna et al, 1971
N. American Indians	30	92.4	Bennion and Li, 1976
Ojibwa Indians	12	182.7	Reed et al, 1976
N. American Indians	17	122.98	Farris and Jones, 1978
Canadian Eskimos	21	109.8	Fenna et al, 1971

ENZYMOLOGY OF ETHANOL DEGRADATION

Ethanol is almost exclusively metabolized in the body by enzyme-catalyzed oxidation processes. The major pathway for the disposition of ethanol is its oxidation to two products—hydrogen and acetaldehyde—to which many of the effects of ethanol can be attributed. Three principal enzymes—the cytosolic alcohol dehydrogenase, the microsomal ethanol oxidizing system (MEOS) located in the endoplasmic reticulum, and catalase located in the peroxisomes—are known to oxidize ethanol (Fig. 1.2). The resulting acetaldehyde is further oxidized to acetate, which is then converted to carbon dioxide via the citric acid cycle. Acetate may also undergo reactions to form fatty acids, ketone bodies, amino acids, and steroids via its activated form, acetyl CoA.

Alcohol Dehydrogenase (ADH)

Alcohol dehydrogenase (ADH: alcohol:NAD$^+$ oxidoreductase, EC 1.1.1.1) is the major oxidative enzyme responsible for initial ethanol metabolism in humans. Ethanol is oxidized to acetaldehyde via hydrogen transfer from the substrate to the cofactor nicotinamide adenine dinucleotide (NAD$^+$), which results in conversion to its reduced form, NADH. ADH is capable of oxidizing a variety of primary, secondary, and tertiary aliphatic alcohols and a limited number of cyclic alcohols to the corresponding aldehydes. ADH has a zero-order kinetics and large amounts of ethanol apparently do not increase the speed of the reaction. Hormonal factors, body weight, and sex influence the rate of alcohol elimination.

Microsomal Ethanol Oxidizing System (MEOS)

A small part of the ingested ethanol (10% or less) is metabolized by alternative pathways. Until recently, the non-ADH ethanol oxidizing activity was usually attributed to a H_2O_2-dependent catalase system. However, recent studies have shown conclusively that the micro-

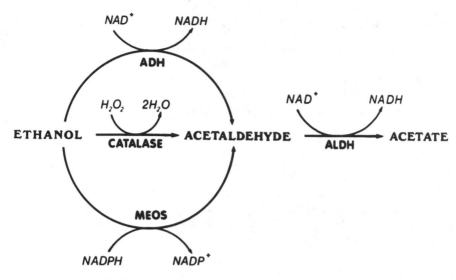

FIGURE 1.2. Enzymatic pathways for ethanol metabolism.

somal metabolism of ethanol accounts for the major non-ADH pathway of ethanol oxidation in the liver. The MEOS is NADPH dependent and is linked to the cytochrome P-450 oxygenases (Lieber and DeCarli, 1972; Teschke et al, 1977; Koop and Coon, 1985). The evidence is based on (1) isolation from the microsomes of a cytochrome P-450-containing fraction devoid of ADH and catalase but showing bulk of the MEOS activity; (2) reconstitution of MEOS with NADPH cytochrome P-450 reductase, phospholipids, and cytochrome P-450, and (3) separation of an ethanol-inducible form of cytochrome P-450 with high activity toward ethanol (Lieber, 1987).

Several lines of evidence also support the role of MEOS in vivo, such as the incomplete inhibition of ethanol metabolism using ADH inhibitors and the increased rate of ethanol metabolism at high ethanol concentrations. Moreover, the persistence of a significant rate of ethanol metabolism in genetically determined ADH-negative deer mice, in association with a high MEOS activity, further illustrates the in-vivo role of MEOS in non-ADH mediated ethanol metabolism (Shigeta et al, 1984).

Chronic ethanol intake leads to an enhanced MEOS activity, which in turn may be responsible for the increased rate of alcohol metabolism commonly observed after prolonged ethanol administration (Lieber, 1977; Teschke et al, 1981). This adaptive increase in ethanol oxidation may play an important role in the hepatotoxicity of a number of drugs, carcinogens, and xenobiotics. Ethanol administration has also been found to increase the rate of metabolism of meprobamate, pentobarbital, aminopyrine, tolbutamide, propanol, and rifamycin (Lieber, 1984).

Catalase

Catalase can react with ethanol in a peroxidase type reaction:

$$\text{cat. } H_2O_2 + CH_3CH_2OH \rightarrow \text{cat. } + CH_3CHO + 2H_2O$$

Most of the catalase in the liver is localized in the peroxisomes, which also contain many other oxidases (glycollate oxidase, amino acid oxidase, urate oxidase, etc.). The main rate limiting factor for catalase activity is the rate of hydrogen peroxide formation. However, the contribution of catalase to non-ADH ethanol oxidation remains controversial (Lieber, 1987).

KINETIC AND STRUCTURAL PROPERTIES OF ADH ISOZYMES

ADH is universally distributed in living organisms such as animals, plants, and microorganisms. It is a dimeric protein consisting of two subunits of a molecular weight of 40,000 daltons each. The enzyme contains two zinc atoms and one active site per unit. At least five different gene loci (ADH$_1$ through ADH$_5$) code for multiple molecular forms of human ADH arising from the association of eight different types of subunits: α, β_1, β_2, β_3, γ_1, γ_2, π, and χ.

Enzyme Classes

The different molecular forms of human ADH can be divided into three major classes or distinct groups (I, II, and III) according to their isoenzyme composition and electrophoretic and kinetic properties (Fig. 1.3). Heterodimers are formed between class I subunits but not between class I and class II subunits.

Class I Isozymes:
The class I isoenzymes are formed by a random association of three types of polypeptide subunits, α, β, and γ, controlled by three separate gene loci, ADH$_1$, ADH$_2$, and ADH$_3$, respectively (Smith et al, 1973). Isozymes are formed through the random combination of these subunits-homodimeric ($\alpha\alpha$, $\beta\beta$, and $\gamma\gamma$) or heterodimeric ($\alpha\beta$, $\alpha\gamma$, $\beta\gamma$) (Fig. 1.4).

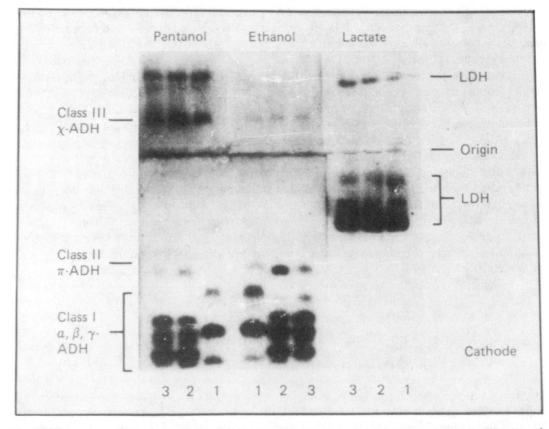

FIGURE 1.3. Starch gel electrophoresis pattern showing class I, class II, and class III ADH isozymes (Bosron and Li, 1987).

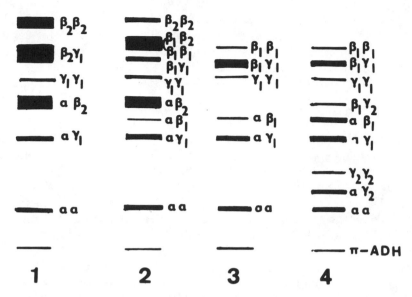

FIGURE 1.4. Homodimeric and heterodimeric subunit combinations of ADH isozymes. 1: ADH_2^2, ADH_3^1; 2: ADH_2^{2-1}, ADH_3^1; 3: ADH_2^1, ADH_3^1; 4: ADH_2^1, ADH_3^{2-1}

Class II Isozymes:

A less-known new molecular form, π-ADH with catalytic properties significantly different from those of other ADH isozymes has been described in human liver (Bosron et al, 1977; 1979). The π-ADH encoded by the ADH_4 locus migrates anodically to the class I isozymes on starch gel electrophoresis. Until now, only a homodimeric molecular form ($\pi\pi$) has been detected in human liver (Ditlow et al, 1984). It was separated from class I isozymes by affinity chromatography using pyrazole-substituted resin Cap–Gap–Sepharose (Bosron et al, 1979). This isozyme has a significantly higher K_m value for ethanol (34 mmol/l) and cannot oxidize methanol.

Class III Isozymes:

Anodic ADH bands on starch gel electrophoresis, showing enzyme staining activity only with long-chain alcohols as a substrate, have been characterized. This enzyme has been designated as χ-ADH and shows widely different catalytic and structural properties as compared to class I and class II molecular forms. It is assumed that this isozyme does not participate in the hepatic ethanol oxidation under physiological conditions.

Immunological Interrelationship

Immunological studies have shown that ADH molecules from different mammalian species share common antigenic determinants and that common structures have been preserved over a long evolutionary period (Adinolfi et al, 1984a, 1984b). Antisera raised against horse ADH cross-react with human ADH isozymes of class I but do not react with human ADH isozymes of classes II and III or with yeast ADH (Adinolfi et al, 1978). Also, antisera raised against the human class III ADH isozyme did not cross-react with human class I ADH isozymes. No cross-reaction was observed between these immune sera and ADH from nonmammalian species. These data suggest that all three classes of human ADH are of separate evolutionary origin (Adinolfi et al, 1984a, 1984b). However, polyclonal antibodies against horse ADH raised in mice were found to react against all the human class I, II, and III ADH forms suggesting some similarities at least concerning certain surface antigenic determinants (Adinolfi et al,

1986; Smith, 1986). Moreover, immunsera raised against denatured horse liver class I isozymes and human placenta class III isozymes cross-reacted with the subunits of other dehydrogenases from various sources, again indicating similarities in the primary structure of some of these isozymes with horse ADH (Adinolfi et al, 1987).

Tissue Distribution

ADH isozymes are widely distributed in human tissues. Although the class I and class II ADH are mainly expressed in liver, they are also present in the kidney, gastrointestinal tract, and lung (Harada et al, 1978; Goedde et al, 1979). During fetal development, ADH_1 is expressed first followed by ADH_2 and ADH_3 (Smith et al, 1971). Stomach ADH is almost exclusively composed of ADH_3 isozymes (γ polypeptides). The π-ADH was noted in the liver only (Parés and Vallee, 1981; Duley et al, 1985). Class III ADH is apparently present in all tissues examined (Adinolfi et al, 1984a; Duley et al, 1985). The enzyme is located in the cytosolic component of the cells.

Immunohistochemical study of the localization of ADH in human tissues revealed that at least some ADH activity could be detected in all tissues investigated (von Wartburg and Bühler, 1984). In some organs, certain cell types exhibited much stronger staining than others within the same organ, indicating that the enzyme is unevenly distributed in many organs. Such an uneven distribution was found in the kidney, the gastrointestinal tract, and also in the liver. In the liver, ADH was present primarily in the pericentral hepatocytes. In the kidney, ADH occurred mainly in the tubular epithelium; in the gastrointestinal tract, ADH was present primarily in the mucosa; and in the brain, Purkinje cells in the cerebellum stained strongly for ADH activity (von Wartburg and Bühler, 1984).

Genetic Variants

Although many genetic variants have been identified at the ADH_2 and ADH_3 loci, no allelic variation has been reported so far for ADH_1 (class I ADH), π-ADH (class II ADH), and χ-ADH (class III ADH). Patterns of class I isozymes vary within and among different racial groups because of allelic polymorphism. A variant enzyme form produced at the polymorphic ADH_2 locus is commonly known as the "atypical ADH" (von Wartburg and Schürch, 1968). The atypical enzyme contains a variant β_2 subunit instead of the usual β_1 subunit and exhibits much higher catalytic activity than the normal enzyme at a relatively physiological pH (pH 8.8) and migrates more cathodic in starch gel electrophoresis. The homodimeric $\beta_2\beta_2$ variant form has significantly higher K_m values for ethanol and NAD^+, and a higher V_{max} for ethanol than $\beta_1\beta_1$ and $\beta_1\beta_2$ forms (Bosron and Li, 1986).

A new enzyme form, resulting from a polymorphism at the ADH_2 locus—designated $ADH_{Indianapolis}$—has been reported in black Americans (Bosron et al, 1983b). As it is the third type of β subunit that has been characterized, it is now called β_3 (Bosron and Li, 1987). This allelic form exhibits a dual pH optimum for ethanol oxidation at pH 7.0 and pH 10.0 as well as a greater electrophoretic mobility toward the cathode.

The multiple molecular forms of class I ADH are identified most clearly on starch gel electrophoresis or isoelectric focusing as a complex set of electrophoretically distinct isoenzymes (Fig. 1.5). Any one particular isoenzyme may be homodimeric, consisting of two identical polypeptides (e.g., $\alpha\alpha$, $\beta\beta$, $\gamma\gamma$) coded by a specific allele at one of the loci, or heterodimeric, consisting of two nonidentical polypeptides (e.g., $\alpha\beta$, $\beta\gamma$) coded by alleles at separate loci, or heterodimeric but coded by different alleles at the same locus (e.g., $\beta_1\beta_2, \gamma_1\gamma_2$).

The characterization of the kinetic and structural properties of the different hetero- and homodimeric isoenzymes containing the β_2 subunits has been reported recently (Yin et al, 1984). Four isozymes containing β_2 subunits were isolated from Japanese livers and identi-

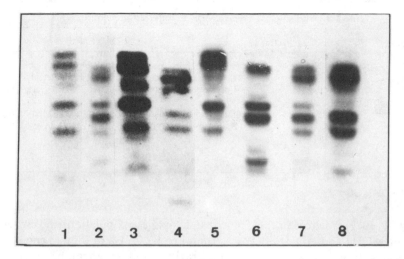

1, 5 : ADH_2 2–1, ADH_3 1.   2, 7 : ADH_2 1, ADH_3 2–1

3   : ADH_2 2, ADH_3 1.   4, 8 : ADH_2 1, ADH_3 1

6   : ADH_2 1, ADH_3 2

FIGURE 1.5. Starch gel electrophoretic pattern of various class I ADH isozymes.

fied as $\beta_2\beta_2$, $\alpha\beta_2$, $\beta_2\gamma_1$, and $\beta_2\beta_1$ after dissociation–recombination studies. The kinetic properties of the three heterodimers, $\beta_1\beta_2$, $\alpha\beta_2$, and $\beta_2\gamma_1$ are intermediate between those of the respective homodimers, suggesting that the two subunits act independently (Yin et al, 1984). The kinetic constants of $\beta_2\beta_2$ differ substantially from those of $\alpha\alpha$, $\beta_1\beta_1$, $\gamma_1\gamma_1$, and $\gamma_2\gamma_2$. At pH 7.5, the V_{max} for ethanol oxidation of $\beta_2\beta_2$ is several times higher than that of other homodimers. The K_m and K_i values of the $\beta_2\beta_2$ isozyme for NAD^+ and NADH are also significantly higher than those of the other homodimers.

Racial Frequency of ADH Alleles

Many population genetic studies have been carried out to estimate the incidence of ADH alleles in different populations using pH-activity ratio (pH 8.8 and pH 11.0) and electrophoretic profiles of the isozyme bands. Livers containing the normal ADH_2 phenotype ($\beta_1\beta_1$ subunits) exhibit a pH optimum at about 10.0 to 11.0, whereas livers with either an atypical heterozygote ($\beta_1\beta_2$) or an atypical homozygote ($\beta_2\beta_2$) show a pH optimum at 8.5. On electrophoresis or isoelectric focusing, the various ADH_2 and ADH_3 phenotypes show typical isozyme patterns. However, it is difficult to separate heterozygous and homozygous forms for the ADH_2^2 allele by using starch gel electrophoresis (Harada et al, 1980).

While about 5 to 10% of the English, 9 to 14% of the German, and 20% of the Swiss populations possess the "atypical" phenotype of ADH (ADH_2 locus), this variant form occurs in at least 85% of the Japanese, Chinese, and other Mongoloid populations (Table 1.3). The $ADH_{2\ Indianapolis}$ variant allele has been found to be present in about 25% of the black American population (Bosron et al, 1980). This variant form was not found in white Americans, Germans, and Japanese (Bosron et al, 1980; Agarwal et al, 1981b).

The frequency of the variant forms of the ADH_3 locus has been found to be relatively higher in Caucasians than in Oriental and African populations (Harada et al, 1980). The frequency of ADH_3^1 and ADH_3^2 alleles in Caucasians was reported to be 0.6 and 0.4, respec-

Table 1.3. Frequency of atypical ADH in different populations

SUBJECT GROUP	% ATYPICAL ADH	REFERENCE
Swiss	20	Von Wartburg and Schürch, 1968
English	5–10	Edwards and Price Evans, 1967; Smith et al, 1971, 1972
Germans	9–14	Käferstein et al, 1976; Schulz et al, 1976; Harada et al, 1980
Japanese	85–98	Fukui and Wakasugi, 1972; Ogata and Mizohata, 1973; Stamatoyannopoulos et al, 1975; Harada et al, 1980
Chinese	89	Teng et al, 1979
Bahia (Brazil)	2.8	Azevêdo et al, 1975
Asian Indians	0	Teng et al, 1979

tively (Smith et al, 1972), whereas in the Chinese and Japanese populations the corresponding frequency of the ADH_3^1 and ADH_3^2 allele was found to be 0.91 and 0.09 (Teng et al, 1979; Harada et al, 1980). In mixed populations from Brazilian and American black populations, the ADH_3^2 allele is relatively less frequent (Azevêdo et al, 1975; Bosron et al, 1983b). However, in a recent study on a few autopsy liver samples of American Indians from New Mexico (Rex et al, 1985), the ADH_3^2 gene frequency was found to be significantly higher (56%) than the ADH_3^1 gene frequency (28%).

Subunit and Molecular Structure of ADH Isozymes

The understanding of the biochemistry of liver ADH has advanced rapidly in the past years. Complete amino acid sequences have been determined for subunits composing the ADH_1, ADH_2, and ADH_3 loci. All subunits consist of 374 residues and have about 10% total amino acid exchanges. The degrees of exchanges in the α, β, and γ subunits are very similar, suggesting separate but comparatively recent gene duplications (Jörnvall et al, 1987).

The ADH₂ Locus

The amino acid data show that the β_2 subunit from Caucasian and Oriental livers is identical but differs from the β_1 subunit by a single amino acid exchange at position Arg-47 in the $NAD^+(H)$ pyrophosphate binding site of β_1 by His-47 in β_2 (Jörnvall et al, 1984; Bühler et al, 1984). The arginine–histidine-47 mutational difference has been found to be responsible for the altered catalytic and functional properties including both a lower pH optimum and higher turnover number of the atypical enzyme.

Full-length cloned cDNAs coding for α, β, and γ subunits of human ADH have been isolated from a human liver lambda gt11 cDNA library. The complete amino acid sequence deduced from the cDNA confirmed that the active site structure of the β_1 subunit should be -Cys-Arg-, and of the atypical β_2 should be -Cys-His- (Ikuta et al, 1985). The amino acid sequence and the coding regions of the cDNAs of the three subunits are very similar except for distinctive differences found in the vicinity of the Zn-binding cysteine residue at position 46 (i.e., Cys-Gly-Thr in the α, Cys-Arg-Thr in the normal type β_1, Cys-His-Thr in the Oriental type β_2, and Cys-Arg-Ser in the γ subunit), reflecting differences in their kinetic properties (Ikuta et al, 1986).

The molecular characterization of the ADH_2^1 allele shows that nine exons are stretched over 15 kilobases (kb) in length (Duester et al, 1985; Duester et al, 1986). The complete nucleotide sequence of all nine exons of the ADH_2^2 allele, which encodes for the β_2 subunit has been determined, using four clones from a human genomic DNA library (Matsuo et al, 1987; personal communication). Nucleotide sequence data indicate that the CGC–CAC substitution responsible for the arginine–histidine exchange is the only nucleotide polymorphism detected between the coding regions of the ADH_2^1 and ADH_2^2 alleles. At the 47th amino acid position, horse, rat, and mouse ADHs and human ADH_3 isozymes have arginine (Yokoyama and Yokoyama, 1987). ADH_2^1 seems to be the original isozyme form in mammals, and the variant ADH_2^2 might have reached its high frequency in Mongoloids through a bottleneck or founder effect. The low level of polymorphism observed at the ADH_2 locus may be due to a smaller population size and/or due to a shorter divergence time between the two alleles (Matsuo et al, 1987).

The ADH_3 Locus

The isozymes determined by the ADH_3 locus are made up of γ polypeptide subunits. ADH_3 is also polymorphic and shows heterodimeric ($\gamma_1\gamma_2$), and homodimeric ($\gamma_2\gamma_2$) allelic forms. The $\gamma_1\gamma_1$ isozyme has a slower electrophoretic mobility than the $\gamma_2\gamma_2$ form.

The differences in γ_1 and γ_2 have also been detected by cDNA and protein analysis. Amino acid sequence analysis of the γ_1 and γ_2 subunits showed that both have the same sequence, Cys-Arg-Ser, at their positions 46–48, but valine at position 276 in γ_1 is replaced by methionine in γ_2 (Ikuta et al, 1986). However, other reports indicate two additional replacements at positions 271 (Arg/Gln) and 349 (Ile/Val) (Bühler et al, 1984; Hempel et al, 1985).

Chromosomal Localization

Chromosome mapping studies using rodent–human somatic cell hybrids have revealed that all three class I ADH genes are located on the long arm of human chromosome 4, between q21 and q24 (Smith, 1986). Also, the gene coding for χ-ADH has been assigned to chromosome 4 (Smith, 1986).

ONTOGENY AND EVOLUTIONARY RELATIONSHIPS OF ADH ISOZYMES

The activity of liver ADH increases during development in humans, rats, mice, and guinea pigs. In humans and mice, different isozymes appear at different developmental stages (Smith et al, 1971; Holmes, 1979). In humans, the ADH activity is low in fetal life and increases to a normal adult level about five years after birth (Pikkarainen and Räihä, 1967). The ADH_1 locus is active in early fetal life followed by the ADH_2 and ADH_3 loci, which show different degrees of expression in different organs at various stages of the fetal development.

The structural differences found in various ADH subunits explain several of the known functional properties of the different isozymes. Single amino acid exchange appears to explain differences in enzymatic properties. The β_2 subunit (atypical ADH form) undergoes an Arg-47 to His-47 exchange, which explains a lower pH optimum, a higher turnover number, and a lower affinity for coenzyme binding. The Arg–Gln exchange at position 271 in the γ_2 subunit may explain the different kinetic constants for γ_1 and γ_2 homodimers (Yin et al, 1984).

By comparing all human class I isozyme differences and horse E-type ADH protein chain, it was revealed that isozyme divergence and species divergence are nonidentical (Jörnvall et al, 1987). There are only six amino acid exchanges in the NAD^+-binding domain of α, β, and γ subunits. The catalytic domain is more variable than the coenzyme-binding domain in the human subunits (Ikuta et al, 1986; Hempel and Jörnvall, 1987).

A summary of the relationship between human class I isozyme (α, β, and γ subunits) differences and species differences (horse E-type) is shown in Figure 1.6 (Jörnvall et al, 1987). These relationships strongly suggest that gene duplication events leading to human class I isozyme differences are different from those leading to differences in horse E and S types. The isozyme divergence in humans is a later event than the species separation of humans and horse. In humans, the α subunit diverges first, and the β and γ subunits diverge later (Fig. 1.6).

PHYSIOLOGICAL ROLE OF ALCOHOL DEHYDROGENASE

The universal distribution of ADH in various living organisms suggests that ADH is physiologically an important enzyme. Dehydrogenation of ethanol or other alcohols is usually visualized as the main function of ADH. At neutral pHs, however, ADH catalyzes irreversible aldehyde reduction. At maximum velocity, the rate of aldehyde reduction is some 40 times greater than the rate of alcohol oxidation. Numerous naturally occurring compounds have been suggested as physiological substrates for ADH. Alcohols arising from foodstuffs and fruits are also metabolized via the ADH pathway. ADH may also play an important role in retinol–retinal interconversion in visual processes. Moreover, ADH has been proposed to be

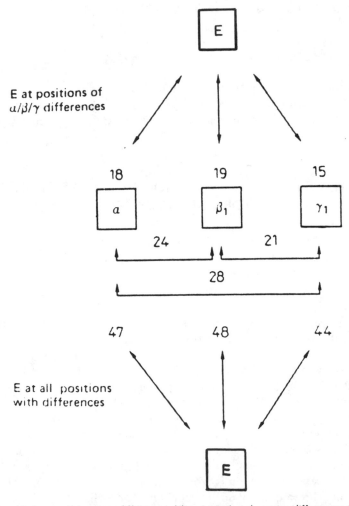

FIGURE 1.6. Relationship between isozyme differences (class I ADH) and species differences (horse E type versus human class I type). Numbers give total amino acid replacement in all the pairwise comparisons, showing the isozyme differences horizontally in the middle, and the species differences above and below. Top scheme gives the number of E differences only at those positions where isozyme differences occur between alpha, beta, and gamma. Bottom scheme shows E differences at all positions (Jörnvall et al, 1987).

involved in the metabolism of steroid and bile acids as well as in the catabolism of short-chain alcohols responsible for food flavors.

The biological importance of the polymorphism of human liver ADH remains undecided. Differences in the kinetic properties of the polymorphic forms of ADH isozymes may contribute to differences in in vivo elimination rate of ethanol. Since the activity of atypical ADH is several times higher than the usual enzyme at relatively physiological pH (pH 8.8), it is possible that individuals with the atypical isozyme forms (ADH_2 locus) metabolize ethanol differently compared with the normal ADH_2 phenotype. Thus, the pharmacokinetic curves for ethanol elimination at higher alcohol concentrations should differ significantly for individuals with the atypical ADH forms (Bosron et al., 1983a). Although alcohol elimination rates in the Japanese and Chinese were found to be higher than in whites (Hanna, 1978), in other studies reported, no significant difference in the rate of alcohol metabolism was found between normal and atypical ADH phenotype carriers (Edwards and Price Evans, 1967; Schulz et al, 1976). Moreover, no atypical ADH form has been detected in autopsy livers from American Indians (Rex et al, 1985), who are generally believed to metabolize ethanol faster than whites (Reed, 1978).

Acute intake of ethanol leads to a significantly high steady-state blood acetaldehyde level in humans. In some individuals, particularly in Mongoloids, this sudden rise in the blood acetaldehyde level may lead to the alcohol intolerance phenomenon (Stamatoyannopoulos et al, 1975). Although some investigators believe that the atypical ADH with higher catalytic activity at relatively physiological pH, found frequently among Japanese and Chinese, may be responsible for the initial higher blood acetaldehyde levels associated with alcohol sensitivity symptoms, the precise role of the ADH isozymes in alcohol intolerance remains obscure (Agarwal et al, 1981a; Goedde et al, 1983; Kogame and Mizoi, 1985; Mizoi et al, 1987). A detailed discussion relating to this aspect of alcohol metabolism is given in Chapter 2.

ALCOHOL DEHYDROGENASE AND ALCOHOL-RELATED DISORDERS

The role of alcohol dehydrogenase in alcoholism and alcohol-related disorders has not been fully understood so far. Altered structure of the genes encoding various ADH isozymes could be determinantal in observed genetic differences in alcoholics and nonalcoholics. Although the rate of ethanol metabolism has been found to be similar in alcoholics and nonalcoholics, elevated serum ADH activity has been noted in alcoholics with liver damage (Kato et al, 1984; Meier-Tackmann et al, 1984). Moreover, the isozymes profile of ADH was found to be altered in alcoholics as compared with nonalcoholics (Coman and Gheorghe, 1981). However, the findings are equivocal (Ricciardi et al, 1983; Tipton et al, 1983).

CONCLUSIONS

There are many contributing factors in the absorption, distribution, and metabolism of ethanol in humans. Microsomal ethanol oxidizing system (MEOS) and alcohol dehydrogenase (ADH) play a major and an important role in the oxidation of ethanol to acetaldehyde in various organs and tissues. ADH occurs in multiple molecular forms and recent studies at the protein and DNA levels have helped us to understand the biochemical and molecular basis of multiplicity of various isozymes. These investigations have also revealed structural as well as evolutionary interrelationships of various isozyme forms in humans, horse and yeast. Genetically determined variation in ADH may partly account for inter- and intraindividual variation observed in the ethanol elimination rate and the acute and chronic pharmacological and pathological consequences of alcohol drinking (Agarwal and Goedde, 1984, 1986).

REFERENCES

Adinolfi A, Adinolfi M, Hopkinson DA, Harris H: Immunological properties of human alcohol dehydrogenase (ADH) isozymes. *J Immunogenet* 1978; 5:283–296.

Adinolfi A, Adinolfi M, Hopkinson DA: Immunological and biochemical characterization of human alcohol dehydrogenase chi ADH isozymes. *Ann Hum Genet* 1984a; 48:1–10.

Adinolfi A, Adinolfi M, Massa O: Immunological cross-reactivity of mouse alcohol dehydrogenase with rabbit immune sera against human alcohol dehydrogenase isozymes. *Exp Clin Immunogenet* 1984b; 1:208–216.

Adinolfi A, Massa O, D'Alessandro G: Immunological cross-reactivity of mouse alcohol dehydrogenase (ADH) isozymes with immune sera against horse and human ADH subunits. *Ann Hum Genet* 1986; 50:197–206.

Adinolfi A, Massa O, D'Alessandro G, Zapponi MC, Bonferoni C: Shared antigenic determinants among alcohol dehydrogenase and other enzymes. *Exp Clin Immunogenet* 1987; 4:115–123.

Agarwal DP, Meier-Tackmann D, Harada S, Goedde HW: A search for the Indianapolis-variant of human alcohol dehydrogenase in liver autopsy samples from Nothern Germany and Japan. *Hum Genet* 1981a; 59:170–171.

Agarwal DP, Harada S, Goedde HW: Racial differences in biological sensitivity to ethanol: The role of alcohol dehydrogenase and aldehyde dehydrogenase isozymes. *Alcohol Clin Exp Res* 1981b; 5: 12–16.

Agarwal DP, Goedde HW; Alkohol metabolisierende Enzyme: Alkoholunverträglichkeit und Alkoholkrankheit, in Zang, KD (ed): *Klinische Genetik des Alkoholismus.* Stuttgart, Verlag W Kohlhammer, 1984, pp 65–89.

Agarwal DP, Goedde HW: Ethanol oxidation: ethnic variation in metabolism and response, in Kalow W, Goedde HW, Agarwal DP (eds): *Ethnic Differences in Reactions to Drugs and Xenobiotics.* New York, Alan R Liss, Inc, 1986, pp 99–111.

Azevêdo ES, Da Silva OMC, Tavares-Neto J: Human alcohol dehydrogenase ADH_1, ADH_2 and ADH_3 loci in a mixed population of Bahia, Brazil. *Ann Hum Genet* 1975; 39:321–327.

Bennion L, Li T-K: Alcohol metabolism in American Indians and whites. *N Engl J Med* 1976; 294:9–13.

Blackmore DJ, Mason JK: Renal clearence of urea, creatinine and alcohol. *Med Sci Law* 1968; 8:50–53.

Bosron WF, Crabb DW, Li T-K: Relationship between kinetics of liver alcohol dehydrogenase and alcohol metabolism. *Pharmacol Biochem Behav* 1983a; 18:223–227.

Bosron WF, Li T-K, Lange LG, Dafaldecker WP, Vallee BL: Isolation and characterization of an anodic form of human liver alcohol dehydrogenase. *Biochem Biophys Res Comm* 1977; 74:85–91.

Bosron WF, Li T-K, Dafeldecker WP, Vallee BL: Human liver π-alcohol dehydrogenase: Kinetic and molecular properties. *Biochemistry* 1979; 18:1101–1105.

Bosron WF, Li T-K, Vallee BL: New molecular forms of liver alcohol dehydrogenase: Isolation and characterization of ADH Indianapolis. *Proc Natl Acad Sci USA* 1980; 77:5784–5788.

Bosron WF, Li T-K: Genetic polymorphism of human liver alcohol and aldehyde dehydrogenases, and their relationship to alcohol metabolism and alcoholism. *Hepatology* 1986; 6:502–510.

Bosron WF, Li-T-K: Catalytic properties of human liver alcohol dehydrogenase isoenzymes. *Enzyme* 1987; 37:19–28.

Bosron WF, Magnes LJ, Li T-K: Human liver alcohol dehydrogenase: ADH Indianapolis results from the genetic polymorphism at the ADH_2 gene locus. *Biochem Genet* 1983b; 21:735–744.

Bühler R, Hempel J, von Wartburg JP, Jörnvall H: Human liver alcohol dehydrogenase: The unique properties of the "atypical" isoenzyme $\beta_2\beta_2$-Bern can be explained by a single base mutation. *Alcohol* 1984; 2:47–51.

Coman M, Gheorghe N: Effects of chronic ethanol intake on isozyme patterns of liver alchol dehydrogenase. *Rev Roumaine Physiologie* 1981; 18:247–249.

Ditlow CC, Holmquist B, Morelock MM, Vallee BL: Physical and enzymatic properties of class II alcohol dehydrogenase isozymes of human liver: π-ADH. *Biochemistry* 1984; 23:6363–6368.

Duester G, Hatfield GW, Smith M: Molecular genetic analysis of human alcohol dehydrogenase. *Alcohol* 1985; 2:53–56.

Duester G, Smith M, Bilanchone V, Hatfield GW: Molecular analysis of the human class I alcohol dehydrogenase gene family and nucleotide sequence of the gene encoding the β subunit. *J Biol Chem* 1986; 162:2027–2033.

Duley JA, Harris O, Holmes RS: Analysis of human alcohol- and aldehyde-metabolising isozymes by electrophoresis and isoelectric focusing. *Alcohol Clin Exp Res* 1985; 9:263–271.

Dundee JW, Isaac M, Wagner JG: Blood ethanol levels following rapid intravenous infusion. *Q J Stud Alcohol* 1971; 32:741–747.

Edwards JA, Price Evans DA: Ethanol metabolism in subjects possessing typical and atypical liver alcohol dehydrogenase. *Clin Pharmacol Therapeut* 1967; 8:824–829.

Erickson CK: Factors affecting the distribution and measurement of ethanol in the body, in Majchrowicz E, Noble EP (eds): *Biochemistry and Pharmacology of Ethanol*, New York, London, Plenum Press, 1979, vol 1, pp 9–26.

Ewing JA, Rouse BA, Pellizzari ED: Alcohol sensitivity and ethnic background. *Am J Psychiatry* 1974; 131:206–210.

Farris JJ, Jones BM: Ethanol metabolism in male American Indians and whites. *Alcohol Clin Exp Res* 1978; 2:77–82.

Feinman L, Baraona E, Matsuzaki S, Korsten M, Lieber CS: Concentration dependence of ethanol metabolism in vivo in rats and man. *Alcohol Clin Exp Res* 1978; 2:381–385.

Fenna D, Mix L, Schaefer O, Gilbert JAL: Ethanol metabolism in various racial groups. *Can Med Assoc J* 1971; 105:472–475.

Fukui M, Wakasugi C: Liver alcohol dehydrogenase in Japanese population. *Jap J Legal Med* 1972; 26:46–51.

Goedde HW, Agarwal DP, Harada S: Alcohol metabolizing enzymes: Studies of isozymes in human biopsies and cultured fibroblasts. *Clin Genet* 1979; 16:29–33.

Goedde HW, Agarwal DP, Harada S: The role of alcohol dehydrogenase and aldehyde dehydrogenase isozymes in alcohol metabolism, alcohol sensitivity and alcoholism, in Rattazzi MC, Scandalios JG, Whitt GS (eds): *Isozymes: Current Topics in Biological and Medical Research*. New York, Alan R Liss Inc, 1983, vol 8, pp 175–193.

Goldberg L: Quantitative studies in alcohol tolerance. *Acta Physiol Scand* 1943; 16 (suppl):1–128.

Goldberg L: Tolerance to alcohol in moderate and heavy drinkers and its significance to alcohol. *Proc 1st International Conf Alcohol and Road Traffic* 1950; Stockholm.

Hanna JM: Metabolic responses of Chinese, Japanese and Europeans to alcohol. *Alcohol Clin Exp Res* 1978; 2:89–92.

Harada S, Agarwal DP, Goedde HW: Human liver alcohol dehydrogenase isozyme variations. Improved separation methods using prolonged high voltage starch gel electrophoresis and isoelectric focusing. *Hum Genet* 1978; 40:215–220.

Harada S, Misawa S, Agarwal DP, Goedde HW: Liver alcohol and aldehyde dehydrogenase in the Japanese: Isozyme variation and its possible role in alcohol intoxication. *Am J Hum Genet* 1980; 32: 8–15.

Hempel J, Holmquist B, Fleetwood L, Kaiser R, Barros-Söderling J, Bühler R, Vallee B, Jörnvall H: Structural relationship among class I isozymes of human liver alcohol dehydrogenase. *Biochemistry* 1985; 24:5303–5307.

Hempel J, Jörnvall H: Functional topology of aldehyde dehydrogenase structures, in Weiner H, Flynn TG (eds): *Enzymology and Molecular Biology of Carbonyl Metabolism*, Progress in Clinical and Biological Research, New York, Alan R Liss Inc, 1987, vol 232, pp 1–14.

Holmes RS: Genetics and ontogeny of alcohol dehydrogenase isoenzymes in the mouse: Evidence for a cis-acting regulator gene (Adt-1) controlling C2 isozyme expression in reproductive tissues and close linkage of Adh-3 and Adt-1 on chromosome 3. *Biochem Genet* 1979; 17:461–472.

Ikuta T, Fuziyoshi T, Kurachi K, Yoshida A: Molecular cloning of a full length cDNA for human alcohol dehydrogenase. *Proc Natl Acad Sci USA* 1985; 82:2703–2707.

Ikuta T, Szeto S, Yoshida A: Three human alcohol dehydrogenase subunits: cDNA structure and molecular and evolutionary divergence. *Proc Natl Acad Sci USA* 1986; 83:634–638.

Jones BM: Circadian variation in the effects of alcohol on cognitive performance. *Q J Stud Alcohol* 1974; 35:1212–1219.

Jones BM, Jones MK: Effects of moderate dose of alcohol on female social drinkers at different times in the menstrual cycle. *Chronobiologia* 1975; Suppl.1:34 (Abstr).

Jörnvall H, Hempel J, Vallee BL, Bosron WF, Li T-K: Human liver alcohol dehydrogenase: Amino acid substitution in the $\beta_2\beta_2$ Oriental enzyme explains functional properties, establishes an active site structure and parallels mutational exchanges in the yeast enzyme. *Proc Natl Acad Sci USA* 1984; 81: 3024–3028.

Jörnvall H, Hempel J, Vallee B: Structures of human alcohol and aldehyde dehydrogenases. *Enzyme* 1987; 37:1–17.

Käferstein H, Berghaus G, Detmer J: "Normale" und "atypische" Alkoholdehydrogenase-Einflußfaktoren auf die Enzymaktivitäten der Leber. *Blutalkohol* 1976; 13:144–155.

Kalant H: Absorption, diffusion, distribution and elimination of ethanol: effects on biological membranes, in Kissin B, Begleiter H (eds): *The Biology of Alcoholism*. New York, Plenum Press, 1971, vol 1, pp 1–62.

Kato S, Ishii H, Kano S, Hagihara S, Todoroki T, Nagata S, Takahashi H, Nagasaka M, Sato J, Tsuchiya M: Improved assay for alcohol dehydrogenase activity in serum by centrifugal analysis. *Clin Chem* 1984; 30:1817–1820.

Keiding S, Christensen NJ, Damgaard SE: Ethanol metabolism in heavy drinkers after massive and moderate alcohol intake. *Biochem Pharmacol* 1983; 32:3097–3102.

Kogame M, Mizoi Y: The polymorphism of alcohol and aldehyde dehydrogenase in the Japanese and its significance in ethanol metabolism. *Jpn J Alcohl Drug Depend* 1985; 20:122–142.

Koop DR, Coon MJ: Role of P-450 oxygenase (APO) in microsomal ethanol oxidation. *Alcohol* 1985; 2:23–26.

Kopun M, Propping P: The kinetics of ethanol absorption and elimination in twins supplemented by repetitive experiments in single subjects. *Eur J Clin Pharmacol* 1977; 11:337–344.

Kricka LJ, Clark, PMS: *Biochemistry of Alcohol and Alcoholism*. Chichester, Great Britain, Ellis Horwood Limited, 1979.

Lehmann WD, Heinrich HC, Leonhardt R, Agarwal DP, Goedde HW, Kneer J, Rating D: ^{13}C-Ethanol and ^{13}C-acetate breath tests in normal and aldehyde dehydrogenase deficient individuals. *Alcohol* 1986; 3:227–231.

Li T-K: Enzymology of human alcohol metabolism. *Adv Enzymol* 1977; 45:427–483.

Li T-K: The absorption, distribution and metabolism of ethanol and its effect on nutrition and hepatic function, in Tabakoff B, Sutker PB, Randall CL (eds): *Medical and Psychological Aspects of Alcohol Abuse*. New York, Plenum Publishing Corp, 1983, pp 47–77.

Lieber, CS: Metabolism of ethanol, in CS Lieber (ed): *Metabolic Aspects of Alcoholism*. Baltimore, University Park Press, 1977, pp 1–29.

Lieber, CS: Metabolism and metabolic effects of alcohol. *Medical Clinics North America* 1984; 68:3–31.

Lieber CS: Effects of chronic alcohol consumption on the metabolism of ethanol, in Goedde HW, Agarwal DP (eds): *Genetics and Alcoholism*, New York, Alan R Liss Inc, 1987, pp 161–172.

Lieber CS, DeCarli LM: The role of hepatic microsomal ethanol oxidizing system (MEOS) for ethanol metabolism in vivo. *J Pharmacol Exp Ther* 1972; 181:279–288.

Lin Y, Weidler DJ, Garg DC, Wagner JC: Effects of solid food on blood levels of alcohol in man. *Res Commun Pathol Pharmacol* 1976; 13:713–722.

Martin NG: Genetic differences in drinking habits, alcohol metabolism and sensitivity in unselected samples of twins, in Goedde HW, Agarwal DP (eds): *Genetics and Alcoholism*, New York, Alan R Liss Inc, 1987, pp 109–120.

Martin E, Moll W, Schmid P, Dettli L: The pharmacokinetics of alcohol in human breath, venous and arterial blood after oral ingestion. *Eur J Pharmacol* 1984; 26:619–626.

Martin NG, Perl J, Oekeshott JG, Gibson, JB, Starmer GA, Wilks AV: A twin study of ethanol metabolism. *Behav Genet* 1985; 15:93–109.

Matsuo Y, Yokoyama R, Yokoyama S: Human alcohol dehydrogenases β_1 and β_2 are specified by a single nucleotide exchange. 1987 (personal communication).

Meier-Tackmann D, Agarwal DP, Harada S, Goedde HW: Plasma alcohol dehydrogenase in normal and alcoholic individuals. *Alcohol Alcohol* 1984; 19:7–12.

Mizoi Y, Adachi J, Fukunaga T, Kogame M, Ueno Y, Nojo Y, Fuziwara S: Individual and ethnic differences in ethanol elimination. *Alcohol Alcoholism* 1987; Suppl.1:389–394.

Mizoi Y, Kogame M, Fukunaga T, Ueno Y, Adachi J, Fuziwara S: Polymorphism of aldehyde dehydrogenase and ethanol elimination. *Alcohol* 1985; 2:393–396.

Moskowitz H, Burns M: Effects of rates of drinking on human performance. *J Stud Alcohol* 1976; 37:598–605.

Mullen PW: The metabolism and pharmacokinetics of alcohol in man. *J Forensic Sci Soc* 1977; 17:49–55.

Nuutinen H, Lindros K, Hekali P, Salaspuro M: Elevated blood acetate as indicator of fast ethanol elimination in chronic alcoholics. *Alcohol* 1985; 2:623–626.

Ogata S, Mizohata M: Studies on atypical human liver alcohol dehydrogenase in Japan. *J Stud Alcohol* 1973; 8:33–44.

Parés X, Vallee BL: New human liver alcohol dehydrogenase forms with unique kinetic characteristics. *Biochem Biophys Res Comm* 1981; 98:122–130.

Payne JP, Hill DW, King NW: Observations on the distribution of alcohol in blood, breath and urine. *Br Med J* 1966; 1:196–202.

Pietruszko R: Alcohol and aldehyde deghydrogenase isozymes from mammalian liver – Their structural and functional differences, in Rattazzi MC, Scandalios JG, Whitt GS (eds): *Isozymes: Current Topics in Biological and Medical Research*. New York, Alan R Liss Inc, 1980, vol 4, pp 107–130.

Pikkarainen PH, Räihä NCR: Development of alcohol dehydrogenase activity in the human liver. *Pediat Res* 1967; 1:165–168.

Reed TE: Racial comparisons of alcohol metabolism: Background, problems and results. *Alcohol Clin Exp Res* 1978; 2:61–69.

Reed TE, Kalant H: Bias in calculated rate of ethanol metabolism due to variation in relative amount of adipose tissue. *J Stud Alcohol* 1977; 38:1773–1776.

Reed TE, Kalant H, Gibbins RJ, Khanna BM: Alcohol and acetaldehyde metabolism in Caucasians, Chinese and Amerinds. *Can Med Assoc J* 1976; 115:851–855.

Rex DK, Bosron WF, Smialek JE, Li T-K: Alcohol and aldehyde dehydrogenase isoenzymes in North American Indians. *Alcohol Clin Exp Res* 1985; 9:147–152.

Ricciardi BR, Saunders JB, Williams R, Hopkinson DA: Identification of alcohol dehydrogenase and aldehyde dehydrogenase isoenzymes in human liver biopsy specimens. *Clin Chim Acta* 1983; 130: 85–94.

Rognstad R, Grunnet N: Enzymatic pathways of ethanol metabolism, in Majchrowicz E, Noble EP (eds): *Biochemistry and Pharmacology of Ethanol*. New York, London, Plenum Press, 1979, vol 1, pp 65–85.

Salaspuro M, Lieber CS: Non-uniformity of blood ethanol elimination: Its exaggeration after chronic consumption. *Ann Clin Res* 1978; 10:294–297.

Schaefer, JM: Alcohol mtabolism and sensitivity among the Reddis of South India. *Alcohol Clin Exp Res* 1978; 2:61–69.

Schulz W, Kreuzberg S, Neymeyer HG, Schwarz U, Pachaly A: Über die Haüfigkeit der atypischen ADH in Leberbiopsiematerial und den Einfluß auf den Äthanolumsatz in vivo. *Kriminalistik und forensische Wissenschaften* 1976; 26:109–111.

Shigeta Y, Nomura F, Lida S, Leo MA, Felder MR, Lieber CS: Ethanol metabolism in vivo by the microsomal ethanol-oxidizing system in deermice lacking alcohol dehydrogenase (ADH). *Biochem Pharamcol* 1984; 33:807–814.

Shumate RP, Crowther RF, Zarafshan M: A study of the metabolism rate of alcohol in the human body. *J Forensic Med* 1967; 14:83–100.

Smith M: Genetics of human alcohol and aldehyde dehydrogenases. In Harris H, Hirschhorn K (eds): *Advances in Human Genetics*. New York, London, Plenum Press, 1986, vol 15, pp 249–290.

Smith M, Hopkinson DA, Harris H: Developmental changes and polymorphisms in human alcohol dehydrogenase. *Ann Hum Genet* 1971; 34:251–271.

Smith M, Hopkinson DA, Harris H: Alcohol dehydrogenase isoenzymes in adult human stomach and liver: Evidence for activity of the ADH$_3$ locus. *Ann Hum Genet* 1972; 35:243–253.

Smith M, Hopkinson DA, Harris H: Studies on the subunit structure and molecular size of the human alcohol dehydrogenase isozymes determined by the different loci ADH$_1$, ADH$_2$, ADH$_3$. *Ann Hum Genet* 1973; 36:401–414.

Stamatoyannopoulos G, Chen SH, Fukui F: Liver alcohol dehydrogenase in Japanese: High population frequency of atypical form and its possible role in alcohol sensitivity. *Am J Hum Genet* 1975; 27: 789–796.

Sturtevant FM, Sturtevant RP, Schevig RP, Pauly JP: Chronopharmacokinteics of ethanol in man. II. Circadian rhythm in rate of blood level decline in a single subject. *Naunyn–Schmiedeberg's Arch Pharmacol* 1976; 293:203–208.

Teng Y-S, Jehan S, Lie-Injo LE: Human alcohol dehydrogenase ADH$_2$ and ADH$_3$ polymorphism in ethnic Chinese and Indians of West Malaysia. *Hum Genet* 1979; 53:87–90.

Teschke R, Matsuzaki S, Ohnishi K, DeCarli LM, Lieber CS: Microsomal ethanol oxidizing system (MEOS): Current status of its characterization and its role. *Alcohol Clin Exp Res* 1977; 1:7–15.

Teschke R, Moreno F, Petrides AS: Hepatic microsomal ethanol oxidizing system (MEOS): Respective roles of ethanol and carbohydrates for the enhanced activity after chronic alcohol consumption. *Biochem Pharmacol* 1981; 30:1745–1751.

Tipton KF, McCrodden, Weir DG, Ward K: Isoenzymes of human liver alcohol dehydrogenase and aldehyde dehydrogenase in alcoholics and non-alcoholic subjects. *Alcohol Alcohol* 1983; 219–225.

Vesell ES, Page JG, Passananti GT: Genetic and environmental factors affecting ethanol metabolism in man. *Clin Pharmacol Ther* 1971; 12:192–201.

Vesell ES: Ethanol metabolism: Regulation by genetic factors in normal volunteers under a controlled environment and the effect of chronic ethanol administration. *Ann N Y Acad Sci USA* 1972; 197: 79–88.

von Wartburg JP, Schürch PM: Atypical human liver alcohol dehydrogenase. *Ann NY Acad Sci USA* 1968; 151:936–946.

von Wartburg JP: The metabolism of alcohol in normals and alcoholics: Enzymes, in Kissin B, Begleiter H (eds): *The Biology of Alcoholism*. New York, Plenum Press, 1971, pp 63–102.

von Wartburg JP, Bühler R: Biology of disease: Alcoholism and aldehydism: New biomedical concepts. *Lab Invest* 1984; 50:5–15.

Wagner, JG, Patel JA: Variations in absorption and elimination rates of ethyl alcohol in a single subject. *Res Commun Chem Pathol Pharmacol* 1972; 4:61–76.

Wagner JG, Wilkinson PK, Sedman AJ, Kay DR, Weidler DJ: Elimination of alcohol from human blood. *J Pharm Sci* 1976; 65:152–154.

Widmark EMP: *Die theoretischen Grundlagen und die praktische Verwendbarkeit gerichtlich-medizinischen Alkoholbestimmung*. Berlin, Urban und Scwarzenberg, 1932.

Wilkinson P: Pharmacokinetics of ethanol: A review. *Alcohol Clin Exp Res* 1980; 4:6–21.

Wilkinson PK, Sedman AJ, Sakmar E, Lin Y-L, Wagner JG: Fasting and non-fasting blood ethanol concentrations following repeated oral administration of ethanol to one adult. *J Pharmacokinet Biopharm* 1977; 5:41–52.

Yin S-J, Bosron WF, Magnes LJ, Li T-K: Human liver alcohol dehydrogenase: Purification and kinetic characteristics of the $\beta_2\beta_2$, $\beta_2\beta_1$, and $\beta_2\gamma_1$ "Oriental" isoenzymes. *Biochemistry* 1984; 23: 5847–5853.

Yokoyama S, Yokoyama R: Molecular evoluation of mammalian class I alcohol dehydrogenases. *Mol Biol Evol* 1987; 4:514–518.

CHAPTER 2

Acetaldehyde Metabolism: Genetic Variation and Physiological Implications

H. Werner Goedde and Dharam P. Agarwal

Institute of Human Genetics, University of Hamburg, Hamburg, F.R. Germany

INTRODUCTION

The direct toxic effects of alcohol and alcohol-related physiochemical alterations have been attributed more to acetaldehyde rather than to ethanol itself and the metabolism of acetaldehyde has received considerable attention in the past years. In this chapter, enzymological aspects of acetaldehyde metabolism are reviewed with particular emphasis on the genetically determined aldehyde dehydrogenase isozyme variation and its functional implications in alcohol sensitivity, alcohol-drinking behavior, and alcohol-related disorders among Orientals and related populations.

METABOLISM OF ACETALDEHYDE

Ethanol is oxidized in human liver to acetaldehyde and further to acetate via hydrogen transfer from the substrate to the cofactor nicotinamide adenine dinucleotide (NAD^+), resulting in the conversion to its reduced form NADH. The oxidative reactions are catalyzed by alcohol dehydrogenase and aldehyde dehydrogenase (cf. Chapter 1). The flavoproteins—aldehyde oxidase and xanthine oxidase—are capable of catalyzing acetaldehyde oxidation, but these enzymes have a broad substrate specificity and a relatively low affinity for acetaldehyde.

The pharmacokinetics of acetaldehyde is characterized by its rate of formation and degradation as well as the localization of these processes. Under normal conditions acetaldehyde is rapidly oxidized to acetate and significant acetaldehyde concentrations can only be found in the liver (Salaspuro and Lindros, 1985). The rate of formation of acetaldehyde being identical with the alcohol elimination rate, a similarly large individual variation in acetaldehyde formation is to be expected as is observed in alcohol elimination rate (cf. Chapter 1). Also, the rate of acetaldehyde elimination does not limit the rate of ethanol metabolism in vivo.

ALDEHYDE DEHYDROGENASES

The oxidation of acetaldehyde in the liver and other organs is mediated mainly by NAD^+-linked nonspecific aldehyde dehydrogenase (ALDH; aldehyde: NAD^+ oxidoreductase, EC 1.2.1.3) as follows:

$$\text{Acetaldehyde} + NAD^+ + H_2O \xrightarrow{\text{ALDH}} \text{acetic acid} + NADH + H^+$$

The ALDH catalyzed reaction is irreversible and a wide range of straight chain- and branched chain- aliphatic and aromatic aldehydes serve as substrates, producing the corresponding keto acids.

Isozyme Composition

The bovine liver ALDH was first purified by Racker (1949) followed by many other studies in different mammalian species (Feldman and Weiner, 1972; Tottmar et al, 1973; Crow et al, 1974; Eckfeldt and Yonetani, 1976; Sugimoto et al, 1976; Sanny, 1985). As a result, two broadly defined groups of ALDH were recognized in rats and mammalians based on their Michaelis constants ("low K_m" and "high K_m" groups).

Human liver ALDH was first studied and partially characterized by Kraemer and Deitrich (1968) and Blair and Bodley (1969). However, there was no clear consensus regarding the existence of multiple molecular forms, molecular weight, and substrate specificity. In recent years, many isozymes of ALDH have been detected and characterized in human organs and tissues (Greenfield and Pietruzsko, 1977; Harada et al, 1978; Goedde et al, 1979a; Harada et al, 1980a; Agarwal et al, 1983; Teng, 1983; Goedde et al, 1983a; Ricciardi et al, 1983a; Forte-McRobbie and Pietruszko, 1985; Duley et al, 1985; Rex et al, 1985; Santisteban et al, 1985; MacKerell et al. 1986). These studies have revealed that in humans there are at least four isozymes of ALDH that differ in their electrophoretic mobility, kinetic properties, and in their cellular and tissue distribution. At the subcellular level, the different isozymes are predominantly located in the cytosolic and mitochondrial fractions.

More recent data indicate that all enzymes capable of oxidizing acetaldehyde are not related to ALDH (Pietruszko et al, 1987). Apparently, the different ALDH isozymes grouped under the Enzyme Commission number, EC 1.2.1.3 are not structurally related and may represent different classes of isozymes (Forte-McRobbie and Pietruszko, 1985; Pietruszko et al, 1987). According to their substrate specificity, subunit composition, and quarternary structure, the aldehyde metabolizing isozymes may be divided into four groups: (1) ALDH (EC 1.2.1.3), (2) succinic semialdehyde dehydrogenase (EC 1.2.1.24), (3) glutamic–gamma–semialdehyde dehydrogenase (EC 1.5.1.12), and (4) glyceraldehyde-3-phosphate dehydrogenase (EC 1.2.1.12).

Nomenclature

The various ALDH isozymes differ in their molecular size, subunit structure, and isoelectric point as well as in their chromosomal assignment. Besides, some of the isozymes show genetic variation. In human liver, two major and two minor ALDH isozymes have been recognized (Greenfield and Pietruszko, 1977; Harada et al, 1978; Goedde et al, 1979a; Harada et al, 1980a). These isozymes are coded by at least four different gene loci.

There has been a considerable confusion regarding their nomenclature. Although some authors prefer the nomenclature used for the horse ALDH isozymes, designating the predominantly cytosolic enzyme as E1 or $ALDH_1$, and the predominantly mitochondrial enzyme as E2 or $ALDH_2$ (Greenfield and Pietruszko, 1977; Impraim et al, 1982), other workers prefer the sequential designation ALDH I, II, III, and IV based on their decreasing anodic electrophoretic mobility and increasing isoelectric point (Harada et al, 1980; Goedde et al, 1983a; Duley et al, 1985; Rex et al, 1985). In this contribution, the latter form of the nomenclature has been adopted for designating various ALDH isozymes.

Organ and Tissue Distribution

Many reports have appeared in the past years regarding the multiple molecular forms of human ALDH isozymes (Harada et al, 1978; Goedde et al, 1979a; Harada et al, 1980b; Agarwal et al, 1981; Goedde et al, 1983a; Jones and Teng, 1983; Ricciardi et al, 1983a;

Pietruszko, 1980; Meier-Tackmann et al, 1984, 1985; Duley et al, 1985; Rex et al, 1985; Santisteban et al, 1985). ALDH isozymes show a considerable heterogeneity in their tissue and organ distribution (Fig. 2.1).

On starch gel electrophoresis and isoelectric focusing, human tissue extracts mainly show isozymes I and II in liver, kidney, scalp skin, and cultured fibroblasts. Isozyme III is present in the stomach, lungs, and testes and, as a weak band in the spleen, liver, and kidney. ALDH IV isozyme band is detected in liver, kidney, and as a weak band in heart, intestine, and skin extracts (Goedde et al, 1979a). A microsomal isozyme designated as ALDH V was detected in liver and kidney (Duley et al, 1985).

Liver

Crude human liver extracts contain at least four different ALDH isozymes (Harada et al, 1978; Forte-McRobbie and Pietruszko, 1985). They may be divided into "low K_m" and "high K_m" classes based on their K_m values, subunit composition, molecular weight, and substrate specificity (Pietruszko et al, 1987). In both biopsy and autopsy liver samples, a large variation in individual and mean values for total ALDH activity expressed per gram fresh tissue was observed (Meier-Tackmann et al, 1988). However, the mean specific activity (per milligram soluble protein) values were found to be very similar in both biopsy and autopsy liver samples (Table 2.1).

On isoelectric focusing (IEF) of crude homogenates, two prominent isozyme bands (ALDH I and ALDH II) were invariably visible. Although an ALDH III isozyme band was not always detectable, a weak ALDH IV band was present in each of the biopsy and autopsy samples. The isozyme profile and activity band intensities from biopsy and autopsy specimens were quite identical (Fig. 2.2).

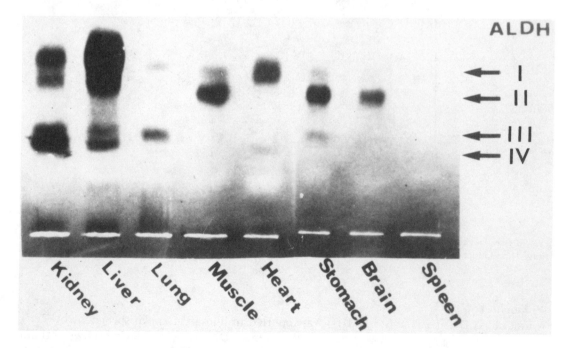

FIGURE 2.1. Distribution profile of ALDH isozymes in various human organ extracts subjected to high-voltage starch gel electrophoresis.

Table 2.1. A comparison of total ALDH activity in autopsy and biopsy liver
extracts (Meier-Tackmann et al, 1988)

| | ALDH ACTIVITY | | | |
| | AUTOPSY LIVER | | BIOPSY LIVER | |
LIVER SPECIMEN	TOTAL (mU/g wet wt)	SPECIFIC (mU/mg protein)	TOTAL (mU/g wet wt)	SPECIFIC (mU/mg protein)
1	832	10.4	749	29.0
2	912	15.8	767	5.7
3	1321	15.7	964	17.7
4	1445	38.4	1322	14.2
5	–	–	1706	13.3
6	–	–	3754	22.0
7	–	–	5336	28.7
Median	1116	15.75	1322	17.5
Mean	1127	20.1	2085	18.6

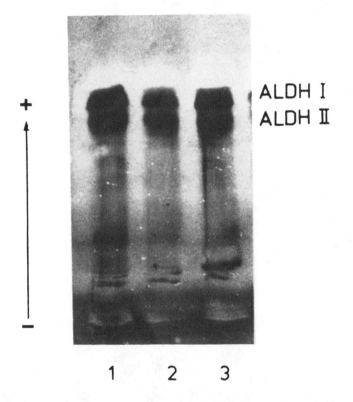

FIGURE 2.2. Polyacrylamide gel isoelectric focusing profile of ALDH isozymes in crude homogenates of autopsy (lane 1) and biopsy (lane 2, 3) livers.

Stomach

A unique ALDH isozyme (ALDHIII) was reported in human stomach specimens by Teng (1981), which is apparently different from the liver ALDH III. This enzyme shows optimal activity with furfuraldehyde and benzaldehyde. The stomach ALDH is a much smaller molecule than the liver enzymes and may be a monomer (Teng, 1981). The stomach isozyme resolves into several bands, which is apparently due to the artefactual formation of secondary isozymes (Meier-Tackmann et al, 1984; Duley et al, 1985). Recently, a stomach-specific ALDH III isozyme has been studied in detail (Santisteban et al, 1985). This stomach-specific ALDH III isozyme appears to be quite different from other ALDH isozymes in its tissue distribution, substrate and coenzyme specificity, and heat stability. Antiserum against a partially purified ALDH III, from the stomach, selectively immunoprecipitated ALDH III isozymes from human tissues but did not react with ALDH I, II, and IV isozymes; also, the immune sera raised against purified human ALDH I and ALDH II did not cross-react with human ALDH III (Santisteban et al, 1985).

Hair Roots

On isoelectric focusing, human hair root follicle extracts showed a prominent ALDH I and a weak ALDH II isozyme band (Goedde et al, 1980). ALDH I and II isozymes isolated from scalp skin showed kinetic properties similar to the corresponding isozymes from the liver (Goedde et al, 1982; 1983a). In the Ouchterlony double diffusion test, a cross-reaction between hair root extracts and antibodies against liver ALDH I was observed. The complete fusion of precipitin arcs from liver and hair root extracts indicates an immunological identity between ALDH I isozymes from the liver and hair roots (Goedde et al, 1985).

Placenta

ALDH I and II isozymes can be visualized in human term placental extracts by isoelectric focusing on polyacrylamide gels and enzyme-specific staining (Meier-Tackmann et al, 1985). Two distinct ALDH isozymes, I and II, were detected in freshly obtained human term placental extracts. Based on placental wet weight, about 80% of the total ALDH activity was found in the cytosolic fraction and about 10% in the mitochondrial fraction. The soluble fraction (cytosol) contained predominantly ALDH II, which suggests that cytosol is the main site for acetaldehyde oxidation in the placenta, but the enzyme activity is apparently too low to prevent the placental passage of the normal concentrations of blood acetaldehyde (<1 μmol) produced by maternal ethanol metabolism (Kouri et al, 1977; Meier-Tackmann et al, 1985). Thus, maternal acetaldehyde metabolism may have important implications concerning possible effects of circulating blood acetaldehyde on the fetus.

Brain

Human brain extracts contain only a small fraction of the ALDH activity present in the liver. At least two distinct ALDH isozymes have been detected in biopsy and autopsy specimens of human brains using acetaldehyde or propionaldehyde as substrate (Harada et al, 1980a; Inoue and Lindros, 1982; Pietruszko et al, 1987).

ALDH was found to be the main enzyme for the metabolism of biogenic aldehydes in human brain (Agarwal et al, 1982). In human autopsy brains, the cerebellum, corpus striatum, and pons showed the highest ALDH activity for 3,4-dihydroxyphenylacetaldehyde (DOPAL). In all regions, the total aldehyde-oxidizing capacity of brain tissue was twice as high for acetaldehyde as for DOPAL (Hafer et al, 1987). Most of the activity was found in the mitochondrial and microsomal fractions. Two activity bands on IEF gels and two K_m values indicate the presence of two distinct isozymes in all the fractions. Enzyme activities from both hemispheres did not differ significantly when expressed as either units/gram wet weight or as units/mg protein. The presence of DOPAC (acid metabolite of DOPAL) did not alter the ALDH activity, which indicates an absence of product inhibition. Pargyline, pyrazole, and ethanol, when present in the assay mixture, did not change the activity pattern either (Hafer et al, 1987).

Erythrocytes

Human blood shows a considerable acetaldehyde-oxidizing capacity (Inoue et al, 1978, 1979, 1984; Hellström et al 1983; Maring et al, 1983; Tottmar and Hellstöm, 1983). ALDH has been found to be present in erythrocytes (Harada et al, 1978; Pietruszko and Vallari, 1978; Inoue et al, 1979; Goedde et al, 1979a; Jones and Teng, 1983). Red cell ALDH is apparently identical with the liver cytosolic enzyme, which shows a relatively high K_m for aldehydes (Inoue et al, 1979). Our recent investigations clearly demonstrate that human erythrocyte and liver cytosolic enzymes are quite similar in their physical and kinetic properties (Agarwal et al, 1983; Goedde et al, 1983a; Agarwal et al, 1987). Both isozymes show a relatively moderate affinity for acetaldehyde. The K_m values with NAD^+ were very low for both enzymes. $NADP^+$ showed a poor coenzyme affinity. The isozymes from both sources are similar in their K_m values, pH optimum, isoelectric point, subunit molecular weight, immunological cross-reaction as well as in their inhibition with divalent cations, disulfiram, and certain drugs (Table 2.2).

Erythrocyte and liver ALDH II isozymes were also found very similar regarding the occurrence of additional bands that could be detected only when IEF was carried out at a very narrow pH range (Agarwal et al, 1987). When red cell hemolysates and liver extracts were subjected to IEF using ampholytes in the range of pH 4.0 to 6.5, ALDH II isozymes focused at about pH 5.1. However, occasionally an additional minor activity band was observed along with the prominent ALDH II band in hemolysates as well as in liver extracts (Fig. 2.3).

A total of four ALDH isozyme bands was detected on isoelectric focusing at narrow pH range. The profile showing additional minor bands was identical for the red cells and liver. The four activity bands were designated as a, b, c, and d according to their ascending isoelectric point. Apparently, band c represents the original prominent ALDH II band. The additional bands could have been generated from band c. Although the origin of these bands is unclear, they apparently represent secondary isozyme bands generated from the primary isozyme band designated as c (Agarwal et al, 1987).

Subcellular Localization

It is generally assumed that the low K_m isozyme (ALDH I) is predominantly localized in the mitochondria, and the high K_m isozymes (ALDH II, II, and IV) in the cytosol (Koivula and Koivusalo, 1975; Pietruszko et al, 1977; Eckfeldt and Yonetani, 1976; Koivula, 1977; Tank et al, 1981; Jenkins and Peters, 1983; Tipton and Henehan, 1984). However, data reported in the literature for the subcellular distribution of human liver ALDH isozymes are equivocal. Although Koivula (1975) reported the presence of the two major isozymes in the mito-

Table 2.2. Comparative biochemical and kinetic properties of human liver and erythrocyte ALDH II isozyme

	ALDH II ISOZYME	
PROPERTY	ERYTHROCYTES	LIVER
Specific activity of purified enzyme (mU/mg protein)	0.443	0.420
K_m (acetaldehyde)	98 μM	93 μM
Immunological cross-reaction with monospecific antibodies	+	+
Subunit molecular weight	51 000	53 000
Isoelectric point (pI)	5.02–5.18	5.05–5.16
pH optimum (0.1 M pyrophosphate)	8.5	8.5
Number of isozyme components after IEF (secondary isozymes)	4	4
K_m values of secondary isozymes	93–105 μM	91–99 μM
Disulfiram	Inhibitory	Inhibitory
Benzylthioisocyanate	Inhibitory	Inhibitory
Lithium	No inhibition	No inhibition

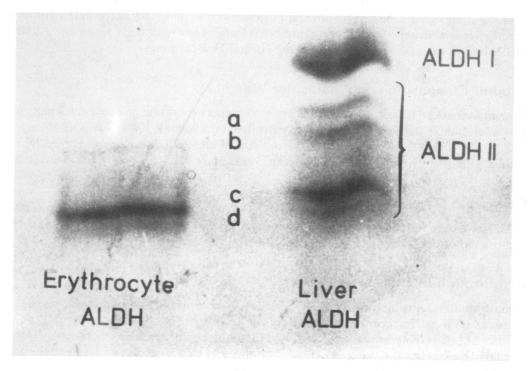

FIGURE 2.3. Polyacrylamide gel isoelectric focusing (pH range 5.0–5.5) pattern of human erythrocyte lysates and liver extracts. Different ALDH II activity bands are designated a to d (Agarwal et al, 1987).

chondrial as well as in the cytosolic fractions, Takada et al (1984) detected both ALDH I and ALDH II isozymes in the cytosol only. Thus, it may be misleading to designate only ALDH I as the mitochondrial isozyme and only ALDH II as the cytosolic isozyme (Meier-Tackmann et al 1988; Sugata et al. 1988).

In a recent study, both ALDH I and II isozymes were detected in soluble and particulate fractions of human autopsy livers (Meier-Tackmann et al 1988). Although both the homogenates and the cytosolic fractions showed strong ALDH I and ALDH II isozyme bands, the mitochondrial and microsomal fractions exhibited a prominent ALDH I and a weak ALDH II isozyme band. The mitochondrial fraction is composed of a very strong ALDH I and a very weak ALDH II band. Although the cytosolic fraction was contaminated with nuclei as was evident from the presence of the marker enzyme NMN-adenylyltransferase (NMNA), there was a negligible contamination from the microsomes and mitochondria. Likewise, the mitochondrial and microsomal fractions were almost free from the cytosolic marker enzyme. Hence, the bulk of ALDH I isozyme present in the cytosolic fraction cannot be accounted for only as being due to a mitochondrial contamination. Apparently, autopsy livers are not suitable for fractionation studies, since during postmortem conditions the lysis of cell membranes occurs, leading to a possible aggregation of the microsomes with the mitochondria (Pietruszko et al 1977).

BIOCHEMICAL CHARACTERISTICS OF ALDH ISOZYMES

Substrate Specificity and Michaelis Constants

All the ALDH isozymes show a broad range of substrate specificity for aliphatic and aromatic aldehydes. Although ALDH I and II both show K_m values in the micromolar range with acetaldehyde and propionaldehyde, the Michaelis constants for ALDH III and IV are millimolar

(Harada et al, 1980a; Goedde et al, 1983a; Forte-McRobbie and Pietruszko, 1985). However, the Michaelis constants for the coenzyme NAD^+ are in the millimolar range for ALDH I and II and in the micromolar range for the III and IV isozymes.

Subunit Composition and Molecular Weight

Human liver ALDH I and II isozymes are homotetramers consisting of unequal subunits with a MW of 54,800 and 54,200 daltons, respectively (Harada et al, 1980b). ALDH IV is a dimer of MW 175,000 daltons having a subunit size of about 70,000 daltons. The ALDH III is similar to or smaller than ALDH IV (Teng, 1983; Forte-McRobbie and Pietruszko, 1985).

Coenzyme Specificity

NAD^+ is the preferred coenzyme for the low K_m ALDH isozymes. The high K_m isozymes can use either NAD^+ or $NADP^+$ (Santisteban et al, 1985).

Disulfiram Inhibition

Disulfiram (tetraethylthiuram disulfide) is widely used clinically under the trade name Antabuse as an aversive agent in the treatment of alcoholism. Disulfiram and its metabolites inhibit ALDH activity in vitro and in vivo (Harada et al, 1982a). The cytoplasmic isozyme (ALDH II) is inhibited at much lower concentrations of disulfiram as compared to the other isozymes. In vitro studies showed that diethylamine is inhibitory to the low K_m mitochondrial enzyme (ALDH I) which may lead to the accumulation of acetaldehyde resulting in aversive reactions (Harada et al, 1982a).

Recent studies indicate that the mitochondrial isozyme (ALDH I) is strongly inhibited by a methanethiol mixed sulfide derivative of the potential physiological metabolite of disulfiram, viz. diethyldithiocarbamic acid (MacKerell et al, 1985). Since methanethiol has been shown to be a normal metabolite of methionine (Cooper, 1983), such mixed disulfides could be produced by reactions with disulfiram and diethyldithiocarbamic acid in vivo.

Stability

Whereas the cytoplasmic isozyme (ALDH II) is the most stable, the high K_m isozymes with benzaldehyde as the preferred substrate are the least stable (Harada et al, 1980a; Santisteban et al, 1985).

Immunological Interrelationship

Immunochemical relationship between various human ALDH isozymes is not conclusive. Although in some studies antibodies produced against human ALDH I and II isozymes precipitate each isozyme form (Pietruszko, 1980; Impraim et al, 1982; Santisteban et al, 1985; McMichael et al, 1986), other studies show a lack of such a cross-reaction (Agarwal et al, 1984; Goedde et al, 1985; Harrington et al, 1987; Johnson et al, 1987).

Structural Interrelationship

The primary structure of the subunits of the cytoplasmic (ALDH II) and mitochondrial (ALDH I) isozymes show that both types of subunits have 500 residues (Jörnvall et al, 1987). Although the cytosolic ALDH is acetylated at the N-terminus, the mitochondrial form has a ragged N-terminus with heterogeneous starting positions. There are extensive subunit differences between the two isozymes with positional identity of only 68% (Hempel et al, 1985).

These dissimilar regions may explain why the subunits from different isozymes do not form hybrid tetrameric molecules. The primary structure data, including the active site residues and coenzyme binding domain, clearly show that the tertiary structure of ALDH is unique and different from other dehydrogenases. The horse and human cytosolic ALDH isozymes are more similar (91% identity) than the human cytosolic and mitochondrial isozymes (68% identity), indicating an older evolutionary divergence of the two human isozymes as compared to the ancestral separation of man and horse (Jörnvall et al, 1987).

MOLECULAR GENETIC CHARACTERISTICS AND CHROMOSOMAL LOCALIZATION

Although the complete genomic structure of ALDH isozymes has yet to be established, the analysis of partial cDNA clones of human ALDH and the corresponding genomic regions have helped in the elucidation of the molecular structure of the ALDH isozymes (Hsu et al, 1985; Goedde and Agarwal, 1986a; Braun et al, 1987a). On the basis of partial cDNA sequencing, about 66% homology was observed between the coding regions of ALDH I and ALDH II isozymes (Hsu et al, 1985).

Partial ALDH I-cDNA Clones

cDNA clones were isolated from a human liver cDNA library constructed in the plasmid expression vector pEX, using monospecific antibodies against the mitochondrial isozyme (ALDH I). Four clones were chosen for further analysis based on the insert size and/or staining intensity. Bacterial clones pEXAL21, pEXAL31, and pEXAL43 expressed proteins of approximately 135 kD size fused with the β-galactosidase of pEX. Western blots showing the specific binding of anti-ALDH I antibody to the cro-β-galactosidase-cDNA fusion proteins synthesized by pEX clones are shown in Figure 2.4. Fusion protein of pEXAL51 gave a very faint signal, but the sequence data demonstrated a strong homology to the ALDH I-cDNA sequence (Goedde and Agarwal, 1986; Braun et al, 1987a).

Direct gel hybridization, as well as Southern blot analysis revealed that inserts of all four clones partly cross-hybridize (Fig. 2.5). The insert of pEXAL21 comprises 861 bp coding for 283 amino acids at the carboxy-terminal end of the protein. The insert of pEXAL43 contains the whole sequence of the cDNA insert of pEXAL21 and additional 330 bp coding for 110 amino acids at its 5'-end.

Restriction maps of the clones are shown in Fig. 2.6 (Braun et al, 1987a). Nucleotide sequence data obtained for pEXAL21 (Braun et al, 1987a) are listed in Fig. 2.7.

The sequences determined for the inserts of pEXAL21 and pEXAL43 showed only minor differences from those reported for the partial ALDH I-cDNA (Hsu et al, 1985) as well as 83% homology to the known amino acid sequence of ALDH II in the compared region (Hempel et al, 1984a).

Full-length ALDH I-cDNA Clone

Using an ALDH I-cDNA fragment, a full-length cDNA clone coding for the mitochondrial isozyme was isolated from a human fetal muscle cDNA library established in the expression vector lambda gt11 (Braun et al, 1987b). DNA was isolated from positive lambda clones and analyzed further by Southern blot hybridization and restriction mapping by the method of Maniatis et al (1982). The inserts were subcloned in M13 mp18 and mp19 and sequenced according to Sanger et al (1977). Full-length ALDH I-cDNA was subcloned downstream of a T3–RNA–polymerase promotor and transcribed in vitro with and without the capping reagent GpppG. The transcription mixture was directly translated in a rabbit reticulocyte ly-

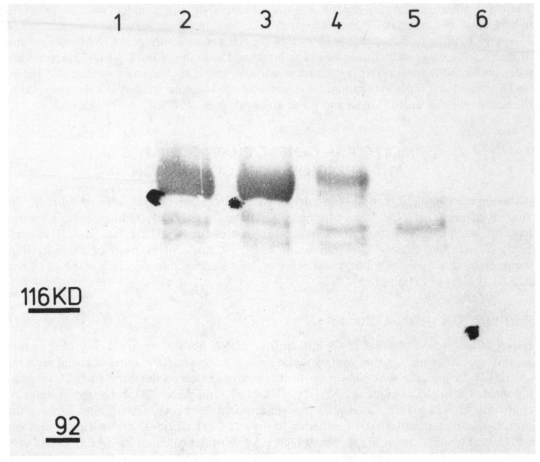

FIGURE 2.4. Specific binding of anti-ALDH antibody to the cro-β-galactosidase–cDNA fusion proteins synthesized by pEX clones indicated at the bottom of the lanes. Lane 1: cro-β-galactosidase protein without cDNA insert; lanes 2 to 6: fusion proteins produced by pEXAL21, pEXAL31, pEXAL43 and pEXAL51 (Braun et al, 1987a).

sate in the presence of ^{35}S-methionine and the synthesized proteins were separated on an SDS-polyacrylamide gel. A limited restriction map of the clone lambda cALI 23 and the sequence strategy is shown in Figure 2.8.

The nucleotide sequence of the insert that corresponds to the entire coding region of ALDH I-mRNA and the adjacent noncoding regions is shown in Fig. 2.9.

The nucleotide sequence showed a good agreement with the previously reported amino acid sequence for the mitochondrial isozyme (Hempel et al, 1985). A considerable homology was also observed in the major part of the enzyme when compared with the known amino acid sequence of the cytoplasmic enzyme (Hempel et al, 1984a) with the exception of the amino-terminal end of both the proteins (Fig. 2.10).

The first 20 amino acids of the deduced ALDH I sequence showed no homology to the corresponding sequence of ALDH I and ALDH II reported by Hempel et al (1984a, 1985). Moreover, an additional 15 residue peptide without a corresponding counterpart in the reported sequence of ALDH I and II was found at the amino-terminal end of the ALDH I. The whole of the 35 residue peptide seems to represent a leader peptide responsible for directing the protein uptake into the mitochondria. Similar to other known mitochondrial leader sequences, this peptide has less acidic residues and a higher than average content of basic residues separated by uncharged residues. However, the actual length of this putative signal peptide remains to be established (Braun et al, 1987b).

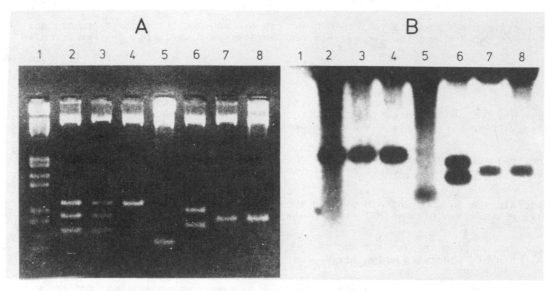

FIGURE 2.5. A: PstI cut plasmid DNAs of different positive clones separated on 1.1% agarose gel and stained with ethidium bromide. B: Autoradiogram of the same gel after hybridization with nick-translated pEXAL31 plasmid DNA. Lane 1: lambda DNA cut with EcoRI and HindIII: lanes 2 to 8: pEXAL51, pEXAL51, pEXAL43, pEXAL41, pEXAL31, pEXAL21, pEXAL21 (Braun et al, 1987a).

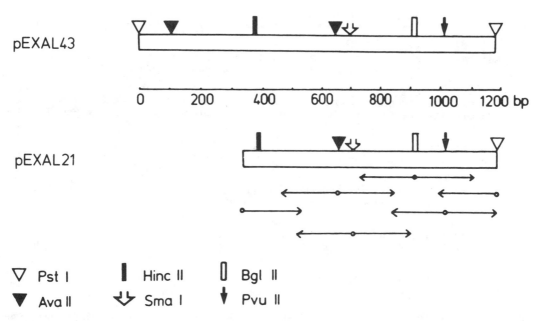

FIGURE 2.6. Partial restriction maps and sequencing strategy of the cDNA inserts of pEXAL21 and pEXAL43. Arrows mark the restriction sites sequenced from and the extent of the individual sequence determinations (Braun et al, 1987a).

mRNA Expression in Tissues

Studies on ALDH-mRNA have helped to understand its expression in fetal and adult liver (Goedde and Agarwal, 1986; Braun et al, 1987a). The messenger RNA of ALDH I was found by Northern blots to contain approximately 2350 nucleotides. Since the mature amino acid sequence of ALDH I accounts for 500 amino acids (Jörnvall et al, 1987), the coding part of

```
                 15                  30                  45                  60
ACA CCC TCC ACC CGC CTC TAT GTG GCC AAC CTG ATC AAG GAG GCT GGC TTT CCC CCT GGT
Thr Pro Ser Thr Arg Leu Tyr Val Ala Asn Leu Ile Lys Glu Ala Gly Phe Pro Pro Gly

                 75                  90                 105                 120
GTG GTC AAC ATT GTG CCT GGA TTT GGC CCC ACG GCT GGG CCG GCC ATT GCC TCC CAT GAG
Val Val Asn Ile Val Pro Gly Phe Gly Pro Thr Ala Gly Pro Ala Ile Ala Ser His Glu

                135                 150                 165                 180
GAT GTG GAC AAA GTG GCA TTC ACA GGC TCC ACT GAG ATT GGC CGC GTA ATC CAG GTT GCT
Asp Val Asp Lys Val Ala Phe Thr Gly Ser Thr Glu Ile Gly Arg Val Ile Gln Val Ala

                195                 210                 225                 240
GCT GGG AGC AGC AAC CTC AAG AGA GTG ACC TTG GAG CTG GGG GGG AAG AGC CCC AAC ATC
Ala Gly Ser Ser Asn Leu Lys Arg Val Thr Leu Glu Leu Gly Gly Lys Ser Pro Asn Ile

                255                 270                 285                 300
ATC ATG TCA GAT GCC GAT ATG GAT TGG GCC GTG GAA CAG GCC CAC TTC GCC CTG TTC TTC
Ile MET Ser Asp Ala Asp MET Asp Trp Ala Val Glu Gln Ala His Phe Ala Leu Phe Phe

                315                 330                 345                 360
AAC CAG GGC CAG TGC TGC TGT GCC GGC TCC CGG ACC TTC GTG CAG GAG GAC ATC TAT GAT
Asn Gln Gly Gln Cys Cys Cys Ala Gly Ser Arg Thr Phe Val Gln Glu Asp Ile Tyr Asp

                375                 390                 405                 420
GAG TTT GTG GTG CGG AGC GTT GCC CGG GCC AAG TCT CGG GTG GTC GGG AAC CCC TTT GAT
Glu Phe Val Val Arg Ser Val Ala Arg Ala Lys Ser Arg Val Val Gly Asn Pro Phe Asp

                435                 450                 465                 480
AGC AAG ACC GAG CAG GGG CCG CAG GTG GAT GAA ACT CAG TTT AAG AAG ATC CTC GGC TAC
Ser Lys Thr Glu Gln Gly Pro Gln Val Asp Glu Thr Gln Phe Lys Lys Ile Leu Gly Tyr

                495                 510                 525                 540
ATC AAC ACG GGG AAG CAA GAG GGG GCG AAG CTG CTG TGT GGT GGG GGC ATT GCT GCT GAC
Ile Asn Thr Gly Lys Gln Glu Gly Ala Lys Leu Leu Cys Gly Gly Gly Ile Ala Ala Asp

                555                 570                 585                 600
CGT GGT TAC TTC ATC CAG CCC ACT GTG TTT GGA GAT GTG CAG GAT GGC ATG ACC ATC GCC
Arg Gly Tyr Phe Ile Gln Pro Thr Val Phe Gly Asp Val Gln Asp Gly MET Thr Ile Ala

                615                 630                 645                 660
AAG GAG GAG ATC TTC GGG CCA GTG ATG CAG ATC CTG GAA GTT CAA GAC CAT AGA GGA GGT
Lys Glu Glu Ile Phe Gly Pro Val MET Gln Ile Leu Glu Val Gln Asp His Arg Gly Gly

                675                 690                 705                 720
TGT TGG GAG AGC CAA CAA TTC CAC GTA CGG GCT GGC GCA GCT GTC TTC GCA CAA AGG ATT
Cys Trp Glu Ser Gln Gln Phe His Val Arg Ala Gly Ala Ala Val Phe Ala Gln Arg Ile

                735                 750                 765                 780
TGG ACA AGG CCA ATT ACC TGT CCC AGC CCT CAG GCG GGC ACT GTG TGG GTC AAC TGC TAT
Trp Thr Arg Pro Ile Thr Cys Pro Ser Pro Gln Ala Gly Thr Val Trp Val Asn Cys Tyr

                795                 810                 825                 840
GAT GTG TTT GGA GCC CAG TCA CCC TTT GGT GGC TAC AAG ATG TCG GGG AGT GGC CGG GAG
Asp Val Phe Gly Ala Gln Ser Pro Phe Gly Gly Tyr Lys MET Ser Gly Ser Gly Arg Glu

                855
TTG GGC GAG TAC GGG CTG CAG
Leu Gly Glu Tyr Gly Leu Gln
```

FIGURE 2.7. Nucleotide sequence of the cDNA insert of pEXAL21. Sequencing was done using the chain terminator method or by chemical cleavage (Braun et al, 1987a).

ALDH-mRNA comprises 1500 nucleotides. The 3'-noncoding part contains 403 nucleotides (Hsu et al, 1985). Because mammalian messages may contain poly (A) tails of 200 nucleotides in length (Lee et al, 1971), it is likely that the remaining 200 nucleotides are not fully covered by the 5'-noncoding region of ALDH-mRNA. Hybridization at high stringency to the heterologic horse liver RNA (Fig. 2.11), as well as length comparison, suggested a very close relationship between horse and humans at RNA level, as also reported at the protein level by von Bahr-Lindström et al (1984).

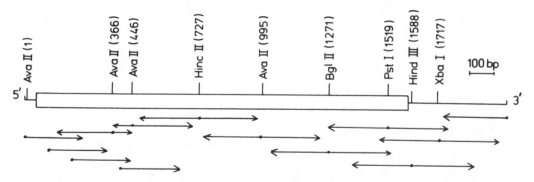

FIGURE 2.8. Partial restriction maps and sequencing strategy of the cDNA inserts of lambda cALI 23. Arrows mark the restriction sites sequenced from and the extent of the individual sequence determinations (Braun et al, 1987b).

Northern blot analysis of human adult and fetal livers revealed four- to fivefold stronger hybridization signals in the adult liver. Generally, a lower transcription level of ALDH I gene was observed in fetal tissues than in the corresponding adult tissues (Fig. 2.12). No signals were detected in fetal cortex even after overexposure.

Chromosomal Localization of ALDH Isozymes

Several reports have appeared in recent years assigning the mitochondrial isozyme (ALDH I) gene to chromosome 12 (Hsu et al, 1985; Smith et al, 1985, 1986; Braun et al, 1986; Goedde and Agarwal, 1986). A cloned 850 bp cDNA fragment corresponding to the 3'-coding part of human ALDH I–mRNA was used as a probe. Southern blot analysis of human–rodent somatic cell hybrids indicated that the human ALDH I gene is localized on chromosome 12 (Fig. 2.13).

The cytoplasmic isozyme (ALDH II) has been reported to be located at chromosome 9 (Hsu et al, 1986) and the less characterized isozyme ALDH III (ALDH3) has been mapped at chromosome 17 (Santisteban et al, 1985).

GENETIC VARIATION IN ALDH ISOZYMES

Although studies reported in recent years have clearly indicated that ALDH exists in more than one molecular form in human organs and tissues, genetic variations in these forms were not detected until recently. Although a widely prevalent genetic polymorphism has been observed for ALDH I, only a few cases of variation in ALDH II have been reported. It is also presumed that the ALDH III isozyme is polymorphic.

Polymorphism of ALDH I

Using simple electrophoretic methods, no variation was observed in ALDH isozymes from Japanese autopsy liver specimens by Stamatoyannopoulos et al (1975). On electrophoresis in starch gel, autopsy liver extracts from Germans showed both the major and minor ALDH bands without any hint of the existence of a polymorphism (Harada et al, 1978). However, when analyzed with modified electrophoretic methods, variation in ALDH I isozyme was found in the liver specimens of Japanese (Goedde et al, 1979b; Harada et al, 1980b; Agarwal et al, 1981). About 50% of the Japanese liver samples analyzed showed a lack of the ALDH I

```
        .         .        30         .         .        60
GCUCUCGGUCCGCUCGCUGUCCGCUAGCCCGCUGCGAUGUUGCGCGCUGCCGCCGCUCGG
                                    MetLeuArgAlaAlaAlaAlaArg

        .         .        90         .         .       120
GCCCCGCCUGGCCGCCGCCUCUUGUCAGCCGCCGCCACCCAGGCCGUGCCUGCCCCCAAC
AlaProProGlyArgArgLeuLeuSerAlaAlaAlaThrGlnAlaValProAlaProAsn

        .         .       150         .         .       180
CAGCAGCCCGAGGUCUUCUGCAACCAGAUUUUCAUAAACAAUGAAUGGCACGAUGCCGUC
GlnGlnProGluValPheCysAsnGlnIlePheIleAsnAsnGluTrpHisAspAlaVal

        .         .       210         .         .       240
AGCAGGAAAACAUUCCCCACCGUCAAUCCGUCCACUGGAGAGGUCAUCUGUCAGGUAGCU
SerArgLysThrPheProThrValAsnProSerThrGlyGluValIleCysGlnValAla

        .         .       270         .         .       300
GAAGGGGACAAGGAAGAUGUGGACAAGGCAGUGAAGGCCGCCCGGGCCGCCUUCCAGCUG
GluGlyAspLysGluAspValAspLysAlaValLysAlaAlaArgAlaAlaPheGlnLeu

        .         .       330         .         .       360
GGCUCACCUUGGCGCCGCAUGGACGCAUCACACAGCGGCCGGCUGCUGAACCGCCUGGCC
GlySerProTrpArgArgMetAspAlaSerHisSerGlyArgLeuLeuAsnArgLeuAla

        .         .       390         .         .       420
GAUCUGAUCGAGCGGGACCGGACCUACCUGGCGGCCUUGGAGACCCUGGACAAUGGCAAG
AspLeuIleGluArgAspArgThrTyrLeuAlaAlaLeuGluThrLeuAspAsnGlyLys

        .         .       450         .         .       480
CCCUAUGUCAUCUCCUACCUGGUGGAUUUGGACAUGGUCCUCAAAUGUCUCCGGUAUUAU
ProTyrValIleSerTyrLeuValAspLeuAspMetValLeuLysCysLeuArgTyrTyr

        .         .       510         .         .       540
GCCGGCUGGGCUGAUAAGUACCACGGGAAAACCAUCCCCAUUGACGGAGACUUCUUCAGC
AlaGlyTrpAlaAspLysTyrHisGlyLysThrIleProIleAspGlyAspPhePheSer

        .         .       570         .         .       600
UACACACGCCAUGAACCUGUGGGGGUGUGCGGGCAGAUCAUUCCGUGGAAUUUCCCGCUC
TyrThrArgHisGluProValGlyValCysGlyGlnIleIleProTrpAsnPheProLeu

        .         .       630         .         .       660
CUGAUGCAAGCAUGGAAGCUGGGCCCAGCCUUGGCAACUGGAAACGUGGUUGUGAUGAAG
LeuMetGlnAlaTrpLysLeuGlyProAlaLeuAlaThrGlyAsnValValValMetLys

        .         .       690         .         .       720
GUAGCUGAGCAGACACCCCUCACCGCCCUCUAUGUGGCCAACCUGAUCAAGGAGGCUGGC
ValAlaGluGlnThrProLeuThrAlaLeuTyrValAlaAsnLeuIleLysGluAlaGly

        .         .       750         .         .       780
UUUCCCCCUGGUGUGGUCAACAUUGUGCCUGGAUUUGGCCCCACGGCUGGGGCCGCCAUU
PheProProGlyValValAsnIleValProGlyPheGlyProThrAlaGlyAlaAlaIle

        .         .       810         .         .       840
GCCUCCCAUGAGGAUGUGGACAAAGUGGCAUUCACAGGCUCCACUGAGAUUGGCCGCGUA
AlaSerHisGluAspValAspLysValAlaPheThrGlySerThrGluIleGlyArgVal

        .         .       870         .         .       900
AUCCAGGUUGCUGCUGGGAGCAGCAACCUCAAGAGAGUGACCUUGGAGCUGGGGGGAAG
IleGlnValAlaAlaGlySerSerAsnLeuLysArgValThrLeuGluLeuGlyGlyLys

        .         .       930         .         .       960
AGCCCCAACAUCAUCAUGUCAGAUGCCGAUAUGGAUUGGGCCGUGGAACAGGCCCACUUC
SerProAsnIleIleMetSerAspAlaAspMetAspTrpAlaValGluGlnAlaHisPhe

        .         .       990         .         .      1020
GCCCUGUUCUUCAACCAGGGCCAGUGCUGCUGUGCCGGCUCCCGGACCUUCGUGCAGGAG
AlaLeuPhePheAsnGlnGlyGlnCysCysCysAlaGlySerArgThrPheValGlnGlu

        .         .      1050         .         .      1080
GACAUCUAUGAUGAGUUUGUGGUGCGGAGCGUUGCCCGGGCCAAGUCUCGGGUGGUCGGG
AspIleTyrAspGluPheValValArgSerValAlaArgAlaLysSerArgValValGly

        .         .      1110         .         .      1140
AACCCCUUUGAUAGCAAGACCGAGCAGGGGCCGCAGGUGGAUGAAACUCAGUUUAAGAAG
AsnProPheAspSerLysThrGluGlnGlyProGlnValAspGluThrGlnPheLysLys

        .         .      1170         .         .      1200
AUCCUCGGCUACAUCAACACGGGGAAGCAAGAGGGGGCGAAGCUGCUGUGUGGUGGGGGC
IleLeuGlyTyrIleAsnThrGlyLysGlnGluGlyAlaLysLeuLeuCysGlyGlyGly

        .         .      1230         .         .      1260
AUUGCUGCUGACCGUGGUUACUUCAUCCAGCCCACUGUGUUUGGAGAUGUGCAGGAUGGC
IleAlaAlaAspArgGlyTyrPheIleGlnProThrValPheGlyAspValGlnAspGly

        .         .      1290         .         .      1320
AUGACCAUCGCCAAGGAGGAGAUCUUCGGGCCAGUGAUGCAGAUCCUGAAGUUCAAGACC
MetThrIleAlaLysGluGluIlePheGlyProValMetGlnIleLeuLysPheLysThr

        .         .      1350         .         .      1380
AUAGAGGAGGUUGUUGGGAGAGCCAACAAUUCCACGUACGGGCUGGCCGCAGCUGUCUUC
IleGluGluValValGlyArgAlaAsnAsnSerThrTyrGlyLeuAlaAlaAlaValPhe

        .         .      1410         .         .      1440
ACAAAGGAUUUGGACAAGGCCAAUUACCUGUCCCACGCCCUCCAGGCGGGCACUGUGUGG
ThrLysAspLeuAspLysAlaAsnTyrLeuSerGlnAlaLeuGlnAlaGlyThrValTrp

        .         .      1470         .         .      1500
GUCAACUGCUAUGAUGUGUUUGGAGCCCAGUCACCCUUUGGUGGCUACAAGAUGUCGGGG
ValAsnCysTyrAspValPheGlyAlaGlnSerProPheGlyGlyTyrLysMetSerGly

        .         .      1530         .         .      1560
AGUGGCCGGGAGUUGGGCGAGUACGGGCUGCAGGCAUACACUGAAGUGAAAACUGUCACA
SerGlyArgGluLeuGlyGluTyrGlyLeuGlnAlaTyrThrGluValLysThrValThr

        .         .      1590         .         .      1620
GUCAAAGUGCCUCAGAAGAACUCAUAAGAAUCAUGCAAGCUUCCUCCCUCAGCCAUUGAU
ValLysValProGlnLysAsnSer

        .         .      1650         .         .      1680
GGAAAGUUCAGCAAGAUCAGCAACAAAACCAAGAAAAAUGAUCCUUGCGUGCUGAAUAUC

        .         .      1710         .         .      1740
UGAAAAGAGAAAUUUUUCCUACAAAAUCUCUUGGGUCAAGAAAGUUCUAGAAUUUGAAUU

        .         .      1770         .         .      1800
GAUAAACAUGGUGGGUUGGCUGAGGGUAAGAGUAUAUGAGGAACCUUUUAAACGACAACA

        .         .      1830         .         .      1860
AUACUGCUAGCUUUCAGGAUGAUUUUUAAAAAAUAGAUUCAAAUGUGUUAUCCUCUCUCU

        .         .      1890         .         .      1920
GAAACGCUUCCUAUAACUCGAGUUUAUAGGGGAAGAAAAAGCUAUUGUUUACAAUUAUAU

        .         .      1950         .         .      1980
CACCAUUAAGGCAACUGCUACACCCUGCUUUGUAUUCUGGGCUAAGAUUCAUUAAAAACU

        .         .      2010
AGCUGCUCUUAAAAAAAAAAAAAAAAAAAAA
```

FIGURE 2.9. Nucleotide sequence of the cDNA insert of lambda cALI 23 (Braun et al, 1987b).

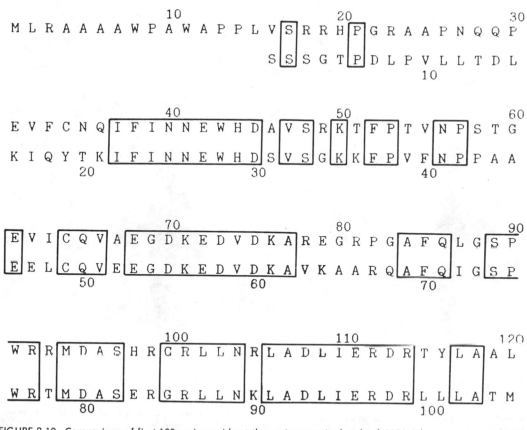

FIGURE 2.10. Comparison of first 100 amino acids at the amino-terminal ends of ALDH I (upper sequence) and ALDH II (lower sequence) (Braun et al, 1987b).

isozyme activity band. A typical ALDH isozyme pattern obtained after isoelectric focusing of the liver extracts from Caucasians and Orientals is shown in Figure 2.14.

Many subsequent reports confirmed that about 50% of the Chinese and Japanese livers show ALDH I isozyme deficiency (Teng 1981; Goedde et al, 1983a; Ricciardi et al, 1983a; Goedde et al, 1985; Rex et al, 1985). When autopsy specimens of Chinese subjects were analyzed, the isozyme deficiency was also found to be prevalent in other organs and tissues of the same individual whose liver was found deficient in ALDH I isozyme (unpublished results).

Incidence of ALDH I Isozyme Deficiency in Different Populations

Since it is not feasible to carry out population genetic studies using liver biopsy and autopsy samples, screening of ALDH I deficiency in diverse populations has been made using hair root follicle extracts as the source of enzyme activity (Goedde et al, 1980). As shown in Figure 2.15, Oriental populations of Mongoloid origin showed varying degrees of isozyme deficiency, whereas none of the Caucasian or Negroid populations have this isozyme abnormality (Goedde et al, 1983b, 1983c, 1984a, 1984b, 1985, 1986; Agarwal and Goedde, 1987a; Goedde and Agarwal, 1986b, 1987a).

Among Native Indians, about 40% of the South American Indian tribes (Mapuche, Atacameños, Shuara) showed ALDH deficiency, while the isozyme deficiency was detected only in a very small percentage of the Sioux, Navajo, and Mestizo tribes (Goedde et al, 1986b; Table 2.3).

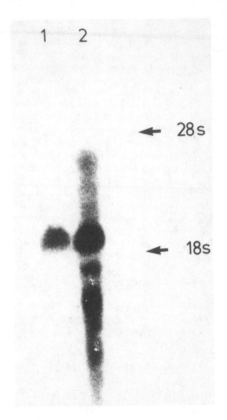

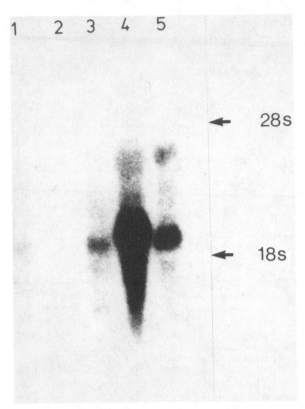

FIGURE 2.11. Northern blot analysis of mRNA from human adult liver (lane 1) and horse liver (lane 2) (Braun et al, 1987a).

FIGURE 2.12. Northern blot analysis of RNAs from different tissues. Lane 1: fetal muscle; lane 2: fetal brain; lane 3: fetal thymus; lane 4: adult liver; lane 5: fetal liver (Braun et al, 1987a).

HUMAN CHROMOSOMES

Hybrids	1	2	3	4	5	6	7	8	9	10	11	12	13	14	15	16	17	18	19	20	21	22	X	Y	ALDH I
RAG GM 194 -7																									
RAG GO 4																									
A9 SU 1-2																									
A9 JT 2-21-14																									
RAG GM 610 5-23																									
RAG GM 610 3-4																									
A9 Call 1-9-9																									
RAG PJ 7-2																									

FIGURE 2.13. Segregation of human ALDH I in a panel of human–mouse somatic cell hybrids. Filled spaces indicate the presence of the chromosome, half-filled spaces indicate that part of the chromosome is present, and empty spaces indicate that the chromosome was not detected by biochemical and cytological analysis. ALDH I segregates concordantly with chromosome 12 (Braun et al, 1986).

In other recent reports, no deficiency of ALDH I isozyme in autopsy livers of American Indians of Northern New Mexico was found (Rex et al, 1985). Only 16% of the Oklahoma Indians were found deficient when their hair roots were analyzed for an ALDH I isozyme activity profile (Zeiner et al, 1984).

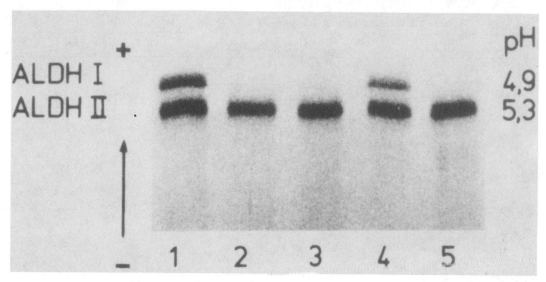

FIGURE 2.14. Isoelectric focusing pattern of ALDH isozymes from Caucasian and Oriental liver extracts. Lanes 1 and 4: normal type; lanes 2, 3, and 5: deficient type.

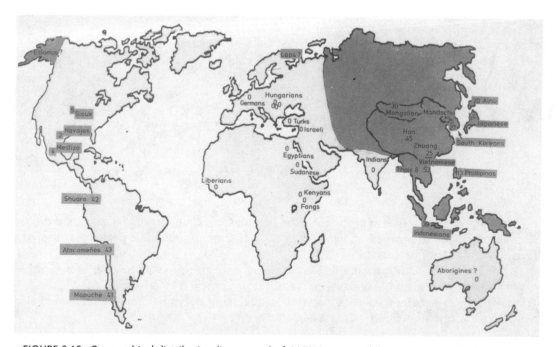

FIGURE 2.15. Geographical distribution (in percent) of ALDH I isozyme deficiency in different populations.

ALDH II Isozyme Abnormality

Variation in ALDH II isozyme has been found to be less common as compared to the wide prevalence of ALDH I deficiency observed so far. Hitherto, only two cases of ALDH II abnormality have been reported in Chinese autopsy livers (Yoshida et al, 1983; Eckey et al, 1986) and in the blood of a Thai subject (Eckey et al, 1986). In a Chinese autopsy liver, while the major isozyme band was nearly absent, several additional minor bands were observed on isoelectric focusing gels (Fig. 2.16).

Table 2.3. Distribution of ALDH I isozyme deficiency in different populations

POPULATION	SAMPLE SIZE	% DEFICIENT
ORIENTALS		
Ainu	80	20
Chinese		
Mongolian	198	30
Zhuang	106	25
Han	120	45
Korean (Mandschu)	209	25
Indonesians	30	39
Japanese	184	44
Koreans (South)	75	27
Philippinos	110	13
Thais (North)	110	8
Vietnamese	138	53
SOUTH AMERICAN INDIANS		
Atachamenos (Chile)	133	43
Mapuche (Chile)	64	41
Shuara (Ecuador)	99	42
NORTH AMERICAN INDIANS		
Navajo (New Mexico)	56	2
Sioux (North Dakota)	90	5
MEXICAN INDIANS		
Mestizo (Mexico City)	43	4
CAUCASIANS AND BLACKS		
Asian Indians	50	0
Egyptians	260	0
Fangs	37	0
Germans	300	0
Hungarians	177	0
Israeli	77	0
Kenyans	23	0
Liberians	184	0
Matyo	106	0
Romai	84	0
Sudanese	40	0
Turks	65	0

A similar pattern was also observed in the hemolysate from a healthy Thai blood donor. Rabbit antibodies to purified human liver ALDH II showed immunological cross-reactivity for the variant enzyme bands (Fig. 2.17).

The existence of additional minor bands indicates the presence of tetramer hybrid forms made up of normal and variant monomers and may represent a heterozygous form of ALDH II variation with a mutant allele leading to the synthesis of enzyme subunits with altered electrophoretic properties (Eckey et al, 1986).

ALDH III Isozyme Polymorphism

The high K_m ALDH III isozyme is not always detectable in human liver extracts and may be polymorphic. The corresponding isozyme in the stomach shows several activity bands and seems to be polymorphic (Teng et al, 1983; Duley et al, 1985; Santisteban et al, 1985). In another study (Meier-Tackmann et al, 1984), the stomach isozyme was found to resolve into several bands when focused at about pH 6.0. While stomach samples from the Germans showed a maximum of four bands, the stomach samples from the Chinese showed up to three such activity bands. Apparently, some of these bands were produced as a result of postmortem alterations leading to the artefactual formation of secondary isozymes (Meier-Tackmann et al, 1984).

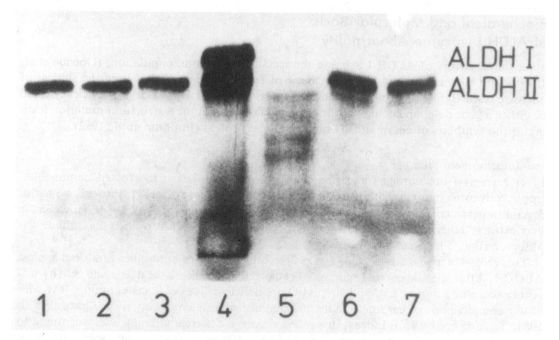

FIGURE 2.16. Isoelectric focusing patterns of ALDH isozymes from erythrocyte hemolysates and liver extract. Samples 1, 2, 3, 6, and 7: hemolysates from healthy blood donors; sample 4: liver extract; sample 5: a hemolysate from a Thai individual showing an atypical ALDH II pattern (Eckey et al, 1986).

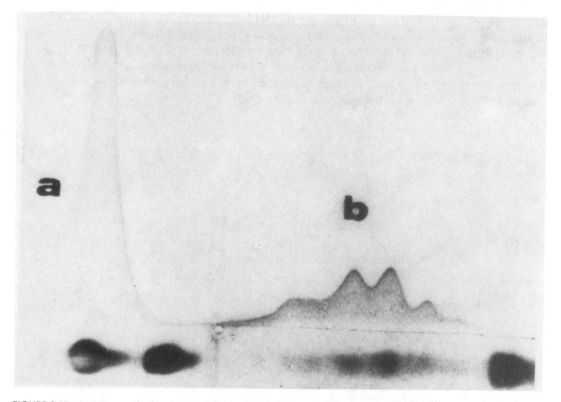

FIGURE 2.17. Antigen–antibody crossed immunoelectrophoresis. First dimension: isoelectric focusing in agarose gel; second dimension; immunoelectrophoresis in agarose gel containing antibodies against ALDH II. Sample a: normal Chinese liver extract; Sample b: Chinese liver with an atypical ALDH II isozyme. The precipitin peaks were stained with Coomassie Brillant Blue R (Eckey et al, 1986).

Biochemical and Molecular Basis of ALDH I Isozyme Abnormality

Since the discovery of ALDH I isozyme abnormality in Oriental populations (Goedde et al, 1979b), the biochemical and molecular basis of enzyme deficiency has been the subject of intensive research in past years. The underlying cause of the ALDH I isozyme deficiency could be either a gene deletion coding for the enzyme (Teng, 1981), or a structural mutation leading to the synthesis of enzymatically nonfunctional protein (Impraim et al, 1982).

Immunochemical Studies

Liver extracts from normal Caucasians and Orientals, subjected to crossed immunoelectrophoresis using a mixture of antibodies against ALDH I and ALDH II, showed two major precipitin peaks corresponding to the respective isozymes (Agarwal et al, 1984). However, in liver extracts deficient in ALDH I, a smaller peak with a minor shift towards the cathode was observed (Fig. 2.18A and B).

This cross-reactive material (CRM) was detectable only with antibodies produced against ALDH I. After specific enzyme staining of the precipitin peaks, a weak enzyme activity was visible corresponding to CRM. Thus, ALDH I-deficient liver extracts contain CRM with nearly complete loss of enzyme activity and diminished antigenic properties (Agarwal et al, 1984; Yoshida et al, 1984). Indeed, in a recent report, a deficient Oriental liver was found to be enzymatically active but showed an altered maximum velocity and isoelectric point (Ferencz-Biro and Pietruszko, 1984). However, other authors do not support the notion that ALDH I-deficient livers contain sufficient enzyme activity (Yoshida and Davé, 1985).

Amino Acid Sequence

The immunological CRM isolated from the ALDH I-deficient Oriental liver has been found to contain an amino acid substitution; glutamic acid at the 14th position from the C-terminus has been substituted in the deficient isozyme by lysine (Hempel et al, 1984b; Hsu et al, 1985). Functionally, a single base mutation at position -14 resulting in a loss of catalytic activity is compatible with the proximity in primary structure between this region and the segment that contains cysteine residues (Hempel et al, 1984b, 1985).

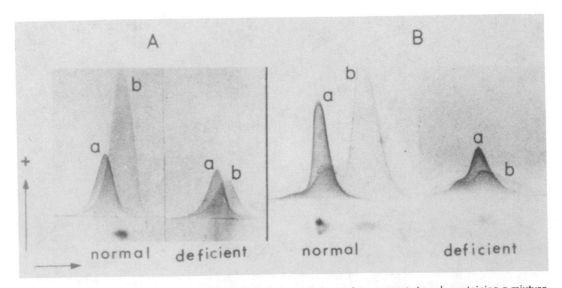

FIGURE 2.18. Crossed immunoelectrophoresis of normal and deficient liver extracts in gels containing a mixture of antibodies against ALDH I and ALDH II. A: electrophoresis in first dimension; B: isoelectric focusing in first direction; a: precipitin peak for ALDH II; b: precipitin peak for ALDH I (Agarwal et al, 1984).

The existence of a single amino acid exchange in the enzymatically inactive ALDH I isozyme has been further confirmed by the nucleotide sequence of a partial cDNA clone for human ALDH I (Hsu et al, 1985).

PHYSIOLOGICAL ROLE AND FUNCTIONAL IMPLICATIONS OF ALDH ISOZYMES

Acetaldehyde-mediated Acute Reactions to Alcohol

Severe hemodynamic changes associated with facial flush are commonly observed after an acute dose of ethanol in certain Orientals. The individual and racial differences in euphoric and dysphoric response to alcohol have been reported in various ethnic and racial groups (Morikawa et al, 1968; Wolff, 1972, 1973; Ewing et al, 1974; Reed et al, 1976; Mizoi et al, 1979; Zeiner et al, 1979). The alcohol sensitivity symptoms include facial flushing, hot feeling in stomach, palpitation, tachycardia, and muscle weakness (Table 2.4).

A greater percentage of Orientals of Mongoloid heritage and American Indians have been found to respond to a mild dose of ethanol when compared to Caucasians. In Figure 2.19, a Japanese female is shown before and after drinking a mild dose of ethanol. As evident, a marked facial flush is visible after alcohol intake.

Acetaldehyde seems to be mainly responsible for most of the severe symptoms of alcohol-related sensitivity. Higher steady-state blood acetaldehyde levels have been noted postdrink in those Japanese and Chinese subjects who show flushing after drinking mild doses of alcohol (Ewing et al, 1974; Reed et al, 1976; Zeiner et al, 1976; Mizoi et al, 1979; Zeiner et al, 1979; Harada et al, 1981).

Several explanations have been given for higher blood acetaldehyde concentrations: (1) differential base rates of alcohol metabolism among different racial groups (2) faster absorption rate of ethanol observed in Chinese and American Indians (3) ethnic differences in clearance of acetaldehyde and (4) genetically determined variant forms of liver ADH and/or ALDH.

The atypical ADH, which is quite frequent in the Japanese, was suggested to produce sensitivity symptoms by rapidly oxidizing ethanol to acetaldehyde (Stamatoyannopoulos et al, 1975). However, no significant difference in the rate of alcohol metabolism has been noted in normal and atypical ADH phenotype carriers (Edwards and Price Evans, 1967). Moreover, no difference in the elimination rate of alcohol was found between flushing and nonflushing subjects (Mizoi et al, 1985).

ALDH I Isozyme Polymorphism and Alcohol Sensitivity

As originally suggested by Goedde et al (1979b), the ALDH I isozyme deficiency commonly found among Orientals could be responsible for the alcohol sensitivity symptoms experienced after alcohol ingestion. Indeed, a positive correlation between alcohol sensitivity and elevated

Table 2.4. Alcohol sensitivity symptoms commonly observed in Orientals after an acute dose of ethanol

SUBJECTIVE SYMPTOMS	OBJECTIVE SYMPTOMS
Cutaneous and facial flushing	Cardiac depression
Blotching of the trunk and arms	Hypotension
Hot feeling in the stomach	Tachycardia
Dizziness/hangover	Bradycardia
Numbness in hands or feet	Peripheral vasodilation
Chest distress/palpitation	Increased skin temperature
Muscular weakness	Augumented flow in arteries

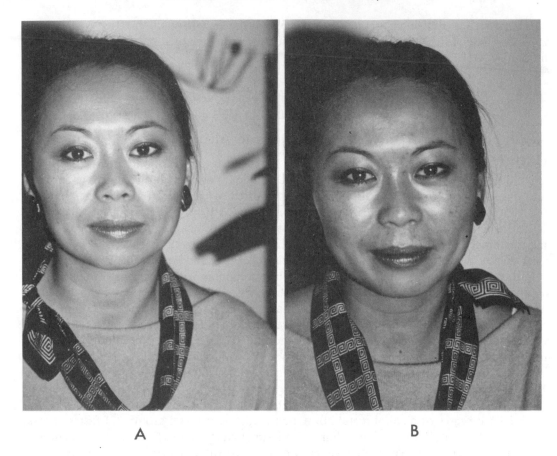

A   B

FIGURE 2.19. A Japanese female before (A) and after (B) drinking a mild dose of ethanol. The facial flush was
visible after about 15 min postdrink.

blood acetaldehyde level in conjunction with ALDH I deficiency was noted in Japanese subjects given an acute dose of alcohol (Harada et al, 1981). In contrast to a near absence of
blood acetaldehyde in nonflushing subjects, individuals who responded by facial flushing and
tachycardia were found to have up to 35 μmoles of blood acetaldehyde after drinking alcohol while the blood ethanol levels were identical in the deficient and normal subjects (Harada
et al, 1981; Goedde et al, 1983a; Mizoi et al, 1983; Inoue et al, 1984). In addition, rise in
plasma level of catecholamines and urinary excretion of catecholamines was also observed in
subjects sensitive to alcohol (Mizoi et al, 1982).

   Thus, the initial vasomotor flushing after alcohol ingestion in Orientals is due to their inability to metabolize acetaldehyde quickly and effectively in the absence of the low K_m
ALDH isozyme I (Goedde et al, 1979b; Agarwal et al, 1981; Harada et al, 1981; Goedde et
al, 1982; Goedde et al, 1983d; Mizoi et al, 1983; von Wartburg and Bühler, 1984; Kogame
and Mizoi, 1985; Lehmann et al, 1986). Thus, impaired oxidation of acetaldehyde, not its
higher-than-normal production through an atypical ADH, may be primarily responsible for
alcohol sensitivity.

   A diagramatic explanation of this hypothesis is shown in Figure 2.20.

   Apparently, slow acetaldehyde oxidation due to ALDH I isozyme abnormality leads to elevated blood acetaldehyde levels resulting in vasodilation associated with dysphoric symptoms.
The enzymatically inactive mitochondrial ALDH isozyme, combined with a rapid ethanol
metabolism catalyzed by the superactive atypical ADH, might be primarily responsible for

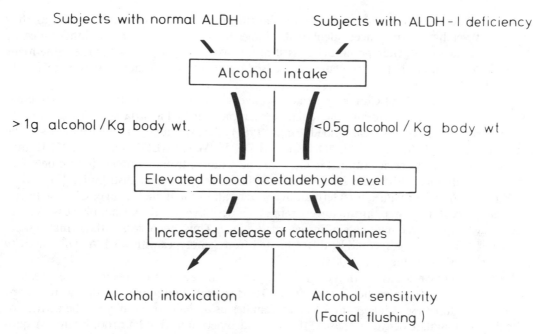

FIGURE 2.20. Hypothetical mechanism of flushing response in ALDH I deficient individuals (Agarwal et al, 1987).

Table 2.5. Frequency of atypical ADH, ALDH deficiency, alcohol sensitivity, and alcohol metabolism rate in different racial groups (Agarwal and Goedde, 1986)

GROUP	ATYPICAL ADH	ALDH DEFICIENCY	ADVERSE RESPONSE	METABOLISM RATE (mg ethanol/kg/h)
		% INCIDENCE		
Caucasians	5–20	0	4–12	93–145
Mongoloids	85–98	20–53	60–85	110–146
Native Americans (North and South)	2–5	2–43	80–90	92–183

the intense aversive reactions commonly observed in Orientals after drinking a small dose of alcohol. Average frequency of ALDH deficiency, atypical ADH, alcohol sensitivity, and alcohol metabolic rate in Caucasians, Orientals, and native Americans are summarized in Table 2.5.

Inheritance of ALDH Deficiency and Flushing Response

Familial resemblances in flushing response to alcohol have also been observed (Schwitters et al, 1982a; Johnson et al, 1984). It was suggested that two types of flushing might exist: fast flush (one or less drinks to evoke flushing) and slow flush (two or more drinks to evoke flushing). Highly significant family resemblances in flushing were found. However, the present knowledge does not permit us to conclude that flushing is controlled by a single autosomal dominant gene.

Family studies regarding ALDH deficiency and alcohol sensitivity are subject to various handicaps. First, it is often difficult to collect hair samples from small children and second, quite often no information is available on the flushing response of the offspring as they might not yet have experienced alcohol drinking. Regarding the mode of inheritance of ALDH deficiency, a genotype model consisting of two common alleles for the same locus expressed codominantly has been suggested based on an analysis of autopsy livers (Yoshida et al, 1983).

In a random sample of Chinese postmortem livers, ALDH I was found completely missing in 45% of the specimens and the remaining samples showed a variable staining intensity ranging from weak to very weak (Goedde et al, 1985). This variability in intensity hints at the existence of two allelic genes, ALDH I^1 and ALDH I^2. When ALDH I and ALDH II antigen concentrations were determined in German and Chinese livers by rocket immunoelectrophoresis, the quotients of ALDH I/ALDH II protein showed a trimodal distribution (Fig. 2.21).

While the quotient values for German livers were all in the highest range, Chinese livers, deficient in ALDH I, were in the lowest range. Chinese livers with normal or weak ALDH I band intensity showed quotients of intermediate range. Thus, genotypes with normal activity of ALDH I (homozygotes) could be differentiated from genotypes with weak ALDH I activity (heterozygotes) (Goedde et al, 1985).

Immunochemical determination of ALDH I protein in hair root lysates may give a reliable estimate of the presence or the absence of ALDH isozymes. Preliminary studies were carried out on some Japanese, Chinese, and Korean families using hair root follicles. The activity of mitochondrial malate dehydrogenase (MDH) was also determined in hair root lysates. A quo-

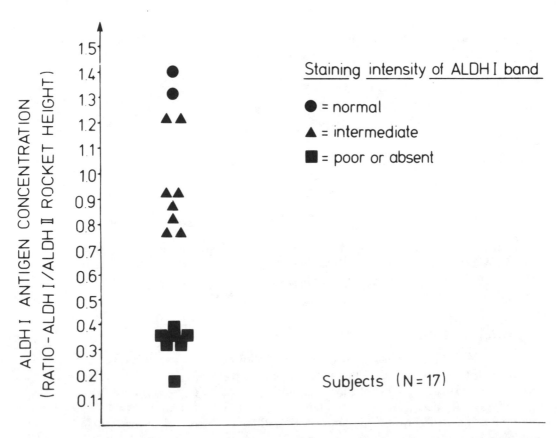

FIGURE 2.21. Distribution of ALDH I/ALDH II ratios in normal and deficient livers of Caucasian and Chinese subjects as determined by rocket immunoelectrophoresis using specific antibodies against human liver ALDH I and ALDH II (Goedde et al, 1985).

tient of ALDH antigen concentration and MDH activity was used as a parameter for the actual values for ALDH activity (Goedde et al, 1985). As shown in Table 2.6, the family members could be divided into three distinct phenotype groups representing normal (homozygotes), intermediate (heterozygotes), and deficient (homozygotes) genotypes.

These results clearly suggested that ALDH protein concentration in tissues is under genetic control and varies according to the genotype of an individual. The distribution of ALDH I deficiency in two typical Oriental families is shown in Fig. 2.22.

An autosomal codominant mode of inheritance for the deficiency is suggested (Goedde et al, 1985, 1986). However, more family studies need to be carried out to confirm these results. Moreover, these data do not allow any conclusion regarding the mode of inheritance of flushing response in families.

The phenotyping method using human hair roots and the genotyping method using autopsie livers are not only difficult to carry out but are sometimes unreliable due to various technical reasons. Recent molecular genetic studies on human ALDH I enzyme have provided DNA sequence information not only in the region of the mutation but also give the nucleotide sequence in the regions flanking the mutation. Thus, appropriate nucleotides can be used to act as primers for the polymerase chain reaction (PCR) in the presence of DNA polymerase and nucleotides. Through successive DNA synthesis cycles, DNA sequence between the outermost oligonucleotides can be greatly amplified, thus allowing the detection of base mismatches at a specific location using sequence-specific nucleotides.

We have applied this DNA amplification and allele-specific oligonucleotide hybridization technique to analyse ALDH I enzyme specific genomic DNA from leukocytes of 200 unrelated South Koreans (Goedde et al, 1989). The ALDH I genotypes (homozygote normal, heterozygote deficient and homozygote deficient) could clearly be determined using this PCR method. On comparing the distribution of genotypes with the distribution of phenotypes in the same population sample, it was found that the 60 apparent deficient phenotypes were a mixture of heterozygote and homozygote deficient genotypes (56 heterozygotes and 4 homozygotes). These preliminary results indicate that the deficient ALDH I gene may be dominating over the normal ALDH I gene by suppressing completely the enzyme activity in the heterozygotes. Family studies, using this genotyping method may help to elucidate the mode of inheritance of ALDH I isozyme deficiency at the genotype level.

Isozyme Abnormality, Alcohol-drinking Habits, and Alcoholism

While alcohol consumption has been found to be quite similar in whites, Latins, and blacks, Asians consume significantly less amounts per capita (Klatsky et al, 1983). Ethnic and cultural factors are generally considered to be mainly responsible for differences in the drinking pattern in a particular society. Variations in drinking norms may be among the strongest determinants of an individuals drinking behavior. However, recent studies clearly hint at a

Table 2.6. Classification of ALDH I deficient subjects into various genotypes and phenotypes

| | PHENOTYPE | | |
GENOTYPE	ALDH ANTIGEN LEVEL/ MDH ACTIVITY RATIO IN HAIR ROOT LYSATES	ALDH I-STAINING INTENSITY	ALCOHOL SENSITIVITY
ALDH I^1/ALDH I^1	High	Normal	Nonflusher
ALDH I^1/ALDH I^2	Intermediate	Intermediate	Nonflusher/light flusher
ALDH I^2/ALDH I^2	Low	Poor or absent	Flusher

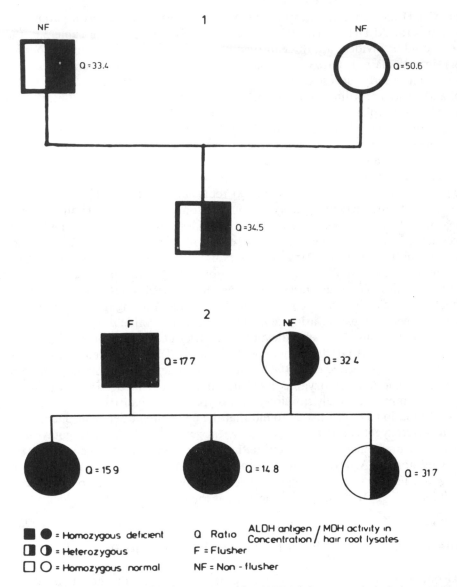

FIGURE 2.22. Pedigree of 2 Japanese families examined for ALDH I deficiency and alcohol sensitivity. A quotient of ALDH I antigen concentration and MDH activity was used to classify homozygotes and heterozygotes (Goedde et al, 1985).

possible involvement of genetic factors in the evolution of alcohol use and abuse (Goedde and Agarwal, 1987b; Agarwal and Goedde, 1987b).

Many investigations have shown that an interesting correlation exists between flushing response and the alcohol drinking habits (Wilson et al, 1978; Schwitters et al, 1982b). For obvious reasons, subjects who are deficient in ALDH I isozyme will experience unpleasant reactions after drinking alcohol and hence may be consuming fewer alcoholic drinks in their daily life. Indeed, a highly significant correlation has been observed among Japanese in the regions of Sendai and Gifu regarding the per capita alcohol consumption, prevalence of alcohol sensitivity, and the frequency of ALDH deficiency (Harada et al, 1985). In Sendai, where the ALDH I deficiency was lower than in the Gifu region, the annual alcohol consumption was found to be significantly higher (Table 2.7).

Similar observations of a large number of Japanese men were reported recently (Ohara et

Table 2.7. Alcohol consumption and incidence of ALDH I isozyme deficiency in alcoholics and healthy persons in Japan (Harada et al, 1985)

Alcohol Consumption and ALDH I deficiency			
DISTRICT	SAMPLE SIZE	ALDH I DEFICIENCY	ALCOHOL CONSUMPTION, LITERS/YEAR PER PERSON
Sendai	47	25.5%	6.25
Gifu	65	52.3%	3.82
Alcoholism and ALDH I isozyme deficiency			
SUBJECTS	SAMPLE SIZE	ALDH I DEFICIENT	ALDH I NORMAL
Alcoholics	261	247 (94.6%)	14 (5.4%)
Healthy	105	61 (58.1%)	44 (41.9%)

al, 1983; Suwaki and Ohara, 1985). Flushers drank small amounts of alcohol compared to nonflushers who frequently drank fairly large amounts of alcohol and suffered from alcohol-related problems. In a large study on Korean and Taiwan Chinese, subjects showing fast flushing consumed substantially smaller amounts of alcohol than those who exhibited no flushing or slow flushing (Park et al, 1984). However, in these studies, the flushing and nonflushing subjects were not tested for ALDH deficiency. In a recent report, multivariate path analysis was used to study flushing after alcohol use and alcohol consumption in nuclear families of Korean, Taiwanese, Hawaiian-Americans of Japanese ancestry, and Hawaiian-Americans of Caucasian ancestry. Although alcohol consumption and flushing response to alcohol varied greatly among the different groups, heritability values as estimated from the familial components were remarkably similar (Nagoshi, 1988).

Alcoholism Among Orientals: Possible Protective Factors

In general, the rate of alcoholism has always been found to be much lower among Japanese, Chinese, and other ethnic groups related to the Mongoloid race (Reed, 1978). As originally suggested by Goedde et al (1979b), individuals sensitive to alcohol by virtue of their genetically controlled deficiency of a key enzyme of alcohol metabolism, viz. ALDH I, may be discouraged from abuse of alcohol due to initial aversive reaction. Indeed, as shown in Table 2.7, in a group of Japanese alcoholics a significantly lower incidence of ALDH I isozyme deficiency was observed than in psychiatric patients, drug dependents, and healthy controls (Harada et al, 1982b; Goedde et al, 1983a, Harada et al, 1985).

Similar findings have also been observed in other psychiatric clinics in a WHO sponsored study in Japan, Taiwan, and the Philippines (Ohmori et al, 1986). Moreover, only 10% of the Japanese chronic alcoholics with liver injury were found to be deficient in ALDH I isozyme activity (Yoshihara et al, 1983).

Native Americans and Alcohol Abuse

Alcohol abuse and alcoholism are major problems among American Indian tribes (Brod, 1975). North and South American and Mexican Indians have been found to metabolize alcohol faster than Caucasian groups (Agarwal and Goedde, 1986). Like the majority of Mongoloids (Japanese, Chinese, Koreans), American Indians are also sensitive to alcohol and exhibit facial flushing associated with various subjective and objective vasomotor symptoms after drinking moderate amounts of alcohol (Wolff, 1972; Zeiner et al, 1976). Although a considerable difference in the drinking habits of native American Indians compared with whites has been observed over centuries, no significant difference between North and South

American Indians regarding drinking pattern and behavioral consequences can be pointed out (Everett et al, 1976).

It remains to be explained why the South American Indian tribes show widespread ALDH isozyme deficiency similar to Mongoloids while their North American counterparts show significantly low incidence of such isozyme abnormality (Goedde et al, 1986). Perhaps, altered social and cultural circumstances make these individuals vulnerable to alcohol abuse despite their inherited intolerance to alcohol drinking. Whether ALDH isozyme deficiency also plays a similar protective role among native Americans has yet to be understood. In order to better understand the evolutionary role of aldehyde dehydrogenase deficiency in alcohol dependence—whether protective or reinforcing—more native American Indian populations need to be investigated concerning ALDH I deficiency, alcohol sensitivity, drinking habits, and the rate of alcoholism.

ALDH ISOZYME CHANGES IN ALCOHOLISM

Hepatic ALDH Isozymes

In recent years, specific alterations in ALDH isozymes in alcohol abuse-related liver damage have been reported. Although a selective reduction of cytosolic isozyme of hepatic ALDH has been observed (Jenkins and Peters, 1980; Palmer and Jenkins, 1982; Thomas et al, 1982; Jenkins et al, 1984), decreased activity of mitochondrial ALDH was noted in the livers of chronic alcoholics (Nuutinen et al, 1983; Yoshihara et al, 1983; Ricciardi et al, 1983b). The pathogenetic role of ALDH isozymes in alcoholic liver damage is further complicated by the lack of reliable data on the subcellular localization of different ALDH isozymes.

In a recent study, human autopsy liver specimens were subjected to subcellular fractionation in order to study the localization and properties of ALDH isozymes (Meier-Tackmann et al, 1988). Appropriate marker enzymes for the nuclei, mitochondria, microsomes, and cytosol were assayed in each subcellular fraction to assess the extent of purity of the fractions. On a tissue wet weight basis, nearly 70% of the total ALDH activity was recovered in the cytosolic fraction, which contained at least two distinct isozymes. Based on densitometric evaluation of isozyme bands after isoelectric focusing, it was estimated that about 65% of the cytosolic activity was due to ALDH II and the rest due to ALDH I isozyme. Only about 5% of the total ALDH activity was found in the mitochondrial fraction (70% ALDH I and 30% ALDH II). A significantly reduced total specific ALDH activity (per milligram soluble protein) was noted in all subcellular fractions of cirrhotic liver specimens. Both ALDH I and ALDH II activities of cytosolic and mitochondrial fractions were decreased (Fig. 2.23).

These results suggest that although ALDH I isozyme in the cytosol and mitochondria may be primarily responsible for the oxidation of small amounts of acetaldehyde normally found in the blood of nonalcoholics after moderate drinking, in alcoholics with higher steady state blood acetaldehyde concentrations, the cytosolic ALDH II isozyme may be of greater physiological significance (Meier-Tackmann et al, 1988).

Erythrocyte ALDH Activity

Erythrocytes show a considerable acetaldehyde-oxidizing capacity. The red cell ALDH is apparently identical with the liver cytosolic isozyme (ALDH II). However, the physiological role of red cell ALDH remains unexplained. Recent studies show significant loss in erythrocyte ALDH activity in the blood of chronic alcoholics, as compared to healthy controls and other nonalcoholic psychiatric and gastrointestinal patients (Agarwal et al, 1982; Goedde et al, 1983a; Lin et al, 1984; Agarwal et al, 1985; Towell et al, 1985). A typical electropherogram showing the comparative intensity of human red cell ALDH isozyme band of alcoholics and healthy controls is shown in Figure 2.24. Thus, erythrocytes may offer a suitable peripheral source of monitoring alcoholics during chronic alcohol abuse as well as in abstinence by measuring red cell ALDH activity.

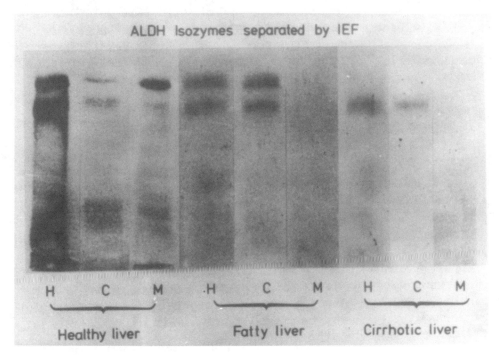

FIGURE 2.23. Comparative pattern of ALDH Isozymes after isoelectric focusing of homogenates (H), mitochondrial (M) and cytosolic fractions of livers from alcoholic and nonalcoholics (Agarwal et al, 1985).

Although it remains undecided whether reduced ALDH activity in the alcoholics represents a genetic trait indicating a risk factor for alcoholism or it represents only a state characteristic, the red cell ALDH activity was found to return to normal values after about 12 weeks of abstinence (Fig. 2.25).

The cause and mechanism of loss in ALDH activity in the erythrocytes of alcoholics was studied (Agarwal et al, 1987) by looking into the following possibilities: chemical or physi-

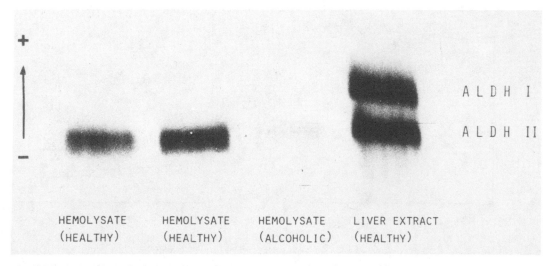

FIGURE 2.24. Isoelectric focusing pattern of ALDH isozymes in hemolysate and liver extracts from alcoholics and healthy controls (Agarwal et al, 1983).

cal alterations in the enzyme protein resulting in the loss of catalytic activity; genetic variation or modification of the preexisting enzyme protein (posttranslational alterations) causing loss in activity; partial or total degradation of the enzyme molecules associated with loss in catalytic activity and/or antigenic properties; or disturbance in protein synthesis resulting from alcohol abuse leads to either a decrease in total protein or a specific decrease in the ALDH protein.

The recent findings show a considerable similarity between the erythrocyte ALDH and the liver cytosolic isozyme regarding electrophoretic, isoelectric, and kinetic characteristics. The red cell ALDH was found to be a specific biochemical marker for alcoholism. However, during abstinence, the ALDH activity remained persistently lower in alcoholics with cirrhotic livers as compared with subjects without an apparent liver damage. The loss in the enzyme activity was not always associated with a corresponding loss in enzyme-related antigen concentration (Agarwal et al, 1987).

SUMMARY AND CONCLUSIONS

The metabolism of acetaldehyde has received considerable attention in the past years owing to its acute and chronic toxic effects in humans. Two major isozymes of hepatic ALDH (ALDH I or E2 and ALDH II or E1) that differ in their structural and functional properties have been characterized in humans. ALDH I with a low K_m for acetaldehyde is predominantly of mitochondrial origin and ALDH II, which has a relatively higher K_m, is mainly of cytosolic origin. An inherited deficiency of ALDH I isozyme, which is primarily responsible

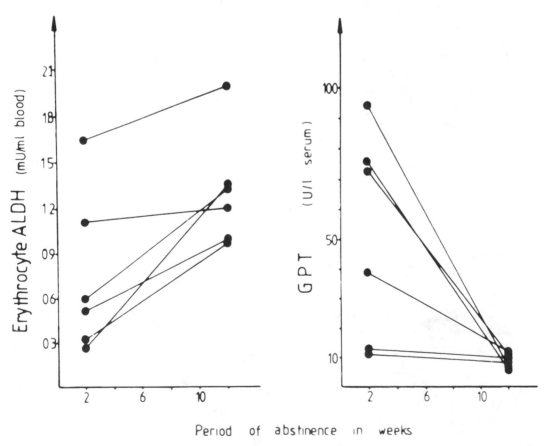

FIGURE 2.25. Changes in erythrocyte ALDH and serum GPT (ALAT) activities in alcoholics during 12 weeks of abstinence.

for producing acute alcohol sensitivity symptoms (flushing response) after drinking mild doses of alcohol, has been found only among Oriental and American Indian populations. Biochemical, immunochemical, and molecular genetics studies concerning this new inborn error of metabolism indicate that a structural mutation in the ALDH I isozyme gene is responsible for the loss in catalytic activity.

Population genetic studies indicate a wide prevalence of ALDH deficiency among individuals of the Mongoloid race. Flushing response to alcohol shows familial resemblances and preliminary data from Japanese, Chinese, and Korean families hint at an autosomal codominant inheritance of ALDH I isozyme deficiency. The ALDH deficiency is apparently responsible for the low incidence of alcoholism in Japanese, Chinese and Koreans. Alcohol-induced sensitivity due to ALDH I isozyme deficiency may act as an inhibitory factor against excessive alcohol drinking thereby imparting a certain protection against alcoholism.

The following conclusions may be drawn:

1. Genetic variations in specific enzymes involved in alcohol metabolism are important determinants of the rates of ethanol metabolism and the resulting physiological responses.

2. Slow acetaldehyde oxidation due to ALDH I isozyme abnormality leads to elevated blood acetaldehyde levels, which results in vasodilation associated with dysphoric symptoms after drinking alcohol.

3. People differ in physiological and morphological features, which influence their drinking behavior and metabolic responses to alcohol.

4. An interesting correlation exists between flushing response and alcohol drinking habits of Japanese, Chinese, and Koreans. Alcohol intolerance results in less consumption of alcohol as compared to the general population average.

5. A significantly lower incidence of ALDH I isozyme deficiency was observed in Japanese alcoholics than in psychiatric patients, drug dependents, and healthy controls. Only about 2% of the alcoholics showed isozyme deficiency against about 40% in the control population.

6. A remarkably low incidence of ALDH I isozyme deficiency was found among North American Indians. A lack of superactive atypical ADH in the autopsy livers of North American Indians excludes the possibility that rapid ethanol metabolism might be responsible for the euphoric responses and reinforcing effects of alcohol.

7. It remains to be explained why the South American Indian tribes show widespread ALDH isozyme deficiency similar to Mongoloids while their North American counterparts show a significantly low incidence of such isozyme abnormality.

Since alcohol abuse and alcoholism are major problems among North and South American Indian tribes, and no significant difference between North and South American Indians regarding their drinking pattern and behavioral consequences can be pointed out, altered social and cultural circumstances possibly make some individuals vulnerable to alcohol abuse despite their inherited intolerance to alcohol.

REFERENCES

Agarwal DP, Harada S, Goedde HW: Racial differences in biological sensitivity to ethanol: The role of alcohol dehydrogenase and aldehyde dehydrogenase isozymes. *Alcoholism: Clin Exp Res* 1981; 5:12–16.

Agarwal DP, Hafer G, Harada S, Goedde HW: Studies on aldehyde dehydrogenase and aldehyde reductase in human brain, in Weiner H, Wermuth B (eds): *Enzymology of Carbonyl Metabolism: Aldehyde Dehydrogenase and Aldo/Keto Reductase*. New York, Alan R Liss Inc, 1982, pp 319–327.

Agarwal DP, Tobar-Rojas L, Harada S, Goedde HW: Comparative study of erythrocyte aldehyde dehydrogenase in alcoholics and control subjects. *Pharmacol Biochem Behav* 1983; 18(Suppl.1):89–95.

Agarwal DP, Eckey R, Harada S, Goedde HW: Basis of aldehyde dehydrogenase deficiency in Orientals: Immunochemical studies. *Alcohol* 1984; 1:111–118.

Agarwal DP, Müller C, Korencke C, Mika U, Harada S, Goedde HW: Changes in erythrocyte and liver aldehyde dehydrogenase isozymes in alcoholics, in Flynn TG, Weiner H (eds): *Enzymology of Carbonyl Metabolism: Aldehyde Dehydrogenase, Aldehyde Reductase, and Alcohol Dehydrogenase*. New York, Alan R Liss Inc, 1985, pp 113–127.

Agarwal DP, Goedde HW: Ethanol oxidation: Ethnic variation in metabolism and response, in Kalow W, Goedde HW, Agarwal DP (eds): Ethnic *Differences in Reactions to Drugs and Xenobiotics*. New York, Alan R Liss Inc, 1986, pp 99–111.

Agarwal DP, Volkens T, Hafer G, Goedde HW: Erythrocyte aldehyde dehydrogenase: Studies of properties and changes in acute and chronic alcohol intoxication, in Weiner H, Flynnn TG (eds): Enzymology and *Molecular Biology of Carbonyl Metabolism: Aldehyde Dehydrogenase, Aldo-Keto Reductase and Alcohol Dehyrogenase*. New York, Alan R Liss Inc, 1987, pp 85–101.

Agarwal DP, Goedde HW: Human aldehyde dehydrogenase isozymes and alcohol sensitivity, in Rattazzi MC, Scandalios JG, Whitt GS (eds): *Isozymes: Current Topics in Biological and Medical Research*. New York, Alan R Liss Inc, 1987a, vol 16, pp 21–48.

Agarwal DP, Goedde HW: Genetic variation in alcohol metabolizing enzymes: Implications in alcohol use and abuse, in Goedde HW, Agarwal DP (eds): *Genetics and Alcoholism*. New York, Alan R Liss Inc, 1987b, pp 121–140.

Blair AH, Bodley FH: Human liver aldehyde dehydrogenase: partial purification and properties. *Can J Biochem* 1969; 47:265–272.

Braun T, Grzeschik KH, Bober E, Agarwal DP, Singh S, Goedde HW: The structural gene for the mitochondrial aldehyde dehydrogenase maps to human chromosome 12. *Hum Genet* 1986; 73:365–367.

Braun T, Bober E, Schaper J, Agarwal DP, Singh S, Goedde HW: Human mitochondrial aldehyde dehydrogenase: mRNA expression in different tissues using a specific probe isolated from a cDNA expression library. *Alcohol & Alcoholism* 1987a (Suppl.1): 161–165.

Braun T, Bober E, Singh S, Agarwal DP, Goedde HW: Evidence for a signal peptide at the amino-terminal end of human mitochondrial aldehyde dehydrogenase. *FEBS Letters* 1987b; 215:233–236.

Brod TM: Alcoholism as a mental health problem of Native Americans: A review of the literature. *Arch Gen Psychiat* 1975; 32:1385–1391.

Cooper AJL: Biochemistry of sulfer-containing amino acids. *Ann Rev Biochem* 1983; 52:187–222.

Crow KE, Kitson TM, MacGibbon AKH, Batt, RD: Intracellular localization and properties of aldehyde dehydrogense from sheep liver. *Biochem Biophys Acta* 1974; 350:121–128.

Duley JA, Harris O, Holmes RS: Analysis of human alcohol- and aldehyde-metabolizing isozymes by electrophoresis and isoelectric focusing. *Alcoholism: Clin Exp Res* 1985; 9:263–271.

Eckey R, Agarwal DP, Saha N, Goedde HW: Detection and partial characterization of a variant form of cytosolic aldehyde dehydrogenase isozyme. *Hum Genet* 1986; 72:95–97.

Eckfeldt JH, Yonetani T: Subcellular localization of the F1 and F2 isozymes of horse liver aldehyde dehydrogenase. *Arch Biochem Biophys* 1976; 175:717–722.

Edwards JA, Evans DAP: Ethanol metabolism in subjects possessing typical and atypical liver alcohol dehydrogenase. *Clin Pharmacol Therapeut* 1967; 8:824–829.

Everett MW, Waddel JO, Heath DB: *Cross-cultural Approaches to the Study of Alcohol*. The Hague, Paris, Mouton Publishers, 1976.

Ewing JA, Rouse BA, Pellizzari ED: Alcohol sensitivity and ethnic background. *Am J Psychiatry* 1974; 131:206–210.

Feldman RI, Weiner H: Horse liver aldehyde dehydrogenase. I. Purification and characterization. *J Biol Chem* 1972; 247:260–269.

Ferencz-Biro K, Pietruszko R: Human aldehyde dehydrogenase: Catalytic activity in Oriental liver. *Biochem Biophys Res Comm* 1984; 118:97–102.

Forte-McRobbie CM, Pietruszko R: Aldehyde dehydrogenase content and composition of human liver. *Alcohol* 1985; 2:375–381.

Goedde HW, Agarwal DP, Harada S: Alcohol metabolizing enzymes: Studies of isozymes in human biopsies and cultured fibroblasts. *Clin Genet* 1979a; 16:29–33.

Goedde HW, Harada S, Agarwal DP: Racial differences in alcohol sensitivity: A new hypothesis. *Hum Genet* 1979b; 51:331–334.

Goedde HW, Agarwal DP, Harada S: Genetic studies on alcohol metabolizing enzymes: Detection of isozymes in human hair roots. *Enzyme* 1980; 25:281–286.

Goedde HW, Agarwal DP, Meier-Tackmann D, Harada S: Physiological role of aldehyde dehydrogenase isozymes, in Weiner H, Wermuth B (eds): *Enzymology of Carbonyl Metabolism: Aldehyde Dehydrogenase and Aldo/Keto Reductase*. New York, Alan R Liss Inc, 1982, pp 347–362.

Goedde HW, Agarwal DP, Harada S: The role of alcohol dehydrogenase and aldehyde dehydrogenase isozymes in alcohol metabolism, alcohol sensitivity and alcoholism, in Rattazzi MC, Scandalios JG, Whitt GS (eds): *Isozymes: Curr Top Biol Med Res*. New York, Alan R Liss Inc, vol 8, 1983a, pp 175–193.

Goedde HW, Agarwal DP, Harada S, Meier-Tackmann D, Ruofu D, Bienzle U, Kroeger A, Hussein L: Population genetic studies on aldehyde dehydrogenase isozyme deficiency and alcohol sensitivity. *Am J Hum Genet* 1983b; 35:769-772.

Goedde HW, Agarwal DP, Paik YK: Frequency of aldehyde dehydrogenase I isozyme deficiency in Koreans. A pilot study. *Korean J Genet* 1983c; 5:88-90.

Goedde HW, Agarwal DP, Harada S: Pharmacogenetics of alcohol sensitivity. *Pharmacol Biochem Behav* 1983d; 18:161-166.

Goedde HW, Benkmann HG, Kriese L, Bogdanski P, Agarwal DP, Ruofu D, Liangzhong C, Meiying C, Yida Y, Jiujin X, Shizhe L, Yongfa W: Aldehyde dehydrogenase isozyme deficiency and alcohol sensitivity in four different Chinese populations. *Hum Hered* 1984a; 34:183-186.

Goedde HW, Rothhammer F, Benkmann HG, Bogdanski P: Ecogenetic studies in Atacameno Indians. *Hum Genet* 1984b; 67:343-346.

Goedde HW, Agarwal DP, Eckey R, Harada S: Population genetic and family studies on aldehyde dehydrogenase deficiency and alcohol sensitivity. *Alcohol* 1985; 2:283-289.

Goedde HW, Agarwal DP: Aldehyde oxidation: Ethnic variation in metabolism and response, in Kalow W, Goedde HW, Agarwal DP (eds): *Ethnic Differences in Reactions to Drugs and Xenobiotics*, New York, Alan R Liss Inc, 1986, pp 113-138.

Goedde HW, Agarwal DP, Harada S, Whittaker JO, Rothhammer F, Lisker R: Aldehyde dehydrogenase polymorphism in North American, South American and Mexican Indians. *Am J Hum Genet* 1986; 38:395-399.

Goedde HW, Agarwal DP: Polymorphism of aldehyde dehydrogenase and alcohol sensitivity. *Enzyme* 1987a; 37:29-44.

Goedde HW, Agarwal DP: Genetics and alcoholism: Problems and perspectives, in Goedde HW and Agarwal DP (eds): *Genetics and Alcoholism*. New York, Alan R Liss Inc, 1987b, pp 3-20.

Goedde HW, Singh S, Agarwal DP, Fritze G, Stapel K, Paik YK: Genotyping of mitochondrial aldehyde dehydrogenase in blood samples using allele-specific oligonucleotides: Comparison with phenotyping in hair roots. *Hum Genet* 1989; 81: 305-307.

Greenfield NJ, Pietruszko R: Two aldehyde dehydrogenases from human liver: Isolation via affinity chromatography and characterization of the isozymes. *Biochem Biophys Acta* 1977; 483:35-45.

Hafer G, Agarwal DP, Goedde HW: Human brain aldehyde dehydrogenase: Activity with dopal and isozyme distribution. *Alcohol* 1987; 4:413-418.

Harada S, Agarwal DP, Goedde HW: Isozyme variations in acetaldehyde dehydrogenase (EC 1.2.1.3) in human tissues. *Hum Genet* 1978; 44:181-185.

Harada S, Agarwal DP, Goedde HW: Electrophoretic and biochemical studies of human aldehyde dehydrogenase isozymes in various tissues. *Life Sci* 1980a; 26:1771-1780.

Harada S, Misawa S, Agarwal DP, Goedde HW: Liver alcohol and aldehyde dehydrogenase in the Japanese: Isozyme variation and its possible role in alcohol intoxication. *Am J Hum Genet* 1980b; 32: 8-15.

Harada S, Agarwal DP, Goedde HW: Aldehyde dehydrogenase deficiency as cause of facial flushing reaction to alcohol in Japanese. *Lancet* 1981; ii:982.

Harada S, Agarwal DP, Goedde HW: Mechanism of alcohol sensitivity and disulfiram–ethanol reaction. *Substance Alcohol Actions/Misuse* 1982a; 3:107-115.

Harada S, Agarwal DP, Goedde HW, Tagaki S, Ishikawa B: Possible protective role against alcoholism for aldehyde dehydrogenase isozyme deficiency in Japan. *Lancet* 1982b; ii:827.

Harada S, Agarwal DP, Goedde HW: Aldehyde dehydrogenase polymorphism and alcohol metabolism in alcoholics. *Alcohol* 1985; 2:391-392.

Harrington MC, Henehan GTM, Tipton KF: The roles of human aldehyde dehydrogenase isozymes in ethanol metabolism, in Weiner H, Flynn TG (eds): *Enzymology and Molecular Biology of Carbonyl Metabolism: Aldehyde Dehydrogenase, Aldo-Keto Reductase and Alcohol Dehydrogenase*. New York, Alan R Liss Inc, 1987, pp 111-125.

Hellström E, Tottmar O, Widerlöv E: Effects of oral administration or implantation of disulfiram on aldehyde dehydrogenase activity in human blood. *Alcohol Clin Exp Res* 1983; 7:231-236.

Hempel J, von Bahr-Lindström H, Jörnvall H: Aldehyde dehydrogenase from human liver. Primary structure of the cytoplasmic isoenzyme. *Eur J Biochem* 1984a; 141:21-35.

Hempel J, Kaiser R, Jörnvall H: Human liver mitochondrial aldehyde dehydrogenase: A C-terminal segment positions and defines the structure corresponding to the one reported to differ in the Oriental enzyme variant. *FEBS Letters* 1984b; 173:367-373.

Hempel J, Kaiser R, Jörnvall H: Mitochondrial aldehyde dehydrogenase from human liver: Primary structure, differences in relation to the cytosolic enzyme and functional correlations. *Eur J Biochem* 1985; 153:13-28.

Hsu LC, Tani K, Fujiyoshi T, Kurachi K, Yoshida A: Cloning of cDNAs for human aldehyde dehydrogenases 1 and 2. *Proc Natl Acad Sci, USA* 1985; 82:3771-3775.

Hsu LC, Yoshida A, Mohandas T: Chromosomal assignment of the genes for human aldehyde dehydrogenase-1 and aldehyde dehydrogenase-2. *Am J Hum Gen* 1986; 38:641–648.

Impraim C, Wang G, Yoshida A: Structural mutation in a major human aldehyde dehyrogenase gene results in loss of enzyme activity. *Am J Hum Genet* 1982; 34:834–837.

Inoue K, Fukunaga M, Kiriyama T, Komura S: Accumulation of acetaldehyde in alcohol sensitive Japanese: Relation to ethanol and acetaldehyde oxidizing capacity. *Alcohol: Clin Exp Res* 1984; 8:319–322.

Inoue K, Lindros KO: Subcellular distribution of human brain aldehyde dehydrogenase. *J Neurochem* 1982; 38:884–888.

Inoue K, Nishimukai H, Yamasawa K: Purification and partial characterization of aldehyde dehydrogenase from human erythrocytes. *Biochem Biophys Acta* 1979; 569:117–123.

Inoue K, Ohbora Y, Yamasawa K: Metabolism of acetaldehyde by human erythrocytes. *Life Sci* 1978; 23:179–184.

Jenkins WJ, Cakebread K, Palmer KR: Effect of alcohol consumption on hepatic aldehyde dehydrogenase activity in alcoholic patients. *Lancet* 1984; i:1048–1049.

Jenkins WJ, Peters TJ: Selectively reduced hepatic acetaldehyde dehydrogenase in alcoholics. *Lancet* 1980; i:628–629.

Jenkins WJ, Peters TJ: Subcellular localization of acetaldehyde dehydrogenase in human liver. *Cell Biochem Funct* 1983; 1:37–40.

Johnson CT, Bosron WF, Harden CA, Li T-K: Purification of human liver aldehyde dehydrogenase by high-performance liquid chromatography and identification of isoenzymes by immunoblotting. *Alcohol: Clin Exp Res* 1987; 11:60–65.

Johnson RC, Nagoshi CT, Schwitters SY, Bowman KS, Ahren FM, Wilson JR: Further investigations of racial/ethnic differences and of familial resemblances in flushing in response to alcohol. *Behav Genet* 1984; 14:171–178.

Jones GL, Teng Y-S: A chemical and enzymological account of the multiple forms of human liver aldehyde dehydrogenase: Implications for ethnic differences in alcohol metabolism. *Biochim Biophys Acta* 1983; 745:162–174.

Jörnvall H, Hempel J, Vallee B: Structures of human alcohol and aldehyde dehydrogenases. *Enzyme* 1987; 37:5–18.

Klatsky AL, Siegelaub AB, Landy C, Friedman GD: Racial patterns of alcohol beverage use. *Alcohol Clin Exp Res* 1983; 7:372–377.

Kogame M, Mizoi Y: The polymorphism of alcohol and aldehyde dehydrogenase in the Japanese and its significance in ethanol metabolism. *Jpn J Alcohol Drug Dependence* 1985; 20:122–142.

Koivula T: Subcellular distribution and characterization of human liver aldehyde dehydrogenase fractions. *Life Sci* 1975; 16:1563–1570.

Koivula T, Koivusalo M: Different forms of rat liver aldehyde dehydrogenase and their subcellular distribution. *Biochem Biophys Acta* 1975; 397:9–23.

Kouri M, Koivula M, Koivusalo M: Aldehyde dehydrogenase activity in human placenta. *Acta Pharmacol Toxicol* 1977; 40:460–464.

Kraemer RJ, Deitrich HA: Isolation and characterization of human liver aldehyde dehydrogenase. *J Biol Chem* 1968; 243:6402–6408.

Lee SY, Mendecki J, Braverman G: A polynucleotide segment rich in adenylic acid in the rapidly labelled polyribosomal RNA component of mouse sarcoma 180 ascites cells. *Proc Natl Acad Sci, USA* 1971; 68:1331–1335.

Lehmann WD, Heinrich HC, Leonhardt R, Agarwal DP, Goedde HW, Kneer J, Rating D: ^{13}C-Ethanol and ^{13}C-acetate breath test in normal and aldehyde dehydrogenase deficient individuals. *Alcohol* 1986; 3:227–231.

Lin CC, Potter JJ, Mezey E: Erythrocyte aldehyde dehydrogenase in alcoholism. *Alcohol Clin Exp Res* 1984; 8:539–542.

MacKerell AD Jr, Vallari RC, Pietruszko R: Human mitochondrial aldehyde dehydrogenase inhibition by diethyldithiocarbamic acid methanethiol mixed disulfide: A derivative of disulfiram. *FEBS Lett* 1985; 179:77–81.

MacKerell AD Jr, Blatter EE, Pietruszko R: Human aldehyde dehydrogenase: Kinetic identification of the isozyme for which biogenic aldehydes and acetaldehyde compete. *Alcohol Clin Exp Res* 1986; 10:266–270.

Maniatis T, Sambrook J, Fritsch EF: *Handbook of Molecular Cloning Techniques*. New York, Cold Spring Harbor Laboratory Press, 1982.

Maring JA, Weigand K, Brenner HD, von Wartburg JP: Aldehyde oxidizing capacity of erythrocytes in normal and alcoholic individuals. *Pharmacol Biochem Behav* 1983; 18:135–138.

McMichael M, Hellström-Lindahl, E, Weiner H: Identification and selective precipitation of human aldehyde dehydrogenase isozymes using antibodies raised to horse liver aldehyde dehydrogenase iso-zymes. *Alcohol Clin Exp Res* 1986; 10:323–329.

Meier-Tackmann D, Agarwal DP, Saha N, Goedde HW: Aldehyde dehydrogenase isozymes in stom-ach autopsy specimens from Germans and Chinese. *Enzyme* 1984; 32:170–177.

Meier-Tackmann D, Korenke GC, Agarwal DP, Goedde HW: Human placental aldehyde dehydroge-nase: Subcellular distribution and properties. *Enzyme* 1985; 33:153–161.

Meier-Tackmann D, Korenke GC, Agarwal DP, Goedde HW: Aldehyde dehydrogenase isozymes: Sub-cellular distribution in livers from alcoholics and healthy subjects. *Alcohol* 1988; 5:73–80.

Mizoi Y, Ijiri I, Tatsuno Y, Kijima T, Fujiwara S, Adachi J: Relationship between facial flushing and blood acetaldehyde levels after alcohol intake. *Pharmacol Biochem Behav* 1979; 10:303–311.

Mizoi Y, Adachi J, Kogame M, Fukunaga T: Polymorphism of aldehyde dehydrogenase and catechol-amine metabolism, in Weiner H, Wermuth B (eds): *Enzymology of Carbonyl Metabolism: Aldehyde Dehydrogenase and Aldo/Keta Reductase*. New York, Alan R Liss Inc, 1982, pp 363–377.

Mizoi Y, Tatsuno Y, Adachi I, Kogame M, Fukunaga T, Fujiwara S, Hishida S, Ijiri I: Alcohol sen-sitivity related to polymorphism of alcohol-metabolizing enzymes in Japanese. *Pharmacol Biochem Behav* 1983; 18:127–133.

Mizoi Y, Kogame M, Fukunaga T, Ueno Y, Adachi J, Fuziwara S: Polymorphism of aldehyde dehy-drogenase and ethanol elimination. *Alcohol* 1985; 2:393–396.

Morikawa Y, Matsuzaka J, Kuratsune M, Tsukamoto S, Makisumi S: Plethysmographic study of effects of alcohol. *Nature* 1968; 220:186–187.

Nagoshi CT, Dixon LK, Johnson RC, Yuen SHL: Familial transmission of alcohol consumption and the flushing response to alcohol in three Oriental groups. *J Stud Alcohol* 1988; 49: 261–267.

Nuutinen H, Lindros KO, Salaspuro M: Determinants of blood acetaldehyde level during ethanol oxi-dation in chronic alcoholics. *Alcohol Clin Exp Res* 1983; 7:163–168.

Ohara H, Suwaki H, Yoshida T, Hisashige A: A study of drinking habits of adult males in Kochi Prefec-ture. *Jpn J Alcohol Stud Drug Depend* 1983: 18:170–183.

Ohmori T, Koyama T, Chen C, Yeh E, Reyes Jr BV, Yamashita I: The role of aldehyde dehydroge-nase isozyme variance in alcohol sensitivity, drinking habits formation and the development of al-coholism in Japan, Taiwan and the Philippines. *Prog Neuro Psychopharmacol Biol Psychiat* 1986; 10:229–235.

Palmer KR, Jenkins WJ: Impaired acetaldehyde oxidation in alcoholics. *Gut* 1982; 23:729–733.

Park JY, Huang Y-H, Nagoshi CT, Yuen S, Johnson RC, Ching CA, Bowman, KS: The flushing re-sponse to alcohol use among Koreans and Taiwanese. *J Stud Alcohol* 1984; 45:481–485.

Pietruszko R, Greenfield NJ, Edson CR: Human liver aldehyde dehydrogenase, in Thurman R, Wil-liamson JR, Drott HR, Chance B (eds): *Alcohol and Aldehyde Metabolizing Systems*. New York, Academic Press, 1977, vol II, pp 195–202.

Pietruszko R, Vallari RC: Aldehyde dehydrogenase in human blood. *FEBS Lett* 1978; 92:89–91.

Pietruszko R: Alcohol and aldehyde dehydrogenase isozymes from mammalian liver-their structural and functional differences, in Rattazzi MC, Scandalios JG, Whitt GS (eds): *Isozymes: Current Topics in Biological and Medical Research*. New York, Alan R Liss Inc, 1980, vol 4, pp 107–130.

Pietruszko R, Ryzlak MT, Forte-McRobbie CM: Multiplicity and identity of human aldehyde dehydrogenases. *Alcohol Alcoholism* 1987; Suppl. 1:175–179.

Racker E: Aldehyde dehydrogenase: A diphosphopyridine nucleotide-linked enzyme. *J Biol Chem* 1949; 177:883–892.

Reed, TE: Racial comparisons of alcohol metabolism: Background, problems and results. *Alcohol Clin Exp Res* 1978; 2:61–69.

Reed TE, Kalant H, Gibbins RJ, Khanna BM: Alcohol and acetaldehyde metabolism in Caucasians, Chinese and Amerinds. *Can Med Assoc J* 1976; 115:851–855.

Rex DK, Bosron WF, Smialek JE, Li TK: Alcohol and aldehyde dehydrogenase isoenzymes in North American Indians. *Alcohol Clin Exp Res* 1985; 9:147–152.

Ricciardi BR, Saunders JB, Williams R, Hopkinson DA: Identification of alcohol dehydrogenase and aldehyde dehydrogenase isoenzymes in human liver biopsy specimens. *Clin Chim Acta* 1983a; 130: 85–94.

Ricciardi BR, Saunders JB, Williams R, Hopkinson DA: Hepatic ADH and ALDH Isoenzymes in dif-ferent racial groups and in alcoholism. *Pharmacol Biochem Behav* 1983b; 18:61–65.

Salaspuro M, Lindros K: Metabolism and toxicity of acetaldehyde, in Seitz HK, Kommerell B (eds): *Alcohol Related Diseases in Gastroenterology*. Berlin, Heidelberg, Springer Verlag, 1985, pp 106–123.

Sanger F, Nicklen S, Coulson AR: DNA sequencing with chain-terminating inhibitors. *Proc Natl Acad Sci USA*. 1977; 74:5463–5467.

Sanny CG: Canine liver aldehyde dehydrogenase: Distribution, isolation, and partial characterization. *Alcohol Clin Exp Res* 1985; 9:255–271.

Santisteban I, Povey S, West LF, Parrington JM, Hopkinson DA: Chromosome assignment, biochemical and immunological studies on a human aldehyde dehydrogenase, ALDH3. *Ann Hum Genet* 1985; 49:87–100.

Schwitters SY, Johnson RC, Johnson SB, Ahren FM: Familial resemblances in flushing following alcohol use. *Behav Genet* 1982a; 12:349–352.

Schwitters SY, Johnson RC, McClearn GE, Wilson JR: Alcohol use and the flushing response in different racial–ethnic groups. *Drug Alcohol Depend* 1982b; 3:147–151.

Smith M, Hiroshige S, Duester G, Saxon P, Carlock L, Wasmuth J: Confirmation of the assignment of the gene coding for mitochondrial aldehyde dehydrogenase (ALDH 2) to human chromosome 12. *Cytogenet Cell Genet* 1985; 40:748–749.

Smith, M: Genetics of human alcohol and aldehyde dehydrogenases, in Harris H, Hirschhorn K (eds): *Advances in Human Genetics*. New York and London, Plenum Press, 1986, pp 249–290.

Stamatoyannopoulos G, Chen SH, Fukui F: Liver alcohol dehydrogenase in Japanese: high population frequency of atypical form and its possible role in alcohol sensitivity. *Am J Hum Genet* 1975; 27: 789–796.

Sugata K, Takada A, Takase S, Tsutsumi M: Determination of aldehyde dehydrogenase isozyme activity in human liver. *Alcohol* 1988; 5:39–43.

Sugimoto E, Takahashi N, Kitagawa Y, Chiba H: Intracellular localization and characterization of beef liver aldehyde dehydrogenase isozymes. *Agr Biol Chem* 1976; 40:2063–2070.

Suwaki H, Ohara H: Alcohol-induced facial flushing and drinking behavior in Japanese men. *J Stud Alcohol* 1985; 46:196–198.

Takada A, Takase S, Nei J, Matsuda Y: Subcellular distribution of ALDH isozymes in the human liver. *Alcohol Clin Exp Res* 1984; 8:123.

Tank AW, Weiner H, Thurman JA: Enzymology and subcellular localization of aldehyde oxidation in rat liver. *Biochem Pharmacol* 1981; 30:3265–3275.

Teng Y-S: Human liver aldehyde dehydrogenase in Chinese and Asiatic Indians: Gene deletion and its possible implications in alcohol metabolism. *Biochem Genet* 1981; 19:107–114.

Teng Y-S: Stomach aldehyde dehydrogenase: Report of a new locus. *Hum Hered* 1983; 31:74–77.

Thomas M, Halsall S, Peters TJ: Role of hepatic aldehyde dehydrogenase in alcoholism: Demonstration of persistent reduction of cytosolic activity in abstaining patients. *Lancet* 1982; ii:1057–1059.

Tipton KF, Henehan GTM: Distribution of aldehyde dehydrogenase activities in human liver. *Alcohol Clin Exp Res* 1984; 8:131.

Tottmar O, Hellström E: Aldehyde dehydrogenase in blood: A sensitive assay and inhibition by disulfiram. *Pharmacol Biochem Behav* 1983; Suppl 1, 18:103–107.

Tottmar O, Pettersson H, Kiessling KH: The subcellular distribution and properties of aldehyde dehydrogenmases in the rat liver. *Biochem J* 1973; 135:577–586.

Towell JF, Townsend WF, Kalbfleisch JH, Wang RIH: Erythrocyte aldehyde dehydrogenase and clinical chemical markers of alcohol abuse and alcoholism. *Alcohol Drug Res* 1985; 6:15–21.

von Bahr-Lindström H, Hempel J, Jörnvall H: The cytoplasmic isoenzyme of horse liver aldehyde dehydrogenase. *Eur J Biochem* 1984; 141:37–42.

von Wartburg JP, Bühler R: Biology of disease. Alcoholism and aldehydism: New biomedical concepts. *Lab Invest* 1984; 50:5–15.

Wilson JR, McClearn GE, Johnson RC: Ethnic variation in the use and effects of alcohol. *Drug Alcohol Depend* 1978; 3:147–151.

Wolff PH: Ethnic differences in alcohol sensitivity. *Science* 1972; 175:449–450.

Wolff PH: Vasomotor sensitivity to alcohol in diverse Mongoloid populations. *Am J Hum Genet* 1973; 25:193–199.

Yoshida A, Wang G, Davé V: Determination of Genotypes of human liver aldehyde dehydrogenase ALDH 2 locus. *Am J Hum Genet* 1983; 35:1107–1116.

Yoshida A, Huang I-Yih, Ikawa M: Molecular abnormality of an inactive aldehyde dehydrogenase variant commonly found in Orientals. *Proc Natl Acad Sci, USA* 1984; 81:258–261.

Yoshida A, Davé V: Enzymatic activity of atypical Oriental types of aldehyde dehydrogenases. *Biochem Genet* 1985; 23:585–590.

Yoshihara H, Sato N, Kamada T, Abe H: Low K_m ALDH isozyme and alcoholic liver injury. *Pharmacol Biochem Behav* 1983; Suppl.1, 18:425–428.

Zeiner AR, Paredes A, Cowden L: Physiologic response to ethanol among the Tarahumara Indians. *Ann N Y Acad Sci* 1976; 273:151–158.

Zeiner AR, Paredes A, Christiansen D: The role of acetaldehyde in mediating reactivity to an acute dose of ethanol among different racial groups. *Alcohol Clin Exp Res* 1979; 3:11–18.

Zeiner AR, Girardot JM, Nichols N, Jones-Saumty D: ALDH I isozyme deficiency among North American Indians. *2nd ISBRA Cong*. Santa Fe, New Mexico. 1984, Abstract 300, p 129.

CHAPTER 3

Toxic and Metabolic Changes Induced by Ethanol

Charles S. Lieber, M.D.

Alcohol Research and Treatment Center
and Section of Liver Disease and Nutrition
Veterans Administration Medical Center, Bronx, New York
and Mount Sinai School of Medicine (CUNY), New York

The toxic and metabolic changes induced by ethanol are extensive and have been summarized in a monograph (Lieber, 1982). In the present review the focus is on progress made in our understanding of the alcohol-induced toxicity, changes in the metabolism of lipids, amino acids, proteins, and carbohydrates as well as associated endocrine alterations.

MECHANISMS OF THE HEPATOTOXICITY OF ETHANOL

Figure 3.1 lists a number of ethanol-related hepatic effects and their relationship either to the induction of the microsomal ethanol oxidizing system (MEOS), alcohol dehydrogenase (ADH) mediated generation of NADH (following oxidation of ethanol), or the product of both pathways, namely acetaldehyde, the metabolism of which is discussed in detail in another chapter.

Microsomal Ethanol Oxidizing System (MEOS)

In addition to the clarification of some metabolic changes related to the oxidation of ethanol via the ADH pathway (vide infra), major insight was gained into the interaction of ethanol with various xenobiotic agents on the basis of the elucidation of the MEOS pathway for ethanol metabolism involving a new ethanol-specific form of cytochrome P450 (P450IIE1). The observation in rats (Iseri et al, 1964, 1966) as well as in man (Lane and Lieber, 1966) that chronic ethanol consumption was associated with proliferation of microsomal membranes prompted the suggestion that liver microsomes could be a site for a distinct and adaptive system of ethanol oxidation. Indeed, such a system was demonstrated in vitro and named the microsomal ethanol oxidizing system (MEOS) (Lieber and DeCarli, 1968, 1970a). Based on various studies, it was concluded that the MEOS is distinct from ADH and catalase and dependent on cytochrome P450. This thesis initiated a decade of research and a lively debate that was finally resolved after (1) isolation of a P450-containing fraction from liver microsomes which, although devoid of any ADH or catalase activity, could still oxidize ethanol as

57

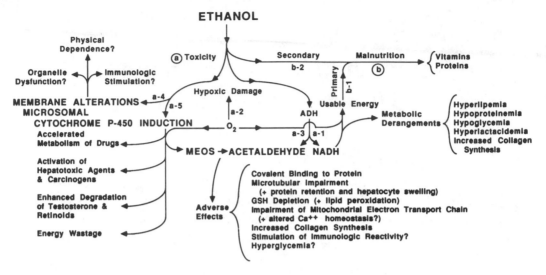

FIGURE 3.1. Hepatic nutritional and metabolic abnormalities after ethanol abuse. Malnutrition (b), whether primary (b-1) or secondary (b-2), has been differentiated from direct toxicity (a). The latter has been attributed, in part, to redox changes (a-1), hypoxia (a-2), acetaldehyde (a-3), direct membrane alterations (a-4), or effects secondary to microsomal induction (a-5). (From Lieber, 1988.)

well as higher aliphatic alcohols (e.g., butanol which is not a substrate for catalase) (Teschke et al, 1972, 1974; Mezey et al, 1973) and (2) reconstitution of ethanol-oxidizing activity using NADPH–cytochrome P450 reductase, phospholipid, and either partially purified or highly purified microsomal P450 from untreated (Ohnishi and Lieber, 1977) or phenobarbital-treated (Miwa et al, 1978) rats. Ohnishi and Lieber (1977) showed that chronic ethanol consumption results in the induction of a unique P450 using a liver microsomal P450 fraction isolated from ethanol-treated rats. An ethanol-inducible form of P450 (LM3a), purified from rabbit liver microsomes (Koop et al, 1982; Ingelman-Sundberg and Johansson, 1984), catalyzed ethanol oxidation at rates much higher than other P450 isozymes and also had an enhanced capacity to oxidize 1-butanol, 1-pentanol, and aniline (Morgan et al, 1982), acetaminophen (Morgan et al, 1983), CCl_4 (Ingelman-Sundberg and Johansson, 1984), acetone (Koop and Cassaza, 1985), and N-nitrosodimethylamine (NDMA) (Yang et al, 1985). Although other compounds can also act as inducers, the specificity of the response to ethanol was demonstrated (Lieber et al, 1988). Similar results have been obtained with cytochrome P450j, a major hepatic P450 isozyme purified from ethanol- or isoniazid-treated rats (Ryan et al, 1985, 1986). Others have also provided evidence for the existence of a P450j-like isozyme in humans (Song et al, 1986; Wrighton et al, 1986). Wrighton et al (1986) employed immunoaffinity chromatography to purify from human liver a protein termed HLj; however, its catalytic activity toward ethanol was not described. Song et al (1986) isolated DNAs complementary to human P450j. The amino acid sequence of human P450j, deduced by sequencing of the cDNA inserts, was reported to be 94% homologous to the published NH_2-termini for HLj (Wrighton et al, 1986) over the first 18 amino acid residues. In a new nomenclature of cytochromes P450, Nebert et al (1987) proposed that the ethanol-inducible form be designated as P450IIEl. We now have succeeded in obtaining the purified human protein (Fig. 3.2) in a catalytically active form, with a high turnover rate for ethanol and other specific substrates (Lasker et al, 1987a) (Table 3.1). The designation P450IIEl should be reserved for this specific P450 alcohol oxygenase. However, other microsomal cytochrome P450 isozymes can also contribute to ethanol oxidation (Lasker et al, 1987b). Thus, the term "microsomal ethanol oxidizing system" (MEOS) should be maintained when one refers to the overall capacity of the microsomes to oxidize ethanol rather than to that fraction of the activity that is specifically catalyzed by P450IIE1. In addition to its role for ethanol metabolism per se, ethanol

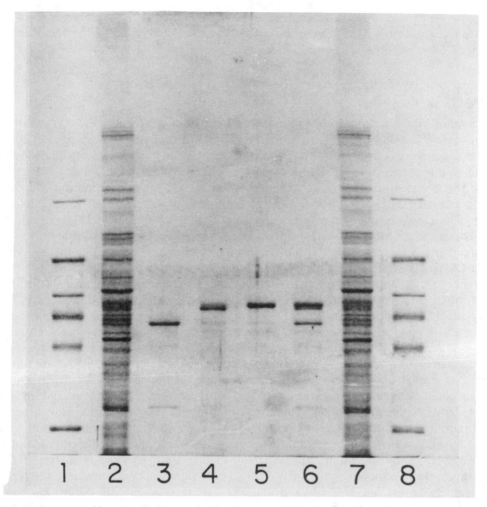

1 2 3 4 5 6 7 8

FIGURE 3.2. SDS-PAGE of human microsomes and purified cytochromes P450. Samples were analyzed on a slab gel 0.75 mm thick containing 7.5% acrylamide using a discontinuous buffer system. Migration proceeds from top to bottom. Lanes 2 and 7, microsomes (10 μg); lanes 3, 4, and 5, cytochrome P450B, P450ALC (P450IIE1) and P450C, respectively, (0.5 μg); lane 6, mix of all three P450s (0.25 μg each); lanes 1 and 8, protein standards with molecular weights of 98,000, 68,000, 58,000, 53,000, 43,000 and 29,000 (0.5 μg each). (From Lasker et al, 1987a.)

Table 3.1. Catalytic activities of purified human liver cytochromes P450

| | SUBSTRATE | | | |
| | ETOH | ANILINE | NDMA | AMINOPYRINE |
HEMEPROTEIN	(nmol product formed/min/nmol P450[a])			
Liver microsomes	12.6	1.6	3.2	16.9
P450ALC	12.2	7.3	2.8 (6.4)[b]	<1.0
P450B	1.2	<0.5	<0.04 (<0.04)	18.0
P450C	1.0	0.7	1.5 (7.0)	3.4

The catalytic activities of human P450ALC, P450B and P450C were determined using 0.1 nmol of each hemeprotein, saturating amounts of human liver Fp (900 units); and optimal concentrations of synthetic dilauroylphosphatidylcholine (50 μM). In reactions containing human liver microsomes (from which the three P450 isozymes were isolated), an amount of protein equivalent to 0.2 nmol P450 was used. Incubations were performed in 1.0 ml of 100 mM potassium phosphate buffer for 10 min at 37°C. (From Lasker et al, 1987a.)

[a]Values represent the mean of at least 3 determinations.

[b]Values in parentheses represent NDMA demethylase activities determined in the presence of 0.4 μmol human liver cytochrome b_5.

oxidation via MEOS may have significant consequences for the pathogenesis of liver injury, either directly (through production of acetaldehyde) or indirectly through the microsomal activation of other xenobiotics.

Hepatotoxicity Directly Associated with the Induction of MEOS Activity

Induction of MEOS activity results in enhanced production of acetaldehyde that exerts a variety of toxic effects at several sites of the hepatocyte, discussed subsequently. In addition, increased generation of acetaldehyde on the surface of the membranes of the endoplasmic reticulum may result in some significant local changes. Indeed, Nomura and Lieber (1981) found that covalent binding of exogenously added acetaldehyde to proteins of liver microsomes; an even greater effect was found with "endogenous acetaldehyde" (when ethanol was used). These results suggested a special capacity of "native" acetaldehyde (generated in situ in the membrane) to form covalent links with associated proteins. Furthermore, this effect was significantly increased after chronic ethanol consumption, in parallel with the induction of MEOS activity. The protein involved in the adduct formation was identified as P450IIE1 (Behrens et al, 1988). It is tempting to postulate that this increased acetaldehyde–protein adduct formation may be responsible, at least in part, for the appearance of antibodies against such adducts. Indeed, using an animal model, Israel et al (1986) demonstrated that acetaldehyde adducts may serve as neoantigens generating an immune response in mice. Our own studies (Hoerner et al, 1986) have shown that antibodies against acetaldehyde adducts (produced in vitro) are present in the serum of most alcoholics (Fig. 3.3). In addition to the acetaldehyde–protein adducts formed in liver microsomes, just referred to, acetaldehyde–protein adducts could be formed in a variety of other tissues and serve as antigens. Indeed, acetaldehyde binds covalently to other hepatic macromolecules (Mauch et al, 1986), hepatic cell membranes (Barry and McGivan, 1985) and other proteins such as human serum albumin (Donohue et al, 1983), hemoglobin (Stevens et al, 1981), red blood cell membrane proteins (Gaines et al, 1977), and tubulin (Baraona and Lieber, 1983). Adduct formation in the endoplasmic reticulum, however, may play a particularly significant role in view of the high level of acetaldehyde generated locally on oxidation of ethanol by the MEOS. Furthermore, acetaldehyde produced by this non-ADH pathway appeared to be degraded more slowly than that produced by the ADH pathway in the liver (Yasuhara et al, 1986), and acceleration of ethanol metabolism via this non-ADH pathway resulted in more severe hepatocytic necrosis. Hepatic injury, in turn, may promote the release of significant amounts of acetaldehyde-altered proteins. Thus, this experimental finding may be relevant to the clinical observation that, in addition to alcohol consumption, severity of liver disease may play a role in the appearance of circulating antibodies against acetaldehyde adducts, not only in alcoholics, but also in some nonalcoholics with liver injury (Hoerner et al, 1988). In turn, complement-binding acetaldehyde, adduct-containing immune complexes may contribute to the perpetuation or exaggeration of liver disease. This may represent one of the immune mechanisms — cell mediated as well as humoral — that would play a role in the pathogenesis of alcoholic liver injury (MacSween, 1984). Other modes of toxicity involve the interference with enzyme activity secondary to acetaldehyde binding with critical -SH groups, as discussed by Sorrell and Tuma (1987). One of the functions most sensitive to acetaldehyde is the repair of alkylated nucleoproteins, which was found to be inactivated by minute concentrations of acetaldehyde (Espina et al, 1988). Further mechanisms of acetaldehyde hepatotoxicity are discussed subsequently in connection with lipid and protein abnormalities.

Hepatotoxicity Through Activation of Xenobiotic Agents

Regardless of its quantitative role in ethanol metabolism per se discussed elsewhere (Lieber et al, 1987), in view of its inducibility and broad substrate specificity, the ethanol-specific form of cytochrome P450 has provided a major clue to the understanding of multiple etha-

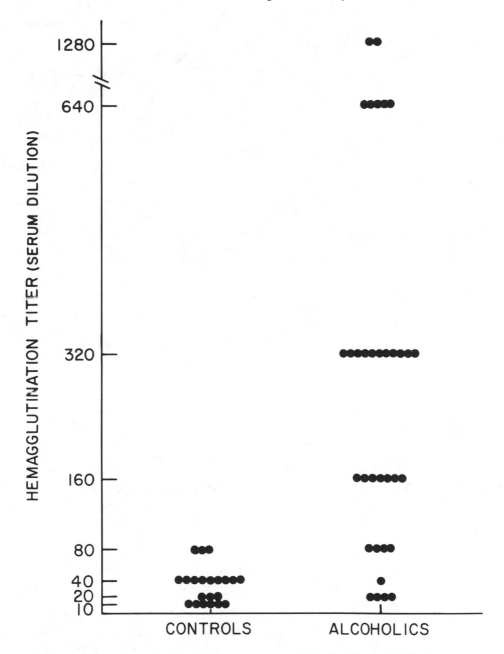

FIGURE 3.3. Hemagglutination titers of antibodies against acetaldehyde adducts in alcoholic patients and control subjects. (From Hoerner et al, 1986.)

nol–drug interactions, particularly with respect to the enhanced susceptibility of alcoholics to the hepatotoxic effects of various xenobiotic agents. Interaction of alcohol and drugs occurs at many sites, as reviewed elsewhere (Lieber, 1982, 1985; Lieber et al, 1987). In this chapter, the focus is on the interaction of ethanol with cytochrome P450-dependent microsomal drug metabolism.

Indeed, chronic alcohol intake has been shown to enhance susceptibility to hepatotoxic agents: the general increase in microsomal enzyme activities after chronic alcohol consumption also applies to those that convert exogenous substrates to toxic compounds and it particularly affects those xenobiotics for which the ethanol-inducible form of cytochrome P450

(P450IIE1) has a high affinity. For instance, CCl_4 exerts its toxicity after conversion to an active metabolite in the microsomes. As discussed before, P450IIE1 is particularly active in that regard and, indeed, alcohol pretreatment remarkably enhances CCl_4 hepatotoxicity (Hasumura et al, 1974). Thus, the clinical observation of the enhanced susceptibility of alcoholics to the hepatotoxic effect of CCl_4 may be due, at least in part, to increased metabolic activation of this compound. Liver toxicity of bromobenzene was also found to increase following chronic alcohol consumption (Hetu et al, 1983). It is likely that a large number of other toxic agents will be found to display a selective injurious action in the alcoholic patient. This pertains not only to industrial solvents but also to a variety of prescribed drugs. For instance, the increased hepatotoxicity of isoniazid observed in alcoholics may well be due to increased microsomal production of an active metabolite of the acetyl derivative of the drug (Timbrell et al, 1980). The capacity of isoniazid to induce the ethanol-specific form of cytochrome P450 has been noted before. Similarly, chronic ethanol administration enhances phenylbutazone hepatotoxicity, possibly because of increased biotransformation (Beskid et al, 1980).

The foregoing mechanism underlying hepatotoxicity also pertains to some over-the-counter medications. Acetaminophen (paracetamol, N-acetyl-p-aminophenol), widely used as an analgesic and an antipyretic, is generally safe when taken in recommended doses. However, large does of acetaminophen, mostly taken in suicide attempts, have been shown to produce fulminant hepatic failure. It is now clear that in addition to glucuronidation and sulfation, acetaminophen is also metabolized in the liver by the microsomal cytochrome P450 system; the latter biotransformation yields an active metabolite highly toxic to the liver. The practical implications are obvious in view of the widespread use of drugs known to be inducers of microsomal drug-metabolizing activities. Because alcohol induces microsomal drug-metabolizing systems, it was to be expected that a history of alcohol consumption might favor the hepatotoxicity of acetaminophen; this has been suggested by various case reports (Wright and Prescott, 1973; Seef et al, 1986). Experimentally, enhanced covalent binding of reactive metabolite(s) of acetaminophen to liver microsomes from ethanol-fed rats was observed to be associated with increased hepatotoxicity (Sato et al, 1981). Furthermore, in a reconstituted system, P450IIE1 was found to have a high capacity to oxidize acetaminophen to a reactive intermediate, which readily formed a conjugate with reduced glutathione (Morgan et al, 1983). For all these reasons, it is likely that the enhanced hepatotoxicity of acetaminophen observed after chronic ethanol consumption is due, at least in part, to increased microsomal production of reactive metabolite(s) of this drug (Timbrell et al, 1980). However, experimentally, unlike pretreatment with alcohol, which (as discussed before) accentuates toxicity, the presence of ethanol in part prevents the acetaminophen-induced hepatotoxicity, most likely because of inhibition of the biotransformation of acetaminophen to reactive metabolites (Sato and Lieber, 1981; Altomare et al, 1984a, 1984b). Thus, the greatest vulnerability of the alcoholic to acetaminophen is not necessarily during drinking, when ethanol may compete with acetaminophen for its microsomal metabolism, but rather after alcohol withdrawal, at which time there is no inhibitory effect of alcohol anymore but the induction of the microsomal metabolism still persists. This is also the period when the need for analgesics may be high because of the well-known withdrawal symptomatology. At that time, amounts of acetaminophen, large but usually still considered safe (2.5–5 g/day), may be taken and cause severe toxic side effects in the alcoholic.

Increased microsomal activation also involves carcinogens. Alcohol abuse is associated with an increased incidence of upper alimentary and respiratory tract cancers and many factors have been incriminated in the cocarcinogenic effect of ethanol (Lieber et al, 1986). One of the mechanisms is the effect of ethanol on enzyme systems involved in cytochrome P450-dependent carcinogen activation. Ethanol's effect on carcinogen activation has been demonstrated by using microsomes derived from a variety of tissues including the liver (the principal site of xenobiotic metabolism), the lungs and intestines (the major portals of entry for tobacco smoke and dietary carcinogens, respectively), and the esophagus (where ethanol consumption is a major risk factor in cancer development). Ethanol has a unique effect on the chemical carcinogen N-nitrosodimethylamine (NDMA): it induces a microsomal NDMA demethylase, which functions at low NDMA concentrations (Garro et al, 1981). This is in contrast to other microsomal enzyme inducers such as phenobarbital, 3-methylcholanthrene and polychlorinated biphenyls. These compounds increase the activity of other NDMA demethylases—the activity of which is detectable only at relatively high NDMA concentrations—while repressing the activity of low K_m NDMA demethylases (Guttenplan and Garro, 1977). Some of these effects may be due to the induction of a unique species of cytochrome P450 by ethanol as described earlier (Ohnishi and Lieber, 1977; Koop et al, 1982), which differentially affects the activation of various carcinogens; indeed, a selective affinity for NDMA has been demonstrated with the ethanol-inducible form of cytochrome P450 (Yang et al, 1985). Alcoholics are also commonly heavy smokers and, epidemiologically, a synergistic effect of alcohol consumption and smoking has been described as reviewed elsewhere (Lieber et al, 1986). Interactions at various levels are possible: chronic ethanol consumption was found to enhance the mutagenicity of tobacco pyrolysates (Garro et al, 1981). More recently benzoflavone, a tobacco-like inducer, was also found to induce a liver cytochrome P450 that is structurally different but catalytically similar to P450EII1. This new P450 could be involved in some of the pathological effects associated with combined habitual alcohol and tobacco use (Lasker et al, 1987b).

Ethanol also affects microsomal metabolism of exogenous and endogenous steroids, as discussed in detail elsewhere (Lieber, 1982); the effects include enhanced testosterone degradation and conversion to estrogens, as well as decreased testicular steroid synthesis. Furthermore, ethanol alters the metabolism of structurally related vitamins, such as Vitamin D (Gascon-Barre, 1982). This and other micronutrients may serve as substrates for the microsomal enzymes and the induction of the microsomal oxidative activities may, therefore, alter vitamin requirements and even affect the integrity of liver and other tissues. It has been found, already at the early fatty liver stage, that alcoholics commonly have very low hepatic vitamin A concentrations despite normal circulating vitamin A levels and the absence of obvious dietary vitamin A deficiency (Leo and Lieber, 1982). In experimental animals, ethanol administration was shown to depress hepatic vitamin A levels, even when administered with diets containing adequate amounts of vitamin A (Sato and Lieber, 1981). When dietary vitamin A was virtually eliminated, the depletion rate of hepatic vitamin A stores was two to three times faster in ethanol-fed rats than in controls, possibly because of accelerated microsomal degradation of vitamin A (Leo et al, 1984). Furthermore, it has been shown, using reconstituted systems with purified forms of cytochrome P450, that retinoic acid can serve as a substrate for microsomal oxidation (Leo at al, 1984). An even greater microsomal metabolism was found for retinol. Indeed, a new pathway of microsomal retinol metabolism, inducible by either ethanol or drug administration and capable of degrading an amount of retinol comparable to the daily intake, has been discovered in the liver (Leo and Lieber, 1985). The hepatic retinoid depletion was strikingly exacerbated when ethanol and drugs were combined (Fig. 3.4) (Leo et al, 1987a), which mimics a common clinical occurrence. A new microsomal NAD-dependent retinol dehydrogenase has also been described (Leo et al, 1987b). Furthermore, ethanol may also contribute to hepatic retinoid depletion by enhanced mobilization of the vitamin (Leo et al, 1986a). Hepatic vitamin A depletion is associated with lysosomal lesions (Leo et al, 1983), decreased NDMA detoxification (Leo et al, 1986b), and probably a score of other adverse effects. For all these reasons, vitamin A supplementation should be given not only to correct the problems of night blindness and sexual dysfunction of the alcoholic but also to alleviate liver dysfunction. The therapeutic administration of vitamin A, however, is complicated by the fact that excessive amounts of this vitamin are known to be hepatotoxic and that the alcoholic has an enhanced susceptibility to this effect (Leo et al, 1982; Leo and Lieber, 1983). There clearly is a narrowed "therapeutic window" for vitamin

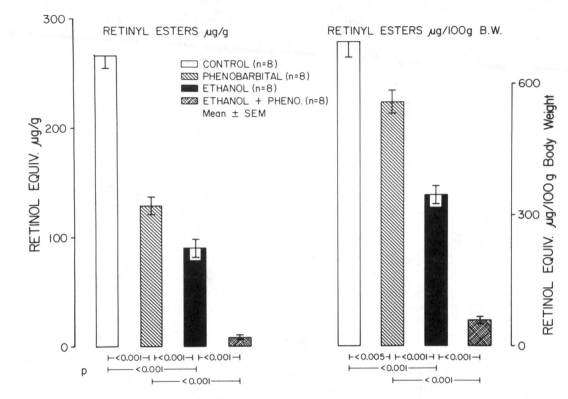

FIGURE 3.4. Effect of phenobarbital and/or ethanol on hepatic retinyl esters. Both drugs resulted in a significant depletion of hepatic retinyl esters. The combination of phenobarbital with ethanol produced a much more striking depletion, resulting in negligible hepatic retinyl ester levels. (From Leo et al, 1987a.)

A in the alcoholic patient who has increased requirements of vitamin A together with enhanced susceptibility to its toxicity.

ADH Mediated Metabolic and Pathologic Effects

In ADH-mediated oxidation of ethanol, hydrogen is transferred from the substrate to the cofactor nicotinamide adenine dinucleotide (NAD^+), converting it to the reduced form (NADH) (Fig. 3.1). As a net result, ethanol oxidation by ADH generates an excess of reducing equivalents as free NADH in hepatic cytosol, primarily because the metabolic systems involved in NADH removal are not able to fully offset the accumulation of NADH. The acetaldehyde produced in this reaction is converted to acetate by aldehyde dehydrogenase. The increased $NADH-NAD^+$ ratio is a sign of a major change in liver metabolism during ethanol oxidation to which several hepatic and metabolic disorders associated with alcohol abuse have been attributed (Lieber et al, 1959; Lieber and Schmid, 1961; Lieber and Davidson, 1962). This concept was useful in furthering our understanding of ethanol-induced changes in lipid, protein, carbohydrate, and uric acid metabolism.

Interaction with Lipid and Amino Acid Metabolism

The interaction of ethanol with lipid metabolism is complex, as discussed in detail elsewhere (Lieber and Pignon, 1989). When ethanol is present, it becomes a preferred fuel for the liver and displaces fat as a source of energy. This block in fat oxidation (Lieber and Schmid, 1961) favors fat accumulation. In addition, the altered redox state secondary to the oxidation of ethanol promotes lipogenesis, for instance, through an increase of α-glycerophosphate and enhanced formation of acylglycerols. The depressed oxidative capacity of the mitochondria injured by chronic alcohol feeding also contributes to the development of the fatty liver. A characteristic feature of liver injury in the alcoholic is the predominance of lesions in the perivenular (also called centrilobular) zone or zone 3 of the hepatic acinus (Edmondson et al, 1967). The mechanism for this zonal selectivity of the toxic effects of ethanol remains unknown. Two distinct but not mutually exclusive hypotheses have been raised: one claims that ethanol can produce hypoxic damage of perivenular hepatocytes, whereas the other postulates that conditions normally prevailing in the perivenular zone enhance the metabolic toxicity of ethanol. The hypoxia hypothesis originated from the observation that liver slices from rats fed alcohol chronically consume more oxygen than those of controls (Videla and Israel, 1970). It was then postulated that the increased consumption of oxygen would increase the gradient of oxygen tensions along the sinusoids to the extent of producing anoxic injury of perivenular hepatocytes (Israel et al, 1975). Such a mechanism was illustrated experimentally when centrilobular liver cell necrosis was induced by hypoxia in chronic ethanol-fed rats (French et al, 1984). Furthermore, both in human alcoholics (Kessler et al, 1954) and in animals fed alcohol chronically (Jauhonen et al, 1982; Sato et al, 1983), decreases in either hepatic venous oxygen saturation (Kessler et al, 1954) or pO_2 (Jauhonen et al, 1982) and in tissue oxygen tensions (Sato et al, 1983) have been found during the withdrawal state. However, this decrease is within the range of values found in normal subjects. Moreover, the differences in hepatic oxygenation found during the withdrawal state disappeared (Shaw et al, 1977; Jauhonen et al, 1982) or decreased (Sato et al, 1983) when alcohol was present in the blood. In addition, ethanol was found to impair oxygen utilization even in the presence of an ample supply (Lieber et al, 1989).

An alternative hypothesis to explain the selective perivenular hepatotoxicity of ethanol postulates that the low oxygen tensions normally prevailing in perivenular zones could exaggerate the redox shift produced by ethanol (Jauhonen et al, 1982). This mechanism was assessed in the baboon (Jauhonen et al, 1982). Acute ethanol administration increased splanchnic oxygen consumption in naïve baboons, but the consequences of this effect on oxygenation in the perivenular zone were offset by increased blood flow resulting in unchanged hepatic venous oxygen tension. In baboons chronically fed alcohol, splanchnic oxygen consumption was not increased in the withdrawal state or after ethanol infusion. To study the magnitude of the shift in redox state induced by ethanol in the perivenular zones, the effects of ethanol on the lactate–pyruvate ratio in hepatic venous blood (an approximation of that in perivenular hepatocytes) were compared with the ratio in total liver. Prior to ethanol infusion, lactate–pyruvate was the same in liver and hepatic venous blood. In contrast, ethanol increased the lactate–pyruvate ratio and decreased pyruvate more in hepatic venous blood than in total liver. In isolated rat hepatocytes, the ethanol-induced redox shift was markedly exaggerated by lowering the oxygen to a tension similar to those found in centrilobular zones. The process was also assessed in the isolated perfused liver, by varying the oxygen supply, to reproduce the oxygen tensions prevailing in vivo along the sinusoid (Jauhonen et al, 1985). Varying the oxygen tensions within the physiological range produced a redox gradient of both cytochrome oxidase and NAD^+. The degree of reduction of cytochrome oxidase at these physiological oxygen tensions was not associated with impairment in the ability of the liver to consume oxygen and to produce ATP, suggesting a lack of cellular anoxia. Twenty-five millimoles of ethanol increased hepatic oxygen consumption, but had no direct effect on the state of reduction of cytochrome oxidase. The effects of ethanol and oxygen tensions on NADH change were additive, indicating that a greater redox shift should occur when ethanol is oxidized at oxygen tensions similar to those normally prevailing in perivenular zones than at those in periportal zones. This dependence of the ethanol-induced redox shift on oxygen tensions may contribute to the selective perivenular hepatotoxicity of alcohol (Jauhonen et al, 1982): the normally low oxygen tension in perivenular zones may exaggerate the ethanol-induced redox shift.

One mechanism that has been invoked to explain liver injury in general and fatty liver in particular has been the peroxidation of lipids. Cysteine is one of the three amino acids that constitute glutathione (GSH). Binding of acetaldehyde with cysteine and/or GSH may contribute to a depression of liver GSH (Shaw et al, 1981), which may reduce the scavenging of toxic free radicals by this tripeptide. Although GSH depletion is not sufficient to cause lipid peroxidation, it is generally agreed that it may favor the peroxidation produced by other factors. GSH is important in the protection of cells against electrophilic drug injury in general and against reactive oxygen species in particular. Morton and Mitchell (1985) determined the turnover of GSH in individual animals by measuring the decrease in specific activity of GSH in bile over time after i.v. administration of $[^{35}S]$ cysteine. Rats chronically fed ethanol had significantly increased rates of GSH turnover associated with increased activity of hepatic GGT. The increase in turnover of GSH was not due to an increase in oxidation of GSH, consistent with the results of Vendemiale et al (1984) who had found evidence for increased synthesis. In contrast to these effects of chronic ethanol consumption, acute ethanol administration inhibited GSH synthesis and produced an increased loss from the liver (Speisky et al, 1985). GSH transferase activity (Kocak-Toker et al, 1985) was decreased by acute ethanol administration and GSH peroxidase after chronic treatment (Morton and Mitchell, 1985). A severe reduction in glutathione favors peroxidation (Wendel et al, 1979), and the damage may possibly be compounded by the increased generation of active radicals by the "induced" microsomes following chronic ethanol consumption. It is well known that the microsomal pathway, which requires O_2 and NADPH, is capable of generating lipid peroxides. Enhanced lipid peroxidation, possibly mediated by acetaldehyde (DiLuzio and Stege, 1977), has been proposed as a mechanism for ethanol-induced fatty liver (DiLuzio and Hartman, 1967).

The capacity of acetaldehyde to cause lipid peroxidation in the liver has been demonstrated in isolated perfused livers (Müller and Sies, 1982). Acetaldehyde may promote lipid peroxidation indirectly, i.e. through depletion of GSH, or by a more direct mechanism. Indeed, peroxidation has been linked to acetaldehyde oxidation (Müller and Sies, 1983). Furthermore, to what extent alcohol administration in vivo results in lipid peroxidation and injury is still uncertain (Hashimoto and Recknagel, 1968; Bunyan et al, 1969; Scheig and Klatskin, 1969; Comporti et al, 1971). Theoretically, increased activity of microsomal NADPH oxidase following ethanol consumption (Lieber and DeCarli, 1970b; Reitz, 1975) could result in enhanced H_2O_2 and O_2^- production, thereby also favoring lipid peroxidation. It has also been claimed that the ethanol-inducible form of rabbit liver microsomal cytochromes P450 is associated with increased hydroxyl radical formation (Ingelman-Sundberg and Johansson, 1984). However, when the effect of chronic alcohol feeding on lipid peroxidation was studied in rat liver microsomes, no correlation with the generation of hydroxyl radicals was observed (Shaw et al, 1984). Studies of Thomas et al (1985) showed that ferritin can provide the iron necessary for initiation of lipid peroxidation. O_2^-, as generated by xanthine oxidase, reductively releases ferritin-bound iron. Once released, this iron can promote the peroxidation of phospholipid liposomes. Catalase markedly stimulates malondialdehyde (MDA) formation in this system, suggesting that initiation is not dependent on H_2O_2. These results were further supported by the use of EPR spin trapping, which demonstrated a negative correlation between OH˙ formation and lipid peroxidation. It is noteworthy that in alcoholics the serum ferritin level was elevated in both groups immediately after a drinking bout, significantly more so in men with, as opposed to those without, biochemical signs of liver injury (Välimäki et al, 1983). The serum iron concentration was equally increased but returned to normal during the first week of ethanol withdrawal. Experimentally, iron and ethanol treatments enhanced liver lipid peroxidation (MDA formation). Since the hepatic MDA formation increased after the joint iron–ethanol treatment, it was suggested that an additive effect on lipid peroxidation occurs under these conditions.

In naïve rats, very large amounts of ethanol (5–6g/kg) are required to produce lipid peroxidation (DiLuzio and Hartman, 1967; MacDonald, 1973), whereas a smaller dose (3g/kg) had no effect (Shaw et al, 1981). By contrast, after chronic ethanol administration, even a smaller dose of ethanol administered acutely induced liver peroxidation and this effect could be prevented, at least partially, by the administration of methionine, a precursor of glutathione (Shaw et al, 1981). In the baboon, the ethanol induced lipid peroxidation was even more striking: administration of relatively small doses of ethanol (1–2g/kg) produced lipid peroxidation and GSH depletion after 5 to 6 hours. In the baboon that was chronically fed alcohol (50% of total calories for 1–4 years), alcoholic liver disease, including cirrhosis in some, developed and such animals showed evidence of enhanced hepatic lipid peroxidation and GSH depletion. These changes were observed following an overnight withdrawal from ethanol and were exacerbated by the readministration of ethanol. Evidence for GSH depletion and lipid peroxidation (enhanced diene conjugates) was found in liver biopsies of alcoholics who were withdrawn from alcohol (Shaw et al, 1983). Experimentally, as discussed before, acute ethanol intake diminished GSH content and enhanced that of GSSG, with a net decrease in the total GSH equivalents (GSH + 2GSSG). Biliary release of total GSH was reduced under these conditions. The combined administration of iron and ethanol further influenced the decrease in hepatic GSH and the increase in GSSG levels elicited by the separate treatments. These data suggest that iron exposure accentuates the changes in lipid peroxidation and in the glutathione status of the liver cell induced by acute ethanol intoxication (Valenzuela et al, 1983).

It is tempting to speculate that the propensity of the baboon to develop more severe lesions than the rat after chronic ethanol consumption may in some way be related, at least in part, to its greater susceptibility to GSH depletion, resulting in the initiation of lipid peroxidation. It is apparent, however, that GSH depletion per se does not suffice to produce liver damage (Siegers et al, 1977). As mentioned before, concomitant enhanced production of active radicals may be required, possibly resulting from the microsomal "induction" (Fig. 3.5) discussed before in this chapter. In addition to cysteine, methionine, and GSH, ethanol also affects other amino acids, as discussed in detail elsewhere (Lieber, 1982).

The accumulation of fat in the liver acts as a stimulus for the secretion of lipoprotein into the bloodstream and the development of hyperlipemia. Clinically, such heavy alcohol consumption is one of the most common (and readily overlooked) factors that promote hyperlipemia. Hyperlipemia may also be caused by the proliferation of the endoplasmic reticulum after chronic ethanol consumption and the associated increase of enzymes involved in the assembly of triglycerides and lipoproteins (Savolainen et al, 1986). The propensity to enhance

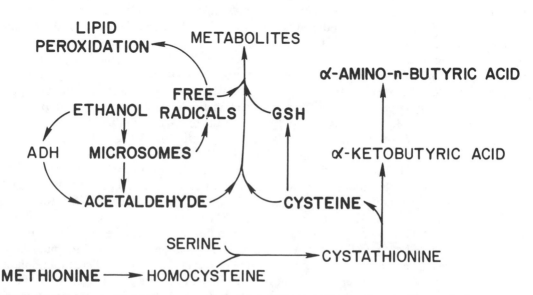

FIGURE 3.5. Hypothetical link between accelerated acetaldehyde production, increased free radical generation by the "induced" microsomes, and enhanced lipid peroxidation. (From Lieber, 1980.)

lipoprotein secretion is offset, at least in part, by a decrease in microtubules and the impairment of the secretory capacity of the liver resulting from liver damage following chronic ethanol consumption (vide infra). The level of blood lipids depends on the balance between these two opposite changes: at the early stage of alcohol abuse, when liver damage is still small, hyperlipemia will prevail, whereas the opposite occurs with severe liver injury (Borowsky et al, 1980). When hyperlipemia occurs, it involves all lipoprotein classes, including HDL. The latter could play a role in opposing the development of atherosclerosis. Prostaglandins may also be involved in the latter process. Indeed, acetaldehyde is a stimulant of vascular production of prostacyclin (Guivernau et al, 1987), a potent vasodilator and platelet antiaggregant agent. This effect may contribute to the flushing and other cardiovascular effects observed after alcohol consumption. After chronic alcohol consumption, ethanol acquires a stimulatory effect on prostacyclin production associated with a marked increase in the response of the vessel to the stimulus provided by HDL (Guivernau et al, 1987).

Alterations of Proteins, Microtubules, and Their Relation to Liver Injury

One of the earliest and most conspicuous features of the hepatic damage produced by alcohol is the enlargement of the liver. This hepatomegaly was traditionally attributed to the accumulation of lipids. However, in animals fed alcohol-containing diets, it was shown that lipids account for only half of the increase in liver dry weight (Lieber et al, 1965), while the other half is almost totally accounted for by an increase in proteins (Baraona et al, 1975). The latter is secondary, in part, to acetaldehyde-induced impairment of microtubular mediated protein secretion. Indeed, hepatic microtubules are significantly decreased in alcoholic liver disease (Matsuda et al, 1979, 1985). Experimentally, feeding rats with diets providing 36% of energy as ethanol resulted in enlargement of hepatocytes, associated with a decrease in the concentration of total tubulin (Baraona et al., 1975, 1977, 1984). Alcohol feeding decreased the difference between total hepatic tubulin and free tubulin by approximately 30% with a proportional increase in the free tubulin fraction. This suggested that alcohol consumption has a major effect on tubulin polymerization to form microtubules (Baraona et al, 1977; Matsuda et al, 1979). The decrease of polymerized tubulin by ethanol was documented in rats (Baraona et al, 1981), baboons (Matsuda et al, 1978), and in alcoholics with liver disease (Matsuda et al, 1983). Morphometric studies by Matsuda et al, (1979) and Okanoue et al (1984) revealed that the ethanol-induced decrease in polymerized tubulin was associated with a decrease in the hepatic microtubular mass. Incubation of hepatocytes isolated from normal rats (Matsuda et al, 1979) with 50 mM ethanol produced accumulation of acetaldehyde (up to 130 μM) and decreased polymerized tubulin and the volume of visible microtubules. In vivo, the acute intravenous administration of ethanol to naïve rats decreased hepatic polymerized tubulin and microtubules. This effect was partially prevented with the ADH inhibitor 4-methylpyrazole. Inhibition of acetaldehyde oxidation by pretreatment of the rats with disulfiram increased the accumulation of acetaldehyde in the liver and produced a further decrease in microtubules (Baraona et al, 1981; Baraona and Lieber, 1983). The acute effects of ethanol were markedly enhanced by prior consumption of ethanol-containing diets (Fig. 3.6).

By inhibiting ADH with pyrazole and maintaining the concentration of acetaldehyde by multiple additions, we observed inhibitory effect of acetaldehyde (approximately 200 μM) on colchicine binding by liver tubulin (Baraona et al, 1981; Baraona and Lieber, 1983). The sulfhydryl groups of cysteine, present in tubulin, are involved in polymerization and colchicine binding. Acetaldehyde also has high affinity for -SH groups and binds to brain tubulin (Baraona et al, 1981). Acetaldehyde binding to tubulin may therefore contribute to the decreased colchicine-binding capacity of tubulin in alcohol-fed animals, but more importantly it may alter the capacity of tubulin to polymerize. The disruption of liver microtubules in alcohol-fed rats and in isolated hepatocytes incubated with ethanol was associated with a prominent accumulation of secretory vesicles (Matsuda et al, 1979). In isolated hepatocytes, the

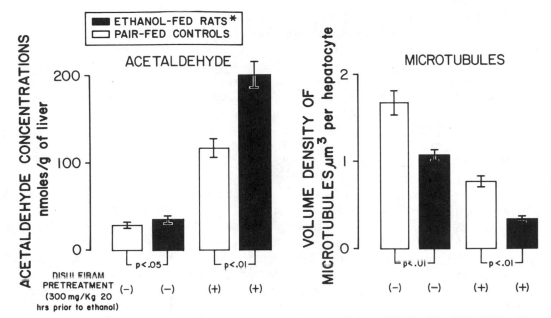

FIGURE 3.6. Acute effects of ethanol (with and without disulfiram) on hepatic acetaldehyde concentrations and microtubules of rats pair-fed with liquid diets containing 36% of calories as either ethanol or additional carbo-hydrate, respectively, for 4 to 6 weeks. Pretreatment with disulfiram increased the ethanol-induced accumulation of acetaldehyde and the decrease in liver microtubules, especially in alcohol-fed rats. (From Baraona et al, 1981.)

increase in volume and surface densities of the secretory vesicles and Golgi apparatus was prevented by pyrazole and reproduced by acetaldehyde and acetate (Matsuda et al, 1979).

The time course of incorporation of labeled leucine into immunoreactive albumin and transferrin revealed a significant delay in the secretion of these newly labeled proteins into the plasma with a corresponding retention in the liver of alcohol-fed rats (Baraona et al, 1977). These effects were associated with a significant accumulation of both albumin and transferrin in the liver. Similar, although less severe, alterations of albumin (Baraona et al, 1980) and glycoproteins (Volentine et al, 1984) were found after acute ethanol administration in rats. Inhibition of secretion was also observed after the addition of ethanol to liver slices (Tuma and Sorrell, 1981; Sorrell et al, 1983) but not to isolated hepatocytes (Mørland et al, 1981); however, in both preparations, inhibitory effects of ethanol on protein synthesis must be taken into consideration.

Transferrin, one of the retained export proteins, was clearly stained in the ballooned hepatocytes of alcoholic liver disease but not in nonalcoholic liver disease (Matsuda et al, 1985). The degree to which transferrin was stained was related to hepatic microtubular contents and also related to the heterogeneity of serum transferrin in alcoholic liver disease. These findings indicate that ballooning of hepatocytes in alcoholic liver disease, but not in nonalcoholic liver disease, is caused by the accumulation of exportable proteins due to impairment of microtubular polymerization. This accumulation might be related to the inhibition of secretion. However, the measured increase in export proteins such as albumin and transferrin accounted for only a relatively small fraction of the total increase in cytosolic protein. This raised the possibility that other export or constituent proteins of the cytosol could also contribute to the increase. Indeed, Pignon et al (1987) found that an increase in fatty acid-binding protein (FABP) accounts for one-sixth to one-third of the increase in cytosolic protein induced by chronic ethanol feeding, thus becoming the largest known contributor to the ethanol-induced increase in these proteins (Fig. 3.7). The results of Pignon et al (1987) also showed a striking discrepancy between the alcohol-induced increase in esterified fatty acids in the liver (mainly as triglycerides) and the modest increase in nonesterified fatty acids. In addition to the ethanol-induced increase in the synthesizing activities (Joly et al, 1974; Savolainen et al, 1984a), the increase of FABP could also favor the esterification of fatty acids, thereby playing a possible role in preventing potentially deleterious accumulation of nonesterified fatty acids (Brenner, 1984) and fatty acyl-CoA esters (Powell et al, 1985) secondary to the ethanol-induced inhibition of their oxidation (vide supra).

The increase in hepatic protein observed after ethanol was not associated with changes in concentration (Baraona et al, 1977), indicating that water was retained in proportion to the increase in protein. The mechanism of the water retention is not fully elucidated, but the rise in both protein and amino acids, plus a likely increase in associated small ions, could retain osmotically a large fraction of the water. The increases in lipid, protein, amino acid, water, and electrolytes result in increased size of the hepatocytes. In the rat, the swelling affects both perivenular and periportal hepatocytes. Similar changes have been observed in baboons fed 50% of dietary energy as ethanol, although in this species the accumulation of fat greatly exceeds that of protein (Savolainen et al, 1984a) and the enlarged hepatocytes have, as in humans, a clear centrilobular distribution (Miyakawa et al, 1985). The number of hepatocytes and the hepatic content of deoxyribonucleic acid (DNA) do not change after alcohol treatment and thus the hepatomegaly is entirely accounted for by the increased cell volume (Baraona et al, 1975, 1977).

One suspects that ballooning and associated increase of the hepatocyte volume may result in severe impairment of key cellular functions. In alcoholic liver disease, some hepatocytes

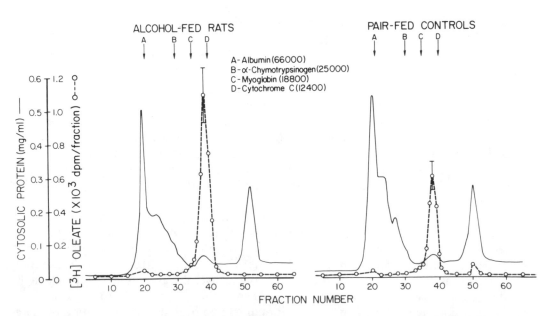

FIGURE 3.7. Identification of the cytosolic fatty acid-binding protein by gel filtration in four ethanol-fed and four pair-fed control rats. Cytosolic protein (4.5 mg) labeled with trace amounts of ^{3}[H] oleate was applied to a Sephacryl 200 S column (1.75 × 48 cm) at 4°C; 2.5 ml fractions were collected and assayed for protein content (solid line) and for radioactivity (broken line). Arrows indicate the elution positions of the calibration proteins. The results shown are the average of four pairs. (From Pignon et al, 1987.)

not uncommonly have a diameter that is increased two to three times, and thereby the volume may be increased more than 10-fold. It is not difficult to image that this type of cellular disorganization, with protein retention and ballooning, may promote progression of the liver injury in the alcoholic. Indeed, other causes of protein retention in the liver, such as alpha$_1$ antitrypsin deficiency, are known to be associated with progression to fibrosis and cirrhosis. By analogy, one can assume that in the alcoholic also, protein retention may in some way favor progression of liver disease to cirrhosis. Alcohol may, of course, promote fibrosis in some other ways, as discussed in detail elsewhere (Lieber and Leo, 1986). One of these mechanisms includes the capacity of acetaldehyde to stimulate collagen synthesis, as demonstrated in cultured hepatic myofibroblasts (Savolainen et al, 1984b). Increased mRNA for collagen in alcohol-fed baboons (Zern et al, 1985) provides further evidence for the role of enhanced collagen synthesis in the process of fibrosis. Other ethanol-induced alterations in protein metabolism have been discussed in detail elsewhere (Lieber, 1982, 1984, 1985).

In summary, ethanol has the potential to inhibit protein synthesis when administered in high doses and when the metabolic derangements associated with ethanol oxidation are experimentally exaggerated. Whether such conditions are relevant to clinical situations that aggravate the effects of alcohol on the liver (such as malnutrition of hypoxia) remains to be documented. Selected areas, such as the perivenular zones, may be adversely affected. Thus far, however, experimental evidence indicates that alcohol consumption can lead to the development of at least the initial stages of liver injury with no apparent impairment in the synthesis of total liver proteins or even with some increase (Baraona et al, 1980). There is scarce information on the synthesis of specific proteins. With progression of alcoholic injury to more severe stages, one would expect various liver functions, including protein synthesis, to be adversely affected.

METABOLIC DISORDERS

Hyperglycemia and Diabetes

In large population studies, alcohol intake correlates with hyperglycemia (Gerard et al, 1977). Aside from patients with chronic pancreatitis and endocrine (insulin) insufficiency, there is no ready explanation for this. It was suspected that ethanol per se impairs glucose tolerance (Phillips and Safrit, 1971; Rehfield et al, 1973) but this is difficult to prove since the elevated insulin levels that accompany alcohol intake could reflect insulin resistance due to alcohol or the augmentation of insulin release that alcohol itself causes (Metz et al, 1969; Dornhorst and Ouyang, 1971; Nikkilä and Taskin, 1975). Insulin resistance caused by alcohol has been demonstrated in healthy subjects using the insulin clamp technique whereby glucose utilization can be measured during glucose infusions at steady blood glucose and insulin levels (Yki-Järvinen and Nikkilä, 1985).

In fed animals and humans, acute alcohol administration results in hyperglycemia (Matunaga, 1942; Forsander et al, 1958). This is caused by the release of glucose from the glycogen reserves of the liver into the blood and is mediated mostly by the adrenal medulla and the sympathetic nervous system (Matunaga, 1942; Ammon and Estler, 1968), although decreased peripheral utilization of glucose may also be contributory (Lochner et al, 1967).

Hypoglycemia

In the fed state, when liver glycogen is abundant, glycogenolysis supports blood glucose levels. In the fasting state, extensive clinical and in vivo studies have established that hypoglycemia following alcohol administration is a normal reaction in humans and experimental animals (Field et al, 1963; Freinkel et al, 1965). Hypoglycemia is due to decreased reserves of hepatic glycogen and the inhibition of hepatic gluconeogenesis from various precursors as a consequence of the increased NADH–NAD$^+$ ratio (Krebs et al, 1969). The following pathways that can support blood glucose are interfered with by concomitant metabolism of alcohol: glucogenesis from amino acids, formation of glucose from glycerol, lactate, and galactose (Madison et al, 1967; Krebs et al, 1969). The increase in NADH–NAD$^+$ ratio due to hepatic metabolism of alcohol is partly responsible for these metabolic changes. Changes in enzyme activities relevant to various metabolic steps of gluconeogenesis have also been described (Stifel et al, 1976; Duruibe and Tejwani, 1981). From a clinical standpoint, hypoglycemia represents a particularly dramatic complication of acute alcohol abuse and may be responsible for some of the unexplained sudden deaths in acute alcoholic intoxication. A prompt diagnosis and initiation of therapy is mandatory in view of the reported mortality rate of 11% in adults and 25% in children (Madison et al, 1967). Hypoglycemia may be present when an alcohol imbiber exhibits an altered mental state (even in the fed state, especially in children). In clinical practice, however, severe alcoholic hypoglycemia is uncommon. In several conditions, refractiveness to alcohol hypoglycemia can be demonstrated: in nondiabetic obese subjects (Arky et al, 1968), in some alcoholics with a diabetic glucose pattern (Hed and Nygren, 1968), and during steroid therapy (Arky and Freinkel, 1966). Refractiveness has also been demonstrated in chronic malnourished alcoholics (Salaspuro, 1970, 1971). This presumably can be related to the attenuation of alcohol-induced hepatic redox changes after chronic alcohol consumption (Salaspuro et al, 1981). Similarly, alcohol-induced hypoglycemia can be suppressed by 4-methylpyrazole (an alcohol dehydrogenase inhibitor) (Salaspuro et al, 1977).

Hyperuricemia

It has long been known that excessive drinking of alcoholic beverages is associated with precipitation of acute gouty arthritis (Newcombe, 1970). The hyperuricemia that accompanies bouts of intense alcohol intake has been shown to occur in patients without known disorders of uric acid metabolism or renal function (Lieber et al, 1962). An important mechanism by which hyperuricemia occurs is decreased urinary excretion of uric acid secondary to elevated serum lactate. Alcoholic hyperuricemia can be readily differentiated from the primary variety because of its reversibility on discontinuation of alcohol abuse. Alcohol-associated ketosis or starvation may also further promote hyperuricemia (MacLachlan and Rodan, 1967).

An increase in urate production (partly explained by an increase in adenosine nucleotide turnover) has been shown to cause hyperuricemia in gouty volunteers (Faller and Fox, 1982). Urinary urate clearance was increased and urinary urate and oxypurines were higher. This mechanism was demonstrated at lower blood alcohol levels than was achieved by those investigating the lactate related renal mechanism, and the levels were also lower than the blood alcohol levels usually seen in patients with alcoholic hyperuricemia. The purine content (guanosine) of some beers may also be a contributing factor for hyperuricemia in alcoholic subjects (Gibson et al, 1984).

Ketoacidosis

Alcohol intake is often accompanied by ketosis with minimal or absent acidosis. Blood glucose is usually normal (Lefevre et al, 1970). Clinically, alcoholic ketosis usually occurs 48 hours or more after the last intake of alcohol and following a period of anorexia and hyperemesis. Decreased, normal or moderately increased blood glucose levels contrasts with the severe ketosis (Cooperman et al, 1974). Levels of β-hydroxybutyrate are typically higher than those of acetoacetate and may be overlooked if blood ketone levels are assessed by the nitroprusside reaction (Acetest, Ketostix), which is insensitive to β-hydroxybutyrate.

Obesity

Theoretically, ethanol may contribute to obesity because ethanol can serve as an energy source. The carbohydrate content of alcoholic beverages is negligible, in the case of whiskey, cognac or vodka; from 2 to 10 g/L for red or dry white wine; 30 g/L for beer or dry sherry; and as much as 120 g/L for sweetened white or port wines (Pekkanen and Forsander, 1977).

The estimated alcohol contribution to the diet of Americans is 4.5% of total calories, based on figures for national consumption (Scheig, 1970). Of course, the heavy drinker may derive as much as half his or her daily calories or more from ethanol. Although the combustion of ethanol in a bomb calorimeter indicates a value of 7.1 Cal/g, we know that its biological value may be less when compared to carbohydrates on a calorie basis. Subjects given additional calories as alcohol under metabolic ward conditions failed to gain weight (Lieber et al, 1965). No additional weight was gained by 17 hospitalized alcoholics who were given 1800 alcohol-derived calories beyond the 2600-calorie diet they had been receiving (Mezey and Faillace, 1971). Under metabolic ward conditions, isocaloric substitution of ethanol for carbohydrate, as 50% of total calories in a balanced diet, resulted in a decline in body weight and, when given as additional calories, ethanol caused less weight gain than calorically equivalent carbohydrate or fat (Pirola and Lieber, 1972). Others have reported variable responses to additional calories as ethanol (Crouse and Grundy, 1984) no weight gain in lean individuals and some weight gain in half the obese individuals.

Support for the view that ethanol increases the metabolic rate was provided by the observation that ethanol ingestion increases oxygen consumption in normal subjects, and that this effect is much greater in alcoholics (Tremolieres and Carre, 1961). Substitution of ethanol for carbohydrate increases the metabolic rate of humans and rodents (Stock et al, 1973; Stock and Stuart, 1974). A 15% increase in thermogenesis was seen in rats that were fed ethanol for 10 days (Stock and Stuart, 1974). In humans, diet-induced thermogenesis was also increased (Stock and Stuart, 1974). Although some of the energy wastage was attributable to brown fat thermogenesis in rats, most of it could not be so explained (Rothwell and Stock, 1984). One postulated mechanism of energy wastage when ethanol is consumed is via oxidation without phosphorylation by the microsomal ethanol oxidizing system (Pirola and Lieber, 1972). This pathway is induced by chronic ethanol consumption, after which the wastage was noted to be aggravated (Pirola and Lieber; 1975, 1976). Others (Israel et al, 1975) have implicated uncoupling of mitochondrial NADH reoxidation, perhaps abetted by catecholamine release or a hyperthyroid state, to explain energy wastage. The hyperthyroid aspect of the mechanism is controversial (Teschke et al, 1983).

In summary, as a calorie source, alcohol is not as adequate as equivalent carbohydrate, particularly when taken chronically in large amounts. Thus, although the caloric value of ethanol may contribute to excess energy intake, ethanol per se is not a common primary cause of obesity. Moderate alcohol intake, alcohol accounting for 16% of total calories (alcohol included), is associated with a slightly elevated energy intake (Gruchow et al, 1985). Despite comparable levels of physical activity, there is no weight gain, perhaps because of the energy considerations already discussed. This level of intake of alcohol, and slightly higher levels (23%) (Hillers and Massey, 1985), is associated with a substitution of alcohol for carbohydrate calories. When the percentage of calories as alcohol exceeds 30%, significant decreases in protein and fat intake occur.

ENDOCRINOLOGICAL COMPLICATIONS

Alcohol interacts with the endocrine system at a number of possible loci, including the hypothalamus, the pituitary, and various target organs. In addition, liver injury may disturb peripheral metabolism of hormones by affecting hepatic blood flow, protein binding, enzymes, cofactors, or receptors.

Clinical and research endocrinologists have shown that many important endocrine inter-actions of alcohol and alcoholic liver disease occur in human beings as well as in experimental animals. Many of the effects attributed to alcohol may be related to other factors as well, such as acquired hepatic dysfunction, malnutrition, drug abuse, sleep disturbances, or psychiatric disease, all of which may have important implications for endocrine function. Nonetheless, a considerable body of research has developed in the last 30 years involving experimental ani-mal models, healthy human volunteers, and alcoholic individuals that suggests that clinically significant alcohol-related endocrine disturbances can occur in humans as a direct toxic effect of alcohol or its metabolites (Cicero, 1981; Lieber, 1982).

The Syndrome of Feminization and Demasculinization

There has been consistent recognition that alcoholic men, particularly those with cirrhosis of the liver, have a well-defined syndrome consisting of features of both feminization and demas-culinization (Mark and Wright, 1978). Feminization features included marked increase in breast size, or gynecomastia, consisting of deposits of fat in the breast area and stimulation of the glandular elements of the breast, also the loss of body and sexual hair. Symptoms of demasculinization involved the decreased need to shave, reduced prostate size, softening and shrinking of the testes, abnormalities in semen, and global sexual dysfunction (decreased libido and erectile and ejaculatory failures) (Van Thiel et al, 1982).

After the discovery of the estrogenic hormones and their clinical application, it became apparent that the symptoms of feminization and demasculinization could be reproduced by estrogen administration to men. The retention theory was proposed, which held that the feminization–demasculinization syndrome was due to the failure of the liver to metabolize and inactivate the normally produced endogenous estrogens. It now seems that the overall met-abolic removal of the estrogenic hormones is not significantly reduced in patients with cir-rhosis. Evidence exists that precursor hormones, that is, androgens of adrenal and gonadal origin, may be converted to active estrogen compounds at a greater-than-normal rate in al-coholic patients (Lieber, 1982). Thus, the hyperestrogenic syndrome is due at least in part to increased hormone production rather than to retention of estrogens produced at a normal rate. Other recently suggested mechanisms include alterations in estrogen-binding protein in the liver, abnormalities in estrogen receptor function, and failure to inactivate xenobiotic estrogenic materials, some of which are contained in beverage alcohols. The pathogenetic mechanism of the hyperestrogenic effect is probably multifactorial. The clinical manifesta-tions may reflect the following alterations in estrogen metabolism—elevated levels of estradiol and estrone (Chopra et al, 1973) and increased conversion of testosterone and androstene-dione to estrogen (Gordon et al, 1975).

Alcohol use also decreases plasma testosterone (Mendelson and Mellow, 1974; Gordon et al, 1978; Mendelson et al, 1978), an effect that reflects both a decrease in production and increased metabolic clearance of the hormone. Depletion of NAD^+ as a result of the metab-olism of alcohol or acetaldehyde or both may lead to decreased conversion of pregnenolone to testosterone (Gordon et al, 1980) and, in part, account for decreases in plasma testoster-one. In addition, alcohol or its oxidation may affect the levels of lutenizing hormone (LH) as well as the receptor for LH in the Leydig cell (Bhalla et al, 1979).

Pituitary Function

This subject has been extensively reviewed (Lieber, 1982) and a detailed discussion would exceed the scope of the present chapter. The highly variable results in this area seem to reflect the complex interrelationship between alcohol, malnutrition, and liver injury. However, at least in terms of the gonadotropins, the hypothalamic–pituitary axis appears defective since gonadotropin levels are in the normal range despite low levels of testosterone (Kent et al,

1973). In addition, the diuretic actions of alcohol are clearly an effect on the posterior pituitary (i.e., a transient suppression of antidiuretic hormone) (Linkola et al, 1978).

Adrenocortical Function

Chronic ethanol abuse increases plasma cortisol (Mendelson and Stein, 1966; Mendelson et al, 1971) and is occasionally associated with physical and biochemical changes resembling those seen in Cushing's syndrome. Patients with alcohol-induced pseudo-Cushing's syndrome may exhibit increased plasma cortisol levels, an abnormal response to dexamethasone, and evidence of pituitary dysfunction. Experimental studies indicate that alcohol activates the hypothalamic–pituitary–adrenal axis resulting in adrenocorticotropic (ACTH) release and cortisol secretion.

Although liver disease (cirrhosis) per se does not consistently alter plasma cortisol levels, plasma aldosterone levels are generally increased (Wolff et al, 1962). The secondary aldosteronism that occurs in liver disease is believed to play a role in the pathogenesis of ascites.

Adronomedullary Function

Considerable evidence in humans indicates that alcohol stimulates adrenal medullary secretion of catecholamines. In addition, the peripheral metabolism of the released catecholamine is altered by alcohol (Davis et al, 1967). Peripheral metabolism of catecholamines shifts from an oxidative (3-methoxy-4-hydroxymadelic acid) to a reductive pathway (3-methoxy-4-hydroxyphenylglycol), a change that may reflect changes in the NADH–NAD ratio or acetaldehyde production (Smith and Gitlow, 1967). The effects of alcohol on adrenomedullary secretion must clearly be considered when evaluating the alcoholic for the presence of a pheochromocytoma.

Catecholamine secretion is markedly stimulated during periods of withdrawal from alcohol, particularly in inexperienced drinkers. These individuals may exhibit tachycardia, hypertension, and tremulousness with sweating, presenting an apparent clinical picture suggestive of pheochromocytoma (Lieber, 1982).

Effects of Alcohol on Thyroid Function

Both alcohol and alcoholic liver injury have effects on thyroid function. Acute administration of ethanol increases the liver to plasma ratio of thyroid hormone (Bleecker et al, 1969; Israel et al, 1973), a finding that may explain some of the metabolic effects of alcohol. In particular, it has been proposed that chronic use of alcohol leads to a hepatic "hypermetabolic" state. In this scheme, hepatic "hyperthyroidism" leads to increased oxygen consumption, local anoxia, and possibly liver injury (Israel et al, 1973; Bernstein et al, 1975). Propylthiouracil has been used to protect against alcohol-induced liver injury on these grounds. Two clinical trials on this question have yielded discrepant findings (Orrego et al, 1979; Halle et al, 1982).

The diagnosis of hyperthyroidism (Grave's disease) may be considered in patients who use alcohol to excess, since they have many of the features suggestive of the disease (tremor, weight loss, tachycardia, stare, palmar erythema). These features are frequently seen during alcohol withdrawal syndrome and are a manifestation of increased catecholamine secretion. Alcoholics exhibit a stare or lack of blinking, suggestive of hyperthyroidism resulting from increased sympathetic tone. Alcoholics also appear to have proptosis because of the wasting of muscle and fat about the face; by measurement, true proptosis is not present.

If an individual is in a dysproteinemic state as a result of alcoholic liver disease, abnormalities in thyroid function may be present, particularly elevated thyroxine levels, leading to an erroneous diagnosis of thyrotoxicosis. In most circumstances, however, the thyroid gland is not palpable and detailed measurements of thyroid function are normal (e.g., free thyroxine level) or discordant (i.e., T_3 resin uptake, which is reduced rather than elevated, as would be seen in true hyperthyroidism).

The diagnosis of hypothyroidism may also be suggested by laboratory findings in some clinical settings. Severely ill patients, including alcoholics, have low triiodothyronine levels, and inappropriately low or normal thyroid-stimulating hormone levels. These low levels may be due to a change in the peripheral metabolism of thyroxine—a decrease in the deiodination of the outer ring of the molecule—leading to increased deiodination of the inner ring structure with increased formation of reverse triiodothyronine. Changes in thyroid-binding proteins due to liver disease may lead to alterations in hormone levels without reflecting primary thyroid disease. The presence of this disorder can often be confirmed by measurement of reverse triiodothyronine or by testing with thyrotropin-releasing hormone.

Other endocrine and metabolic abnormalities associated with alcoholism or alcoholic liver disease are discussed in detail elsewhere (Lieber, 1982).

ACKNOWLEDGMENTS

Original studies reviewed in this chapter were supported, in part, by DHHS Grants #AA03508, #DK23810, #AA05934 and the Veterans Administration. The author wishes to thank Ms. Patricia Walker for expert secretarial assistance.

REFERENCES

Altomare E, Leo MA, Lieber CS: Interaction of acute ethanol administration with acetaminophen metabolism and toxicity in rats fed alcohol chronically. *Alcohol Clin Exp Res* 1984a; 8:405–409.

Altomare E, Leo MA, Sato C, Vendemiale G, Lieber CS: Interaction of ethanol with acetaminophen metabolism in the baboon. *Biochem Pharmacol* 1984b; 33:2207–2212.

Ammon HPT, Estler CJ: Inhibition of ethanol-induced glycogenolysis in brain and liver by adrenergic Δ-blockade. *J Pharm Pharmacol* 1968; 20:164–165.

Arky RA, Abramson EZ, Freinkel N: Alcohol hypoglycemia. VII. Further studies on the refractoriness of obese subjects. *Metabolism* 1968; 17:977–987.

Arky RA, Freinkel N: Alcohol hypoglycemia. V. Alcohol infusion to test gluconeogenesis in starvation with special reference to obesity. *N Engl J Med* 1966; 274:426–433.

Baraona E, Finkelman F, Lieber CS: Reevaluation of the effects of alcohol consumption on rat liver microtubules. *Res Commun Chem Path Pharmacol* 1984; 44:265–278.

Baraona E, Leo MA, Borowsky SA, Lieber CS: Alcoholic hepatomegaly: Accumulation of protein in the liver. *Science* 1975; 190:794–795.

Baraona E, Leo MA, Borowsky SA, Lieber CS: Pathogenesis of alcohol-induced accumulation of protein in the liver. *J Clin Invest* 1977; 60:546–554.

Baraona E, Lieber CS: Effects of ethanol on hepatic protein metabolism. In: Alcohol and Protein Synthesis: Ethanol, Nucleic Acids and Protein Synthesis in the Brain and Other Organs. *NIAAA Research Monograph*, 1983, No. 10, DHHS Publication No. (ADM) 83-1198, pp. 75–95.

Baraona E, Matsuda Y, Pikkarainen P, Finkelman F, Lieber CS: Effects of ethanol on hepatic protein secretion and microtubules. Possible mediation by acetaldehyde. *Curr Alcohol* 1981; 8:421–434.

Baraona E, Pikkarainen P, Salaspuro M, Finkelman F, Lieber CS: Acute effects of ethanol on hepatic protein synthesis and secretion in the rat. *Gastroenterology* 1980; 79:104–111.

Barry RE, McGivan JD: Acetaldehyde alone may initiate hepatocellular damage in acute alcoholic liver disease. *Gut* 1985; 26:1065–1069.

Behrens UJ, Hoerner M, Lasker JM, Lieber CS: Formation of acetaldehyde adducts with ethanol-inducible P450IIE1 in vivo. *Biochem Biophys Res Commun* 1988; 154:584–590.

Bernstein J, Videla L, Israel Y: Hormonal influences in the development of the hypermetabolic state of the liver produced by chronic administration of ethanol. *J Pharmacol Exp Ther* 1975; 192:583–591.

Beskid M, Bialek J, Dzieniszewski D, Sadowski J, Tlalka J: Effect of combined phenylbutazone and ethanol administration on rat liver. *Exp Path* 1980; 18:487–491.

Bhalla VK, Chen CJ, Gyanprakasam MS: Effect of in vivo administration of human chorionic gonadotropin and ethanol on the process of testicular receptor depletion and replenishment. *Life Sci* 1979; 24:1315–1324.

Bleecker M, Ford DH, Rhines RK: A comparison of ^{131}I-triiodothyronine accumulation and degradation in ethanol-treated and control rats. *Life Sci* 1969; 8:267–275.

Borowsky SA, Perlow W, Baraona E, Lieber CS: Relationship of alcoholic hypertriglyceridemia to stage of liver disease and dietary lipid. *Dig Dis Sci* 1980; 25:22–27.

Brenner RR: Effects of unsaturated acids on membrane structure and enzyme kinetics. *Prog Lipid Res* 1984; 23:69.

Bunyan J, Cawthrone MA, Diplock AT, Green J: Vitamin E and hepatotoxic agents. 2. Lipid peroxidation and poisoning with orotic acid, ethanol and thioacetamide in rats. *Br J Nutr* 1969; 23:309–317.

Chopra IJ, Tulchinsky D, Greenway F: Estrogen–androgen imbalance in hepatic cirrhosis. *Ann Int Med* 1973; 79:198–203.

Cicero TJ: Neuroendocrinological effects of alcohol. *Ann Rev Med* 1981; 32:123.

Comporti M, Burdino E, Raja F: Fatty acids composition of mitochondrial an microsomal lipids of rat liver after acute ethanol intoxication. *Life Sci* 1971; 10:855–866.

Cooperman MT, Davidoff F, Spark R, Pallotta J: Clinical studies of alcoholic ketoacidosis. *Diabetes* 1974; 23:433–439.

Crouse JR, Grundy SM: Effects of alcohol on plasma lipoproteins and cholesterol and triglyceride metabolism in man. *J Lipid Res* 1984; 25:486–496.

Davis VE, Brown H, Huff JA, Cashaw JL: Ethanol-induced alterations of norepinephrine metabolism in man. *J Lab Clin Med* 1967; 69:787–799.

DiLuzio NR, Hartman AD: Role of lipid peroxidation on the pathogenesis of the ethanol-induced fatty liver. *Fed Proc* 1967; 26:1436–1442.

DiLuzio NR, Stege TE: The role of ethanol metabolites in hepatic lipid peroxidation, in Fisher MM, Rankin JG (eds): *Alcohol and the Liver*. New York. Plenum Press, 1977, vol 3, pp 45–62.

Donohue TM Jr, Tuma DJ, Sorrell MF: Binding of metabolically derived acetaldehyde to hepatic proteins in vitro. *Lab Invest* 1983; 49:226.

Dornhorst A, Ouyang A: Effect of alcohol on glucose tolerance. *Lancet* 1971; ii:957–959.

Duruibe V, Tejwani GA: The effect of ethanol on the activities of the key gluconeogenic and glycolytic enzymes of rat liver. *Mol Pharmacol* 1981; 20:621–630.

Edmondson HA, Peters RL, Frankel HH, Borowsky S: The early stage of liver injury in the alcoholic. *Medicine* 1967, 46:119–129.

Espina N, Lima V, Lieber CS, Garro AJ: In vitro and in vivo inhibitory effect of ethanol and acetaldehyde on D-methylguanine transferase. *Carcinogenesis* 1988; 9:761–766.

Faller J, Fox IH: Ethanol-induced hyperuricemia: Evidence for increased urate production by activation of adenine nucleotide turnover. *N Engl J Med* 1982; 307:1598–1602.

Field JB, Williams HE, Mortimore GE: Studies on the mechanism of ethanol induced hypoglycemia. *J Clin Invest* 1963; 42:497–506.

Forsander OA, Vartia KO, Krusius FE: Experimentelle Studien über die biologische Wirkung von Alcohol. A. Alcohol und Blutzucker. *Annales Medicinsere Experimentalis et Biologiae Fenniae* 1958; 36:416–434.

Freinkel N, Arky RA, Singer DL, Cohen AK, Bleicher SJ, Anderson JB: Alcohol hypoglycemia: IV. Current concepts of its pathogenesis. *Diabetes* 1965; 14:350–361.

French SW, Benson NC, Sun PS: Centrilobular liver necrosis induced by hypoxia in chronic ethanol-fed rats. *Hepatology* 1984; 4:912–917.

Gaines KC, Salhany JM, Tuma DJ, Sorrell MF: Reaction of acetaldehyde with human erythrocyte membrane proteins. *FEBS Lett* 1977; 75:115–117.

Garro AJ, Seitz HK, Lieber CS: Enhancement of dimethylnitrosamine metabolism and activation to a mutagen following chronic ethanol consumption. *Cancer Res* 1981; 41:120–124.

Gascon-Barre M: Interrelationships between vitamin A_3 and 25-hydroxy-vitamin D_3 during chronic ethanol administration in the rat. *Metabolism* 1982; 31:67–72.

Gerard MJ, Klatsky AL, Siegelaub AB, Friedman GD, Feldman R: Serum glucose levels and alcohol-consumption habits in a large population. *Diabetes* 1977; 26:780–785.

Gibson T, Rodgers AV, Simmonds HA, Toseland P: Beer drinking and its effect on uric acid. *Br J Rheumatology* 1984; 23:203–209.

Gordon GG, Olivo J, Rafi F, Southren AL: Conversion of androgens to estrogens in cirrhosis of the liver. *J Clin Endocr Metab* 1975; 40:1018–1026.

Gordon GG, Southern AL, Lieber CS: The effects of alcoholic liver disease and alcohol ingestion on sex hormone levels. *Alcohol Clin Exp Res* 1978; 2:259–263.

Gordon GG, Vittek J, Southren AL, Munnangi P, Lieber CS: Effect of chronic alcohol ingestion on the biosynthesis of steroids in rat testicular homogenate in vitro. *Endocrinology* 1980; 106:1880–1885.

Gruchow HW, Sobocinski KA, Barboriak JJ, Scheller JG: Alcohol consumption, nutrient intake and relative weight among US adults. *Am J Clin Nutr* 1985; 42:289–295.

Guivernau M, Baraona E, Lieber CS: Acute and chronic effects of ethanol and its metabolites on vascular production of prostacyclin in rats. *J Pharmacol Exp Ther* 1987; 240:59–64.

Guttenplan JB, Garro AJ: Factors affecting the induction of dimethylnitrosamine by Aroclor 1254. *Cancer Res* 1977; 37:329–330.

Halle P, Pari P, Kapstein E, Kanel G, Redeker AG, Reynolds TB: Double-blind, controlled trial of propylthiouracil in patients with severe acute alcoholic hepatitis. *Gastroenterology* 1982; 82:925–931.

Hashimoto S, Recknagel RO: No chemical evidence of hepatic lipid peroxidation in acute ethanol toxicity. *Exp Mol Pathol* 1968; 8:225–242.

Hasumura Y, Teschke R, Lieber CS: Increased carbon tetrachloride hepatotoxicity, and its mechanism after chronic ethanol consumption. *Gastroenterology* 1974; 66:415–422.

Hed R, Nygren A: Alcohol induced hypoglycemia in chronic alcoholics with liver disease. *Acta Medica Scand* 1968; 183:507–510.

Hetu C, Dumont A, Joly JG: Effect of chronic ethanol administration on bromobenzene liver toxicity in the rat. *Toxicol Appl Pharmacol* 1983; 67:166–177.

Hillers VN, Massey LK: Interrelationships of moderate and high alcohol consumption with diet and health status. *Am J Clin Nutr* 1985; 41:356–362.

Hoerner M, Behrens UJ, Worner TM, Blacksberg I, Braly LF, Schaffner F, Lieber CS: The role of alcoholism and liver disease in the appearance of serum antibodies against acetaldehyde adducts. *Hepatology* 1988; 8:569–574.

Hoerner M, Behrens UJ, Worner TM, Lieber CS: Humoral immune response to acetaldehyde adducts in alcoholic patients. *Res Commun Chem Path Pharmacol* 1986; 54:3–12.

Ingelman-Sundberg M, Johansson I: Mechanisms of hydroxyl radical formation and ethanol oxidation by ethanol-inducible and other forms of rabbit liver microsomal cytochromes P-450. *J Biol Chem* 1984; 259:6447–6458.

Iseri OA, Gottlieb LS, Lieber CS: The ultrastructure of ethanol-induced fatty liver. *Fed Proc* 1964; 23: 579.

Iseri OA, Lieber CS, Gottlieb LS: The ultrastructure of fatty liver induced by prolonged ethanol ingestion. *Am J Path* 1966; 48:535–555.

Israel Y, Hurwitz E, Niëmelä O, Arnon R: Monoclonal and polyclonal antibodies against acetaldehyde-containing epitopes in acetaldehyde-protein adducts. *Proc Soc Natl Acad Sci* 1986; 83:7923–7927.

Israel Y, Kalant H, Orrego H, Khanna JM, Videla I, Phillips JM: Experimental alcohol-induced hepatic necrosis: Suppression by propythiouracil. *Proc Natl Acad Sci USA* 1975; 72:1137–1141.

Israel Y, Videla L, MacDonald A, Bernstein J: Metabolic alterations produced in the liver by chronic ethanol administration. Comparison between the effects produced by ethanol and by thyroid hormones. *Biochem J* 1973; 134:523–529.

Jauhonen P, Baraona E, Lieber CS, Hassinen IE: Dependence of ethanol-induced redox shift on hepatic oxygen tensions prevailing in vivo. *Alcohol* 1985; 2:163–167.

Jauhonen P, Baraona E, Miyakawa H, Lieber CS: Mechanism for selective perivenular hepatotoxicity of ethanol. *Alcohol Clin Exp Res* 1982; 6:350–357.

Joly JG, Feinman L, Ishii H, Lieber CS: Effect of chronic ethanol feeding on hepatic microsomal glycerophosphate acyltransferase activity. *J Lipid Res* 1974; 14:337–343.

Kent JR, Scaramuzzi RJ, Lauwers W, et al: Plasma testosterone estradiol and gonadotropoins in hepatic insufficiency. *Gastroenterology* 1973; 64:111–115.

Kessler BJ, Liebler JB, Bronfin GJ, Sass M: The hepatic blood flow and splanchnic oxygen consumption in alcoholic fatty liver. *J Clin Invest* 1954; 33:1338–1345.

Kocak-Toker N, Uysal M, Aykac G, Sivas A, Yalcin S, Oz H: Influence of acute ethanol administration on hepatic glutathione peroxidase and glutathione transferase activities in the rat. *Pharmacol Res Commun* 1985; 17:233–239.

Koop DR, Cassaza JP: Identification of ethanol-inducible P-450 isozyme 3a as the acetone and acetol monooxygenase of rabbit microsomes. *J Biol Chem* 1985; 260:13,607–13,612.

Koop DR, Morgan ET, Tarr GE, Coon MJ: Purification and characterization of a unique isozyme of cytochrome P-450 from liver microsomes of ethanol-treated rabbits. *J Biol Chem* 1982; 257:8472–8480.

Krebs HA, Freedland RA, Hems R, Stibbs M: Inhibition of hepatic gluconeogenesis by ethanol. *Biochem J* 1969; 112:117–124.

Lane BP, Lieber CS: Ultrastructural alterations in human hepatocytes following ingestion of ethanol with adequate diets. *Am J Pathol* 1966; 49:593–603.

Lasker JM, Raucy J, Kubota S, Bloswick BP, Black M, Lieber CS: Purification and characterication of human liver cytochrome P-450ALC. *Biochem Biophys Res Comm* 1987a; 148:232–238.

Lasker JM, Tsutsumi M, Bloswick BP, Lieber CS: Characterization of a benzoflavone (BF)-inducible hamster liver cytochrome P-450 isozyme catalytically similar to cytochrome P-450-ALC. *Hepatology* 1987b; 7:432.

Lefevre A, Adler H, Lieber CS: Effects of ethanol on ketone metabolism. *J Clin Invest* 1970; 49:1775–1782.

Leo MA, Arai M, Sato M, Lieber CS: Hepatotoxicity of moderate vitamin A supplementation in the rat. *Gastroenterology* 1982; 82:194–205.

Leo MA, Iida S, Lieber CS: Retinoic acid metabolism by a system reconstituted with cytochrome P-450. *Arch Biochem Biophys* 1984; 234:305–312.

Leo MA, Kim C, Lieber CS: Increased vitamin A in esophagus and other extrahepatic tissues after chronic ethanol consumption in the rat. *Alcohol Clin Exp Res* 1986a; 10:487–492.

Leo MA, Kim C, Lieber CS: NAD$^+$-dependent retinol dehydrogenase in liver microsomes. *Arch Biochem Biophys* 1987b; 259:241–249.

Leo MA, Lieber CS: Hepatic vitamin A depletion in alcoholic liver injury in man. *N Engl J Med* 1982; 307:597–601.

Leo MA, Lieber CS: Hepatic fibrosis after long term administration of ethanol and moderate vitamin A supplementation in the rat. *Hepatology* 1983; 3:1–11.

Leo MA, Lieber CS: New pathway of retinol metabolism in liver microsomes. *J Biol Chem* 1985; 260: 5228–5231.

Leo MA, Lowe N, Lieber CS: Interaction of drugs and retinol. *Biochem Pharmacol* 1986b; 35:3949–3953.

Leo MA, Lowe N, Lieber CS: Potentiation of ethanol-induced hepatic vitamin A depletion by phenobarbital and butylated hydroxytoluene. *J Nutr* 1987a; 117:70–76.

Leo MA, Sato M, Lieber CS: Effect of hepatic vitamin A depletion on the liver in men and rats. *Gastroenterology* 1983; 84:562–572.

Lieber CS: *Medical Disorders of Alcoholism: Pathogenesis and Treatment.* Philadelphia; W B Saunders Company, 1982.

Lieber CS: Alcohol and the liver: 1984 update. *Hepatology* 1984; 4:1243–1260.

Lieber CS: Alcohol and the liver: Metabolism of ethanol, metabolic effects and pathogenesis of injury. *Acta Med Scand Suppl* 1985; 703:11–55.

Lieber CS: Metabolic effects of ethanol and its interaction with other drugs, hepatotoxic agents, vitamins and carcinogens (1988 Update). *Semin Liver Dis* 1988; 8:47–68.

Lieber CS, Davidson CS: Some metabolic effects of ethyl alcohol. *Am J Med* 1962; 33:319–327.

Lieber CS, DeCarli LM: Ethanol oxidation by hepatic microsomes: adaptive increase after ethanol feeding. *Science* 1968; 162:917–918.

Lieber CS, DeCarli LM: Hepatic microsomal ethanol oxidizing system: In vitro characteristics and adaptive properties in vivo. *J Biol Chem* 1970a; 245:2505–2512.

Lieber CS, DeCarli LM: Reduced nicotinamide–adenine dinucleotide phosphate oxidase: Activity enhanced by ethanol consumption. *Science* 1970b; 170:78–80.

Lieber CS, DeCarli LM, Schmid R: Effects of ethanol on fatty acid metabolism in liver slices. *Biochem Biophys Res Commun* 1959; 1:302–306.

Lieber CS, Garro A, Leo MA, Mak KM, Worner T: Alcohol and cancer. *Hepatology* 1986; 6:1005–1009.

Lieber CS, Jones DP, DeCarli LM: Effects of prolonged ethanol intake: Production of fatty liver despite adequate diets. *J Clin Invest* 1965; 44:1009–1020.

Lieber CS, Jones DP, Losowsky MS: Interrelation of uric acid and ethanol metabolism in man. *J Clin Invest* 1962; 41:1863–1870.

Lieber CS, Lasker JM, Alderman J, Leo MA: The microsomal ethanol oxidizing system and its interaction with other drugs, carcinogens, and vitamins. *Ann NY Acad Sci* 1987; 492:11–24.

Lieber CS, Leo MA: Interaction of alcohol and nutritional factors with hepatic fibrosis, in Popper H, Schaffner F (eds): *Progress in Liver Disease.* New York, Grune and Stratton 1986; vol. 8, pp. 253–272.

Lieber CS, Pignon JP: Ethanol and Lipids, in Fruchart JC, Shepherd J (eds): *Human Plasma Lipoproteins: Chemistry, Physiology and Pathology.* Berlin-New York, Walter de Gruyter and Co., 1989; (in press).

Lieber CS, Schmid R: The effect of ethanol on fatty acid metabolism: Stimulation of hepatic fatty acid synthesis in vitro. *J Clin Invest* 1961; 40:394–399.

Lieber CS, Lasker JM, DeCarli LM, Saeli J, Wojtowicz T: Role of acetone, dietary fat and total energy intake in the induction of the hepatic microsomal oxidizing system. *J Pharmacol Exp Ther* 1988; 247:791–795.

Lieber CS, Baraona E, Hernandez-Munoz R, Kubota S, Sato N, Kawano S, Matsumura T, Inatomi N: Impaired oxygen utilization: A new mechanism for the hepatotoxicity of ethanol in sub-human primates. *J Clin Invest* 1989; (in press).

Linkola J, Ylikhari R, Fyhrquist F, Wallenius M: Plasma vasopressin in ethanol intoxication and hangover. *Acta Physiol Scand* 1978; 104:180–187.

Lochner A, Wulff J, Madison LL: Ethanol-induced hypoglycemia. I. The acute effects of ethanol on hepatic glucose output and peripheral glucose utilization in fasted dogs. *Metabolism* 1967; 16:1–18.

MacDonald CM: The effect of ethanol on hepatic lipid peroxidation and on the activities of glutathione reductase and peroxidase. *FEBS Letters* 1973; 35:227–230.

MacLachlan MJ, Rodan GP: Effect of food, fast, and alcohol on serum uric acid and acute attacks of gout. *Am J Med* 1967; 42:38–57.

MacSween RNM: Alcohol and liver injury: Genetic and immunologic factors. *Acta Med Scand* 1984; 703:57–65.

Madison LL, Lochner A, Wulff J: Ethanol induced hypoglycemia II. Mechanism of suppression of hepatic gluconeogenesis. *Diabetes* 1967; 16:252–258.

Mark V, Wright J: Metabolic effects of alcohol. *Clin Endocrinol Metab* 1978; 7:247.

Matsuda Y, Baraona E, Salaspuro M, Lieber CS: Pathogenesis and role of microtubular alterations in alcohol induced liver injury. *Fed Proc* 1978; 37:402.

Matsuda Y, Baraona E, Salaspuro M, Lieber CS: Effects of ethanol on liver microtubules and Golgi apparatus. *Lab Invest* 1979; 41:455–463.

Matsuda Y, Takada A, Kanayama R, Takase S: Changes of hepatic microtubules and secretory proteins in human alcoholic liver disease. *Pharmacol Biochem Behav* 1983; 18:479–482.

Matsuda Y, Takada A, Sato H, Lieber CS: Comparison between ballooned hepatocytes occurring in human alcoholic and nonalcoholic liver diseases. *Alcohol Clin Exp Res* 1985; 9:366.

Matunaga H; Experimentelle Untersuchungen über den Einfluss des Alkohols auf den Kohlenhydratstoffwechsel. I. Über die Wirkung des Alkohols auf den Blutzuckerspiegel und den Glykogehalt der Leber, mit besonderer Berucksichtigung seines Wirkungsmechanismus. *Tohoku J Exp Med* 1942; 44:130–157.

Mauch TJ, Donohue TM, Zetterman RK, Sorrell MF, Tuma DJ: Covalent binding of acetaldehyde selectively inhibits the catalytic activity of lysine-dependent enzymes. *Hepatology* 1986; 6:263–269.

Mendelson JH, Ellingboe J, Mellow NK, Kuehnle J: Effects of alcohol on plasma testosterone and luteinizing hormone levels. *Alcohol Clin Exp Res* 1978; 2:255–258.

Mendelson JH, Mellow NK: Alcohol aggression and androgens, in Frazier SH (ed): *Aggression*. Baltimore, The Williams and Wilkins Co., 1974, pp 225–247.

Mendelson JH, Ogata M, Mello NK: Adrenal function and alcoholism I. Serum cortisol, *Psychosomatic Med* 1971; 33:145–157.

Mendelson JH, Stein S: Serum cortisol levels in alcoholic and nonalcoholic subjects during experimentally induced alcohol intoxication. *Psychosomatic Med* 1966; 28:616–626.

Metz R, Berger S, Mako M: Potentiation of the plasma insulin response to glucose by prior administration of alcohol. *Diabetes* 1969; 18:517–522.

Mezey E, Faillace LA: Metabolic impairment and recovery time in acute ethanol intoxication. *J Nerv Ment Dis* 1971; 153:445–452.

Mezey E, Potter JJ, Maddrey WC: Collagen turnover in alcoholic liver disease. *Gastroenterology* 1973; 65:560.

Miwa GT, Levin W, Thomas PE, Lu AYH: The direct oxidation of ethanol by catalase- and alcohol dehydrogenase-free reconstituted system containing cytochrome P-450. *Arch Biochem Biophys* 1978; 187:464–475.

Miyakawa H, Iida S, Leo MA, Greenstein RJ, Zimmon DS, Lieber CS: Pathogenesis of precirrhotic portal hypertension in alcohol-fed baboons. *Gastroenterology* 1985; 88:143–150.

Morgan ET, Koop DR, Coon MJ: Catalytic activity of cytochrome P-450 isozyme 3a isolated from liver microsomes of ethanol-treated rabbits. *J Biol Chem* 1982; 257:13951–13957.

Morgan ET, Koop DR, Coon MJ: Comparison of six rabbit liver cytochrome P-450 isozymes in formation of a reactive metabolite of acetaminophen. *Biochem Biophys Res Commun* 1983; 112:8–13.

Mørland J, Rothschild MA, Oratz M, Mongelli J, Donor D, Schreiber SS: Protein secretion in suspensions of isolated rat hepatocytes: No influence of acute ethanol administration. *Gastroenterology* 1981; 80:159–165.

Morton S, Mitchell MC: Effects of chronic ethanol feeding on glutathione turnover in the rat. *Biochem Pharmacol* 1985; 34:1559–1563.

Müller A, Sies H: Role of alcohol dehydrogenase activity and of acetaldehyde in ethanol induced ethane and pentane production by isolated perfused rat liver. *Biochem J* 1982; 206:153–156.

Müller A, Sies H: Inhibition of ethanol and aldehyde induced release of ethane from isolated perfused rat liver by pargyline and disulfiram. *Pharmacol Biochem Behav* 1983; 18:429–432.

Nebert DW, Adesnik M, Coon MJ, Estabrook RW, Gonzalez FJ, Guengerich FP, Gunsalus IC, Johnson EF, Kemper B, Levin W, Phillips IR, Sato R, Waterman MR: The P450 gene superfamily: recommended nomeclature. *DNA* 1987; 6:1–11.

Newcombe DS: Ethanol metabolism and uric acid. *Metabolism* 1970; 21:1193–1203.

Nikkilä EA, Taskin MR: Ethanol-induced alterations of glucose tolerance, postglucose, hypoglycemia, and insulin secretion in normal, obese, and diabetic subjects. *Diabetes* 1975; 24:933–943.

Nomura F, Lieber CS: Binding of acetaldehyde to rat liver microsomes: Enhancement after chronic alcohol consumption. *Biochem Biophys Res Commun* 1981; 100:131–137.

Ohnishi K, Lieber CS: Reconstitution of the microsomal ethanol-oxidizing system: qualitative and quantitative changes of cytochrome P-450 after chronic ethanol consumption. *J Biol Chem* 1977; 252: 7124–7131.

Okanoue T, Ou O, Ohta M, Yoshida J, Horishi M, Yuki T, Okuno T, Takino T: Effect of chronic ethanol administration on the cytoskeleton of rat hepatocytes, including morphometric analysis. *Acta Hepatologica Japonica* 1984; 25:210–313.

Orrego H, Kalant H, Israel Y, Blake J, Medline A, Rankin JG, Armstrong A, Kapur B: Effect of short-term therapy with propylthiouracil in patients with alcoholic liver disease. *Gastroenterology* 1979; 76:105–115.

Pekkanen L, Forsander O: Nutritional implications of alcoholism. *Nutr Bull* 1977; 4:91–102.

Phillips GB, Safrit HF: Alcoholic diabetes: Induction of glucose intolerance with alcohol. *JAMA* 1971; 217:1513–1519.

Pignon JP, Bailey NC, Baraona E, Lieber CS: Fatty acid-binding protein: A major contributor to the ethanol-induced increase in liver cytosolic proteins in rat. *Hepatology* 1987; 7:865–871.

Pirola R, Lieber CS: The energy cost of the metabolism of drugs including alcohol. *Pharmacology* 1972; 7:185–196.

Pirola R, Lieber CS: Energy wastage in rats given drugs that induce microsomal enzymes. *J Nutr* 1975; 1544–1548.

Pirola RC, Lieber CS: Hypothesis: energy wastage in alcoholism and drug abuse: Possible role of hepatic microsomal enzymes. *Am J Clin Nutr* 1976; 29:90–93.

Powell GL, Tippett PS, Kiorpes TC, McMillin-Wood J, Coll KE, Schulz H, Tanaka K, Kang ES, Shrago E. Fatty acyl-CoA as an effector molecule in metabolism. *Fed Proc* 1985; 44:81–84.

Rehfield JF, Juhl E, Hilden M: Carbohydrate metabolism in alcohol-induced fatty liver (evidence for an abnormal insulin response to glucagon in alcoholic liver disease). *Gastroenterology* 1973; 64:445–451.

Reitz RC: A possible mechanism for the peroxidation of lipids due to chronic ethanol ingestion. *Biochim Biophys Acta* 1975; 380:145–154.

Rothwell NJ, Stock MJ: Influence of alcohol and sucrose consumption on energy balance and brown fat activity in rat. *Metabolism* 1984; 33:768–771.

Ryan DE, Koop DR, Thomas PE, Coon MJ, Levin W: Evidence that isoniazid and ethanol induce the same microsomal cytochrome P-450 in rat liver, and isozyme homologous to rabbit liver cytochrome P-450 isozyme 3a. *Arch Biochem Biophys* 1986; 246:633–644.

Ryan DE, Ramathan L, Iida S, Thomas PE, Haniu M, Shively JE, Lieber CS, Levin W: Characterization of a major form of rat hepatic microsomal cytochrome P-450 induced by isoniazid. *J Biol Chem* 1985; 260:6385–6393.

Salaspuro MP: Influence of the unchanged redox state of the liver during ethanol oxidation on galactose and glucose metabolism in protein deficiency, in Gerok W, Sickinger K, Hennekeuser HH (eds) *Alcohol and the Liver.* Stuttgart and New York, Schattauer Verlag, 1970, pp 58–64.

Salaspuro MP: Influence of ethanol on the metabolism of the pathological liver, in Israel Y, Mardones J (eds), *Biological Basis of Alcoholism.* New York and London, John Wiley, 1971, pp 163–182.

Salaspuro MP, Pikkarainen P, Lindros K: Ethanol-induced hypoglycemia in man: Its suppression by the alcohol dehydrogenase inhibitor 4-methylpyrazole. *Eur J Clin Invest* 1977; 7:487–490.

Salaspuro MP, Shaw S, Jayatilleke E, Ross WA, Lieber CS: Attenuation of the ethanol induced hepatic redox change after chronic alcohol consumption in baboons: Metabolic consequences in vivo and in vitro. *Hepatology* 1981; 1:33–38.

Sato C, Matsuda Y, Lieber CS: Increased hepatotoxicity of acetaminophen after chronic ethanol consumption in the rat. *Gastroenterology* 1981; 80:140–148.

Sato M, Lieber CS: Hepatic vitamin A depletion after chronic ethanol consumption in baboons and rats. *J Nutr* 1981; 111:2015–2023.

Sato N, Kamada T, Kawano S, Hayashi N, Kishida Y, Meren H, Yoshihara H, Abe H: Effect of acute and chronic ethanol consumption on hepatic tissue oxygen tension in rats. *Pharmacol Biochem Behav* 1983; 18:443–447.

Savolainen MJ, Baraona E, Leo MA, Lieber CS: Pathogenesis of the hypertriglyceridemia at early stages of alcoholic liver injury in the baboon. *J Lipid Res* 1986; 27:1073–1083.

Savolainen MJ, Baraona E, Pikkarainen P, Lieber CS: Hepatic triacylglycerol synthesizing activity during progression of alcoholic liver injury in the baboon. *J Lipid Res* 1984a; 25:813–820.

Savolainen ER, Leo MA, Timpl R, Lieber CS: Acetaldehyde and lactate stimulate collagen synthesis of cultured baboon liver myofibroblasts. *Gastroenterology* 1984b; 87:777–787.

Scheig R: Effects of ethanol on the liver. *Am J Clin Nutr* 1970; 23:467–473.

Scheig R, Klatskin G: Some effects of ethanol and carbon tetrachloride on lipoperoxidation in rat liver. *Life Sci* 1969; 8:855–865.

Seef LB, Cuccherini BA, Hyman MPH, Zimmerman J, Adler E, Benjamin SB: Acetaminophen hepatotoxicity in alcoholics: A therapeutic misadventure. *Ann Int Med* 1986; 104:399–404.

Shaw S, Heller E, Friedman H, Baraona E, Lieber CS: Increased hepatic oxygenation following ethanol administration in the baboon. *Proc Soc Exp Biol Med* 1977; 156:509–513.

Shaw S, Jayatilleke E, Lieber CS: The effect of chronic alcohol feeding on lipid peroxidation in microsomes: Lack of relationship to hydroxyl radical generation. *Biochem Biophys Res Commun* 1984; 118:233–238.

Shaw S, Jayatilleke E, Ross WA, Gordon ER, Lieber CS: Ethanol induced lipid peroxidation: Potentiation by long-term alcohol feeding and attenuation by methionine. *J Lab Clin Med* 1981; 98:417–425.

Shaw S, Rubin KP, Lieber CS: Depressed hepatic glutathione and increased diene conjugates in alcoholic liver disease: evidence of lipid peroxidation. *Dig Dis Sci* 1983; 28:585–589.

Siegers CP, Schutt A, Strubelt O: Influence of some hepatotoxic agents on hepatic glutathione levels in mice. *Proc Eur Soc Toxicol* 1977; 18:160–162.

Smith AA, Gitlow S: Effect of disulfiram and ethanol on the catabolism of norepinephrine in man, in Maickel RP (ed): *Biochemical Factors in Alcoholism*. New York, Pergamon Press, 1967, pp 53–55.

Song BJ, Gelboin HV, Park SS, Yand CS, Gonzales FJ: Complementary DNA and protein sequences of ethanol-inducible rat and human cytochrome P-450s. *J Biol Chem* 1986; 261:16689–16697.

Sorrell MF, Nauss JM, Donohue TM, Tuma DJ: Effects of chronic ethanol administration on hepatic glycoprotein secretion in the rat. *Gastroenterology* 1983; 84:580–586.

Sorrell MF, Tuma DJ: The functional implications of acetaldehyde binding to cell constituents. *Anal NY Acad Sci* 1987; 492:51–62.

Speisky H, MacDonald A, Giles G, Gunasekara A, Israel Y: Increased loss and decreased synthesis of hepatic glutathione after acute ethanol administration. *Biochem J* 1985; 225:565–572.

Stevens VJ, Fantl WJ, Newman CB, Sims RV, Cerami A, Peterson CM: Acetaldehyde adducts with hemoglobin. *J Clin Invest* 1981; 67:361–369.

Stifel FB, Green HL, Lufkin EG, Wrensch MR, Hagler L, Herman RH: Acute effects of oral and intravenous ethanol on rat hepatic enzyme activities. *Biochim Biophys Acta* 1976; 428:633–638.

Stock AL, Stock MJ, Stuart JA: The effect of alcohol (ethanol) on the oxygen consumption of fed and fasting subjects. *Proc Nutr Soc* 1973; 32:40A–41A.

Stock MJ, Stuart JA: Thermic effects of ethanol in the rat and man. *Nutr Metabol* 1974; 17:297–305.

Teschke R, Hasumura Y, Joly JG, Ishii H, Lieber CS: Microsomal ethanol-oxidizing system (MEOS): Purification and properties of a rat liver system free of catalase and alcohol dehydrogenase. *Biochem Biophys Res Commun* 1972; 49:1187–1193.

Teschke R, Hasumura Y, Lieber CS: Hepatic microsomal alcohol oxidizing system. Solubilization, isolation and characterization. *Arch Biochem Biophys* 1974; 163:404–415.

Teschke R, Moreno F, Heinen E, Herrmann J, Kruskemper HL, Strohmeyer G: Is there any evidence of a hyperthyroid hepatic state following chronic alcohol intake? *Alcohol and Alcohol* 1983; 18:151–155.

Thomas CE, Morehouse LA, Aust SD: Ferritin and superoxide-dependent lipid peroxidation. *J Biol Chem* 1985; 260:3275–3280.

Timbrell JA, Mitchell JR, Snodgrass WR, Nelson SD: Isoniazid hepatotoxicity: The relationship between covalent binding and metabolism in vivo. *J Pharmacol Exp Ther* 1980; 23:364–369.

Tremolieres J, Carre L: Etudes sur les modalités d'oxydation de l'alcool chez l'homme normal et alcoolique. *Rev Alcoolisme* 1961; 7:202.

Tuma DJ, Sorrell MF: Effects of ethanol on the secretion of glycoproteins in rat liver slices. *Gastroenterology* 1981; 80:273–278.

Valenzuela A, Fernandez F, Videla LA: Hepatic and biliary levels of glutathione and lipid peroxides following iron overload in the rat: Effect of simultaneous ethanol administration. *Toxicol Appl Pharmacol* 1983; 70:87–95.

Välimäki M, Härkönen M, Ylikahri R: Serum ferritin and iron levels in chronic male alcoholics before and after ethanol withdrawal. *Alcohol and Alcoholism* 1983; 18:255–260.

Van Thiel DH, Gavaler JS, Sanghvi A: Recovery of sexual function in abstinent alcoholic men. *Gastroenterology* 1982; 84:677–684.

Vendemiale G, Jayatilleke E, Shaw S, Lieber CS: Depression of biliary glutathione excretion by chronic ethanol feeding in the rat. *Life Sci* 1984; 34:1065–1073.

Videla L, Israel Y: Factors that modify the metabolism of ethanol in rat liver and adaptive changes produced by its chronic administration. *Biochem J* 1970; 118:275–281.

Volentine GD, Tuma DJ, Sorrell MF: Acute effects of ethanol on hepatic glycoprotein secretion in the rat in vivo. *Gastroenterology* 1984; 88:225–229.

Wendel A, Fenerstein S, Konz KH: Acute paracetamol intoxication of starved mice leads to lipid peroxidation in vivo. *Biochem Pharmacol* 1979; 28:2051–2055.

Wolff HP, Lommer D, Torbica M: Studies in plasma aldosterone metabolism in some heart, liver and kidney disease. *Schweiz Med Wschr* 1962; 95:387–395.

Wright N, Prescott LF: Potentiation by previous drug therapy of hepatotoxicity following paracetamol overdosage. *Scot Med J* 1973; 18:56–58.

Wrighton SA, Campanele C, Thomas PE, Maines SL, Watkins PB, Parker G, Mendez-Picon G, Haniu M, Shively JE, Levin W, Guzelian PS: Identification of a human liver cytochrome P-450 homologous to the major isosafrole-inducible cytochrome P-450 in the rat. *Mol Pharmacol* 1986; 29:405–410.

Yang CS, Tu YY, Koop DR, Coon MJ: Metabolism of nitrosamines by purified rabbit liver cytochrome P-450 isozymes. *Cancer Res* 1985; 45:1140–1145.

Yasuhara M, Matsuda Y, Takada A: Degradation of acetaldehyde produced by the nonalcohol dehydrogenase pathway. *Alcohol Clin Exp Res* 1986; 10:545–549.

Yki-Järvinen H, Nikkilä EA: Ethanol decreases glucose utilization in healthy man. *J Clin Endocrin Metab* 1985; 61:941–945.

Zern MA, Leo MA, Giabrone MA, Lieber CS: Increased type I procollagen mRNA levels and in vitro protein synthesis in the baboon model of chronic alcoholic liver disease. *Gastroenterology* 1985; 89: 1123–1131.

Section 2

Neuropsychopharmacological Effects

CHAPTER 4

Alcohol and Biological Membranes

Dora B. Goldstein

Department of Pharmacology
Stanford University School of Medicine
Stanford, California, USA

After 10 years of investigation with spectrometric methods, the membrane-disordering effect of ethanol has been well characterized and the development of tolerance to this effect is obvious. But the relationship of these observations to the mechanism of action of ethanol still eludes us. Is disorder important? Are membrane lipids the primary site of action? Is genetic vulnerability to alcoholism a property of membranes? These questions guide much of the current research on ethanol and cell membranes. Partial answers elicit new questions and we are far from an acceptable understanding.

This chapter includes some comments on the hydrophobic interactions of aliphatic alcohols with membranes, a discussion of the pharmacological relevance of disordered membranes and some consideration of chronic effects of ethanol on membrane structure. Recent reviews of similar scope include those by Taraschi and Rubin (1985) and Goldstein (1984). For reviews that focus on the chemical composition of membrane lipids, see Sun and Sun (1985) and Chin and Goldstein (1985).

THE HYDROPHOBIC PHASE

Some things we do know. There are indeed reasons to believe that cell membranes are sites of action of ethanol and of other anesthetic drugs whose actions depend on their hydrophobic properties. It is worth noting in passing that anesthetics are not the only drugs for which hydrophobic properties are important; the potency of many other drugs can be modified by changing their hydrophobicity, indicating that their sites of action are hydrophobic in nature. An example is the series of pyrazoles that inhibit a water-soluble enzyme, alcohol dehydrogenase (Cornell et al, 1983).

The hydrophobic effect is an expulsion from water (Tanford, 1980). Water molecules are

Supported by U.S. Public Health Service, grant AA01066, and by the Alcoholic Beverage Medical Research Foundation.

connected by an ever-shifting but cohesive network of hydrogen bonds. Hydrocarbons and acyl chains, which cannot form hydrogen bonds with water, will distort the network; this requires energy. Forced out, they cluster together in ordered formations away from water. Thus, vesicles, micelles, and bilayers will form spontaneously when any such compound is dispersed in water. Hydrophobic drugs in contact with a lipid suspension will quickly be drawn into the hydrophobic phase, rather than remaining uncomfortably in water.

Increase in Potency with Chain Length as a Characterization of the Site of Action

Partition Coefficients of a Homologous Series of Alcohols

The evidence provided long ago that anesthetics vary in potency according to their oil–water partition coefficients remains valid and still guides much of our thinking. Ethanol's low lipid solubility matches its weak potency as an anesthetic or intoxicant.

The partition of any solute between two solvents is related to the free energy of the compound in the two phases. It will seek the lowest-energy location. The equation relating the free energy change (relative ease of transfer) to the relative partition coefficients of a homologous series is:

$$\Delta(\Delta G°)_{Me} = -RT \ln (K_n/K_{(n-1)}),$$

where $(\Delta G°)$ is the change in standard free energy on transfer to a new phase, and $\Delta(\Delta G°)_{Me}$ is the difference between transfer energies of two adjacent compounds in a homologous series. K_n and $K_{(n-1)}$ are the partition coefficients for chains with n or $n - 1$ carbon atoms, respectively; R is the gas constant and T the absolute temperature. Since the data are ratios of two partition coefficients, molal or mole fraction units are equally acceptable (Kamaya et al, 1981). For isotropic solvents such as octanol (a good model for biomembranes (Leo et al, 1971; Diamond and Katz, 1974)), the change in free energy per methylene group is about 750 cal/mole (Lyon et al, 1981). This is equivalent to an increase in the octanol–water partition coefficient of about 3.5-fold per methylene group.

Relationship of Potency to Partition Coefficient

The common finding that potencies of alcohols increase with chain length hints only rather feebly at a hydrophobic effect. If the potency increases *by a constant factor* with each additional carbon atom, then the partition of the alcohols into their site of action (rather than chemically specific binding) may control their action. This is useful information indeed. Furthermore, a factor close to 3.5 suggests that partition of the alcohols into an octanol-like site initiates their effects. Factors other than 3.5, for some particular actions of alcohols, may indicate that these responses occur at hydrophobic sites with different properties from the usual plasma membrane. Therefore, even without knowing the absolute partition coefficients of the alcohols we can guess whether different actions are initiated in different environments. In addition, the same actions observed in animals of different genetic background or history of alcohol treatment may take place in membranes with unusual properties, giving new values for differential potencies of a series of alcohols.

To examine this point, I have compiled data from the literature (Table 4.1). For each system, the fold increase in potency of a series of straight-chain aliphatic alcohols was calculated. (The series did not always include ethanol.) If a cutoff effect (see below) was evident, only the shorter-chain compounds were included.

Apparently there is a set of alcohol effects, those in the middle of the list, occurring in a phase that resembles octanol, but other actions may require microenvironments with different physical properties. Functions that are neighbors in Table 4.1 may have sites of action in common. For example, ataxia or hypnosis in intact animals more closely resemble partition in dimyristoylphosphatidylcholine than in octanol, whereas a few other functions suggest a more

Table 4.1. Effect of chain length on potencies or partition coefficients of homologous series of alcohols

N	ALCOHOLS	FOLD ± SE	SYSTEM	REF
6	C1–C6	1.93 ± 0.09	RBC[a], calcium binding	Seeman et al, 1971a
4	C1–C4	2.24 ± 0.33	Tortoise heart, narcosis	Vernon, 1912
6	C1–C6	2.33 ± 0.15	Rats, ataxia	McCreery and Hunt, 1978
5	C1–C5	2.34 ± 0.11	Brain, enkephalin binding	Hiller et al, 1981
5	C2–C6	2.43 ± 0.15	Mouse, hypnosis	Lyon et al, 1981
4	C1–C4	2.53 ± 0.11	DMPC, partition	Katz and Diamond, 1974
5	C1–C7	2.70 ± 0.09	Frog heart, block	Führner, 1921
6	C1–C8	2.87 ± 0.15	Nonsynaptic nerve block	Brink and Posternak, 1948
6	C3–C8	3.03 ± 0.16	RBC, disorder	Paterson et al, 1972
3	C2–C6	3.16 ± 0.00	Brain, transmitter release	Carmichael and Israel, 1975
6	C1–C6	3.23 ± 0.07	Gut brush border, disorder	Boigegrain et al, 1984
5	C1–C5	3.25 ± 0.26	Goose RBC, respiration	Warburg, 1921
5	C1–C5	3.29 ± 0.22	Frog muscle, block	Kochmann, 1923
5	C4–C8	3.30 ± 0.13	Heart microsomes, disorder	Zavoico and Kutchai, 1980
5	C5–C10	3.36 ± 0.18	RBC membranes, partition	Seeman et al, 1971b
8	C1–C10	3.52 ± 0.27	Firefly luciferase, inhibition	Franks and Lieb, 1984
4	C2–C5	3.53 ± 0.08	Octanol, partition	Lyon et al, 1981
5	C2–C6	3.67 ± 0.35	Egg PC, swelling	Jain et al, 1973
8	C2–C10	3.83 ± 0.09	Tadpoles, loss reflex	Meyer and Hemmi, 1935
8	C1–C8	3.85 ± 0.13	Bacteria, luminescence	Taylor, 1933
6	C2–C8	3.86 ± 0.10	SPM, disorder	Lyon et al, 1981
8	C1–C8	3.88 ± 0.17	Tadpoles, stop movement	Vernon, 1913
7	C4–C10	3.99 ± 0.21	RBC, antihemolysis	Roth and Seeman, 1972
5	C1–C5	4.00 ± 0.07	Olive oil, partition	Lindenburg, 1951
6	C1–C8	4.07 ± 0.91	Synaptic transmission	Brink and Posternak, 1948
6	C2–C7	4.20 ± 0.23	DPPC, partition	Kamaya et al, 1981
5	C2–C6	4.62 ± 0.25	Sodium channel, block	Mullin and Hunt, 1985
5	C2–C6	4.92 ± 0.45	Synaptosomes, Ca^{++} uptake	Stokes and Harris, 1982

Published data were converted to a regression of ln(potency) on number of carbon atoms. The natural antilog of this slope gives the factor by which potencies increase with chain length, and the standard error of this estimate is computed from the standard error of the slope. A few measured partition coefficients are included for comparison. The number of compounds, range of chain lengths, fold increases in potency per carbon atom, biological systems, and references are shown.

[a] Abbreviations: RBC, red blood cells; SPM, synaptosomal plasma membranes; PC, phosphatidylcholine; DMPC, dimyristoylphosphatidylcholine; DPPC, dipalmitoylphosphatidylcholine.

ordered environment, like dipalmitoylphosphatidylcholine. Although some of these calculations may be misleading because of the different techniques and the doubtful purity of the alcohols in early experiments (Vernon, 1913), they demonstrate that hitherto-unused information inheres in studies of homologous series, even when absolute partition coefficients are not available.

Absolute Value of the Ethanol Partition Coefficient

The partition coefficient for ethanol in biomembranes has been measured only recently (Rottenberg et al, 1981). Most of the ethanol in a membrane pellet remains in the trapped water and the necessary correction has proved difficult. Rottenberg et al (1981) reported values of 1.0 for synaptosomal membranes (recently confirmed by Nordmann's group (1987)) and 3.6 for mitochondrial membranes. These are surprisingly high partition coefficients compared to the usually accepted estimate of 0.14, which Seeman calculated for erythrocyte membranes by extrapolation (1972). However, estimates of the partition coefficient of ethanol are known to vary more among solvents than do those of higher alcohols (Meyer and Hemmi, 1935; Leo et al, 1971), either because of experimental difficulties or because extrapolation is not valid when complex biological membranes are used. The measured partition coefficients for ethanol cited by Leo et al (1971) vary over 40-fold, from 0.043 to 1.9, in various isotropic solvents.

Hydrophobic Sites on Proteins

The possibilities for hydrophobic sites of action include not only membrane bilayers but also the surfaces of proteins. Patches of hydrophobic amino acid residues on the surfaces of folded proteins provide potential receptor-like harbors for ethanol. Most such proteins reside within membranes, and any lipid-soluble compounds that partition into membranes will equilibrate with these sites, with likely effects on the function of the proteins. There will be a secondary partition between the bulk lipid and the intramembrane surface of the protein, leading to different chain-length effects for different proteins. It is entirely unknown whether such effects are physiologically significant at relevant concentrations of ethanol in membranes. An interesting possibility that has recently been raised is that alcohols may bind to hydrophobic sites on *water-soluble* proteins. Franks and Lieb (1984) have demonstrated that alcohols inhibit firefly luciferase, a water-soluble enzyme, competitively with the substrate luciferin. This may be a useful model for mammalian aqueous proteins that have hydrophobic binding sites, such as albumin or the many specific transport proteins that carry steroids and other water-insoluble molecules throughout the body. Interference with these transport processes could well be among the important actions of ethanol.

MEMBRANE DISORDERING

When ethanol becomes incorporated into a membrane, what follows? A possibility is that the alcohol molecules, simply by their presence in the phospholipid bilayer, might disrupt the structure of the membrane, changing the packing of phospholipids and the environment of proteins. This notion is also under scrutiny in the search for the mechanism of action of inhalation anesthetics. The evident importance of partition coefficients plus the apparent irrelevance of specific chemical structures for drugs of this class is the basis for such a hypothesis. Space occupancy within a membrane might be the driving force for anesthetic action. By extension, other actions of the same drugs (including some chronic effects) might derive from physical disruption of membranes.

The physical properties of isolated cell membranes can be examined by spectroscopic methods such as NMR, EPR, or fluorescence polarization, as well as calorimetric and optical methods. The results are reported in terms of order parameters, fluorescence anisotropy, phase transition temperatures, etc. and are sometimes interpreted as measures of membrane fluidity, a poorly defined term that includes a variety of molecular motions such as lateral diffusion, wobble of acyl chains, rotation of chains, and bends or kinks in the acyl chains. The mobility of a spin label or fluorescent dye incorporated nonspecifically into a membrane reflects the properties of the membrane lipids.

The different spectroscopic methods have provided a gratifying degree of agreement on the basic observation; anesthetic drugs disrupt the structure of membranes. They reduce membrane order determined by EPR (Chin and Goldstein, 1977b; Lyon et al, 1981) or fluorescence anisotropy (Harris and Schroeder, 1981; Beaugé et al, 1985; Gonzales et al, 1987). They decrease phase transition temperatures (Rowe, 1982), thereby (at some temperatures) increasing the proportion of lipid that is fluid. These effects are seen in liposomes made of defined phospholipids (Johnson et al, 1979; Beaugé et al, 1985; Taraschi et al, 1986) (ruling out a necessary role for proteins), in erythrocyte membranes (Chin and Goldstein, 1977b), enterocyte brush borders (Boigegrain et al, 1984), and the plasma membranes of neurons (Chin and Goldstein, 1977b; Harris and Schroeder, 1981; Lyon et al, 1981), of liver (Schüller et al, 1984), and of cultured hepatoma cells (Polokoff et al, 1985), thus apparently in all types of biological membranes. Intracellular membranes such as those of microsomes (Ponnappa et al, 1982; Taraschi et al, 1985; Taraschi et al, 1986b) and mitochondria (Waring et al, 1981) are affected. The sensitivity of synaptosomal membranes to ethanol-induced disordering varies among brain regions, being most intense for cerebellar membranes (Gonzales et al, 1987).

Little attention has been given to the effects of ethanol on the ability of phospholipids to diffuse rapidly in the plane of the membrane but a recent paper by Treistman et al (1987) shows that ethanol and butanol accelerate the diffusion of fluorescent-labeled PE in membranes of *Aplysia* neurons. The diffusion of labeled PC was not affected.

Is Membrane Disorder the Cause of Intoxication?

An impressive magnitude of disordering by ethanol can only be seen at concentrations far above those that cause anesthesia. To credit disorder with clinical relevance, one must assume that it signals a similar but much stronger effect at some particularly sensitive site or that there are pockets where ethanol accumulates. With that caveat we can examine the functional disruption that correlates with disordering.

Evidence for Disorder as the Mechanism of Intoxication

Experimental findings that implicate increased membrane fluidity include correlations between the behavioral response of animals and the sensitivity of their membranes to disordering by ethanol in vitro. For example, mice that have been selectively bred for resistance to the hypnotic effects of ethanol ("Short-Sleep" mice) have synaptosomal plasma membranes that are less sensitive to ethanol in vitro than are membranes from ethanol-sensitive "Long-Sleep" mice (Goldstein et al, 1982). Among individual mice of a genetically heterogeneous stock, those animals that were relatively sensitive to ethanol-induced ataxia had relatively ethanol-sensitive membranes, as measured by the reduction in EPR order parameter by ethanol in vitro (Goldstein et al, 1982). Furthermore, as discussed below, animals that are tolerant to behavioral effects of ethanol after chronic treatment have brain membranes that are relatively resistant to ethanol-induced disordering (Chin and Goldstein, 1977a).

If simple physical disordering is the cause of intoxication, then a warm environment should make ethanol more potent and a high hydrostatic pressure (increasing membrane order) should have a sobering effect. Both statements are true. Mice are more sensitive to ethanol at high than at low body temperatures (Dinh and Gailis, 1979; Wenger and Alkana, 1984). Furthermore, Alkana and his group (Malcolm and Alkana, 1982) have shown that increased hydrostatic pressure can counteract the intoxicating effects of ethanol. The pressures used in these studies, about 12 atmospheres, are far below those used in Miller's earlier studies of pressure reversal of anesthesia (Miller et al, 1973), about 100 atmospheres. The partition coefficient of ethanol increases with temperature (Katz and Diamond, 1974), although probably not enough to account for these results. Thus, the significance of the temperature and pressure effects is still unclear; they are, however, in the right direction for a putative mechanism of action of ethanol by disordering membranes. Attempts to use the temperature dependence of local anesthetic action to rule out lipid mechanisms (Richards et al, 1978; Bradley and Richards, 1984) are confounded by the temperature effects on the partition coefficients of the drugs and on nerve block itself and do not yield interpretable results.

Evidence Against Disorder as the Mechanism of Intoxication

Disorder fails to correlate with intoxication when age of the animals is a variable. As they grow older, animals become increasingly sensitive to ethanol but their membranes become less and less vulnerable to disordering (Armbrecht et al, 1983). The sensitivity of synaptosomal plasma membranes to ethanol-induced disordering remains constant during a developmental period when behavioral sensitivity to ethanol increases strikingly (Hitzemann and Harris, 1984; Rydberg and Goldstein, 1986).

A more powerful argument against the disordering hypothesis is that the reduction in EPR order parameter or in fluorescence anisotropy of membranes at anesthetic concentrations of ethanol can be mimicked by a tiny rise in temperature, only about half a degree. The ratio of ethanol effect to temperature effect varies somewhat according to the method of determining order, but all such comparisons make clear that ethanol cannot work by a simple over-all change in membrane order such as that caused by warming.

Warming and ethanol sometimes have opposite effects. For example, uptake of glucose by isolated adipocytes is inhibited by ethanol at membrane-disordering concentrations but is stimulated when a similar disordering is induced by warming (Sauerheber et al, 1982). Because warming directly accelerates any enzymatic process, temperature and ethanol cannot be expected to have additive effects in enzymatic systems that are inhibited by ethanol.

Furthermore, different alcohols sometimes have opposite effects even though they all disorder membranes. For example, hexanol stimulates calcium uptake by sarcoplasmic reticulum, whereas ethanol and butanol are inhibitory (Almeida et al, 1986). In cultured L6 cells (Rabin et al, 1986), actions of ethanol and butanol differ even though both disorder plasma membranes and both activate adenylate cyclase, and even though butanol is more potent in both actions. The difference is that the increase in cyclase activity per unit change in fluorescence anisotropy is greater for ethanol than for butanol. Whether these examples of dissociation between disorder and function are generalizable remains to be determined.

Cutoff

The potencies of homologous series of anesthetic compounds increase with chain length only up to a point, after which they are no longer anesthetic. This cutoff phenomenon has puzzled investigators for decades, especially in searches for the primary mechanism of anesthetic action, and has sometimes been used to argue against a lipid site of action of anesthetic agents (Richards et al, 1978). There seem to be several reasons for cutoff effects. Sometimes the insolubility of the drugs in water prevents their incorporation into membranes in adequate concentrations (Pringle et al, 1981) or their effective administration to animals (Lyon et al, 1981). Cutoff effects have also been ascribed to the inability of long-chain molecules to fit into a postulated binding site on a protein (Pringle et al, 1981).

Factors that Affect Sensitivity to Disordering

Are there indeed pockets of sensitivity within membranes where ethanol equilibrates easily and has greater effect than on the bulk lipids? Indeed, the response of isolated membranes to ethanol varies somewhat according to location in the bilayer and the lipid composition of the membranes. With fatty acid spin labels, the interior of the bilayer (monitored by 12-doxylstearic acid, for example) is more sensitive to disordering than is the region near the surface (5-doxylstearic) (Chin and Goldstein, 1981). The ethanol molecules presumably remain near the aqueous interface, but their effect may be magnified near the ends of the dangling acyl chains. Probes that monitor different depths in the membrane often differ in their ability to pick up certain effects of ethanol; this undoubtedly accounts for some discrepancies in the literature. For example, membranes from Long Sleep and Short Sleep mice differ in sensitivity to ethanol when they are observed by a surface probe such as 5-doxylstearic acid (Goldstein et al, 1982) or trimethylammonium-diphenylhexatriene (Harris et al, 1987) but not with a deep probe such as diphenylhexatriene. The pertinent line difference seems to reside near the surface.

Cholesterol

The disordering produced by ethanol is generally greatest in the membranes that are intrinsically most fluid. Thus, the effect is strongest at high temperatures and in the deepest parts of the membrane. Cholesterol counteracts the disordering effect of ethanol, presumably because of cholesterol's ability to increase membrane order. The protective effect of cholesterol can be seen in liposomes (Chin and Goldstein, 1981), in cholesterol-enriched synaptosomal plasma membranes, and in erythrocytes of Japanese quail treated with dietary cholesterol (Chin and Goldstein, 1984).

Gangliosides

An intriguing possibility is that surface carbohydrates affect the sensitivity of membranes to disordering. Harris and co-workers (1984b) have shown that addition of gangliosides to a brain lipid extract greatly increases disordering by ethanol. Further, Beaugé et al (1985) found reduced amounts of sialic acid and galactose in the ethanol-tolerant red cell membranes of alcoholic subjects. Removal of these compounds from normal erythrocyte membranes induces an ethanol-resistant state similar to tolerance (Stibler et al, 1984). Changes in surface sugars may well accompany tolerance (although Harris et al found no such changes in tolerant animals (1984b)) or mediate genetically determined differences in sensitivity to ethanol, but they cannot explain the resistance to disordering that is seen in the extracted phospholipids of tolerant animals.

Contaminants as Disordering Artifacts

Ethanol should be distilled before use in studies on membranes. A variety of plasticizers have been found as contaminants in a batch of ethanol (Goldstein et al, 1987). These plasticizers were strongly disordering compounds that must have been introduced inadvertently by the manufacturer or distributor during storage or transport of ethanol.

HOW DO CELLS REACT TO ETHANOL OVER TIME?

Membrane Tolerance

Virtually all studies agree that tolerance develops to the membrane-disordering effects of ethanol. A few days' exposure to ethanol suffice, whether administered by inhalation, liquid diet, or injection. Tolerance is seen in synaptosomal membranes (Chin and Goldstein, 1977a; Lyon and Goldstein, 1983a; Harris et al, 1984a), in erythrocytes (Chin and Goldstein, 1977a; Rottenberg et al, 1981), in microsomes of brain (Aloia et al, 1985) and liver (Taraschi et al, 1986b), and in hepatic mitochondria (Waring et al, 1981). Tolerance is evident with EPR (with 5- or 12-doxylstearic acid spin labels) or fluorescence polarization methods (with diphenylhexatriene but not with trimethylammonium diphenylhexatriene) (Harris et al, 1984), and it appears in the extracted lipids of membranes (Johnson et al, 1979; Waring et al, 1981; Harris et al, 1984; Taraschi et al, 1986), as well as in the intact membranes themselves. This rules out a necessary role for membrane proteins or carbohydrates, although these may participate in determining the magnitude of tolerance.

The erythrocytes of alcoholic patients, whether observed by fluorescence polarization (Beaugé et al, 1985) or by EPR (Wood et al, 1987), are resistant to the disordering effect of ethanol. This state persists at least a month after withdrawal (Wood et al, 1987), which raises the question whether a genetically determined abnormality in membrane fluidity predates the onset of alcoholism. Behavioral tolerance to ethanol-induced ataxia (Goldstein and Zaechelein, 1983) and membrane tolerance (Lyon and Goldstein, 1983; Taraschi et al, 1986a) both disappear within a day after withdrawal.

During chronic administration of ethanol, the membrane lipid composition must have changed in such a way as to decrease the ethanol partition coefficient or to make the membranes less vulnerable to disordering. We should find out which is true. The existence of tolerance in the membrane lipids lends some weight to the view that membrane lipid disorder is an important component of intoxication, because it greatly extends the range of correlations that link disorder and behavioral effects of ethanol.

However, behavioral tolerance to ethanol cannot be simply equated to decreased overall partition coefficients or to reduced sensitivity of membranes because tolerance to different effects develops with different magnitudes and rates. Furthermore, tolerance to hypnosis develops best at warm ambient temperatures, whereas tolerance to hypothermia develops most strongly in a relatively cool environment (Alkana et al, 1987). Thus other physiological adaptive processes must interact with the development of tolerance.

Possible Role of Phosphatidylinositol in Tolerance

Taraschi et al (1986b), attempting to identify the particular lipid that may have changed in the tolerant state, have reported that phosphatidylinositol is the relevant type. Using fluorescence polarization, they demonstrated tolerance to ethanol-induced disordering in the extracted phospholipids of rat liver microsomes after treating the animals chronically with ethanol. After separating and recombining the lipids from normal and tolerant animals, they showed tolerance only in mixtures that contained phosphatidylinositol from tolerant animals. The other phospholipids, although present in much larger amounts, had no such effect. No unusual fatty acyl composition of this phosphatidylinositol has been reported. Whereas it would not seem unusual for a particular species of phospholipid (e.g., a novel species of phosphatidylinositol) to be insensitive to disordering, this goes far beyond. Here it appears that the phosphatidylinositol from ethanol-treated rats actually prevents the other lipids in the vesicle from being disordered. This intriguing observation needs repeating.

Hydrophobic Metabolites of Ethanol

A newly reported class of hydrophobic metabolites of ethanol might contribute either to membrane tolerance or to the toxicity of chronic ethanol administration. Lange and co-workers discovered ethyl esters of long-chain fatty acids as metabolites of ethanol in human brain in vitro (Laposata et al, 1987) and in tissues of human alcoholics (Laposata and Lange, 1986). The responsible enzyme has been isolated and characterized (Mogelson and Lange, 1984; Mogelson et al, 1984). These esters have also been found in liver and brain of mice exposed chronically to ethanol (Hungund et al, 1988). They are of interest to investigators of membranes because the ethyl esters of palmitic, oleic, and linoleic acids (which are among those found in vivo), are strongly disordering in vitro as measured by fluorescence polarization (Hungerland et al, 1988). When the slope of the disordering curve is defined as change in fluorescence anisotropy vs. the concentration of esters in the aqueous suspension of membranes, the esters appear about four orders of magnitude more potent than ethanol. When we take the partition coefficients into account, however, assuming that the esters are entirely incorporated into the available membrane, and correcting for the ratio of lipid to water in vivo and in the cuvette, it seems that the esters, molecule for molecule, are not much more potent than ethanol. Presumably these esters attach themselves to hydrophobic proteins such as albumin and are thus transported throughout the body, equilibrating with membranes in many organs.

Another hydrophobic substance that may appear after chronic treatment with ethanol is phosphatidylethanol (Alling et al, 1984). Although the compound forms nonenzymatically when tissues are stored in the presence of ethanol (Anggård et al, 1984), the artifact does not account for all the observed phosphatidylethanol. Its concentrations and physiological or toxic effects have not yet been elucidated. It is another hydrophobic compound likely to find its way into membranes.

Dependence

Somewhat less often than the appearance of membrane tolerance, it is observed that membranes of ethanol-treated animals are more rigid than those of controls. This might be interpreted as another facet of a postulated adaptation to the disordering caused by ethanol—the cells had stiffened their membranes to counteract the physiological disruption caused by the too-fluid membranes. However, this result is not uniformly seen, and it depends on the type of probe that is used. In our hands, mouse synaptosomal plasma membranes from ethanol-treated animals are more ordered than controls when 12-doxylstearic acid is the spin label but not with 5-doxylstearic acid (Lyon and Goldstein, 1983a). That is, the increased order is seen deep in the membrane, not at the surface; it must be a property of the acyl chains. When membrane fluidity is assessed with diphenylhexatriene, also a deep probe, the increased order is seen in synaptosomal membranes from chronically treated mice (Perlman and Goldstein, 1983; Harris et al, 1984a) or rats (Le Bourhis et al, 1987) and in erythrocyte membranes of human alcoholics (Beaugé et al, 1985). Harris et al (1984a) reported increased order in membranes of alcohol-treated mice, when the probe was trimethylammonium-diphenylhexatriene (as well as with *cis*- and *trans*-parinaric acid), but they did not observe increased membrane order in lipid extracts of membranes, suggesting that a change in the membrane proteins was responsible. The temperature of the in vitro assay may also affect the difference in baseline order between control and ethanol-treated membranes, as in the experiments of Waring et al (1981) where increased membrane order was seen with 5-doxylstearic acid as spin label at 15°C but not at 35°C.

Membrane "dependence" (i.e.; the increased order of membranes from ethanol-treated animals), cannot be explained by changes in partition coefficients. Conversely, increased order may reduce the partition coefficient, but we lack data on the quantitative relationship between order and partition coefficients.

Liver Plasma Membranes

Hepatocyte plasma membranes may behave differently from those of neurons or erythrocytes after chronic exposure to ethanol. Experiments with fluorescence polarization show that liver plasma membranes are more, rather than less, fluid after treatment of the animals with ethanol (Yamada and Lieber, 1984). This occurs even with membranes that are acutely disordered by ethanol in vitro and can develop tolerance to the disordering effect (Polokoff et al, 1985), an observation that dissociates membrane tolerance from membrane dependence. Inhibition of ethanol metabolism (in cultured hepatocytes) blocked the long-term disordering effect of ethanol (Polokoff et al, 1985). Thus, it appears that the liver responds differently from other organs because of its ability to metabolize ethanol. Acetaldehyde or other metabolites of ethanol in the liver may have their own chronic effects on lipid composition and fluidity.

CONCLUSION

The question of the primary site of action of ethanol, whether lipid or protein, has not been answered, but surely the target is likely to be in membranes. The only alternative is the untested hypothesis (Franks and Lieb, 1984) that hydrophobic sites on water-soluble proteins are important. Assuming that membranes are crucial, we should ascertain partition coefficients for the exact site of a particular action of ethanol. Since this cannot be done directly with present methods, an alternative approach is to measure the increase in potency (for a particular effect) as the chain length increases. This gives useful information about relative partition coefficients of the acyl portion of the molecules, a measure of the free energy change for admitting a methylene group. In turn, this indicates similarity or differences among the sites of particular responses to the alcohols. For this purpose, ethanol, *n*-butanol and *n*-hexanol form a useful series; two 10-fold steps of increase in potency are seen for sites that resemble octanol. Physically different sites will give steps of 7- and 16-fold, indicating events that will bear further examination in seeking the causes of differential responses of membranes to ethanol. Either the responses to alcohol of genetically different organisms or the temporally changing response due to tolerance or aging may be ascribable to altered lipid environments at specific sites within membranes.

Tolerance certainly develops to the disordering effect of ethanol on membranes of all sorts. This tells us that the chemical composition of the bilayer has changed in some way. But the causal relation to behavioral tolerance is unknown. Is it only a matter of partition coefficients?

REFERENCES

Alkana RL, Bejanian M, Syapin PJ, Finn DA: Chronic functional ethanol tolerance in mice influenced by body temperature during acquisition. *Life Sci* 1987; 41:413–420.

Alling C, Gustavsson L, Månsson JE, Benthin G: Phosphatidylethanol formation in rat organs after ethanol treatment. *Biochim Biophys Acta* 1984; 793:119–122.

Almeida LM, Vaz WLC, Stümpel J, Madeira VMC: Effect of short-chain primary alcohols on fluidity and activity of sarcoplasmic reticulum membranes. *Biochemistry* 1986; 25:4832–4839.

Aloia RC, Paxton J, Daviau JS, van Gelb O, Mlekusch W, Truppe W, Meyer JA, Brauer FH: Effect of chronic alcohol consumption on rat brain microsome lipid composition, membrane fluidity and Na^+-K^+-ATPase activity. *Life Sci* 1985; 36:1003–1017.

Anggård E, Benthin G, Gustavsson L, Alling C: Factors affecting phosphatidyl ethanol (PEt) formation in kidneys from ethanol treated rats. *Alcoholism (NY)* 1984; 8:251.

Armbrecht HJ, Wood WG, Wise RW, Walsh JB, Thomas BN, Strong R: Ethanol-induced disordering of membranes from different age groups of C57BL/6NNIA mice. *J Pharmacol Exp Ther* 1983; 226:387–391.

Beaugé F, Stibler H, Borg S: Abnormal fluidity and surface carbohydrate content of the erythrocyte membrane in alcoholic patients. *Alcoholism (NY)* 1985; 9:322–326.

Boigegrain RA, Fernandez Y, Massol M, Mitjavila S: Thermodynamic interpretation of effects of alcohols on membrane lipid fluidity. *Chem Phys Lipids* 1984; 35:321–330.

Bradley DJ, Richards CD: Temperature-dependence of the action of nerve blocking agents and its relationship to membrane-buffer partition coefficients: Thermodynamic implications for the site of action of local anaesthetics. *Br J Pharmacol* 1984; 81:161–167.

Brink F, Posternak JM: Thermodynamic analysis of the relative effectiveness of narcotics. *J Cell Comp Physiol* 1948; 32:211–233.

Carmichael FJ, Israel Y: Effects of ethanol on neurotransmitter release by rat brain cortical slices. *J Pharmacol Exp Ther* 1975; 193:824–834.

Chin JH, Goldstein DB: Drug tolerance in biomembranes: A spin label study of the effects of ethanol. *Science* 1977a; 196:684–685.

Chin JH, Goldstein DB: Effects of low concentrations of ethanol on the fluidity of spin-labeled erythrocyte and brain membranes. *Mol Pharmacol* 1977b; 13:435–441.

Chin JH, Goldstein DB: Membrane-disordering action of ethanol: Variation with membrane cholesterol content and depth of the spin label probe. *Mol Pharmacol* 1981; 19:425–431.

Chin JH, Goldstein DB: Cholesterol blocks the disordering effects of ethanol in biomembranes. *Lipids* 1984; 19:929–935.

Chin JH, Goldstein DB: Effects of alcohols on membrane fluidity and lipid composition, in Aloia RC, Boggs JM (eds): *Membrane Fluidity in Biology*. New York, Academic Press, 1985, vol. 3, pp 1–58.

Cornell NW, Hansch C, Kim KH, Henegar K: The inhibition of alcohol dehydrogenase *in vitro* and in isolated hepatocytes by 4-substituted pyrazoles. *Arch Biochem Biophys* 1983; 227:81–90.

Diamond JM, Katz Y: Interpretation of nonelectrolyte partition coefficients between dimyristoyl lecithin and water. *J Membrane Biol* 1974; 17:121–154.

Dinh TKH, Gailis L: Effect of body temperature on acute ethanol toxicity. *Life Sci* 1979; 25:547–552.

Franks NP, Lieb WR: Do general anaesthetics act by competitive binding to specific receptors? *Nature* 1984; 310:599–601.

Franks NP, Lieb WR: Mapping of general anaesthetic target sites provides a molecular basis for cutoff effects. *Nature* 1985; 316:349–351.

Führer H: Die Wirkungsstärke der Narkotica. *Biochem Z* 1921; 120:143–163.

Goldstein DB: The effects of drugs on membrane fluidity. *Annu Rev Pharmacol Toxicol* 1984; 24:43–64.

Goldstein DB, Chin JH, Lyon RC: Ethanol disordering of spin-labeled mouse brain membranes: Correlation with genetically determined ethanol sensitivity of mice. *Proc Natl Acad Sci USA* 1982; 79: 4231–4233.

Goldstein DB, Feistner GJ, Faull KF, Tomer KB: Plasticizers as contaminants in commercial ethanol. *Alcoholism (NY)*, 1987; 11:521–524.

Goldstein DB, Zaechelein R: Time course of functional tolerance produced in mice by inhalation of ethanol. *J Pharmacol Exp Ther* 1983; 227:150–153.

Gonzales RA, Ganz N, Crews FT: Variations in membrane sensitivity of brain region synaptosomes to the effects of ethanol *in vitro* and chronic *in vivo* treatment. *J Neurochem* 1987; 49:158–162.

Harris RA, Baxter DM, Mitchell MA, Hitzemann RJ: Physical properties and lipid composition of brain membranes from ethanol tolerant-dependent mice. *Mol Pharmacol* 1984a; 25:401–409.

Harris RA, Burnett R, McQuilkin S, McClard A, Simon FR: Effects of ethanol on membrane order: Fluorescence studies. *Ann NY Acad Sci* 1987; 492:125–135.

Harris RA, Groh GI, Baxter DM, Hitzemann RJ: Gangliosides enhance the membrane actions of ethanol and pentobarbital. *Mol Pharmacol* 1984b; 25:410–417.

Harris RA, Schroeder F: Ethanol and the physical properties of brain membranes. Fluorescence studies. *Mol Pharmacol* 1981; 20:128–137.

Hiller JM, Angel LM, Simon EJ: Multiple opiate receptors: Alcohol selectively inhibits binding to delta receptors. *Science* 1981; 214:468–469.

Hitzemann RJ, Harris RA: Developmental changes in synaptic membrane fluidity: A comparison of 1,6-diphenylhexatriene (DPH) and 1-[4-(trimethylamino)phenyl]-6-phenyl-1,3,5 hexatriene (TMA-DPH). *Dev Brain Res* 1984; 14:113–120.

Jain MK, Touissaint DG, Cordes EH: Kinetics of water penetration into unsonicated liposomes. Effects of *n*-alkanols and cholesterol. *J Membrane Biol* 1973; 14:1–16.

Johnson DA, Lee NM, Cooke R, Loh HH: Ethanol-induced fluidization of brain lipid bilayers: Required presence of cholesterol in membranes for the expression of tolerance. *Mol Pharmacol* 1979; 15:739–746.

Kamaya H, Kaneshina S, Ueda I: Partition equilibrium of inhalation anesthetics and alcohols between water and membranes of phospholipids with varying acyl chain-lengths. *Biochim Biophys Acta* 1981; 646:135–142.

Katz Y, Diamond JM: Thermodynamic constants for nonelectrolyte partition between dimyristoyl lecithin and water. *J Membrane Biol* 1974; 17:101–120.

Kochmann M: Einfluss der Narkotica der Fettreihe auf den Quellungszustand der Zellkolloide. *Biochem Z* 1923; 136:49 65.

Laposata EA, Lange LG: Presence of nonoxidative ethanol metabolism in human organs commonly damaged by ethanol abuse. *Science* 1986; 231:497–500.

Laposata EA, Scherrer DE, Mazow C, Lange LG: Metabolism of ethanol by human brain to fatty acid ethyl esters. *J Biol Chem* 1987; 262:4653–4657.

Le Bourhis B, Beaugé F, Aufrère G, Nordmann R: Membrane fluidity and alcohol dependence. *Alcohol Clin Exp Res* 1987; 10:337–342.

Leguicher A, Beaugé F, Nordmann R: Concomitant changes in ethanol partitioning and disordering capacities in rat synaptic membranes. *Biochem Pharmacol* 1987; 36:2045–2048.

Leo A, Hansch C, Elkins D: Partition coefficients and their uses. *Chem Rev* 1971; 71:525–616.

Lindenberg BA: Sur la solubilité des substances organiques amphipatiques dans les glycérides neutres et hydroxylés. *J Chim Phys* 1951; 48:350–355.

Lyon RC, Goldstein DB: Changes in synaptic membrane order associated with chronic ethanol treatment in mice. *Mol Pharmacol* 1983a; 23:86–91.

Lyon RC, Goldstein DB: Restoration of synaptic membrane order following chronic ethanol treatment in mice. *Biophys J* 1983b; 198a.

Lyon RC, McComb JA, Schreurs J, Goldstein DB: A relationship between alcohol intoxication and the disordering of brain membranes by a series of short-chain alcohols. *J Pharmacol Exp Ther* 1981; 218:669–675.

Malcolm RD, Alkana RL: Hyperbaric ethanol antagonism: Role of temperature, blood and brain ethanol concentrations. *Pharmacol Biochem Behav* 1982; 16:341–346.

McCreery MJ, Hunt WA: Physico-chemical correlates of alcohol intoxication. *Neuropharmacology* 1978; 17:451–461.

Meyer KH, Hemmi H: Beiträge zur Theorie der Narkose. *Biochem Z* 1935; 277:39–71.

Miller KW, Paton WDM, Smith RA, Smith EB: The pressure reversal of general anesthesia and the critical volume hypothesis. *Mol Pharmacol* 1973; 8:131–143.

Mogelson S, Lange LG: Nonoxidative ethanol metabolism in rabbit myocardium: Purification to homogeneity of fatty acyl ethyl ester synthase. *Biochemistry* 1984; 23:4075–4081.

Mogelson S, Pieper SJ, Lange LG: Thermodynamic bases for fatty acid ethyl ester synthase catalyzed esterification of free fatty acid with ethanol and accumulation of fatty acid esters. *Biochemistry* 1984; 23:4082–4087.

Mullin MJ, Hunt WA: Actions of ethanol on voltage-sensitive sodium channels: Effects on neurotoxin-stimulated sodium uptake in synaptosomes. *J Pharmacol Exp Ther* 1985; 232:413–419.

Paterson SJ, Butler KW, Huang P, Labelle J, Smith, ICP, Schneider H: The effects of alcohols on lipid bilayers: A spin label study. *Biochim Biophys Acta* 1972; 266:597–602.

Perlman BJ, Goldstein DB: Ethanol and sodium valproate disordering of membranes from chronic ethanol treated mice. *Fed Proc* 1983; 42:2123.

Polokoff MA, Simon TJ, Harris RA, Simon FR, Iwahashi M: Chronic ethanol increases liver plasma membrane fluidity. *Biochemistry* 1985; 24:3114–3120.

Ponnappa BC, Waring AJ, Hoek JB, Rottenberg H, Rubin E: Chronic ethanol ingestion increases calcium uptake and resistance to molecular disordering by ethanol in liver microsomes. *J Biol Chem* 1982; 257:10141–10146.

Pringle MJ, Brown KB, Miller KW: Can the lipid theories of anesthesia account for the cutoff in anesthetic potency in homologous series of alcohols? *Mol Pharmacol* 1981; 19:49–55.

Rabin RA, Bode DC, Molinoff PB: Relationship between ethanol-induced alterations in fluorescence anisotropy and adenylate cyclase activity. *Biochem Pharmacol* 1986; 35:2331–2335.

Richards CD, Martin K, Gregory S, Keightley CA, Hesketh TR, Smith GA, Warren GB, Metcalfe JC: Degenerate perturbations of protein structure as the mechanism of anaesthetic action. *Nature* 1978; 276:775–779.

Roth S, Seeman P: The membrane concentrations of neutral and positive anesthetics (alcohols, chlorpromazine, morphine) fit the Meyer–Overton rule of anesthesia: Negative narcotics do not. *Biochim Biophys Acta* 1972; 255:207–219.

Rottenberg H, Waring A, Rubin E: Tolerance and cross-tolerance in chronic alcoholics: Reduced membrane binding of ethanol and other drugs. *Science* 1981; 213:583–585.

Rowe ES: The effects of ethanol on the thermotropic properties of dipalmitoylphosphatidylcholine. *Mol Pharmacol* 1982; 22:133–139.

Rydberg US, Goldstein DB: Synaptosomal membrane fluidity and response to ethanol in developing mice. *Alcohol Alcohol* 1986; 21:A74.

Sauerheber RD, Esgate JA, Kuhn CE: Alcohols inhibit adipocyte basal and insulin-stimulated glucose uptake and increase the membrane lipid fluidity. *Biochim Biophys Acta* 1982; 691:115–124.

Schüller A, Moscat J, Diez E, Fernandez-Checa C, Gavilanes FG, Municio AM: The fluidity of plasma membranes from ethanol-treated rat liver. *Mol Cell Biochem* 1984; 64:89–95.

Seeman P: The membrane actions of anesthetics and tranquilizers. *Pharmacol Rev* 1972; 24:583–655.

Seeman P, Chau M, Goldberg M, Sauks T, Sax L: The binding of Ca^{2+} to the cell membrane increased by volatile anesthetics (alcohols, acetone, ether) which induce sensitization of nerve or muscle. *Biochim Biophys Acta* 1971a; 225:185–193.

Seeman P, Roth S, Schneider H: The membrane concentrations of alcohol anesthetics. *Biochim Biophys Acta* 1971b; 225:171–184.

Stibler H, Beaugé F, Borg S: Changes in $(Na^+ + K^+)$ATPase activity and the composition of surface carbohydrates in erythrocyte membranes in alcoholics. *Alcoholism (NY)* 1984; 8:522–527.

Stokes JA, Harris RA: Alcohols and synaptosomal calcium transport. *Mol Pharmacol* 1982; 22:99–104.

Sun GY, Sun AY: Ethanol and membrane lipids. *Alcoholism (NY)* 1985; 9:164–180.

Tanford C: *The Hydrophobic Effect: Formation of Micelles and Biological Membranes*, ed 2. New York, Wiley, 1980, pp 1–4.

Taraschi TF, Ellingson JS, Wu A, Zimmerman R, Rubin E: Membrane tolerance to ethanol is rapidly lost after withdrawal: A model for studies of membrane adaptation. *Proc Natl Acad Sci USA* 1986a; 83:3669–3673.

Taraschi TF, Ellingson JS, Wu A, Zimmerman R, Rubin E: Phosphatidylinositol from ethanol-fed rats confers membrane tolerance to ethanol. *Proc Natl Acad Sci USA* 1986b; 83:9398–9402.

Taraschi TF, Rubin E: Effects of ethanol on the chemical and structural properties of biologic membranes. *Lab Invest* 1985; 52:120–131.

Taraschi TF, Wu A, Rubin E: Phospholipid spin probes measure the effects of ethanol on the molecular order of liver microsomes. *Biochemistry* 1985; 24:7096–7101.

Taylor GW: The effects of narcotics on respiration and luminescence in bacteria with special reference to the relation between the two processes. *J Cell Comp Physiol* 1933; 4:329. Cited in Brink and Posternak, 1948.

Treistman SN, Moynihan MM, Wolf DE: Influence of alcohols, temperature, and region on the mobility of lipids in neuronal membrane. *Biochim Biophys Acta* 1987; 898:109–120.

Vernon HM: The action of homologous alcohols and aldehydes on the tortoise heart. *J Physiol* 1912; 43:325–342.

Vernon HM: The changes in the reactions of growing organisms to narcotics. *J Physiol* 1913; 47:15. Cited in Ref 17.

Warburg O: Physikalische Chemie der Zellatmung. *Biochem Z* 1921; 119:134–166.

Waring AJ, Rottenberg H, Ohnishi T, Rubin E: Membranes and phospholipids of liver mitochondria from chronic alcoholic rats are resistant to membrane disordering by alcohol. *Proc Natl Acad Sci USA* 1981; 78:2582–2586.

Wenger JR, Alkana RL: Temperature dependence of ethanol depression in C57BL/6 and BALB/c mice. *Alcohol* 1984; 1:297–303.

Wood WG, Lahiri S, Gorka C, Armbrecht HJ, Strong R: In vitro effects of ethanol on erythrocyte membrane fluidity of alcoholic patients: An electron spin resonance study. *Alcohol Clin Exp Res* 1987; 11:332–335.

Yamada S, Lieber CS: Decrease in microviscosity and cholesterol content of rat liver plasma membranes after chronic ethanol feeding. *J Clin Invest* 1984; 74:2285–2289.

Zavoico GB, Kutchai H: Effects of *n*-alkanols on the membrane fluidity of chick embryo heart microsomes. *Biochim Biophys Acta* 1980; 600:263–269.

CHAPTER 5

Adaptive Responses to Ethanol in the Central Nervous System

Boris Tabakoff and Paula L. Hoffman

National Institute on Alcohol Abuse and Alcoholism
Bethesda, Maryland, USA

NEUROADAPTATION AND "ADDICTION" TO ETHANOL

Studies of neuroadaptation in response to the ingestion of ethanol are, in many cases, ostensibly directed at generating information on why individuals consume ethanol in quantities that are injurious to themselves and to those around them. It is assumed that changes in neuronal structure and/or function produced by ethanol are responsible for phenomena such as tolerance and dependence and that tolerance and dependence in turn are contributors to the actualization of addiction. Clearly, "addiction" to a substance such as ethanol may never be adequately defined (circumscribed) by the concepts of tolerance and dependence, even though these concepts are currently undergoing a rapid metamorphosis. A host of social, cultural, and personal variables need to be considered when discussing addictions and considering the reasons why some persons drink alcohol in a self-destructive manner. On the other hand, the concept of an alcohol dependence syndrome (Edwards, 1968) has proven to be a valuable tool in beginning to provide operational definitions for substantive portions of the spectrum of alcohol addiction in humans, as well as providing a framework for categorizing various observations regarding pathologic drinking behavior and its concomitants. Although the alcohol dependence syndrome as defined by Edwards (1968) and others contains some elements that are distinctly human (e.g., salience), many of the elements (tolerance, withdrawal symptoms, and need for relief drinking) are amenable to modeling with the use of infrahuman species. Such models are valuable not only for validating and better describing the components of the syndrome but also allow for assessment of the biological and molecular mechanisms that underlie each particular component.

CONCEPTUALIZATION OF ALCOHOL TOLERANCE

Tolerance is defined as an acquired resistance to the physiological and behavioral effects of ethanol. Although tolerance to the effects of ethanol is an integral part of the definition of alcoholism (WHO, 1952), the importance of tolerance in the etiology or the expression of alcoholism has been often debated. For example, although Cappell and Le Blanc (1979) stated that "Perhaps the most important question about tolerance to ethanol . . . is whether it affects [the] probability of [ethanol] self-administration," they also argued that the relationship between tolerance and alcohol consumption "resists empirical documentation with our present scientific capability." Current work, however, is demonstrating that selective breeding of animals for preference for ethanol also produces animals that rapidly develop toler-ance to the sedative effects of ethanol (Waller et al, 1983). Furthermore, there are indications that, in animals, significant periods of prior consumption of ethanol are necessary in order to demonstrate the reinforcing properties of ethanol (Numan, 1981; Reid et al, 1985).

Tolerance may be classified as acute (within-session) or chronic (between-session) tolerance. Whereas acute tolerance can be evidenced within the time that a single dose of alcohol is cleared from an individual, chronic tolerance develops after repeated dosing with ethanol. Chronic tolerance has, classically, been divided into pharmacokinetic (metabolic) and phar-macodynamic (functional) tolerance. Although metabolic tolerance can contribute to changes in duration of ethanol's actions, functional tolerance is primarily responsible for changes in the intensity of ethanol's effects.

Recently, alcohol tolerance has been recognized to be even more multifactorial. Tolerance in certain instances has been likened to learning, in that it represents an adaptive response of the central nervous system (CNS) to external and internal stimuli produced by the "ritual" of drug administration and the physiological effects of the drug (Lê et al, 1979; Crowell et al, 1981). A Pavlovian conditioning model of tolerance has been proposed by a number of inves-tigators (Tabakoff et al, 1982). This type of tolerance has been designated in our studies as "conditioned" or "environment-dependent" tolerance (Melchior and Tabakoff, 1981), to dis-tinguish it from "environment-independent" tolerance, which can be demonstrated regardless of the testing environment (Tabakoff et al, 1982).

CONCEPTUALIZATION OF ALCOHOL DEPENDENCE

Although parsimony in the past has generated unitary concepts to explain both tolerance and physical dependence, experiments utilizing neurotoxins (Tabakoff and Ritzmann, 1977) and selective breeding for withdrawal seizure-prone and withdrawal seizure-resistant (WSP and WSR) mice (Crabbe and Kosobud, 1986) dictate a need for conceptual dissociation of toler-ance and physical dependence.

Dependence on ethanol has also been subclassified on many occasions into "psychologi-cal" and "physical" dependence. The presence of a withdrawal reaction has been used as a priori evidence that an individual was physically dependent on ethanol. In neurochemical terms, the presence of high amounts of ethanol in the body for prolonged periods would pro-mote neuronal adaptation. The altered neuronal function would produce the signs and symp-toms of the ethanol withdrawal syndrome on cessation of ethanol ingestion. Psychological dependence is a term that is used to describe the difficult-to-quantify concepts of "need" or "craving" (Edwards, 1968). The terms "need" or "craving" indicate that during chronic consumption of alcohol there develops some underlying biologic necessity for ethanol in the "psychologically dependent" individual. In the past, there have been few, if any, means of modeling "psychological dependence" in subhuman species. Recent work utilizing the con-ditioned place preference paradigm (Reid et al, 1985) may, however, provide the initial oppor-tunities for exploring the phenomenon of "psychological dependence" even in rodents.

FACTORS THAT INFLUENCE ETHANOL TOLERANCE

A concept that has been applied both to the neurobiology of learning and to tolerance (Tabakoff and Ritzmann, 1977; Squire and Davis, 1981; Hoffman and Tabakoff, 1984) is that of extrinsic and intrinsic neural systems. Intrinsic systems encode specific information, such as tolerance to a particular effect of ethanol, possibly by changes in synaptic efficacy. An example of such a change, related to learning, is the phenomenon of long-term potenti-ation (Schwartzkroin and Wester, 1975). Extrinsic systems, on the other hand, can influence the development, maintenance, or expression of tolerance but do not encode tolerance in themselves (Tabakoff and Ritzmann, 1977; Squire and Davis, 1981). Current evidence from our laboratories, and laboratories of others, indicates that both intrinsic characteristics of certain neurons and extrinsic neurochemical events modulate the rates and extents of development of various forms of tolerance and of physical dependence. Underlying the propensity of an animal to develop tolerance to or dependence on ethanol are genetic variables, which may control both the intrinsic and extrinsic determinants of tolerance and dependence (Grieve et al, 1979; Tabakoff and Ritzmann, 1979; Tabakoff et al, 1980; Crabbe et al, 1985).

EXTRINSIC SYSTEMS: NEUROTRANSMITTER EFFECTS ON TOLERANCE

Two candidates for the extrinsic systems modulating ethanol tolerance are the noradrenergic and serotonergic neuronal pathways of the brain. One approach to studying the roles of these neurotransmitter systems in tolerance has been to specifically modify the activity of the neurotransmitter systems and to determine the effect of the modification on the development or maintenance of ethanol tolerance. In rats, depletion of brain serotonin was shown to delay the development of tolerance to the hypothermic and motor-impairing effects of ethanol (Frankel et al, 1975; Frankel et al, 1978; Lê et al, 1980). The specific serotonergic pathway involved was the one connecting the median raphe nucleus to the hippocampus (Lê et al, 1981).

In mice, partial destruction of catecholaminergic neurons by 6-hydroxydopamine (6 OHDA) blocked the development of tolerance to the hypnotic and hypothermic effects of ethanol (Tabakoff and Ritzmann, 1977). In animals treated with desmethylimipramine prior to administration of 6-OHDA, noradrenergic systems were protected, and tolerance developed as usual (Tabakoff and Ritzmann, 1977). Recent data (Szabó et al, 1988) indicate that interaction of norepinephrine with beta-adrenergic receptors coupled to adenylate cyclase may be important for the development of tolerance in mice. Although partial depletion of brain norepinephrine by 6-OHDA blocked the development of tolerance, daily intracerebroventricular treatment with forskolin, an activator of adenylate cyclase, overcame this blockade. It has also been shown that ethanol, in vitro, enhances isoproterenol stimulation of adenylate cyclase activity (Saito et al, 1985) and alters agonist (isoproterenol) binding to beta-adrenergic receptors in cerebral cortical membrane preparations (Valverius et al, 1987). These effects were observed at low concentrations of ethanol that could be attained in vivo. The data suggest that ethanol specifically affects the function of G_s, the stimulatory guanine nucleotide binding protein (Saito et al, 1985; Valverius et al, 1987) and are consistent with the postulate that ethanol enhancement of norepinephrine-stimulated adenylate cyclase activity may be important for the development of ethanol tolerance. It is of interest that norepinephrine, as well as forskolin and dibutyryl cyclic AMP, were also reported to enhance the magnitude, duration, and probability of induction of long-term potentiation in hippocampal slices (Hopkins and Johnston, 1984, 1986). Interaction of norepinephrine with beta-adrenergic receptors, and the consequent increase in intracellular cyclic adenosine monophosphate (AMP) levels, may therefore be important for neuroadaptive processes in general.

In rats, depletion of norepinephrine (NE) did not block the development of tolerance to the hypnotic effects of ethanol (Lê et al, 1981; Wood and Laverty, 1979), although it altered the initial response of the animals to ethanol (Wood and Laverty, 1979). On the other hand, development of tolerance to the *hypothermic* effects of ethanol in rats was blocked by administration of the NE neuron toxin DSP-4 (Trzaskowska et al, 1986). It was also found that, although partial destruction of brain noradrenergic neurons did not block the development of tolerance to the hypnotic effect of ethanol in rats, combined destruction of both NE and serotonin systems could completely block tolerance development, whereas destruction of serotonergic neurons only delayed tolerance development (Lê et al, 1981). Additional studies aimed at understanding the interactions between noradrenergic and serotonergic systems in various areas of brain (e.g., locus coeruleus) could certainly amplify and clarify these observations. There is much evidence, from inbred strains and selected lines of animals, for genetic variability with respect to the neurochemistry of serotonergic and noradrenergic systems in brain (Li et al, 1979). Thus, although the influence of genetic factors on the role of the extrinsic systems (i.e., noradrenergic, serotonergic) with respect to ethanol tolerance has not been specifically investigated, it is possible that genetically based differences in an animal's noradrenergic and serotonergic pathways contribute to differences in rate and extent of tolerance development [cf. differences in serotonergic systems in P and NP rats (Kakihana and Butte, 1980)].

In certain studies just described, neurotransmitters were depleted prior to ingestion of ethanol, but the animals ingested equivalent amounts of ethanol during the period of chronic ethanol intoxication. An important conclusion that can be drawn, therefore, is that the presence of ethanol in the CNS is necessary, but not sufficient, to produce ethanol tolerance. In addition to the presence of ethanol, the activity of certain neuronal pathways seems to be required in order for tolerance to be manifest. This requirement was also quite clearly demonstrated using a model system of an identified synapse in *Aplysia*. Ethanol accelerated the decay of posttetanic potentiation at this synapse, and, with repeated exposure, the ethanol effect diminished (i.e., tolerance developed (Traynor et al, 1976)). However, the development of tolerance was strictly dependent on adequate stimulation of the presynaptic terminal in the presence of ethanol (Traynor et al, 1980). Such invertebrate model systems of synaptic plasticity have been used to great advantage in studies of the biochemistry and electrophysiology of learning and may provide further insights into mechanisms of ethanol tolerance.

EXTRINSIC SYSTEMS: NEUROPEPTIDE EFFECTS ON TOLERANCE

Arginine vasopressin (AVP) is another compound that has been found to be important for expression or maintenance of ethanol tolerance. Mice made functionally tolerant to various physiological effects of ethanol were found to remain tolerant, even without further ethanol ingestion, for as long as they received once-daily subcutaneous or intracerebroventricular injections of AVP (Hoffman et al, 1979; Hung et al, 1984). In mice, depletion of brain norepinephrine prevented the maintenance of tolerance by AVP, suggesting a role for noradrenergic systems in this action of the hormone (Hoffman et al, 1983). An analog of AVP (des-9-glycinamide AVP [DGAVP]) also maintained tolerance to the motor-incoordinating effect of ethanol in rats (Lê et al, 1982). In these animals, depletion of serotonin prevented the action of DGAVP (Lê et al, 1982). Specifically, DGAVP could no longer maintain tolerance after chemical denervation of the dorsal serotonergic afferent pathways to the hippocampus (Speisky and Kalant, 1981; Lê et al, 1982). Thus, AVP appears to modulate the activity of the extrinsic neurotransmitter systems that influence ethanol tolerance development.

Recently, AVP receptors have been identified in hippocampus and other brain areas (Barberis, 1983; Dorsa et al, 1983; Costantini and Perlmutter, 1984; Bugon et al, 1984; Audigier and Barberis, 1985). Hippocampal AVP receptors appear to have characteristics in common with V_1 vasopressin receptors as defined in peripheral tissues (Jard, 1983; Costantini and Perlmutter; Audigier and Barberis, 1985). V_1 receptors mediate vasopressin-induced mobilization of intracellular calcium, and the first step in this process is stimulation of phosphatidylinositol metabolism (Jard, 1983). Vasopressin has been reported to enhance the metabolism of inositol phospholipids in hippocampal slices (Stephens and Logan, 1985). In contrast, the interaction of vasopressin with V_2 receptors, located in the kidney (Jard, 1983), results in stimulation of adenylate cyclase activity and cyclic AMP production. Using agonists and antagonists selective for V_1 or V_2 receptors (Sawyer and Manning, 1985), it has been demonstrated that the ability of vasopressin to maintain ethanol tolerance is mediated by a CNS receptor with V_1 characteristics. Thus, [2-Phe,3-Ile,8-Orn] vasopressin, a V_1-specific agonist, given intracerebroventricularly, was more potent than AVP in maintaining tolerance, whereas a V_2-specific agonist, [1-deamino,4-Val,8-D-Arg] vasopressin (dVDAVP), given at the same dose as AVP, was ineffective (Szabó et al, 1988). Furthermore, antagonists selective for V_1 receptors were more potent than a V_2-selective antagonist at blocking the ability of AVP to maintain ethanol tolerance (Szabó et al, 1988).

Although extrahypothalamic vasopressin-containing neuronal networks have been located in the brain, and evidence has been presented for independent control of CNS and peripheral vasopressin rhythms, few studies have investigated whether *endogenous* AVP in the brain is important for the maintenance of ethanol tolerance. Recent results indicate that intracerebroventricular administration of V_1-selective antagonists *alone* facilitates the loss of ethanol tolerance. A V_2-selective antagonist did not have this effect (Szabó et al, 1988). These findings are consistent with the hypothesis that endogenous AVP, acting at CNS V_1 receptors, may play a role in neuroadaptation to ethanol. In addition, Pittman et al (1982) reported that ethanol tolerance did not develop in Brattleboro rats given ethanol chronically, in contrast to control animals. Brattleboro rats do not produce active arginine vasopressin because of a mutation that interferes with the translation of mRNA for the vasopressin precursor molecule (Schmale et al, 1984). These findings not only suggest a role for endogenous vasopressin in ethanol tolerance but also indicate a further mechanism by which genetic variability can influence ethanol tolerance.

INTRINSIC SYSTEMS INVOLVED IN ETHANOL TOLERANCE

As discussed above, intrinsic neural systems are those that encode tolerance to specific effects of ethanol. It has been proposed that neuronal membranes represent the initial site of action of ethanol (Seeman, 1972; Chin and Goldstein, 1976; Harris and Schroeder, 1981; Goldstein et al, 1982) and it has been implied that adaptive changes in the structure of these membranes could be responsible for ethanol tolerance (Chin and Goldstein, 1976; Lyon and Goldstein, 1983; Harris et al, 1984). Thus, by the use of sensitive techniques such as electron paramagnetic resonance (EPR) and fluorescence polarization, relatively low concentrations of ethanol have been shown to perturb the structure (increase the "fluidity") of neuronal membrane lipids (Chin and Goldstein, 1976, 1977; Harris and Schroeder, 1981) as well as the membrane lipids from other cells (Chin and Goldstein, 1977; Waring et al, 1981). Although a great deal of attention has been focused on generalized membrane "disordering" effects of ethanol, current studies using nuclear magnetic resonance (NMR) techniques have supported the contention that the effects of ethanol are not equivalent throughout the neuronal membrane. Hitzemann et al (1986) presented evidence that ethanol (0.1% and 0.2%) may actually produce an "ordering" effect at the membrane surface.

When neuronal membranes are obtained from animals that are chronically administered ethanol, the membranes are resistant to the fluidizing effects of ethanol (Chin and Goldstein, 1976; Harris et al, 1984). In some cases, the membranes from ethanol-tolerant animals also display decreased baseline fluidity (increased "rigidity"). The demonstrations of changes in baseline fluidity depend both on the probe used to assess fluidity (i.e., the area of the membrane examined) (Lyon and Goldstein, 1983; Harris et al, 1984) and the tissue origin of the membranes. Liver membranes from animals treated chronically with ethanol have in some studies been reported to be *more* fluid than those of controls (Yamada and Lieber, 1984; Polokoff et al, 1985). Changes in the partition coefficient for ethanol have been suggested (Rottenberg et al, 1981; Rubin and Rottenberg, 1986) to be responsible for membrane resistance to the disordering effects of ethanol, but inherent difficulties in measuring the partition coefficient of ethanol by tracer distribution methods make direct demonstrations of this phenomenon difficult (Rottenberg, 1986).

Resistance to the membrane-fluidizing effects of ethanol can be defined as "tolerance" at the molecular level, but there is currently little evidence that such a change is associated with tolerance to the physiological effects of ethanol in the whole animal. Before such a conclusion can be reached, consideration should be given to factors such as the relationship between the time course for development and dissipation of physiological manifestations of tolerance and of changes in membrane properties. For example, it was recently reported that resistance to the lipid-perturbing effect of ethanol in membranes of liver microsomes and erythrocytes obtained from rats that had been chronically fed ethanol was lost within one to four days of withdrawal (Taraschi et al, 1986). Although physiological signs of tolerance were not assessed in this study, tolerance generally dissipates with a longer time course after cessation of chronic ethanol ingestion (Ritzmann and Tabakoff, 1976). The source of membranes that are used for such correlational studies should also be carefully considered.

Currently the most consistent changes in membrane *chemistry* that accompany resistance to ethanol's membrane perturbing actions are in the fatty acid substituents of particular classes of phospholipids. The two phospholipids, phosphatidylserine and phosphatidylinositol, are present in low abundance in membranes but are of major importance in the function of membrane proteins (Charnock et al, 1973; Mandersloot et al, 1978) and as reservoirs of second messengers (inositol trisphosphate [IP$_3$] and diacylglycerol [DAG]) and hormone precursors (arachidonic acid) (Majerus et al, 1986). Chronic ethanol ingestion has been reported to diminish the levels of polyunsaturated fatty acid substituents (20:4, arachidonate and 22:6, docosahexaenoate) in phosphatidylinositol (Aloia et al, 1985) and phosphatidylserine (Harris et al, 1984; Aloia et al, 1985), respectively. Such changes in acyl composition may contribute to changes in membrane functional properties produced by chronic ingestion of ethanol. However, given the contention (Taraschi et al, 1986) that significant periods (several days to weeks) of *high levels* of ethanol intake are necessary to produce the witnessed membrane changes, one has to inquire whether all types of tolerance (environment dependent as well as environment independent) can be ascribed to changes in neuronal membrane lipid composition.

There are some other candidates for intrinsic systems mediating ethanol tolerance, such as the various ion channels that control neuronal excitability (Leslie, 1986), but, again, there is little evidence linking changes in these systems to physiological aspects of tolerance. The ethanol-induced changes in ion channels will be discussed under the heading "Extrinsic and Intrinsic Systems Influencing Ethanol Dependence."

MODEL CELLULAR SYSTEMS FOR STUDIES OF ETHANOL TOLERANCE

In a search for the molecular mechanisms of tolerance development, the attention of several laboratories has been focused on cells of neural origin grown in culture. Neuroblastoma cells or neuroblastoma–glioma hybrids (NG108-15, N1E-115) have been grown in the presence of ethanol, and the characteristics of several receptors, effectors, and ionophores in the cell membranes have been examined. These studies have, in general, demonstrated that the presence of ethanol in the culture medium leads to an altered function of a number of membrane receptors and ionophores. Theoretically, the findings could be viewed as a developed tolerance to the acute effects of ethanol on these systems. The extrapolation of results obtained in such model systems to in vivo neuronal systems is not without difficulty, but there are some indications that certain systems (e.g., receptor-regulated adenylate cyclase) may respond similarly in vivo and in the cultured cell systems (Tabakoff and Hoffman, 1979; Gordon et al, 1986; Richelson et al, 1986; Saito et al, 1987). A number of caveats have to be dealt with when such model systems are used to investigate alcohol tolerance at the level of the cell membrane. The membrane lipid characteristics of hybrid cells depend on the composition of the medium in which the cells are grown and, as a result, may well differ from either neurons or glia in situ (McGee, 1981). Cultured cell membrane physical properties or membrane lipid chemistry have not been examined after chronic ethanol treatment. The cells in culture exist in the absence of many of the functional interactions with other cell types that occur in the

CNS, and there is no a priori reason to assume that the receptor–effector systems examined in these cells are specifically important in tolerance. On the other hand, if testable hypotheses can emanate from such studies, the use of the cells in culture may facilitate elucidation of the mechanism(s) underlying ethanol tolerance.

ATTEMPTS TO LINK IN VIVO CHANGES IN BRAIN ELECTROPHYSIOLOGY AND TRANSMITTER FUNCTION TO TOLERANCE

There are currently numerous studies that examine various aspects of neuronal function (particularly neurotransmitter metabolism and electrophysiologic responses) after chronic ethanol administration to animals (see Hoffman and Tabakoff, 1985 for review). There may be relevance of reported findings to the processes of alcohol-induced neuroadaptation, but much work needs to be completed before any of the witnessed changes can be looked on as candidates for the determinants of tolerance to the physiologic and/or behavioral effects of ethanol.

FACTORS THAT INFLUENCE ETHANOL DEPENDENCE

As for ethanol tolerance, it may be postulated that extrinsic and intrinsic neural systems contribute to physical and/or psychological dependence. The systems associated with ethanol dependence are not necessarily the same as those that influence tolerance, since ethanol tolerance and dependence appear to be dissociable phenomena (Tabakoff and Ritzmann, 1977). In addition, recent data indicate that classical conditioning does not influence ethanol withdrawal as it does ethanol tolerance (Numan, 1986). It does appear that, as for tolerance, genetic factors underlie an individual's susceptibility to ethanol-induced physical dependence. The most direct evidence for a genetic influence on ethanol dependence derives from studies of ethanol withdrawal in inbred strains and selected lines of mice. Selected lines of mice have been bred that have high (WSP) and low (WSR) susceptibility to ethanol withdrawal seizures. These animals have been shown not to differ in sensitivity to various treatments, unrelated to alcohol withdrawal, which produce generalized seizures (electroconvulsive shock, strychnine, flurothyl, picrotoxin, bicuculline, and pentylenetetrazole), supporting the hypothesis that the lines of mice differ specifically in the degree of seizure susceptibility produced by ethanol withdrawal (physical dependence) (McSwigan et al, 1984). These types of animals promise to provide a valuable model for assessing the biochemical basis of withdrawal seizures that accompany physical dependence on ethanol.

EXTRINSIC AND INTRINSIC SYSTEMS INFLUENCING ETHANOL PHYSICAL DEPENDENCE

Prior to discussing neuronal systems that influence the development or expression of ethanol physical dependence, one has to note that current definitions of physical dependence rely on events occurring *after* termination of ethanol ingestion to describe neuroadaptive phenomena that presumably occur during the course of ethanol ingestion.

The evidence for extrinsic and intrinsic neuronal systems that influence ethanol dependence is rather sparse. The postulate that changes in neuronal membrane fluidity (i.e., decreased fluidity) produce ethanol withdrawal symptomatology has been tested in the WSP and WSR mice described above. Fluidity was decreased to the same degree in WSP and WSR mice after chronic ethanol ingestion, indicating that the genetic differences in ethanol withdrawal seizures in these lines of mice could not be attributed to differential changes in neuronal membrane properties (Harris et al, 1984).

The processes that underlie the ethanol-induced CNS hyperexcitability that results in ethanol withdrawal seizures have been likened to the processes that underlie the development of spontaneous seizures by prior periodic brain stimulation (i.e., kindling [Ballenger and Post, 1978]). Kindling has been postulated to produce alterations in brain cholinergic receptors (McNamara, 1978) and to increase the responsiveness of brain cells to ionophoretically applied acetylcholine (Burchfiel et al, 1979). When muscarinic cholinergic receptors were assessed in brains of C57BL mice or rats that had ingested ethanol chronically, it was observed that the number of receptors in the hippocampus and cortex (Tabakoff et al, 1979; Rabin et al, 1980; Nordberg et al, 1985), but not in the striatum, was increased. In mice, the increase in receptor number was apparent at the time of withdrawal and at 8 hours after withdrawal, the time of peak withdrawal symptomatology. Receptor number had reverted to normal by 24 hours after withdrawal, a time when ethanol withdrawal seizures and tremors had also dissipated (Tabakoff et al, 1979; Rabin et al, 1980). The increase in muscarinic receptor number in the cortex of ethanol-fed C57BL mice was also accompanied, in one study (Hoffman et al, 1986), by an increased sensitivity of phosphatidylinositol turnover to stimulation by carbachol. The increased functional response to the muscarinic cholinergic agonist, with concomitant changes in inositol trisphosphate (IP_3) production and in the consequent mobilization of calcium from intracellular stores (Abdel-Latif, 1986) may contribute to the signs of ethanol withdrawal.

THE ROLE OF CALCIUM IN ETHANOL-INDUCED NEUROADAPTATION AND DEPENDENCE

Intracellular concentrations of calcium are controlled by a substantial number of regulators. In addition to the above-mentioned IP_3-sensitive microsomal calcium sequestration systems, voltage-sensitive calcium channels (VSCC) are of major importance in altering intracellular calcium levels and coupling signal conduction to transmitter release as well. A number of VSCCs with different physiologic and pharmacologic properties have been described (Miller, 1987). These include T, L, and N channels. Little is yet known about T channels, which are activated by low levels of depolarization and give rise to small transient calcium currents. L channels are activated by substantial neuronal membrane depolarization and their activity is modulated by dihydropyridine (DHP) agonists and antagonists (e.g., nitrendipine, nifedipine, and BAY k 8644). The L channels are found in neuronal preparations but do not appear to be linked to neurotransmitter release. N channels, which are not sensitive to DHPs, have been suggested to be localized in neuron terminals and to mediate neurotransmitter release, whereas L channels have been postulated to be localized on neuronal cell bodies (Miller, 1987). Although controversy had, in the past, surrounded the question of whether ethanol affected depolarization-induced calcium uptake into synaptosomes, recent work clarified the need to use short depolarization times to study ethanol's actions. Measures of calcium uptake over periods of 1 to 3 seconds demonstrated that ethanol was a potent inhibitor of synaptosomal depolarization-induced calcium uptake (Leslie et al, 1983). Interestingly, the acute effects of ethanol and certain other anesthetics on depolarization-dependent calcium uptake were not clearly related to the anesthetics' membrane disordering effects (Harris and Bruno, 1985). Fast-phase calcium uptake has been reported to be associated with phasic neurotransmitter release (Leslie et al, 1983; Daniell and Leslie, 1986). However, although ethanol clearly inhibited this calcium uptake, ethanol did not alter norepinephrine release from a crude synaptosomal preparation. It was suggested that ethanol might alter calcium uptake into neurons that release transmitters other than norepinephrine, since the synaptosomal preparation is heterogeneous (Daniell and Leslie, 1986). Another reasonable explanation may be that ethanol, at least in part, alters calcium uptake by L channels located on non-terminal-vesicular elements present in the "synaptosomal" preparation.

The chronic ingestion of ethanol by rats over a period of several weeks produced resistance to the ethanol-induced inhibition of synaptosomal depolarization-dependent calcium uptake

(Leslie et al, 1983). Studies of ^{3}H-nitrendipine binding have indicated that the chronic presence of ethanol in the medium bathing cells of neural crest origin (PC12 cells) increases the number of nitrendipine (a dihydropyridine)-sensitive calcium channels (Messing et al, 1986) and increases depolarization-dependent calcium influx (Greenberg et al, 1987). Chronic ethanol administration, as well as administration of opiates or neuroleptics, was also reported to increase the number of ^{3}H-DHP binding sites in *brain* membranes (Bolger et al, 1985; Lucchí et al, 1985). The binding sites for nitrendipine and DHP are believed to represent L channels, as discussed above, and the characteristics of the increased calcium flux in PC12 cells (e.g., modulation by DHPs) were also consistent with an increased number of L channels (Greenberg et al, 1987). One could consider that calcium channel proliferation in cells in culture or in brain promotes a resistance to ethanol's actions and/or generates a neuronal hyperexcitability. Although an increased depolarization-induced, calcium-dependent release of dopamine from striatal slices of chronically ethanol-treated rats was demonstrated in one study (Lynch et al, 1986), such a change was not observed under different experimental conditions (Leslie et al, 1986) and is not necessarily related to an increase in the number of L channels, which contribute little to neurotransmitter release (Miller, 1987). The studies of Lynch et al (1986) demonstrated that the release of dopamine from striatal slices of the ethanol-treated rats was also more sensitive to A-23187 (a calcium ionophore). One can, thus, conclude that the sensitivity of the intracellular transmitter release mechanisms to calcium may become enhanced during chronic treatment with ethanol, rather than, or in addition to, ethanol inducing increases in VSCC. The physiologic significance of changes in the L channel number is currently being debated, but reports indicating that DHP calcium channel blockers reduce certain signs of ethanol withdrawal (Little et al, 1986) make further investigations of ethanol's effects on sensitivity to calcium and on various types of VSCC most important.

Very recent studies suggest that the N-methyl-D-asparate (NMDA) receptor-gated ion channel, which, when open, is permeable to monovalent cations and calcium, may be a key system involved in the actions of ethanol. Ethanol, *in vitro*, has been found to be a selective and very potent inhibitor of the biochemical (i.e., stimulation of calcium uptake and cyclic GMP production) (Hoffman et al, 1989a) and electrophysiological (stimulation of ion current) (Lovinger et al, 1989) effects of NMDA in neuronal cells. After chronic ethanol ingestion, NMDA receptors in brain were increased (Hoffman et al, 1989b). Furthermore, administration of NMDA increased ethanol withdrawal seizure severity, while administration of an antagonist at the NMDA receptor/channel complex reduced withdrawal seizures (Grant and Tabakoff, 1989). Because NMDA receptors, which represent one subtype of brain glutamate receptors, have been implicated in long-term potentiation, synaptic plasticity and epileptiform seizures, the results suggest that certain acute pharmacological effects of ethanol, including cognitive deficits, as well as ethanol withdrawal seizures, may involve specific alterations of the function of the NMDA receptor-gated cation channel.

PROTEIN MODIFICATION AS A DETERMINANT
OF NEUROADAPTATION

The processes by which chronic ethanol ingestion can alter the function of neuronal membrane proteins (e.g., VSCC or receptors) are diverse. Although it has been contended that changes in protein function are secondary to changes in the properties of membrane lipids, phosphorylation or other direct modifications of protein structure and function need to be considered as possible mediators of ethanol-induced neuroadaptation. For instance, ethanol potentiates transmitter-stimulated generation of cyclic AMP in various areas of brain (Rabin and Molinoff, 1981; Luthin and Tabakoff, 1984; Saito, 1985). This event may initiate a cascade by which membrane protein phosphorylation is enhanced after ethanol ingestion. The decreased ability to induce in vitro phosphorylation of neuronal membrane proteins of ethanol-treated animals (Rius et al, 1986) may indicate increased protein phosphorylation in vivo.

This change may be related to the increased number of DHP binding sites and calcium flux observed after chronic ethanol treatment (Lucchi et al, 1985; Messing et al, 1986; Greenberg et al, 1987). The dihydropyridine-sensitive calcium channel has been reported to be a substrate for cyclic AMP-dependent protein kinase, and phosphorylation alters this channel's properties (Miller, 1987). Furthermore, in certain neuronal cell lines, cyclic AMP has been found to induce DHP binding sites (Miller, 1987). In light of the evidence just discussed for the apparent role of ethanol- and beta-adrenergic agonist-stimulated cyclic AMP production in the development of ethanol tolerance, it is of interest that administration of the DHP calcium channel antagonist—nifedipine—was recently reported to delay the acquisition of ethanol tolerance (Wu et al, 1987). These data are consistent with the possibility that cyclic AMP-dependent alterations in calcium channel activity in brain may influence the development of ethanol tolerance. Additionally, calcium–calmodulin-dependent phosphorylation of membrane proteins has been reported to be altered by chronic ethanol treatment (Shanley et al, 1985; Rius et al, 1986).

In addition to phosphorylation, other posttranslational modifications of membrane-bound proteins may be produced by chronic ethanol ingestion. In mice made tolerant to and physically dependent on ethanol, stimulation of adenylate cyclase activity in cerebral cortical membranes by the beta-adrenergic agonist, isoproterenol, and by the nonhydrolyzable guanine nucleotide, Gpp(HN)p, was reduced (Saito et al, 1987). Furthermore, when agonist (isoproterenol) binding to cerebral cortical beta-adrenergic receptors was measured, the data were best fit by a one-site model in the absence of guanine nucleotides (Valverius et al, 1987). Such data are indicative of an uncoupling of the three major protein constituents of the receptor-coupled adenylate cyclase system and are similar to data on ligand binding and adenylate cyclase activation that are obtained under conditions where agonist-induced heterologous desensitization occurs (Sibley and Lefkowitz, 1985). The findings are compatible with a change in the quantity or function of the guanine nucleotide binding protein, G_s, which, as discussed previously, represents a site of the acute actions of ethanol in the brain (Luthin and Tabakoff, 1984; Saito et al, 1985). The results of recent investigations (Nhamburo, PT, Tabakoff, B, and Hoffman, PL) indicate that there is decreased G_s available for cholera toxin-induced ADP-ribosylation in cortical membranes of ethanol-withdrawn animals. The amount of other guanine nucleotide binding proteins (i.e., G_i and/or G_o), as measured by pertussis toxin-induced ribosylation, appears to be unaltered, although small changes in these proteins are more difficult to detect. The change in G_s may represent a decrease in the amount of protein, since in NG108-15 cells exposed to ethanol, the function, as well as the amount of G_s as measured by Western blot analysis, and the mRNA for G_s were decreased (Mochly-Rosen et al, 1988). Alternatively, since G proteins have been reported to undergo endogenous ribosylation (Jacquemin et al, 1986), and it is possible that ethanol-induced changes in ribosylation, in concert with changes in phosphorylation, may be of importance in neuroadaptation to ethanol. Selective changes in the function of G proteins in the brain may have profound effects on the actions of neurotransmitters (Codina et al, 1984) as well as on the properties of ion channels, including calcium channels, whose functions are directly affected by G proteins as well by cyclic AMP (Gray and Johnston, 1979; Grega and Macdonald, 1987; Hescheler et al, 1987). As more sophisticated techniques (e.g., two-dimensional gel electrophoresis, immunoblotting, etc.) are applied to the separation and identification of membrane proteins, definitive statements regarding the role of ethanol-induced membrane protein modifications in the development of tolerance and/or physical dependence will be possible.

REFERENCES

Abdel-Latif AA: Calcium mobilizing receptors, polyphosphoinositides and the generation of second messengers. *Pharmacol Rev* 1986; 38:227–272.

Aloia RC, Paxton J, Daviau JS, van Gelb O, Mlekusch W, Truppe W, Meyer JA, Brauer FS: Effect of chronic alcohol consumption on rat brain microsome lipid composition, membrane fluidity and Na$^+$K$^+$-ATPase activity. *Life Sci* 1985; 36:1003–1017.

Audigier S, Barberis C: Pharmacological characterization of two specific binding sites for neurohypophyseal hormones in hippocampal synaptic plasma membranes of the rat. *EMBO Journal* 1985; 4: 1407–1412.

Ballenger JC, Post RM: Kindling as a model for alcohol withdrawal syndromes. *Brit J Psych* 1978; 133: 1–14.

Barberis C: [^{3}H]Vasopressin binding to rat hippocampal synaptic plasma membrane. Kinetic and pharmacological characterization. *FEBS Lett* 1983; 162:400–405.

Biegon A, Terlou M, Voorhuis ThD, de Kloet ER: Arginine vasopressin binding sites in rat brain: A quantitative autoradiographic study. *Neurosci Lett* 1984; 44:229–234.

Bolger GT, Rafftery MF, Skolnick P: Phencyclidine increases the affinity of dihydropyridine calcium channel antagonist binding in rat brain. *N-S Arch Pharmacol* 1985; 330:227–234.

Burchfiel JL, Suchawny MS, Duffy FH: Neuronal supersensitivity to acetylcholine induced by kindling in the rat hippocampus. *Science* 1979; 204:1096–1098.

Cappell H, LeBlanc AE: Tolerance to, and physical dependence on, ethanol: Why do we study them? *Drug Alc Dep* 1979; 4:15–31.

Charnock JS, Cook DA, Almeida AF, To R: Activation energy and phospholipid requirements of membrane-bound adenosine triphosphatases. *Arch Biochem Biophys* 1973; 159:393–399.

Chin JH, Goldstein DB: Drug tolerance in biomembranes: A spin-label study of the effects of ethanol. *Science* 1976; 196:684–685.

Chin JH, Goldstein DB: Effects of low concentrations of ethanol on the fluidity of spin-labeled erythrocyte and brain membranes. *Mol Pharmacol* 1977; 13:435–441.

Codina J, Hildebrandt J, Sunyer T, Sekura RD, Manclark CR, Iyengar R, Birnbaumer L: Mechanisms in the vectorial receptor-adenylate cyclase signal transduction. *Adv Cyclic Nucl Protein Phos Res* 1984; 17:111–125.

Costantini MG, Pearlmutter AF: Properties of the specific binding site for arginine vasopressin in rat hippocampal synaptic membranes. *J Biol Chem* 1984; 259:11739–11745.

Crabbe JC, Kosobud A: Sensitivity and tolerance to ethanol in mice bred to be genetically prone or resistant to ethanol withdrawal seizures. *J Pharmacol Exptl Ther* 1986; 239:327–333.

Crabbe JC, McSwigan JD, Belknap JK: The role of genetics in substance abuse, in Galizio M, Maisto SA (eds): *Determinants of Substance Abuse*. New York: Plenum Press, 1985, pp 13–64.

Crowell CR, Hinson RE, Siegel S: The role of conditioned drug responses in tolerance to the hypothermic effect of ethanol. *Psychopharmacol* 1981; 73:51–54.

Daniell LC, Leslie SW: Inhibition of fast phase calcium uptake and endogenous norepinephrine release in rat brain region synaptosomes by ethanol. *Brain Res* 1986; 377:18–28.

Dorsa DM, Majumdar LA, Petracca FM, Baskin DG, Cornett LE: Characterization and localization of ^{3}H-arginine^8-vasopressin binding to rat kidney and brain tissue. *Peptides* 1983; 4:699–706.

Edwards G: The alcohol dependence syndrome: A concept as stimulus to inquiry. *Brit J Addiction* 1968; 81:171–183.

Frankel D, Khanna JM, Kalant H, LeBlanc AE: Effect of p-chlorophenylalanine on the acquisition of tolerance to the hypothermic effects of ethanol. *Psychopharmacologia* 1978; 57:239–242.

Frankel D, Khanna JM, LeBlanc AE, Kalant H: Effect of p-chlorophenylalanine on the acquisition of tolerance to ethanol and phenobarbital. *Psychopharmacologia* 1975; 44:247–252.

Goldstein DB, Chin JH, Lyon RC: Ethanol disordering of spin-labelled mouse brain membranes: Correlation with genetically-determined ethanol sensitivity of mice. *Proc Natl Acad Sci USA* 1982; 79: 4231–4233.

Gordon AS, Collier K, Diamond I: Ethanol regulation of adenosine receptor-stimulated cAMP levels in a clonal neural cell line: An *in vitro* model of cellular tolerance to ethanol. *Proc Natl Acad Sci USA* 1986; 83:2105–2108.

Grant KA, Tabakoff B: Blockade of seizures in ethanol dependent mice by the NMDA receptor antagonist MK-801. *Alcohol Clin Exp Res* 1989; in press.

Gray R, Johnston D: Noradrenaline and beta-adrenoceptor agonists increase activity of voltage-dependent calcium channels in hippocampal neurons. *Nature* 1979; 327:620–622.

Greenberg DA, Carpenter CL, Messing RO: Ethanol-induced component of ^{45}Ca^{2+} uptake in PC12 cells is sensitive to Ca^{2+} channel modulating drugs. *Brain Res* 1987; 410:143–146.

Grega DS, Macdonald RS: Activators of adenylate cyclase and cyclic AMP prolong calcium-dependent action potentials of mouse sensory neurons in culture by reducing a voltage-dependent potassium conductance. *J Neurosci* 1987; 7:700–707.

Grieve SF, Griffiths PJ, Littleton JM: Genetic influences on the rate of development of ethanol tolerance and the ethanol physical dependence syndrome in mice. *Drug Alc Dep* 1979; 4:77–86.

Harris RA, Baxter DM, Mitchell MA, Hitzemann RJ: Physical properties and lipid composition of brain membranes from ethanol tolerant-dependent mice. *Mol Pharmacol* 1984; 25:401–409.

Harris RA, Bruno P: Membrane disordering by anesthetic drugs: Relationship to synaptosomal sodium and calcium fluxes. *J Neurochem* 1985; 44:1274–1281.

Harris RA, Crabbe JC, McSwigan JD: Relationship of membrane physical properties to alcohol dependence in mice selected for genetic differences in alcohol withdrawal. *Life Sci* 1984; 35:2601–2608.

Harris RA, Schroeder F: Ethanol and the physical properties of brain membranes: Fluorescence studies. *Mol Pharmacol* 1981; 20:128–137.

Hescheler J, Rosenthal W, Trautwein W, Schultz G: The GTP-binding protein, G_o, regulates neuronal calcium channels. *Nature* 1987; 325:445–447.

Hitzemann RJ, Schueler HE, Graham-Brittain C, Kreishman GP: Ethanol-induced changes in neuronal membrane order. An NMR Study. *Biochim Biophys Acta* 1986; 859:189–197.

Hoffman PL, Melchior CL, Tabakoff B: Vasopressin maintenance of ethanol tolerance requires intact brain noradrenergic systems. *Life Sci* 1983; 32:1065–1071.

Hoffman PL, Moses F, Luthin GR, Tabakoff B: Acute and chronic effects of ethanol on receptor-mediated phosphatidylinositol 4,5-bisphosphate breakdown in mouse brain. *Mol Pharmacol* 1986; 30:13–18.

Hoffman PL, Rabe CS, Moses F, Tabakoff B: NMDA receptors and ethanol: inhibition of calcium flux and cyclic GMP production. *J Neurochem* 1989a; in press.

Hoffman PL, Moses F, Hudspith M, Tabakoff B: Ethanol: potent and selective inhibitor of NMDA-stimulated cyclic GMP production. *Alcohol Clin Exp Res* 1989b, in press.

Hoffman PL, Ritzmann RF, Walter R, Tabakoff B: Arginine vasopressin maintains ethanol tolerance. *Nature* 1979; 276:614–616.

Hoffman PL, Tabakoff B: Neurohypophyseal peptides maintain tolerance to the incoordinating effects of ethanol. *Pharmacol Biochem Behav* 1984; 21:539–543.

Hoffman PL, Tabakoff B: Ethanol's action on brain biochemistry, in RE Tarter and DH van Thiel (eds): *Alcohol and the Brain: Chronic Effects*. New York, Plenum Press, 1985, pp 19–68.

Hopkins WF, Johnston D: Frequency-dependent noradrenergic modulation of long-term potentiation in the hippocampus. *Science* 1984; 226:350–352.

Hopkins WF, Johnston D: Noradrenergic enhancement of long-term potentiation in disinhibited hippocampal slices. *Soc Neurosci Abst* 1986; 12:508.

Hung C-R, Tabakoff B, Melchior CL, Hoffman PL: Intraventricular arginine vasopressin maintains ethanol tolerance. *Eur J Pharmacol* 1984; 106:645–648.

Jacquemin C, Thibout H, Lambert B, Correze C: Endogenous ADP-ribosylation of G_s subunit and autonomous regulation of adenylate cyclase. *Nature* 1986; 323:182–184.

Jard S: Vasopressin isoreceptors in mammals: Relation to cyclic AMP-dependent and cyclic AMP-independent transduction mechanisms. *Current Topics Memb Transp* 1983; 18:255–285.

Kakihana R, Butte JC: Biochemical correlates of inherited drinking in laboratory animals, in K Eriksson, JD Sinclair and K Kiianmaa (eds): *Animal Models in Alcohol Research*. New York, Academic Press, 1980, pp 21–33.

Lê AD, Kalant H, Khanna JM: Interaction between desglycinamide[9]-[Arg[8]]vasopressin and serotonin on ethanol tolerance. *Eur J Pharmacol* 1982; 80:337–345.

Lê AD, Khanna JM, Kalant H, Le Blanc AE: Effect of 5,7-dihydroxytryptamine on the development of tolerance to ethanol. *Psychopharmacol* 1980; 67:143–146.

Lê AD, Khanna JM, Kalant H, Le Blanc AE: Effect of modification of brain serotonin (5-HT), norepinephrine (NE) and dopamine (DA) on ethanol tolerance. *Psychopharmacol* 1981; 75:231–235.

Lê AD, Khanna JM, Kalant H, Le Blanc AE: The effect of lesions in the dorsal, median and magnus raphe nuclei on the development of tolerance to ethanol. *J Pharmacol Exptl Ther* 1981; 218:525–529.

Lê AD, Poulos CS, Cappell H: Conditioned tolerance to the hypothermic effect of ethyl alcohol. *Science* 1979; 206:1109–1110.

Leslie SW: Sedative-hypnotic drugs: Interaction with calcium channels. *Alcohol Drug Res* 1986; 6:371–377.

Leslie SW, Barr E, Chandler J, Farrar RP: Inhibition of fast and slow phase depolarization-dependent synaptosomal calcium uptake by ethanol. *J Pharmacol Exptl Ther* 1983; 225:571–575.

Leslie SW, Woodward JJ, Wilcox RE, Farrar RP: Chronic ethanol treatment uncouples striatal calcium entry and endogenous dopamine release. *Brain Res* 1986; 368(1):174–177.

Li T-K, Lumeng L, McBride WJ, Waller MB, Hawkins TD: Progress toward a voluntary consumption model of alcoholism. *Drug Alcohol Dep* 1979; 4:45–60.

Little HJ, Dolin SJ, Halsey MJ: Calcium channel antagonists decrease the ethanol withdrawal syndrome. *Life Sci* 1986; 39:2059–2065.

Lovinger DM, White G, Weight FF: Ethanol inhibits NMDA-activated ion current in hippocampal neurons. *Science* 1989; in press.

Lucchi L, Govoni S, Battaini F, Pasinetti G, Trabucchi M: Ethanol administration *in vivo* alters calcium ions control in rat striatum. *Brain Res* 1985; 332:376–379.

Luthin GR, Tabakoff B: Activation of adenylate cyclase by alcohol requires the nucleotide binding protein. *J Pharmacol Exptl Ther* 1984; 228:579–587.

Lynch MA, Archer ER, Littleton JM: Increased sensitivity of transmitter release to calcium in ethanol tolerance. *Biochem Pharmacol* 1986; 35:1207–1209.

Lyon RC, Goldstein DB: Changes in synaptic membrane order associated with chronic ethanol treatment in mice. *Mol Pharmacol* 1983; 23:86–91.

Majerus PW, Connolly TM, Deckmyn H, Ross TS, Bross TE, Ishii H, Bansal VS, Wilson DB: The metabolism of phosphoinositide-derived messenger molecules. *Science* 1986; 234:1519–1526.

Mandersloot JG, Roelofson B, de Gier J: Phosphatidylinositol as the endogenous activator of the (Na^+K^+)-ATPase in microsomes of rabbit kidney. *Biochim Biophys Acta* 1978; 508:478–485.

McGee R Jr: Membrane fatty acid modification of the neuroblastoma x glioma hybrid, NG108-15. *Biochim Biophys Acta* 1981; 663:314–328.

McNamara JO: Muscarinic cholinergic receptors participate in the kindling model of epilepsy. *Brain Res* 1978; 154:415–420.

McSwigan JD, Crabbe JC, Young ER: Specific ethanol withdrawal seizures in genetically selected mice. *Life Sci* 1984; 35:2119–2126.

Melchior, CL, Tabakoff B: Modification of environmentally cued tolerance to ethanol in mice. *J Pharmacol Exptl Ther* 1981; 219:175–180.

Messing RO, Carpenter CL, Diamond I, Greenberg DA: Ethanol regulates calcium channels in clonal neural cells. *Proc Natl Acad Sci USA* 1986; 83:6213–6215.

Miller RJ: Multiple calcium channels and neuronal function. *Science* 1987; 235:46–52.

Mochly-Rosen D, Chang F-H, Cheever L, Kim M, Diamond I, Gordon AS: Chronic ethanol causes heterologous desensitization of receptors by reducing α_s messenger RNA. *Nature* 1988; 333:848–850.

Nordberg A, Wahlstrom G, Eriksson B: Relations between muscimol, quinuclidinyl benzilate and nicotine binding sites in brain after very long treatment with ethanol in rats. *Eur J Pharmacol* 1985; 115:301–304.

Numan R: Multiple exposures to ethanol facilitates intravenous self-administration of ethanol by rats. *Pharmacol Biochem Behav* 1981; 15:101–108.

Numan R: Effects of Pavlovian conditioning on the ethanol withdrawal syndrome in rats. *Pharmacol Biochem Behav* 1986; 25:1111–1115.

Pittman QJ, Rogers J, Bloom FE: Arginine vasopressin deficient Brattleboro rats fail to develop tolerance to the hypothermic effects of ethanol. *Regul Pept* 1982; 4:33–41.

Polokoff MA, Simon TJ, Harris RA, Simon FR, Iwahashi M: Chronic ethanol increases liver plasma membrane fluidity. *Biochem J.* 1985; 24:3114–3120.

Rabin RA, Molinoff PB: Activation of adenylate cyclase by ethanol in mouse striatal tissue. *J Pharmacol Exp Ther* 1981; 216:129–134.

Rabin RA, Wolfe BB, Dibner MD, Zahniser NR, Melchior C, Molinoff PB: Effects of ethanol administration and withdrawal on neurotransmitter receptor systems in C57 mice. *J Pharmacol Exp Ther* 1980; 213:491–496.

Reid LD, Hunter GA, Beaman CM, Hubbell CL: Toward understanding ethanol's capacity to be reinforcing: A conditioned place preference following injections of ethanol. *Pharmacol Biochem Behav* 1985; 22:483–487.

Richelson E, Stenstrom S, Forray C, Enloe L, Pfenning M: Effects of chronic exposure to ethanol on the prostaglandin E_1 receptor-mediated response and binding in a murine neuroblastoma clone (N1E-115). *J Pharmacol Exp Ther* 1986; 239:687–692.

Ritzmann RF, Tabakoff B: Body temperature in mice: A quantitative measure of alcohol tolerance and physical dependence. *J Pharmacol Exp Ther* 1976; 199:158–170.

Rius RA, Govoni A, Battaini F, Trabucchi M: Cyclic AMP-dependent protein phosphorylation is reduced in rat striatum after chronic ethanol treatment. *Brain Res* 1986; 365:355–359.

Rius RA, Govoni S, Onagno L, Araujo ACP, Trabucchi M: Altered calcium signal transduction after chronic ethanol consumption. *Alcohol* 1986; 3:233–238.

Rottenberg H: Membrane solubility of ethanol in chronic alcoholism. The effect of ethanol feeding and its withdrawal on the protection by alcohol of red blood cells from hypotonic hemolysis. *Biochim Biophys Acta* 1986; 855:211–222.

Rottenberg H, Waring A, Rubin E: Tolerance and cross-tolerance in chronic alcoholics: Reduced membrane binding of ethanol and other drugs. *Science* 1981; 213:583–585.

Rubin E, Rottenberg H: Ethanol-induced injury and adaptation in biological membranes. *Federation Proc* 1986; 41:2465–2471.

Saito T, Lee JM, Hoffman PL, Tabakoff B: Effects of chronic ethanol treatment on the beta-adrenergic receptor-coupled adenylate cyclase system of mouse cerebral cortex. *J Neurochem* 1987; 48:1817–1822.

Saito T, Lee JM, Tabakoff B: Ethanol's effects on cortical adenylate cyclase activity. *J Neurochem* 1985; 44: 1037–1044.

Sawyer WH, Manning M: Development of selective agonists and antagonists of vasopressin and oxytocin, in Schrier RW (ed): *Vasopressin*. New York, Raven Press, 1985, pp 131–144.

Schmale H, Ivell R, Breindl M, Darmer D, Richter D: The mutant vasopressin gene from diabetes insipidus (Brattleboro) rats is transcribed but the message is not efficiently translated. *EMBO Journal* 1984; 3:3289–3293.

Schwartzkroin PA, Wester K: Long-lasting facilitation of a synaptic potential following tetanization in the *in vitro* hippocampal slice. *Brain Res* 1975; 89:107–119.

Seeman P: The membrane actions of anesthetics and tranquilizers. *Pharmacol Rev* 1972; 24:583–655.

Shanley B, Gurd J, Kalant H: Ethanol tolerance and enhanced calcium/calmodulin-dependent phosphorylation of synaptic membrane proteins. *Neurosci Lett* 1985; 58:55–59.

Sibley DR, Lefkowitz RJ: Molecular mechanisms of receptor desensitization using the beta-adrenergic receptor-coupled adenylate cyclase system as a model. *Nature* 1985; 317:214–229.

Speisky MB, Kalant H: Site of interaction of serotonin and desglycinamide-arginine-vasopressin in maintenance of ethanol tolerance. *Brain Res* 1981; 326:281–290.

Squire LR, Davis HP: The pharmacology of memory: A neurobiological perspective. *Ann. Rev. Pharmacol Toxicol* 1981; 21:323–356.

Stephens LR, Logan SD: Arginine vasopressin stimulates inositol phospholipid metabolism in rat hippocampus. *J Neurochem* 1985; 46:649–651.

Szabó G, Hoffman PL, Tabakoff B: Forskolin promotes the development of ethanol tolerance in 6-hydroxydopamine-treated mice. *Life Sci* 1988; 42:615–621.

Szabó G, Tabakoff B, Hoffman PL: Receptors with V_1 characteristics mediate the maintenance of ethanol tolerance by vasopressin. *J Pharmacol Exp Ther* 1988; 247:536–541.

Tabakoff B, Hoffman PL: Development of functional dependence on ethanol in dopaminergic systems. *J Pharmacol Exptl Ther* 1979; 208:216-222.

Tabakoff B, Melchior CL, Hoffman PL: Commentary on ethanol tolerance. *Alcohol Clin and Exptl Res* 1982; 6:252–259.

Tabakoff B, Munoz-Marcus M, Fields JZ: Chronic ethanol feeding produces an increase in muscarinic cholinergic receptors in mouse brain. *Life Sci* 1979; 25:2173–2180.

Tabakoff B, Ritzmann RF: The effects of 6-hydroxydopamine on tolerance to and dependence on ethanol. *J Pharmacol Exp Ther* 1977; 203:319–332.

Tabakoff B, Ritzmann RF: Acute tolerance in inbred and selected lines of mice. *Drug Alc Dep* 1979; 4:87–90.

Tabakoff B, Ritzmann RF, Raju TS, Deitrich RA: Characterization of acute and chronic tolerance in mice selected for inherent differences in sensitivity to ethanol. *Alcoholism: Clin Exptl Res* 1980; 4: 70–73.

Taraschi TF, Ellingson JS, Wu A, Zimmerman R, Rubin E: Membrane tolerance to ethanol is rapidly lost after withdrawal: A model for studies of membrane adaptation. *Proc Natl Acad Sci USA* 1986; 83:3669–3673.

Traynor ME, Schlapfer WT, Barondes SH: Stimulation is necessary for the development of tolerance to a neuronal effect of ethanol. *J Neurobiol* 1980; 11:633–637.

Traynor ME, Woodson PBJ, Schlapfer WT, Barondes SH: Sustained tolerance to a specific effect of ethanol in post-tetanic potentiation in *Aplysia*. *Science* 1976; 193:510–511.

Trzaskowska E, Pucilowski O, Dyr W, Kostowski W, Hauptmann M: Suppression of ethanol tolerance and dependence in rats treated with DSP-4, a noradrenergic neurotoxin. *Drug Alc Dep* 1986; 18: 349–353.

Valverius P, Hoffman PL, Tabakoff B: Effect of ethanol on mouse cerebral cortical beta-adrenergic receptors. *Mol Pharmacol* 1987; 32:217–222.

Waller MB, McBride WJ, Lumeng L, Li T-K: Initial sensitivity and acute tolerance to ethanol in the P and NP lines of rats. *Pharmacol Biochem Behav* 1983; 19:683–686.

Waring AJ, Rottenberg H, Ohnishi T, Rubin E: Membranes and phospholipids of liver mitochondria from chronic alcoholic rats are resistant to membrane disordering by alcohol. *Proc Natl Acad Sci USA* 1981; 78:2582–2586.

Wood JM, Laverty R: Effect of depletion of brain catecholamines on ethanol tolerance and dependence. *Eur J Pharmacol* 1979; 58:285–293.

World Health Organization Expert Committee on Mental Health, Alcoholism Subcommittee: Second Report. WHO Technical Report Series No. 48, 1952.

Wu PH, Pham T, Naranjo CA: Nifedipine delays the acquisition of tolerance to ethanol. *Eur J Pharmacol* 1987; 139:233–236.

Yamada S, Lieber CS: Decreases in microviscosity and cholesterol content of rat liver plasma membranes after chronic ethanol feeding. *J Clin Invest* 1984; 74:2285–2289.

CHAPTER 6

Neurobehavioral Disorders Associated with Chronic Alcohol Abuse[1]

Ralph E. Tarter, Ph.D,[2] Amelia M. Arria, B.S.,[2]
and David H. Van Thiel, M.D.[3]

University of Pittsburgh School of Medicine

The chronic consumption of alcoholic beverages is commonly associated with life threatening injury to vital organs and systems. Cognitive impairment and behavioral disturbance are also very prevalent, and for the most part, are due to the disruption of central nervous system integrity (Tarter and Alterman, 1984).

Ethanol is a powerful neurotoxin. Not all aspects of psychological disorder, however, are directly the product of ethanol neurotoxicity. For example, endocrine changes in men concomitant to excessive and chronic alcohol consumption cause disturbances in both sexual drive and in the capacity for performance; these impairments in turn can induce significant emotional disruption and further exacerbate an existing psychologic disorder. Disease or injury to other organ systems consequential to chronic alcohol excess can likewise trigger major psychological disturbance. For example, pain from pancreatitis or gastritis as well as digestion and elimination disturbances can cause significant emotional and social disruption.

Furthermore, cognitive disturbances are common also in a variety of medical conditions that are frequently found in conjunction with alcohol abuse. Liver disease, cardiovascular disease, and endocrine disturbances are prevalent in alcoholics and, independently of alcoholism, are associated with cognitive disturbances. The point to be underscored is that the psychological disturbances in alcoholics may be mediated in large part by alcohol-induced damage to various organ systems, which in turn causes both neurologic and psychologic disorders.

Several neurologic syndromes have been documented in alcoholics. Dementia, Wernicke–Korsakoff syndrome, and pontine myelinolysis, corpus callosum degeneration (Marchiafava–Bignami disease) have been well described (Freund, 1985) and so are not reviewed again here. Other neurologic sequelae of longstanding alcohol abuse include malnutrition, subdural hematoma, multiple infarction, hepatic encephalopathy and cerebellar degeneration. These latter neurologic disorders are not mutually exclusive from each other and each apparently has a multifactorial etiology; that is, they are not due solely to ethanol's action on the brain.

---

[1]Supported by grants AA07453, AA06601, AA06936, and AM32556.
[2]Department of Psychiatry.
[3]Department of Medicine.

Because of the multiplicity of etiological factors underlying the various neurologic syndromes and their unique interaction within the individual, the manifest behavioral disturbances concomitant with alcoholism are quite variable. Hence, in describing the psychological characteristics of alcoholics, it is important to be cognizant that while distinctive typologies of impairment have been documented, there is substantial interindividual variability with respect to both the causes and overt expression of psychological disturbance.

It is essential also to emphasize that the behavioral disturbances concomitant with alcoholism are the product of the interaction between the individual and the physical and social environments. For example, as alcohol abuse assumes a central focus in the life of the alcoholic, hygiene neglect, irresponsible behavior, and inadequate nutrition all may occur. These factors individually and in combination increase the individual's susceptibility to infectious disease, accidental injury, and systemic illness. The risks and potential consequences of "closet" drinking are very different from saloon drinking. Thus, social contextual factors strongly influence the natural history of the neuropsychologic and psychopathologic syndromes of alcoholism.

It is important to recognize the possibility that certain cognitive deficits and behavioral disturbances commonly demonstrated in alcoholics may precede the onset of drinking. These disturbances may reflect either a heritable predisposition or emerge as the result of living in a disruptive home environment. In view of the observation that alcoholism runs in families, it is likely that many of the disturbances found in alcoholics emanate from being raised by one or more alcoholic parents. Thus, genetic predisposition exacerbated by adverse environmental circumstances may conjointly also influence the development of behavioral problems and cognitive deficits. In one study (Tarter et al, 1984), for example, it was found that adolescent sons of alcoholics with delinquent behavior histories had been more frequently physically and sexually abused than offspring of nonalcoholics. The former individuals also experienced a higher prevalence of head injury and loss of consciousness and exhibited more severe social maladjustment. Thus, both genetic and environmental factors may synergistically operate to produce psychological disturbance prior to the onset of alcohol abuse.

Finally, as a consequence of the teratologic effects of alcohol, there may be neurologic injury, physical abnormality, and concomitant psychological disturbance that is present in childhood and persists into adulthood. Thus, there is the strong likelihood that certain of the neurologic and behavioral disturbances observed in many alcoholics may actually predate the onset of drinking and have their origin in disturbed embryogenesis.

This chapter reviews the research literature pertaining to the causes, characteristics, and significance of the psychological disturbances associated with chronic alcoholism. Emphasis is placed on illustrating that the manifest psychological disturbances have a multifactorial etiology involving conjointly biological and psychological factors. The biopsychological processes are discussed within the context of the natural history of alcoholism. The relationship between biopsychological disturbance and treatment are also discussed. Suggested future directions for research conclude this chapter.

NEUROBEHAVIORAL IMPAIRMENT IN CHRONIC ALCOHOLICS

Cognitive Status

Alcoholics who are evaluated while in treatment commonly demonstrate impairments on neuropsychological tests measuring cerebral integrity (Parsons and Farr, 1981; Tarter, 1981). Whereas a deficit is not observed in all individuals, there is substantial evidence indicating that the majority of alcoholics are cognitively impaired during the first several weeks or months following detoxification. Where deficits are found, they typically are in the mild to moderate ranges of severity and generally are not as debilitating as those found in unselected patients who are in treatment for acute neurologic diseases or injury. Deficits on tests evaluating visuospatial capacity, memory, abstracting ability, and learning ability have been reported frequently (Tarter, 1973, 1975).

The cognitive processes disrupted encompass the specific abilities necessary for adaptive living. For instance, with respect to abstracting ability, impairments have been noted in cognitive flexibility (Tarter, 1973), the ability to form hypotheses in problem solving (Klisz and Parsons, 1977), the capacity to sustain a cognitive or mental set (Tarter, 1973) and the ability to identify general principles or rules (Pishkin et al, 1972). Memory deficits, although not routinely detected on clinically standardized tests, are nonetheless prevalent among alcoholics, even among those whose drinking career is relatively brief (Wilkinson and Carlen, 1980). Typically, the memory deficits are not severe and are found only when effortful information processing is required. Nonetheless, the magnitude of impairment is significant and of sufficient degree so as to impede efficient learning and retention of new information. The nature of the material to be learned (e.g., verbal lists, faces, etc.) or the sensory modality through which the information is acquired (visual, auditory) are unrelated to the manifestation of the deficit (Oscar-Berman, 1987). Visuospatial disturbances are also observed commonly and are manifest in various ways. For example, alcoholics have been shown in numerous studies to be impaired in the ability to perceptually analyze a complex figure, organize the elements of a picture or design into a Gestalt, and efficiently perform tasks requiring spatial analysis and concentration (Tarter, 1975; Parsons and Farr, 1981). Moreover, deficits have been reported on constructional praxis tasks where visual perception is not required, suggesting that the spatial disorder is not due simply to a disturbance in visual perception (Fitzhugh et al, 1965).

Not all cognitive processes are impaired in alcoholics. For instance, linguistic capacities are invariably normal with respect to both verbal comprehension and expression. Also, motor speed and eye–hand coordination are intact in alcoholics who have been completely detoxified (Tarter, 1985). To date, neuropsychologic investigations have not been conducted to evaluate the association between peripheral neuropathy and perceptual-motor functioning in alcoholics; it may be that this particular subgroup of impaired alcoholics do, in fact, have psychomotor impairments.

Significantly, psychometric tests of intelligence do not reveal the presence of global intellectual decline. IQ indices do not differentiate unselected samples of alcoholics from nonalcoholics. Intellectual deficits have, however, been reported on nonverbal intelligence tests (Jones, 1971). The previously described impairments in the higher cognitive processes reflect specific aspects of intellectual impairment. However, most alcoholics are not globally deteriorated.

Conclusions regarding impairments in cognitive capacity in alcoholics are based on group differences. Alcoholics as a group perform more poorly than nonalcoholics as a group. It should be noted that substantial variability, with respect to both the pattern and history of abusive drinking, as well as comorbid psychopathology and medical history, characterize the alcoholic population. Thus, inferences about the cognitive status of a particular alcoholic individual cannot be made in lieu of a comprehensive neuropsychologic and psychiatric examination. Alcoholics are different from nonalcoholics in many ways besides their excessive alcohol beverage consumption; how these factors affect neuropsychologic test performance remains unknown. For instance, cognitive deficits, particularly attentional problems and learning disabilities are common in men having an antisocial disorder. Since an antisocial personality is frequently a comorbid characteristic of alcoholics, the impairments observed on neuropsychologic tests may not be attributable entirely to alcoholism effects. The point to be made is that even though alcoholics as a group are impaired on tests of cognitive capacity, it is not valid to assume that all alcoholics are impaired; indeed even where deficits are observed they may be causally unrelated to the alcoholism.

It should also be noted that the prevalence of cognitive disorder is difficult to estimate. Virtually every study conducted to date recruited alcoholics from treatment programs. However, each type of treatment program attracts individuals who are most suitable for rehabilitation at the particular facility. For instance, alcoholics with severe medical complications of their drinking (e.g., hepatitis, gastritis, malnutrition, etc.) are sharply different from alcoholics who seek treatment because of the psychiatric, vocational, social, or legal consequences of their drinking. Because socioeconomic status, medical morbidity, and the presence of comorbid psychopathology can influence the type and severity of cognitive impairment, estimates of the prevalence of cognitive deficit in alcoholics derived from clinical populations are nonrepresentative of the whole population of alcoholics.

The importance of sampling parameters in estimating the prevalence of cognitive deficit cannot be overemphasized. For example, 80% of alcoholics treated in Veterans Administration hospitals in the United States have been found to exhibit impairments (Goldstein and Shelly, 1980). In contrast, no deficits have been found in alcoholics who are medically intact (Grant et al, 1979) or who are recruited from private hospitals serving a financially secure and socially adjusted clientele (Tarter et al, 1975).

In summary, cognitive impairments have been observed frequently in unselected samples of alcoholics who are in treatment. These findings must be interpreted cautiously inasmuch as they reflect the presence of impairment in recently detoxified individuals. Moreover, not all alcoholics exhibit deficits on cognitive tests measuring cerebral pathology or dysfunction. Indeed, in the absence of epidemiologic research, it is not possible to advance conclusions about the prevalence of cognitive deficits in the nontreated chronic alcohol abusing population. These latter lacunae do not mitigate the results demonstrating the presence of cognitive deficits, but rather they underscore the need for population based research in which drinking history and other compounding factors could be analyzed within a multivariate framework.

Subtypes of Cognitive Impairment

In view of the multifaceted injury to vital organs and systems caused by the chronic abuse of alcoholic beverages and the range of concurrent exacerbating events common to alcoholics (e.g., trauma, infectious disease, etc.), it is unlikely that pure neuropsychologic syndromes can be detected. That is, the neuropsychologic deficits exhibited by any given alcoholic individual most probably reflects the interactive and cumulative effects of numerous etiologic factors. Neuroradiologic and neuropsychologic techniques have revealed that alcoholics comprise a heterogeneous population but, however, can be divided into two general subtypes. First, there is extensive documentation indicating that the Wernicke–Korsakoff syndrome, present in a minority of chronic alcoholics, is characterized by a number of specific differentiating neuropsychologic features. These alcoholics are readily diagnosed upon interview, mental and neurologic status examination and assisted by informant report about the individual's drinking history and general behavior. The neurologic and psychologic characteristics of Wernicke–Korsakoff patients have been previously reviewed in detail (Butters and Cermak, 1980; Freund, 1985) and so will not be discussed again here; however, it is noteworthy that the most profound impairments relate to information processing memory storage, ability to form new associations, as well as access for retrieval from memory previously acquired associations (Butters and Cermak, 1980; Butters and Granholm, 1987).

An amnesic syndrome or subclinical Korsakoff syndrome has also been identified in less severe cases using neuropsychological tests to detect a memory disorder. As is the case in its florid manifestation, the less severe amnesic alcoholic or subclinical variation is featured by impaired learning and memory capacity (Ryan and Butters, 1980). Specifically, an anterograde amnesia is evidenced. The ability to encode semantic information is diminished whereas the capacity to learn and remember how to perform motor tasks (procedural memory) is otherwise intact (Butters and Granholm, 1987). These findings aptly illustrate that memory is not a unitary process but rather is highly specific to the type of information to be stored. On tasks that do not have memory demands such as reading, speaking, and psychomotor performance, the amnesic alcoholic typically performs within the normal ranges. Tests that require "working memory," that is, the concurrent allocation of attention and memory resources are, however, performed poorly.

The second type of cognitive disorder in alcoholism is dementia (Wilkinson and Paulos, 1987). Affected individuals demonstrate a general decline in specific cognitive processes and superficially at least, may suggest the presence of premature aging. For example, on neuropsychological tests of abstraction and memory capacity, young alcoholics perform comparably to normal controls who are 10 to 15 years older than themselves (Brandt et al, 1983). There is also suggestive evidence that the greatest amount of deterioration occurs during the early stages of alcoholism, suggesting perhaps that progressive and cumulative brain injury in tandem with chronic alcohol consumption does not occur. Rather, the intriguing possibility is raised that because of the early manifestation of the neuropsychologic deficit, some individuals may be particularly susceptible to neurologic disruption.

Etiology of Cognitive Disturbances in Alcoholism

The demonstration that there are at least two categories of neuropsychologic sequelae of chronic alcohol excess, and additionally that there are several other neurologic syndromes that have not yet been submitted to psychological study (e.g., pontine myelinolysis, cerebellar degeneration), underscores the point that there are multiple pathologic mechanisms underlying the manifest central nervous system (CNS) disturbances. Furthermore, the observation that drinking pattern and history do not predict the specific type of neurologic pathology suggests that as yet undetermined individual differences in the vulnerability to the effects of alcohol beverage consumption contributes to the specific adverse effects. Hence, a susceptibility, perhaps genetically mediated, may influence the particular type of neuropsychologic and neurologic presentation. The most striking and clear example of a specific vulnerability is the absence of the thiamine requiring enzyme, transketolase, in individuals with Korsakoff's syndrome (Blass and Gibson, 1977). To date, research has not been conducted that systematically attempts to delineate the nature of the vulnerability to neurologic pathology or the interaction between alcohol beverage consumption and the neurologic vulnerability.

Mechanisms Underlying the Cognitive Deficits in Alcoholics

The most obvious single cause of neurologic pathology is ethanol toxicity. Neurotoxicity of alcohol has been conclusively established in controlled studies with animals in which potentially confounding factors (e.g., nutrition) were controlled (Riley and Walker, 1978). Pathologic changes at the synapse and particularly the dendritic tree at the synaptic junction have been clearly documented. In addition, a wealth of information has accumulated describing the multifaceted adverse effects of alcohol on neuronal metabolism and membrane structural integrity. Furthermore, there is substantial evidence illustrating that ethanol can directly cause neuronal demyelination. Controlling for the potentially confounding effects of nutritional disturbance and hepatic injury, it has been shown that learning and memory capacity are impaired in rodents after chronic exposure to ethanol (Walker et al, 1981). It can thus be safely concluded that ethanol is a neurotoxin and that in controlled animal studies causes both histopathologic and behavioral disruption.

The generalizability of the results from animal research for explaining the etiology of cognitive impairments in humans remains uncertain. Alcohol consumption is self-regulated in humans with respect to pattern, quantity, and induced level of intoxication. In animals, alcohol is not a naturally preferred substance, thus oral intake must be induced by manipulating the animal's natural food preferences. Furthermore, in studies where ethanol is directly administered into the vascular system or the brain, the doses given to the animal typically exceed comparable human levels of consumption. Moreover, the social and motivational context of alcohol ingestion in animals is greatly different from that of humans. In humans, many factors could influence the development of neurologic pathology. For example, alcoholic beverages all contain congeners, that is, additives and artificial flavors, as well as residual by-products of the distillation process. These impurities in alcoholic beverages have active metabolic effects (Murphree and Price, 1970) and may potentially have lasting neurotoxic effects as well.

Systemic disease, malnutrition and advanced liver disease are prevalent in alcoholics. With respect to liver disease, it has been shown that alcoholics with cirrhosis are not statistically distinguishable from nonalcoholics with cirrhosis on most neuropsychological tests (Tarter et al, 1988). Furthermore, certain biochemical measures of liver injury have been found to correlate with the level of neuropsychological test performance in alcoholics (Tarter et al, 1986). These latter findings suggest that advanced liver disease is an important etiological factor underlying the neuropsychological impairments in alcoholics.

It is interesting to note that nonalcoholics with cirrhosis exhibit impairments on the same types of cognitive tests as alcoholics with cirrhosis (Tarter et al, 1984). In addition, the morphologic brain changes observed in patients who died while in hepatic coma resemble closely the alterations found in alcoholics at autopsy (Courville, 1955; Hoyumpa and Schenker, 1985). In both alcoholics and nonalcoholics with liver disease, the gross morphologic and histopathologic manifestations consist of generalized cortical atrophy with relatively greater injury to the anterior cerebrum accompanied by atrophy in the subcortical periventricular region. These findings suggest that advanced liver disease is a major factor contributing to the manifest neuropsychologic deficits found commonly in alcoholics, and indeed may be the single most important factor underlying the observed impairments.

Nutritional deficiency may also contribute substantially to the neurologic and cognitive disturbances found in alcoholics. Inadequate nutrient intake, particularly in alcoholics of low socioeconomic status, can produce major neuropsychiatric disturbances. Nutritional deficiency, due either to insufficient intake or absorption of B_1 causes Wernicke's encephalopathy, which if untreated in alcoholics, culminates in Korsakoff's syndrome. Deficiencies in other water soluble B-complex vitamins such as niacin and folate additionally have been reported in alcoholics (Anatow and McClain, 1985), which, if chronic, can result in an organic brain syndrome.

Diseases of the digestive system, common in alcoholics, disrupt the optimal absorption of vitamins and other nutrients. Significantly, a vitamin E deficiency is prevalent in alcoholics with chronic cholestasis. A study recently completed in our laboratory (Arria et al, in preparation) indicates that approximately 50% of alcoholics with cholestasis also have a chronically severe vitamin E deficiency. Furthermore, the presence of this vitamin E deficiency is strongly associated with deficits in psychomotor performance. Thus, for a substantial proportion of alcoholics, hepatobiliary disease accompanied by an absorption deficiency may contribute to the neuropsychological deficits in alcoholics. Significantly, alcoholics rated to be nutritionally deficient clinically perform more poorly on tests of cognitive capacity than alcoholics classified as nutritionally normal (Guthrie and Elliott, 1977).

A number of other medical factors also appear to contribute to the neuropsychological disturbances seen in alcoholics. For example, Adams and Grant (1986) developed an index of general neuromedical risk that consisted of ratings of head injury severity, systemic disease, nutritional status, use of drugs, and developmental disability. They found that the severity of ratings on these factors predicted the level of neuropsychological test performance in alcoholics. Notably, alcoholics without a history of neuromedical disturbance performed similar to normal controls, suggesting that alcohol beverage consumption without complicating medical sequelae does not impact adversely on cognitive functioning. However, this finding should not be construed to indicate that the CNS is unaffected in medically intact alcoholics. Rather, the data illustrate only that cognitive capacity is not compromised using rather general cognitive tests of cerebral integrity. Perhaps more demanding tasks or tasks that are more specific for measuring particular cognitive processes, would reveal the presence of neuropsychologic impairment in medically intact alcoholics. The obvious importance of the findings presented by Grant and his colleagues lies in demonstrating that comorbid features of alcoholism are important determinants of neuropsychologic impairment, and perhaps may even be more important than the pattern and quantity of alcohol beverage consumption.

In summary, the neurobehavioral findings underscore the multifactorial etiology of the cognitive impairments demonstrated by alcoholics. Medical status, especially the presence of nutritional deficiencies and advanced liver disease, have been shown to be related to neuropsychological test performance. Other potential contributing factors—the coexistence of cerebrovascular disease, subdural hematoma, closed head injury, polysubstance abuse, and the complications of systemic diseases concomitant with alcoholism—may also contribute to the cognitive disturbance commonly observed on neuropsychological assessment. The latter factors have, however, not yet been submitted to systematic empirical analysis. The point to be emphasized is that whereas, at the descriptive level, the pattern and severity of neuropsychologic deficit has been well documented (see Ryan and Butters, 1983; Tarter and Edwards, 1985 for reviews), the underlying mechanisms and pathways to these overt disturbances remain to be delineated.

Localization of CNS Lesion in Alcoholics

The cognitive disturbances concomitant with each of the two previously described neuropsychologic subtypes are associated with distinct morphologic brain injury as determined by quantification of the CT scan image. This literature has already been reviewed in detail (Wilkinson, 1985) and so are only succinctly summarized here.

The available data suggest that alcoholic dementia is featured by diffuse cortical atrophy with possibly more severe pathology in the anterior region of the brain (Wilkinson, 1985). The pattern of psychological deficit demonstrated points to an anterior brain injury as revealed by deficits on tasks requiring cognitive persistence and flexibility, visuospatial organization, and short-term memory. The neuroradiologic and behavioral findings in unselected alcoholics concur with histologic studies showing generalized cortical atrophy with relatively greater necrosis in the frontal region (Ron, 1987).

The second type of neuropsychologic disorder—the amnesic or Korsakoff's syndrome—is characterized on the computed tomography (CT) scan by pronounced subcortical pathology that is most visible as enlarged ventricles and accompanying cortical atrophy (Wilkinson and Carlen, 1980; Wilkinson, 1985). Histopathologic studies reveal lesions in the hippocampus, fornix, and mammillary bodies; these limbic system structures have been strongly implicated to be crucial for the consolidation of short-term memory into long-term storage.

Behavioral Disturbances in Chronic Alcoholics

In view of the widespread cortical and subcortical damage, it is to be expected that behavioral disturbances, besides the cognitive impairments just described, will be manifest. Neuropsychological research has not been directed to systematically elucidating the emotional and motivational concomitants of disrupted neurological functioning. In a comprehensive review of the literature, Gorenstein and Newman (1980) theorize that alcoholics demonstrate a "disinhibitory psychopathology"; that is, they are unable to restrain from behavioral excess. Consequently, they are easily aroused, primed toward impulsive and sensation seeking behavior and essentially are unable to exercise cognitive control in monitoring goal-directed behavior.

The neurologic pathology underlying the incapacity to regulate goal-directed behavior has been hypothesized to lie along the frontal–midbrain neuroaxis (Pribram, 1969). These same neural systems have also been implicated to underlie the cognitive impairments in alcoholics (Tarter and Parsons, 1972; Tarter, 1975). Interestingly, a body of evidence has been independently accumulated indicating that the same neural substrate may underlie antisocial personality disorder (Yeudall and Fromm-Auch, 1979; Miller, 1987). The latter disorder is found frequently in conjunction with alcoholism.

Disturbances in emotional and affective regulation have been reported frequently in alcoholics. Depression, anxiety, phobia, and panic disorders are frequently comorbid psychiatric conditions in alcoholism. Indeed, virtually every psychiatric disorder has been found in conjunction with alcoholism. The point is that excessive alcohol consumption, defined clinically as alcoholism, is often associated with psychiatric disturbances. The neurochemical lesions underlying these psychiatric disorders have yet to be specified, however, it should be noted that these comorbid psychopathologic conditions are often amenable to pharmacotherapeutic intervention. As will be discussed subsequently, certain of these disturbances may actually antedate the onset of alcoholism as well as emerge consequential to chronic excessive alcohol beverage consumption.

BEHAVIORAL ALTERATIONS VIEWED IN THE CONTEXT OF THE NATURAL HISTORY OF ALCOHOLISM

Neurobehavioral Disturbances Predating Alcoholism

Behavioral Characteristics Presaging Alcoholism

A number of deviant behavioral characteristics have been identified in children who subsequently developed alcoholism. These characteristics include impulsivity, high behavioral activity level, conduct disorder, sensation- or novelty-seeking motivation, and emotional instability (Tarter, 1988). These features appear to be more prevalent in males than in females who are at risk, and where present, are typically found in conjunction with a conduct disorder.

To date, studies aimed at clarifying the pathways to specifically an alcoholism outcome have not been conducted. Thus, the differentiating characteristics of the psychological vulnerability for alcoholism from other adult disorders of excess (e.g., drug use, eating, gambling, etc.) remains to be ascertained. Furthermore, how the behavioral deviations present in children who subsequently develop alcoholism interact with the environment to result in a drinking problem remains to be established. Finally, the extent to which environmental factors, such as alcohol beverage availability, social stress, and cultural sanctions, can influence the behavioral vulnerability to attenuate the risk for alcoholism remains to be studied.

To date, research has focused on elucidating the vulnerability characteristics associated with alcoholism risk without examining the processes and pathways leading to an adverse outcome. It has been hypothesized, for example, that certain temperament traits, that is inherited behavioral dispositions, place the child at increased risk for an alcoholism disorder in adulthood. These psychological traits include low attention or concentration capacity, high behavioral activity, low sociability, high emotionality, and low soothability (Tarter et al, 1985). Certain personality variants, specifically high novelty seeking, low reward dependence, and poor avoidance learning, have also been speculated to portend an alcoholism outcome (Cloninger, 1987). The latter temperament and personality traits have been theorized to reflect the overt behavioral expression of the genetic predisposition to alcoholism. Interestingly, in the one epidemiologic study in which psychological measures were obtained, it was observed that the trait of "subsolidity" in interaction with neurotic excitability best predicted an alcoholism outcome (Hagnell et al, 1986). Individuals characterized by subsolidity have a rapid behavioral tempo, exhibit intense behavioral expression to the most immediate salient stimulus, are emotionally labile, and interpersonally are superficial and self-centered.

One behavioral trait that best exemplifies the behavior–genetic approach to alcoholism vulnerability is hyperactivity. Behavioral activity is strongly determined by genetics and in animals this trait can be selectively bred. Differences in activity level are readily observable in human neonates; for example, males are more active than females. It is interesting to note that several investigators have reported that hyperactive children have a high prevalence of biological, but not adoptive, fathers who are alcoholics (Cantwell, 1972; Morrison and Stewart, 1973). Children of alcoholic men have also been reported to demonstrate more hyperactivity characteristics than children of nonalcoholics (Goodwin et al, 1975). Furthermore, familial alcoholics, that is, alcoholics who have alcoholism in other family members, are more hyperactive as children compared to nonfamilial alcoholics (Tarter et al, 1977; Alterman et al, 1982, 1985). Finally, there is indication that hyperactive adolescents are more inclined towards alcohol abuse and other forms of drug use than normal children (Blowin et al, 1978).

Thus, there is emerging evidence suggesting that hyperactivity in childhood may be a predisposing trait for alcoholism. Note, however, that the biological mechanisms underlying hyperactivity remain unknown. Also, hyperactivity is typically found in conjunction with a conduct disorder in high risk children, suggesting that it may be only one component of a more broadly encompassing disorder of behavioral disinhibition or dysregulation. As such, hyperactivity is most likely to be found in the alcoholic with comorbid antisocial tendencies, or in whom Cloninger (1987) refers to as the Type II alcoholic.

Cognitive Impairment Presaging Alcoholism

Investigations of children who are at known risk for developing alcoholism have tentatively indicated that a high percentage may have cognitive impairments. Risk status is usually based on the presence of paternal alcoholism since sons of alcoholic men, even if raised by adoptive parents, are at fourfold greater risk for developing alcoholism than offspring of nonalcoholic fathers (Cloninger et al, 1981). Compared to offspring of normal parents, it has been found that sons of alcoholics perform more poorly on certain tests of intelligence, language ability, spatial capacity, and perceptual motor coordination (Gabrielli and Mednick, 1983; Ervin et al, 1984; Tarter et al, 1984). For reasons that have yet to be clarified, offspring of alcoholics exhibit deficits on certain tasks that are not performed deficiently by alcoholics. Adult first-degree relatives of alcoholics, who themselves are not alcoholic, have also been found to perform more poorly on tests of abstracting and psychomotor efficiency than men without an alcoholic family member (Schaeffer et al, 1984). These deficits most likely have a multifactorial etiology of which compromised environmental circumstance is undoubtedly a major factor. To date, data have not been accrued that point to heritable cognitive deficits in children at risk for alcoholism even though numerous cognitive abilities have been shown to be strongly influenced by genetic factors. Moreover, although the latter findings raise the intriguing possibility that cognitive impairment may comprise features of alcoholism vulnerability, it should be noted that not all investigators have observed a lower level of cognitive capacity in sons of alcoholics. The sample selected for study may be a critical factor that determines whether a cognitive disorder will be observed. Alcoholics selected from treatment programs, these presumably being the most severe alcoholics, are more likely to have offspring who exhibit cognitive impairments. For example, in one study of community-dwelling alcoholic men, it was found that their children evidenced no systematic cognitive deficits although subtle impairments were observed on tests measuring planning ability and impulse control (Tarter et al, 1988).

While still awaiting further empirical confirmation, the evidence suggests that the cognitive deficits are most pronounced in persons for whom there is a coexistent antisocial disorder. Significantly, the cognitive deficits seen in children of alcoholics are qualitatively similar to the types of impairments exhibited by antisocial individuals, suggesting perhaps that the cognitive characteristics may not be specific to alcoholism. Also, it should be emphasized that in the absence of longitudinal studies, there is no basis to assume that the deficits found in high-risk children actually increase the risk for alcoholism. The possibility remains that the manifest cognitive deficits found in high-risk children are merely epiphenomena and unrelated to the risk for an adverse outcome. Nonetheless, there are important practical considerations bearing on impaired cognitive capacity in children of alcoholics. For instance, children of alcoholics do not progress as rapidly as other children in school (Knop, 1985) and perform less competently on standardized tests of academic achievement (Hegedus et al, 1984). There is also a higher prevalence of school maladjustment in children of alcoholics compared to off-spring of nonalcoholics (Knop et al, 1984). These findings suggest that the potential for academic achievement is lower in children of alcoholics, a deficiency that could have lifelong consequences. Thus, whereas the cognitive deficits in high-risk children remain uncertain with respect to their etiology and impact on outcome, the impairments nonetheless have important ramifications on academic achievement and adjustment.

Neurophysiologic Disturbance Presaging Alcoholism

Preliminary evidence suggests that a neurophysiologic disorder may also characterize children who are at risk for alcoholism. Quantitative analysis of the electroencephalogram (EEG) has revealed that children of alcoholics are differentiable from children of nonalcoholics, particularly with respect to the alpha bandwidth frequency (Gabrielli et al, 1982; Pollack et al, 1983). Children of alcoholics can also be discriminated from children of nonalcoholics in stimulus information processing. Particularly, the P300 wave component of the visual evoked response has been shown to be attenuated in children of alcoholics (Begleiter et al, 1984). Although the precise meaning or significance of these findings is unclear, there is evidence linking this neurophysiologic parameter to the regulation of cognitive processes, specifically attention and memory capacities. Multidisciplinary studies using neuropsychologic and psychologic measurements on children of alcoholics have, however, not yet been conducted. Also note that other clinical disorders are also characterized by P3 voltage attenuation, thereby indicating that this neurophysiologic risk parameter may be sensitive but not specific to the risk for alcoholism.

Neurologic Disturbance Presaging Alcoholism

There is tentative indication that a neurologic disorder may contribute to the risk for developing alcoholism in some individuals. For example, an essential or familial tremor has been linked to alcoholism (Nasrallah et al, 1982; Schroeder and Nasrallah, 1982) although the results in this regard are not entirely consistent (Koller, 1982). A higher prevalence of left handedness in alcoholic men compared to normal men has also been reported (Bakan, 1973) pointing to the possibility of a laterality shift in alcoholism (Nasrallah et al, 1983). In several studies, children and other first-degree relatives of alcoholics have been shown to be more ataxic than offspring of normal parents (Hegedus et al, 1984; Lester and Carpenter, 1985; Hill et al, 1987). In one study, sons of alcoholics were discriminated from children of depressed and normal fathers on a quantified measure of ataxia, suggesting that this disorder in the children of alcoholics may be specific to alcoholism and not merely reflect a general manifestation of risk for psychopathology (Hegedus et al, 1984). Whereas the available findings implicate static ataxia as a potential risk marker for alcoholism, it should be pointed out that the results of the studies conducted to date are not entirely consistent. For example, although several investigators have observed that children and young adult offspring of alcoholics are dispositionally differentiable from children of normal controls, other investigators have reported that differences are manifest only after an acute alcohol challenge (Schuckit, 1985).

In summary, evidence is accumulating indicating that behavioral, cognitive, neurologic, and neurophysiological disturbances may predate the onset of alcoholism in some individuals. The results of these studies should be viewed as preliminary especially since there is no evidence causally linking such deficits to alcoholism. Longitudinal investigations are needed to clarify the prevalence of neurobehavioral disturbance in high-risk children and to determine how the putative vulnerability features interact with the environment to culminate in an alcoholism outcome.

Factors Influencing Neurobehavioral Disturbance Concomitant With Alcohol Abuse

Life-style

The life-style of alcohol abusers can potentially influence the risk for developing cognitive and behavioral disturbances. Drinking, occurring in the company of socially deviant and antisocial individuals, is associated with violence and injury-prone behavior. Craniocerebral trauma due to fights and falls are also likely to occur while intoxicated which, independent of the direct effects of ethanol consumption, could produce neuropsychological impairment. Poor diet, use of other psychoactive drugs, and poor hygiene additionally increase the susceptibility to disease and ultimately neuropsychologic impairment consequent to neurologic injury.

Drinking Parameters

One phenomenon that has been repeatedly demonstrated concerns the absence of robust correlations between chronicity of alcohol consumption and magnitude of neuropsychologic impairment. Lifetime quantity of alcohol beverage consumption has also not been found to correlate strongly or consistently across studies with neuropsychologic deficit. A modest association between quantity consumed per drinking occasion and cognitive performance has been reported, but like other drinking variables this factor has not been shown to be strongly predictive of cognitive and behavioral disorder. The general thrust of the available evidence suggests that the neuropsychologic deficits commonly observed in alcoholics cannot be explained on the basis of the cumulative neurotoxic effects of ethanol. Furthermore, the observation that cognitive deficits are exhibited by young alcoholics who have a relatively short history of drinking excess, illustrates that the deficits are revealed rather early in the drinking career. Alternatively, these latter findings raise the question that the deficits are unrelated to ethanol consumption or that some individuals may be especially susceptible to the deleterious effects of alcohol such that neuropsychologic impairment is rapidly induced.

Preliminary evidence has been offered suggesting that the amount of alcohol consumed per drinking occasion may be correlated with neuropsychological test performance in social drinkers (Parker and Noble, 1977). The latter variable does not, however, account for a major proportion of cognitive test score variance. Also, the possibility cannot be discounted that the observed correlation is spurious and related to certain moderating variables (e.g., developmental disability, systemic disease, etc.) that were not considered in the latter studies. The prevailing evidence obtained to date suggests that the relationship between social drinking and cognitive capacity, if such an association even exists, is weak and of unknown etiology or significance (Hill and Ryan, 1985). Thus, whereas social drinking and impaired cognitive performance may be related, the basis for this relationship is unknown, and in all likelihood, is not due primarily to ethanol toxicity since no significant association has been reliably observed between lifetime quantity of ethanol consumption and neuropsychologic test performance.

Coexistent Systemic Disease

As discussed previously, hepatic disease and nutritional deficiency are frequent concomitants with chronic alcohol abuse. Other systemic diseases are also common in alcoholics that may influence cognitive capacity and behavioral adjustment. Certain medical conditions (e.g., hypertension, pancreatitis) can cause psychological disorder independently of alcoholism. Thus, these medical conditions — when present in chronic alcohol abusers — may contribute to the overall disturbance. Furthermore, disturbances of immune and endocrine function are frequently observed in alcoholics. Cardiomyopathy and infectious disease are more common in alcoholics than in the nonalcoholic population. However, little is known about how these latter diseases impact on psychological processes. The paucity of investigations notwithstanding, it is reasonable to conclude that the neuropsychological disturbances revealed by alcoholics are the end-point of the disruption of multiple synergistic biological systems.

REVERSIBILITY OF NEUROPSYCHOLOGIC DISTURBANCE

The presence of neuropsychologic impairments in a substantial proportion of the alcoholic population is well established. Less well understood is the degree to which the cognitive disturbances observed in alcoholics can be ameliorated by treatment or reverse spontaneously on abstinence from alcohol consumption. Investigations aimed at clarifying cognitive recovery are difficult to implement because of the need for serial assessments while simultaneously controlling for the confounding effects of practice on the test results. Moreover, it is difficult to verify alcohol consumption behavior during the follow-up period of recovery. Also, the time of measurement of cognitive capacity will greatly influence the results obtained; for example, neuropsychologic testing conducted in the early postalcohol withdrawal period will reveal performance deficits due to persisting metabolic disruption and malnutrition. Further complicating research into cognitive recovery is that medical treatments, including vitamin supplements and tranquilizers, can obscure the natural course of cognitive improvement. Finally, the heterogeneity of manifest cognitive deficits and the multiplicity of their underlying causal mechanisms militate against elucidating in a straightforward manner the rate and level of cognitive improvement. For these reasons, any conclusions drawn about cognitive recovery in alcoholics should be regarded as general and preliminary. In view of the established association between impaired performance on neuropsychological tests and social and vocational maladjustment (Heaton and Pendleton, 1981), it is nonetheless very important to clarify the extent to which alcoholics can recover from cognitive deficits following detoxification.

Alcoholics generally demonstrate substantial improvement in neuropsychological test performance following alcohol abstinence of one year or longer (Parsons and Leber, 1981; Donovan et al, 1987). The learning and visuospatial deficits commonly observed within the first month after detoxification ameliorate but do not completely resolve even after several years of sobriety (Berglund et al, 1977). It is also interesting to note that cognitive recovery does not proceed at the same rate across cognitive processes. For example, it was found in one study that alcoholics reevaluated after at least five years of sobriety manifest residual impairments on tests of visuospatial analysis and association learning whereas performance on tests of psychomotor, attention and spatial ability returned to normal (Brandt et al, 1983).

Alcoholics who drink during the postdetoxification period, even when the alcohol consumption is moderate and intermittent, demonstrate greater impairment than alcoholics who are totally abstinent (Yohman et al, 1985). Somewhat surprising, however, is the finding that alcoholics who resume drinking are more impaired neuropsychologically in the immediate postdetoxification period, suggesting perhaps that the magnitude of cognitive deficit may be a useful prognostic indicator where sobriety is the index of treatment outcome (Parsons, 1987).

Effects of Cognitive Rehabilitation on Reversing the Manifest Deficits

Goldman (1987) in an innovative program of research, has investigated the efficacy of cognitive rehabilitation procedures for facilitating cognitive recovery. By giving alcoholics repeated practice on tasks that assess a specific functional capacity (e.g., visuospatial problem solving), improvements are observed on other tasks requiring the same functional capacities. These improvements are significantly greater than those found in alcoholics who receive no intervention. The extent to which these improvements are sustained relates to psychosocial adjustment, or treatment outcome remains unknown.

Mechanisms Underlying Cognitive Improvement

Treatment of the sequelae of liver disease by reducing the putative neurotoxins responsible for hepatic encephalopathy has been tentatively shown to improve cognitive capacity in alcoholics (McClain et al, 1984). Alcoholics with cirrhosis who receive a regimen of Lactulose demonstrate relatively greater improvement on cognitive tests than alcoholics who do not receive treatment. This finding raises the possibility that aggressive medical management of the alcoholic could facilitate the rate and ultimate level of cognitive recovery. Also, data have been presented recently indicating that over 50% of alcoholics entering a medical service for treatment of the medical complications of alcoholism meet criteria for a vitamin E deficiency (A. Arria, R. Tarter, V. Warty, D. Van Thiel, in preparation.) This deficiency has been found to covary with the magnitude of psychomotor impairment. Because of the protective effects on membranes afforded by the antioxidant properties of vitamin E, it is reasonable to conjecture that this nutritional deficit may be a particularly important cofactor underlying the neuropsychological deficits. As yet, no investigations have been conducted linking nutritional therapy with improvement in cognitive capacity in alcoholics. Nonetheless, it appears that the concerted medical management of systemic disease in alcoholics may facilitate cognitive recovery.

Neuropsychologic Capacity and Treatment Outcome

Neuropsychological test performance in alcoholics has been reported to be correlated with therapist's predictions of treatment prognosis (Leber et al, 1985). Alcoholics rated as having a poor prognosis score lower on tests measuring abstracting, memory, verbal skills, and cognitive flexibility. In another study (Boon, 1982), it was observed that alcoholics who were classified by their therapists as good problem solvers obtained significantly higher scores than poor problem solvers on ratings assessing future orientation, insight, therapeutic benefit, vocational status, and quality of life.

In addition to therapist judgment, there is some indication that cognitive capacity is related also to the actual treatment process. Several reports have been published demonstrating that alcoholics who have cognitive deficits remember less treatment relevant information presented to them in the course of their rehabilitation than cognitively intact alcoholics (Parsons, 1987). The latter findings suggest that the didactic forms of counseling directed toward the acquisition of insight into personal psychodynamics, conscious restructuring of life-style, and improved interpersonal problem solving are best suited for the more cognitively intact alcoholic.

The likelihood of persisting in a treatment program appears from tentative findings to also be related to cognitive ability. O'Leary et al (1979) found that clinicians rated alcoholics with good problem-solving abilities as responding better to treatment than less capable problem solvers. Additionally, the latter alcoholics were also less likely to complete an inpatient treatment program.

There is suggestive evidence implicating a relationship between cognitive status measured during treatment and posttreatment outcome status. Gregson and Taylor (1977) found that cognitive status is a more robust factor than drinking parameters or psychosocial variables in predicting treatment outcome. Other researchers have also demonstrated that alcoholics with good cognitive capacity were most likely to sustain posttreatment sobriety (Berglund et al, 1977; Guthrie and Elliott, 1977; O'Leary et al, 1979). It should be noted, however, that although cognitive impairment has been implicated to be a predictor of poor treatment outcome, it is only one of many personal and treatment-related factors affecting prognosis and, by itself, does not strongly portend outcome (Wilkinson and Sanchez-Craig, 1981).

FURTHER RESEARCH DIRECTIONS

As discussed in this chapter, neuropsychological investigations can substantially contribute to clarifying the etiology of alcoholism, determine the impact of alcohol related systemic disease on adaptive cognitive and behavioral functioning, and help elucidate who is most likely to benefit from treatment. However, several major issues still need to be examined in order to comprehensively delineate the psychological course, correlates, and consequences of alcoholism.

With respect to alcoholism etiology, it remains to be determined whether the behavioral and cognitive impairments found in high-risk individuals reflect the end-point of a genetically determined biological disturbance. In addition, it is important to characterize the neuropsychologic deficits present in children at risk more precisely and comprehensively so as to derive empirically based psychological subtypes of alcoholism vulnerability. Neuropsychologic methods thus need to be incorporated into prospective longitudinal investigations addressing the multiple developmental pathways to an alcoholism outcome.

With respect to the neuropsychologic correlates of alcoholism, it remains still to be determined whether there are additional subtypes of impairment besides the dementia and amnesic manifestations. Future research also must focus on the explication of the causal mechanisms underlying the neuropsychologic deficits. In this regard, the biological processes, both within and outside the central nervous system, need to be systematically analyzed insofar as they determine the overall impairments. Notably absent to date are studies evaluating the neurochemical basis of cognitive impairment in alcoholics. Clarifying the association between the neurochemical and systemic mechanisms underlying the neuropsychologic deficits would enable the implementation of more effective rehabilitation interventions. In addition, in view of the available evidence demonstrating that treatment persistence and outcome are influenced by cognitive capacity, it would appear essential to design specialized rehabilitation procedures for alcoholics who are not cognitively adept or where improvement in cognitive capacity is unlikely. Furthermore, the utility of psychological tests to predict employment and social adjustment, particularly for determining whether the person should engage in risk-prone activity (e.g., drive a car, use power machinery) has not been studied empirically. Finally, based on the promising early findings it is important to ascertain the efficacy of cognitive rehabilitation procedures and to determine whether intensive medical management of nutritional and hepatic disturbance can accelerate the rate and maximize the ultimate level of cognitive recovery.

REFERENCES

Adams K, Grant J: The influence of premorbid risk factors on neuropsychological performance in alcoholics. *J Clin Exp Neuropsych* 1986; 8:362–376.

Alterman A, Petrarulo E, Tarter R, McCowen J: Hyperactivity and alcoholism: Familial and behavioral correlates. *Addict Behav* 1982; 7:413–421.

Alterman A, Tarter R, Baughman T, Bober B, Fabian S: Differentiation of alcoholics high and low in childhood hyperactivity. *Drug Alcohol Depend* 1985; 15:111–121.

Antanow D, McClain C: Nutrition and alcoholism, in Tarter R, Van Thiel D (eds): *Alcohol and the Brain: Chronic Effects*. New York, Plenum Press, 1985, pp 81–120.

Arria A, Tarter R, Warty V, Van Thiel D: The prevalence of serum vitamin E deficiency in alcoholic and nonalcoholic cirrhosis. (in preparation).

Bakan P: Left-handedness and alcoholism. *Percept Mot Skills* 1973; 36:514.

Begleiter H, Porjesz B, Kissin B: Event-related brain potentials in children at risk for alcoholism. *Science* 1984; 225:1493–1496.

Berglund M, Leijonquist H, Horlea M: Prognostic significance and reversibility of cerebral dysfunction in alcoholics. *J Stud Alcohol* 1977; 38:1761–1769.

Blass J, Gibson G: Abnormality of a thiamin-requiring enzyme in patients with Wernicke–Korsakoff syndrome. *New Engl J Med* 1977; 297:1367–1370.

Blowin A, Bornstein R, Trites R: Teenage alcohol use among hyperactive children: A four-year follow-up study. *J Pediatr Psychol* 1978; 3:188–194.

Boon J: Real life implications of problem solving deficits in alcoholics. Unpublished doctoral dissertation. Vanderbilt University, Nashville, TN, 1982.

Brandt J, Butters N, Ryan C, Bayog R: Cognitive loss and recovery in long-term alcohol abusers. *Arch Gen Psychiatry* 1983; 40:435–442.

Butters N, Cermak L: *Alcoholic Korsakoff's Syndrome: An Information Processing Approach to Amnesia*. New York, Academic Press, 1980.

Butters N, Granholm E: The continuity hypothesis: Some conclusions and their implications for the etiology and neuropsychology of alcoholic Korsakoff Syndrome, in Parsons O, Butters N, Nathan P (eds): *Neuropsychology of Alcoholism: Implications for Diagnosis and Treatment*. New York, Guilford, 1987; pp 176–207.

Cantwell D: Psychiatric illness in the families of hyperactive children. *Arch Gen Psychiatry* 1972; 27: 414–417.

Cloninger C: Neurogenetic adaptive mechanisms in alcoholism. *Science* 1987; 236:410–416.

Cloninger R, Bohman M, Sigvardson S: Inheritance of alcohol abuse: Cross-fostering analysis of adopted men. *Arch Gen Psychiatry* 1981; 38:861–867.

Courville C: *Effects of Alcohol on the Nervous System of Man*. Los Angeles, San Lucas Press, 1955.

Donovan D, Walker D, Kivlahan D: Recovery and remediation of neuropsychological functions: Implications for alcoholism rehabilitation process and outcome, in Parsons O, Butters N, Nathan P (eds): *Neuropsychology of Alcoholism: Implications for Diagnosis and Treatment*. New York, Guilford, 1987.

Ervin C, Little R, Streissguth A, Beck D: Alcoholic fathering and its relation to child's intellectual development. *Alcohol Clin Exp Res* 1984; 8:362–365.

Fitzhugh L, Fitzhugh K, Reitan R: Adaptive abilities and intellectual functioning of hospitalized alcoholics. *Quart Stud Alcohol* 1965; 26:402–411.

Freund G: Neuropathology of alcohol aubse, in Tarter R, Van Thiel D (eds): *Alcohol and the Brain: Chronic Effects*. New York, Plenum, 1985, pp 3–18.

Gabrielli W, Mednick S: Intellectual performance in children of alcoholics. *J Nerv Ment Dis* 1983; 171: 444–447.

Gabrielli W, Mednick S, Volavka J, Pollack V, Schulsinger F, Itil T: Electroencephalograms in children of alcoholic fathers. *Psychophysiology* 1982; 19:404–407.

Goldman M: The role of time and practice in recovery of function in alcoholics, in Parsons O, Butters N, Nathan P (eds): *Neuropsychology of Alcoholism. Implications for Diagnosis and Treatment*. New York, Guilford, 1987, pp 291–322.

Goldstein G, Shelly C: Neuropsychological investigation of brain lesion localization in alcoholism, in Begleiter H (ed): *Biological Effects of Alcohol*. New York, Plenum, 1980, pp 731–743.

Goodwin D, Schulsinger F, Hermansen L, Guze S, Winokur G: Alcoholism and the hyperactive child syndrome. *J Nerv Ment Dis* 1975; 160:349–353.

Gorenstein E, Newman J: Disinhibitory psychopathology: A new perspective and model for research. *Psychol Rev* 1980; 87:301–315.

Grant I, Adams K, Reed R: Normal neuropsychological abilities of alcoholic men in their late thirties. *Am J Psychiatry* 1979; 136:1263–1269.

Gregson R, Taylor G: Prediction of relapse in men alcoholics. *J Stud Alcohol* 1977; 38:1749–1759.

Guthrie A, Elliott W: The nature and reversibility of cerebral impairment in alcoholism: Treatment implications. *Quart J Studies Alcohol* 1977; 41:147–155.

Hagnell O, Larke J, Rosman B, Ohman R: Predictors of alcoholism in the Lundby study. ii. Personality traits as risk factors for alcoholism. *Eur Arch Psychiatry Neurol Sci* 1986; 235:192–196.

Heaton R, Pendleton M: Use of neuropsychological tests to predict adult patients' everyday functioning. *J Consult Clin Psychol* 1981; 49:807–821.

Hegedus A, Alterman A, Tarter R: Learning achievement in sons of alcoholics. *Alcohol Clin Exp Res* 1984; 8:330–333.

Hegedus A, Tarter R, Hill S, Jacob R, Winsten N: Static ataxia: A possible marker for alcoholism. *Alcohol Clin Exp Res* 1984; 8:580–582.

Hill S, Armstrong J, Steinhauer S, Baughman T, Zubin J: Static ataxia as a psychological marker for alcoholism. *Alcohol Clin Exp Res* 1987; 11:345–348.

Hill S, Ryan C: Brain damage in social drinkers—Reasons for caution, in Galanter M (ed): *Recent Developments in Alcoholism (Vol 3)*. New York, Plenum Press, 1985, pp 277–288.

Hoyumpa A, Schenker S: Hepatic encephalopathy, in Berk E, Haubrich W, Kalser M, Roth J (eds): *Gastroenterology*. Philadelphia, WB Saunders, 1985, Vol. 5, pp 3083–3120.

Jones B: Verbal and spatial intelligence in short- and long-term alcoholics. *J Nerv Ment Dis* 1971; 153: 292–297.

Klisz D, Parsons O: Hypothesis testing in younger and older alcoholics. *J Stud Alcohol* 1977; 38:1718–1729.

Knop J: Premorbid assessment of young men at high risk for alcoholism, in Galanter M (ed): *Recent Developments in Alcoholism (Vol. 3)*. New York, Plenum Press, 1985, pp 53–64.

Knop J, Goodwin D, Teasdale T, Mikkelsen U, Schulsinger F: A Danish prospective study of young adult males at high risk for alcoholism, in Goodwin D, Van Dusen K, Mednick S (eds): *Longitudinal Research in Alcoholism*. Boston, Kluven-Nijhoff, 1984, pp 107–124.

Koller W: Alcoholism in essential tremor. *Neurology* 1983; 33:1074–1076.

Leber W, Parsons O, Nichols N: Neuropsychological tests are related to ratings of alcoholics' therapeutic progress. A replicated study. *J Stud Alcohol* 1985; 46:116–121.

Lester D, Carpenter J: Static ataxia in adolescents and their parents. *Alcohol Clin Exp Res* 1985; 9:212.

McClain C, Potter T, Kromhout J, Zieve L: The effect of lactulose on psychomotor performance tests in alcohlic cirrhotics without overt hepatic encephalopathy. *J Clin Gastroenterol* 1984; 6:325–329.

Miller L: Neuropsychology of the aggressive psychopath: An integrative review. *Aggressive Behavior* 1987; 13:119–148.

Morrison J, Stewart M: The psychiatric status of the legal families of adopted hyperactive children. *Arch Gen Psychiatry* 1973; 28:888–891.

Murphree H, Price L: Electroencephalographic effects of some alcoholic beverages, in Popham R (ed): *Alcohol and Alcoholism*. Toronto, University of Toronto Press, 1970; pp 57–62.

Nasrallah H, Keelor K, McCalley-Whitters M: Laterality shift in alcoholic males. *Biol Psychiatry* 1983; 18:1065–1067.

Nasrallah H, Schroeder D, Petty F: Alcoholism secondary to essential tremor. *J Clin Psychiatry* 1982; 4:163–164.

O'Leary M, Donovan D, Chaney E, Walker R: Cognitive impairment and treatment outcome with alcoholics: Preliminary findings. *J Clin Psychiat* 1979; 40:397–398.

Oscar-Berman M: Neuropsychological consequences of alcohol abuse: Questions, hypotheses and models, in Parsons O, Butters N, Nathan P (eds): *Neuropsychology of Alcoholism: Implications for Diagnosis and Treatment*. New York, Guilford, 1987; pp 256–273.

Parker E, Noble E: Alcohol consumption and cognitive functioning in social drinkers. *J Stud Alcohol* 1977; 38:1224–1232.

Parsons O: Do neuropsychological deficits predict alcoholics' treatment course and post treatment recovery?, in Parsons O, Butters N, Nathan P (eds): *Neuropsychology of Alcoholism. Implications for Diagnosis and Treatment*. New York, Guilford, 1987; pp 273–291.

Parsons O, Farr S: The neuropsychology of alcohol and drug use, in Filskov S, Boll T (eds): *Handbook of Clinical Neuropsychology*. New York, Wiley, 1981.

Parsons O, Leber W: The relationship between cognitive dysfunction and brain damage in alcoholics: Causal, interactive or epiphenomenal. *Alcohol Clin Exp Res* 1981; 5:326–343.

Pishkin V, Fishkin S, Stahl M: Concept learning in chronic alcoholics: Psychophysiological and set functions. *J Clin Psychol* 1972; 28:328–334.

Pollack V, Volavka J, Goodwin D, Mednick S, Gabrielli W, Knop J, Schulsinger F: The EEG after alcohol administration in men at risk for alcoholism. *Arch Gen Psychiatry* 1983; 40;857–861.

Pribram K: The primate frontal cortex. *Neuropsychologia* 1969; 7:259–266.

Riley J, Walker D: Morphological alterations in hippocampus after long-term alcohol consumption in mice. *Science* 1978; 201:646–648.

Ron M: The brain of alcoholics: An overview, in Parsons O, Butters N, Nathan P (eds): *Neuropsychology of Alcoholism: Implications for Diagnosis and Treatment*. New York, Guilford, 1987; pp 11–20.

Ryan C, Butters N: Further evidence for a continuum-of-impairment encompassing male alcoholic Korsakoff patients and chronic alcoholics. *Alcohol Clin Exp Res* 1980; 4:190–198.

Ryan C, Butters N: Cognitive deficits in alcoholics, in Kissin B, Begleiter H (eds): *The Pathogenesis of Alcoholism*. New York, Plenum Press, 1983.

Schaeffer K, Parsons O, Yohman J: Neuropsychological differences between male familial alcoholics and nonalcoholics. *Alcohol Clin Exp Res* 1984; 8:347–351.

Schroeder D, Nasrallah H: High alcoholism rate in patients with essential tremor. *Am J Psychiatry* 1982; 139:1471–1473.

Schuckit M: Ethanol induced changes in body sway in men at high alcoholism risk. *Arch Gen Psychiatry* 1985; 42:375–379.

Tarter R: An analysis of cognitive deficits in chronic alcoholics. *J Nerv Ment Dis* 1973; 157:139–147.

Tarter R: Psychological deficit in chronic alcoholics. A review. *Int J Addict* 1975; 10;327–368.

Tarter R: Brain damange in chronic alcoholics: A review of the psychological evidence, in Richter D (ed): *Addiction: Biochemical Aspects of Dependence and Brain Damage*. London, Crown Helm, 1981.

Tarter R: Neuropsychology of alcoholism, in Tarter R, Van Thiel D (eds): *Alcohol and the Brain: Chronic Effects*. New York, Plenum Press, 1985, pp 217–244.

Tarter R: Are there inherited behavioral traits which predispose to substance abuse? *J Consult Clin Psychol* 1988; 56:189–196.

Tarter R, Alterman A: Neuropsychological deficits in alcoholics. Etiological considerations. *J Stud Alcohol* 1984; 45:1–9.

Tarter R, Alterman A, Edwards K: Vulnerability to alcoholism in men: A behavior–genetic perspective. *J Stud Alcohol* 1985; 46:329–356.

Tarter R, Buonpane N, Wynant C: Intellectual competence of alcoholics. *J Stud Alcohol* 1975; 36:381–386.

Tarter R, Edwards K: Neuropsychology of alcoholism, in Tarter R, Van Thiel D (eds): *Alcohol and the Brain: Chronic Effects*. New York, Plenum Press, 1985.

Tarter R, Hegedus A, Goldstein G, Shelly C, Alterman A: Adolescent sons of alcoholics: Neuropsychological and personality characteristics. *Alcohol Clin Exp Res* 1984; 8:216–222.

Tarter R, Hegedus A, Van Thiel D: Neuropsychiatric sequelae of portal systemic encephalopathy: A review. *Int J Addict* 1984; 24:203–216.

Tarter R. Hegedus A, Van Thiel D: Association between hepatic dysfunction and neuropsychological test performance in alcoholics with cirrhosis. *J Stud Alcohol* 1986; 47:74–77.

Tarter R, Hegedus A, Winsten N, Alterman A: Neuropsychological, personality and familial characteristics of physically abused juvenile delinquents. *J Acad Child Psychiatry* 1984; 27:668–674.

Tarter R, Jacob T, Bremer D: Cognitive status of sons of alcoholic men. (Unpublished manuscript, Department of Psychiatry, University of Pittsburgh). 1988.

Tarter R, McBride H, Buonpane N, Schneider D: Differentiation of alcoholics: Childhood history of minimal brain dysfunction, family history, and drinking pattern. *Arch Gen Psychiatry* 1977; 34:668–674.

Tarter R, Parsons O: Conceptual shifting in chronic alcoholics. *J Abnorm Psychol* 1972; 77:71–75.

Tarter R, Van Thiel D, Arria A, Moss H: Impact of cirrhosis on the neuropsychologic test performance of alcoholics. *Alcohol Clin and Exp Res* 1988; 12:619–621.

Walker D, Hunter B, Abraham W: Neuroanatomical and functional deficits subsequent to chronic ethanol administration in animals. *Alcohol Clin Exp Res* 1981; 5:267–282.

Wilkinson DA: Neuroradiologic investigations of alcoholism, in Tarter R, Van Thiel D (eds): *Alcohol and the Brain: Chronic Effects* New York, Plenum Press, 1985, pp 183–216.

Wilkinson DA, Carlen P: Relationship of neuropsychological test performance to brain morphology in amnesic and non-amnesic chronic alcoholics. *Acta Psychiat Scand* 1980; 62:89–102.

Wilkinson D, Paulos C: The chronic effects of alcohol on memory: A contrast between a unitary and dual system approach, in Galanter M (ed): *Recent Developments in Alcoholism*. New York, Plenum, 1987, vol 5, pp 5–26.

Wilkinson A, Sanchez-Craig M: Relevance of brain dysfunction to treatment objectives: Should alcohol-related cognitive deficits influence the way we think about treatment? *Addict Behav* 1981; 6: 253–268.

Yeudall L, Fromm-Auch D: Neuropsychological impairments in various psychopathological populations, in Gruzelier J, Flor-Henry P (eds): *Hemisphere Asymmetries of Function in Psychopathology*. New York, Elsevier/North Holland, 1979; pp 401–430.

Yohman J, Parsons O, Leber W: Lack of recovery in alcoholics' neuropsychological performance one year after treatment. *Alcohol Clin Exp Res* 1985; 9:114–117.

Section 3

Clinical Aspects

CHAPTER 7

The Organ Pathogenesis of Alcoholism: Liver and Gastrointestinal Tract

Mikko Salaspuro, M.D.

Research Unit of Alcohol Diseases
University Central Hospital of Helsinki
Helsinki, Finland

LIVER

Epidemiology

Mortality and Prevalence

The majority of heavy drinkers and alcoholics will develop hepatomegaly and fatty infiltration of the liver. However, only one-fifth to one-third develop a more severe liver injury, alcoholic hepatitis, or liver cirrhosis (Lelbach, 1966; Leevy 1968). According to autopsy data, the prevalence of cirrhosis in alcoholics is about 18%; in series based on liver biopsy it ranges from 17 to 30.8% (Lelbach, 1966, 1967; Leevy, 1968).

In the early 1960s, the worldwide annual mortality rate from cirrhosis was at least 310,000 (Steiner, 1964). Since then, cirrhosis mortality has increased considerably. For instance, in West Germany cirrhosis mortality, which was 6:100,000 in 1950 increased to 27:100,000 in 1980 (Lelbach, 1985). Similar trends have been documented in most European countries (Lelbach, 1985, Morgan, 1985), in Australia (Rankin et al, 1985), in the United States (Galambos, 1985), and in Japan (Ohnishi and Okuda, 1985). In many countries, as for instance, in England, alcoholic cirrhosis is now the most common form of liver injury (Saunders et al, 1981). The considerable underreporting of liver cirrhosis (up to 47.9%) in death certificates, however, significantly hampers the interpretation of epidemiological data (Blake et al, 1988).

In the majority of cases, cirrhosis of the liver remains undetected during life (Schubert et al, 1982b). Accordingly, morbidity from all types of alcoholic liver diseases is much higher than mortality, but no valid data about exact numbers are available. However, in Wuppertal and Tübingen, the postmortem prevalence of cirrhosis of the liver was shown to be increased from about 2% in 1939 to 11% in 1975 (Schubert et al, 1982a).

Relation of Liver Cirrhosis to Alcohol Consumption

The close relationship between alcohol consumption and liver cirrhosis mortality has been demonstrated in many studies. One of the classical examples is the effect of wine rationing in France during World War II (Lelbach, 1985). From 1941 to 1946, alcohol consumption dropped there drastically and this was associated with a similar decrease in cirrhosis mortality (Fig. 7.1). Similarly, the subsequent rise in alcohol consumption from 1946 to 1955 resulted

133

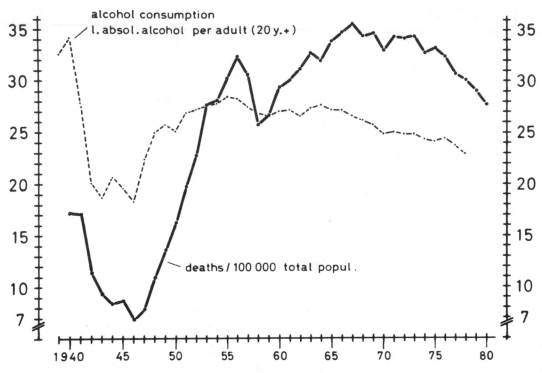

FIGURE 7.1. Alcohol consumption (adults) and cirrhosis mortality in France 1939–1980 (Lelbach, 1985).

in an even more pronounced increase in mortality caused by liver cirrhosis. From 1965 there has been a decreasing trend in alcohol consumption in France with an equal trend in cirrhosis mortality (Fig. 7.1).

In 1972, the mortality for cirrhosis was 7.5:100,000 in Finland as compared to 57.2:100,000 in France. Corresponding per capita alcohol consumptions were 5.1 and 16.8 liters of absolute alcohol, respectively. The termination of alcohol rationing in Sweden in 1955 was followed by an increase in deaths attributable to cirrhosis (Norström, 1987). On the other hand decrease in alcohol consumption from 1976 was associated with at least an equal decrease in cirrhosis mortality (Romelsjö and Ågren, 1985; Romelsjö, 1987).

For males, the relative risk of cirrhosis has been estimated to be six times greater at 40 to 60 g alcohol/day than at 0 to 20 g/day and 14 times greater at 60 to 80 g/day (Pequignot et al, 1978). The average "cirrhogenic" dose was calculated to be 180 g ethanol/day consumed regularly for approximately 25 years. According to Lelbach (1976), the probability of developing cirrhosis for an individual consuming about 210 g of ethanol daily for 22 years is 50% and increases to 80% after 33 years. In a case control study, risk for cirrhosis in males was 1.83 for men consuming 40 to 59 g absolute alcohol/day compared to men consuming less than 40 g/day, rising to 100 for men consuming over 80 g/day (Coates et al, 1986). Similar trends were found in women and in the risk of developing fatty liver (Coates et al, 1986). Confirming results demonstrating that the severity of alcohol-related liver injury correlates positively both with the total amount of alcohol consumed daily as well as with the duration of excessive consumption (drinking life) has been obtained in many other recent studies (Poikolainen, 1980; Kendell, 1984; Smith and Burvill, 1985; Rush, 1986; Norton et al, 1987; Skog, 1987), too.

Pequignot found that the average cirrhogenic dose and the threshold doses are lower in females than in males (Pequignot et al, 1978). This suggestion is supported by most, but not by all, studies (Morgan and Sherlock 1977; Mendenhall, 1985; Morgan 1985). There is no valid epidemiological or clinical evidence to suggest that drinking habits — continuous versus periodic — or the type of alcoholic beverage influence mortality from cirrhosis (Schmidt, 1975).

The availability of alcoholic beverages; licensing laws; and economic, cultural, and environmental conditions have all been shown to influence both per capita alcohol consumption and mortality from cirrhosis (for ref. see Lieber and Salaspuro, 1985). It is now generally accepted that both the consumption of alcohol and the incidence of alcohol related health problems can be regulated by means of various restrictions and tax policies. In Canada and Finland both the potential usefulness of the many diverse restrictions through which control can be exercised has been examined in great detail (Bruun et al, 1975; Popham et al, 1976).

Patterns and Pathology of Alcoholic Liver Injury

The spectrum of alcoholic liver injury involves hepatic steatosis (fatty liver), perivenular and perisinusoidal fibrosis, alcoholic hepatitis, and cirrhosis.

Fatty Liver

Fat accumulation in the liver cells is the earliest and most common response to alcohol, and alcohol is its most common etiological factor (Leevy, 1962; Brunt et al, 1974). In electron microscopy, the early fat droplets are membrane bound, but later on they fuse and form clear intracytoplasmic vacuoles. In massive steatosis the hepatocytes are uniformly filled by large fat droplets, the cell nucleus may be eccentrically placed, and, when the cell membranes between adjacent hepatocytes rupture, fatty cysts are formed. Increased hepatic lipid content may be demonstrated by biochemical measurements before it becomes histologically apparent. Evidence of necrosis is usually sparse, but sometimes hepatocytes are surrounded by mononuclear cells, indicating a mild inflammatory response. When pronounced, these formations are called "lipogranulomas." In a prospective evaluation fatty liver, despite its potential reversibility, has been shown to be causally associated with alcoholic cirrhosis (Fig. 7.2) (Sörensen et al, 1984).

Perivenular Fibrosis

In light microscopy, the earliest deposition of fibrous tissue is generally seen around the efferent central veins and venules (terminal venules). This necrotizing process was earlier described in alcoholic hepatitis and was called *sclerosing hyaline necrosis* (Edmondson et al, 1963). In electronmicroscopy this is preceded by an increased amount of activated perisinusoidal cells and collagen (Horn et al, 1985, 1986), which may occur anywhere in the acinus. At the same time, there is a loss of fenestrae in sinusoidal walls and the development of basement-membrane material (Mak et al, 1984; Horn et al, 1987).

Perivenular fibrosis can be seen in the absence of widespread inflammation and necrosis. In its most severe form, it may obliterate central veins and lead to postsinusoidal portal hypertension with ascites prior to the development of cirrhosis. In baboons, the degree of perivenular fibrosis correlates with an increase in portal pressure (Miyakawa et al, 1985). The progression of alcoholic liver injury has been suggested to be more rapid in the patients with perivenular fibrosis as compared to those with simple fatty liver (Nakano et al, 1982).

Alcoholic Hepatitis

This is a morphological diagnosis characterized by hepatocellular degeneration and necrosis with an associated neutrophil polymorph infiltrate (Baptista et al, 1981). The long-term incidence of cirrhosis in patients with alcoholic hepatitis is nine times higher than in those with fatty liver (Sörensen et al, 1984). Mallory bodies are frequently seen in ballooned hepatocytes, but their presence is not obligatory for the diagnosis.

Mallory's alcoholic hyaline was first defined by Mallory (1911) as an irregular, coarse, hyaline meshwork that stains deeply with eosin (Fig. 7.3). Hepatocytes containing these bod-

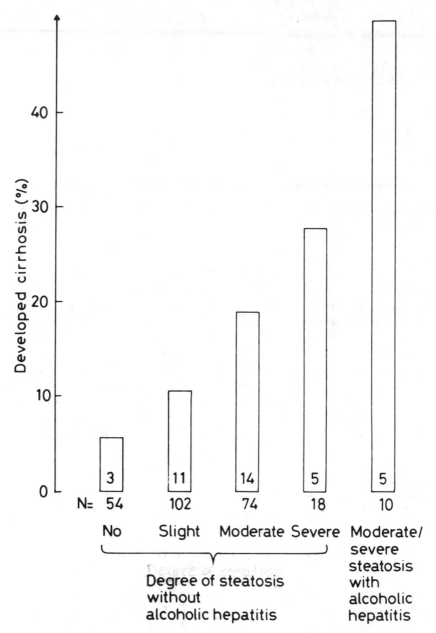

FIGURE 7.2. Steatosis and alcholic hepatitis on initial biopsy in relation to subsequent development of cirrhosis (Sörensen et al, 1984).

ies are often surrounded by polymorphonuclear leucocytes. Although alcoholic hyaline is characteristic of alcoholic hepatitis, it is by no means specific; it has been described in association with a variety of liver damage of different etiology (for ref. see Hall, 1985; Lieber and Salaspuro, 1985). Alcoholic hyaline is found in approximately 30% of patients with alcoholic hepatitis (Lischner et al, 1971). Its appearance does not correlate mortality rates either retrospectively (Harinasuta and Zimmerman, 1971) or prospectively (Birschbach et al, 1974), but it is accompanied by more severe degree of necrosis, cholestasis and steatosis.

Three morphologically distinct forms of *Mallory bodies* have been described: I—bundles of filaments in parallel arrays, II—clusters of randomly orientated fibrils, and III—granular

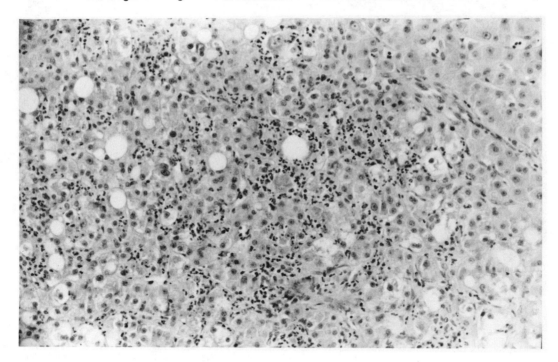

FIGURE 7.3. Alcoholic hepatitis. Note the ballooning of hepatocytes, which furthermore often are surrounded by inflammatory cells. Many of the enlarged hepatocytes contain alcoholic hyaline.

or amorphous substance containing only scattered remains of fibrils (Yokoo et al, 1972). The formation of alcoholic hyaline is considered to be a manifestation of derangement of the cytoskeleton of the hepatocyte. It has been suggested to represent intermediate filaments of the cell (Denk et al, 1981; French, 1981). Intermediate filaments are of the prekeratin type and antibodies to the prekeratin components of the hepatocyte react with Mallory bodies (Denk et al, 1979, 1981; Morton et al, 1981). The formation of Mallory bodies have been related to microtubular failure, preneoplasia, and vitamin A deficiency (Denk et al, 1981; French, 1983; Denk, 1985), but none of these hypotheses is particularly convincing.

Cirrhosis
Micronodular–Laennec's cirrhosis is characterized by regeneration nodules of hepatocytes that are surrounded by fibrous tissue. The size of the micronodules is usually less than 3 mm in diameter. Portal tracts and central veins are difficult to demonstrate. Variable amounts of bile duct proliferation and inflammatory cells are seen. Macronodular or a mixed cirrhosis may develop in those surviving longer after the cessation of drinking (Rubin et al, 1973).

Pathophysiology of Alcoholic Liver Damage

In the late 1940s, the pathogenesis of alcoholic liver injury was associated almost exclusively with a secondary protein and choline deficiency (Best et al, 1949). Since then, a block of evidence strongly relates the pathogenesis of alcohol-related liver damage to the direct toxicity of ethanol, its metabolism, and its metabolites (Chapter 3; Salaspuro, 1987a).

Animal Models of Alcohol-Related Organ Damage
A lot of evidence supporting the direct hepatotoxicity of ethanol has been obtained from experiments done with animal models of alcohol-induced organ damage (Salaspuro and Lieber, 1980; Lieber, 1984). One of the major advances has been the introduction of a technique

of feeding ethanol to rats as a part of nutritionally adequate totally liquid diet (Lieber et al, 1963, 1965; lieber and DeCarli, 1982; Israel et al, 1984). However, even with the "liquid diet model" the rat will not consume more than 36% of total calories as ethanol. Consequently, more advanced liver lesions than fatty livers cannot be produced in rats.

This difficulty has been overcome by applying the same feeding technique to baboons (Lieber and DeCarli, 1974). The alcohol intake of these animals can be increased to 50% of total calories, they are phylogenetically close to man, and furthermore their life span is long enough for the development of cirrhosis to occur. In this animal model, the biochemical and morphological alterations in the liver — even liver cirrhosis — are comparable to those seen in humans despite the fact that a complete histological spectrum of alcoholic hepatitis as seen in man has not been produced in baboons (Popper and Lieber, 1980).

Hepatotoxic Factors Associated with Ethanol Oxidation

Ethanol. Ethanol, like other general anesthetics, causes physical changes in all biologic membranes (Chapter 4) including hepatic mitochondrial and endoplasmic reticulum membranes (Goldstein and Chin, 1981; Taraschi and Rubin, 1985). Ethanol directly "fluidizes" membrane lipid bilayers, and it has been proposed that during chronic alcohol consumption, cell surface membranes may resist this effect of ethanol (i.e., "adapt") by changing their membrane lipid composition (Chapter 4).

As for the liver, the results obtained mainly in experimental animals are controversial. Some results have found an increase in membrane unesterified cholesterol (Mendenhall et al, 1969) and some an increase in membrane phospholipid content (French, 1967; Mendenhall et al, 1969), while others have reported no changes in these lipids in total liver (Takeuchi et al, 1974), in hepatic microsomes, or in mitochondria (French et al, 1970). The cholesterol-phospholipid ratio was recently reported to be unaltered in liver plasma membrane fractions (LPM) of mice exposed to chronic ethanol (Wing et al, 1983). This was confirmed in another study in which an increased cholesteryl ester content of LPM was found, however (Zysset et al, 1985). Increased LPM cholesteryl ester content has been proposed to mediate changes in membrane fluidity.

In addition to the alterations of LPM lipid composition, changes in the enzyme activities of liver membranes have also been reported (Wing et al, 1983). These include a decrease in cytochrome a and b, succinic dehydrogenase, cytochrome oxidase, as well as in the total respiratory capacity of the mitochondria (Taraschi and Rubin, 1985). The changes in enzyme activities may be due to the effects of both acute and chronic ethanol on either the synthesis of membrane proteins or on the transport of amino acids or both (Tarashi and Rubin, 1985).

Ethanol-Induced Shift in the Redox State of the Liver. The ethanol-induced increase in the NADH/NAD$^+$ (nicotinamide adenine dinucleotide [reduced form]/nicotinamide adenine dinucleotide) ratio is a sign of major change in hepatic metabolism during ethanol oxidation (Chapter 3). Many of the acute secondary changes in the intermediary metabolism of the liver can be explained by the action of ethanol on the hepatic redox state. These include, for instance, the inhibition of tricarboxylic acid cycle and gluconeogenesis. The redox-related inhibition of fatty acid oxidation and the enhancement of triglyceride synthesis are the main pathogenetic mechanisms in the development of *alcoholic fatty liver* as described in detail in Chapter 3.

In baboons chronically fed an alcohol-containing liquid diet, ethanol-induced shift in the hepatic redox state, however, is attenuated (Salaspuro et al, 1981). This is associated with the attenuation of the accumulation of hepatic triglycerides (Fig. 7.4). This "adaptation" during chronic alcohol consumption may explain why only a few alcoholics or heavy drinkers develop a more severe fatty liver despite continuous abuse of alcohol.

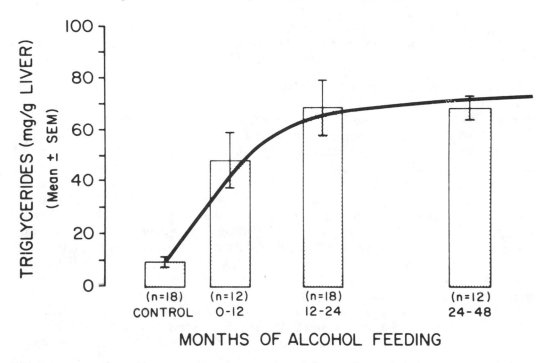

FIGURE 7.4. Attenuation of hepatic triglyceride accumulation following chronic alcohol consumption in baboons (Salaspuro et al, 1981).

Acetaldehyde. The metabolism and possible hepatotoxicity of acetaldehyde has recently been reviewed (Salaspuro and Lindroos, 1985; Salaspuro, 1987a; Chapter 3). The organ toxicity of acetaldehyde has been related to its capability to bind covalently (to form adducts) with phospholipids, nucleic acids, and proteins. Furthermore, acetaldehyde may cause lipid peroxidation by at least two mechanisms (Salaspuro, 1987a) (1) by enhancing the production of free radicals and (2) by binding to cysteine and glutathione or both, which may contribute to the depression of liver glutathione associated with ethanol administration (Vina et al, 1980; Shaw et al, 1981). The effect of acetaldehyde on the liver cytoskeleton (microtubules) and protein retention is discussed in detail in Chapter 3.

Hepatotoxicity Associated with MEOS. The existence of a nonalcohol dehydrogenase, cytochrome P450-dependent pathway of ethanol metabolism (MEOS), is at present well established (Lieber, 1984; Chapter 3). Theoretically, MEOS may cause enhanced hepatotoxicity by several means. MEOS contributes to the production of the potentially hepatotoxic agent, acetaldehyde. MEOS may enhance oxygen consumption, which at least in part may potentiate hypoxia in the centrilobular hepatocytes. MEOS may activate hepatotoxic agents, for instance, such as carbon tetrachloride (Hasumura et al, 1974) or acetaminophen (Teschke et al, 1979). In accordance with this hypothesis the history of ethanol consumption in humans has been shown to increase the hepatotoxicity of acetaminophen (Seeff et al, 1986).

Both in experimental animals and in humans, chronic alcohol consumption has been shown to be associated with vitamin A depletion (Sato and Lieber, 1981; Leo and Lieber, 1982). This may be caused by the induction of a new pathway of microsomal retinol oxidation, which is inducible by ethanol and which may degrade an amount of retinol comparable to the daily intake (Leo and Lieber, 1985). Decreased hepatic vitamin A levels may lead to some functional and structural abnormalities in the liver (Leo et al, 1983). Vitamin A deficiency may be a triggering factor in aggregation of cytokeratin filaments (Ray et al, 1988). However, the possible therapeutic use of vitamin A in alcohol-related liver diseases is complicated by its own potential hepatotoxicity (Leo et al, 1982; Leo and Lieber, 1983).

Lipid Peroxidation. An enhanced lipid peroxidation as a mechanism of alcoholic liver injury was proposed already in 1966 by Kalish and DiLuzio. Since then, several studies have been published on this topic and they have been reviewed recently (Videla and Valenzuela, 1982; Comporti, 1985; Dianzani, 1985). The ethanol-induced lipid peroxidation can be linked (1) to the formation of oxygen free radicals, (2) to the direct impact of ethanol-derived free radicals, and (3) to acetaldehyde (Dianzani, 1985), which may cause lipid peroxidation by at least two mechanisms (Salaspuro, 1987a).

In acute experiments with rats, large amounts of ethanol (5–6 g/kg) are required to produce lipid peroxidation (DiLuzio and Hartman, 1967; MacDonald, 1973), whereas a smaller dose has no effect (Hashimoto and Recknagel, 1968; Shaw et al, 1981). After chronic alcohol consumption, however, even smaller doses of ethanol administered acutely produce lipid peroxidation, which can be partly prevented by the glutathione precursor, methionine (Shaw et al, 1981). In rats, chronic ethanol feeding increases glutathione (GSH) turnover (Morton and Mitchell, (1985) and the cellular requirements for GSH (Pierson and Mitchell, 1986).

In chronic alcoholics, there is an increase both in serum and liver lipoperoxide levels (Suematsu et al, 1981). The content of hepatic-reduced GSH is decreased especially in patients with histological liver necrosis (Videla et al, 1984). As an integral part of the enzyme glutathione peroxidase, selenium has a central role in the protection against the tissue damage caused by lipid peroxides. In this respect, the decrease not only in blood but also in liver selenium in patients with alcoholic liver injury is worth mentioning (Välimäki et al, 1987).

Selective Perivenular Hepatotoxicity of Ethanol

Alcoholic liver injury starts and predominates in the perivenular (also called centrolobular) region – zone 3 of the hepatic acinus (Popper and Lieber, 1980), which is exposed to lowest oxygen tension. The enhanced injurious effect of ethanol at this site has been postulated to be due to hypoxia, resulting from ethanol-induced stimulation of hepatic oxygen consumption (Israel et al, 1975). The low oxygen tensions existing in perivenular zones may exaggerate the ethanol-induced redox shift (Chapter 3) on this area, a change that may contribute to the exacerbation of the damage in the perivenular area of the hepatic lobule (Jauhonen et al, 1982).

The activities of ethanol and acetaldehyde metabolizing enzymes, alcohol dehydrogenase, and low K_m aldehyde dehydrogenase have been shown to be evenly distributed within hepatic acinus (Väänänen et al, 1984). Furthermore, the distribution is unaffected by chronic ethanol treatment (Väänänen et al, 1984). Hepatocytes in zone 3, however, contain more smooth endoplasmic reticulum and cytochrome P450 than hepatocytes of other zones, suggesting that zone 3 is the region of maximal drug and alcohol metabolism (Väänänen, 1986). The role of the uneven distribution of the multiple microsomal functions in the pathogenesis of alcohol-related perivenular hepatotoxicity has not yet been resolved.

Alcohol and Fibrogenesis

Alcohol-induced necrosis and inflammation may trigger the scarring and the development of cirrhosis. In addition, ethanol itself, its metabolism, and/or metabolites may have significant effects on collagen metabolism and fibrogenesis (Chapter 3). This might explain why alcoholic hepatitis is not always a necessary intermediate step in the development of cirrhosis (Popper and Lieber, 1980; Nakano et al, 1982; Takada et al, 1982; Lieber, 1984). The pathophysiology of collagen metabolism in the liver and fibrogenesis has been recently reviewed in detail (Hahn and Schuppan, 1985, 1987; Rojkind, 1985). Consequently, only a short summary covering the most important approaches will be given here.

The induction and proliferation of various perisinusoidal cells has been documented in alcoholic liver injury. These mesenchymal cells, which may belong to the same cell family include *Ito cells* (fat storing cells, lipocytes), *myofibroplasts*, *fibroplasts*, and *transitional cells*. The most common of these are Ito cells. Electronmicroscopy shows that they contain lipid droplets and bundles of microfilaments, but they can also be demonstrated by light microscopy (Bronfenmajer et al, 1966; Hall et al, 1982). Their number increases in alcoholic liver injury and they have been suggested to produce increased amounts of Type III collagen (Kent et al, 1976). The process of hepatic fibrosis is associated with a shift from Ito cells to transitional cells (Mak and Lieber 1988).

Both perisinusoidal and perivenular cells show morphological transition between Ito cells and myofibroblasts (Okanoue et al, 1983). Myofibroblasts were first demonstrated in cirrhotic human livers (Bhathal, 1972). Later they were isolated from baboon liver biopsies (Savolainen et al, 1984a) and shown to produce type I, III, and IV collagen and laminin. Myofibroblasts are actively contractile cells and may contribute to scar contraction and portal hypertension in liver cirrhosis (Rudolph et al, 1979). They are predominantly present around the terminal venules and they increase in number before the development of perivenular and pericellular fibrosis (Nakano and Lieber, 1982; Nakano et al, 1982). Myofibroblasts processes extend into the Disse space, although the most common cell there is the Ito cell. A part of the Ito cells is replaced by transitional cells after chronic alcohol consumption (Mak et al, 1984).

The basic mechanisms by which chronic alcohol consumption stimulates the mesenchymal cells to produce collagen and induces their proliferation are still largely unresolved. Possible candidates are mononuclear inflammation (Nakano et al, 1982) and hyperlactacidemia (Savolainen et al, 1984b).

In any case, the increased collagenization of the Disse space associated with the reduction of fenestrations between sinusoids and the Disse space (Mak and Lieber, 1984; Horn et al, 1987) may isolate the hepatocytes from its blood supply. Furthermore, these changes increase the resistance of blood flow, thereby contributing to the increased portal pressure (Miyakawa et al, 1985) often seen in the early stage of liver injury.

Effect of Alcohol on Hepatocyte Regeneration

In most of the studies on partially hepatectomized rats, acute ethanol administration (1–6 days) has been shown to inhibit the incorporation of tritiated thymidine into hepatic DNA (see Joly and Duguay, 1985). This indicates that both a short-term and continuous presence of ethanol during the regeneration retards hepatic DNA synthesis and cell division. However, at the end of the experiment, total liver mass and DNA content are the same as in the controls (Frank et al, 1979; Pösö et al, 1980; Orrego et al, 1981), indicating that liver regeneration is not inhibited. A direct impairment of DNA synthesis by alcohol in rat hepatocyte cultures has recently been reported (Carter and Wands, 1988).

Observations in the model of chronic alcohol administration to partially hepatectomized rats generally agree with those received with the "acute model" (Wands et al, 1979; Frank and Houck, 1980; Duguay et al, 1981). There is no evidence that the inhibition of hepatic regeneration might play a role in the pathogenesis of alcoholic liver damage in humans.

Role of Immune Mechanisms

So far, most of the immunological alterations as well as changes in cellular immunity seen in patients with alcoholic liver diseases have been thought to be secondary to the primary hepatocellular injury (MacSween and Anthony, 1985; Paronetto, 1985). The information that alcohol or its metabolites might have a direct damaging effect on the cells and organs responsible for the immune responses in human is also scarce. However, there is some evidence that cytotoxic reactions mediated by mononuclear cells may take place in some patients with alcoholic liver injury.

Genetic Factors. The association of alcoholic cirrhosis with blood group A (Billington, 1956) and color blindness (Cruz-Coke, 1965) has not been confirmed in later studies (Fialkow et al, 1966; Reid et al, 1968; Ranek and Julh, 1970). The evidence implicating the association between human lymphocyte antigens (HLA) and the predisposition of alcoholic liver disease is weak (Eddleston and Davis, 1982). Normally hepatocytes do not express HLA class I antigens on their surface, which make them poor targets to immunological attacks after hepatic transplantation. However, in alcoholic hepatitis and in some other liver diseases, such HLA expression may develop (Barbatis et al, 1981).

Hypergammaglobulinemia. In all alcohol-related liver diseases, immunoglobulin A (IgA) is increased and the levels correlate with the degree of injury (Iturriaga et al, 1977). The increase in serum IgA may either reflect the hepatocellular damage (MacSween, 1978) or be due to the interference with the transport of immunoglobulins at the bile duct level (Nagura et al, 1981; Kuttch et al, 1982). IgA deposits along the sinusoidal walls appear to be a specific phenomenon in alcoholic liver injury (Kater et al, 1979). Hyperglobulinemia in alcohol-related liver disease may also be contributed by increased synthesis from both antigen-specific (monoclonal) and antigen nonspecific (polyclonal) activation of B-cells (MacSween and Anthony, 1985). Recently alcoholic liver disease has been called "an IgA-associated disorder" (van de Wiel et al, 1987).

Autoantibodies and Immune Complexes. In alcohol-related liver diseases, there is a significant increase in the prevalence of antinuclear and antismooth muscle antibodies (Gluud et al, 1981). Profiles of antinuclear antibodies can be used in the differentiation of chronic active hepatitis and primary biliary cirrhosis from alcoholic liver diseases (Kurki et al, 1983). Furthermore, patients with alcoholic cirrhosis have higher levels of ss-DNA- and poly(A)-antibodies than patients with other alcoholic liver diseases (Kurki et al, 1983). The demonstration of high titers of antibodies to enterobacterial common antigen in patients with alcoholic cirrhosis suggest that endotoxins may play a role in the pathophysiology of alcoholic cirrhosis (Turunen et al, 1981).

In alcoholic liver injury, circulating antibodies to liver-specific protein and to liver membranes have been found in about one-third of the patients (Manns et al, 1980; Perperas et al, 1981; Burt et al, 1982). The latter finding, however, was not confirmed in another laboratory (Krogsgaard et al, 1982). The presence of antibodies directed against alcoholic hyaline is equally controversial (Kanagasundram et al, 1977; Kehl et al, 1981).

An increased prevalence of antibodies to microtubules has been demonstrated in patients with alcoholic liver disease but not in nonalcoholic liver diseases (Kurki et al, 1984). The production of these cytoskeleton antibodies may be due to the destruction or reorganization of the cytoskeletal structures of the liver. Furthermore, 69% of patients with alcoholic liver injury have antibodies to cytokeratin filaments (Kurki et al, 1984). Immune complexes are frequent in alcoholics (Thomas et al, 1978; Brown et al, 1983) and alcoholic hyaline has been suggested to be a component of these particles (Govindarajan et al, 1982). The nature of immunoglobulin G (IgG) complexes in alcoholic liver disease has recently been resolved (Stoltenberg and Soltis, 1984).

Cellular Immune Mechanisms. Nonspecific derangements in cellular immunity, akin to many autoimmune diseases of unknown etiology, have been described in patients with alcoholic cirrhosis (Berenyi et al, 1974). Organ-specific changes such as lymphocyte-mediated cytotoxicity to autologous liver cells in tissue cultures have also been reported (Paronetto and Lieber, 1976; Cochrane et al, 1977). Alcohol-dependent changes in either antigenicity of liver structures or reactivity of immune reflector cells may contribute to alcoholic liver injury.

Although the neutrophilic granulocytes usually predominate in the inflammatory lesions of alcoholic liver injury, mononuclear cells are frequently seen in mild alcoholic liver damage (French et al, 1979) and the sequestration of sensitized T cells in the liver has been suggested (French et al, 1979).

Lymphocytes with T8 (Si et al, 1983) and T4 phenotype (Bergroth et al, 1986) are present in alcoholic hepatitis. The frequency of Ia(HLA-DR) positive cells in mild alcoholic liver disease varies between 15% and 30% of all mononuclear cells, which indicates the activation of the local T cells (Bergroth et al, 1986). This implies that T cells in alcoholic fatty liver are not only innocent bystanders but may actively participate in the local inflammatory process. Both K and T cells have been demonstrated to be involved in cytotoxicity against autologous hepatocytes (Actis et al, 1983b; Izumi et al, 1983; Hütteroth et al, 1983).

Nutritional Factors

Although the direct hepatotoxic effect of ethanol has been indisputably proven (Chapter 3), the role of potentiating nutritional factors has not been fully excluded. If the fat content of ethanol-containing liquid diet is decreased from 32% to 25%, hepatic triglyceride accumulation significantly decreases (Lieber and DeCarli, 1970). On the other hand, replacement of dietary triglycerides containing long-chain fatty acids by fat containing medium-chain fatty acids (MCT) markedly reduces the capacity of alcohol to produce fatty liver in rats (Lieber et al, 1967).

Deficiencies in lipotrophic factors (choline and methionine) can produce fatty liver and cirrhosis in growing rats (Daft et al, 1941; Best et al, 1949). However, hepatic injury induced by choline deficiency has been suggested to be primarily an experimental disease of rats with little, if any, relevance to alcoholic liver injury, particularly in humans (Lieber, 1982).

The results in subhuman primates are controversial. The entire spectrum of alcoholic liver disease (steatosis, mild alcoholic hepatitis, and cirrhosis) has been produced in baboons by Lieber and co-workers (Lieber and DeCarli 1974; Popper and Lieber, 1980). Two other groups, however, have failed to produce fibrosis and cirrhosis in monkeys (Rogers et al, 1981; Mezey et al, 1983). The discrepancy in the results has been related to the differences in the choline contents of the diets. It was suggested that chronic alcohol feeding may exaggerate choline requirements by the monkeys (Mezey et al, 1983). However, in subsequent studies, additional choline failed to prevent the development of fibrosis in baboons (Lieber et al, 1985). The failure to produce cirrhosis in monkeys was related to the small number of animals studied, species differences, and a relatively lower alcohol intake of the monkeys as compared to baboons (Lieber et al, 1985).

Information about the nutritional status of alcoholics and of patients with alcoholic liver injury are equally controversial. This is largely due to the difficulties associated with reliable dietary assessments, especially in chronic alcoholics. Without doubt, however, heavy alcohol consumption has profound effects on nutrient economy and may produce nutritional imbalances in subjects eating normal diets (Morgan, 1982; World et al, 1985; Galambos, 1987).

It has been claimed that alcoholic liver disease is frequently recognized among well nourished alcoholic individuals manifesting no nutritional deficiency (Fallon, 1982). On the other hand, cirrhotic alcoholics were reported to have a significantly lower total food calorie intake and a significantly lower daily protein intake than noncirrhotic chronic alcoholics (Patek et al, 1975). Using established criteria to diagnose and classify protein calorie malnutrition, 248 patients with alcoholic liver disease were shown to have some evidence of malnutrition (Mendenhall et al, 1984b, 1985). The prevalence of the malnutrition correlated closely with the severity of the liver disease, with a 72% incidence of both kwashiorkor and marasmus with severe disease (Mendenhall et al, 1985). It should, however, be noted that in neither study the cause-relationship between malnutrition and liver disease was established; malnutrition at least in part might have been secondary to the liver injury and not its cause.

Data on the nutritional status of heavy middle-class drinkers is also controversial. Only subtle nutritional alterations have been documented in several studies (Neville et al, 1968; Hurt et al, 1981; Goldsmith et al, 1983; Rissanen et al, 1987). Nevertheless, these drinkers also frequently develop laboratory signs of alcoholic liver injury (Rissanen et al, 1987). In some other studies, a significantly decreased protein, fat, and cholesterol intake has been documented in heavy drinkers (Jones et al, 1982; Hillers and Massey, 1985). There is some epidemiological evidence pointing to the possible protective effect of high protein diet on alcohol-induced cirrhosis (Raymond et al, 1985).

Role of Enteric Bacteria

Liver injury, morphologically identical to alcoholic hepatitis, often follows jejunoileal bypass surgery (Moxley et al, 1974: Peters et al, 1975; Craig et al, 1980). In accordance with alcoholic liver injury, in these patients histologic evidence of pericentral fibrosis also identifies the ones at risk to develop steatonecrosis and cirrhosis (Haines et al, 1981). In addition to parenteral or enteral hyperalimentation (Heimburger et al, 1975; Ames et al, 1976; Galambos, 1976; Lockwood et al, 1977) these patients have successfully been treated with antibiotics, chloramphenicol, and metronidazole (Baker et al, 1980; Drenick et al, 1982). On this basis, the pathogenesis of the liver injury associated with jejunoileal bypass has also been related to bacterial overgrowth in the excluded segment.

It has recently been suggested that acetaldhyde produced by overgrowth of intestinal bacteria might cause subtle changes in the plasma membranes of hepatocytes, which could contribute to cell necrosis. In fact, the role of bacterial overgrowth in the production of acetaldehyde from endogenous alcohol in the small intestine is well documented (Fig. 7.5) (Baraona et al, 1986). Blind loop microorganisms have been demonstrated to be able to oxidize ethanol both in aerobic and anaerobic conditions (Baraona et al, 1986). It was concluded that bacterial overgrowth in the intestine could aggravate the direct hepatotoxicity of alcohol and should be considered as an additional risk factor for alcoholic liver disease (Baraona et al, 1986).

Hepatitis B Infection and Alcoholic Liver Injury

Several studies have revealed the higher prevalence of markers of hepatitis B virus (HBV) in alcoholics than in matched controls (Mills et al, 1979; Hislop et al, 1981; Periente et al, 1981; Gluud et al, 1982a; Chevilotte et al, 1983).

An increased prevalence of anti-HBV antibodies has also been observed both in outpatient alcoholics and in hospitalized patients with alcoholic liver disease (Gluud et al, 1982b). In some studies, the highest prevalence of HBV has been found in cirrhotics (Milles et al, 1979; Hislop et al, 1981). In a prospective study in Italy, the HBV carriers were found to have a greater risk of developing hepatomegaly and raised liver enzymes when drinking less than 80 g alcohol daily than controls, suggesting that the presence of HBV could be a contributing factor in the development of alcoholic liver injury (Villa et al, 1982). However, contradictory results have been reported from Japan (Ishii et al, 1985).

Eight of 51 subjects with alcoholic liver disease were shown to have HBV DNA in the liver and in five of these the DNA was integrated into the genome (Bréchot et al, 1982). This and some other evidence may suggest in alcoholics a relationship between viral hepatitis and hepatocellular carcinoma (Bréchot et al, 1982; Shafritz et al, 1981). An enhanced hepatocarcinogenesis from drinking as compared to nondrinking HBV carriers has been reported (Ohnishi et al, 1982), but this is not supported by an earlier study in which there was no difference in the prevalence of hepatitis infection in alcoholic cirrhotics with or without hepatocellular carcinoma (Omata et al, 1979).

Clinical Aspects

In this chapter it is impossible to deal with all the clinical aspects of alcoholic liver diseases. On the other hand, the clinical manifestations, natural course, diagnosis, differential diagnosis, treatment, and prognosis of alcoholic fatty liver, alcoholic hepatitis, and cirrhosis are

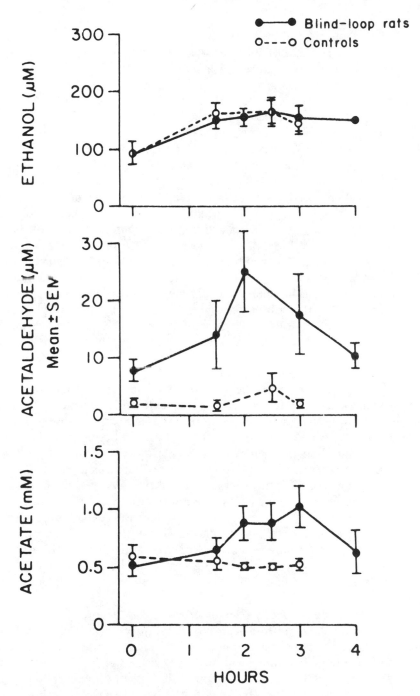

FIGURE 7.5. Portal concentrations of ethanol and its metabolites after intragastric administration of sucrose to the control rats and to the rats with jejunal blind loops (Baraona et al, 1986).

well presented in the main medical textbooks and in some recent reviews (Pimstone and French, 1984; Hall 1985; Ishii et al, 1985; Lieber and Salaspuro, 1985; Mendenhall and the VA Cooperative Study of Alcoholic Hepatitis 1985; Galambos, 1987; Salaspuro, 1987b). Some of the most recent advances in the diagnosis and treatment of alcoholic liver diseases will be shortly reviewed here.

Clinical Assessment of Fibrosis

At each stage of alcoholic liver disease (fatty liver, hepatitis, or cirrhosis), the clinician must distinguish between the acute reversible forms of alcoholic liver disease and the chronic, mainly irreversible, cirrhosis. Therefore, the assessment of the degree of fibrosis (the presence of excess connective tissue), fibrogenesis (the formation of excess connective tissue), and fibrolysis (the resolution of excess connective tissue) is of great importance. So far, the liver biopsy has been the method of choice in the evaluation of the disease process in the liver. However, liver biopsy is an invasive method, which cannot be repeated too often. Consequently, the search for new methods for assessing the various aspects of liver fibrogenesis has been very active during the recent years (Rojkind and Kershenobich, 1983; Hahn and Schuppan, 1985, 1987; Risteli and Risteli 1986).

Enzymes and metabolic products of collagen and other proteins may be used to quantitate altered connective tissue metabolism in alcoholic liver diseases. These parameters can be measured in liver biopsies, serum or plasma and in urine (Hahn and Schuppan, 1987). So far, the most promising blood test for clinical purposes has been the radioimmunoassay of the aminoterminal procollagen type III peptide (PIIIP) (Rohde et al, 1979; Schuppan et al, 1986). Several clinical studies have demonstrated that the determination of serum PIIIP may be helpful in monitoring fibrogenesis in alcoholic liver injury (Nakano et al, 1983; Niemelä et al, 1983; Savolainen et al, 1984a). Serum propeptide concentrations correlate with the degree of liver fibrosis and also with the degree of hepatic inflammation. Highest values were observed in patients with alcoholic hepatitis in whom numerous Mallory bodies have been found. In another study, a good correlation was found only between the degree of hepatocellular necroinflammation but not with hepatic fibrosis (Colombo et al, 1985). PIIIP distinguishes between alcoholic fatty liver and alcoholic hepatitis with a very high efficacy (Fig. 7.6). Moderately increased values are, however, found less frequently in patients with simple fatty liver (Savolainen et al, 1984a), and the test does not differentiate patients with simple fatty liver from those with fatty liver and early fibrosis. PIIIP has also been reported to be increased in 33% of patients with idiopathic hemochromatosis (Colombo et al, 1985). Consequently, liver biopsy is still necessary in the establishment of the diagnosis in most of the cases.

Specific radioimmunoassays for the determination of type IV collagen and laminin-related antigens in human serum in alcoholic liver disease have also been developed (Niemelä et al, 1985). These tests appear to differentiate patients with alcoholic hepatitis and cirrhosis from those with inactive cirrhosis or with fatty liver (Niemelä et al, 1985), but the true clinical value of these tests has not yet been fully examined. Recently, a modified PIIIP assay using Fab fragments of the antibody has been shown to discriminate between simple fatty liver and perivenular fibrosis in a significant number of subjects (Sato et al, 1986; Nouchi et al, 1987).

Clinical Assessment of the Alcoholic Etiology of the Liver Disease

In addition to the establishment of the degree of liver injury, the clinician must also distinguish between alcoholic and nonalcoholic causes of liver injury. This is important for the subsequent treatment of the patient, as exemplified by a case of chronic active hepatitis in an alcoholic (Goldberg et al, 1977). In the evaluation of the patient with either an incidental finding of pathological laboratory values pointing to the liver damage or with more advanced symptomalogy requiring hospitalization, the history of heavy alcohol intake for weeks or months before hospital admission is strongly suggestive of an alcoholic etiology for the liver injury. For this purpose, simplified screening questions and various questionnaires have been developed (for ref. see Salaspuro, 1986, 1988). These questionnaires rather well identify severe alcoholism with its dismal social consequences, but in the evaluation of a heavy drinker's personal drinking history they often are unreliable. Therefore the search for laboratory markers of excessive alcohol consumption (Chapter 11; Salaspuro 1986, 1988) and/or for the differentiation between alcohol and nonalcoholic liver injury (Salaspuro, 1987b) has been active during the recent years.

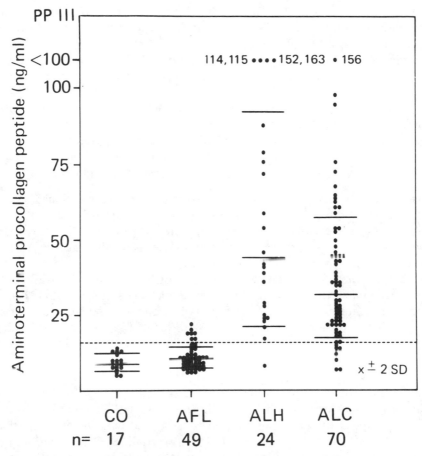

FIGURE 7.6. Serum concentrations of aminoterminal type III procollagen peptide (PIIIP) in 143 patients with alcoholic liver disease as compared to 17 controls (Hahn and Schuppan, 1985).

Serum Enzymes in the Diagnosis of Alcohol-related Liver Injury. Elevated levels of serum enzymes are frequently associated not only with alcohol-related liver injury (Salaspuro, 1987b) but also with excessive alcohol consumption and alcoholism without significant tissue injury (Chapter 11; Salaspuro 1986, 1988). In most cases, it is possible to determine the tissue from which the elevated enzyme is derived, but only occasionally enzyme changes reflect the quantity of tissue injury.

It is generally believed that an elevated level of serum aspartate aminotransferase (ASAT) and alanine aminotransferase (ALAT) in an alcoholic or a heavy consumer indicates alcohol-induced organ damage. However, they are frequently slightly elevated also in apparently healthy male populations with normal drinking habits (unpublished observation in a general health screening of 2931 men). In patients with histologically proven liver injury, the most characteristic finding in favor of the alcoholic etiology of the liver injury is an inverted ASAT–ALAT ratio (Deritis et al, 1972; Cohen and Kaplan 1979). An ASAT–ALAT ratio greater than 1.5 can be considered as suggestive of alcoholic liver disease, and a ratio greater than 2 is indicative (Cohen and Kaplan, 1979; Correia et al, 1981). Pyridoxal 5-phosphate depletion has been found to be at least in part responsible for the low serum ALAT–ASAT ratio (Matloff, 1980).

Still better discrimination between alcoholic and nonalcoholic origin of the liver disease may be achieved by determining the ratio of gamma-glutamyltransferase (GGT) to alkaline phosphatase. If the ratio exceeds 1.4, the specificity of the finding in favor of alcoholic liver disease is 78% (Lai et al, 1982). GGT so far is the most widely used laboratory marker of alcoholism and heavy drinking. Its significance in this field is reviewed in detail elsewhere (Chapter 11; Salaspuro, 1986, 1987b).

The determination of the mitochondrial isoenzyme of ASAT improves the diagnostic value of ASAT determination. The ratio of mitochondrial isoenzyme to total enzyme over 4 is highly suggestive for alcohol-related liver injury (Nalpas et al, 1984, 1986).

In general, the determination of serum activities of other enzymes such as ornithine carbamyl transferase, lactate dehydrogenase, isocitrate dehydrogenase, sorbitol dehydrogenase, alcohol dehydrogenase, guanase, aldolase, alkaline phosphatase, glutathione S-transferase, or beta-hexosaminidase do not significantly improve the diagnostic information obtained with more conventional laboratory markers of liver injury (Salaspuro, 1987b).

Other Tests in the Diagnosis of Alcohol-related Liver Disease. As mentioned, the incidence of serum nonorgan- and organ-specific antibodies has been reported to be either increased or normal in alcoholic liver diseases. However, the prevalences, as well as titers, are generally low. On this basis, the occurrence of tissue antibodies is highly suggestive of a nonalcoholic etiology or pathogenetic mechanism. Serum IgA is infrequently increased in patients with alcoholic liver injury. The magnitude of increase of IgA and IgA–IgG ratio can be used to differentiate alcoholic from non-alcoholic liver diseases (Iturriaga et al, 1977).

New laboratory markers for the early detection of alcoholism and heavy drinking are currently widely evaluated (Chapter 11; Salaspuro 1986, 1987b, 1988). Their clinical value as well as that of various test combinations in the differential diagnosis of liver diseases will be available in the near future.

Approaches in the Treatment of Alcoholic Liver Diseases

Prognosis for acute and chronic alcoholic liver disease is dramatically improved by abstinence from alcohol, whereas continued consumption is associated with increased morbidity and mortality (Brunt et al, 1974; Galambos, 1974; Tygstrup et al, 1976). In addition, new drugs and treatment models have been actively tried especially for alcoholic hepatitis and for the inhibition of fibrogenesis in alcoholic cirrhosis.

Hormones. The most extensively tested drugs for alcoholic hepatitis have been steroids, with at least 10 randomized double-blind trials with either prednisolone or prednisone being performed since 1971 (Conn, 1985). Some controlled prospective studies reported significantly improved survival of patients with severe alcoholic hepatitis but not in those with milder illness (Hellman et al, 1971). Several subsequent studies, however, have not confirmed these findings (Porter et al, 1971; Schlichting et al, 1976; Lesesne et al, 1978; Maddrey et al, 1978). Indeed, in one of the controlled studies an increased risk of fungal infections associated with corticosteroid therapy was reported (Blitzer et al, 1977).

Anabolic steroids have been found to be efficacious in the treatment of alcoholic fatty liver in two studies (Jabbari and Leevy, 1967; Mendenhall, 1968), but not in a third one (Fenster, 1966). In alcoholic hepatitis and cirrhosis, androgens have been demonstrated to be ineffective (Mendenhall et al, 1984a; Gluud, 1985).

Intravenous infusion of insulin and glucagon has been shown to be effective in alcoholic hepatitis (Baker et al, 1981), but confirming results are still needed from other trials.

Nutritional Factors. Daily infusion of 70 to 85 g of amino acids has been reported to improve the symptoms of alcoholic hepatitis and to decrease mortality (Nasrallah and Galambos, 1980). Similar results have been obtained in severe alcoholic hepatitis with the combination of amino acid hyperalimentation, testosterone, and prednisolone (Gill et al, 1984). The addition of lipotrophs such as choline to the diet had no beneficial value in treating alcoholic fatty liver (Post et al, 1952). Carnitine deficiency has been documented in liver cirrhosis (Rudman et al, 1977), but controlled trials about its effectiveness are not available.

Propylthiouracil. Chronic alcohol consumption has been suggested to create in experimental animals hepatic hypermetabolic state akin to hyperthyroidism (Israel et al, 1973; Bernstein et al, 1975). On this basis, propylthiouracil was suggested for the treatment of alcoholic liver disease (Orrego et al, 1979). The beneficial effects of propylthiouracil reported by Orrego et al were not, however, confirmed by another subsequent study (Halle et al, 1982). Most recently the administration of propylthiouracil was reported to reduce significantly mortality due to alcoholic liver disease (Orrego et al, 1987).

Penicillamine. Penicillamine has been shown to reduce the active deposition of collagen in alcoholic hepatitis (Resnick et al, 1974). However, as compared to a placebo, penicillamine had no effect on mortality.

Colchicine. In one randomized study with 43 patients with alcoholic cirrhosis, colchicine, which was given to patients for as long as four years, was shown to produce a remarkable decrease in liver fibrosis (Kershenobich et al, 1979). As compared to controls, a better clinical improvement was also documented, but the difference in mortality did not reach statistical significance with this rather small sample. Further studies on this interesting area are warranted.

Catechin, thioctic acid, silymarin (Legalon), and malotilate. Catechin (+)-cyanidol-3 and thioctic acid have been found to be ineffective in the treatment of alcohol-related liver disease (Colman et al, 1980; Marshall et al, 1982); silymarin and malotilate are still agents under the evaluation.

PANCREAS

Chronic heavy alcohol consumption is associated with a spectrum of pancreatic manifestations that include acute hemorrhagic, edematous, relapsing, chronic relapsing, and painless pancreatitis. As in the case of the liver, the natural courses, clinical manifestations, and treatment of these diseases are well described in all main gastroenterological textbooks and in some recent reviews (Sarles and Laugier, 1981; Lieber, 1982; Geokas, 1984; Sarles, 1985, 1986; Singer, 1985; Singer and Goebell, 1985; Malagelada, 1986; Singh, 1986). Therefore, only the main pathogenetic associations between alcohol and pancreas are included in this chapter.

Acute Effects of Alcohol on Pancreas

Alcohol and Pancreatic Exocrine Secretion
The effects of ethanol on the secretory functions of the pancreas are greatly modified by the experimental conditions and animal model used (Singer and Goebell, 1985; Singh, 1986). Ethanol given intragastrically or intraduodenally has been reported not to alter (Madding et al, 1968), stimulate (Tiscornia et al, 1973, 1974; Korsten et al, 1979, 1981), or inhibit pancreatic secretion (Mott et al, 1972; Marin et al, 1973; Tiscornia et al, 1977). Similar controversial results have been obtained after intravenous administration of ethanol (Dreiling et al, 1952; Solomon et al, 1974; Lowenfels et al, 1968). From these studies it can be concluded that intravenous ethanol inhibits secretin-stimulated pancreatic secretion, but in the absence of secretin, pancreatic secretion is either unchanged or stimulated. Recently, a physiopathogenetic hypothesis of alcoholic pancreatitis—supranormal ecbolic stimulation of the "pancreon" units secondary to the loss of the negative component of pancreas innervation—was presented (Tiscornia and Dreiling, 1987).

Alcohol and Gastrointestinal Hormones
Gastrin, which stimulates pancreatic enzyme secretion, is insignificantly or only slightly effected by oral or intravenous ethanol (Cooke, 1972; Becker et al, 1974). Beer and red wine, but not whisky and pure ethanol, are potent stimulants of gastrin (Singer et al, 1983a).

Studies on the effects of alcohol on secretin release are controversial. Vodka has been shown to increase plasma secretin levels (Straus et al, 1975), whereas intragastric and intra-duodenal administration of pure alcohol had no effect (Fahrenkrug et al, 1977; Llanos et al, 1977; Demol et al, 1982).

In humans, oral alcohol had no effect on serum levels of pancreatic polypeptide (PP) (Singer et al, 1983b). In dogs, only a high dose of intragastric ethanol increased plasma PP levels, but the change was only 12% of the PP response to meal (Singer et al, 1983b).

Metabolic Effects of Alcohol on the Pancreas

Pancreatic involvement in ethanol oxidation has been suggested as a possible pathogenetic mechanism leading to histological changes observed in the pancreas after alcohol consumption (Darle et al, 1970; Nizze et al, 1979). Only low activities of alcohol dehydrogenase have been found in the pancreas (Clemente et al, 1977; Guynn et al, 1982). In rat pancreas there is a small amount of ethanol acyltransferase responsible for the esterification of fatty acids with ethanol and also some aldehyde dehydrogenase (Estival et al, 1981). An acute dose of ethanol increases pancreatic lactate and decreases the cytoplasmic free NAD^+-NADH ratio (Guynn et al, 1982). Evidently, pancreas is able to metabolize ethanol at least to some extent, but how this might contribute to pancreatic functions or to the pathogenesis of alcohol-related pancreas injury is still unclear.

Many human organs including pancreas metabolize ethanol through a recently described nonoxidative pathway to form fatty acid ethyl esters. This nonoxidative pathway of ethanol metabolism has recently been related to the pathophysiology of alcoholic pancreatitis (Laposata and Lange, 1986). There is a lot of evidence suggesting that in the pathogenesis of alcoholic pancreatitis, oxygen-derived free radicals, generated by activated xanthine oxidase, may play a central role as in the case of alcoholic liver injury (Sanfey et al, 1986).

It has been suggested that ethanol causes a spasm of the sphincter of Oddi, resulting in obstruction of the flow of pancreatic juice. However, the reported changes in the pressure of the sphincter of Oddi have been small and, in part, also controversial (Pirola and Davis, 1970; Becker and Sharp, 1985). Abnormalities of the function of the sphincter of Oddi have also been associated with both biliary-pancreatic and duodeno-pancreatic reflux. These factors have been suggested to initiate the intrapancreatic autodigestion of the pancreatic tissue. However, the evidence in favor of the existence of these pathogenetic mechanisms behind acute alcoholic pancreatitis is rather scanty (Pirola and Davis, 1970).

Chronic Effects of Alcohol on the Pancreas

Pancreatic Steatosis. The earliest histological change in the pancreas of alcoholic patients is fat accumulation in acinar cells (Bordalo et al, 1977; Dreiling and Bordalo, 1977). The deposition of intracellular lipid droplets within the rough endoplasmic reticulum occurs both in experimental animals and in patients with chronic pancreatitis (Darle et al, 1970; Bordalo et al, 1977; Singh et al, 1982). These findings suggest profound ethanol-induced changes in the metabolism of pancreatic cells.

Chronic feeding of ethanol to rats as a part of a totally liquid diet produces pancreatic steatosis in three weeks (Wilson et al, 1982). Lipid vesicles are localized principally at the basis of pancreatic acinar cells. There is also a significant increase in the pancreatic content of cholesteryl ester and serum cholesterol without changes in other lipids (Wilson et al, 1982, 1984).

Pancreatic Protein Secretion; Protein Plugs. The first morphological change in chronic pancreatitis is the precipitation of normal proteins in the ducts to form plugs, which later calcify and form stones (Sarles, 1985, 1986; Sarles et al, 1971). This results in irregular dilatation of pancreatic ducts associated with loss of the lining epithelium and pancreatic cysts and disappearance of acini and ducts in the territory drained by a blocked duct (Nakamura et al, 1972).

Chronic alcohol consumption produces hyperconcentration of proteins in pancreatic juice of experimental animals and humans (Sarles et al, 1971; Harada et al, 1979; Jalovaara, 1979; Sahel and Sarles, 1979; Renner et al, 1980; Noel-Jorand et al, 1981). As a consequence of a high output of pancreatic proteins, ductular protein plugs and acinar atrophy similar to those seen in patients with chronic alcoholic pancreatitis occurs also in animal models of chronic alcoholic pancreatitis (Sarles et al, 1977). However, histological changes, protein plug formation, and protein hypersecretion were not found in rats fed ethanol as 36% of the total calories (Singh et al, 1982; Singh, 1983). This study demonstrated complex and nonparallel changes in the secretion of the pancreatic enzymes especially in the presence of a high-fat diet (LaSure et al, 1986). Interestingly, in some epidemiological studies on human chronic pancreatitis, there is an association between high-lipid intake and risk of developing pancreatitis (Durbec and Sarles, 1978), although contradictory results also exist (Wilson et al, 1985).

Chronic feeding of ethanol to dogs results in increased protein and decreased bicarbonate concentration in pure pancreatic juice (Tiscornia et al, 1975; Schmidt et al, 1982). This is associated with the secretion of white protein plugs with a crystal core containing desquamated ductal and acinar cells.

In human alcoholics without evidence of pancreatic disease, there is an increased concentration of protein and trypsinogen in endoscopically collected pure pancreatic juice (Sahel and Sarles, 1979; Renner et al, 1980; Planche et al, 1982). In addition there is an increase in albumin, immunoglobulins, and hexosamine, which may increase the viscosity of the pancreatic juice (Clemente et al, 1971; Harada et al, 1980; Harada et al, 1981). Complexes of chymotrypsin and alfa-1-proteinase inhibitor have been found in the pancreatic juice of patients with chronic pancreatitis (Misczuk-Jamska et al, 1983).

Some alcoholics and patients with chronic pancreatitis have *protein plugs* in pancreatic juice. These contain clusters of epithelial cells, leucocytes, and lactoferrin (Figarella and Sarles, 1975; Harada et al, 1981; Cuy et al, 1983; Bockman et al, 1985). In electronmicroscopy, protein plugs are amorphous or fibrillar (Bockman et al, 1973, 1985). Plugs contain two fractions: (1) proteins of the pancreatic juice and (2) so-called "stone protein" (mol. weight 13.500) located in the endoplasmic reticulum and zymogen granules (De Caro et al, 1979; Lechene de La Porte et al, 1981). A messenger RNA coding for stone protein has been demonstrated in the human pancreas (Bernard et al, 1984). Most recently, this stone protein has been characterized in detail (Sarles, 1986). It has also been suggested that the stone protein is a degradation product of trypsinogen (Figarella et al, 1984). So far, the basic pathogenetic mechanisms leading to the formation of protein plugs and their relationship to ethanol are still unclear.

GASTROINTESTINAL TRACT

Esophagus

Acute Effects of Alcohol

High ethanol concentrations (40%) cause mucosal damage of the esophagus in canine and rabbits whereas lower concentrations are less harmful (Shirazi and Platz, 1978; Salo 1983). This injury may be potentiated by bile acids and hydrogen ions (Chung et al, 1977).

Acute application of ethanol reduces lower esophageal sphincter pressure (LESP) and its response to pentagastrin and protein stimulation (Hogan et al, 1972; Mayer et al, 1978). This is associated with a reduction of primary esophageal peristalsis and the amplitude of esophageal contractions. Both of these effects increase the ethanol-induced acid reflux (Kaufmann and Kaye, 1979). The harmful local effects of ethanol on esophageal mucosa may be potentiated by ethanol caused decrease in saliva secretion (Wienbeck and Berges, 1985).

Chronic Effects of Alcohol

Esophageal dysfunction is common in alcoholics (Winship et al, 1968) even in the absence esophagitis and neuropathy (Keshavarzian et al, 1987). This may be potentiated by vagal damage, which is a feature of alcoholic polyneuropathy (Duncan et al, 1980). Both the acute and chronic effects of alcohol may contribute to the development of esophagitis, Barrett's syndrome, and esophageal carcinoma (Wienbeck and Berges, 1985).

Stomach

Effects of Alcohol

Gastric Motility and Secretion. In most studies, ethanol has been shown to delay gastric emptying (Bode, 1980; Wienbeck and Berges, 1985). This is neither caused by the ethanol-induced suppression of gastric motility (Keshavarzian et al, 1986) nor by a spasm of pylorus (Phaosawasdi et al, 1979).

Low ethanol concentrations stimulate acid secretion, whereas concentrations above 20% may be inhibitory (Davenport, 1967). Beer and wine but not pure alcohol increase serum gastrin (Singer et al, 1983a). Histamine release, cAMP (cyclic adenylic acid), prostaglandins, and an increase in the activity of gastric adenylate cyclase have all been related to the effects of ethanol on the regulation of gastric secretion (Dinoso et al, 1976; Puurunen, 1978; Seitz et al, 1983; Reichstein et al, 1986). Chronic consumption of alcohol may decrease or increase gastric acid secretion; the end result probably depends on test conditions (Chey, 1972; Kuo and Shanbour, 1983).

Mucosal Damage. Acute ingestion of ethanol causes erythema, mucosal hemorrhage, and eosinophilic infiltration (Gottfried et al, 1978; Ito and Lacy, 1985). These changes are associated with a drop in gastric mucosal potential difference (Caspary, 1975; Morris et al, 1984) and with the disruption of gastric mucosal barrier (Dawson and Cooke, 1978). Bicarbonate leakage through the damaged mucosa occurs and has been suggested to protect against further injury (Dayton et al, 1983; Takeuchi and Okabe, 1983). Mucosal damage is associated with early vascular injury and increased vascular permeability (Szabo, 1985). The end stage of the mucosal damage is either acute or chronic gastritis the details of which have been recently reviewed (Bode, 1980; Lieber, 1982; Wienbeck and Berges, 1985). During the last few years several drugs have been suggested for the prevention and treatment of acute alcoholic gastritis (Hollander et al, 1985; Ohno et al, 1985; Robert et al, 1985; Tarnawski et al, 1985).

Intestine

Chronic alcoholism is often associated with steatorrhea, malnutrition, or simple diarrhea (Mezey, 1975). These conditions may be derived from abnormal pancreatic and hepatobiliary secretion, disturbed intestinal function, or from the combination of all the above. There are many reviews on the acute and chronic effects of ethanol on the morphology and function of small intestine (Wilson and Hoyumpa, 1979; Bode, 1980; Beck and Dinda, 1981; Lieber, 1982; Mezey, 1985) and some of the effects are mentioned here.

The mean mucosal surface per square millimeter of jejunum is decreased in alcoholics (Bode et al, 1982) and this damage may be potentiated by simultaneous folate deficiency (Hermos et al, 1972). Acute ingestion of ethanol may produce minor injuries in the jejunal villi both in man and experimental animals (Baraona et al, 1974; Gottfried et al, 1978; Zucoloto and Rossi, 1979; Millan et al, 1980). These changes may be associated with decreases in the activities of intestinal enzymes such as lactase and sucrase (Perlow et al, 1977; Madzarova-Nohejlova, 1971). However, controversial results have been obtained in some studies on experimental animals (Mezey, 1985; Zarling et al, 1986).

As a final consequence of the slight morphological and secretory abnormalities in the intestine caused by acute and chronic consumption of alcohol, minor deficiencies in the absorption of amino acids, glucose, water, sodium, fat, minerals, drugs, and vitamins are frequently seen in alcoholics (for ref. see Bode, 1980; Lieber, 1982; Mezey, 1985).

REFERENCES

Actis G, Mieli-Vergani G, Portmann B, Eddlestone ALWF, Williams DM: Lymphocyte cytotoxicity to autologous hepatocytes in alcoholic liver disease. *Liver* 1983; 3:8–12.

Ames FC, Copeland EM, Leeb DC, Moore DL, Dudrick SJ: Liver dysfunction following small-bowel bypass for obesity. Nonoperative treatment of fatty metamorphosis with parenteral hyperalimentation. *JAMA* 1976; 235:1249–1252.

Baker AL: Management of liver failure in a patient following jejunoileal bypass. *Gastroenterology* 1980; 78:1593–1601.

Baker AL, Jaspan JB, Haines NW, Hartfield GE, Krager PS, Schneider JF, The University of Chicago Medical House Staff: A randomized clinical trial of insulin and glucagon infusion for treatment of alcoholic hepatitis. Progress report in 50 patients. *Gastroenterology* 1980; 80:1410–1414.

Baptista A, Bianchi L, de Groote J, Desmet VJ, Gedigk P, Korb G, MacSween RNM, Popper H, Poulsen H, Scheuer PJ, Schmid M, Thaler H, Wepler W: Alcoholic liver disease: Morphological manifestations. Review by an International Group. *Lancet* 1981; i:707–711.

Baraona E, Julkunen R, Tannenbaum L, Lieber CS: Role of intestinal bacterial overgrowth in ethanol production and metabolism in rats. *Gastroenterology* 1986; 90:103–110.

Baraona E, Pirola RL, Lieber CS: Small Intestinal damage and changes in cell population produced by ethanol ingestion in the rat. *Gastroenterology* 1974; 66:226–234.

Barbatis C, Woods J, Morton JA, Fleming KA, McMichael A, McGee JO'D: Immunohistochemical analysis of HLA (A,B,C) antigens in liver disease using a monoclonal antibody. *Gut* 1981; 22:985–991.

Beck IT, Dinda PK: Acute exposure of small intestine to ethanol; Effects on morphology and function. *Dig Dis Sci* 1981; 9:817–838.

Becker HD, Reeder DD, Thompson JC: Gastrin release by ethanol in man and dogs. *Ann Surg* 1974; 906:1979.

Becker JM, Sharp SW: Effect of alcohol on cyclical myoelectric activity of the opossum sphincter of Oddi. *J Surg Res* 1985; 38:343–349.

Berenyi MR, Straus B, Cruz D: In vitro and in vivo studies of cellular immunity in alcoholic cirrhosis. *Am J Dig Dis* 1974; 19:199–205.

Bergroth V, Konttinen YT, Segerberg-Konttinen M, Ollikainen V, Salaspuro M: Phenotypic in situ characterization of lymphocytes in mild alcoholic liver disease. *Acta Path Microbiol Immunol Scand* Sect A, 1986; 94:337–341.

Bernard JP, De Caro A, Giorgi D, Multigner R, Lapointe R, Sarles H, Dagorn JC: A messenger RNA from human pancreas code for the pancreatic stone protein. *Dig Dis Sci* 1984; 29:941.

Bernstein J, Videla L, Israel Y: Hormonal influences in the development of the hypermetabolic state of the liver produced by chronic administration of ethanol. *J Pharmacol Exp Ther* 1975; 192:583–591.

Best CH, Hartroft WS, Lucas SS, Ridout JH: Liver damage produced by feeding alcohol or sugar and its prevention by choline. *Br Med J* 1949; 2:1001–1006.

Bhathal PS: Presence of modified fibroblasts in cirrhotic livers in man. *Pathology* 1972; 4:139–144.

Billington BP: A note on the distribution of ABO blood groups in bronchiectasis and portal cirrhosis. *Aust Ann Med* 1956; 5:20–22.

Birschbach HR, Harinasuta U, Zimmerman JH: Alcoholic steatonecrosis. II. Prospective study of prevalence of Mallory bodies in biopsy specimens and comparison of severity of hepatic disease in patients with and without this histological feature. *Gastroenterology* 1974; 66:1195–1202.

Blake JE, Compton KV, Schmidt RNW, Orrego H: Accuracy of death certificates in the diagnosis of alcoholic liver cirrhosis. *Alcoholism Clin Exp Res* 1988; 12:168–172.

Blitzer BL, Mutchnick MG, Joshi PH, Phillips MM, Fessel JM, Conn HO: Adrenocorticosteroid therapy in alcoholic hepatitis. A prospective double-blind randomized study. *Am J Dig Dis* 1977; 22: 477–484.

Bockman DE, Schiller WR, Suriyapa C, Mutschler JHW, Anderson MC: Fine structure of early experimental acute pancreatitis in dogs. *Lab Invest* 1973; 28:584–592.

Bockman DE, Singh M, Laugier H, Sarles H: Alcohol and the integrity of the pancreas. *Scand J Gastroenterol* 1985; 20(Suppl. 112):106–113.

Bode JCH: Alcohol and the gastrointestinal tract, in Frick P, von Harnack G-A, Martini GA, Prader A (eds): *Advances in Internal Medicine and Pediatrics.* Berlin, Heidelberg, Springer-Verlag, 1980, pp 1–75.

Bode JCH, Knüppel H, Schwerk W, Lorenz-Meyer H, Dürr HK: Quantitative histomorphometric study of the jejunal mucosa in chronic alcoholics. *Digestion* 1982; 23:265–270.

Bordalo O, Concalves D, Noronha M, Cristina ML, Salgadinho A, Dreiling DA: Newer concept for the pathogenesis of chronic alcoholic pancreatitis. *Am J Gastroenterol* 1977; 68:278–285.

Bréchot C, Nalpas B, Courouce A-M, Duhamel G, Callard P, Carnot F, Tiollais P, Berthelot P: Evidence that hepatitis B virus has a role in liver-cell carcinoma in alcoholic liver disease. *N Engl J Med* 1982; 306:1384–1387.

Bronfenmajer S, Schaffner F, Popper H: Fat storing cells (lipocytes) in human liver. *Arch Pathol* 1966; 82:447–453.

Brown SE, Steward MW, Viola L, Howard CR, Murray-Lyon IM: Chronic liver disease: The detection and characterization of circulating immune complexes. *Immunology* 1983; 49:673–683.

Brunt PW, Kew MC, Scheuer PJ, Sherlock S: Studies in alcoholic liver disease in Britain. I. Clinical and pathological patterns related to natural history. *Gut* 1974; 15:52–58.

Bruun K, Edwards G. Lumio M. Mäkelä K, Pan L, Popham RE, Room R, Schmidt W, Skog O-J, Sulkunen P, Österberg E: Alcohol control policies in public health perspective. *Report of an International Working Group.* Helsinki, The Finnish Foundation for Alcohol Studies vol. 25, 1975.

Burt AD, Anthony RS, Hislop WS, Bouchier IAD, MacSween RNM: Liver membrane antibodies in alcoholic liver disease. I. Prevalence and immunoglobulin class. *Gut* 1982; 23:221–225.

Carter EA, Wands JR: Ethanol-induced inhibition of liver cell function: I. Effect of ethanol on hormone stimulated hepatocyte DNA synthesis and the role of ethanol metabolism. *Alcoholism Clin Exp Res* 1988; 12:555–562.

Caspary WF: Einfluss von Aspirin, Antacida, Alkohol und Gallensäuren auf die elektrische Potential-differenz des menschlichen Magens. *Dtsch Med Wochenschr* 1975; 100:1263–1268.

Castelli WP, Doyle JT, Gordon T, Hames OG, Hjortland MC, Hulley SB, Kagan A, Zukel WJ: Alcohol and blood lipids. The cooperative lipoprotein phenotyping study. *Lancet* 1977; ii:153–155.

Chevilotte G, Durber JP, Gerolami A, Berthezene P, Bidart JM, Camatte R: Interaction between hepatitis B virus and alcohol consumption in liver cirrhosis. *Gastroenterology* 1983; 85:141–145.

Chey WY: Alcohol and gastric mucosa. *Digestion* 1972; 7:239–251.

Chung RSK, Johnson GM, DenBesten L: Effect of sodium taurocholate and ethanol on hydrogen ion absorption in rabbit esophagus. *Am J Dig Dis* 1977; 22:582–588.

Clemente F, Durand S, Laval J, Thouvenot JP, Ribet A: Metabolisme de l'éthanol par le pancréas de rat. I. Recherche des éventuelles enzymes impliquées et étude de leurs variations de niveau. *Gastroenterol Clin Biol* 1977; 1:39.

Clemente F, Ribeiro T, Colomb E, Figarella C, Sarles H: Comparaison des protéines de sucs pancréatiques humains normaux et pathologiques. Dosage protéines sériques et mise en évidence d'une protéine particuliére dans la pancréatite chronique calcifiante. *Biochim Biophys Acta* 1971; 251:456–466.

Coates RA, Halliday ML, Rankin JG, Feinman SV, Fisher MM: Risk of fatty infiltration or cirrhosis of the liver in relation to ethanol consumption: A case-control study. *Clin Invest Med* 1986; 9:26–32.

Cochrane AMG, Moussouros A, Portman B, McFarlane OG, Thomson AD, Eddleston ALWF, Williams R: Lymphocyte cytotoxicity for isolated hepatocytes in alcoholic liver disease. *Gastroenterology* 1977; 72:918–923.

Cohen JS, Kaplan MM: The SGOT/SGPT ratio—An indicator of alcoholic liver disease. *Am J Dig Dis* 1979; 24:835–838.

Colman JC, Morgan MY, Scheuer PJ, Sherlock S: Treatment of alcohol-related liver disease with (+)-cyanidanol-3: A randomized double blind trial. *Gut* 1980; 21:965–969.

Colombo M, Annoni G, Donato MF, Conte D, Martines D, Zaramella MG, Bianchi PA, Piperno A, Tiribelli C: Serum type III procollagen peptide in alcoholic liver disease and idiopathic hemochromatosis: Its relationship to hepatic fibrosis, activity of the disease and iron overload. *Hepatology* 1985; 5:475–479.

Comporti M: Lipid peroxidation and cellular damage in toxic liver injury. *Lab Invest* 1985; 53:599–622.

Conn HO: The rational management of alcoholic liver disease, in Hall P (ed): *Alcoholic Liver Disease; Pathobiology, Epidemiology and Clinical Aspects.* London, Edward Arnold Ltd, 1985, pp 266–289.

Cooke AR: Ethanol and gastric acid secretion. *Gastroenterology* 1979; 69:501–559.

Correia JP, Alves PS, Camilo EA: SGOT-SGPT ratios. *Dig Dis Sci* 1981; 26:284.

Craig RM, Neumann T, Jeejeebhoy KN, Yokoo H: Severe hepatocellular reaction resembling alcoholic hepatitis with cirrhosis after massive small bowel resection and prolonged total parenteral nutrition. *Gastroenterology* 1980; 79:131–137.

Cruz-Coke R: Colour-blindness and cirrhosis of the liver. *Lancet* 1965; 1:1131–1133.

Cuy O, Robles-Diaz G, Adrich Z, Sahel J, Sarles H: Protein content of precipitates present in pancreatic juice of alcoholic subjects and patients with chronic calcifying pancreatitis. *Gastroenterology* 1983; 84:102–107.

Daft FS, Sebrell WH, Lillie RD: Production and apparent prevention of a dietary liver cirrhosis in rats. *Proc Soc Exp Biol Med* 1941; 48:228–29.

Darle N, Ekholm R, Edlund Y: Ultrastructure of the rat exocrine pancreas after long term intake of ethanol. *Gastroenterology* 1970; 58:62–72.

Davenport HW: Ethanol damage to canine glandular mucosa. *Proc Soc Exp Biol Med* 1967; 126:657–662.

Dawson DC, Cooke AR: Parallel pathways for ion transport across gastric mucosa: Effect of ethanol. *Am J Physiol* 1978; 235:E7–19.

Dayton MT, Kauffman GL, Schlegel JF, Code CF, Steinbach JH: Gastric bicarbonate appearance with ethanol ingestion. Mechanism and significance. *Dig Dis Sci* 1983; 23:449–455.

De Caro A, Lohse J, Sarles H: Characterization of a protein isolated from pancreatic calculi of men suffering from chronic calcifying pancreatitis. *Biochem Biophys Res Commun* 1979; 87:1176–1182.

Demol P, Singer MV, Hotz J, Hoffman U, Goebell H: Wirkung von intragastralem Alkohol auf die exokrine Pankressekretion und die interdigestive Motilität des oberen Gastrointestinaltraktes beim Menschen. *Z Gastroenterol* 1982; 20:531.

Denk H: Ethanol, Mallory bodies and microtubular system, in Seitz HK, Kommerell B (eds.): *Alcohol Related Diseases in Gastroenterology*. Berlin, Springer-Verlag, 1985, pp 154–171.

Denk H, Franke WW, Dragosics B, Zeiler I: Pathology of cytoskeleton of liver cells; Demonstration of Mallory bodies (alcoholic hyalin) in murine and human hepatocytes by immunofluorescence microscopy using antibodies to cytokeratin polypeptides from hepatocytes. *Hepatology* 1981; 1:9–20.

Denk H, Franke WW, Eckerstorfer R, Schmid E, Kerjaschki D: Formation and involution of Mallory bodies ("alcoholic hyalin") in murine and human liver revealed by immunofluorescence microscopy with antibodies to prekeratin *Proc Nat Acad Sci* 1979; 76:4112–4116.

Denk H, Franke WW, Kerjaschi D: Mallory bodies: New facts and findings, in Berk PD, Chalmers TC (eds): *Frontiers in Liver Disease*. New York, Stuttgart, Thieme-Stratton Inc, 1981, pp 93–105.

Deritis F, Coltorti M, Giusti G: Serum transaminase activities in liver disease. *Lancet* 1972; i:685.

Dianzani MU: Lipid peroxidation in ethanol poisoning: A critical reconsideration. *Alcohol Alcohol* 1985; 20:161–173.

DiLuzio NR, Hartman AD: Role of lipid peroxidation on the pathogenesis of the ethanol-induced fatty liver. *Fed Proc* 1967; 26:1436–1442.

Dinoso VP Jr, Chuang J, Murthy SNS: Changes in mucosal and venous histamine concentrations during instillation of ethanol in the canine stomach. *Am J Dig Dis* 1976; 21:93–97.

Dreiling DA, Bordalo O: A toxic-metabolic hypothesis of pathogenesis of alcoholic pancreatitis. *Alcoholism* 1977; 1:293–299.

Dreiling DA, Richman A, Fradkin NF: The role of alcohol in the etiology of pancreatitis: A study of the effect of intravenous ethyl alcohol on the external secretion of the pancreas. *Gastroenterology* 1952; 20:636–646.

Drenick EJ, Fisler J, Johnson D: Hepatic steatosis after intestinal bypass—prevention and reversal by metronidazole, irrespective of protein–calorie malnutrition, *Gastroenterology* 1982; 82:535–548.

Duguay L, Coutu D, Hetu C, Joly J-G: Inhibition of liver regeneration by chronic alcohol administration. *Gut* 1981; 23:3–13.

Duncan G, Johnson RH, Lambie DG, Whiteside EA: Evidence of vagal neuropathy in chronic alcoholics. *Lancet* 1980; ii:1053–1057.

Durbec JP, Sarles H: Multicenter survey of the etiology of pancreatic disease: Relationship between the relative risk of developing chronic pancreatitis and alcohol, protein and lipid consumption. *Digestion* 1978; 18:337–350.

Eddleston ALWF, Davis M: Histocompability antigens in alcoholic liver disease. *Br Med Bull* 1982; 38:13–16.

Edmondson HA, Peters RL, Reynolds TB, Kuzma OT: Sclerosing hyaline necrosis of the liver. A recognizable clinical syndrome. *Ann Int Med* 1963; 59:646–673.

Estival A, Clemente F, Ribet A: Ethanol metabolism by the rat pancreas. *Toxicol Appl Pharmacol* 1981; 61:155–165.

Fahrenkrug J, Schaffalitzky de Muckadell OB: Plasma secretin concentration in man: Effect of intraduodenal glucose, fat, amino acids, ethanol, HCL, or ingestion of a meal. *Eur J Clin Invest* 1977; 7:201–203.

Fallon HJ: Alcoholic hepatitis, in Schiff L, Schiff ER (eds): *Diseases of the Liver*. Philadelphia, JB Lippincott, 1982, pp 693–708.

Fenster LF: The nonefficacy of short-term anabolic steroid therapy in alcoholic liver disease. *Ann Int Med* 1966; 65:738–744.

Fialkow PJ, Thuline HC, Fenster LF: Lack of association between cirrhosis and the common types of colour blindness. *N Engl J Med* 1966; 275:548–587.

Figarella C, Amouric M, Cuy-Crotte O: Proteolysis of human trypsinogen. 1. Pathogenic implication of chronic pancreatitis. *Biochem Biophys Res Commun* 1984; 118:154–161.

Figarella C, Sarles H: Lactoferrin, a protein of human pancreatic external secretion. *Scand J Gastroent* 1975; 10:449–451.

Frank WO, Houck C: Does chronic ethanol consumption impair hepatic regeneration. *Gastroenterology* 1980; 78:1167.

Frank WO, Rayyes AN, Washington A, Holt PR: Effect of acute ethanol administration upon hepatic regeneration. *J Lab Clin Med* 1979; 93:402–413.

French SW: Effect of chronic feeding of ethanol on rat liver phospholipids. *J Nutr* 1967; 91:292–298.

French SW: The Mallory body: Structure, composition and pathogenesis. *Hepatology* 1981; 1:76–83.

French SW: Present understanding of the development of Mallory's body. *Arch Pathol Lab Med* 1983; 107:445–450.

French SW, Burbige EJ, Tarder G, Bourke E, Harkin OG: Lymphocyte sequestration by the liver in alcoholic hepatitis. *Arch Pathol Lab Med* 1979; 103:146–152.

French SW, Ihrig TJ, Morin RJ: Lipid composition of RBC ghosts, liver mitochondria and microsomes of ethanol-fed rats. *Q J Stud Alcohol* 1970; 31:801–809.

Galambos JT: Alcoholic hepatitis, in Schaffner F, Sherlock S, Leevy CM (eds): *The Liver and its Diseases.* New York, Intercontinental Medical Books, 1974, pp 255–267.

Galambos JT: Jejunoileal bypass and nutritional liver injury. *Arch Pathol Lab Med* 1976; 100:229–231.

Galambos JT: Epidemiology of alcoholic liver disease in United States of America, in Hall P (ed): *Alcoholic Liver Disease; Pathobiology, Epidemiology and Clinical Aspects.* London, Edward Arnold Ltd, 1985, pp 230–249.

Galambos JT: Natural history of cirrhosis due to alcohol, in Tygstrup N, Orlandi F (eds): *Cirrhosis of the liver: Methods and Fields of Research.* Amsterdam, Elsevier, 1987, 307–322.

Geokas MC: Ethanol and the pancreas. *Med Clin North America* 1984; 68:57–75.

Gill R, Zieve L, Logan G: Severe alcoholic hepatitis improved by combined treatment with prednisolone, testosterone and an aminoacid supplement. *Hepatology* 1984; 4:1013.

Gluud C: Effect of testosterone treatment in men with alcoholic cirrhosis. Copenhagen Study Group for Liver Diseases. *J Hepatol* 1985; (Suppl. 1):S59.

Gluud C, Aldershvile J, Henriksen J, Kryger P, Mathiesen L: Hepatitis B and A virus antibodies in alcoholic steatosis and cirrhosis. *J Clin Pathol* 1982b; 35:693–697.

Gluud C, Gluud B, Aldershvile J, Jacobsen A, Dietrichson O: Prevalence of hepatitis B virus infection in out-patient alcoholics. *Infection* 1982a; 12:72–74.

Gluud C, Tage-Jensen U, Bahnsen M, Dietrichson O, Svejgaard A: Autoantibodies, histocompatibility antigens and testosterone in males with alcoholic liver cirrhosis. *Clin Exp Immunol* 1981; 44: 31–37.

Goldberg SI, Mendenhall CL, Connell AM, Chedid A: "Non-alcoholic" chronic hepatitis in the alcoholic. *Gastroenterology* 1977; 72:598–604.

Goldsmith RH, Iber FL, Miller BA: Nutritional status of alcoholics of different socioeconomic class. *J Am Coll Nutr* 1983; 2:215–220.

Goldstein DP, Chin JH: Interaction of ethanol with biological membranes. *Fed Proc* 1981; 40:2073–2076.

Gottfried EB, Korsten MA, Lieber CS: Alcohol-induced gastric and duodenal lesions in man. *Am J Gastrenterol* 1978; 70:587–592.

Govindarajan S; Tinberg H, Radvan G: Circulating immune complexes in alcoholic hepatitis. *Clin Res* 1982; 30:995A.

Guynn RW, Kuo Y-J, Shanbour LL: Acute effect of ethanol on metabolite concentrations of dog pancreas *in vivo. Alcoholism Clin Exp Res* 1982; 6:469–474.

Hahn EG, Schuppan D: Ethanol and fibrogenesis in the liver, in Seitz HK, Kommerell B (eds): *Alcohol Related Diseases in Gastroenterology.* Berlin, Springer-Verlag, 1985, pp 124–153.

Hahn EG, Schuppan D: Pathogenic mechanisms: Fibrosis, fibrogenesis and fibrolysis, in Tygstrup N, Orlandi F (eds): *Cirrhosis of the Liver: Methods and Fields of Research.* Amsterdam, Elsevier, 1987, pp 63–82.

Haines NW; Baker AL, Boyer JL, Glagov S, Schneir H, Jaspan J, Ferguson DJ: Prognostic indicators of hepatic injury following jejunoileal bypass performed for refractory obesity: A prospective study. *Hepatology* 1981; 1:161–167.

Hall P (ed): *Alcoholic Liver Disease; Pathobiology, Epidemiology and Clinical Aspects.* London, Edward Arnold Ltd, 1985, pp 3–319.

Hall P: Pathology and pathogenesis of alcoholic liver disease, in Hall P (ed): *Alcoholic Liver Disease; Pathobiology, Epidemiology and Clinical Aspects.* London, Edward Arnold Ltd, 1985, pp 41–68.

Hall P, Smith RD, Gormley BM: Routine stains on osmicated resin embedded hepatic tissue. *Pathology* 1982; 4:73–74.

Hall P, Pare P, Kaptein E, Kanel G, Redeker AG, Reynolds TB: Double-blind, controlled trial of propylthiouracil in patients with severe acute alcoholic hepatitis. *Gastroenterology* 1982; 82:925–931.

Harada H, Takeda M, Yabe H, Hanafusa E, Hayashi T, Kunichika K, Kochi F, Mishima K, Kimura I, Ubuga T: The hexosamine concentration and output in human pure pancreatic juice in chronic pancreatitis. *Gastroenterol Jpn* 1980; 15:520–526.

Harada H, Ueda O, Kochi F, Kobayashi T, Komazawa M: Comparative studies on viscosity and concentrations of protein and hexosamine in pure pancreatic juice. *Gastroenterol Jpn* 1981; 16:623–626.

Harada H, Ueda O, Yasuoka M, Nakamura T, Kunichika K, Ikubo I, Kochi F, Shigetoshi M, Yabe H, Hanafusa E, Hayashi T, Takeda M, Mishima K, Kimura I, Tanaka T: Histochemical studies on protein plugs obtained by endoscopic retrograde catheterization of the papilla. *Gastroenterol Jpn* 1981; 16:563–567.

Harada H, Yabe H, Hanafusa E, Ikubo I, Takeda M, Hayashi T, Negron A, Ono A, Yamamoto N, Mishima K, Kimura I: Analysis of pure pancreatic juice in patients with chronic alcoholism. *Gastroenterol Jpn* 1979; 14:458–466.

Harinasuta U, Zimmerman HJ: Alcoholic steatonecrosis. I. Relationship between severity of hepatic disease and presence of Mallory bodies in the liver. *Gastroenterology* 1971; 60:1036–1046.

Hashimoto S, Recknagel RO: No chemical evidence of hepatic lipid peroxidation in acute ethanol toxicity. *Exp Mol Pathol* 1968; 8:225–242.

Hasumura Y, Teschke R, Lieber CS: Increased carbon tetrachloride hepatotoxicity, and its mechanism, after chronic ethanol consumption. *Gastroenterology* 1974; 66:415–422.

Heimburger SL, Steiger E, Lo Gerfo P, Biel AG, Williams MJ: Reversal of severe fatty hepatic infiltration after intestinal bypass for morbid obesity by calorie-free amino acid infusion. *Am J Surg* 1975; 129:229–235.

Hellman RA, Temko MH, Nyc SW, Fallon HJ: Alcoholic hepatitis: Natural history and evaluation of prednisolone therapy. *Ann Intern Med* 1971; 74:311–321.

Hillers VN, Massey LK: Interrelationships of moderate and high alcohol consumption with diet and health status. *Am J Clin Nutr* 1985; 41:356–362.

Hislop WS, Follett EAC, Bouchier IAD, MacSween RNM: Serological markers in hepatitis B in patients with alcoholic liver disease: A multicenter survey. *J Clin Pathol* 1981; 34:1017–1019.

Hogan WJ, Viegas de Andrade SR, Winship DH: Ethanol induced acute esophageal motor dysfunction. *J Appl Physiol* 1972; 32:755–760.

Hollander D, Tarnawski A, Krause WJ, Gergely H: Protective effect of sucralfate against alcohol-induced gastric mucosal injury in the rat. *Gastroenterology* 1985; 88:366–374.

Horn T, Henriksen JH, Christoffersen P: Alcoholic liver injury: Defenestration of sinusoidal lining cells. An SEM investigation: *Hepatology* 1987; 7:77–82.

Horn T, Junge J, Christoffersen P: Early alcoholic liver injury: Changes of the Disse space in acinar zone 3. *Liver* 1985: 5:301–310.

Horn T, Junge J, Christoffersen P: Early alcoholic injury: Activation of lipocytes and collagenization of the Disse space in acinar zone 3. *J Hepatol* 1986; 3:333–340.

Hurt RD, Higgins JA, Nelson RA, Morse RM, Dickson ER: Nutritional status of a group of alcoholics before and after admission to an alcoholism treatment unit. *Am J Clin Nutr* 1981; 34:386–392.

Hütteroth TH; Poralla T, Meyer zum Büschenfelde KH: Cellular cytotoxicity against autologous hepatocytes in alcoholic liver disease. *Hepatology* 1983; 3:842.

Ishii H, Okazaki I, Tsuchiya M: Pathology of alcoholic liver disease with speical emphasis on alcoholic hepatitis, in Seitz HK, Kommerell B (eds): *Alcohol Related Diseases in Gastroenterology.* Berlin, Springer-Verlag, 1985, pp 282–303.

Israel Y, Oporto B, MacDonald AD: Simultaneous pair-feeding system for the administration of alcohol-containing liquid diets. *Alcoholism Clin Exp Res* 1984; 8:505–508.

Israel Y, Videla L, Bernstein J: Liver hypermetabolic state after chronic alcohol consumption: Hormonal interrelations and pathogenic implications. *Fed Proc* 1975; 34:1052–1059.

Israel Y, Videla L, MacDonald A, Bernstein J: Metabolic alterations produced in the liver by chronic ethanol administration. Comparison between the effects produced by ethanol and by thyroid hormones. *Biochem J* 1973; 134:523–529.

Ito S, Lacy ER: Morphology of rat mucosal damage, defense, and restitution in the presence of luminal ethanol. *Gastroenterology* 1985; 88:250–260.

Iturriaga H, Pereda T, Esterez A, Ugarte G: Serum immunoglobulin A changes in alcoholic patients. *Ann Clin Res* 1977; 9:39–43.

Izumi N, Hasumura Y, Takeuchi J: Lymphocyte cytotoxicity for autologous human hepatocytes in alcoholic liver disease. *Clin Exp Immunol* 1983; 53:219–224.

Jabbari M, Leevy CM: Protein anabolism and fatty liver of the alcoholic. *Medicine* 1967; 46:131–139.

Jalovaara P: Pancreatic exocrine secretion in the rat after chronic alcohol ingestion: Nonparallel secretion of proteins and pancreatic secretory trypsin inhibitor. *Scand J Gastroent* 1979; 14:57–63.

Jauhonen P, Baraona E, Miyakawa H, Lieber CS: Mechanism of selective perivenular hepatotoxicity of ethanol. *Alcoholism Clin Exp Res* 1982; 6:350–357.

Joly J-G, Duguay L: Ethanol and hepatic cell regeneration, in Seitz HK, Kommerell B (eds): *Alcohol Related Diseases in Gastroenterology*. Berlin, Springer-Verlag, 1985, pp 253–268.

Jones BR, Barrett-Connor E, Criqui MH, Holdbrook MJ: A community study of calorie and nutrient intake in drinkers and nondrinkers of alcohol. *Am J Clin Nutr* 1982; 35:135–139.

Kalish GH, Di Luzio NR: Peroxidation of liver lipids in the pathogenesis of the ethanol-induced fatty liver. *Science* 1966; 152:1390–1392.

Kanagasundaram N, Kakumu S, Chen T, Leevy CM: Alcoholic hyaline antigen (AHAg) and antibody (AHAb) in alcoholic hepatitis. *Gastroenterology* 1977; 73:1368–1373.

Kater L, Jöbsis AC, de la Faille-Kuyper EHB, Vogten AJM, Grijm R: Alcoholic hepatic disease: Specificity of IgA deposits in liver. *Am J Clin Pathol* 1979; 71:51–57.

Kaufmann SE, Kaye MD: Effect of ethanol upon gastric emptying. *Gut* 1979; 20:688–692.

Kehl A, Schober A, Junge U, Winckber K: Solid-phase radioimmunoassay for detection of alcoholic hyalin antigen (AHAH) and antibody (anti-AH). *Clin Exp Immunol* 1981; 43:215–221.

Kendell RE: The beneficial consequences of the United Kingdom's declining per capita consumption of alcohol in 1979–82. *Alcohol Alcohol* 1984; 19:271–276.

Kent G, Gay S, Inouye T, Bahu R, Minick OT, Popper H: Vitamin A-containing lipocytes and formation of type III collagen in liver injury. *Proc Nat Acad Sci* 1976; 73:3719–3722.

Kershenobich D, Uribe M, Suarez GI, Mata JM, Pérez-Tamayo R, Rojkind M: Treatment of cirrhosis with colchicine. A double-blind randomized trial. *Gastroenterology* 1979; 77:532–536.

Keshavarzian A, Iber FL, Ferguson Y: Esophageal manometry and radionuclide emptying in chronic alcoholics. *Gastroenterology* 1987; 92:651–657.

Keshavarzian A, Iber FL, Greer P, Wobbleton I: Gastric emptying of solid meal in male chronic alcoholics. *Alcoholism Clin Exp Res* 1986; 10:432–435.

Korsten MA, Hodes SE, Saili JF, Seitz HK, Lieber CS: Effects of ethanol on pancreatic secretion: Roles of gastric acid and exogenous secretin. *Gastroenterology* 1979; 76:1175.

Korsten MA, Seitz H, Hodes SF, Klingenstein J, Lieber CS: The effect of intravenous ethanol on pancreatic secretion in the conscious rat. *Dig Dis Sci* 1981; 26:790–795.

Krogsgaard K, Tage-Jensey U, Gluud C: Liver membrane antibodies in alcoholic liver disease. *Lancet* 1982; i:1365–1366.

Kuo Y-J, Shanbour LL: Route of ethanol administration and gastric acid output during chronic conditions. *Dig Dis Sci* 1983; 28:820–826.

Kurki P, Miettinen A, Salaspuro M, Virtanen I, Stenman S: Cytoskeleton antibodies in chronic active hepatitis, primary biliary cirrhosis and alcoholic liver disease. *Hepatology* 1983; 3:297–302.

Kurki P, Virtanen I, Lehto V-P, Alfthan O, Salaspuro M: Antibodies to cytokeratin filaments in patients with alcoholic liver disease. *Alcohol Clin Exp Res* 1984; 8:212–215.

Kuttch WH; Prince SJ, Philips JH, Spenney JG, Mestecky J: Properties of immunoglobulin A in serum of individuals with liver diseases and in hepatic bile. *Gastroenterology* 1982; 82:184–193.

Lai CL, Ng RP, Lok ASF: The diagnostic value of the ratio of serum gamma-glutamyltranspeptidase to alkaline phosphatase in alcoholic liver disease. *Scand J Gastroent* 1982; 17:41–47.

Laposata EA, Lange LG: Presence of nonoxidative ethanol metabolism in human organs commonly damaged by ethanol abuse. *Science* 1986; 231:497–499.

LaSure MM, Perez-Jimenez F, Singh M: Interaction of chronic alcohol administration and diet on pancreatic acinar cell metabolism in the rat. *Dig Dis Sci* 1986; 31:1073–1080.

Lechene de La Porte P, De Caro A, Amouric M, Sarles H: Localisation immunocytochimique de la proteine majoritaire des calculus pancreatiques humains. *Nouv Presse Med* 1981; 10:3851.

Leevy CM: Fatty liver: A study of 270 patients with biopsy proven fatty liver and a review of the literature. *Medicine* 1962; 41:249–276.

Leevy CM: Cirrhosis in alcoholics. *Med Clin North Amer* 1968; 52:1445–1451.

Lelbach WK: Leberschäden bei chronischem Alkoholismus. I–III. *Acta Hepatosplenologica* 1966; 13: 321–349.

Lelbach WK: Leberschäden bei chronischem Alkoholismus. *Acta Hepatosplenologica* 1967; 14:9–39.

Lelbach WK: Epidemiology of alcoholic liver disease, in Popper H, Schaffner F (eds): *Progress in Liver Diseases*. New York, Grune & Stratton, 1976, pp 494–515.

Lelbach WK: Epidemiology of alcoholic liver disease; Continental Europe, in Hall P (ed): *Alcoholic Liver Disease*. London, Edward Arnold Ltd, 1985, pp 130–166.

Leo MA, Arai M; Sato M, Lieber CS: Hepatotoxicity of moderate vitamin A supplementation in the rat. *Gastroenterology* 1982; 82:194–205.

Leo MA, Lieber CS: Hepatic vitamin A depletion in alcoholic liver injury in men. *N Engl J Med* 1982; 37:597–601.

Leo MA, Lieber CS: Hepatic fibrosis after long term administration of ethanol and moderate vitamin A supplementation in the rat. *Hepatology* 1983; 2:1–11.

Leo MA, Lieber CS: New pathway for retinol metabolism in liver microsomes. *J Biol Chem* 1985; 260: 5228–5231.

Leo MA, Sato M, Lieber CS: Effect of hepatic vitamin A depletion on the liver in humans and rats. *Gastroenterology* 1983; 84:562–572.

Lesesne HR, Bozymski EM, Fallon HJ: Treatment of alcoholic hepatitis with encephalopathy. Comparison of prednisolone with caloric supplements. *Gastroenterology* 1978; 74:169–173.

Lieber CS (ed): *Medical Disorders of Alcoholism: Pathogenesis and Treatment*. Philadelphia, Pennsylvania, WB Saunders Company, 1982.

Lieber CS: Alcohol and the liver: 1984 Update. *Hepatology* 1984; 6:1243–1260.

Lieber CS, DeCarli LM: Quantitative relationship between the amount of dietary fat and the severity of alcoholic hepatitis. *Am J Clin Nutr* 1970; 23:2505–2512.

Lieber CS, DeCarli LM: An experimental model of alcohol feeding and liver injury in the baboon. *J Med Primatol* 1974; 3:153–163.

Lieber CS, DeCarli LM: The feeding of alcohol in liquid diets: Two decades of applications and 1982 update. *Alcoholism Clin Exp Res* 1982; 4:523–531.

Lieber CS, Jones DP, DeCarli LM: Effects of prolonged ethanol intake: Production of fatty liver despite adequate diets. *J Clin Invest* 1965; 44:1009–1021.

Lieber CS, Jones DP, Mendelson J. DeCarli LM: Fatty liver, hyperlipemia, and hyperuricemia produced by prolonged alcohol consumption, despite adequate dietary intake. *Trans Assoc Am Phys* 1963; 76: 289–300.

Lieber CS, Lefevre A, Spritz N, Feinman L, DeCarli LM: Difference in hepatic metabolism of long- and medium chain fatty acids: The role of fatty acid chain length in the production of the alcoholic fatty liver. *J Clin Invest* 1967: 46:1451–1460.

Lieber CS, Leo MA, Mak K, DeCarli LM, Sato S: Choline fails to prevent liver fibrosis in alcohol-fed baboons but causes toxicity. *Hepatology* 1985; 5:561–572.

Lieber CS, Salaspuro M: Alcoholic liver disease, in Wright R, Millward-Sadler GH, Alberti KGMM, Karran S (eds): *Liver and Biliary Disease; Pathophysiology, Diagnosis, Management*. Bailliere Tindall, WB Saunders, London, Philadelphia, Toronto, 1985, pp 881–947.

Lischner MW, Alexander JF, Galambos JT: Natural history of alcoholic hepatitis. I. The acute disease. *Am J Dig Dis* 1971; 16:481–494.

Llanos OL, Swierczek JS, Teichmann RK, Rayford PL, Thompson JC: Effect of alcohol on the release of secretin and pancreatic secretion. *Surgery* 1977; 81:661.

Lockwood DH, Amatruda JM, Moxley RT et al: Effect of oral amino acid supplementation on liver disease after jejunoileal bypass for morbid obesity. *Am J Clin Nutr* 1977; 30:58–63.

Lowenfels AB, Masih B, Lee TCY, Rohman M: Effect of intravenous alcohol on the pancreas. *Arch Surg* 1968; 96:440–441.

MacDonald CM: The effect of ethanol on hepatic lipid peroxidation and on the activities of glutathione reductase and peroxidase. *FEBS Lett* 1973; 35:227–230.

MacSween RNM: Alcoholic liver disease, in Anthony PP, Woolf N (eds): *Recent Advances in Histopathology*. Edinburgh, London, New York, Churchill Livingstone, 1978, pp 193–212.

MacSween RNM, Anthony RS: Immune mechanisms in alcoholic liver disease, in Hall P (ed): *Alcoholic Liver Disease*. London, Edward Arnold Ltd, 1985, pp 69–89.

Madding GF, Tueller EE, Kennedy PA: Oral and intravenous administration of alcohol and the pancreas. *JAMA* 1968; 205; 116.

Maddrey WC, Boitnott JK, Bedine MS, Weber FL, Mezey E, White RIJr: Corticosteroid therapy of alcoholic hepatitis. *Gastroenterology* 1978; 75:193–199.

Madzarovora-Nohejlova J: Intestinal disaccharidase activity in adults and chronic Pilsen beer drinkers. *Biol Gastroenterol* 1971: 4:325–332.

Mak KM, Leo MA, Lieber CS: Alcoholic liver injury in baboons: transformation of lipocytes to transitional cells. *Gastroenterology* 1984; 87:188–200.

Mak KM, Lieber CS: Alterations in endothelial fenestrations in liver sinusoids of baboons fed alcohol: A scanning electronmicroscopic study. *Hepatology* 1984; 4:386–391.

Mak KM, Lieber CS: Lipocytes and transitional cells in alcoholic liver disease: a morphometric study. *Hepatology* 1988; 3:1027–1033.

Malagelada JR: The pathophysiology of alcoholic pancreatitis. *Pancreas* 1986; 1:270–278.

Mallory FB: Cirrhosis of the liver: Five different types of lesions from which it may arise. *Bull Johns Hopkins Hosp* 1911; 22:69–75.

Manns M, Meyer zum Büschenfelde KH, Hess G: Autoantibodies against liver specific membrane lipoprotein in acute and chronic liver diseases: Studies on organ-, species-, and disease-specificity. *Gut* 1980: 21:955–961.

Marin GA, Ward NL, Fischer R: Effect of ethanol on pancreatic and biliary secretions in humans. *Am J Dig Dis* 1973; 18:825–833.

Marshall AW, Graul RS, Morgan MY, Sherlock S: Treatment of alcohol-related liver disease with thioctic acid: A six-month randomized double-blind trial. *Gut* 1982; 23:1088–1093.

Matloff DS, Selinger MJ, Kaplan MM: Hepatic transaminase activity in alcoholic liver disease. *Gastroenterology* 1980; 78:1389–1392.

Mayer EM, Grabowski CJ, Fisher RS: Effect of graded doses of alcohol upon esophageal motor function. *Gastroenterology* 1978; 76:1133–1136.

Mendenhall CL: Anabolic steroid therapy as an adjunct to diet in alcoholic hepatic steatosis. *Am J Dig Dis* 1968; 13:783–791.

Mendenhall CL and the VA Cooperative Study Group on Alcoholic Hepatitis: Clinical and therapeutic aspects of alcoholic liver disease, in Seitz HK, Kommerell B (eds): *Alcohol Related Diseases in Gastronenterology.* Berlin, Springer-Verlag 1985, pp 304–323.

Mendenhall CL, Anderson S, Garcia-Pont P, Goldberg S, Kiernan T, Seeff L, Sorrell M, Tamburro C, Weesner RE, Zetterman R, Chedid A, Chen T, Rabin L: Short-term and long-term survival in patients with alcoholic hepatitis treated with oxandrolone and prednisolone. *N Engl J Med* 1984a; 311:1464–1470.

Mendenhall CL, Anderson S, Weesner RE, Goldberg SJ, Crolic KA: Protein-calorie malnutrition associated with alcoholic hepatitis. Veterans Administration Cooperative Study Group on Alcoholic Hepatitis. *Am J Med* 1984b; 76:211–222.

Mendenhall CL, Bradford RH, Furman RH: Effect of ethanol on glycerolipid metabolism in rat liver. *Biochim Biophys Acta* 1969; 187:501–509.

Mezey E: Effect of ethanol on intestinal morphology, metabolism and function, in Seitz HK, Kommerell B (eds): *Alcohol Related Diseases in Gastroenterology.* Berlin, Springer-Verlag, 1985, pp 342–360.

Mezey E, Potter JJ, French SW, Tamura T, Halsted CH: Effect of chronic ethanol feeding on hepatic collagen in monkeys. *Hepatology* 1983; 3:41–44.

Millan MS, Morris GP, Beck IT, Henson JT: Villous damage induced by suction biopsy and by acute ethanol intake in normal human small intestine. *Dig Dis Sci* 1980; 25:513–525.

Mills JR, Pennington TH, Kay P, MacSween RNM, Watkinson G: Hepatitis Bs antibody in alcoholic cirrhosis. *J Clin Pathol* 1979; 32:778–782.

Miszczuk-Jamska B, Guy O, Figarella C: Alfa-1-proteinase inhibitor in pure human pancreatic juice. Characterization of a complex form in patients with chronic calcifying pancreatitis and its significance. *Hoppe Seyler's Z Physiol Chem* 1983; 254:1597–1601.

Miyakawa H, Iida S. Leo MA, Greenstein R, Zimmon D, Lieber CS: Pathogenesis of precirrhotic portal hypertension in alcohol-fed baboons. *Gastroenterology* 1985; 88:143–150.

Morgan MY: Alcohol and nutrition. *Br Med Bull* 1982; 38:21–29.

Morgan MY: Epidemiology of alcoholic liver disease; United Kingdom, in Hall P (ed): *Alcoholic Liver Disease.* London, Edward Arnold Ltd, 1985, pp 193–229.

Morgan MY, Sherlock S: Sex-related differences among 100 patients with alcoholic liver disease. *Br Med J* 1977; 1:939–941.

Morris GP, Wallace JL, Hardwig PL: Correlations between changes in indicators of gastric mucosal barrier integrity at time of exposure to "barrier brakers" and extent of hemorrhagic erosions one hour later. *Dig Dis Sci* 1984; 29:6–11.

Morton JA, Bastin J, Fleming KA, McMichael A, McGee JO'D: Mallory bodies in alcoholic liver disease: Identification of cytoplasmic filament/cell membrane and unique antigenic determinants by monoclonal antibodies. *Gut* 1981; 22:1–7.

Morton S, Mitchell MC: Effects of chronic ethanol feeding on glutathione turnover in the rat. *Biochem Pharmacol* 1985; 34:1559–1563.

Mott C, Sarles H, Tiscornia O, Gullo L: Inhibitory action of alcohol on human exocrine pancreatic secretion. *Am J Dig Dis* 1972; 17:902–910.

Moxley RT, Pozesky T, Lockwood DH: Protein nutrition and liver disease after jejunoileal bypass for morbid obesity. *N Engl J Med* 1974; 290:921–926.

Nagura H, Smith PD, Nakane PK, Brown WR: IgA in human bile and liver. *J Immunol* 1981; 126: 587–595.

Nakamura K, Sarles H, Payan H. Three-dimensional reconstruction of the pancreatic ducts in chronic pancreatitis. *Gastroenterology* 1972; 69:942–949.

Nakano H, Kawasaki T, Miyamura M, Fukuda Y, Imura H: Serum levels of N-terminal type III procollagen peptide in normal subjects and comparison to hepatic fibrosis. *Acta Hepatol Jpn* 1983; 24: 1230–1234.

Nakano M, Lieber CS: Ultrastructure of initial stages of perivenular fibrosis in alcohol-fed baboons. *Am J Pathol* 1982; 106:145–155.

Nakano M, Worner TM, Lieber CS: Perivenular fibrosis in alcoholic liver injury: Ultrastructure and histologic progression. *Gastroenterology* 1982; 83:777–785.

Nalpas B; Vassault A, Charpin S, Lacour B, Berthelot P: Serum mitochondrial aspartate aminotransferase as a marker of chronic alcoholism: Diagnostic value and interpretation in a liver unit. *Hepatology* 1986; 6:608–614.

Nalpas B, Vassault A, Le Guillou A, Lesgourgues B, Ferry N, Lacour B, Berthelot P: Serum activity of mitochondrial aspartate aminotransferase: A sensitive marker of alcoholism with or without alcoholic hepatitis. *Hepatology* 1984; 5:893–896.

Nasrallah SM, Galambos JT: Amino acid therapy of alcoholic hepatitis. *Lancet* 1980; ii:1276–1277.

Neville JN, Eagles JA, Samson G, Olson RE: Nutritional status of alcoholics. *Am J Clin Nutr* 1968; 21:1329–1340.

Niemelä O, Risteli L, Sotaniemi EA, Risteli J: Aminoterminal propeptide of type III procollagen in serum in alcoholic liver disease. *Gastroenterology* 1983; 85:254–259.

Niemelä O, Risteli L, Sotaniemi EA, Risteli J: Type IV collagen and laminin-related antigens in human serum in alcoholic liver disease. *Eur J Clin Invest* 1985; 15:132–137

Nizze H, Lapis K, Kovacks I : Allyl alcohol-induced changes in the rat exocrine pancreas. *Digestion* 1979; 19:359–369.

Noel-Jorand MC, Colomb E, Astier JP, Sarles H: Pancreatic basal secretion in alcohol-fed and normal dogs. *Dig Dis Sci* 1981; 26:783–789.

Norström T: The abolition of the Swedish alcohol rationing system: Effects on consumption distribution and cirrhosis mortality. *Br J Addict* 1987; 82:633–641.

Norton R, Batey R, Dwyer T, MacMahon S: Alcohol consumption and the risk of alcohol related cirrhosis in women. *Br Med J* 1987; 295:80 82.

Nouchi T, Worner TM, Sato S, Lieber CS: Serum procollagen type III n-terminal peptides and laminin P1 peptide in alcoholic liver disease. *Alcoholism Clin Exp Res* 1987; 11:287–291.

Ohnishi K, Iida S, Iwama S, Goto N, Nomura F, Takashi M, Mishima A, Kono K, Kimura K, Musha H, Kotota, K, Okuda K: The effect of chronic habitual alcohol intake on the development of liver cirrhosis and hepatocellular carcinoma: Relation to hepatitis B surface antigen carriage. *Cancer* 1982; 49:672–677.

Ohnishi K, Okuda K: Epidemiology of alcoholic liver disease; Japan, in Hall P (ed): *Alcoholic Liver Disease*. London, Edward Arnold Ltd, 1985, pp 167–183.

Ohno T, Ohtsuki H, Okabe S: Effects of 16,16-dimethyl prostaglandin E2 on ethanol-induced and aspirin-induced gastric damage in the rat. *Gastroenterology* 1985; 88:353–361.

Okanoue T, Burbige EJ, French SW: The role of the Ito cell in perivenular and intralobular fibrosis in alcoholic hepatitis. *Arch Pathol Lab Med* 1983; 107:456–463.

Omata M, Ashcavai M, Liew C-T, Peters RL: Hepatocellular carcinoma in the USA: Etiologic consideration. *Gastroenterology* 1979; 76:279–287.

Orrego H, Blake JE, Blendis LM, Compton KV, Israel Y: Long-term treatment of alcoholic liver disease with propylthiouracil. *N Engl J Med* 1987; 312:1421–1427.

Orrego H, Crossley IR, Saldivia V, Medline A, Varghese G, Israel Y: Long-term ethanol administration and short- and long-term liver regeneration after partial hepatectomy. *J Lab Clin Med* 1981; 97:221–230.

Orrego H, Kalant H, Israel Y, Blake J, Medline A, Rankin JG, Armstrong A, Kapur B: Effect of short-term therapy with propylthiouracil in patients with alcoholic liver disease. *Gastroenterology* 1979; 76:105–115.

Paronetto F: Ethanol and the immune system, in Seitz HK, Kommerell B (eds): *Alcohol Related Diseases in Gastroenterology*, Berlin, Springer-Verlag, 1985, pp 269–281.

Paronetto F, Lieber CS: Cytotoxicity of lymphocytes in experimental liver injury in the baboon. *Proc Soc Exp Biol Med* 1976; 153:495–497.

Patek AJ Jr, Toth IG, Saunders MG, Castro GAM, Engel JJ: Alcohol and dietary factors in cirrhosis. An epidemiological study of 304 alcoholic patients. *Arch Intern Med* 1975; 135:1053–1057.

Pequignot G, Tuyns AJ, Berta JL: Ascitic cirrhosis in relation to alcohol consumption. *Int J Epidemiol* 1978; 7:113–120.

Periente E-A, Degott C, Martin J-P, Feldman G, Potet F, Benhamou J-P: Hepatocyte PAS-positive diatase-resistant inclusions in the absence of alpha-I-antitrypsin deficiency—High prevalence in alcoholic cirrhosis. *Am J Clin Pathol* 1981; 76:299–302.

Perlow W, Baraona E, Lieber CS: Symptomatic intestinal disaccharidase deficiency in alcoholics. *Gastroenterology* 1977; 77:680–684.

Perperas A, Tsantoulas D, Portmann B, Eddleston ALWF, Williams R: Autoimmunity to liver membrane protein and liver damage in alcoholic liver disease. *Gut* 1981; 22:149–152.

Peters RL, Gay T, Reynolds TB: Postjejunoileal bypass hepatic disease. *Am J Clin Pathol* 1975; 63: 318–331.

Phaosawasdi K, Tolin R, Mayer E, Fisher RS: Effects of alcohol on pyloric sphincter. *Dig Dis Sci* 1979; 24:934–939.

Pierson JL, Mitchell MC: Increased hepatic efflux of glutathione after chronic ethanol feeding. *Biochem Pharmacol* 1986; 35:1533–1537.

Pimstone NR, French SW: Alcoholic liver disease. *Med Clin North Am* 1984; 68:39–56.

Pirola RC, Davis AE: The sphincter of Oddi and pancreatitis. *Am J Dig Dis* 1970; 15:583–588.

Planche NE, Palasciano G, Meullenent J, Laugier R, Sarles H: Effects of intravenous alcohol on pancreatic and bilary secretion in man. *Dig Dis Sci* 1982; 27:449–453.

Poikolainen K: Increase in alcohol-related hospitalizations in Finland 1969–1975. *Br J Addict* 1980; 75: 281–291.

Popham RE, Schmidt W, DeLint JE: The effect of legal restraint on drinking, in Kissin B, Begleiter H(eds): *Biology of Alcoholism*. New York, Plenum Press, 1976, vol 4, pp 579–625.

Popper H, Lieber CS: Histogenesis of alcoholic fibrosis and cirrhosis in the baboon. *Am J Pathol* 1980; 98:695–716.

Porter HP, Simon FR, Pope CE, Volwiler W, Fenster FL: Corticosteroid therapy in severe alcoholic hepatitis: A double-blind drug trial. *N Engl J Med* 1971; 284:1350–1355.

Pösö H, Väänänen H, Salaspuro MP, Pösö AR: Effects of ethanol on liver regeneration after partial hepatectomy in rats. *Med Biol* 1980; 58:329–336.

Post J, Benton J, Breakstone R, Hoffman J: The effects of diet and choline on fatty infiltration of the human liver. *Gastroenterology* 1952; 20:403–410.

Puurunen J: Studies on the mechanism of the inhibitory effect of ethanol on the gastric acid output in the rat. *Naunyn Schmiedebergs Arch Pathol* 1978; 303:87–93.

Ranek L, Juhl E: Copenhagen Study Group for Liver Diseases. Blood group distribution in patients with cirrhosis of the liver. *Scand J Gastroenterol* 1970; 7:203–206.

Rankin JG, Halliday ML, Corey PNJ, Coates RA, de Lint JE: Epidemiology of alcoholic liver diseas Australia, in Hall P (ed): *Alcoholic Liver Disease*. London, Edward Arnold Ltd, 1985, pp 115–1'

Ray MB, Mendenhall CL, French SW, Gartside PS, The VA Cooperative Study Group: Serum min A deficiency and increased expression of cytokeratin antigen in alcoholic liver disease. *tology* 1988; 8:1019–1028.

Raymond L, Infante F, Voirol M, Hollenweger V, Zurkirch-Conti M-Ch, Loizeau E: Interaction des facteurs alcool et nutrition dans l'étiologie de la cirrhose hépatique, chez les hommes. *Schweiz med Wschr* 1985; 115:998–1000.

Reichstein BJ, Okamoto C, Forte JG: Effect of ethanol on acid secretion by isolated gastric glands from rabbit. *Gastroenterology* 1986; 91:439–447.

Reid NRCW, Brunt PW, Bias WB, Maddrey WC, Alonso BA, Iber FL: Genetic characteristics and cirrhosis: a controlled study of 200 patients. *Br Med J* 1968; 2:463–465.

Renner IG, Rinderknecht H, Valenzuela JE, Douglas AP: Studies of pure pancreatic secretions in chronic alcoholic subjects without pancreatic insufficiency. *Scand J Gastroenterol* 1980; 15:241–244.

Resnick RH, Boitnott J, Iber JL, Makapour H, Cerda JJ: Preliminary observations of d-penicillamine therapy in acute alcoholic liver disease. *Digestion* 1974; 11:257–265.

Rissanen A, Sarlio-Lähteenkorva S, Alfthan G, Gref C-G, Keso L, Salaspuro M: Employed problem drinkers: A nutritional risk group? *Am J Clin Nutr* 1987; 45:456–461.

Risteli L, Risteli J: Radioimmunoassays for monitoring connective tissue metabolism. *Rheumatology* 1986; 10:216–245.

Robert A, Lancaster L, Davis JP, Field SO, Wickremasinha AJ, Thornburgh BA: Cytoprotection by prostaglandin occurs in spite of penetration of absolute ethanol into the gastric mucosa. *Gastroenterology* 1985; 88:328–333.

Rogers AE, Fox JG, Gottlieb LS: Effect of ethanol and malnutrition on nonhuman primate liver, in Berk PD, Chalmers T Ch (eds): *Frontiers in Liver Disease*. New York, Georg Thieme Verlag, 1981, pp 167–175.

Rohde H, Vargas L, Hahn EG, Kalbfleisch H, Bruguera M, Timpl R: Radioimmunoassay for type III procollagen peptide and its application to human liver disease. *Eur J Clin Invest* 1979; 9:451–459.

Rojkind M: Collagen metabolism in the liver, in Hall P (ed): *Alcoholic Liver Disease*. London, Edward Arnold Ltd, 1985, pp 90–112.

Rojkind M, Kershenobich D: Diagnostic procedures for liver fibrosis, in Becker S (ed): *Diagnostic Procedures in the Evaluation of Hepatic Disease*. New York, AR Liss, 1983, pp 73–78.

Romelsjö A: Decline in alcohol-related in-patient care and mortality in Stockholm county. *Br J Addict* 1987; 82:653–663.

Romelsjö A, Ågren G: Has mortality related to alcohol decreased in Sweden? *Br Med J* 1985; 291:167–170.

Rubin E, Krus S. Popper H: Pathogenesis of postnecrotic cirrhosis in alcoholics. *Arch Pathol* 1973; 73: 40–51.

Rudman D, Sewell CW, Ansley JT: Deficiency of carnitine in cachectic cirrhotic patients. *J Clin Invest* 1977; 60:716–723.

Rudolph R, McClure WJ, Woodward M: Contractile fibroblasts in chronic alcoholic cirrhosis. *Gastroenterology* 1979; 76:704–709.

Rush B, Steinberg M, Brook R: The relationships among alcohol availability, alcohol consumption and alcohol-related damage in the province of Ontario and the State of Michigan 1955–1982. *Adv Alc Subst Abuse* 1986; 5:33–44.

Sahel J, Sarles H: Modifications of pure human pancreatic juice induced by chronic alcohol consumption. *Dig Dis Sci* 1979; 24:897–905.

Salaspuro M: Conventional and coming laboratory markers of alcoholism and heavy drinking. *Alcoholism Clin Exp Res* 1986; 10:5S–12S.

Salaspuro M: Mechanism of liver cell damage leading to cirrhosis from alcohol, in Tygstrup N, Orlandi F (eds): *Cirrhosis of the Liver: Methods and Fields of Research.* Amsterdam, Elsevier Publishers, 1987a, pp 3–16.

Salaspuro M: Use of enzymes for the diagnosis of alcohol-related organ damage. *Enzyme* 1987b; 37: 87–107

Salaspuro M: Early identification of excessive drinking; conventional methods and the future. *Alabama J Med* 1988, in press.

Salaspuro M, Korri U-M, Nuutinen H, Roine R: Blood acetate and urinary dolichols—New markers of heavy drinking and alcoholism, in Goedde HW, Agarwal DP (eds): *Genetics and Alcoholism.* New York, Alan R Liss, Inc, 1987, vol 241, pp 231–240.

Salaspuro M, Lieber CS: Comparison of the detrimental effects of chronic alcohol intake in humans and animals, in Eriksson K, Sinclair JD, Kiianmaa K (eds): *Animal Models in Alcohol Research.* London, New York, Academic Press, 1980, p 359–376.

Salaspuro M, Lindroos K: Metabolism and toxicity of acetaldehyde, in Seitz HK, Kommerell B (eds): *Alcohol Related Diseases in Gastroenterology.* Berlin, Springer-Verlag, 1985; pp 106–123.

Salaspuro M, Shaw S, Jayatilleke E, Ross WA, Lieber CS: Attenuation of the ethanol induced hepatic redox change after chronic alcohol consumption in baboons: Metabolic consequences in vivo and in vitro. *Hepatology* 1981; 1:33–38.

Salo JA: Ethanol-induced mucosal injury in rabbit oesophagus. *Scan J Gastroenterol* 1983; 18:713–721.

Sanfey H, Sarr MG, Bulkley GB, Cameron JL: Oxygen derived free radicals and acute pancreatitis. *Acta Physiol Scand* 1986; 548:109–118.

Sarles H: Alcohol and pancreas. *Acta Med Scand* 1985; 703 (Suppl):235–249.

Sarles H: Etiopathogenesis and definition of chronic pancreatitis. *Dig Dis Sci* 1986; 31 (Suppl 9):91S–107S.

Sarles H, Laugier R: Alcoholic pancreatitis. *Clin Gastroenterol* 1981; 10:401–415.

Sarles H, Lebreuil G, Tasso F, Figarella C, Clemente F, Devaux MA, Fagonde B, Payan H: A comparison of alcoholic pancreatitis in rat and man. *Gut* 1971; 12:377–388.

Sarles H, Tiscornia O, Palasciano G: Chronic alcoholism and canine exocrine pancreas secretion: A long term follow-up study. *Gastroenterology* 1977; 72:238–248.

Sato M, Lieber CS: Hepatic vitamin A depletion after chronic ethanol consumption in baboons and rats. *J Nutr* 1981; 111:2015–2023.

Sato S, Nouchi T, Worner TM, Lieber CS: Liver fibrosis in alcoholics. Detection by fab radioimmunoassay of serum procollagen III peptides. *JAMA* 1986; 256; 1471–1473.

Saunders JB, Walters JRF, Davies P, Paton A: A 20-year prospective study of cirrhosis. *Br Med J* 1981; 282:263–266.

Savolainen ER, Goldberg B, Leo MA, Velez M, Lieber CS: Diagnostic value of serum procollagen peptide measurements in alcoholic liver disease. *Alcoholism Clin Exp Res* 1984a; 8:384–389.

Savolainen ER, Leo MA, Timple R; Lieber CS: Acetaldehyde and lactate stimulate collagen synthesis of cultured baboon liver myofibroblasts. *Gastroenterology* 1984b; 87:777–787.

Schlichting P, Juhl E, Poulsen H, Winkel P and the Copenhagen Study Group for Liver Diseases: Alcoholic hepatitis superimposed cirrhosis: Clinical significance and effect of long-term prednisolone treatment. *Scand J Gastroenterol* 1976; 11:305–312.

Schmidt DN, Sarles H, Devaux MA: Early increased pancreatic secretory capacity during alcohol adaptation in the dog. *Scand J Gastroenterol* 1982; 17:49–55.

Schmidt KL, Henagan JM, Smith GS, Hilburn PJ, Miller TA: Prostaglandin cytoprotection against ethanol-induced gastric injury in the rat. *Gastroenterology* 1985; 88:649–659.

Schmidt W: Agreement and disagreement in experimental, clinical and epidemiological evidence on the etiology of alcoholic liver cirrhosis: A comment, in Khanna JM, Israel Y, Kalant H (eds): *Alcoholic Liver Pathology.* Toronto, Addiction Research Foundation, 1975, pp 19–30.

Schubert GE, Bethke-Bedurftig BA, Bujnoch AW, Diehm A: Die Leberzirrhose in Autopsiegut von 48 Jahren. I. Häufigkeitsänderungen, regionale Unterschiede. *Zschr Gastroent* 1982a; 20:213–220.

Schubert GE, Bethke-Bedurftig BA, Bujnoch AW, Diehm A: Die Leberzirrhose in Autopsiegut von 48 Jahren. II. Todesursachen, Leberkarzinome, Leber- und Milzgewichte. *Zschr Gastroent* 1982b; 20: 221–227.

Schuppan D, Dumont JM; Kim JK, Hennings G, Hahn EG: Serum concentration of the aminotermi-nal procollagen type III peptide in the rat reflects early formation of connective tissue in experimental liver cirrhosis. *J Hepatol* 1986; 3:27–37.

Seeff LB, Cuccherini BA, Zimmerman HJ, Alder E, Benjamin SB: Acetaminophen hepatotoxicity in alcoholics (clinical review). *Ann Int Med* 1986; 106:399–404.

Seitz HK, Simon B, Czygan P, Veith S, Kommrell B: Effect of chronic ethanol ingestion on the cyclic AMP system of the upper gastrointestinal tract in the rat. *Alcoholism* 1983; 7:369–371.

Shafritz DA, Shouval D, Zern MA: Recombinant DNA and the liver: studies with albumin, alpha-fetoprotein, hepatitis B virus, and other DNA probes, in Popper H, Schaffner F (eds): *Progress in Liver Diseases.* New York, Grune & Stratton, 1982, vol VII, pp 429–449.

Shaw S, Jayatilleke E, Ross WA, Gordon ER, Lieber CS: Ethanol induced lipid peroxidation: Poten-tiation by long-term alcohol feeding and attenuation by methionine. *J Lab Clin Med* 1981; 98:417–424.

Shirazi SS, Platz CE: Effect of alcohol on canine esophageal mucosa. *J Surg Res* 1978; 25:373–379.

Si L, Whiteside TL, Van Thiel DH: Lymphocyte subsets studied with monoclonal antibodies in liver tissue of patients with alcoholic liver disease. *Alcoholism* 1983; 7:431–435.

Singer MV: Pankreas und Alkohol. *Schw Med Wschr* 1985; 115:973–987.

Singer MV, Eysselein V, Goebell H: Beer and wine but not whisky and pure ethanol do stimulate release of gastrin in humans. *Digestion* 1983a; 26:73–79.

Singer MV, Eysselein V, Goebell H: Pancreatic polypeptide response to intragastric ethanol in humans and dogs. *Regul Pept* 1983b; 6:13–23.

Singer MV, Goebbel H: Acute and chronic actions of alcohol on pancreatic exocrine secretion in humans and animals, in Seitz HK, Kommerell B (eds): *Alcohol Related Diseases in Gastroenterology.* Springer-Verlag Berlin, 1985, pp 376–414.

Singh M: Effect of chronic ethanol feeding on pancreatic enzyme secretion in rats in vitro. *Dig Dis Sci* 1983; 28:117–123.

Singh M: Ethanol and pancreas, in Go LW, et al (eds): *The Exocrine Pancreas, Pathobiology and Dis-eases.* New York, Raven Press, 1986, pp 423–442.

Singh M, LaSure MM, Bockman DE: Pancreatic acinar cell function and morphology in rats chroni-cally fed an ethanol diet. *Gastroenterology* 1982; 82:425–434.

Skog O-J: Trends in alcohol consumption and deaths from diseases. *Br J Addict* 1987; 82:1033-1041.

Smith DI, Burvill PW: Epidemiology of liver cirrhosis morbidity and mortality in western Australia, 1971–82: Some preliminary findings. *Drug Alc Dep* 1985; 15:35–45.

Solomon N, Solomon TE, Jacobson ED, Shanbour LL: Direct effects of alcohol on in vivo and in vitro exocrine pancreatic secretion and metabolism. *Am J Dig Dis* 1974; 19:253–260.

Sörensen TIA, Orholm M, Bentsen KD, Hoyby G, Eghoje K, Christoffersen P: Prospective evaluation of alcohol abuse and alcoholic liver injury in man as predictors of development of cirrhosis. *Lancet* 1984, ii:241–244.

Steiner PE: World problem in the cirrhotic diseases of the liver. Their incidence, frequency, types and aetiology. *Trop Geograph Med* 1964; 16:175–205.

Stoltenberg PH, Soltis RD: The nature of IgG complexes in alcoholic liver disease. *Hepatology* 1984; 4:101–106.

Straus E, Urbach H-J, Yalow RS: Alcohol-stimulated secretion of immunoreactive secretin. *N Engl J Med* 1975; 293:1031–1032.

Suematsu T, Matsumura T, Sato N, Miyamoto T, Ooka T, Kamada T, Abe H: Lipid peroxidation in alcoholic liver disease in humans. *Alcoholism Clin Exp Res* 1981; 5:427–436.

Szabo S, Trier JS, Brown A, Schnoor J: Early vascular injury and increased vascular permeability in gastric mucosal injury caused by ethanol in the rat. *Gastroenterology* 1985; 88:228–236.

Takada A, Nei J, Matsuda Y, Kanayama R: Clinicopathological study of alcoholic fibrosis. Am J Gas-troenterol 1982; 77:660–666.

Takeuchi N, Ito M, Yamamura Y: Esterification of cholesterol and hydrolysis of cholesteryl ester in alcohol-induced fatty liver of rats. *Lipids* 1974; 9:353–357.

Takeuchi K, Okabe S: Role of luminal alkalinization in repair process of ethanol-induced mucosal dam-age in rat stomach. *Dig Dis Sci* 1983; 28:993–1000.

Taraschi TF, Rubin E: Biology of disease. Effects of ethanol on the chemical and structural properties of biologic membranes. *Lab Invest* 1985; 52:120–131.

Tarnawski A, Hollander D, Stachura J, Krause WJ, Gergely H: Prostaglandin protection of the gastric mucosa against alcohol injury — A dynamic time-related process. *Gastroenterology* 1985; 88:334–352.

Teschke R; Stutz G, Strohmeyer G: Increased paracetamol-induced hepatoxicity after chronic alcohol consumption. *Biochem Biophys Res Commun* 1979; 91:368–374.

Thomas HC, De Villiers D, Potter B, Hodgson H, Jain S. Jewell DP, Sherlock S: Immune complexes in acute and chronic liver disease. *Clin Exp Immunol* 1978; 31:150–157.

Tiscornia OM, Dreiling DA: Physiopathogenic hypothesis of alcoholic pancreatitis: Supranormal ecbolic stimulation of "pancreon" units secondary to the loss of the negative component of pancreas innervation. *Pancreas* 1987; 2:604–612.

Tiscornia OM, Gullo L, Barros Mott C de, Devaux MA, Palasciano G, Hage G, Sarles H: The effects of intragastric ethanol administration upon canine exocrine pancreas secretion. *Digestion* 1973; 9: 490–501.

Tiscornia OM, Gullo L, Sarles H, Barros Mott C de, Brasca A, Devaux MA, Palasciano G, Hage G: Effects of intragastric and intraduodenal ethanol on canine exocrine pancreatic secretion. *Digestion* 1974; 10:52–60.

Tiscornia OM, Leveskue D, Sarles H, Bretholtz A, Voirol M, de Oliviera M, Sluger M, Demol P: Canine exocrine pancreatic secretory changes induced by an intragastric ethanol test meal. *Am J Gastroenterol* 1977; 67:121–130.

Tiscornia OM, Palasciano G, Sarles H: Atropine and exocrine pancreatic secretion in alcohol fed dogs. *Am J Gastroenterol* 1975; 63:33–36.

Turunen U, Malkamäki M, Valtonen VV, Larinkari U, Pikkarainen P, Salaspuro MP, Mäkelä PH: Endotoxin and liver diseases. High titres of enterobacterial common antigen antibodies in patients with alcoholic cirrhosis. *Gut* 1981; 22:949–953.

Tygstrup N, Juhl E and the Copenhagen Study Group for Liver Diseases: The Treatment of alcoholic cirrhosis. The effect of continued drinking and prednisone on survival, in Gerok W (ed): *Alcohol and the Liver*. International Symposium 2-4. Stuttgart, FK Schattauer Verlag, 1970, pp 519–536.

Väänänen H: The distribution of cytochrome P-450-mediated drug oxidation and glutathione in periportal and perivenous rat hepatocytes after phenobarbital treatment. *J Hepatol* 1986; 2:174–181.

Väänänen H, Salaspuro M, Lindros K: The effect of chronic ethanol ingestion on ethanol metabolizing enzymes in isolated periportal and perivenous rat hepatocytes. *Hepatology* 1984; 4:862–866.

Välimäki M, Alfthan G, Pikkarainen J, Ylikahri R, Salaspuro M: Blood and liver selenium concentrations in patients with liver diseases. *Clin Chim Acta* 1987; 166:171–176.

van de Wiel A, Schuurman HJ, Kater L: Alcoholic liver disease: An IgA associated disorder. *Scand J Gastroenterol* 1987; 22:1025–1030.

Videla LA, Iturriaga H, Pino ME, Bunout D, Valenzuela A, Ugarte G: Content of hepatic reduced glutathione in chronic alcoholic patients: Influence of the length of abstinence and liver necrosis. *Clin Sci* 1984; 66:283–290.

Videla LA, Valenzuela A: Alcohol ingestion, liver glutathione and lipoperoxidation: Metabolic interrelations and pathological implications. *Life Sci* 1982; 31:2395–2407.

Villa E, Rubbiani L, Barchi T, Ferretti I, Grisendi A, De Palma M, Bellentani S. Manenti F: Susceptibility of chronic symptomless HBsAg carriers to ethanol-induced hepatic damage. *Lancet* 1982; ii:1243–1244.

Vina J, Esterela M, Guerri C, Romero FJ: Effect of ethanol on glutathione concentration in isolated hepatocytes. *Biochem J* 1980; 188:549–552.

Wands JR, Carter EA, Bücher NLR, Isselbacher KJ: Inhibition of hepatic regeneration in rats by acute and chronic ethanol intoxication. *Gastroenterol* 1979; 77:528–531.

Wienbeck M, Berges W: Esophageal and gastric lesions in the alcoholic, in Seitz HK, Kommerell B (eds): *Alcohol Related Diseases in Gastroenterology*. Berlin, Springer-Verlag, 1985, pp 361–375.

Wilson FA, Hoyumpa AM: Ethanol and small intestinal transport. *Gastroenterol* 1979; 76:388–403.

Wilson ID, Onstad G, Williams RC: Serum immunoglobulin concentrations in patients with alcoholic liver disease. *Gastroenterol* 1969; 57:59–67.

Wilson JS, Bernstein L, McDonald C, Tait A, McNeil D, Pirola RC: Diet and drinking habits in relation to the development of alcoholic pancreatitis. *Gut* 1985; 26:882–887.

Wilson JS, Fracp BS, Colley PW, Sosula L, Pirola RC, Chapman BA, Somer JB: Alcohol causes a fatty pancreas. A rat model of ethanol-induced pancreatic steatosis. *Alcoholism Clin Exp Res* 1982; 6: 117–121.

Wilson JS, Somer JB, Pirola RC: Chronic ethanol feeding causes accumulation of serum cholesterol in rat pancreas. *Exp Molec Pathol* 1984; 41:289–297.

Wing DR, Harvey DJ, Hughes J, Dunbar PG, McPherson KA, Paton WDM: Effects of chronic ethanol administration on the composition of membrane lipids in the mouse. *Biochem Pharmacol* 1983; 31:3431–3439.

Winship DH, Callish CR, Zboralske FF, Hogan WJ: Deterioration of esophageal peristalsis in patients with alcoholic neuropathy. *Gastroenterol* 1968; 55:173–178.

World MJ, Ryle PR, Thomson AD: Alcoholic malnutrition and the small intestine. *Alcohol Alcohol* 1985; 20:89–124.

Yokoo H, Minick OT, Batti F, Kent G: Morphologic variants of alcoholic hyalin. *Am J Pathol* 1972; 69:25–40.

Zarling EJ, Mobarhan S, Donahue PE: Effect of moderate prolonged ethanol ingestion on intestinal disaccharidase activity and histology. *J Lab Clin Med* 1986; 108:7–10.

Zucoloto S, Rossi MA: Effect of chronic ethanol consumption on mucosal morphology and mitotic index in the rat small intestine. *Digestion* 1979; 19:277–283.

Zysset T, Polokof MA, Simon FR: Effect of chronic ethanol administration on enzyme and lipid properties of liver plasma membranes in long and short sleep mice. *Hepatology* 1985; 5:531–537.

CHAPTER 8

Cardiovascular Functions in Alcoholism and After Acute Administration of Alcohol: Heart and Blood Vessels

Burton M. Altura and Bella T. Altura

Department of Physiology, State University of New York
Health Science Center at Brooklyn, New York, USA

INTRODUCTION

Excessive consumption of alcohol is now known to affect various bodily functions. Among these are synthetic and degradative metabolic processes, central nervous system functions, behavior, endocrine glands, hormones, host defense mechanisms and immune functions, bone and skeletal muscles, and various aspects of cardiac and circulatory function, to name a few. Alcohol is considered by many to be the most abused drug in the United States. Alcoholism is, of course, not a new disease entity. Numerous references to the effects of wine are found in the Bible, beginning with Noah. The cardiomyopathic effects of alcohol were recognized more than a century ago (Bollinger, 1884).

Alcohol is apparently ingested because it often produces pleasant psychopharmacologic effects. However, it exerts devastating and adverse effects on gastrointestinal function, absorption of nutrients, energy, endocrine functions, body metabolism, vitamin metabolism, and mineral and fluid electrolyte balance (Lieber, 1982).

Alcohol abuse leads to primary malnutrition, that is, deficient utilization of nutrients. Alcoholic beverages provide what is termed "empty" calories because ethanol does not contain significant amounts of protein, vitamins, or minerals.

Table 8.1 indicates that an individual who drinks from 5 to 30 ounces of an 86-proof beverage will consume from 375 to 2,250 empty calories. In other terms, this represents from as little as 15% of the normal daily caloric requirement to 100%. The end result of such intake is a decreased intake of other foods and results in an imbalance of daily nutrient ingestion.

Secondary malnutrition, that is, deficient nutrient utilization, is also produced by a host of multiple factors such as ethanol-induced gastrointestinal damage, deficiency-induced maldigestion and malabsorption, decreased activation or increased inactivation of nutrients, and energy wastage. The mechanism(s) for the latter are not known (Li, 1979; Lieber, 1982).

Since ethanol is metabolized primarily by the liver (Lieber, 1982), it profoundly affects the metabolism of many nutrients. In this way, ethanol can alter the storage, activation, and metabolism of numerous nutrients, particularly vitamins, amino acids, and proteins. Vitamin metabolism demonstrates numerous levels at which alcohol can impair nutrition (Table 8.2).

Table 8.1. Influence of alcohol intake on empty caloric intake in humans

AMOUNT OF 86-PROOF BEVERAGE CONSUMED	EMPTY CALORIES INGESTED*	PERCENTAGE OF NORMAL DAILY CALORIC REQUIREMENT
5 oz. (146.5 ml)	375	12.5–17
10 oz. (293 ml)	750	25–33
20 oz. (586 ml)	1500	50–67
30 oz. (879 ml)	2250	75–100

86-proof = 43 percent v/v ethanol.

*Each gram of ethanol provides 7.1 calories.

Impairment in folate metabolism often results in anemias. Introduction of thiamine deficiency by excessive alcohol intake has been linked to increased neurologic-cerebrovascular abnormalities seen in alcoholics, including Wernicke's encephalopathies. In addition to effects on vitamin metabolism, alcohol can also produce adverse effects on plasma levels of amino acids and albumin. Brain protein synthesis has also been shown to be impaired (Kricka and Clark, 1979; Li, 1979; Lieber, 1982).

In addition to the vitamins already mentioned, alcohol also is known to result in deficiencies of nicotinic acid, vitamin B_{12}, vitamin A, and vitamin K. Deficiencies of these additional vitamins are known to be associated with hematological disorders and impairments in energy metabolism, red blood cell metabolism, and vision (Kricka and Clark, 1979; Li, 1979; Lieber, 1982).

Of particular interest, in the present context, vitamins, in addition to being pivotal in synthetic and degradative processes, play key roles in the metabolism of ethanol and its major metabolites, acetate, and acetaldehyde. So, deficiencies in these vitamins will often result in high levels of ethanol, acetate, and acetaldehyde in body tissues.

In recent years, abuse of alcohol has been shown to produce several mineral deficiencies, such as zinc, magnesium, phosphate, and iron deficiency syndromes. Hypercalcitoninemia and metabolic acidosis are frequently seen in alcoholics (Kricka and Clark, 1979; Li, 1979; Lieber, 1982).

More recent studies show that alcoholics also are deficient in potassium, calcium, and the trace elements, selenium and cobalt (Li, 1979).

In relation to specific disease states, both clinical and epidemiological studies have implicated the excessive use of alcohol and, in particular, spirits in the risk of developing cirrhosis of the liver, central nervous system disorders, and metabolic disorders, among others (Table 8.3). The question which should be addressed is how many and how much of these disorders, and in particular, cardiovascular problems, are direct consequences of problems with vitamin and mineral metabolism?

Table 8.2. Effects of alcohol on vitamin and protein metabolism

1. Impaired folate metabolism and absorption-amenia commonly seen in alcoholics.
2. Thiamine deficiency
3. Vitamin B_6 deficiency–pyridoxal phosphate deficiency
4. Vitamin D metabolism impairment
5. Decrease in plasma amino acids (e.g., α-amino-n-butyric acid, leucine, valine, isoleucine*)
6. Reduction in hepatic albumin synthesis
7. Impairment of brain protein synthesis

*Chronic alcohol consumption appears to be associated with elevations in these branched amino acids.

Table 8.3. Alcohol-related disorders

1. Alcoholism itself
2. Liver disease, e.g., cirrhosis, etc.
3. Central nervous system degeneration
4. Acute and chronic muscle disorders
5. Peripheral neuropathies
6. Metabolic disorders (e.g., hypoglycemia, ketosis, hyperuricemia, gout)
7. Alterations in drug metabolism
8. Increased susceptibility to infections
9. Malnutrition
10. Dietary deficiencies
11. Fetal malformations
12. Cardiovascular disorders

It has long been known that both acute and chronic ingestion of alcohol can exert profound pharmacological as well as pathological effects on the cardiovascular system (Walshe, 1873). Excessive consumption of alcohol is now known to affect various aspects of cardiac and circulatory functions (Khetarpal, 1981; Alderman and Coltart, 1982; Altura BM, 1982; Altura BM and Altura BT, 1984a). Chronic administration is thought to play important roles in the etiology of high blood pressure, cardiac arrhythmias, ischemic heart disease, angina, degeneration of heart muscle (cardiomyopathy), coronary vasospasm, atherosclerosis, congestive heart failure, cerebrovascular diseases, strokes, and increased incidence of sudden death, among others.

However, during recent years, some evidence, particularly data gathered by epidemiologists, has suggested that moderate, daily ingestion of alcohol may actually produce beneficial effects on the coronary circulation and the myocardium (Khetarpal and Volicer, 1981; Klatsky et al, 1981b; Turner et al, 1981; Klatsky, 1985). Such findings have led some physicians to suggest that daily or thrice weekly ingestion of small amounts of alcohol (for example, 1–2 ounces) may be beneficial to the heart. Currently, this remains a matter of much controversy, particularly since (1) a great deal of the data is difficult to analyze, (2) human, controlled studies are not available, and (3) other epidemiologists and clinicians suggest from their human studies that alcohol ingestion even in small doses may be harmful to the cardiovascular system (Harburg et al, 1980; Khetarpal and Volicer, 1981; Alderman and Coltart, 1982; Altura BM, 1982; Kittner et al, 1983; Ireland et al, 1984; Hillbom et al, 1985).

Assuming small doses of alcohol are beneficial to the cardiovascular system, how could alcohol exert such salutory actions? Some of these possibilities are shown in Table 8.4. A leading protective mechanism has been suggested by alcohol's ability to produce changes in plasma lipid levels. A number of clinical investigations have now shown an action of alcohol on plasma triglycerides and plasma lipoproteins, particularly the low (VDL) and high (HDL) lipoproteins (see below) (Criqui et al, 1981; Barboriak et al, 1983). Increases in plasma levels

Table 8.4. Mechanisms by which moderate alcohol consumption* could exert protection against ischemic heart disease and cardiac arrhythmias

1. Anti-atherogenic effect of alcohol-induced high-density lipoproteins
2. Inhibitory actions of alcohol on blood coagulation
3. Coronary vasodilator actions
4. Anti-spasmodic actions on blood vessels

*Assumes up to 4 standard drinks (containing 0.6 oz of absolute alcohol) per day could be consumed. A standard drink would be 1.5 oz of distilled spirits (40% v/v), 12 oz of beer (5% v/v) or 5 oz of table wine (12% v/v).

of the HDLs are often associated with reductions in prevalence of coronary artery disease. It is believed by several groups of investigators that daily ingestion of low doses of alcohol may enhance the level of these HDLs.

It is also thought that alcohol can exert beneficial actions on the blood clotting system (Lieber, 1982). Coronary artery and cerebrovascular diseases are often associated with increased blood clotting, coagulation of blood platelets in the coronary and cerebral blood vessels, and generation of thromboxane B_2 (TXB_2). Theoretically, low doses of alcohol might prevent the latter diverse effects in blood vessels. However, it has been demonstrated recently that even low doses of ethanol can enhance aggregation of blood platelets and lead to generation of TXB_2 (Hillbom et al, 1984; Hillbom et al, 1985).

It has been suggested that spasm of coronary arteries and cerebral blood vessels can play important roles in the etiology of ischemic heart disease, angina, and stroke. It has also been suggested that low doses of alcohol might prevent or attenuate such spasms (Altura BM and Altura BT, 1984a). However, recent findings make this doubtful (see below).

Although the possible beneficial or salutory, circulatory actions of ethanol remain to be elucidated, it is clear that chronic ingestion of alcohol exerts very detrimental actions on the cardiovascular system (Rubin E, 1979; Regan and Haider, 1981; Altura BM, 1982; Lieber, 1982; Lowenstein et al, 1983; Altura BM and Altura BT, 1984a; Potter et al, 1984; Taylor and Combs-Orme, 1985; Altura BM, 1987). The association of excessive alcohol consumption with hypertension (Harburg et al, 1980; Khetarpal and Volicer, 1981; Turner et al, 1981; Klatsky et al, 1981b; Altura BM, 1982; Altura BM and Altura BT, 1984a; Potter et al, 1984; Klatsky, 1985) and death from cardiovascular disease is clear (Alderman and Coltart, 1982; Ashley, 1982; Potter et al, 1984; Hillbom et al, 1985; Taylor and Combs-Orme, 1985; Altura BM, 1987). However, it is not clear to what extent alcohol causes hypertension nor how this is brought about (see below) (Khetarpal and Volicer, 1981; Klatsky et al, 1981b; Altura BM and Altura BT, 1982b; Altura BM and Altura BT, 1984a; Ireland et al, 1984; Potter et al, 1984; Altura BM and Altura BT, 1987). Ongoing clinical studies in several clinics and laboratories in the U.S.A., Scandinavia, and the Soviet Union, in particular, indicate a higher than normal incidence of hemorrhagic stroke and aneurysmal subarachnoid hemorrhage among heavy users of alcohol (Kagan et al, 1981; Ashley, 1982; Altura BM and Altura BT, 1984a; Hillbom et al, 1984; Hillbom et al, 1985; Taylor and Combs-Orme, 1985). Such stroke-like episodes often appear to occur within 24 hours of a drinking binge. Several investigators have suggested that excessive alcohol consumption predisposes humans to stroke and sudden death (Altura BM et al, 1983; Altura BM and Altura BT, 1984a; Hillbom et al, 1985; Taylor and Combs-Orme, 1985). Abuse of alcohol is also associated with a higher than normal incidence of chronic pulmonary disorders, atherosclerosis, and hematological disturbances (Khetarpal and Volicer, 1981; Altura BM, 1982; Ashley, 1982; Lieber, 1982; Altura BM and Altura BT, 1984a; Hillbom et al, 1985).

It is rather interesting to note that morbidity and mortality from most causes are significantly greater among heavy drinkers than among the general population, and almost 50% of the excess deaths appear to be attributed to circulatory causes (Table 8.5) (Ashley and Rankin, 1980; Ashley, 1982). In view of the latter, it is extremely important to determine precisely, under properly controlled conditions, what actions the acute and chronic ingestion of alcohol exert on the heart, peripheral blood vessels, and the blood vessels in the brain.

In addition to possible direct actions on blood vessels and the heart (Altura BM, 1982; Altura BM and Altura BT, 1982b; Altura BM et al, 1983; Potter et al, 1984; Altura BM and Altura BT, 1984a; Altura BM and Altura BT, 1987), alcohol probably alters circulatory function by affecting the release and actions of endogenous hormones and humoral substances (Morvai et al, 1979a; Khetarpal and Volicer, 1981; Altura BM, 1982; Altura BM and Altura BT, 1982b; Pohorecky, 1982; Altura BM and Altura BT, 1983; Bannan et al, 1984; Hillbom et al, 1984; Ireland et al, 1984; Altura BM and Altura BT, 1984a; Noe et al, 1985; Howes and Reid, 1986; Altura BM and Altura BT, 1987).

Table 8.5. Percent of excess mortality in alcoholics and heavy users attributed to different causes*

CAUSE OF DEATH	% OF (Range)
Suicide	3–27
Accidents	3–23 (leading cause among youth)
Liver cirrhosis	3–28
Pneumonia	0–20
Neoplasms	0–28
Cardiovascular diseases	14–36 ⎫
	⎬ 16–50 combined
Cerebrovascular disorders	2–14 ⎭

*Adapted from Ashley and Rankin (1980) and based on epidemiologic studies of more than 20 different groups of investigators around the globe.

Alcohol can result in the release into the blood stream of diverse hormones and humoral-vasoactive substances such as catecholamines, aldosterone, cortisol, dopamine, angiotensin II, renin, eicosanoids, and cyclic AMP, among others. Excessive amounts of these substances, together with other circulating (and released) agents, can interact with cardiac and vascular smooth muscle cells to alter cardiac activity, blood pressure, blood flow, vascular homeostasis, etc. In addition, it is likely that excessive, continued amounts of such hormones could result in cardiac and vascular damage. What precise pathways are involved when these hormones interact with alcohol in regional organs or vasculatures will have to await further investigation.

It is hoped that the sections of this chapter that follow this brief introduction will help to shed light on some of the problems and questions which must be addressed. Although an attempt has been made to focus on recent work, which may unfortunately have overlooked some older, relevant work in the literature, the reader should consult other reviews which have focused on older findings and some recent work which was omitted due to space limitations (see refs Rubin E, 1979; Khetarpal and Volicer, 1981; Alderman and Coltart, 1982; Altura BM, 1982; Lieber, 1982; Potter et al, 1984; Segel et al, 1984; Howes and Reid, 1986; Trell et al, 1986; Altura BM, 1987; Regan and Morvan, 1987).

EPIDEMIOLOGY OF RELATIONSHIP OF ALCOHOL CONSUMPTION TO CARDIOVASCULAR DISEASE

Historically, there has been a long interest in the health effects of alcohol. In 1926, Pearl observed a "U"-shaped relationship between alcohol ingestion and total mortality which remains an enigma to this day (Pearl, 1926). At low consumption of alcohol, there is a higher heart death rate; at moderate intake levels ($\cong 2$ drinks/day), a lower death rate, and at high intake (> 5 drinks per day), there is a high death rate. In the past decade, numerous reviews devoted to the beneficial health effects of moderate intake on cardiovascular disease have appeared in the literature (Stason et al, 1976; Rhoads et al, 1978; Hennekens et al, 1979; LaPorte et al, 1980; Criqui et al, 1981; Dyer et al, 1981; Gordon et al, 1981; Kagan et al, 1981; Khetarpal and Volicer, 1981; Turner et al, 1981; Wallace et al, 1981; Klatsky et al, 1981a; Klatsky et al, 1981b; Barboriak et al, 1983; Kittner et al, 1983; Colditz et al, 1985; Klatsky, 1985; LaPorte et al, 1985; Criqui, 1986; Klatsky et al, 1986). However, it is important to point out that all of these epidemiological data are based on prospective, not retrospective, studies. And most importantly, these studies also found, collectively, that subjects who *did not* develop coronary heart disease had concomitantly high intakes of starch and calories along with moderate alcohol intake. A careful analysis of these studies also indicates that they were not able to determine precise intakes of vitamins, minerals, and proteins, all factors that could have individually or collectively accounted solely for the so-called observed "beneficial action of moderate alcohol intake."

Another problem with a number of these epidemiological studies is that, surprisingly, the people who had the highest death rates were those subjects who abstained completely from alcohol after exhibiting a history of drinking moderate to high amounts of alcohol. Additionally, in all fairness to the reader and to investigators in the field, it must be pointed out that a number of the above studies do not show very impressive drops in total mortality with moderate ingestion of alcohol. The latter suggests that death from other causes confounds the data analysis with moderate drinkers. In this context, it is quite clear that death from other causes becomes quite striking with heavy consumption of alcohol (Table 8.5) (Rhoads et al, 1978; Ashley and Rankin, 1980; Ashley, 1982; Criqui, 1987). Lastly, although there may be, statistically, a beneficial effect of moderate alcohol ingestion on CHD mortality, there is no such protection observed in stroke cases. In fact, the evidence, so far, suggests a positive correlation between degree of alcohol consumption and stroke incidence.

Even since Castelli and coworkers reported in 1977, on the basis of epidemiologic prospective findings in 3800 subjects, that there appeared to be a significant relationship between alcohol consumption and the serum levels of HDL, other epidemiologists have rushed to support this conclusion (Barboriak et al, 1979; Danielsson, 1979; Ricci and Angelico, 1979; Williams et al, 1979; Ernst et al, 1980; Criqui et al, 1981; Gordon et al, 1981; Barboriak et al, 1983). The presumption here is that over the past three decades, evidence has accumulated to indicate that elevation in the serum HDL component of cholesterol is associated with protection against CHD and atherosclerosis due to its two major functions: (1) normal clearance of blood cholesterol, thereby keeping tissue cholesterol levels in check; and (2) inhibition of the tissue uptake of LDL-cholesterol, which would enhance atherogenesis and CHD. Although on the surface this seems like a viable hypothesis for the so-called protective action of moderate drinking on CHD, it is flawed in our opinion for a number of reasons: (1) From the studies done so far on human subjects, it appears that there is a strong positive correlation between alcohol consumption and serum HDL levels (Barboriak et al, 1979; Danielsson, 1979; Ricci and Angelico, 1979; Williams et al, 1979; Ernst et al, 1980; Criqui et al, 1981; Gordon et al, 1981; Barboriak et al, 1983; Criqui, 1986; Criqui, 1987); yet moderate to heavy drinking of alcohol is associated with a higher total mortality from CHD than is low to moderate ingestion of alcohol, which clearly is associated with lower serum HDL levels. (2) Autopsy studies on several thousand human subjects have revealed less atherosclerosis in coronary arteries of heavy and moderate drinkers than in abstainers (see Kittner et al, 1983 for review). (3) No relationship exists between sudden cardiac death and alcohol consumption (Dyer et al, 1981; Kozarevic et al, 1982). (4) A number of studies now exist in which it is difficult to find an inverse correlation between alcohol-induced elevation of HDL-2 (the sub-fraction of HDL most negatively associated with CHD incidence) and CHD (Kittner et al, 1983; Criqui, 1986; Criqui, 1987). (5) Surprisingly, alcohol intake appears to be a significant discriminator between subjects with or without prior myocardial infarction (AMI), independent of the degree of coronary atherosclerosis (Barboriak et al, 1979). (6) In women, no consistent negative association between alcohol consumption, lipoprotein levels, and risk for CHD can be found (Criqui, 1986; Criqui, 1987). In conclusion, if indeed the negative association between moderate drinking of alcohol and CHD is free of confounding problems, it is doubtful that lipoproteins are prime factors in this protection.

One must, therefore, look to other factors as causative agents in the alcohol-induced protection against CHD, such as those suggested above (e.g., Table 8.4), i.e., actions on blood coagulation and platelets, possible coronary vasodilatory actions and/or anti-spasmodic actions on blood vessels (Altura BM and Altura BT, 1982b; Altura BM, 1987). Action of alcohol on generation and/or release of numerous vasoactive neurohumoral substances may also prove to be a useful investigative endeavor.

CARDIAC ACTIONS OF ALCOHOL

Introduction

An association of alcohol and heart disease was recognized in 1873 by Walshe; and Osler's (1912) and Price's (1922) early textbooks of medicine indicated that longterm alcohol usage resulted in degenerative changes (e.g., fatty infiltration, fatty degeneration, chronic interstitial myocarditis, hypertrophy, and dilatation of the myocardium). Such knowledge was forgotten or overlooked, however, when beri-beri–induced heart failure was reported in the late 1920s and 1930s in malnourished, thiamine-deficient alcoholics (Wenckebach, 1928; Weiss and Wilkins, 1937). This latter work provoked the idea that thiamine deficiency was solely responsible for heart disease in alcoholics until alcoholic cardiomyopathy was rediscovered in the late 1950s by Brigden (1957) and Burch (1960). A review of the literature, consisting of studies of 50 patients, by Brigden and Robinson (1964), suggested that alcoholic heart disease could be brought about in ways other than by thiamine deficiency, e.g., arrhythmias (particularly atrial fibrillation) as well as poorly contracting ventricles which contained normal main coronary arteries (a congestive type of cardiomyopathy). Although such a compendium has led over the past quarter of a century to the generation of considerable data on alcoholic cardiac myopathy and the effects of chronic alcohol intake on the myocardium (for reviews, see below and Morvai et al, 1979a; Rubin, 1979; Anonymous, 1980; Khetarpal and Volicer, 1981; Regan and Haider, 1981; Alderman and Coltart, 1982; Ashley, 1982; Segel et al, 1984; Altura BM, 1987; Regan and Morvan, 1987) much of this body of information is difficult to evaluate, and much more quantitative information has been published on the acute effects of alcohol administration.

Acute Actions of Alcohol on the Myocardium

Chronotropicity in Humans and Intact Animals

A review of the literature suggests strongly that oral ingestion of ethanol (i.e. blood alcohol = 15–30 mM) in non-alcoholic human subjects produces inconsistent effects on heart rate, e.g., acceleration (Juchems and Klobe, 1969; Riff et al, 1969; Blomqvist et al, 1970; Delgado et al, 1975), deceleration (Gould et al, 1973), or no change (Ahmed et al, 1973). Blood levels of alcohol lower than 15 mM consistently fail to alter heart rate in normal human subjects (Gould et al, 1971; Mendoza et al, 1971; Gould et al, 1972). Although it is difficult to draw definitive conclusions, it would appear that, at most, ethanol exerts minimal effects on heart rate in nonalcoholic human subjects after acute ingestion to blood levels of 30–40 mM.

Although there appears to be a great tendency of alcoholic subjects, or subjects with decompensated hearts, to exhibit more sensitivity to acute administration of ethanol, it is not clear whether this tendency toward depressed heart rate has been examined as thoroughly as it demands (Alderman and Coltart, 1982; Lieber, 1982; Segel et al, 1984). This area appears in need of a complete reexamination using more sophisticated, advanced instruments.

In contrast to these data in compromised human subjects, studies with intact normal animals show variable results on heart rate with alcohol blood levels = 20–70 mM. Using anesthetized dogs with different anesthetic agents, several groups of investigators found that heart rate exhibited no significant change from control levels (Ganz, 1963; Regan et al, 1966; Mendoza et al, 1971; Wong, 1973). Other investigators, however, have reported increases at similar blood alcohol concentrations (BAC) followed by decreases in heart rate at levels higher than 65 mM (Nakano and Prancan, 1972). However, using conscious dogs, Horowitz and Atkins failed to detect any changes at BAC = 26 mM, but observed acceleration at high BAC (e.g., 68 mM) (Horowitz and Atkins, 1974). Overall, it would appear that BACs which are accepted as the legal definition of intoxication for driving a motor vehicle (i.e., 100 mg/dl) do not seem to be associated with any consistent effect on heart rate. However, the "true effect" may be naturally masked by the built-in compensatory mechanisms in the organism (e.g., sympathetic nervous system reflexes) (Nakano and Prancan, 1972; Wong, 1973). The latter may be true to some degree, but work with isolated heart preparations and cells in culture do not necessarily support such a concept.

Chronotropicity in Isolated Heart Preparations and in Cultured Cells

Although the use of isolated perfused hearts, perfused sinus node, atria, and ventricular muscle strips as well as cultured atrial and ventricular muscle cells have revealed, collectively, that ethanol can exert direct actions on myocardial muscle cells independent of nervous inerations, release of hormones, ethanol's major metabolites (e.g., acetaldehyde), or hyperosmolarity (James and Bear, 1967; Lochner et al, 1969; Gailis and Verdy, 1971; Okarma et al, 1972; Schreiber et al, 1972; Martinez et al, 1977; Kobayashi et al, 1979; Ikeda et al, 1984; Mashimo, 1985), these data exhibit considerable variability in response to ethanol from one preparation to another. For example, Schreiber and coworkers (1972), using guinea pig hearts, observed no change in heart rate at ethanol concentrations up to 54 mM and from 280 to 370 mM. Ikeda et al (1984), however, using isolated bullfrog hearts, found a concentration-dependent decrease in heart rate going from 22 to 1100 mM ethanol. James and Bear (1967), using perfusion of the sinus node of the anesthetized dog, failed to find any effect at BAC = 20 mM and deceleration at high BAC (e.g., 200 mM). Using isolated, perfused canine atria, Kobayashi et al (1979) observed concentration-dependent negative chronotropicity at BAC up to 200 mM and biphasic effect (i.e., initial decrease followed by increase) at high concentrations of ethanol, e.g., 1,000 mM. Although others have reported positive chronotropic responses in isolated perfused rat hearts using 100 and 200 mM ethanol (Lochner et al, 1969), these findings could not be confirmed (Gailis and Verdy, 1971).

Concerning single myocardial cells in culture, only a limited number of studies have been published (Okarma et al, 1972; Martinez et al, 1977; Mashimo, 1985). Okarma and coworkers (1972) found that very low concentrations of ethanol (i.e., 1 mM) failed to affect heart rate, whereas others utilizing a similar preparation have reported that 17 and 35 mM ethanol induced positive responses (Martinez et al, 1977). The most thorough and elegant of these studies was recently reported by Mashimo in 1985, who utilized mouse atrial and ventricular myocardial cells and concentrations of ethanol going from 12.5 to 200 mM. This study demonstrates several new and potentially important findings. Mashimo (1985) found that atrial cells were affected and arrested much more readily by ethanol than were the ventricular cells (e.g., Fig. 8.1). Myocardial cells which remained viable continued beating in ethanol media and exhibited chronotropic responses in a concentration-dependent manner. Atrial cells exhibited negative chronotropicity to high concentrations of ethanol (50 and 200 mM), whereas ventricular cells demonstrated transient positive responses. Mashimo also reported, in this interesting study, that low concentrations of acetaldehyde could partially mimic some of the chronotropic effects of ethanol on the atrial cells but not those on the ventricular cells; in addition, the chronotropic effects of ethanol did not appear to be due to hyperosmolarity of ethanol.

Cardiodynamics and Coronary Blood Flow

Human Subjects. Although there is often an impression that acute single-dose ingestion of alcohol has a deleterious effect on cardiac performance in non-alcoholic humans (Khetarpal and Volicer, 1981; Alderman and Coltart, 1982), the literature is replete with controversy on this point (Regan et al, 1966; Juchems and Klobe, 1969; Riff et al, 1969; Gould et al, 1971; Mendoza et al, 1971; Gould et al, 1972; Ahmed et al, 1973; Gould et al, 1973; Wong, 1973; Horowitz and Atkins, 1974; Delgado et al, 1975; Turner et al, 1981; Lieber, 1982; Segel et al, 1984; Howes and Reid, 1986; Altura BM, 1987). In spite of this large body of data, recent reviewers still state that "acute alcohol administration causes a dose-dependent impairment

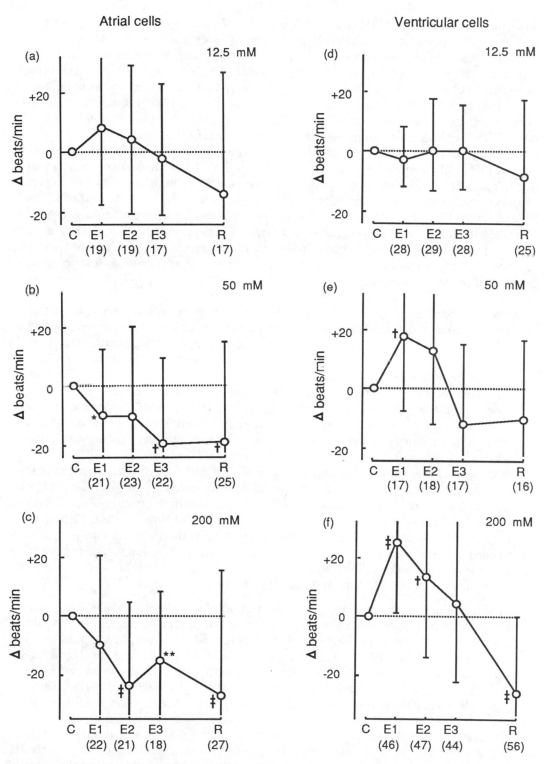

FIGURE 8.1. Chronotropic effects of addition of ethanol on atrial (a, b, c) and ventricular (d, e, f) myocardial cells. The concentrations of ethanol were 12.5 mM (a, d), 50 mM (b, e), and 200 mM (c, f). Graphs are expressed by the time course of changes in beat rates of myocardial cells from control values (before ethanol addition; C) (mean ± S.D.; each number of evaluated cells indicated by parentheses): about 0.3–1 h (E1), about 1–2 h (E2), and about 2–3 h (E3) after ethanol addition, and 1–1.8 hr after removal of ethanol from the medium (R). *$p < 0.05$, **$p < 0.02$, †$p < 0.01$, ‡$p < 0.001$. (Taken from Mashino, 1985, by permission.)

of cardiac function in man" (Howes and Reid, 1986). This is certainly not borne out by the studies to date. For example, a fairly large number of investigators, using doses of ethanol which result in BAC = 4–40 mM (i.e., low dose to intoxication), have reported either a dose-dependent increase in cardiac output, stroke volume, ejection fraction and overall cardiac index, or no change in these parameters, depending upon dose and time of examination of each cardiac parameter (Juchems and Klobe, 1969; Riff et al, 1969; Blomqvist et al, 1970; Gould et al, 1971; Horowitz and Atkins, 1974; Kupari, 1983; Kupari et al, 1983). It is thus difficult to dismiss such findings obtained in normal human subjects.

An examination of other reports reveals that some workers, using similar BAC, have observed signs of depressed myocardial function, such as decline in cardiac output, reduction in ejection fraction, and a worsening of the systolic time ratio (i.e., preinjection period per left ventricular ejection time) (Gould et al, 1971; Gould et al, 1972; Ahmed et al, 1973; Delgado et al, 1975; Timmis et al, 1975; Child et al, 1979). But before accepting such data, we should recall that some measurements, for example, cardiac output, are reflections of both heart rate and cardiac loading, while systolic time ratios are, at best, indirect indices of left ventricular contractility, and without correction for changes in afterload can lead to an exaggeration of myocardial depression (Gould et al, 1971; Ahmed et al, 1973; Van Voorhees et al, 1981).

Although one might be tempted to conclude, from the above, that the net acute effects of ethanol on cardiac function are minimal in normal human subjects, because sympathoadrenal reflex mechanisms compensate for any alteration in myocardial function (Segel et al, 1974), it seems to the present reviewers that this is a dangerous statement, particularly in view of the types of studies and well-established investigators who carried them out. Obviously, there is a need for more studies carried out with the new types of non-invasive techniques now available, e.g., nuclear magnetic resonance imaging (NMRI), ^{31}P-NMR, reflectance spectroscopy, radio-labeled isotope scans, etc. Quantitative information on the effects of ethanol administration on coronary blood flow in normal human subjects appears to be sorely lacking.

We are also of the opinion that since nonalcoholic patients with cardiac disease appear to demonstrate almost consistent signs of myocardial depression (e.g., falls in stroke work, cardiac output, and increased ST-segment depression) after acute administration of ethanol (Conway, 1968; Gould et al, 1971; Gould et al, 1972; Khetarpal and Volicer, 1981; Lieber, 1982; Segel et al, 1984), the notion must be entertained that some of the above, seemingly contradictory data may be reflections of non-homogeneous patient populations (e.g., some having unknown or undiagnosed cardiac disease; possible subclinical abnormalities of cardiac function; chronic social users of alcohol) (Spodick et al, 1972; Levi et al, 1977).

Animals. Turning to intact animals and administration of ethanol (10–65 mM BAC), except for a limited number of exceptions in which increments in cardiac output and stroke volume have been reported (Webb and Degeleri, 1965; Nakano and Kessinger, 1972), it is clear that acute alcohol (11–44 mM BAC) administration results in deleterious and concentration-dependent effects on the myocardium, irrespective of whether the animal is conscious or anesthetized (Regan et al, 1966; Mendoza et al, 1971; Newman and Valcienti, 1971; Mierzwiak et al, 1972; Wong, 1973; Horowitz and Atkins, 1974; Goodkind et al, 1975; Jones et al, 1975; Friedman et al, 1979; Abel, 1980; Khetarpal and Volicer, 1981; Stratton et al, 1981; Altura BM, 1982; Altura BM, 1987). Collectively, these data indicate that alcohol, in a concentration-dependent manner, results in significant depression of dp/dt^2, elevation of left ventricular filling pressures, increases in left ventricular dimension (cardiac dilatation), stroke volume, and declines in ejection fraction.

With respect to the effects of ethanol on coronary blood flow or coronary vascular resistance, the available data do not allow one to draw firm conclusions. Several investigators, working with anesthetized or conscious dogs, have reported that ethanol (BAC = 10–45 mM) decreases coronary vascular resistance in a concentration-dependent manner, most likely as a consequence of a direct effect on coronary vascular smooth muscle (Lasker et al, 1955; Ganz, 1963; Pitt et al, 1970; Gailis and Verdy, 1971; Mendoza et al, 1971; Friedman et al, 1979; Abel, 1980; Friedman, 1981; Lieber, 1982; Pescio et al, 1983; Altura BM, 1987). Other investigators, working with dogs and rats, have demonstrated that similar blood levels of alcohol produce reductions in coronary blood flow or increases in coronary vascular resistance concomitant with reductions or elevations in cardiac output (Webb and Degerli, 1965; Regan et al, 1966; Segel et al, 1978). Since the experimental conditions used in most of these studies do not preclude a number of variables (e.g., coronary O_2 supply, release of metabolites and vasoactive mediators, sympathodrenal reflexes and neurohumors, extravascular compression, etc.) that are known to alter coronary blood flow and coronary vascular resistance, it is difficult to for us to pinpoint exact reasons for the opposite and contrasting data.

Isolated Heart Preparations. In order to study the "pure" actions of acute ethanol administration of the myocardium, divorced from in-vivo homeostatic influences (above), isolated atrial and ventricular preparations as well as perfused hearts and heart lung preparations have been studied (Loeb, 1905; Dixon, 1907; Sulzer, 1924; Loomis, 1952; Gimeno et al, 1962; Webb et al, 1967; Spann et al, 1968; Lochner et al, 1969; Gailis and Verdy, 1971; Nakano and Moore, 1972; Fisher and Kavaler, 1975; Hirota et al, 1976; Lake et al, 1978; Mason et al, 1978; Altura BM, 1982; Lieber, 1982; Segel et al, 1984). Evidence seems to be persuasive that ethanol, in concentrations from 10 to 60 mM, causes dose-related depression in contractile function of isolated atrial (Loomis, 1952; Gimeno et al, 1962; Lake et al, 1978) and ventricular (Nakano and Moore, 1972; Fisher and Kavaler, 1975; Hirota et al, 1976; Mason et al, 1978; Segel et al, 1978) cardiac muscle measured as tension and rate of tension developed. Use of isolated, perfused rat and rabbit hearts or canine heart-lung preparations does not seem to yield as clear-cut results. Except for one study on perfused rat hearts (Lochner et al, 1969), most of these studies demonstrate that concentrations of ethanol from 10 to 60 mM result in dose-related enhancement of cardiac function (as assessed by cardiac output, stroke volume, or LVEDP), whereas concentrations of ethanol greater than 60 mM seem to produce depression of these parameters (Loeb, 1905; Dixon, 1907; Sulzer, 1924; Webb and Degerli, 1965; Webb et al, 1967; Gailis and Verdy, 1971; Mierzwiak et al, 1972; Wong, 1973). In conclusion, the work on isolated atrial and ventricular tissues makes it clear that ethanol can exert direct depressant actions on cardiac contractility in low and intoxicating BAC, but that studies on perfused hearts and/or heart-lung preparations may yield equivocal results at similar BAC since many intrinsic factors (e.g., cardiac metabolism, coronary circulation, etc.) make interpretation often impossible.

With respect to coronary blood flow, at least two studies, performed on isolated, perfused rat (Abel, 1980) and dog (Pescio et al, 1983) hearts, collectively, suggest rather strongly that ethanol can produce coronary vasodilatation and a dose-related decrease in total coronary vascular resistance which do not appear to be reflections of neurohumoral, metabolic, or cardiac mechanical factors (e.g., extravascular compression). Although these studies point to a direct coronary vasodilator action for ethanol, other newer work, done directly on coronary vascular muscle, questions such an interpretation (see below for further discussion) (Altura BM et al, 1983a).

Mechanisms and Role of Ethanol Metabolites
Although some previous reviewers have suggested that ethanol exerts exclusively depressant actions on the myocardium (Rubin, 1979; Regan and Haider, 1981; Alderman and Coltart, 1982; Segel et al, 1984), a thorough review of the literature seriously questions such a tenet. Rather, it seems that depending upon the pathophysiologic state of the subject and myocardium (whether animal or human subject), BAC concentration, coronary vascular actions, and

degree of autonomic nervous function, ethanol can enhance or depress a number of cardiac electrophysiologic and contractile parameters. Thus, any suggested mechanism(s) for ethanol's action on the myocardium must carefully take the latter into consideration. Overall, it seems clear that, at the present time, the cardiac cellular mechanisms for ethanol's acute excitatory and depressant actions are not known. Obviously, there are considerable data available indicating that acute ethanol administration can alter cardiac lipid metabolism (Kikuchi and Kako, 1970; Kako et al, 1973; Wong, 1974; Kricka and Clark, 1979), mitochondrial respiration, sarcoplasmic reticulum (SR) calcium ion (Ca^{2+}) transport, elevate Ca^{2+}, and produce slight modifications in adenosine triphosphate (ATP) levels (Swartz et al, 1974; Salerno and Ohrisini, 1976; Retig et al, 1977; Segel and Mason, 1979; Auffermann et al, 1988); intracellular pH (pHi), phosphocreatine, and inorganic phosphate (Pi) levels do not, however, appear to change (Auffermann et al, 1988). Most of these cellular actions of ethanol appear to be directed at membranes (both external and internal). Since acute ethanol in increasing concentration is well-known to disorder membranes (Lieber, 1982; Li et al, 1979; Kricka and Clark, 1979), it seems reasonable to conclude that both the cardiac excitatory and depressant actions of acute ethanol are reflections of effects at the plasma and internal cardiac cell membranes (e.g., SR, endoplasmic reticular, mitochondrial, and lysosomal). An attractive hypothesis, to us, appears to be actions of ethanol on transcellular movement and translocation of Ca^{2+} and Mg^{2+}, particularly since normal cardiac electrophysiologic and contractile events are dependent upon these two divalent cations, and cellular contents of these cations are known to be affected by ethanol (Altura BM, 1986; Altura BM, 1987; Altura BM and Altura BT, 1987). Acute Mg deficiency in cardiac and coronary vascular muscle can mimic most, if not all, the electrophysiologic, cardiac, and coronary vascular effects observed after acute ethanol administration; many of these effects are attributed to actions on cellular movement and translocation of Ca^{2+} (Peng et al, 1972; Turlapaty and Altura BM, 1978; Turlapaty and Altura BM, 1980; Altura BM and Altura BT, 1981b; Altura BM and Altura BT, 1981c; Altura BM, 1982; Altura BM and Altura BT, 1983; Altura BM et al, 1984c; Altura BM and Altura BT, 1985a; Altura BM and Altura BT, 1985b; Altura BM, 1986; Altura BM and Altura BT, 1987; Regan and Morvan, 1987).

With respect to ethanol's major metabolites, acetaldehyde and acetate, both of these molecules can exert potent, acute effects on the myocardium and coronary blood flow in human subjects and animals, in vivo as well as on in-vitro preparations (James and Bear, 1967; Walsh et al, 1969; Nakano and Prancan, 1972; Schreiber et al, 1972; Kirkendol et al, 1978; Friedman et al, 1979; Kobayashi et al, 1979; Rubin, 1979; Williams et al, 1980; Stratton et al, 1981; Altura BM, 1982; Lieber, 1982; Rubin and Rubin, 1982; Vincent et al, 1982; Altura BM and Altura BT, 1982b; Altura BM and Altura BT, 1983; Brien and Loomis, 1983; Altura BM et al, 1982a; Altura BM and Altura BT, 1987; Condouris and Havelin, 1987). However, it is important to point out that, in the main, acetaldehyde, in concentrations found in the blood after acute ethanol administration (i.e., 30–50 μM), acts as a sympathomimetic agent primarily (i.e., arterial blood pressure, heart rate, myocardial contractile force, and cardiac output all become elevated), depression of the myocardium is only obtained at doses of acetaldehyde which are severely toxic (e.g., 20–40 mg/kg). In addition, unlike ethanol, the sympathomimetic effects of acetaldehyde on the heart can be completely abrogated either by adrenergic blockade or agents that deplete tissues of catecholamines (James and Bear, 1967; Walsh et al, 1969; Gailis and Verdy, 1971; Nakano and Prancan, 1972; Lieber, 1982; Brien and Loomis, 1983; Condouris and Havelin, 1987). On the other hand, except for one report in dogs (Liang and Lowenstein, 1978), blood levels of acetate, observed after acute administration of ethanol in intact animals, isolated heart preparations, and human subjects, appear to induce consistent myocardial depressant actions (Kirkendol et al, 1978; Lieber, 1982; Vincent et al, 1982). Although the excitatory and depressant actions of acetaldehyde and acetate, respectively, may obscure and confound the acute myocardial actions of ethanol, it is doubtful that either substance, or both acting in concert, can account for the acute actions of alcohol on the heart.

Chronic Actions of Repeated Ingestion of Alcohol on the Myocardium

Chronotropicity in Humans and Intact Animals

Despite the fact that chronic consumption of alcohol can lead to progressive losses in cardiac functions, and eventually to alcoholic cardiomyopathy (a type of congestive cardiomyopathy), coronary heart disease, and stroke, there is only one prospective study available in human subjects (on one patient) (Regan et al, 1977) and a handful of controlled experimental studies in animals in which alcohol was administered over periods of several months in duration (Maines and Aldinger, 1967; Knott and Beard, 1972; Pachinger et al, 1973; Regan et al, 1974; Morvai et al, 1979b; Segel et al, 1981; Chan and Sutter, 1982; Noren et al, 1983; Hepp et al, 1984; Tepper et al, 1986; Posner et al, 1987). In the one study on one human (a "well-compensated" alcoholic studied for 5 1/2 months), heart rate clearly increased, leading to a ventricular gallop rhythm at 16 weeks which continued until the ethanol (16 oz. scotch whiskey per day) was discontinued. With respect to the animal studies, rats, turkeys, and dogs were utilized, receiving alcohol (4 to 18 g/kg body wt daily, depending upon the study) for periods of from 12 weeks (Morvai et al, 1979b) to as long as 22 months (Regan et al, 1974). However, it is important to point out that although some of these studies lasted 6–22 months (Maines and Aldinger, 1967; Regan et al, 1974; Tepper et al, 1986; Posner et al, 1987), the amount of alcohol taken in per day was often less than 4 gm/kg and less than 36% of the total calories (Maines and Aldinger, 1967; Regan et al, 1974). Also, the diets were often not controlled, thus making conclusions for the present reviewers difficult. Several of these long-term studies fail to demonstrate any significant changes in heart rate (Maines and Aldinger, 1967; Knott and Beard, 1972; Pachinger et al, 1973; Morvai et al, 1979b; Segel et al, 1981; Chan and Sutter, 1982; Noren et al, 1983; Hepp et al, 1984; Posner et al, 1987). Only the recent study in rats by Tepper et al. (1986) demonstrates a slight, significant fall (380 ± 12.5 to 335 ± 11.3 bpm, after 30 wks) in heart rate. However, the BAC at the time of measurement was 398 mg/dl or about 90 mM. This BAC seems rather high in comparison to levels observed in alcoholic patients. We must, therefore, conclude that, collectively, the data seem to suggest that chronic treatment with alcohol, at least under controlled laboratory conditions, fails to alter heart rate or chronotropicity. Obviously, it is distinctly possible that an intact autonomic nervous system and hormonal mechanisms compensate for any temporary alteration in HR.

Long-term, sequential studies on the effects of ethanol administration on isolated hearts, cardiac preparations, or cardiac myocytes are not available. Such studies are obviously sorely needed.

Cardiodynamics and Coronary Blood Flow in Humans and Animals

By now, it is clear that chronic ingestion of alcohol will most likely lead to progressive and marked impairment of cardiac function and often development of cardiomyopathy in animals and human subjects (Walshe, 1873; Bollinger, 1884; Brigden, 1957; Burch and Walsh, 1964; Maines and Aldinger, 1967; Knott and Beard, 1972; Spodick et al, 1972; Pachinger et al, 1973; Regan et al, 1974; Levi et al, 1977; Regan et al, 1977; Rubin, 1979; Morvai et al, 1979b; Anonymous, 1980; Khetarpal and Volicer, 1981; Regan and Haider, 1981; Segel et al, 1981; Alderman and Coltart, 1982; Altura BM, 1982; Chan and Sutter, 1982; Rubin and Rubin, 1982; Noren et al, 1983; Hepp et al, 1984; Segel et al, 1984; Howes and Reid, 1986; Tepper et al, 1986; Altura BM, 1987; Posner et al, 1987; Regan and Morvan, 1987). A syndrome termed "alcoholic heart disease" is now well-recognized, characterized by depressed myocardial function and frequent arrhythmias (Anonymous, 1980; Alderman and Coltart, 1982; Lieber, 1982). If alcohol consumption is aborted within a reasonable time (dependent upon dose and subject sensitivity), all of the pathophysiological manifestations can be reversed; however, if a certain duration of alcohol exposure has been obtained, then cardiomyopathy and death may ensue. Of particular interest, clinically, is that a stage prior to heart failure can be detected (Asokan et al, 1972; Spodick et al, 1972; Levi et al, 1977; Anonymous, 1980). Depressed cardiac function has been observed in chronic alcoholics who often lack overt clinical signs of heart disease. Exactly why some alcoholic patients go on to develop cirrhosis of the liver rather than cardiomyopathy is a mystery.

Although a number of reports have appeared documenting some of the hemodynamic changes observed in alcoholic cardiomyopathy (Burch and Walsh, 1960; Brigden and Robinson, 1964; Wendt et al, 1965; Hamby et al, 1970; Asokan et al, 1972; Spodick et al, 1972; Parker, 1974; Regan et al, 1977; Rubin, 1979; Anonymous, 1980; Regan and Haider, 1981; Alderman and Coltart, 1982; Lieber, 1982; Noren et al, 1983; Hepp et al, 1984; Tepper et al, 1986; Posner et al, 1987; Regan and Morvan, 1987), the available studies on the early states, either in animal or human subjects, are sparse and are difficult to compare, primarily due to different levels of alcohol intoxication and many dietary variables (Brigden and Robinson, 1964; Maines and Aldinger, 1967; Knott and Beard, 1972; Pachinger et al, 1973; Regan et al, 1974; Regan et al, 1975; Sarma et al, 1976; Morvai et al, 1979b; Segel et al, 1981; Chan and Sutter, 1982; Noren et al, 1983; Hepp et al, 1984; Segel et al, 1984; Tepper et al, 1986; Posner et al, 1987; Regan and Morvan, 1987). In addition, few data exist on coronary blood flow, per se (Regan et al, 1975; Morvai et al, 1979b; Alderman and Coltart, 1982; Lieber, 1982; Segel et al, 1984). Most of the precise data have to do with different parameters of mechanical performance. Due to these pitfalls, we are limited to qualitative, overall impressions rather than precise appraisals of the meaning of the available literature, particularly with respect to the effect of chronic ethanol on progressive changes in cardiac hemodynamics and coronary blood flow.

Overall, exposure to chronic dosing with alcohol, either self-administered or through laboratory experimentation, is associated with several types of arrhythmias, atrial as well as ventricular—the latter being seen more frequently (Burch and Walsh, 1960; Brigden and Robinson, 1964; Hamby et al, 1970; Spodick et al, 1972; Parker, 1974; Regan et al, 1975; Regan et al, 1977; Morvai et al, 1979b; Regan and Haider, 1981; Alderman and Coltart, 1982; Lieber, 1982; Lowenstein et al, 1983; Segel et al, 1984; Posner et al, 1987; Regan and Morvan, 1987). Alcoholics, who may not present with any signs of heart failure, often have abnormal systolic time intervals, elevated left ventricular end-diastolic pressures (LEDPs), depressed cardiac outputs, and sporadic signs of atrial fibrillation, as well as abnormal increases in LEDPs when the myocardium is stressed by rises in systemic arterial blood pressure (Regan et al, 1969; Asokan et al, 1972; Spodick et al, 1972; Demakis et al, 1974; Levi et al, 1977; Regan et al, 1977; Fink and Rosalki, 1979; Levi et al, 1979; Regan and Haider, 1981; Lieber, 1982; Lowenstein et al, 1983; Noe et al, 1985). In animals, particularly dogs made to imbibe ethanol chronically, sudden death is often observed, which is thought to be due to arrhythmias (Ettinger et al, 1976; Regan and Haider, 1981; Lieber, 1982; Regan and Morvan, 1987). The threshold for ventricular fibrillation in animals appears to be often decreased by ethanol administration (Regan et al, 1975; Lieber, 1982; Segel et al, 1984; Regan and Morvan, 1987).

In this context, arrhythmias are often precipitated in alcoholic human volunteers given alcohol orally (Singer and Lundberg, 1972). Bouts of heavy drinking ("binge drinking") clearly are associated with a higher than normal frequency of cardiac arrhythmias, often followed by sudden death (Anonymous, 1980; Alderman and Coltart, 1982; Lieber, 1982). The latter is often observed in the so-called "holiday heart" syndrome, which is usually due to atrial arrhythmias, together with life-threatening ventricular arrhythmias (e.g., ventricular tachycardia) (Ettinger et al, 1978; Greenspon et al, 1979).

To the foregoing must be added the growing number of experimental studies in animals which clearly show that prolonged exposure to ethanol results in progressive deficits in many types of cardiac mechanical functions (e.g., inotropic functions, time to peak tension, developed tension, time to half maximal relaxation, time to peak shortening, velocity of shortening, depressed force-velocity relationships, cardiac hypertrophy, decrease in number of β-adrenergic receptors (Maines and Aldinger, 1967; Pachinger et al, 1973; Swartz et al, 1974; Sarma et al, 1976; Weishaar et al, 1977; Maruyama et al, 1978; Tindall, 1980; Segel et al, 1981; Chan and Sutter, 1982; Hepp et al, 1984; Tepper et al, 1986; Hirst and Adams, 1987; Kwast et al, 1987; Posner et al, 1987).

Mechanisms

The biochemical and molecular mechanisms responsible for the foregoing impairments in cardiac functions, observed with prolonged exposure of the heart to ethanol, are at present unknown. Since a number of previous reviewers have provided considerable speculation already, the reader should consult these reviews for various hypotheses, bearing in mind that some of the above data may be in need of considerable revision (Regan et al, 1975; Regan et al, 1977; Kricka and Clark, 1979; Rubin, 1979; Morvai et al, 1979a; Regan and Haider, 1981; Altura BM, 1982; Leiber, 1982; Segel et al, 1984; Howes and Reid, 1986; Altura BM, 1987; Regan and Morvan, 1987).

CEREBRAL VASCULAR ACTIONS OF ALCOHOL

Introduction

In today's hospital population, vascular disorders of the nervous system are among the most frequent cases seen. More than half of all neurological admissions are for cerebrovascular disorders (Tindall, 1980). Included among these disorders involving the cerebral vasculature are occlusions by emboli, i.e., blood clots, rupture of cerebral vessels, obliteration of cerebral vessel lumens, and increased cerebral vascular permeability. Whatever the exact process, the result is one of transient brain ischemia, an ischemic stroke syndrome, or a hemorrhagic stroke syndrome. Since stroke is also a major contributor to disability and its treatment is often unlikely to restore a patient to his original prestroke state, prevention would appear to be the most realistic approach to stroke morbidity and mortality. But in order to accomplish this latter task, we must understand fully the etiologies of stroke syndromes. Germane to our discussion is the growing body of evidence which suggests that excessive alcohol consumption or "binge drinking" predisposes humans to strokes and sudden deaths (Bengesser and Weiser, 1974; Berlaga, 1975; Burtsev, 1975; Tarasyuk, 1976; Hillbom and Kaste, 1978; Lee, 1979; Lee et al, 1979; Ashley and Rankin, 1980; Anonymous, 1981; Hillbom and Kaste, 1981; Ashley, 1982; Taylor, 1982; Hillbom et al, 1983; Hillbom and Kaste, 1983; Altura BM and Altura BT, 1984a; Hillbom et al, 1985; Taylor and Combs-Orme, 1985; Anonymous, 1986; Donahue et al, 1986; Altura BM, 1987; Hillbom, 1987).

Chronic abuse of alcohol is known to produce atrophy of cortical, subcortical, and cerebral areas in the brain, including blackouts, functional neuronal deficits, and psychoses (Cala et al, 1978; Carlen et al, 1978; Riley and Walker, 1978; Lee et al, 1979; Walker et al, 1980; Anonymous, 1981; Cala and Mastaglia, 1981; Carlen et al, 1981; Lieber, 1982; Porjesz and Begleiter, 1983; Altura BM and Altura BT, 1984a; Lishman, et al, 1987), which may be related to reductions in cerebral blood flow (Altura BM and Altura BT, 1984a). Therefore, it is important to determine precisely whether acute administration and chronic abuse of alcohol result in alterations in blood flow to different areas in the brain. One must keep in mind that gross measurements of cerebral blood flow rather than discrete, localized measurements, will not provide critical and important information (Altura BM and Altura BT, 1984a). Unfortunately, most of the available studies on humans and animals did not employ sophisticated techniques nor control for ventilation (e.g., pCO_2) which would have provided such answers (Thomas, 1937; Goldfarb et al, 1940; Sohler et al, 1941; Battey et al, 1953; Fazekas et al, 1955; Eisenberg, 1968; Moskow et al, 1968; Marx et al, 1975). In addition, and most important, it must be borne in mind that most of the animal studies have employed diverse anesthetics and other drugs (Thomas, 1937; Fuhrman and Field, 1948; Hadji-Dimo et al, 1968; Hemmingsen et al, 1979; Hemmingsen and Barry, 1979; Barry and Hemmingsen, 1984), which not only exert direct actions on cerebral vascular smooth muscle (Altura BM et al, 1980; Altura BM et al, 1983c; Altura BM et al, 1984; Altura BT and Altura BM, 1984a; Altura BM and Altura BT, 1984b; Altura BM and Halevy, 1986), and interact in bizarre ways with ethanol on blood vessels (Altura BM and Altura BT, 1979b), but which impair normal autoregulation of cerebral blood flow (Altura BM and Halevy, 1986), thus compromising the data obtained with ethanol.

Effects of Ethanol on Cerebral and Regional Brain Blood Flow

Gross Cerebral Blood Flow Measurements in Humans

With the advent of the nitrous oxide technique devised by Kety and Schmidt in 1948 to assess cerebral blood flow (CBF) a number of studies were initiated by several clinic investigators in human subjects (Battey et al, 1953; Fazekas et al, 1955). Collectively, these studies by Battey et al (1953) and Fazekas et al (1955) indicated that mild ethanol intoxification (BAC = 68–140 mg/dl) did not cause reproducible changes in either CBF or cerebral oxygen consumption (CMRO$_2$), whereas patients admitted during severe alcohol intoxication (BAC = 320 mg/dl) exhibited 30% increases in CBF and about 30% decreases in CMRO$_2$. However, patients who presented with the Wernicke-Korsakoff Syndrome exhibited severe depression in CBF and CMRO$_2$ which persisted for several weeks (Shimojyo et al, 1967; Berglund and Ingvar, 1976; Berglund, 1981). We must keep in mind that the Kety-Schmidt technique is invasive and does not allow assessment of regional blood flow changes in the brain.

Regional Cerebral Blood Flow Measurements in Humans

With the advent of a new technique, whereby radioactive 133 Xenon is inhaled or injected in the internal carotid artery, it became possible to monitor discrete changes in regional cerebral blood flow (rCBF) (Raichle et al, 1976). Utilizing such a technique, a number of interesting and important observations have been made concerning alcohol's effect on rCBF in light to moderate drinkers and alcoholics. No studies, however, have been reported with a wide range of alcohol doses in naive human subjects. Utilizing subjects with histories of light to moderate drinking, Newlin et al (1982) found that subjects who consumed, acutely, 0.75 g/kg body weight of ethanol (in the form of 80-proof vodka mixed 1:3 with chilled fruit juice), which resulted in a BAC of approximately 50 mg/dl, exhibited increases in blood flow in the cortical gray matter (e.g., ~ 20% over controls) but not the white matter; flow seemed to increase more in the right than left anterior areas. Two of these eight subjects exhibited decreases in cortical blood flow upon ingestion of the alcohol.

With respect to chronic alcoholics, a number of investigators have clearly shown that such human subjects exhibit significant deficits in blood flow to the gray and white matter, as well as deficits in blood flow to the frontal and parietal regions of the brain (Berglund and Sonnessen, 1976; Berglund and Risberg, 1977; Heiss, 1977; Berglund, 1981). It is noteworthy that most of these studies seemed to demonstrate a correlation of alcohol abuse, degree of confusion, and degree of rCBF deficit. Patients who presented with Korsakoff's psychoses exhibited the greatest deficits in rCBF (Berglund and Ingvar, 1976; Berglund, 1981). These latter, more recent observations of Berglund and Ingvar (1976) thus support and extend the earlier findings of Shimojyo et al (1967) discussed above, who used less rigorous techniques.

Cerebral Blood Flow Measurements in Animals

Several in-vivo studies, employing rats, cats and dogs, have been performed to elucidate the effects of ethanol on CBF (Moskow et al, 1968; Hemmingsen and Barry, 1979; Hemmingsen et al, 1979; Friedman et al, 1981; Friedman et al, 1982; Goldman et al, 1973). Only two of these studies assessed rCBF in conscious animals (Friedman, 1981; Goldman et al, 1973). Both of these latter investigations, utilizing rats and dogs, demonstrated that when the acute administration of ethanol results in BAC levels = > 150 mg/dl, deficits in regional CBF are seen, particularly in the cortical and hippocampal areas. Barry and his coworkers, using halo-thane-anesthetized rats, have noted reductions in total CBF and $CMRO_2$ when BAC = 200–300 mg/dl (Hemmingsen and Barry, 1979; Hemmingsen et al, 1979; Barry and Hemmingsen, 1984); transient increases in CBF were noted when BAC < 100 mg/dl. In earlier studies in which rCBF was assessed with the ^{85}Krypton clearance technique, in nitrous-oxide- and pen-tobarbital-anesthetized cats, Hadji-Domo and colleagues (1968) demonstrated several inter-esting phenomena: (1) low doses of ethanol (BAC = 55 mg/dl) produced a transient 30% increase in cortical blood flow in N_2O-anesthetized animals, but no effect in pentobarbital-anesthetized cats; (2) BAC approaching approximately 135 mg/dl after two hours resulted in 30% decreases in rCBF in N_2O—as well as in pentobarbital-anesthetized animals; (3) in-terestingly, mean blood pressure levels often fell sharply with low and high BAC; and (4) a transient increase in rCBF observed with low BAC was accompanied by a desynchronization in the N_2O-anesthetized animals but not the pentobarbital-treated cats, leading to the specu-lation that CBF changes are linked to EEG changes. Since respiration was carefully monitored in these latter experiments and the others above (Friedman et al, 1981; Goldman et al, 1973), in which ethanol was found to produce decreases in rCBF, it is doubtful whether alterations in ventilation, per se, could have been responsible for the observed constrictor actions of al-cohol. It is also unlikely that the declines in mean arterial blood pressure could have been responsible, primarily, for the deficits in rCBF, since the former was observed even when low doses of ethanol produced transient increases in CBF (Hadji-Dimo et al, 1968).

Direct In-situ Studies on the Cerebral (Cortical) Microcirculation

Early qualitative studies by Thomas (1937) and Sohler et al (1941), performed more than 40 years ago using anesthetized cats and conscious rabbits or monkeys, respectively, suggested that small doses of ethanol, when intravenously-intracarotidally-, or intragastrically-admin-istered, could produce increases in the diameters of pial arteries. Unfortunately, these early studies did not control for respiration or pCO_2, nor were the brain preparations, visualized through cranial windows made by considerable trauma, what could be termed physiologic. These investigators unfortunately did not employ blood-free vascular fields—bleeding must perforce produce cerebrovasospasm (Tindall, 1980). In addition, the failure to examine a range of alcohol doses, together with the lack of any quantification, make such observations highly questionable and suspect.

In order to determine precisely alcohol's effect on cerebral arterioles and venules, the ultimate regulatory vessels, we had to devise an experimental animal model which would allow us to examine directly the cortical microscopic blood vessels in the brain after removal of select areas of the cranium without producing any vascular damage (Lassoff et al, 1982). Our technique results in a bloodless and atraumatic vascular field, as well as well-controlled ventilation and respiration (e.g., arterial pH = 7.42; $paCO_2$ = 35–43 mm Hg; PaO_2 = 98–108 mm Hg). In addition, the development of a sophisticated TV-image intensification micro-scope recording system allows us to make 30 measurements per minute of wall/lumen sizes of microvessels with an accuracy of 0.02 μm (Lassoff et al, 1982; Altura BM et al, 1983). The use of a local carbon clearance technique allows us to assess transit time or blood flow, locally, from an arteriole to a venule.

Utilizing the in-situ rat brain preparation, ethanol produced graded contractile responses in cortical arterioles (16–60 μm in diameter) and venules (22–75 μm in diameter) at a concen-tration range (10–500 mg/dl) which parallels that needed for its graded effects of euphoria, mental haziness, muscular incoordination, stupor, and coma in humans. These observations were noted irrespective of how the ethanol was administered, e.g., intravenously, intraperi-toneally, intracarotidally, or perivascularly (Altura BM and Altura BT, 1981a; Altura BM and

Altura BT, 1982b; Altura BM et al, 1982b; Altura BM et al, 1983; Altura BM et al, 1983b). Some of the data are illustrated in Figures 8.2 and 8.3 and Table 8.6. Doses of alcohol that resulted in perivascular or blood concentrations greater than 300 mg/dl usually resulted in arteriolar spasms that were irreversible and often followed by rupture within 5–10 minutes, leading to focal hemorrhages. Perivascular or intracarotid administration of 0.01% to 1% ethanol produced a concentration-related vasoconstriction of cortical venules, with an 8% to 60% reduction in vessel diameter (Altura BM and Altura BT, 1981a; Altura BM and Altura BT; 1982b; Altura BM et al, 1982b; Altura BM et al, 1983b; Altura BM and Altura BT, 1987); doses of ethanol above 0.3% often resulted in irreversible spasm and rupture. Using bolus intracarotid injections of doses of colloidal carbon (C1431a, Pellikan-Werke, Hanover, Germany), we have observed that blood flow in cortical arterioles to venules is reduced, in a concentration-dependent manner, 20%–60%, concomitant with the ethanol-induced micro-vascular spasms. As yet, no known pharmacologic antagonist or cyclo-oxygenase inhibitor can prevent, block, or attenuate the ethanol-induced vasospasms (Fig. 8.4) (Altura BM and Altura BT, 1981a; Altura BM, 1982; Altura BM et al, 1982b; Altura BM et al, 1983b). Since the arterial blood gases and pH were well within the normal ranges, and the animal was well ventilated, it is difficult to believe that these in-vivo microvascular cerebral spasms are due to local metabolic suppression, as has been suggested recently by Barry and Hemmingsen (1984). Moreover, a variety of drugs which we have used to induce metabolic suppression do not mimic the pronounced and sustained spasmogenic actions of ethanol. Other studies on

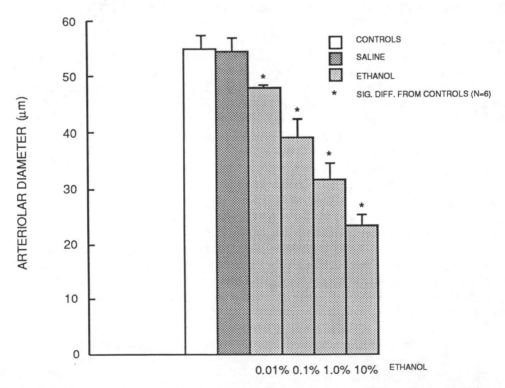

FIGURE 8.2. Alcohol-induced vasoconstriction of rat cortical arterioles in vivo. Different doses of alcohol were infused through the carotid artery at a constant rate of 0.02 ml/min. Observations were recorded for 30 to 45 seconds every 2 minutes over a period of 30 minutes beginning with each infusion. Vessel diameters were affected by alcohol within seconds. All experimental values are significant at $P < .0001$. Values are mean ± standard errors for six rats per group. Similar results were obtained irrespective of whether sodium pentobarbital or ketamine hydrochloride was used as the anesthetic. (Reprinted with permission of the American Association of Science, see Altura BM et al, 1983b).

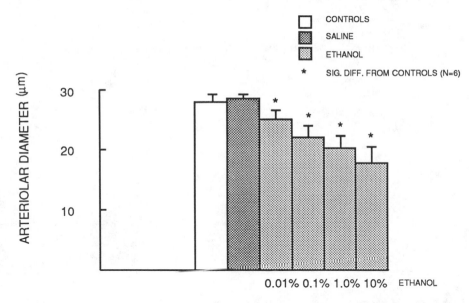

FIGURE 8.3 Perivascular application of alcohol to cortical surface of rat brain produces concentration-dependent constriction of arterioles.

Table 8.6. Alcohol-induced vasoconstriction of rat cortical arterioles in vivo*

ROUTE OF ADMINISTRATION AND DOSE	ARTERIOLAR DIAMETER (um)		
	BEFORE ALCOHOL	AFTER ALCOHOL	(%)
Perivascular			
Cerebrospinal fluid (0.01 ml)	27.4 ± 0.57	27.5 ± 0.56	0
10 mg/dl	27.5 ± 0.56	24.0 ± 0.50	12.7
25 mg/dl	27.4 ± 0.52	22.5 ± 0.42	17.8
100 mg/dl	27.3 ± 0.53	21.7 ± 0.38	20.5
250 mg/dl	27.3 ± 0.53	20.8 ± 0.35	23.8
1000 mg/dl	27.5 ± 0.56	20.2 ± 0.34	26.5
Systemic			
Saline	38.2 ± 0.72	38.4 ± 0.73	0
0.5 g/kg	38.0 ± 0.72	34.2 ± 0.66	10
1.0 g/kg	38.4 ± 0.74	30.4 ± 0.58	20.8
2.0 g/kg	38.2 ± 0.72	26.2 ± 0.46	31.4
4.0 g/kg	38.0 ± 0.71	24.6 ± 0.42	35.2

*Alcohol was administered to the surface of the brain in 0.1 ml volumes or intraperitoneally in doses of 0.5, 1.0, 2.0 or 4.0 g/kg. Observations were made 30 to 60 minutes after systemic (intraperitoneal) administration of alcohol. All experimental values are significantly different from the corresponding control values ($p < 0.001$, paired t-test). Values are means ± standard errors for eight rats per group.

isolated cerebral blood vessels lend support to our tenet (see below) (Toda et al, 1983; Altura BM et al, 1983b).

Ethanol Produces Spasms of Isolated Cerebral Arteries

Using isolated canine middle cerebral and basilar arteries (Fig. 8.5), we have clearly demonstrated that ethanol, in a concentration as little as 37 mg/dl (8 mM), produces contraction (Altura BM and Altura BT, 1981a; Altura BM et al, 1982b; Altura BM et al, 1983b). Thus

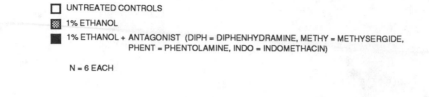

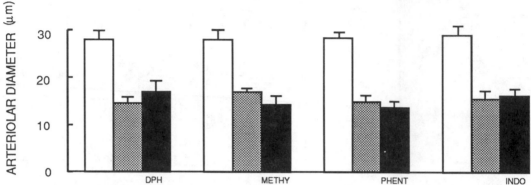

FIGURE 8.4. Failure of a variety of pharmacologic antagonists to prevent spasmogenic actions of alcohol on in-situ cortical arterioles.

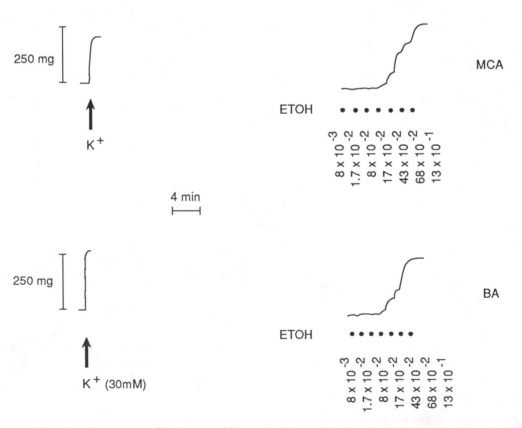

FIGURE 8.5. Typical responses of a canine middle cerebral artery (MCA) and a basilar artery (BA) to addition of KCl and alcohol. (Reprinted with permission of the American Association of Science, see Altura BM et al, 1983b.)

the threshold concentrations for cerebral arterioles in-vivo and isolated cerebral arteries are similar. Others have confirmed these observations on isolated cerebral arteries (Toda et al, 1983). In humans, blood alcohol concentrations of 35–40 mg/dl appear after the ingestion of less than 1 ounce of whiskey, producing some degree of euphoria, light-headedness, mental haziness, and talkativeness, with little impairment in memory or arithmetic problem-solving. The higher vasoactive levels of alcohol (> 250 mg/dl), which produce intense spasm of cerebral microvessels and arteries (Figs. 8.2–8.5, Table 8.6) (Altura BM and Altura BT, 1981a; Altura BM and Altura BT, 1982b; Altura BM et al, 1982b; Altura BM and Altura BT, 1983; Altura BM et al, 1983b) and often rupture of cortical arterioles and venules, are identical to those concentrations found in the blood of humans with alcohol-induced stupor, coma, and stroke-like episodes (Berlaga, 1975; Hillbom and Kaste, 1978; Ashley and Rankin, 1980; Hillbom and Kaste, 1981; Taylor, 1982; Hillbom and Kaste, 1983; Hillbom et al, 1983; Hillbom, 1987).

Calcium Antagonists and the Mimic-Calcium Antagonist, Magnesium, Prevent and Reverse Alcohol-induced Cerebrovasospasms

Since all contractile events in muscle tissues, including vascular smooth muscle, are mediated by an elevation in the cytoplasmic level of calcium-ions (Ca^{2+}) (Karaki and Weiss, 1988), it was of great interest to determine whether synthetic Ca^{2+} antagonists or the naturally-occurring mimic-Ca^{2+} antagonist, Mg^{2+} (Altura BM and Altura BT, 1981b; Altura BM and Altura BT, 1981c; Altura BM and Altura BT, 1985b), could reverse or prevent the in-vivo and in-vitro cerebrovasospasms. Use of several different Ca^{2+} antagonists, e.g., verapamil, nimodipine, nitrendipine and nisoldipine (10^{-9} to 10^{-5}M), known to act on microvessels (Altura BM et al, 1983c; Altura BM and Altura BT, 1984b; Altura BM et al, 1984a; Altura BM et al, 1987), completely reversed or prevented spasms in all isolated canine cerebral arteries tested (Altura BM et al, 1983b; Altura and Altura, 1987). Mg^{2+} (10^{-4} to 10^{-2}M) was also found to be an effective in-vitro antagonist of the ethanol-induced vasospasms (Altura BT and Altura BM, 1982; Altura BT and Altura BM, 1984b; Altura BM et al, 1986; Ema et al, 1988). Recent in-vivo findings, using the intact rat brain preparation, indicate that the systemic administration of synthetic Ca^{2+} antagonists as well as the natural Ca^{2+} antagonist, Mg^{2+}, are also effective in reversing or preventing arteriolar and venular spasms (Altura BT and Altura BM, 1982; Altura BM et al, 1983b; Altura BT and Altura BM, 1984b; Altura BM et al, 1986; Altura BM and Altura BT, 1987; Ema et al, 1988).

Conclusions Concerning CBF

Collectively, the bulk of the human and animal studies seem to indicate that ingestion of ethanol (> 150 mg/dl) can produce deficits in regional CBF, particularly in the cortical and hippocampal areas. Ingestion of small amounts of ethanol (e.g., < 75 mg/dl) may produce transient increases in CBF. There appears to be no question, however, that long-term ingestion of ethanol will result in deficits in rCBF in human subjects; the Korsakoff-type syndrome seems to result in the greatest deficits in rCBF. A great deal of the literature, unfortunately, has been confounded by the use of crude techniques, anesthetics, and drugs which affect $CMRO_2$ and rCBF, and a failure to explore a range of alcohol concentrations. At this point, one must seriously entertain the probability that ethanol produces direct effects on cerebral vascular smooth muscle. It is anticipated that refinements in rCBF measurements in human subjects will result from the direct application of positron emission tomography and nuclear magnetic resonance imaging techniques in the near future.

Significance of Ethanol-induced Cerebral Vasoconstriction: Possible Relationship to Stroke Etiology, Sudden Death, Hypertension and Hallucinations

Hillbom and Kaste have reported that of 100 patients who presented with ischemic brain infarction, 40% were directly associated with heavy usage of alcohol 72 hours prior to the stroke-like events (1983). It is interesting to note here that young, middle-aged men, as opposed to women, appear to be susceptible to alcohol-related cerebral infarctions. Overall, when this persuasive evidence is viewed in light of previous and more recent reports (Bengesser and Weiser, 1974; Berlaga, 1975; Burtsev, 1975; Tarasyuk, 1976; Hillbom and Kaste, 1978; Lee, 1979; Lee et al, 1979; Ashley and Rankin, 1980; Anonymous, 1981; Hillbom and Kaste, 1981; Taylor, 1982; Hillbom et al, 1983; Anonymous, 1986; Donahue et al, 1986; Hillbom, 1987; Lishman et al, 1987), one must entertain the probability that a number of stroke-like events and strokes are directly due to the spasmogenic actions of ethanol on the brain. The question is whether or not these stroke-like incidents can, indeed, be related directly to the actions of alcohol on cerebral blood vessels and/or local and systemic effects on blood pressure.

Our observations in-vivo and in-vitro support the suggestion made earlier by Goldman and coworkers (1973) that ethanol produces anoxia in the brain by affecting the cerebral circulation. The tenet would fit in well with the reported effects of ethanol on $CMRO_2$. These observations also may explain in part the hallucinations often observed in a number of chronic alcoholics, e.g., Korsakoff syndrome in particular. A number of psychotomimetic agents have recently been reported to reduce cerebral blood flow and to produce spasmogenic effects on cerebral arteries, arterioles, and venules (Altura BT and Altura BM, 1981; Altura BT and Altura BM, 1983b; Altura BT et al, 1983; Altura BT et al, 1984; Altura BT and Altura BM, 1984a). Several of these psychotomimetic agents, e.g., Phencyclidine (PCP), LSD, Mescaline, etc., have also been found to produce stroke-like effects in a number of human subjects (Altura BT and Altura BM, 1981; Altura BT and Altura BM, 1984a).

We believe that our findings, indicating spasmogenic actions of ethanol on cerebral blood vessels, may also have direct bearing on the higher than normal incidence of hypertension in chronic alcoholics and the higher than normal incidence of cerebrovascular accidents and sudden death in binge drinkers. The previously observed adverse actions of ethanol on sludging of blood flow (Moskow et al, 1968), blood viscosity (Stefanelli and Ronge, 1978; Hillbom et al, 1983; Hillbom, 1987), and platelet-derived eicosanoid products (Kangasho et al, 1983; Hillbom et al, 1984; Hillbom et al, 1985; Hillbom, 1987) could act in concert with the spasmogenic actions of ethanol on cerebral blood vessels to produce cerebral infarctions. So far, it has been difficult to account for the elevation in blood pressure observed in chronic alcoholics on the basis of age, sex, obesity, smoking, plasma high-density lipoproteins, catecholamines, or heredity (Beevers, 1977; Mathews, 1979; Ashley and Rankin, 1980; Potter et al, 1984; Howes and Reid, 1986; Trell et al, 1986). Likewise, none of these factors can account for the incidence of stroke in binge drinkers, particularly among the young (Hillbom and Kaste, 1978; Hillbom and Kaste, 1981; Taylor, 1982; Hillbom and Kaste, 1983; Hillbom et al, 1983; Anonymous, 1986; Hillbom, 1987). Because curtailment of blood flow to the central nervous system may result in hypertension (Folkow, 1982), and because prolonged cerebral vasospasm can lead to brain ischemia and rupture of cerebral vessels (Altura BT and Altura BM, 1982; Altura BT and Altura BM, 1984b), our findings when taken in concert with other observations (Edgarian and Altura BM, 1976; Altura BM et al, 1979; Altura BM, 1982; Altura BM et al, 1982a; Altura BM and Altura BT, 1982b; Altura BM et al, 1982c; Altura BM et al, 1982b; Altura BM and Altura BT, 1983; Toda et al, 1983; Altura BT and Altura BM, 1983a; Altura BM et al, 1983b; Potter et al, 1984; Howes and Reid, 1986; Altura BM and Altura BT, 1987) may cast light on the etiology of alcohol-induced hypertension (see also below) and stroke, particularly since both are often associated with one another.

PERIPHERAL VASCULAR ACTIONS OF ALCOHOL

Introduction

In terms of peripheral circulatory effects, acute systemic administration of ethanol (EtOH) can produce vasodilatation and lower arterial blood pressure (Khetarpal and Volicer, 1981; Altura BM, 1982). Until recently, it was thought that such effects were due primarily to the actions of EtOH on the heart, respiratory system, central nervous system (CNS), and autonomic nervous system (Ritchie, 1975; Rix, 1977). There are also some reports, both in humans and experimental animals, which indicate that systemic administration of EtOH may induce profound vasoconstriction or biphasic effects on peripheral blood flow (Fewings et al, 1966; Nakano and Kessinger, 1972; Jones et al, 1981; Khetarpal and Volicer, 1981; Altura BM, 1982; Friedman et al, 1982; Friedman et al, 1983; Goldman et al, 1983; Kettunen et al, 1983; Friedman et al, 1984; Altura BM and Altura BT, 1984a; Howes and Reid, 1986). The mechanism(s) of these effects does not appear to be attributable to actions of EtOH on the heart, CNS, or autonomic nervous system. It should be recalled here that tone and reactivity of intact peripheral blood vessels can be affected by numerous homeostatic (physiologic), pharmacologic, and experimental factors (Table 8.7).

Since ethanol's major metabolites (i.e., acetaldehyde and acetate) can exert actions on the heart (see above) and peripheral vascular system (Egle et al, 1973; Gallis, 1975; Altura BM and Altura BT, 1982b), the idea must be entertained that these molecules may play roles in the seemingly diverse actions EtOH exerts on the cardiovascular system. It is also possible, however, that EtOH exerts differential actions on peripheral and cerebral blood vessels due to its indirect actions on the vascular effects of circulating neurohumoral substances (Edgarian and Altura BM, 1976; Altura BM et al, 1979; Turlapaty et al, 1979b; Altura BM and Altura BT, 1981b; Dionigi et al, 1982; Altura BM and Altura BT, 1982b; Altura BM and Altura BT, 1983; Altura BT and Altura BM, 1983a; Eisenhofer et al, 1984; Howes and Reid, 1986). One must also consider the fact that vascular smooth muscle cells in different regions of the circulation could respond differently to identical concentrations of EtOH (Altura BM et al, 1976; Edgarian and Altura BM, 1976; Altura BM et al, 1980; Altura BM and Altura BT, 1981b; Altura BM et al, 1982a; Altura BM and Altura BT, 1982b; Altura BM et al, 1982c; Altura BM and Altura BT, 1983; Altura BM et al, 1983a; Altura BM et al, 1983b; Altura BM and Altura BT, 1984a). A number of diverse physiological and pharmacological factors have been suggested to account for the heterogeneous response of regional blood vessels to EtOH (Altura and Altura, 1982a).

Table 8.7. Physiological, pharmacological and experimental factors which can modify the tone and actions of vasoactive agents on blood vessels

PHYSIOLOGICAL	PHARMACOLOGICAL AND EXPERIMENTAL
Heterogeneity of smooth muscle elements	Anesthetic (presence and type)
Endothelial cell integrity	Analgesics
Aging	Buffers
Sex hormones	Solvents, preservatives
Innervation	Presence of certain drugs
Ionic milieu	Route of drug administration
Physical	Purity of agonist
a. Length-tension (e.g., blood pressure, wall thickness, geometry, etc.)	Surgical manipulation
b. Temperature	
Tissue metabolism and osmolarity	
Local chemicals and hormones	
Species, strain	
Physiologic state of host	
Diet	

Since the chronic effects of EtOH on the cardiovascular system appear to be pivotal in some unknown way(s) in the etiology of hypertension, coronary heart disease(s) (CHD), and strokes, it is important to elucidate and understand the effects of chronic alcohol abuse and its mechanisms of action on the peripheral blood vessels.

This section will review recent evidence which suggests that EtOH alters peripheral blood flows, as well as arterial blood pressure, both acutely and chronically, by virtue of its direct actions on vascular smooth muscle cells, circulating and released neurohumoral substances, and on movement and translocation of divalent cations (Ca^{2+}, Mg^{2+}) across the diverse vascular muscle membranes.

Influence of Ethanol on Spontaneous Contractions and Basal Tone of Blood Vessels

In vitro, low to intermediate concentrations of ethanol (e.g., 1–100 mM) cause a dose-dependent inhibition of spontaneous mechanical activity in venous and arterial smooth muscles as well as lower resting tension in arteries (Fig. 8.6) (Altura BM and Altura BT, 1976; Altura BM et al, 1976; Edgarian and Altura BM, 1976; Altura BT and Altura BM, 1978; Turlapaty et al, 1979b; Altura BM et al, 1980; Altura BM and Altura BT, 1981b; Altura BM and Altura BT, 1982a; Altura BM and Altura BT, 1982b; Altura BM and Altura BT, 1983; Altura BT and Altura BM, 1983). In all cases, the greater the concentration of alcohol (up to approximately 150 mM), the more rapid the inhibition, and the more the resting tension is lowered. Threshold inhibitory effects can be observed with blood alcohol levels of 1–20 mM, depending upon blood vessels; these concentrations are what one would expect in the blood of man after oral ingestion of only 1–2 ounces of ethanol (Altura BM et al, 1976). These concentration-dependent changes in mechanical activity are not tachyphylactic and are not all-or-none responses (Altura BM and Altura BT, 1976; Altura BM et al, 1976; Edgarian and Altura BM, 1976; Altura BT and Altura BM, 1978; Turlapaty et al, 1979b; Altura BM et al, 1980; Altura BM and Altura BT, 1981b; Altura BM and Altura BT, 1982a; Altura BM and Altura BT, 1982b; Altura BM and Altura BT, 1983; Altura BT and Altura BM, 1983a). None of these

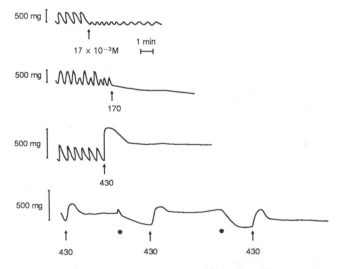

FIGURE 8.6. Influence of various concentrations of ethanol on the development of spontaneous mechanical activity and base-line tension in isolated rat aortic strips. The arrows indicate the points at which the tissues were exposed to ethanol (mM). The bars on the left represent developed tension. Dots in figure indicate point at which strips were washed (and relaxed) in normal Krebs-Ringer bicarbonate solution. Adapted from Altura BM et al, 1976.

ethanol-induced inhibitory (relaxation) responses can be mimicked, attenuated, or prevented with known pharmacologic antagonists, nor are they due to release of prostaglandins or to actions on beta-adrenergic receptors (Altura BM and Altura BT, 1976; Altura BM et al, 1976; Edgarian and Altura BM, 1976; Altura BT and Altura BM, 1978; Turlapaty et al, 1979a; Altura BM et al, 1980; Altura BM and Altura BT, 1981b; Altura BM and Altura BT, 1982a; Altura BM and Altura BT, 1982b; Altura BM and Altura BT, 1983; Altura BT and Altura BM, 1983a). Such data suggest that these vasodepressant effects of ethanol may be due to some direct actions on the vascular smooth muscles. It is of interest to note that these effects of ethanol on basal tension and spontaneous activity resemble rather closely the effects of reduction in the concentration of extracellular calcium ions ($[Ca^{2+}]_o$) on these vessels (Altura BM et al, 1970; Altura BM et al, 1980; Altura BM and Altura BT, 1981b; Karaki and Weiss, 1988). It may be of further interest that similar observations have been seen on other types of smooth muscle (Goldie et al, 1984).

With respect to higher concentrations of ethanol (>100 mM), one usually finds that this alcohol will evoke dose-dependent contractile effects on isolated blood vessels (Fig. 8.6) (Altura BM et al, 1976; Edgarian and Altura BM, 1976a; Edgarian and Altura BM, 1976b; Altura BM et al, 1979; Turlapaty et al, 1979b; Altura BM et al, 1980; Altura BM and Altura BT, 1981b; Lassoff et al, 1982; Altura BM and Altura BT, 1982a; Altura BM et al, 1982a; Altura BM and Altura BT, 1982b; Altura BM et al, 1982c; Altura BM and Altura BT, 1983; Toda et al, 1983; Altura BT and Altura BM, 1983a; Altura BM et al, 1983a; Altura BM et al, 1983b; Chand and Altura BM, 1984; Karanian and Salem, 1986; Yang et al, 1986), including those obtained from coronary, renal, pulmonary, umbilical-placental, and skeletal muscle vasculatures. Like the effects seen with lower concentrations of ethanol, these contractile actions are not due to release of any known vasoactive mediator nor to actions of any known distinct receptor which subserves contractile events (Altura BM et al, 1976; Edgarian and Altura BM, 1976a; Altura BM et al, 1979; Turlapaty et al, 1979b; Altura BM et al, 1980; Altura BM and Altura BT, 1981a; Altura BM and Altura BT, 1981b; Altura BM, 1982; Altura BM and Altura BT, 1982a; Altura BM et al, 1982a; Altura BM and Altura BT, 1982b; Altura BM et al 1982b; Altura BM et al, 1982c; Altura BM and Altura BT, 1983; Toda et al, 1983; Altura BT and Altura BM, 1983a; Altura BM et al, 1983a; Altura BM et al, 1983b; Chand and Altura BM, 1984; Altura BM and Altura BT, 1984a). Such findings may aid in explaining why one often sees potent constriction of blood vessels in the forearm of humans upon intra-arterial administration of ethanol (Fewings et al, 1966), as well as pulmonary hypertension (Kettunen et al, 1983), and coronary arterial ischemia (and arrhythmias) after administration of ethanol (Regan and Haider, 1981; Alderman and Coltart, 1982; Altura BM and Altura BT, 1983; Lowenstein et al, 1983; Altura BT and Altura BM, 1983a; Takizawa et al, 1984). The umbilical-placental vessel vasoconstriction noted after administration of ethanol (Altura BM et al, 1982a) may be linked to production of the fetal alcohol syndrome and fetal mortality during pregnancy (Lieber, 1982).

Ethanol Differentially Affects Eicosanoid-Induced Contractions of Blood Vessels

Another important peripheral vascular effect of ethanol is that it interacts with prostaglandin compounds (PG) in bizarre ways. For example, addition of low concentrations of ethanol (e.g., only 1 $\mu g/ml$) can markedly inhibit the contractile action of PGE_1 on isolated rat and canine arteries and veins. In contrast to what is seen for PGE_1, these same low concentrations of ethanol can enhance contractions induced by PGE_1 and PGA_1 on isolated rat blood vessels (Altura BM and Altura BT, 1976; Edgarian and Altura BM, 1976a; Altura BM and Altura BT, 1982a; Karanian and Salem, 1986). High concentrations of ethanol, however, can markedly attenuate contractions induced by all eicosanoid compounds (i.e., As, Bs, Ds, Fs, PGI_2, thromboxanes, endoperoxides) so far investigated (Altura BM and Altura BT, 1976;

Edgarian and Altura BM, 1976a; Altura BM and Altura BT, 1982a; Karanian and Salem, 1986). Exactly how are these differential actions induced by the alcohol? Are these effects also linked in some way to actions on ionized calcium levels (see below)?

Ethanol Interacts with Contractile Substances on Blood Vessels

Other substances, in addition to PGs, are also differentially affected by the concentration of ethanol and the particular neurohumoral agent. For example, low concentrations of ethanol potentiate vasopressin and catecholamines (e.g., epinephrine, norepinephrine), while higher concentrations attenuate contractions induced by these two classes of circulating neurohumors (Fig. 8.7) (Altura BM et al, 1976; Edgarian and Altura BM, 1976a; Altura BM et al, 1979; Turlapaty et al, 1979b; Altura BM et al, 1980; Altura BM and Altura BT, 1981a; Altura BM and Altura BT, 1981b; Altura BM, 1982; Altura BM and Altura BT, 1982a; Altura BM et al, 1982a; Altura BM and Altura BT, 1982b; Altura BM et al, 1982b; Altura BM et al, 1982c; Altura BM and Altura BT, 1983; Toda et al, 1983; Altura BT and Altura BM, 1983a; Altura BM et al, 1983a; Altura BM et al, 1983b; Chand and Altura BM, 1984; Altura BM and Altura BT, 1984a). As with the PGs, higher concentrations of ethanol can attenuate, markedly and in a concentration-dependent manner, contractions induced by all other types of vasoactive mediators (e.g., angiotensin II, serotonin, histamine, kinins, acetylcholine, etc.) so far examined (Altura BM et al, 1976; Edgarian and Altura BM, 1976a; Altura BM et al, 1979; Turlapaty et al, 1979b; Altura BM et al, 1980; Altura BT et al, 1980; Altura BM and Altura BT,

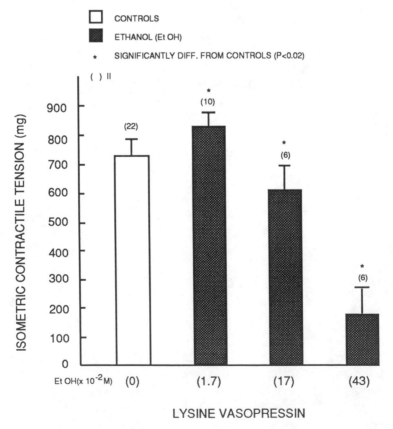

FIGURE 8.7. Effects of ethanol on vasopressin (2 mU/ml)-induced concentrations of rat aortic strips. Adapted from Altura BM et al, 1976.

1981a; Altura BM and Altura BT, 1981b; Altura BM, 1982; Altura BM and Altura BT, 1982a; Altura BM et al, 1982a; Altura BM and Altura BT, 1982b; Altura BM et al, 1982b; Altura BM et al, 1982c; Toda et al, 1983; Altura BT and Altura BM, 1983a; Altura BM et al, 1983a; Altura BM et al, 1983b; Chand and Altura BM, 1984; Altura BM and Altura BT, 1984a). It should be pointed out that these neurohumoral substances are normally responsible for controlling vascular tone, blood flow, and blood pressure (Altura BM, 1971; Altura BM, 1981).

Non-specificity of Ethanol's Inhibitory Actions on Isolated Blood Vessels

The above described direct inhibitory actions on myogenic tone and neurohumoral-induced contractile responses suggest that ethanol might produce vasodilatation and hypotention by some non-specific, direct action on vascular smooth muscle. In support of this concept are recent findings which indicate that contractile concentration-effect curves obtained for a variety of neurohumoral substances, and potassium ions in the presence of increasing concentrations of ethanol are shifted rightward to higher concentration concomitant with dose-dependent reductions in maximum responses (Figs. 8.8 and 8.9) (Altura BM et al, 1976; Edgarian and Altura BM, 1976a; Altura BT and Altura BM, 1978; Altura BM et al, 1979; Altura BM et al, 1980; Altura BM and Altura BT, 1981b; Dionigi et al, 1982; Altura BM and Altura BT, 1982a; Altura BM and Altura BT, 1982b; Altura BM and Altura BT, 1983; Altura BT and Altura BM, 1983a; Karanian and Salem, 1986; Yang et al, 1986).

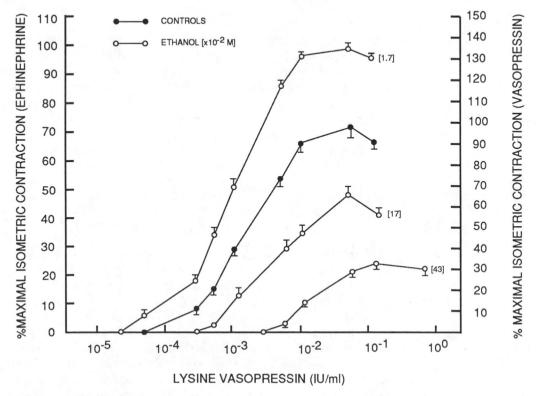

FIGURE 8.8. Influence of ethanol on vasopressin concentration-effect curves on isolated rat aortic strips. Values are means ± SEM, N = 28. Maximal control isometric response = 839 ± 57 mg. Adapted from Altura BM et al, 1976.

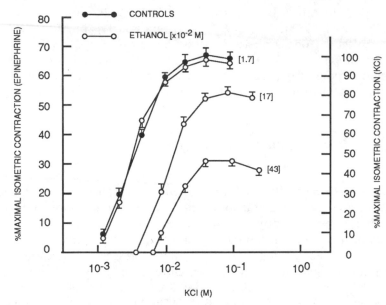

FIGURE 8.9. Influence of ethanol on KCl concentration-effect curves in isolated rat aortic strips. Values are means ± SEM. Maximal isometric response = 713 ± 21 mg. Adapted from Altura BM et al, 1976.

Similarity of Ethanol's Inhibitory Action to Those Observed for General Anesthetics on Vascular Smooth Muscles

In vitro, most of the commonly used general anesthetics (e.g., halothane, diethyl ether, chloroform, barbiturates, ketamine, urethane, propanidid, steroids, etc.) also cause a dose-dependent inhibition of spontaneous mechanical activity in venous and arterial smooth muscle and lower resting tension in arteries, as well as attenuate the contractile responses of isolated blood vessels to catecholamines, serotonin, angiotensin II, vasopressin, PGs, and potassium ions. Again, these actions suggest that these anesthetics produce vasodepressant effects on blood vessels by some nonspecific action on the vascular smooth muscle cells (Altura BM et al, 1970; Altura BT and Altura BM, 1975; Altura BT and Altura BM, 1978; Altura BM and Weinberg, 1979; Altura BM et al, 1980; Altura BM, 1981; Altura BM and Altura BT, 1981b; Altura BM and Altura BT, 1982a; Altura BT and Altura BM, 1984a).

Influence of Ethanol on Calcium-induced Contractions, Calcium Exchange, and Content of Vascular Muscle

If ethanol can exert the above actions on isolated arterial and venous smooth muscle, how does the alcohol bring about the inhibitory actions? Since ethanol (1) does not cause its vasodepressant (or contractile, or potentiating) effects by releasing (or inhibiting) any known endogenous substances or vasoactive mediator; (2) acts on isolated blood vessels and several other types of smooth muscle (Heiss, 1977; Clement, 1980; Goldie et al, 1984), even some devoid of sympathetic innervation (e.g., umbilical arteries and veins, precapillary sphincters, metarterioles), and (3) acts nonspecifically on spontaneous vasomotor (or myogenic) tone, neurohumoral contractions, and ion-induced responses, it is more than likely that ethanol inhibits and potentiates contractility, depending upon concentration (and tissue) of vascular smooth muscle (and maybe smooth muscle, in general) cells by a common mechanism. A likely point of action might be the availability of activator Ca^{2+} for the contractile process.

Ethanol could interfere with the mobility of Ca^{2+} both at the vascular membranes and intracellularly, since it penetrates both membranes and cells rapidly (Seeman, 1972; Smith, 1977). If so, one would anticipate that Ca^{2+}-induced contractions of K^+-depolarized vascular muscles would be most sensitive to ethanol inhibition, as is exactly the case (e.g., Fig. 8.10) (Altura BM et al, 1976; Edgarian and Altura BM, 1976b; Altura BT and Altura BM, 1978; Turlapaty et al, 1979b; Altura BM et al, 1980; Altura BM and Altura BT, 1981b; Altura BM and Altura BT, 1982a; Altura BM and Altura BT, 1982b; Altura BM and Altura BT, 1983; Yang et al, 1986). The observed shifts of the log concentration-response curves for the agonists (e.g., Figs. 8.8, 8.9), as well as for Ca^{2+}, together with the reduction in maximum tensions and the inhibition of $[Ca^{2+}]_o$-dependent spontaneous mechanical activity in the presence of ethanol would all be consistent with the hypothesis that this membrane-active agent interferes with the mobility of Ca^{2+} both at the vascular membranes and intracellularly. Recent direct experiments, using ^{45}Ca and isolated rat aortas and portal veins, indicate that ethanol can indeed significantly inhibit membrane-bound Ca by 30% to 40%; total exchangeable Ca is also significantly attenuated (Table 8.8) (Turlapaty et al, 1979a; Turlapaty et al, 1979b; Altura BM and Altura BT, 1981b).

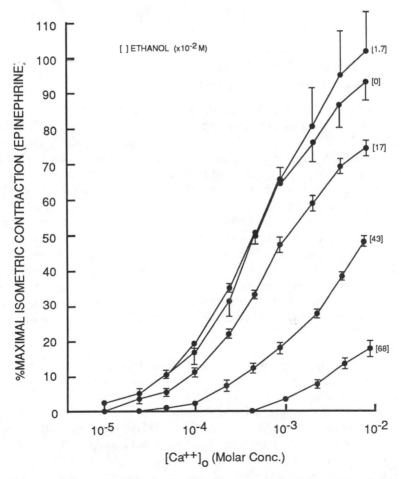

FIGURE 8.10. Influence of ethanol on calcium chloride-induced contractions of potassium-depolarized rat aorta. N = 5 to 6 each. Values are means ± SEM. Mean 100% response = 1,020 ± 71 mg. Adapted from Altura BM et al, 1976.

Table 8.8. Influence of an anesthetic concentration of ethanol on total exchangeable and cellular calcium in rat aortas and portal veins*

VESSEL TREATMENT	TOTAL EXCHANGEABLE CALCIUM	2-MIN LA^{3+} WASH CALCIUM FRACTION (membrane-bound)	5-MIN LA^{3+} WASH CALCIUM FRACTION (cellular fraction)
Aorta			
Control	4.22 ± 0.11 (33)+	2.27 ± 0.10 (24)	0.80 ± 0.04 (12)
Ethanol‡	3.46 ± 0.11^{ss} (6)	1.53 ± 0.14^{ss} (6)	0.78 ± 0.09 (6)
Portal Vein			
Control	3.07 ± 0.18 (31)+	2.17 ± 0.08 (19)	1.40 ± 0.14 (10)
Ethanol‡	2.51 ± 0.17^{ss} (5)	1.55 ± 0.12^{ss} (6)	1.64 ± 0.17 (5)

*Values are expressed as mMoles/kg wet wt. Adapted from Turlapaty et al (148, 149).

+Number of different animals examined.

‡170 mM.

^{ss}Significantly different from control (p < 0.005).

Effects of Acute Ethanol Administration on Arterioles and Venules in the Peripheral Circulation: Direct In vivo Studies on Microcirculation

Despite the numerous attempts for the past 100 years to define precisely the peripheral vascular actions of ethanol, using intact animals and human subjects (Walshe, 1873; Steell, 1893; Dixon, 1907; Price, 1922; Ritchie, 1975; Rix, 1977; Khetarpal and Volicer, 1981; Altura BM, 1982; Friedman et al, 1982; Howes and Reid, 1986), it has been difficult to find a solution to this dilemma. Part of the problem resides in the complex effects of EtOH on the autonomic and central nervous systems. But a major problem has been to find a method(s) which would allow one to discern instantaneously, or after chronic treatment, what a particular concentration of EtOH does to basal tone and blood flow in the effector microscopic resistance and capacitance vessels, viz., the arterioles and venules in different regions of the microvasculature. Use of quantitative in vivo television microscope recording systems allows one to resolve 10 times the power of the light microscope, i.e., 6,000 times normal size, and make 30–60 measurements per minute. Thus, the observer can quantify the effects of various drug molecules in arterioles (12–40 μm) and venules (15–80 μm) in different regions of the microcirculation (Altura BM, 1971; Altura BM et al, 1979; Altura BM, 1981; Altura BM et al, 1982c; Altura BM et al, 1983b).

Splanchnic Microcirculation: Intestinal Wall and Mesentery

Recent in vivo, quantitative observations on the splanchnic microvasculature, using high-resolution closed circuit television microscopy (up to 3000× magnification), have revealed that irrespective of the route of administration (i.e., topical, intravenous, intra-arterial), ethanol dilates precapillary sphincters (4–6 μm), arterioles (17–35 μm) and muscular venules (35–70 μm) in a concentration-dependent manner (e.g., Figs. 8.11 and 8.12) (Altura BM, 1978; Altura BM et al, 1979; Altura BM, 1981). In addition, irrespective of the route of administration, ethanol can non-specifically inhibit constrictions caused by neurohumoral agonists (e.g., norepinephrine, epinephrine, angiotensin, serotonin, vasopressin, prostaglandins, etc.) and Ba^{2+} ions (Fig. 8.13) (Altura BM, 1978; Altura BM et al, 1979; Altura BM, 1981), results very similar to those noted above in isolated arteries and veins. These direct in-situ stud-

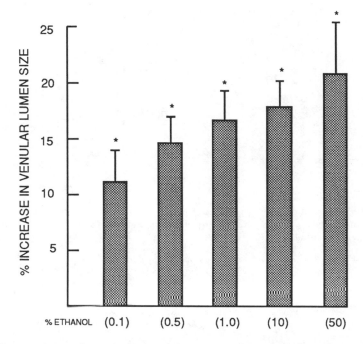

FIGURE 8.11. Influence of topically applied ethanol on rat mesenteric terminal venules. N = 39. Small bars = SEM. The control lumen sizes were 15–23 μm. Each large bar represents the mean percent change in lumen size obtained from measurements on vessels of different male rats. Adapted from Altura BM et al, 1979.

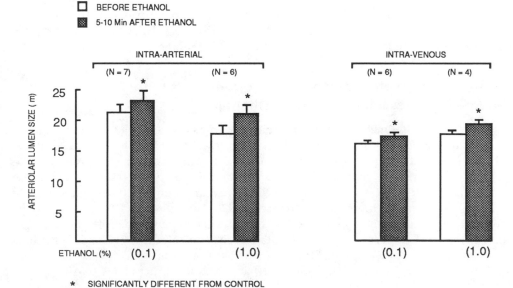

FIGURE 8.12. Influence of intra-arterial and intravenous infusion of ethanol on arteriolar lumen sizes (μm) in rat mesentery. Small bars = SEM. Adapted from Altura BM et al, 1979.

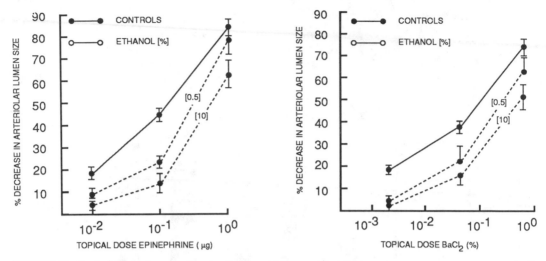

FIGURE 8.13. Topical ethanol application (--- 0.5% and 10%) and its effect on dose-response curves to topically administered epinephrine and barium on terminal arterioles. Note rightward shift of agonist dose-response curves in presence of ethanol. Adapted from Altura BM et al, 1979.

ies on microscopic blood vessels provide good evidence for common mechanisms of action for ethanol on peripheral blood vessels.

Skeletal Muscle Microcirculation

Using in vivo quantitative TV-imaging observations on the cremasteric muscle microvasculature, we have recently found, in marked contrast to the splanchnic vasculature, that irrespective of the route of administration (i.e., topical, intravenous, intra-arterial), EtOH produces spasms (constrictions) of arterioles (12–40 μm) and venules (15–60 μm) in a concentration-dependent manner (Altura BM et al, 1982c). No amine or opiate pharmacologic antagonist or cyclooxygenase inhibitor could attenuate or prevent EtOH from eliciting constrictor responses on these skeletal muscle microvessels. These results seem to substantiate the ideas that (1) intra-arterial infusions of EtOH in humans can produce constriction in forearm skeletal muscle arterioles (Fewings et al, 1966), and (2) the precise effects EtOH exerts on peripheral blood vessels are dependent on the region of the circulation and concentration of EtOH.

Do Metabolites, Acetaldehyde, and Acetate Contribute to the Regional Vascular Actions of Ethanol?

Acetaldehyde or acetate, metabolites of ethanol, could possibly play roles in the stimulatory, depressant, and vasodilator actions ethanol is known to exert on peripheral, intact, and isolated blood vessels. It has long been known that (1) acetaldehyde can exert pressor effects on intravenous administration, increase heart rate, and decrease coronary resistance in perfused rat and guinea pig hearts (Gailis and Verdy, 1971; Brien and Loomis, 1983); and (2) acetate can induce vasodilatation (Liang and Lowenstein, 1978; Vincent et al, 1982); therefore, it is indeed possible that either or both of these metabolites could play some role in the vascular actions of ethanol. However, recent direct studies on isolated blood vessels and on the intact microcirculation do not convince one that either or both of these metabolites could account for most of the peripheral vascular actions of ethanol (Altura BM et al, 1978; Altura BM et al, 1980; Altura BM and Gebrewold, 1981; Altura BM and Altura BT, 1982b; Altura BM et al, 1982c; Altura BM and Altura BT, 1983; Toda et al, 1983; Altura BT and Altura BM, 1983a; Altura BM et al, 1983d; Carmichael et al, 1987).

Although both acetaldehyde and acetate can attenuate, in a dose-dependent manner, spontaneous mechanical activity in isolated arterial smooth muscles (Altura BM et al, 1978; Altura BM et al, 1980; Altura BM and Altura BT, 1982b), the relative concentrations required to do this are much higher than one would expect in the blood from ethanol metabolism. In addition, unlike ethanol, low concentrations of acetaldehyde enhance (potentiate) spontaneous contractions in hepatic-portal-mesenteric veins (Altura BM et al, 1978). Like ethanol, both acetaldehyde and acetate can also attenuate, in a dose-dependent manner, contractions of isolated arteries and veins induced by catecholamines, angiotensin II, serotonin, prostanoids, and KCl; however, the concentrations of acetaldehyde and acetate necessary for the latter are, again, higher than one would expect from the metabolism of ethanol (Altura BM et al, 1978; Altura BM et al, 1980; Altura BM and Altura BT, 1982b; Altura BM et al, n.d.a). Unlike ethanol, neither acetaldehyde nor acetate (no matter how small the dose) can potentiate PG-, catecholamine-, or vasopressin-induced contractions on arterial and venous smooth muscle (Altura BM et al, 1978; Altura BM and Altura BT, 1982b; Altura BM et al, 1983d; Altura BM et al, n.d.a).

Studies of the in vivo microcirculation of the splanchnic vasculature in the male rat do not provide any evidence that the dilator and/or vasodepressant effects of ethanol can be attributed to either acetaldehyde or acetate (Altura BM and Gebrewold, 1981). To illustrate, no concentration of either acetaldehyde or sodium acetate (high, intermediate, or low) can dilate arterioles (15–30 μm) or muscular venules (30–70 μm) in the splanchnic microvasculature. Acetaldehyde and acetate induce only potent, and concentration-dependent, vasoconstriction. In addition, unlike ethanol, neither acetaldehyde nor acetate can inhibit the constrictor actions of neurohumoral substances (regardless of the route of administration).

With respect to other regional microvasculatures of the rat, e.g., skeletal muscle and cortical (brain), where EtOH exerts vasoconstrictor (spasmogenic) actions, acetaldehyde and acetate, surprisingly, seem to exert vasodilator actions (Altura BM et al, 1982c; Altura BM et al, 1983d). It is rather intriguing, therefore, to note in the rat that where EtOH is a vasodilator, acetaldehyde and acetate are vasoconstrictors, whereas in those microvasculatures where EtOH is a vasoconstrictor, acetaldehyde and acetate possess vasodilator properties. We are, thus, tempted to speculate that a balance between the opposing vascular actions of EtOH versus its major metabolites in different regions of the circulation might normally mask the specific vascular actions of ethanol. Therefore, depending upon the rate of formation of acetaldehyde and acetate, one could see diverse effects of ethanol on hemodynamics. Moreover, such an intriguing idea might also account for the varying results from one species to another, seen in the literature, as well as some of the differences noted in human subject studies.

In conclusion, although some of the actions exerted by both acetaldehyde and acetate on isolated arterial and venous smooth muscle mimic in some respects — but not all — the actions of ethanol, the microcirculatory actions of the latter's major metabolites do not, in themselves, account for the direct vascular actions of ethanol. Nevertheless, the opposite, regional vascular actions of acetaldehyde and acetate might act to modulate the overall hemodynamic actions of ethanol.

Chronic Ethanol Administration on Function and Divalent Cation Content of Vascular Smooth Muscle: Possible Relationship to Alcohol-induced Hypertension and Coronary Ischemia

Although recent epidemiologic studies on several thousand human subjects suggest that alcoholics of longstanding have a high incidence of hypertensive vascular disease (D'Alonzo and Pell, 1968; Beevers, 1977; Mathews, 1979; Saunders et al, 1979; Harburg et al, 1980; Klatsky et al, 1981b; Kittner et al, 1983; Arkwright et al, 1984; Beilin and Puddey, 1984; Clark, 1984; Ireland et al, 1984; Potter and Beevers, 1984; Potter et al, 1984; Gruchow et al, 1985; Klatsky, 1985; Criqui, 1986; Friedman et al, 1986; Anonymous, 1987), the mechanism(s) for this is not known. Moreover, although the incidence of sudden cardiac death from binge-drinking is high (Ettinger et al, 1978; Hillbom and Kaste, 1978; Anonymous, 1980; Hillbom and Kaste, 1981; Khetarpal and Volicer, 1981; Alderman and Coltart, 1982; Ashley, 1982; Altura BM and Altura BT, 1983; Taylor and Combs-Orme, 1985), as is the incidence of variant angina and cardiac fibrillation (Regan and Haider, 1981; Alderman and Coltart, 1982; Lowenstein et al, 1983; Takizawa et al, 1984), the mechanisms for these cardiac ischemic events are also not understood. The precise peripheral vascular effects are evoked in animals and humans that ingest alcohol chronically, and are tolerant to ethanol, are also uncertain. However, some recent studies on rats maintained on liquid diets of ethanol may provide some insights into these important problems (Altura BT et al, 1980; Altura BT and Altura BM, 1982; Altura BM and Altura BT, 1982b; Altura BT and Altura BM, 1984b; Altura BM et al, 1986; Ema et al, 1988; Altura BM et al, unpublished findings).

Vascular Smooth Muscle Function in Ethanolized Rats

Using aortae and portal veins, excised from male Wistar rats maintained on liquid diets containing ethanol (6.8% v/v) or sucrose (controls) for periods of 2, 6, 12, and 24 weeks, we have found that chronic ingestion of ethanol can influence, directly, normal vasomotor tone, reactivity of blood vessels to stimuli, and permeability of vascular membranes to divalent cations, i.e., Ca^{2+} and Mg^{2+} (Altura BT et al, 1980; Altura BT and Altura BM, 1982; Altura BM and Altura BT, 1982b; Altura BT and Altura BM, 1984b; Altura BM et al, 1986; Ema et al, 1988; Altura BM et al, unpublished findings). To date, our results indicate that chronic treatment of rats with ethanol can induce a progressive tolerance in excitable tissues (e.g., aorta and portal vein) other than those associated with the central or autonomic nervous systems. Furthermore, these findings suggest that peripheral vascular muscle from rats, and maybe mammals in general, can adapt to the presence of certain plasma levels of ethanol for prolonged periods of time (at least 24 weeks), thus preventing hypotension and cardiovascular collapse. Moreover, the findings indicate that prolonged ethanol feeding (i.e., 12–24 weeks) produces a hypersensitivity of vascular muscle to several types of stimuli.

Our data also indicate that in vitro administration of massive amounts of ethanol (170, 430 mM) to blood vessels excised from rats maintained on ethyl alcohol do not evoke the vasodepressant actions which are usually noted on vessels from normal animals (e.g., Fig. 8.14, Table 8.9). Since tolerance is by definition a reduced effectiveness of alcohol that develops after repeated intake, a state of tolerance of these peripheral vessels to the depressant actions of ethanol use, therefore, exists. Furthermore, since the ability of the excised blood vessels to respond to added doses of ethanol is far less after 6 to 24 weeks of ethanol (e.g., Table 8.9) (Altura BT et al, 1980; Altura BM and Altura BT, 1982b; Altura BM et al, unpublished findings), the tolerance is progressive. It is of considerable interest that as the degree of ethanolization progresses from 6 to 24 weeks, vascular muscle excised from these rats becomes progressively hypersensitive (i.e., greater contractile tensions are noted) to contractile stimulants such as potassium, catecholamines, and angiotensin II (e.g., Table 8.4) (Altura BM et al, unpublished findings).

Vascular muscle contractions induced by stimulants such as angiotensin II and potassium ions, which are normally markedly attenuated by high pharmacologic doses of ethanol, e.g., 170–430 mM, are not inhibited at all when tested against aortae and portal veins excised from rats maintained on this alcohol for periods of 6 to 24 weeks (Table 8.9). Moreover, the contractile concentration-effect curves induced by angiotensin II, potassium or catecholamine stimulation on these vessels, obtained from 6-week ethanol-maintained animals, were not shifted to higher concentrations when compared to similar responses obtained in sucrose-treated or normal vessels (Altura BT et al, 1980). However, at 12 to 24 weeks of ethanol feeding, the concentration-effect curves for these contractile stimulants were shifted to the left of controls (i.e., to lower effective concentrations) or, in other words, a supersensitivity was observed to the contractile stimulants (Altura BM et al, unpublished findings).

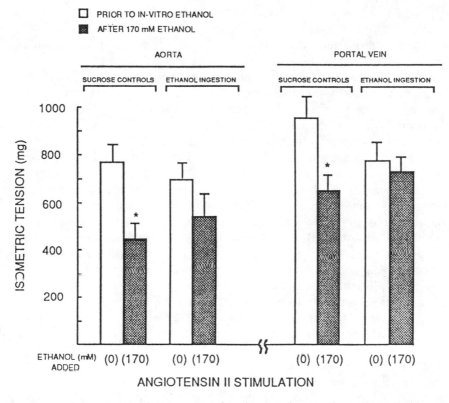

□ PRIOR TO IN-VITRO ETHANOL
▨ AFTER 170 mM ETHANOL

FIGURE 8.14. In-vitro demonstration of tolerance to ethanol in vascular smooth muscle excised from rats chronically treated with ethanol for 2 weeks. Open bars represent results (mg ± SEM) obtained for angiotensin II (2 ng/ml) prior to in-vitro addition of 170 mM ethanol. Hatched bars represent results for angiotensin II stimulation in the presence of 170 mM ethanol. Asterisk indicates mean experimental values which are significantly different from control values (before ethanol addition, p < 0.01). Adapted from Altura BM et al, 1980.

Table 8.9. Comparative inhibitory actions of acute in-vitro additions of ethanol on potassium chloride-induced contractions of portal veins excised from rats chronically treated with sucrose and ethanol*

		TENSION (mg ± SEM)		
DURATION TREATMENT	N	PRIOR TO ETHANOL ADDITION	AFTER ETHANOL (170 mM)	% INHIBITION
2 Weeks				
Sucrose controls	5	990.0 ± 102	330.5 ± 47.5+	67
Ethanol	6	795.5 ± 68	575.4 ± 52.6	28‡
6 Weeks				
Sucrose controls	4	1015 ± 136	342.8 ± 92.6+	66
Ethanol	4	1267 ± 144	1300 ± 148	0ss
12 Weeks				
Sucrose controls	4	1112 ± 142	420.5 ± 48.6+	62
Ethanol	4	1620 ± 146‡	1595 ± 122	0ss
24 Weeks				
Sucrose controls	5	1262 ± 138	410.8 ± 52.5+	67
Ethanol	5	1826 ± 158‡	1924 ± 162	0ss

*20 mM KCl was used as the stimulant concentration. Methods used similar to those found in Altura BT et al, 1980.

+Significantly different from values prior to ethanol addition (p < 0.01).

‡Significantly different from sucrose controls (p < 0.02).

ssSignificantly different from all other values (p < 0.01).

Chronic Ethanol Treatment Alters Divalent Cation Content of Vascular Smooth Muscle

Since the effects of chronic alcohol administration result in similar nonspecific and progressive effects on arterial and venous smooth muscle, as well as intact microvascular smooth muscle, the mechanism(s) responsible for the production of ethanol tolerance in these different tissues must be similar and somewhat nonspecific. Since the vasodepressant effects observed from acute administration of ethanol appear to be linked to effects on Ca^{2+} uptake, binding, and distribution in vascular smooth muscle, the progressively reduced inhibitory-increased excitability effects of chronic ethanol administration on excised and intact peripheral blood vessels could be explained by an alcoholic-induced shift in Ca^{2+} binding (and permeability) in the vascular muscle cells as the exposure to the blood ethanol concentration is increased progressively. In support of this are recent findings which indicate that (1) Ca^{2+}-induced contractile responses on blood vessels obtained from alcohol-maintained rats are shifted to higher concentrations progressively *less* as the duration of the ethanol ingestion is lengthened (Altura BT et al, 1980; Altura BM et al, unpublished findings), and (2) there is a progressive increase in the total exchangeable and intracellular Ca^{2+} concentration of the vascular muscle cells as the duration of the ethanol ingestion is lengthened (Tables 8.10 and 8.11) (Altura BM et al, unpublished findings).

It has long been known that (1) ethanol ingestion in humans results in hypomagnesemia and magnesium (Mg^{2+}) wasting (loss) (Flink et al, 1954), (2) membrane $[Mg^{2+}]$ controls entry of Ca^{2+}, tone, and reactivity of vascular smooth muscle (Turlapaty and Altura BM, 1978; Turlapaty et al, 1980; Altura BM and Altura BT, 1981b; Altura BM and Altura BT, 1981c), and (3) dietary deficiency of Mg^{2+} can result in hypertension and spasms of arterioles, precapillary sphincters, and venules in the microcirculation (Altura BM et al, 1984a). In view of these facts, it was of considerable interest to determine whether chronic ingestion of 6.8% v/v ethanol by rats would alter Mg content of vascular muscle (Altura BM et al, n.d.a). Our preliminary data (utilizing atomic absorption spectroscopy) shown in Table 8.11 clearly indicate that progressive exposure of rats to ethanol results in progressive, significant reduction in total Mg content of arterial and venous smooth muscle. At this junction, one might ask, does the loss in $[Mg^{2+}]$ precede the increase in cellular and membrane $[Ca^{2+}]$ or do both events take place simultaneously? In either event, the resultant alterations in Ca and Mg content and cellular binding could, in themselves, account for the development of alco-

Table 8.10. Total exchangeable and cellular calcium-45 in aortas of rats which ingested ethanol for 2, 6, and 24 weeks

DURATION TREATMENT	TOTAL EXCHANGEABLE CALCIUM	2-MIN La^{3+} WASH CALCIUM FRACTION (membrane-bound)	5-MIN La^{3+} WASH CALCIUM FRACTION (cellular fraction)
2 Weeks			
Sucrose controls	4.08 ± 0.16	1.82 ± 0.12	0.82 ± 0.06
Ethanol*	4.16 ± 0.22	1.78 ± 0.16	0.81 ± 0.05
6 Weeks			
Sucrose controls	3.82 ± 0.16	2.04 ± 0.18	0.77 ± 0.07
Ethanol	$4.76 \pm 0.18**$	2.42 ± 0.14	$0.99 \pm 0.05**$
12 Weeks			
Sucrose controls	4.36 ± 0.22	2.32 ± 0.19	0.83 ± 0.05
Ethanol	$5.64 \pm 0.26**$	$3.12 \pm 0.16**$	$1.32 \pm 0.08**$
24 Weeks			
Sucrose controls	4.42 ± 0.26	2.45 ± 0.18	0.84 ± 0.04
Ethanol	$5.96 \pm 0.24**$	$3.43 \pm 0.19**$	$1.46 \pm 0.06**$

*6.8% (v/v) N = 5–8 each. See Turlapaty et al, 1979a, 1979b, for methods.

**Significantly different from controls ($p < 0.01$).

Table 8.11. Total calcium, magnesium and water content of aortas and portal veins freshly excised from rats ingesting ethanol chronically

DURATION OF TREATMENT, PARAMETERS	AORTAS (mM/Kg wet weight) (means ± SEM)*		PORTAL VEINS (mM/Kg wet weight) (means ± SEM)*	
	SUCROSE CONTROLS	ETHANOL	SUCROSE CONTROLS	ETHANOL
2 Weeks				
Calcium	7.62 ± 0.38	7.76 ± 0.42	7.06 ± 0.26	7.28 ± 0.32
Magnesium	3.62 ± 0.12	3.40 ± 0.14	3.11 ± 0.34	2.92 ± 0.28
Water+	717 ± 127	725 ± 132	606 ± 116	612 ± 38
6 Weeks				
Calcium	7.64 ± 0.32	8.86 ± 0.38**	7.28 ± 0.27	8.32 ± 0.29**
Magnesium	3.46 ± 0.14	2.98 ± 0.12**	3.13 ± 0.26	2.58 ± 0.14**
Water	727 ± 149	771 ± 112	618 ± 117	622 ± 125
12 Weeks				
Calcium	8.29 ± 0.47	10.52 ± 0.48**	7.54 ± 0.27	9.48 ± 0.35**
Magnesium	3.84 ± 0.12	2.88 ± 0.18**	3.79 ± 0.32	2.42 ± 0.12**
Water	739 + 128	791 ± 112	622 ± 119	632 ± 45

*N = 5-8 each.

**Significantly different from controls (p < 0.02).

+ml/kg wet weight.

hol-induced hypertensive disease. In this context, we have recently found that coronary vasospasms, which are known to be induced by Mg^{2+} deficiency (Turlapaty and Altura BM, 1980; Altura BM and Altura BT, 1981c; Altura BM and Altura BT, 1985a; Altura BM and Altura BT, 1985b), can be potentiated or set into motion by low levels of ethanol, e.g., 8–17 mM/L (Altura BM et al, 1988; Altura BM et al, 1989). We are thus tempted to speculate that alcohol-induced Mg^{2+} loss from vascular smooth muscle cells, coupled with an increased uptake and binding of Ca^{2+}, might predispose alcoholics and binge drinkers to coronary ischemia, cardiac arrhythmias, and sudden cardiac death.

Not only may our new findings provide a rationale for the etiology of alcohol-induced hypertension and sudden cardiac death, but they may also help to shed some light on why alcoholics often show hypocalcemia (Peng et al, 1972; Avery et al, 1983); an increased membrane permeability of vascular, cardiac, and other tissues to calcium might aid in explaining why urinary excretion alone cannot account for the alcohol-induced loss of plasma calcium. Our findings on vascular muscle lend considerable support to other findings which indicate that alcohol ingestion leads to decreased brain (Ross, 1976) and red blood cell Ca^{2+} (Meltzer and Alexopoulos, 1982).

If our hypothesis, which is testable, is correct, then, as the duration of ethanol ingestion (and concentration in tissues) is lengthened (and increased), causing greater and greater shifts in reciprocal cellular movements of Ca^{2+} and Mg^{2+}, alcoholic animals and humans could develop hypertension by several different pathways acting in concert: (1) an increase in vascular tone solely due to loss of Mg^{2+} from, and an increase of Ca^{2+} movement into, the peripheral vascular smooth muscle cells; (2) a supersensitivity of blood vessels to endogenously circulating neurohumoral constrictor substances (e.g., catecholamines, angiotensin II, serotonin, etc.) (a loss of membrane Mg^{2+} is well-known in itself to cause the latter supersensitivity [Turlapaty and Altura BM, 1978; Turlapaty and Altura BM, 1980; Altura BM and Altura BT, 1981b; Altura BM and Altura BT, 1981c; Altura BM et al, 1984a; Altura BM and Altura BT, 1985a; Altura BM and Altura BT, 1985b]; and (3) a decreased responsiveness of blood vessels to endogenous vasodilators (e.g., adenosine, PGs, neuropeptides, etc.) (a reduction in Mg^{2+} [Turlapaty and Altura BM, 1978; Turlapaty and Altura BM, 1980; Altura BM and Altura BT, 1981b; Altura BM and Altura BT, 1981c; Altura BM et al, 1984a; Altura BM and Altura BT, 1985a; Altura BM and Altura BT, 1985b] and an increase in vascular muscle Ca^{2+} are known to produce hyporesponsiveness to vasodilators). It is thus of considerable interest that alcoholic-hypertensives have recently been shown to have decreased red blood cell concentrations of Mg^{2+} (Adeniyi, 1986).

It may be of further interest that development of tolerance of rats to other drugs of abuse, e.g., barbiturates and morphine, has been shown to induce supersensitivity of excised arterial smooth muscle to catecholamines and potassium ions (Altura BM and Altura BT, 1979a; Weinberg and Altura BM, 1980). It is thus possible that the hypertensive episodes associated with patients undergoing barbiturate, narcotic, and alcohol withdrawal may all be linked to alterations in Ca^{2+} and Mg^{2+} binding in arterial and arteriolar smooth muscle cells induced by chronic administration of drugs of abuse. If the latter turns out to be true, it could suggest a way to reverse or prevent these cardiovascular manifestations. In this context, the preliminary studies with rats mentioned above suggest that Ca^{2+} antagonists and the "mimic" Ca^{2+} antagonist, Mg^{2+}, can ameliorate and reverse the stroke-like effects in the brain observed after ethanol administration (Altura BT and Altura BM, 1982; Altura BM et al, 1983b; Altura BT and Altura BM, 1984b; Altura BM and Altura BT, 1985a; Altura BM and Altura BT, 1985b; Altura BM et al, 1986; Ema et al, 1988).

CONCLUSIONS

In as much as ethanol is thought to exert its major effects in the autonomic and central nervous systems, it is important to determine whether acute versus chronic ingestion of this abused substance exerts any direct actions on the heart as well as the peripheral and cerebral blood vessels. Since the chronic effects of ethanol on the cardiovascular system appear to be pivotal in the etiology of hypertension, cardiac arrhythmias, coronary heart disease, congestive heart failure, and stroke-like events, it is important to elucidate and understand the effects of chronic ethanol abuse and its mechanism(s) of action on the cardiovascular system. Data are presented which provide insights into cardiac, cerebral, and peripheral vascular effects of acute and chronic ingestion (or administration) of ethanol.

Although the direct effects of ethanol on vascular smooth muscle appear to be the most precise type of information obtained so far, the cardiac and cerebral vascular data in contrast are often confusing, confounded by many variables, and difficult to interpret. Little in the way of precise information appears to exist with respect to the chronic actions of ethanol on the heart and blood vessels under well-controlled conditions, either with respect to retrospective patient studies or laboratory animals. Despite the latter drawback, a number of studies are beginning to yield important and useful information, particularly on isolated cardiac myocytes and vascular smooth muscle cells. The need for new, powerful, sophisticated, non-invasive techniques for assessing cardiovascular parameters over prolonged periods of time is apparent. Overall, the available data seem to be overwhelmingly in favor of the idea that ethanol exerts adverse, not beneficial, actions on the heart, cerebral, and regional blood vessels. Some of these data are beginning to provide a rational, scientific basis for the etiology of alcohol-induced hypertension, ischemic heart disease, and stroke-like events.

ACKNOWLEDGMENTS

The authors are grateful to the USPHS for Research Grants DA-02339 and HL-29600 which provided support for the original studies reported here. We are also grateful to our colleagues, A. Carella, M. Ema, Q. Huang, T. Murakawa, A. Nishio, L. A. Pohorecky, P.D.M.V. Turlapaty and J. Weinberg, whose help was invaluable in our studies.

REFERENCES

Abel FL: Direct effects of ethanol on myocardial performance and coronary resistance. *J Pharmacol Exp Ther* 1980; 212:28–33.

Adeniyi FAA: Interactive roles of monovalent and divalent cations in pathogenesis of hypertension caused by alcohol. *J Clin Pathol* 1986; 39:1264–1268.

Ahmed SS, Levinson GF, Regan TJ: Depression of myocardial contractility with low doses of ethanol in normal man. *Circulation* 1973; 48:378–385.

Alderman EL, Coltart DJ: Alcohol and the heart. *Brit Med Bull* 1982; 38:77–80.

Altura BM: Chemical and humoral regulation of blood flow through the precapillary sphincter. *Microvasc Res* 1971; 3:361–384.

Altura BM, Altura BT: Vascular smooth muscle and prostaglandins. *Federation Proc* 1976; 35:2360–2366.

Altura BM, Edgarian H: Ethanol-prostaglandin interactions in contraction of vascular smooth muscle. *Proc Soc Exp Biol Med* 1976; 152:334–336.

Altura BM, Edgarian H, Altura BT: Differential effects of ethanol and mannitol on contraction of arterial smooth muscle. *J Pharmacol Exp Ther* 1976; 197:352–361.

Altura BM: Pharmacology of venular smooth muscle: New insights. *Microvasc Res* 1978; 16;91–117

Altura BM, Carella A, Altura BT: Acetaldehyde on vascular smooth muscle: Possible role in vasodilator action of ethanol. *Eur J Pharmacol* 1978; 52:73–83.

Altura BM, Ogunkoya A, Gebrewold A, Altura BT: Effects of ethanol on terminal arterioles and muscular venules: Direct observations on the micro-circulation. *J Cardiovasc Pharmacol* 1979; 1:97–113.

Altura BM, Weinberg J: Urethane and contraction of vascular smooth muscle. *Brit J Pharmacol* 1979; 67:255–263.

Altura BM, Altura BT: Barbiturate tolerance and hypersensitivity of arterial smooth muscle. *Drug Alcohol Depend* 1979a; 4:467–473.

Altura BM, Altura BT: Ethanol-barbiturate synergism in arterial and venous smooth muscle. *Alcohol Clin Exp Res* 1979b; 3:166.

Altura BM, Altura BT, Carella A: Effects of ketamine on vascular smooth muscle function. *Brit J Pharmacol* 1980; 70:257–267.

Altura BM, Altura BT, Carella A, Turlapaty PDMV, Weinberg J: Vascular smooth muscle and general anesthetics. *Federation Proc* 1980; 39:1584–1591.

Altura BM: Pharmacology of venules: Some current concepts and clinical potential. *J Cardiovasc Pharmacol* 1981; 3:1413–1428.

Altura BM, Gebrewold A: Failure of acetaldehyde or acetate to mimic the splanchnic arteriolar or venular dilator actions of ethanol: Direct in-situ studies on the microcirculation. *Brit J Pharmacol* 1981; 73:580–582.

Altura BM, Altura BT: Alcohol induces cerebral arterial and arteriolar vasospasm by a direct action. *Circulation* 1981a; 64 (Part II):231.

Altura BM, Altura BT: General anesthetics and magnesium ions as calcium antagonists on vascular smooth muscle, in Weiss GB (ed): *New Perspectives on Calcium Antagonists*. Wash, D.C., Am Physiol Soc, 1981b, pp. 131–145.

Altura BM, Altura BT: Magnesium ions and contraction of vascular smooth muscle: Relationship to some vascular diseases. *Federation Proc* 1981c; 40:2672–2679.

Altura BM (ed): Symposium Am Soc for Pharmacology and Exptl Therapeutics. Cardiovascular effects of alcohol and alcoholism. *Federation Proc* 1982; 41:2437–2464.

Altura BM, Altura BT: Factors affecting responsiveness of blood vessels to prostaglandins and other chemical mediators of injury and shock, in McConn R (ed): *Role of Chemical Mediators in the Pathophysiology of Acute Illness and Injury*. New York, Raven Press, 1982a; p 45.

Altura BM, Altura BT, Carella A, Chatterjee M, Halevy S, Tejani N: Alcohol produces spasms of human umbilical blood vessels: Relationship to fetal alcohol syndrome (FAS). *Eur J Pharmacol* 1982a; 86:311–312.

Altura BM, Altura BT: Microvascular and vascular smooth muscle actions of ethanol, acetaldehyde, and acetate. *Federation Proc* 1982b; 41:2447–2451.

Altura BM, Altura BT, Gebrewold A: Alcohol produces spasms of cerebral and coronary arteries and arterioles. *Federation Proc* 1982b; 41:1465.

Altura BM, Altura BT, Gebrewold A: Comparative in-vivo effects of ethanol, acetaldehyde and acetate on arterioles and venules in skeletal muscle. *Alcoholism: Clin and Exp Res* 1982c; 6:134.

Altura BM, Altura BT: Peripheral vascular actions of ethanol and its interaction with neurohumoral substances. *Neurobehav Toxicol Teratol* 1983; 5:211–220.

Altura BM, Altura BT, Carella A: Ethanol produces coronary vasospasm: Evidence for a direct action of ethanol on vascular muscle. *Brit J Pharmacol* 1983a; 78:260–262.

Altura BM, Altura BT, Gebrewold A: Alcohol-induced spasms of cerebral blood vessels: Relation to cerebrovascular accidents and sudden death. *Science* 1983b; 220:331–333.

Altura BM, Altura BT, Gebrewold A: Comparative microvascular actions of Ca^{2+} antagonists, in Merrill RM, Weiss HR (eds): *Calcium Antagonists, Adenosine and Neurohumors*. Baltimore, Urban & Schwarzenberg, 1983c, pp 155–175.

Altura BM, Altura BT, Gebrewold A: Failure of acetaldehyde or acetate to mimic the cerebral arteriolar and venular constrictor actions of ethanol: Direct in-situ microcirculatory studies. *Alcohol Clin Exp Res* 1983d; 7:104.

Altura BM, Altura BT: Alcohol, the cerebral circulation and strokes. *Alcohol* 1984a; 1:325–331.

Altura BM, Altura BT, Gebrewold A, Ising H, Günther T: Magnesium deficiency and hypertension: Correlation between magnesium-deficient diets and microcirculatory changes in situ. *Science* 1984a; 223:1315–1317.

Altura BM, Altura BT: Microcirculatory actions and uses of naturally-occurring (magnesium) and novel synthetic calcium channel blockers. *Microcirculation Endothelium and Lymphatics* 1984b; 1:185–220.

Altura BM, Gebrewold A, Altura BT: Regional arteriolar and venular dilator actions of dihydropyridines vs verapamil: Direct in-vivo studies on the microcirculation, in Scriabine A, Vanov S, Deck K (eds): *Nitrendipine*. Baltimore, Urban & Schwarzenberg, 1984b, pp 219–236.

Altura BM, Altura BT: New perspectives on the role of magnesium in the pathophysiology of the cardiovascular system: I. Clinical aspects. *Magnesium* 1985a; 4:226–244.

Altura BM, Altura BT: New perspectives on the role of magnesium in the pathophysiology of the cardiovascular system: II. Experimental aspects. *Magnesium* 1985b; 4:227–271.

Altura BM (ed): Vitamins, minerals and alcohol. *Alcohol Clin Exp Res* 1986; 10:570–594.

Altura BM, Altura BT, Gebrewold A: Alcohol-induced vascular damage can be ameliorated by administration of magnesium. *Federation Proc* 1986; 45:570.

Altura BM, Halevy S: *Cardiovascular Actions of Anesthetic Agents and Drugs Used in Anesthesia*, Vols 1 and 2. Basel, Karger, 1986.

Altura BM (ed): Cardiovascular effects of ethanol. *Alcohol Clin Exp Res* 1986; 10:557–564.

Altura BM, Altura BT: Peripheral and cardiovascular actions of ethanol, acetaldehyde, and acetate: Relationship to divalent cations. *Alcohol Clin Exp Res* 1987; 11:99–126.

Altura BM, Altura BT: Peripheral and cerebrovascular actions of ethanol, acetaldehyde and acetate: Relationship to divalent cations. *Alcohol Clin Exp Res* 1987; 11:99–111.

Altura BM, Altura BT, Carella A, Gebrewold A, Murakawa T, Nishio A: Mg^{2+}-Ca^{2+} interaction in contractility of vascular smooth muscle: Mg^{2+} versus organic calcium channel blockers on myogenic tone and agonist-induced responsiveness of blood vessels. *Canad J Physiol Pharmacol* 1987; 65:729–745.

Altura BM, Carella A, Altura BT: Magnesium deficiency potentiates coronary arterial spasms induced by ethanol. *Proc Fifth International Magnesium Symposium*, Kyoto, Japan, 1988.

Altura BM, Carella A, Altura BT: Coronary arterial spasms induced by alcohol are potentiated by withdrawal of magnesium. *Fase BJ*, 1989; A 433.

Altura BM, Carella A, Gebrewold A, Altura BT: unpublished findings.

Altura BT, Altura BM: Barbiturates and aortic and venous smooth muscle function. *Anesthesiol* 1975; 43:432–445.

Altura BT, Altura BM: Intravenous anesthetic agents and vascular smooth muscle function, in Vanhoutte PM, Leusen I (eds): *Mechanism of Vasodilatation*. Basel, Karger, 1978; pp 165–172.

Altura BT, Pohorecky LA, Altura BM: Demonstration of tolerance to ethanol in non-nervous tissue: Effects on vascular smooth muscle. *Alcohol Clin Exp Res* 1980; 4:62–69.

Altura BT, Altura BM: Phencyclidine, lysergic acid diethylamide and mescaline: Cerebral artery spasms and hallucinogenic activity. *Science* 1981; 212:1051–1053.

Altura BT, Altura BM: The role of magnesium in etiology of strokes and cerebrovasospasm. *Magnesium: Exp Clin Res* 1982; 1:277–291.

Altura BT, Quirion R, Pert CB, Altura BM: Phencyclidine ("angel dust") analogs and σ-opiate benzomorphans cause cerebral arterial spasm. *Proc Nat Acad Sci USA* 1983; 80:865–869.

Altura BT and Altura BM: Alcohol and cardiovascular function, in Smith J et al (eds): *Stokely-Van Camp Annual Symposium: Food in Contemporary Society. Its Role in the Treatment of and Recovery from Disease, May 18–20, 1983*. Knoxville, Univ of Tennessee, 1983a, pp 102–133.

Altura BT, Altura BM: Cerebrovasospasms induced by phencyclidine are prevented by calcium antagonists and magnesium ions. *Magnesium: Exp Clin Res* 1983b; 2:52–56.

Altura BT, Altura BM: Effects of barbiturates, phencyclidine, ketamine and analogs on cerebral circulation and cerebrovascular muscle. *Microcirculation Endothelium and Lymphatics* 1984a; 1:169–184.

Altura BT, Altura BM: Interactions of Mg and K on cerebral vessels. Aspects in view of stroke: Review of present status and new findings. *Magnesium* 1984b; 3:195–221.

Altura BT, Altura BM, Quirion R: Identification of benzomorphan - K opiate receptors in cerebral arteries which subserve relaxation. *Brit J Pharmacol* 1984; 82:459–466.

Anonymous: Alcoholic heart disease. *Lancet* 1980; i:961–962.

Anonymous: Alcoholic brain damage. *Lancet* 1981; i:477–478.

Anonymous: Alcohol and haemorrhagic stroke. *Lancet* 1986; ii:256–257.

Anonymous: Alcohol: An important cause of hypertension. *Brit Med J* 1987; 294:1045–1046.

Arkwright P, Beilin LJ, Vandangen R, Armstrong BK, Masarei JRL: Alcohol and hypertension. *Austr NZ J Med* 1984; 14:463–469.

Ashley MJ, Rankin JG: Hazardous alcohol consumption and diseases of the circulatory system. *J Stud Alcohol* 1980; 41:1040–1070.

Ashley MJ: Alcohol consumption, ischemic heart disease and cerebrovascular disease. *J Stud Alcohol* 1982; 43:869–887.

Asokan SK, Frank MJ, Witham AC: Cardiomyopathy without cardiomegaly in alcoholics. *Am Heart J* 1972; 84:13–18.

Auffermann W, Wu S, Parmley WW, Higgins CB, Sievers R, Wikman-Coffelt J: Reversibility of acute alcohol cardiac depression: ^{31}P-NMR in hamsters. *FASEB J* 1988; 2:256–263.

Avery DH, Overall JE, Calil HM, Hollister LE: Plasma calcium and phosphate during alcohol intoxication. Alcoholics versus nonalcoholics. *J Stud Alcohol* 1983; 44:205–214.

Bannan LT, Potter JF, Beevers DG, Saunders JB, Walters JRF, Ingram MC: Effect of alcohol withdrawal on blood pressure, plasma renin activity, aldosterone, cortisol and dopamine-hydroxylase. *Clin Sci* 1984; 66:659–663.

Barboriak JJ, Anderson AJ, Hoffman RG: Interrelationships between coronary artery occlusion, high density lipoprotein, cholesterol and alcohol intake. *J Lab Clin Med* 1979; 94:348–353.

Barboriak JJ, Gruchow HW, Anderson AJ: Alcohol and the diet-heart controversy. *Alcohol Clin Exp Res* 1983; 7:31–34.

Barry DI, Hemmingsen R: Cerebral blood flow autoregulation during acute ethanol intoxication in the rat. *Acta Pharmacol et Toxicol* 1984; 54:227–232.

Battey LL, Heyman A, Patterson JL: Effects of ethyl alcohol on cerebral blood flow and metabolism. *J Am Med Assn* 1953; 152:6–10.

Beevers DG: Alcohol and hypertension. *Lancet* 1977; 2:114–115.

Beilin LJ, Puddey IB: Alcohol and essential hypertension. *Alcohol Alcohol* 1984; 19:191–195.

Bengesser G, Weiser G: Schlaganfalle bei Alkoholikern im fruhen Erwachsenalter. *Wien Med Wschr* 1974; 124:733–734.

Berglund M, Ingvar DH: Cerebral blood flow and its regional distribution in alcoholism and in Korsakoff's psychosis. *J Stud Alcohol* 1976; 37:586–597.

Berglund M, Sonnessen B: Personality impairment in alcoholism. Its relation to regional cerebral blood flow and psychometric performance. *J Stud Alcohol* 1976; 37:298–310.

Berglund M, Risberg J: Regional cerebral blood flow during alcohol withdrawal related consumption and symptomology. *Acta Neurol Scand Suppl* 1977; 64:480–481.

Berglund M: Cerebral blood flow in chronic alcoholics. *Alcohol Clin Exp Res* 1981; 5:293–303.

Berlaga ML: Some clinical characteristics of acute disorders of cerebral blood circulation in alcohol misusers. *Zh Nevropat Psikhiat* 1975, 75:857–860.

Blomqvist G, Saltin B, Mitchell JH: Acute effects of ethanol ingestion on the response to submaximal and maximal exercise in man. *Circulation* 1970; 42:463–470.

Bollinger O: Uber die Haufigkeit und Uraschen der idiopathischen Herzhypertrophic in Munchen, *Dtsch Med Wochenschr* 1884; 10:180–181.

Brien JF, Loomis VW: Pharmacology of acetaldehyde. *Canad J Physiol Pharmacol* 1983; 68:1–22.

Brigden W: Uncommon myocardial diseases: The non-coronary cardiomyopathies. *Lancet* 1957; ii:1243–1249.

Brigden W, Robinson J: Alcoholic heart disease. *Brit Med J* 1964; ii:1283–1289.

Burch GE, Walsh JJ: Cardiac insufficiency in chronic alcoholism. *Am J Cardiol* 1960; 6:864–874.

Burtsev E: On the provocative role of alcohol in the pathogenesis underlying cerebral circulation disturbances in young persons. *Sov Med* 1975; 12:19–95.

Cala LA, Jones B, Mastaglia FL, Wiley B: Brain atrophy and intellectual impairment in heavy drinkers — A clinical, psychometric and tomography study. *Austr NZ J Med* 1978; 8:147–153.

Cala LA, Mastaglia FL: Computerized tomography in chronic alcoholics. *Alcohol Clin Exp Res* 1981; 5:283–294.

Carlen PL, Wortzman G, Holgate RC, Wilkinson DA, Rankin JG: Reversible cerebral atrophy in recently abstinent chronic alcoholics measured by computed tomography scans. *Science* 1978; 200: 1076–1078.

Carmichael FJ, Israel Y, Saldiva V, Giles HG, Meggiorini S, Orrego H: Blood acetaldehyde and the ethanol-induced increase in splanchnic circulation. *Biochem Pharmacol* 1987; 36:2673–2678.

Castelli WP, Gordon T, Hjortland MC, Kagan A, Doyle JT, Hames CG, Huiley SB, Zukel WJ: Alcohol and blood lipids. The cooperative Lipoprotein Phenotyping Study. *Lancet* 1977; ii:153–155.

Chan TC, Sutter MC: The effects of chronic ethanol consumption on cardiac function in rats. *Canad J Physiol Pharmacol* 1982; 60:777–782.

Chand N, Altura BM: Contractile responses of isolated pulmonary and renal arteries to alcohol: Implication in hypertensive states. *Am Rev Resp Dis* 1984; 129:A338.

Child JS, Kovick RB, Leviman JA, Pearce ML: Cardiac effects of acute ethanol ingestion unmasked by autonomic blockade. *Circulation* 1979; 59:120–125.

Clark LT: Alcohol use and hypertension. Clinical considerations and implications. *Postgr Med* 1984; 75:273–276.

Clement JG: Investigations into the mechanisms of morphine and ethanol inhibition in the guinea pig ileum longitudinal strip. *Can J Physiol Pharmacol* 1980; 58:265–270.

Colditz GA, Branch LG, Lipnick RJ, Willett WC, Rosner B, Posner B, Hennekens CH: Moderate alcohol and decreased cardiovascular mortality in an elderly cohort. *Am Heart J* 1985; 109:886–889.

Condouris GA, Havelin DM: Acetaldehyde and cardiac arrhythmias. *Arch Intern Pharmacodyn Ther* 1987; 285:50–59.

Conway N: Haemodynamic effects of ethyl alcohol in patients with coronary heart disease. *Brit Heart J* 1968; 30:638–644.

Criqui MH, Wallace RB, Mishkel M, Barrett-Connor E, Heiss G: Alcohol consumption and blood pressure. The lipid research clinics prevalence study. *Hypertension* 1981; 3:557–565.

Criqui MH: Alcohol consumption, blood pressure, lipids and cardiovascular mortality. *Alcohol Clin Exp Res* 1986; 10:564–569.

Criqui MH: The role of alcohol in the epidemiology of cardiovascular diseases. *Acta Med Scand* 1987; Suppl 717:73–85.

D'Alonzo CA, Pell S: Cardiovascular disease among problem drinkers. *J Occupat Med* 1968; 10:344–350.

Danielsson B: Changes in plasma high density lipoproteins and coronary risk factors in normal men. *Lancet* 1979; i:72–75.

Delgado CE, Fortuin NJ, Ross RS: Acute effects of low doses of alcohol on left ventricular function by echocardiography. *Circulation* 1975; 51:535–540.

Demakis JG, Proskey A, Rahimtoola SH, Jamil M, Sutton GC, Rosen KM, Gunnar RM, Tobin JR, Jr. The natural course of alcoholic cardiomyopathy. *Ann Intern Med* 1974; 80:293–297.

Dionigi AR, Lanza E, Piccinini F: The effects of ethanol on the responses of the vascular musculature to norepinephrine. *Arch Intern Physiol Biochem* 1982; 90:179–184.

Dixon WE: Action of alcohol on the circulation. *J Physiol (London)* 1907; 35:346–366.

Donahue RP, Abbott RD, Reed DM, Yano K: Alcohol and hemorrhagic stroke. The Honolulu heart program. *J Am Med Assn* 1986; 255:2311–2314.

Dyer AR, Stamler J, Paul O, Berkson DM, Shekelle RB, Lepper MH, McKean H, Lindberg HA, Garside D, Tokich T: Alcohol, cardiovascular risk factors and mortality. The Chicago experience. *Circulation* 1981; 64 (Suppl III):III-20–26.

Edgarian H, Altura BM: Differential effects of ethanol on prostaglandin responses of arterial and venous smooth muscle. *Experientia* 1976a; 32:618–619.

Edgarian H, Altura BM: Ethanol and contraction of venous smooth muscle. *Anesthesiol* 1976b; 44:311–317.

Egle Jr. JL, Hudgins PM, Lai FM: Cardiovascular effects of intravenous acetaldehyde and propionaldehyde in the anesthetized rat. *Toxicol Appl Pharmacol* 1973; 24:636–644.

Eisenberg S: Cerebral blood flow and metabolism in patients with delirium tremens. *Clin Res* 1968; 16:71.

Eisenhofer G, Lambie DG, Johnson RH: Effects of ethanol ingestion on adrenoceptor-mediated circulatory responses in man. *Brit J Clin Pharmacol* 1984; 18:581–586.

Ema M, Altura BT, Gebrewold A, Altura BM: Alcohol-induced damage of brain can be ameliorated by administration of magnesium. *Proc Fifth International Magnesium Symposium*, Kyoto, Japan, 1988.

Ernst N, Fisher M, Smith W, Gordon T, Rifkind BM, Little JA, Mishkel MA, Williams OD: The association of plasma HDL cholesterol with dietary intake and alcohol consumption. *Circulation* 1980; 62 (Suppl IV) IV-41–52.

Ettinger PO, Lyons M, Oldewurter HA, Regan TJ: Cardiac conduction abnormalities produced by chronic alcoholism. *Am Heart J* 1976; 91:66–78.

Ettinger PO, Wu CF, De La Cruz C, Weisse AB, Ahmed SS, Regan TJ: Arrhythmias and the "holiday heart"; Alcohol-associated cardiac rhythm disorders. *Am Heart J* 1978; 95:555–562.

Fazekas JF, Albert SN, Alman RW: Influence of chlorpromazine and alcohol on cerebral hemodynamics and metabolism. *Am J Med Sci* 1955; 230:128–132.

Fewings JD, Hanna MJD, Walsh JS, Whelan RF: The effects of ethyl alcohol on the blood vessels of the hand and forearm of man. *Brit J Pharmacol* 1966; 27:93–106.

Fink RS, Rosalki SB: Observations on the incidence of alcoholic cardiomyopathy. *Brit J Alcohol Alcoholism* 1979; 14:245–252.

Fisher VJ, Kavaler F: The action of ethanol upon the action potential and contraction of ventricular muscle, in Fleckenstein A, Dhalla NS (eds): *Basic Functions of Cations in Myocardial Activity*. Baltimore, Univ. Park Press, 1975, p 415–422.

Flink EB, Stutzman FL, Anderson AR, Konig T, Fraser R: Magnesium deficiency after prolonged fluid administration and after chronic alcoholism complicated by delirium tremens. *J Lab Clin Med* 1954; 43:169–183.

Folkow B: Physiology of hypertension. *Physiol Rev* 1982; 62:347–504.

Friedman HS: Acute effect of ethanol on myocardial blood flow in the nonischemic and ischemic heart. *Am J Cardiol* 1981; 47:61–67.

Friedman HS, Geller SA, Lieber CS: The effect of alcohol on the heart, skeletal, and smooth muscles, in Lieber CS (ed): *Medical Disorders of Alcoholism. Pathogenesis and Treatment*. Philadelphia, W.B. Saunders, 1982, pp 436–479.

Friedman HS, Lowrey R, Archer M, Scorza J: The effects of ethanol on brain blood flow in awake dogs. *Clin Res* 1981; 29:192.

Friedman HS, Lowery R, Archer M, Shaughnessy E, Scorza J: The effects of ethanol on brain blood flow in awake dogs. *J Cardiovasc Pharmacol* 1984; 6:344–348.

Friedman HS, Matsuzaki S, Choe SS, Fernando HA, Celis A, Zaman O, Lieber CS: Demonstration of dissimilar acute hemodynamic effects of ethanol and acetaldehyde. *Cardiovasc Res* 1979; 13:477–487.

Friedman HS, Vasavada BC, Malec AM, Hassan KK, Shah A, Siddiqui S: Cardiac function in alcohol-associated hypertension. *Am J Cardiol* 1986; 57:227–231.

Friedman HS, Lowery R, Shaughnessy E, Scorza J: The effects of ethanol on pancreatic blood flow in awake and anesthetized dogs. *Proc Soc Exp Biol Med* 1983; 174:377–382.

Fuhrman FA, Field J: Inhibition of brain respiration by ethanol at varied temperature levels. *Proc Soc Exp Biol Med* 1948; 69:331–332.

Gailis L, Verdy M: The effect of ethanol and acetaldehyde on the metabolism and vascular resistance of the perfused heart. *Canad J Biochem* 1971; 49:227–233.

Gallis L: Cardiovascular effects of acetaldehyde: Evidence for the involvement of tissue SH groups, in Lindros KO, Eriksson CJP (eds): *The Role of Acetaldehyde in the Actions of Ethanol*. Helsinki, Kauppakirjapaino, 1975, p 135.

Ganz V: The acute effect of alcohol on the circulation and the oxygen metabolism of the heart. *Am Heart J* 1963; 66:494–497.

Gimeno AL, Gimeno MF, Webb JL: Effects of ethanol on cellular membrane potentials and contractility of isolated rat atrium. *Am J Physiol* 1962; 203:194–196.

Goldfarb W, Bowman KM, Wortis H: The effect of alcohol on cerebral metabolism. *Am J Psychiatry* 1940; 97:384–387.

Goldie RG, Ellis GM, Paterson JW: Ethanol and isoprenaline-induced responses in pig parenchymal lung tissue. *J Pharmacy Pharmacol* 1984; 36:53–56.

Goldman H, Sapirstein LA, Murphy S, Moore J: Alcohol and regional blood flow in brains of rats. *Proc Soc Exp Biol Med* 1973; 144:983–988.

Goodkind MJ, Gerber NH, Jr, Mellen JR, Kostis JB: Altered intracardiac conduction after acute administration of ethanol in the dog. *J Pharmacol Exp Ther* 1975; 194:633–638.

Gordon R, Kagan A, Garcia-Palmieri MR, et al: Diet and its relation to coronary heart disease and death in three populations. *Circulation* 1981; 63:500–515.

Gould L, Zahr M, DeMartino A, Gomprecht RF: Cardiac effects of a cocktail. *J Am Med Assoc* 1971; 218:1799–1802.

Gould L, Jaynal F, Zahr M, Gomprecht RF: Effects of alcohol on the systolic time intervals. *Quart J Stud Alcohol* 1972; 33:451–463.

Gould L, Reddy CVR, Goswami K, Venkataraman K, Gomprecht RF: Cardiac effects of two cocktails in normal man. *Chest* 1973; 63:943–947.

Greenspon AJ, Stang JM, Lewis RP, Schaal SF: Provocation of ventricular tachycardia after consumption of alcohol. *New Engl J Med* 1979; 301:1049–1050.

Gruchow HW, Sobocinski KA, Barboriak JJ: Alcohol, nutrient intake, and hypertension in US adults. *JAMA* 1985; 253:1567–1570.

Hadji-Dimo AA, Ekberg R, Ingvar DH: Effects of ethanol on EEG and cortical blood flow in the cat. *J Stud Alcohol* 1968; 29A:828–838.

Hamby RI, Catangay P, Apiado O, Khan AH: Primary myocardial disease. Clinical hemodynamic and angiographic correlates in fifty patients. *Am J Cardiol* 1970; 25:625–634.

Harburg E, Ozgoren F, Hawthorne VM, Schork MA: Community norms of alcohol usage and blood pressure: Tecumseh, Michigan. *Am J Public Health* 1980; 70:813–820.

Heiss WD: Regional cerebral blood flow measurement with scintillation camera. *Int J Neurology, Montevideo* 1977; 11:144–161.

Hemmingsen R, Barry DI: Adaptive changes in cerebral blood flow and oxygen consumption during ethanol intoxication in the rat. *Acta Physiol Scand* 1979; 106:249–255.

Hemmingsen R, Barry DI, Hertz MM, Klinken L: Cerebral blood flow and oxygen consumption during ethanol withdrawal in the rat. *Brain Res* 1979; 173:259–269.

Hennekens CH, Willet W, Rosner B, Cole DS, Mayrent SL: Effects of beer, wine and liquor in coronary deaths. *JAMA* 1979; 242:1973–1974.

Hepp A, Rudolph T, Kochsiek K: Is the rat a suitable model for studying alcoholic cardiomyopathy? Hemodynamic studies at various stages of alcohol ingestion. *Basic Res Cardiol* 1984; 79:230–237.

Hillbom E: What supports the role of alcohol as a risk factor for stroke? *Acta Med Scand* 1987; Suppl 717:93–106.

Hillbom ME, Kangasaho M, Hjelm-Jager M: Platelet aggregation and thromboxane B_2 formation after ethanol abuse: Is there a relationship to stroke? *Acta Neurol Scand* 1984; 70:432–437.

Hillbom M, Kangasaho M, Kaste M, Numminen H, Vapaatalo H: Acute ethanol ingestion increases platelet reactivity: Is there a relationship to stroke? *Stroke* 1985; 16:19–23.

Hillbom M, Kaste M: Does ethanol intoxication promote brain infarction in young adults? *Lancet* 1978; ii:1181–1183.

Hillbom M, Kaste M: Ethanol intoxication: A risk factor for ischemic brain infarction in adolescents and young adults. *Stroke* 1981; 12:422–524.

Hillbom M, Kaste M: Ethanol intoxication: A risk factor for ischemic brain infarction. *Stroke* 1983; 14:694–699.

Hillbom M, Kaste M, Rasi V: Can ethanol intoxication affect hemocoagulation to increase the risk of brain infarction in young adults? *Neurology* 1983; 33:381–384.

Hirota Y, Bing OHL, Abelman WH: Effect of ethanol on contraction and relaxation of isolated rat ventricular muscle. *J Mol Cell Cardiol* 1976; 8:727–732.

Hirst M, Adams MA: Ethanol-induced cardiac hypertrophy: Effects of peripheral sympathectomy. *Canad J Physiol Pharmacol* 1987; 65:2363–2367.

Horowitz LD, Atkins JM: Acute effects of ethanol on left ventricular performance. *Circulation* 1974; 49:124–128.

Howes LG, Reid JL: The effects of alcohol on local, neural and humoral cardiovascular regulation. *Clin Science* 1986; 71:9–15.

Ikeda K, Hachisuga M, Goto M: Effects of alcohol on the myocardium. I. An analysis of the effects of ethanol on the bullfrog myocardium. *Fukuoka Igaku Zasshi* 1984; 75:64–71.

Ireland MA, Vandongen R, Davidson L, Beilin LJ, Rouse IL: Acute effects of moderate alcohol consumption on blood pressure and plasma catecholamines. *Clin Sci* 1984; 66:643–648.

James TN, Bear ES: Effects of ethanol and acetyladehyde on the heart. *Am Heart J* 1967; 74:243–255.

Jones PJH, Leichter J, Lee M: Placental blood flow in rats fed alcohol before and during gestation. *Life Sci* 1981; 29:1153–1159.

Jones RD, Kleinerman JI, Luria MH: Observations on left ventricular failure induced by ethanol. *Cardiovasc Res* 1975; 9:286–294.

Juchems R, Klobe R: Hemodynamic effects of ethyl alcohol in man. *Am Heart J* 1969; 78:133–135.

Kagan A, Yano K, Rhoads GG, McGee DL: Alcohol and cardiovascular disease: The Hawaiian experience. *Circulation* 1981; 64 (Suppl III):III-27–33.

Kako KJ, Liu MS, Thornton MJ: Changes in fatty acid composition of myocardial triglyceride following a single administration of ethanol to rabbits. *J Molec Cell Cardiol* 1973; 5:473–489.

Kangasho M, Hillbom M, Kaste M, Wuorela H, Vapaatalo H: Formation of thromboxane B_2 by platelets and concentrations of thromboxane B_2 and 6-keto-prostaglandin F_1 in plasma after acute ethanol ingestion, in Samuelsson B, Paoleti R, Ramwell P (eds): *Advances in Prostaglandin, Thromboxane and Leukotriene Research*. New York, Raven Press, 1983, pp 223–228.

Karaki H, Weiss GB: Calcium release in smooth muscle. *Life Sci* 1988, 42:111–122.

Karanian JW, Salem N, Jr.: Effects of acute and chronic ethanol exposure on the response of rat aorta to a thromboxane mimic, U 46619. *Alcohol Clin Exp Res* 1986; 10:171–176.

Kettunen R, Timisjarvi J, Saukko P, Koskela M: Influence of ethanol on systemic and pulmonary hemodynamics in anesthetized dogs. *Acta Physiol Scand* 1983; 118:209–214.

Kety SS, Schmidt CF: The nitrous oxide method for the quantitative determination of cerebral blood flow in man: Theory, procedure and normal values. *J Clin Invest* 1948; 27:476–483.

Khetarpal VK, Volicer L: Alcohol and cardiovascular disorders. *Drug Alcohol Dep* 1981; 7:1–30.

Kikuchi T, Kako KJ: Metabolic effects of ethanol on the rabbit heart. *Circ Res* 1970; 26:625–634.

Kino M, Thorp KA, Bing OM, Abelmann WH: Impaired myocardial performance and response to calcium in experimental alcoholic cardiomyopathy. *J Mol Cell Cardiol* 1981; 13:981–989.

Kirkendol PL, Pearson JE, Bowler JD, Holbert RD: Myocardial depressant effects of sodium acetate. *Cardiovasc Res* 1978; 12:127–136.

Kittner SJ, Garcia-Palmieri MR, Costas R, Jr., Cruz-Vidal M, Abbott RD, Havlik RJ: Alcohol and coronary heart disease in Puerto Rico. *Am J Epidemiol* 1983; 117:538–550.

Klatsky AL: Blood pressure and alcohol consumption, in Bulpitt CJ (ed): *Handbook of Hypertension, Vol. 6: Epidemiology and Hypertension*. Amsterdam Elsevier Science Publ, 1985, p 159–174.

Klatsky AL, Armstrong MA, Friedman GD: Relation of alcoholic beverage use to subsequent coronary artery disease hospitalization. *Am J Cardiol* 1986; 58:710–714.

Klatsky AL, Friedman GD, Siegelaub AB: Alcohol and mortality: The ten-year Kaiser-Permanente experience. *Ann Intern Med* 1981a; 95:139–145.

Klatsky AL, Friedman GD, Siegelaub AB: Alcohol use and cardiovascular disease: The Kaiser-Permanente experience. *Circulation* 1981b; 64 (Suppl III):32–41.

Knott DH, Beard JD: Changes in cardiovascular activity as a function of alcohol intake, in Kissin B, Begleiter H (eds): *The Biology of Alcoholism, Vol. 2*. New York, Plenum Press, 1972, pp 348–365.

Kobayashi M, Furukawa Y, Chiba S: Effects of ethanol acetaldehyde on the isolated, blood-perfused canine atrium. *Arch Intern Pharmacodyn* 1979; 239:109–120.

Kozarevic D, Demirovic J, Gordon T, et al: Drinking habits and coronary heart disease. The Yugoslavia Cardiovascular Disease Study. *Am J Epidemiol* 1982; 116:748–758.

Kricka LJ, Clark PMS: *Biochemistry of Alcohol and Alcoholism*. New York, John Wiley and Sons, 1979.

Kupari M: Drunkenness, hangover, and the heart. *Acta Med Scand* 1983; 213:84–90.

Kupari M, Eriksson CJP, Heikkila J, Ylikahri R: Alcohol and the heart. *Acta Med Scand* 1983; 213: 91–98.

Kwast M, Tabakoff B, Hoffman P: Effect of ethanol on cardiac B-adrenoceptors. *Eur J Pharmacol* 1987; 142:441–445.

Lake DA, Chilian WM, Roberts LA: Ethanol increases rate of isolated atria. *Alcohol Clin Exp Res* 1978; 2:271–275.

LaPorte RE, Cresanta JL, Kuller LM: The relationship of alcohol consumption to atherosclerotic heart disease. *Prev Med* 1980; 9:22–40.

LaPorte RE, Cauley JA, Kuller LH, Fiegal K, Gavaler JS, Van Thiel D: Alcohol, coronary heart disease, and total mortality. *Recent Adv Alcohol* 1985; 3:157.

Lasker N, Sherrod TR, Killam KF: Alcohol on the coronary circulation of the dog. *J Pharmacol Exp Ther* 1955; 113:414–420.

Lassoff S, Gebrewold A, Altura BM: A new method of craniotomy in the rat: In-vivo investigation of the pial microcirculation. *Microcirculation* 1982; 2:345–353.

Lee K: Alcoholism and cerebrovascular thrombosis in the young. *Acta Neurol* 1979; 59:270–274.

Lee K, Moller L, Hardt F, Haubek A, Jensen E: Alcohol-induced brain damage and liver damage in young males. *Lancet* 1979; ii:759–761.

Levi GF, Quadri A, Ratti S, Rasagni M: Preclinical abnormality of left ventricular function in chronic alcoholics. *Brit Heart J* 1977; 39:35–37.

Li T-K, Schenker S, Lumeng L: *Alcohol and Nutrition*. DHEW Publication No. (ADM) 79-780. Washington, D.C., NIAAA, 1979.

Liang CS, Lowenstein JM: Metabolic control of the circulation. Effects of acetate and pyruvate. *J Clin Invest* 1978; 62:1029–1038.

Lieber CS: *Medical Disorders of Alcoholism: Pathogenesis and Treatment*. Baltimore, Univ. Park Press, 1982.

Lishman A, Jacobson RR, Acker C: Brain damage in alcoholism: Current concepts. *Acta Med Scand* 1987; Suppl 717:5–17.

Lochner A, Cowley R, Brink AJ: Effect of ethanol on metabolism and function of perfused rat heart. *Am Heart J* 1969; 78:770–780.

Loeb O: Die Wirkung des Alkohols auf das Warmbluterherz. *Arch Exp Pathol Pharmakol* 1905; 52: 459–480.

Loomis TA: The effect of alcohol on myocardial and respiratory function; The influence of modified respiratory function on the cardiac toxicity of alcohol. *Q J Stud Alcohol* 1952; 13:459–480.

Lowenstein SR, Gabow PA, Cramer J, Oliva PB, Ratner K: The role of alcohol in new-onset atrial fibrillation. *Arch Intern Med* 1983; 143:1882–1885.

Maines JE, Aldinger EE: Myocardial depression accompanying chronic consumption of alcohol. *Am Heart J* 1967; 73:55–63.

Martinez TT, Collins GA, Walker MJA: The effects of prostaglandins on the beating activity of cultured heart cells. *Prostaglandins* 1977; 14:449–461.

Maruyama Y, Bing RJ, Sarma JSM, Weishaar R: The effect of alcohol on active and passive stiffness, and on isometric contractions of glycerinated heart muscle in rats. *Jap Heart J* 1978; 19:513–521.

Marx P, Neundorfer B, Potz G, Hoyer S: Cerebral blood flow and amino acid metabolism in chronic alcoholism, in Harper AM et al (eds): *Blood Flow and Metabolism in the Brain*. Edinburgh, Churchill Livingstone, 1975.

Mashimo K: Chronotropic responses to ethanol of mouse atrial and ventricular myocardial cells in culture. *Jap J Physiol* 1985; 35:659–671.

Mason DT, Spann JF Jr, Miller RR et al: Effects of acute ethanol on the contractile state of normal and failing cat papillary muscles. *Eur J Cardiol* 1978; 7:311–316.

Mathews JD: Alcohol and hypertension. *Austr NZ J Med* 1979; 9:158–169.

Meltzer HL, Alexopoulos G: Increased erythrocyte calcium in alcoholism. *J Clin Pharmacol* 1982; 22: 466–469.

Mendoza LC, Hellberg K, Rickart A, Tillich G, Bing RJ: The effect of intravenous ethyl alcohol on the coronary circulation and myocardial contractility of the human and canine heart. *J Clin Pharmacol* 1971; 11:165–176.

Mierzwiak DS, Wildenthal K, Mitchell JH: Acute effects of ethanol on the left ventricle in dogs. *Arch Intern Pharmacodyn* 1972; 199:43–52.

Morvai V, Donath T, Unguary GY: Effect of long-term alcohol intake on the innervation of the rat myocardium. *Acta Morphol Acad Sci Hung* 1979a; 27:315–322.

Morvai V, Varga UK, Albert K, Folly G: Effects of long-term alcohol intake on the cardiovascular system of the rat. *Acta Physiol Acad Sci Hung* 1979b; 54:369–379.

Moskow HA, Pennington RC, Knisely MH: Alcohol, sludge and hypoxic areas of nervous system, liver and heart. *Microvasc Res* 1968; 1:174–185.

Nakano J, Kessinger JM: Cardiovascular effects of ethanol, its congeners and synthetic bourbon in dogs. *Eur J Pharmacol* 1972; 17:195–201.

Nakano J, Moore SE: Effect of different alcohols on the contractile force of the isolated guinea pig myocardium. *Eur J Pharmacol* 1972; 20:266–270.

Nakano J, Prancan AV: Effects of adrenergic blockade on cardiovascular responses to ethanol and acetaldehyde. *Arch Int Pharmacodyn* 1972; 196:259–268.

Newlin DB, Golden CJ, Quaife M, Graber B: Effect of alcohol ingestion on regional cerebral blood flow. *Int J Neuroscience* 1982; 17:145–150.

Newman WH, Valcienti JF Jr: Ventricular function following acute alcohol administration: A strain-gauge analysis of depressed ventricular dynamics. *Am Heart J* 1971; 81:61–68.

Noe M, Oliva D, Corsini A, Soma M, Fumagalli R, Nicosia S: Differential effects of in-vitro ethanol on prostaglandin E_1-sensitive adenylate cyclase activity from smooth muscle cells and platelets. *J Cyclic Nucleotide Pr Phosph Res* 1985; 10:293–308.

Noren GR, Staley NA, Einzig S, Mikell FL, Asinger RW: Alcohol-induced congestive cardiomyopathy: An animal model. *Cardiovac Res* 1983; 17:81–87.

Okarma TB, Tramell P, Kalman SM: The surface interaction between digoxin and cultured heart cells. *J Pharmacol Exp Ther* 1972; 183:559–576.

Osler W: *The Principles and Practice of Medicine*. New York, D. Appleton, 1912.

Pachinger OM, Tillmann H, Mao JC, Fauvel JM, Bing RJ: The effect of prolonged administration of ethanol on cardiac metabolism and performance in the dog. *J Clin Invest* 1973; 52:2690–2696.

Parker BM: The effects of ethyl alcohol on the heart. *J Am Med Assn* 1974; 228:741–742.

Pearl R: *Alcohol and longevity*. New York, Knopf, 1926.

Peng T-C, Cooper CW, Munson PL: The hypocalcemic effects of ethyl alcohol in rats and dogs. *Endocrinol* 1972; 91:586–593.

Pescio S, Macho P, Penna M, Domenech PJ: Changes in total and transmural coronary blood flow induced by ethanol. *Cardiovasc Res* 1983; 17:604–607.

Pitt B, Sugishita Y, Green HL, Freisinger GC: Coronary hemodynamic effect of ethyl alcohol in the conscious dog. *Am J Physiol* 1970; 219:175–177.

Pohorecky LA: Influence of alcohol on peripheral neurotransmitter function. *Federation Proc* 1982; 41:2452–2455.

Porjesz B, Begleiter H: Brain dysfunction and alcohol, in Kissin B and Begleiter H (eds): *The Pathogenesis of Alcoholism*, vol 7. New York, Plenum, 1983, pp 415–483.

Posner P, Baker SP, Hunter B, Walker DW: Chronotropic and inotropic effects on atria of chronic ethanol ingestion in the aging rat. *Alcohol and Drug Res* 1987; 7:273–277.

Potter JF, Beevers DG: The possible mechanisms of alcohol associated hypertension. *Ann Clin Res* 1984; 16 (Suppl 43):97–102.

Potter JF, Bannan LT, Beevers DG: Alcohol and hypertension. *Brit J Addiction* 1984; 79:365–372.

Price F: *A Textbook of the Practice of Medicine*. London, Oxford Medical Publications, 1922.

Raichle ME, Grubb RL, Gado MD, Eichling JO, Ter-Pogossian MT: Correlation between regional cerebral blood flow, blood flow and oxidative metabolism. *Arch Neurol* 1976; 8:523–526.

Regan TJ, Koroxenidis G, Moschos CB, Oldewurtel HA, Lehan PH, Hellems HK: The acute metabolic and hemodynamic responses of the left ventricle to ethanol. *J Clin Invest* 1966; 45:270–280.

Regan TJ, Levinson GE, Oldewurtel HA, Frank MJ, Weisse AB, Moschos CB: Ventricular function in non-cardiacs with alcoholic fatty liver: Role of ethanol in the production of cardiomyopathy. *J Clin Invest* 1969; 48:397–407.

Regan TJ, Khan MI, Ettinger PO, Haider B, Lyons MM, Oldewurtel HA: Myocardial function and lipid metabolism in the chronic alcoholic animal. *J Clin Invest* 1974; 54:740–752.

Regan TJ, Ettinger PO, Oldewurtel MA, Haider B: Heart cell responses to ethanol. *Ann NY Acad Sci* 1975; 252:250–263.

Regan TJ, Ettinger PO, Lyons MM et al: Ethyl alcohol as a cardiac risk factor. *Curr Probl Cardiol* 1977; 2.

Regan TJ, Haider B: Ethanol abuse and heart disease. *Circulation* 1981; 64 (Suppl. III):14–19.

Regan TJ, Morvan F: Experimental models for studying the effects of ethanol on the myocardium. *Acta Med Scand* 1987; Suppl 717:107–113.

Retig JN, Kirchberger MA, Rubin E, et al: Effects of ethanol on calcium transport by microsomes phosphorylated by cyclic AMP-dependent protein kinase. *Biochem Pharmacol* 1977; 26:393–396.

Rhoads GG, Blackwelder WC, Stemmerman GN, Hayashi T, Kagan A: Coronary risk factors and autopsy findings in Japanese-American men. *Lab Invest* 1978; 38:304–311.

Ricci G, Angelico F: Alcohol consumption and coronary heart disease. *Lancet* 1979; i:1404.

Riff DP, Jain AC, Doyle JJ: Acute hemodynamic effects of ethanol on normal human volunteers. *Am Heart J* 1969; 78:592–597.

Riley JN, Walker DW: Morphologic alterations in hippocampus after long-term alcohol consumption in mice. *Science* 1978; 201:646–648.

Ritchie JM: The aliphatic alcoholics, in Goodman LS, Gilman A (eds): *The Pharmacological Basis of Therapeutics*, 5th ed. New York, McMillan, 1975, p 139.

Rix KJB: *Alcohol and Alcoholism*. Montreal, Eden, 1977.

Ross DH: Selective action of alcohols on cerebral calcium levels. *Ann NY Acad Sci* 1976; 273:280–294.

Rubin E: Alcoholic myopathy in heart and skeletal muscle. *New Engl J Med* 1979; 301:28–33.

Rubin JI, Rubin E: Myocardial toxicity of alcohols, aldehydes, and glycols, including alcoholic cardiomyopathy, in Van Stee EW (ed): *Cardiovascular Toxicity*. New York, Raven Press, 1982, pp 353–363.

Salerno JC, Ohrisini T: Effects of ethanol and acetaldehyde on iron-sulfur centers in the mitochondrial respiratory chain. *Arch Biochem Biophys* 1976; 176:757–765.

Sarma JSM, Ikeda S, Fischer R, Maruyama Y, Weishaar R, Bing RJ: Biochemical and contractile properties of heart muscle after prolonged alcohol administration. *J Mol Cell Cardiol* 1976; 8:951–972.

Saunders JB, Beevers DG, Paton A: Factors influencing blood pressure in chronic alcoholics. *Clin Sci* 1979; 57:295S–298S.

Schreiber SS, Briden K, Oratz M, Rothschild MA: Ethanol, acetaldehyde, and myocardial protein synthesis. *J Clin Invest* 1972; 51:2820–2826.

Seeman P: The membrane actions of anesthetics and tranquilizers. *Pharmacol Rev* 1972; 24:583–655.

Segel LD, Miller RR, Mason DT: Depressive effects of acute ethanol exposure on function of isolated working rat hearts. *Cardiovasc Med* 1978; 3:211–213.

Segel LD, Mason DT: Acute effects of acetaldehyde and ethanol on rat heart mitochondria. *Res Comm Chem Pathol Pharmacol* 1979; 25:461–474.

Segel LD, Rendig SV, Mason DT: Alcohol-induced cardiac hemodynamics and CA^{2+} flux and dysfunctions are reversible. *J Mol Cell Cardiol* 1981; 13:443–455.

Segel LD, Klausner SC, Gnadt JTH, Amsterdam EA: Alcohol and the heart. *Med Clin North Am* 1984; 68:147–161.

Shimojyo S, Scheinberg P, Reinmuth O: Cerebral blood flow and metabolism in the Wernicke-Korsakoff syndrome. *J Clin Invest* 1967; 46:849–854.

Singer K, Lundberg WB: Ventricular arrhythmias associated with ingestion of alcohol. *Ann Intern Med* 1972; 77:241–248.

Smith CM: The pharmacology of sedatives/hypnotics, alcohol, and anesthetics: Sites and mechanisms of action, in Martin AR (ed): *Handbook of Experimental Pharmacology, Vol. 45, Part I*, New York, Springer-Verlag, 1977; pp 413–587.

Sohler TP, Lothrop GN, Forbes HS: The pial circulation of normal, nonanesthetized animals. II. Effects of drugs, alcohol and carbon dioxide. *J Pharmacol Exp Ther* 1941; 71:331–375.

Spann JF, Mason DT, Beiser GD, Gold HK: Actions of ethanol on the contractile state of the normal and failing cat papillary muscle. *Clin Res* 1968; 16:249 (Abstr).

Spodick DH, Pigott VM, Chirife R: Preclinical cardiac malfunction in chronic alcoholism: Comparison with matched normal controls with alcoholic cardiomyopathy. *New Engl J Med* 1972; 287:677–680.

Stason WB, Neff RK, Miettinen OS, Jick H: Alcohol consumption and nonfatal myocardial infarction. *Am J Epidemiol* 1976; 104:603–608.

Steell G: Heart failure as a result of chronic alcoholism. *Med Chron* 1893; 18:1–22.

Stefanelli N, Ronge H: Andereung der Vereformbarkeite und des viskosimetrischen Verhaltens von Erythrozyten unter Athanoleinwirkung. *Wien Klin Wschr* 1978; 90:806–808.

Stott DJ, Ball SG, Inglis GC, Davies DL, Fraser R, Murray GD, McInnes GT: Effects of a single moderate dose of alcohol on blood pressure, heart rate and associated metabolic and endocrine changes. *Clin Sci* 1987; 73:411–416.

Stratton R, Dormer K, Zeimer A: The cardiovascular effects of ethanol and acetaldehyde in exercising dogs. *Alcohol Clin Exp Res* 1981; 5:56–63.

Sulzer R: The influence of alcohol on the isolated mammalian heart. *Heart* 1924; 14:141–150.

Swartz MH, Repke DI, Katz AM et al: Effects of ethanol on calcium binding and calcium uptake by cardiac microsomes. *Biochem Pharmacol* 1974; 23:2369–2376.

Takizawa A, Yasue H, Omote S, Nagao M, Hyon M, Nishida S, Horie M: Variant agina induced by alcohol ingestion. *Am Heart J* 1984; 107:25–27.

Tarasyuk IK: The effect of alcohol misuse on the development and course of acute brain circulation disorders. *Zh Nevropat Psikhiat* 1976; 76:1177–1180.

Taylor JR: Alcohol and strokes. *New Engl J Med* 1982; 306:1111.

Taylor JR, Combs-Orme T: Alcohol and strokes in young adults. *Am J Psychiat* 1985; 142:116–118.

Tepper D, Capasso JM, Sonnenblick EH: Excitation-contraction coupling in rat myocardium: Alterations with long-term consumption. *Cardiovasc Res* 1986; 20:369–374.

Thomas BC: The cerebral circulation. 31. Effect of alcohol on cerebral vessels. *Arch Neurol Psychiat* 1937; 38:321–339.

Timmis GG, Ramos RC, Gordon S, Parikh R, Gangadharan V: The basis for differences in ethanol-induced myocardial depression in normal subjects. *Circulation* 1975; 51:1144–1148.

Tindall AS: Cerebrovascular disease, in Rosenberg RN (ed): *Neurology*. New York, Grune and Stratton, 1980, p 41.

Toda N, Kodishi M, Miyazaki M, Komura S: Responses of arterial smooth muscle to ethanol and acetaldehyde. *J Stud Alcohol* 1983; 44:1–16.

Trell E, Henningsen NC, Petersson B, Westin L, Hood B: Alcohol and the vascular system. *Acta Med Scand* 1986; Suppl 703:281–290.

Turlapaty PDMV, Altura BM: Extracellular magnesium ions control calcium exchange and content of vascular smooth muscle. *Eur J Pharmacol* 1978; 52:421–423.

Turlapaty PDMV, Altura BM: Magnesium deficiency produces spasms of coronary arteries: Relationship to etiology of sudden death ischemic heart disease. *Science* 1980; 208:198–200.

Turlapaty PDMV, Altura BT, Altura BM: Ethanol reduces Ca^{2+} concentrations in arterial and venous smooth muscle. *Experientia* 1979a; 35:639–640.

Turlapaty PDMV, Altura BT, Altura BM: Interactions of Tris buffer and ethanol on agonist-induced responses of vascular smooth muscle and on calcium-45 uptake. *J Pharmacol Exp Ther* 1979b; 211:59–67.

Turner TB, Bennett VL, Hernandez H: The beneficial side of moderate alcohol use. *Johns Hopkins Med J* 1981; 145:53–63.

Van Voorhees L, Gottdiener J, Gay J, DiBianco R, Maloney D, Fletcher R: The effects of alcohol on left ventricular (LV) relaxation and systolic LV function in normal subjects: Echocardiography assessment by computer-assisted analysis of LV wall velocity. *Clin Res* 1981; 29:248A.

Vincent J-L, Vanherweghem J-L, Degaute J-L, Berre J, Dufaye P, Kahn RJ: Acetate-induced myocardial depression during hemodialysis for acute renal failure. *Kidney Intl* 1982; 22:653–657.

Walker DW, Barnes DE, Zornetzer SF, Hunter BE, Kubanis P: Neuronal loss in hippocampus induced by prolonged ethanol consumption in rats. *Science* 1980; 209:711–713.

Wallace RB, Lynch CF, Pomrehn PR, Criqui MH, Heiss G: Alcohol and hypertension: Epidemiologic and experimental considerations. *Circulation* 1981; 64 (Suppl III):III-41–47.

Walsh MJ, Hollander PB, Truit EB: Sympathomimetic effects of acetaldehyde on the electrical and contractile characteristics of isolated left atia of guinea pig. *J Pharmacol Exp Ther* 1969; 167:173–186.

Walshe WH: *A Practical Review of the Diseases of the Heart and Great Vessels, including the Principles of Their Physical Diagnosis*. London, Smith, Elder, 1873.

Webb WR, Degerli IU: Ethyl alcohol and the cardiovascular system: Effects on coronary blood flow. *J Am Med Assoc* 1965; 191:77–80.

Webb WR, Gupta DN, Cook WA, Sugg WL, Bashour FA, Unal MO: Effects of alcohol on myocardial contractility. *Dis Chest* 1967; 52:602–605.

Weinberg J, Altura BM: Morphine pretreatment influences reactivity of isolated rat arterial smooth muscle. *Subst Alcohol Actions/Misuse* 1980; 7:71–81.

Weishaar R, Sarma JSM, Maruyama Y, Fischer R, Bertuglia S, Bing RJ: Reversibility of mitochondrial and contractile changes in the myocardium after cessation of prolonged ethanol intake. *Am J Cardiol* 1977; 40:556–562.

Weiss S, Wilkins RW: The nature of the cardiovascular disturbances in nutritional deficiency states (beriberi). *Ann Intern Med* 1937; 11:104.

Wenckebach KF: St. Cyre's lecture: The heart and circulation in tropical avitaminosis (beri-beri). *Lancet* 1928; ii:265–268.

Wendt WE, Wu C, Balcon R, Doty G, Bing RJ: Hemodynamic and metabolic effects of chronic alcoholism in man. *Am J Cardiol* 1965; 15:175–184.

Williams ER, Mirro MJ, Bailey JC: Electrophysiologic effects of ethanol, acetaldehyde and acetate on cardiac tissues from dog and guinea pig. *Circ Res* 1980; 47:473–478.

Williams P, Robinson D, Bailey A: High-density lipoprotein and coronary risk factors in normal men. *Lancet* 1979; 1:72–75.

Wong M: Depression of cardiac performance by ethanol unmasked during autonomic blockade. *Am Heart J* 1973; 86:508–515.

Wong M: In-vivo sampling of cardiac triglyceride from dogs during ethanol infusion. *J Lipid Res* 1974; 15:50 55.

Yang H-Y, Shum AY-C, Ng H-T, Chen CF: Effect of ethanol on human umbilical artery and vein in vitro. *Gynecol Obstet Invest* 1986; 21:131–135.

CHAPTER 9

Alcoholism and Psychiatric Disorders

Joel Solomon, M.D.

Department of Psychiatry
Columbia University
College of Physicians and Surgeons
New York, USA

Historically, the relationship between alcoholism and psychiatric disorders has created much confusion, conjecture and polarization in the medical/mental health field. Whether alcoholism is a symptom, a disease, or merely evidence of moral weakness has been raised as a question since professionals began to write about this condition.

Dr. Benjamin Rush, the founder of modern psychiatry, first defined alcoholism as a disease in 1786. His writings conveyed an early understanding of the disease concept, loss of control, and the psychiatric complications that can result from alcoholism. However, he also described the alcoholic as a "weak-willed sinner and degenerate" (Levin, 1978), a clear expression of the ambivalence felt toward the alcoholic by the psychiatric community of that time.

Much of the psychiatric literature dealing with alcoholism that followed attempted to show how alcohol was responsible for most cases of insanity and used by fundamentalist temperance groups to support their moralistic position regarding alcohol and the people who consumed it. This early psychiatric literature has been comprehensively reviewed by Bowman and Jellinek (1941).

It was not until the 1930s that a small group of psychoanalysts led by Fenichel (1945), Knight (1937), and Rado (1933), among others, began to take a more enlightened, yet still limited, look at alcoholism and some of the underlying dynamics. Most of this early psychoanalytic writing described alcoholism as merely symptomatic of more severe underlying psychopathology rather than a disease in and of itself. Knight, in particular, felt there was "always an underlying personality disorder evidenced by obvious maladjustment, neurotic character traits, emotional immaturity of infantilism and often by other neurotic symptoms. In some, if not all, thinly veiled psychotic trends, especially paranoid and schizoid features are discovered" (1937).

At about the same time that Knight and colleagues were developing their approach, Dr. Bob Smith, an active alcoholic, and Bob Wilson, a recovering alcoholic, developed a relationship that eventually led to the founding of the fellowship of Alcoholics Anonymous, an organization based on the tenet that alcoholism is a disease that is constantly in the process of recovery, and for which there is no "cure."

Present psychiatric thinking has tried to encompass aspects of both of these approaches. There are indeed, many, if not most, alcoholics for whom alcoholism is the primary and only diagnosis, and once they have stopped drinking, any secondary psychopathology that may be a reversible complication of the alcoholism generally clears. However, there are a number of alcoholics who are using alcohol in an attempt to medicate painful and disturbing affects and thoughts. These people may indeed have developed their alcoholism secondary to a psychiatric disorder.

Although this primary-secondary dimension is important from both a theoretical as well as a practical perspective, the disease of alcoholism makes little distinction between them. The disease is a pathologic condition that eventually becomes autonomous from the factors that may have contributed to it and develops a life of its own. The loss of control found in alcoholism makes little distinction between the alcoholic who may have been trying to medicate a depression from the alcoholic who is basically free of severe psychopathology other than the alcoholism.

Although the diagnosis of alcoholism as a primary psychiatric disorder and the generalization that all alcoholics suffer from severe underlying psychopathology has been the subject of much controversy, a more enlightened psychiatric position has recently been taken with the American Psychiatric Association's publication of the *Diagnostic and Statistical Manual of Mental Disorders* (Third Edition) (DSM-III) (1987), which describes specific areas of dysfunction associated with pathological patterns of alcohol consumption. The DSM-III describes two general categories under which diagnostic criteria for alcohol-related problems are found. Under "Substance Use Disorders" are Alcohol Dependence and Alcohol Abuse. The former incorporates the concepts of loss of control, tolerance, withdrawal, and the development of social, psychological, and physical problems. The latter focuses on maladaptive patterns of alcohol use that do not meet the criteria for the former.

The second category of diagnostic criteria is found under the "Alcohol Induced Organic Mental Disorders." It includes:

Acute Alcohol Intoxication is usually a self-limiting event and requires little intervention other than protecting the individual from dangerous situations. It rarely manifests either severe or prolonged psychiatric symptoms, but in some cases must be differentiated from acute neurological, metabolic, or psychiatric illness, such as catatonia or hysteria. For alcohol intoxication to be diagnosed as a mental disorder, some maladaptive behavior must occur.

Idiosyncratic or Pathological Intoxication can be defined as behavioral changes of a violent or psychotic nature that occur under the influence of even small amounts of alcohol and are considered atypical for the individual. There is usually little or no recall of the event once the patient is sober. Pathological intoxication was first described by Krafft-Ebing in 1869 and subsequently reviewed by several other authors (Banay, 1944; May and Ebaugh, 1953).

In a recent review of the subject, Coid (1979) thought of it as having no clinical or forensic value and thought it should be discarded from the literature as a diagnostic classification. May and Ebaugh (1953) also felt that, based on their review of the literature and clinical studies, "there is no justification for the use of pathological intoxication as a special diagnostic term . . . and both the concept and term should be abandoned." They concluded that it was always possible to demonstrate a clear relationship between the effect of alcohol intoxication, personality structure, current conflicts, and the symptoms of the reaction.

Maletsky (1978), on the other hand, found that in the group of patients that he studied, those who demonstrated dangerous, psychotic, or other types of pathological behavior during drinking episodes and were amnesic for the event also demonstrated a high incidence of abnormal electroencephalograms during these periods of intoxication. These periods of pathological behavior can be easily confused with temporal lobe epilepsy, schizophrenia, or other acute psychosis. This differential diagnosis is particularly important if medication is begun, which can further complicate the clinical picture.

The results of other studies differed from those of Maletsky. Coid (1979), for example, saw Maletsky's study as uncontrolled and thought his subjects were not acting any differently from when they were not intoxicated. Bach-y-Rita et al (1970) found no seizure activity in 10 patients with the presumptive diagnosis of pathological intoxication when they were intravenously given an alcohol solution.

Although there continues to be disagreement as to whether the distinct entity of pathological intoxication actually exists, there is little question that there are some people who manifest a variety of psychotic symptoms after consuming even small amounts of alcohol. This condition may or may not be related to temporal lobe epilepsy or specific psychiatric diagnoses, but, nevertheless, these relationships await clarification.

Alcohol Withdrawal Syndromes is another area that has presented some diagnostic confusion. Much of the work of Gross et al (1963) has been devoted to the clarification and systematization of these syndromes. Mild to moderate withdrawal, not complicated by psychiatric illness, should be easy to recognize and manage. Many symptoms of more severe withdrawal may also be present during and confused with a variety of psychiatric diagnoses. Anxiety, depression, sleep disturbance, hallucinations, and delusions, as well as other forms of psychoses are not uncommon in more severe withdrawal.

Alcohol Hallucinosis is frequently mentioned, occasionally seen, and poorly understood. Several authors have examined the relationship between this diagnosis and schizophrenia. Alpert and Silvers (1970) compared the perceptual characteristics of the hallucinations in schizophrenics and in alcoholics and found the former's hallucinations were more like thoughts that had become audible, were poorly localized in space, and showed more sensitivity to emotional arousal. The latter's hallucinations were characterized by more sensory factors, were specifically localized in space, and were of greater frequency.

Mott et al (1965) compared the hallucinations of patients suffering from a variety of psychiatric, neurological, and toxic states. The schizophrenic and alcoholic patients both reported more persecutory and instructive hallucinations but differed on the localization of them; schizophrenics perceived them internally, alcoholics externally.

Goodwin et al (1971) evaluated hallucinations in several psychiatric disorders and found no diagnostic significance in the type of hallucinations reported. Both visual as well as auditory hallucinations were common in all of the disorders evaluated.

Alcohol Amnesic Disorder or, more commonly, Korsakoff's psychosis, is associated with prolonged, heavy drinking and thiamine deficiency. Usually manifested by signs of cerebellar involvement, peripheral neuropathy, and memory impairment, this condition has been extensively reviewed by Victor et al (1971).

Alcoholic Dementia is somewhat controversial and is manifest by global cognitive deficits and perceptual and personality deterioration.

It is generally accepted that anyone can develop alcoholism. No one is immune. However, certain people develop alcoholism with more frequency, rapidity, and intensity than others. This selectivity seems to be based on a variety of biological, psychological, and social factors. These factors also seem to play a role in the development of complications. In examining these various factors, Kissin (1982) proposed a bio-psych-social model of alcoholism that takes into consideration the biological, psychological, psychiatric, and social elements that predispose certain people to develop the disease; increase the intensity and rapidity with which certain people develop tolerance and dependence; and determine to what extent and degree certain people develop which particular complications of alcoholism.

This model is also helpful in understanding the various relationships that can develop between alcoholism and the gamut of psychiatric disorders. For both theoretical reasons as well as obvious treatment implications, it is important to determine the primacy of the alcoholism or the psychiatric disorder.

This primary-secondary (or essential-reactive) dimension has been an important one for the field of psychiatry. Simply recognizing that psychiatric disorders occur more frequently in alcoholics and vice versa, although important, sheds little light on whether these psychiatric disorders predisposed the individual to the development of alcoholism, arose as a result of the alcoholism, or predated the alcoholism and was independent of its development. An attempt to clarify this issue was undertaken by Winokur et al (1971) who hypothesized that based on clinical findings that there are actually three major groups of alcoholics: the primary alcoholic, the primary depressive alcoholic, and the primary sociopathic alcoholic. These three groups were found to be different in a number of ways, such as family histories, grouping by sex, age of onset of drinking, and years of abusing alcohol and risk of suicide.

Other authors have attempted to develop a typology of alcoholism based on family history of alcoholism and psychopathology. Frances et al (1980), for example, found that of a large group of men admitted to a naval residential alcoholism treatment facility, those who reported at least one family member with a possible drinking problem also showed more antisocial behavior and worse academic, social, and employment performance. The authors suggest that this group of alcoholics might be related to the "essential" alcoholic described by Knight (1937) and were felt to be more severe and therefore more difficult to treat.

Others (Tarter et al, 1977) have suggested that there may be a subgroup of alcoholics who as children displayed symptoms of minimal brain dysfunction and began to consume excessive quantities of alcohol at an early age but had no other psychiatric symptoms. These were described as primary alcoholics. These authors also suggest that the secondary alcoholics were normal children who in adult life became psychiatrically impaired and used alcohol for relief of symptoms.

The primary alcoholic frequently has a biological parent who is alcoholic (Goodwin, 1973), has more medical, psychological, and social complications of their drinking (Frances et al, 1980), and is generally thought to suffer the more severe form of alcoholism with a poorer prognosis than the alcoholic who is drinking secondary to psychiatric symptoms.

The secondary or reactive alcoholic, although less clearly defined, appears to have a variety of psychiatric disorders on which the alcoholism has been superimposed. It is, of course, difficult, if not impossible, to make this distinction when the alcoholic is actively drinking since both the acute as well as chronic effects of alcohol can both mask or mimic a wide range of psychiatric disorders.

Many psychiatric patients also have alcoholism. These alcoholics are seen in a variety of psychiatric facilities. Crowley et al (1974) examined alcohol problems in 50 consecutive admissions to an adult inpatient psychiatric ward and found that alcohol contributed to over one-fourth of the admissions. "Character problems" were found to be the most common diagnostic category in this group.

Using DSM-III criteria, Hesselbrock et al (1985) assessed the prevalence of lifetime psychopathology among a group of hospitalized alcoholics and found that antisocial personalities and substance-use disorders were common among the males and depression and phobia were more frequent among the females. Also of interest in this study was that the onset of psychopathologies preceded the abuse of alcohol among the women but not the men, with the exception of antisocial personality and panic disorder, where it also preceded the alcohol abuse.

This gender difference is also important from the perspective of treatment outcome as reported by Rounsaville et al (1987) who found that while coexistant psychiatric diagnosis generally predicted poorer treatment outcome, there were significant differences between men and women. For men, having an additional diagnosis of major depression, antisocial personality, or drug abuse was associated with poorer outcome. For women, having a major depression was associated with a better outcome in drinking-related measures, whereas antisocial personality and drug abuse were associated with poorer prognosis.

Other factors, such as the location at which a study is being carried out, can influence the rate at which alcoholism is found. For example, at a Veterans Administration hospital, Fowler et al (1977) found that 53% of the admissions he studied met the diagnostic criteria for alcoholism.

Psychiatric emergency facilities are also commonly used by alcoholics. In a large study, Idestrom (1974) found that at the Karolinska Hospital in Sweden, 35% of the patients using the emergency services were diagnosed as alcoholic. He also felt that this number was probably an underestimate. Another report by Schwarz and Fjeld (1969) also concluded that it is usually the end-stage alcoholic with multiple problems who uses these psychiatric facilities, rather than the younger, healthier alcoholic who may be a better candidate for treatment.

As might be expected, psychiatric outpatient clinics also see large numbers of alcoholic patients. Bahn and Chandler (1961) found that among all Maryland residents discharged from psychiatric outpatient clinics during a one-year period, 25% of the men and 9% of the women had been diagnosed as alcoholic. They also found that as the age increased, the diagnosis of alcoholism also increased and the diagnosis of personality disorders decreased.

Thus, whether it be in psychiatric inpatient, outpatient, or emergency room facilities, alcoholics comprise a minimum of one-fifth of the patients and, most likely, this percentage is much higher.

From the other perspective, Tyndal (1974) found that among 1000 alcoholic patients, 100% of them could be psychiatrically diagnosed according to DSM-II criteria. He concluded that the development of alcoholism is not possible without underlying psychopathology and is the "outcome of a prolonged process of continuous or repeated attempts to deal with the discomfort caused by psychopathological processes and their associated social difficulties."

Several attempts have been made to develop a general theory regarding the relationship between alcoholism and psychiatric disorders. They have met with little success. For just as there are psychiatric patients who have no problem with alcohol, there are alcoholics who have no psychiatric problems other than their alcoholism. Additionally, the psychopathology associated with alcoholism may be a cause, a consequence, or independent of the abuse of alcohol. Defining psychiatric disorders among alcoholics is obviously more than a theoretical issue. Panepinto et al (1970) showed that it can also act as an indicator of participation in treatment if the treatment was based on the diagnostic findings. They found that patients diagnosed as schizophrenic and put into treatment employing primarily a medical model had more doctor visits over a longer period of time than did patients with various character disorders.

The following sections review these relationships and a variety of specific psychiatric disorders.

ALCOHOLISM AND SCHIZOPHRENIA

As clinicians generally acknowledge, patients sharing the duel diagnoses of alcoholism and schizophrenia are notoriously among the most difficult to treat. Surprisingly however, there has been a paucity of literature about this vexatious problem. Freed (1975) did an extensive review of the subject and found little consistency among authors on a number of issues. For example, in looking at the prevalence of schizophrenia among populations of alcoholics, studies have found a range of from 1% (Gillis and Keet, 1969) to 49% (Tomsovic and Edwards, 1970) among patients in alcoholism treatment programs.

From the other perspective, the prevalence of alcoholism among schizophrenic patients is also variable. Parker et al (1960) found that 22% of 150 hospitalized schizophrenics were abusing alcohol while Johanson (1958) found that 35% of his sample were also problem drinkers. In a group of 30 hospitalized Irish schizophrenic patients, Opler (1957) found that 63% were alcohol abusers while finding only 3% of Italian schizophrenics carrying the additional diagnosis of alcoholism.

On average, it appears that about 10 to 15% of alcoholics have also been diagnosed to be suffering from schizophrenia and a similar number of hospitalized schizophrenics also have a serious drinking problem.

In an attempt to clarify these topics, there have also been some studies that look at the rates of alcoholism in the families of schizophrenics. As might be expected, the families of schizophrenic probands will have higher rates of alcoholism if the family members themselves are afflicted with the disease. Bleuler (1950) found a range of from 3 to 24% of the fathers of schizophrenic alcoholics also suffered from alcoholism. In a recent more sophisticated study, Rimmer and Jacobsen (1977) compared schizophrenic adoptees and their biological relatives with control adoptees and their biological relatives and concluded that neither schizophrenics nor their relatives had higher rates of alcoholism than did the controls. In a recent study of this issue, Kesselman et al (1982) found that an alcohol–schizophrenic group lay between pure alcoholics and pure schizophrenics in giving a positive family history for alcohol abuse.

One part of the difficulty in trying to evaluate the relationship and make the diagnosis between these two entities is that they may share many similar symptoms, particularly during a state of pathological intoxication or withdrawal. Hallucinations, delusions, loss of control, agitation, and disorganization may be present in both conditions. Whether a clinician is faced with an alcoholic schizophrenic patient, a schizophrenic with superimposed alcoholism, or one who independently has these two conditions will depend on the prominence and persistence of specific symptoms, the longitudinal history, and perhaps most important, the theoretical orientation of the clinician making the diagnosis.

Among the most troublesome patients to evaluate are those who present with chronic hallucinations or delusions, which are precipitated by alcohol but do not resolve when the alcohol has been discontinued. Victor and Hope (1958) felt that there was a small group of alcoholics in whom hallucinations persist for long periods of time and who occasionally follow a deteriorating course independent of continued drinking and who begin to look more like chronic schizophrenic patients but without a clearcut formal thought disorder.

Although many clinicians attempted to delineate a causal relationship between these two conditions, Kesselman et al (1982) believed that based on their findings, the conditions were merely two unrelated entities. Kesselman et al felt that anything other than a chance relationship that may have been found was a function of attributing a patient's drinking to "nervousness" or their "nervousness" to their drinking. This clinical impression puts in question, a number of articles that describe how alcohol has an ameliorating effect on schizophrenic symptoms (Halley, 1940).

Very little information exists on the long-term prognosis and course of patients with these two diagnoses. Part of the difficulty may be that they are frequently segregated at an early stage of treatment by the system into which they happen to fall based on the definition of the predominant problem by the treating source. This is unfortunate since schizophrenic alcoholics may present problems that neither schizophrenics nor alcoholics alone do. For example, disulfiram treatment has been found to precipitate relapse in some of these patients with the combined diagnosis (Ban, 1977).

The increased recognition of the need for specialized treatment programs for these patients has led to a number of authors making recommendations for these type of programs (Gottheil et al, 1980) where specialized staff would be capable of assessing and evaluating the specific treatment needs of these patients as well as developing more systematic research.

ALCOHOLISM AND AFFECTIVE ILLNESS

The association between the use and abuse of alcohol and affective illness has been the subject of study by many authors and from many perspectives, yet there are few generalizations that can be drawn about this relationship. Even the rates at which these two conditions coexist is fraught with marked disparity. Winokur et al (1971), for example, reporting on structured interviews with alcoholics, found that 3% of them also had a primary affective illness. Shaw et al (1975), on the other hand, found that depression as measured on the Zung Self-Rating Depression Scale, the Beck Depression Inventory, and the Minnesota Multiphasic Personality Inventory (MMPI) was present in 98% of the alcoholics on whom these evaluations were performed. One possible explanation has been put forth by Gibson and Becker (1973), who suggested that alcoholics may interpret physical distress cognitively as depression. In addition to the possibility of alcoholics misinterpreting their subjective state, the wide range of prevalence may also be an indication of that depression in alcoholics is particularly susceptible to the variation of the instrument or the diagnostic criteria that is being used to measure both the alcoholism as well as the depression.

A review of these methodological considerations can be found elsewhere (Solomon, 1982).

A variety of direct and indirect factors have been proposed as possible causes of depression in alcoholics. Among them are the effect of alcohol on neurotransmitters, personality factors, physical illness, psychosocial stressors, familial and hereditary factors, and psychiatric disorders to name just a few. The direct depressive effect of alcohol has been examined by a number of authors. Tamerin and Mendelson (1969) in a controlled setting found that prolonged drinking led to progressive depression with rapid relief of symptoms and little recall when they became sober.

Mayfield and Montgomery (1972) also described a depressive syndrome of chronic intoxication where they found profound depression following extended periods of intoxication. This would also be supported by the work of Keeler et al (1979) who felt that any work that looks at alcohol and affective illness must consider that "a significant factor may be that the sequelae of chronic alcoholism and/or a recent prolonged spell of excessive drinking and/or withdrawal can produce signs and symptoms similar to those of depression and invalidate self-administered tests" (p. 588).

In addition to the direct depressive effects of chronic intoxication, the severe physical deterioration caused by the direct toxic effects of alcohol as well as the malnutrition that accompanies the alcoholic life-style may be at least partly responsible for the depression. The loss of family, friends, and employment may also precipitate or at least contribute to a depression. If these physical and social consequences are absent, it may take longer for depression in the alcoholic to develop. This phenomenon might then account for the low rate of depression in younger alcoholics as reported by Hamm et al (1979).

A number of authors have attempted to divide people who suffer from alcoholism and affective illness into two groups: one in which the alcoholism predated and possibly gave rise to the depression, the primary alcoholic with a secondary depression, and another in which the depression predated the alcoholism. Unfortunately, the temporal relationship is rarely clear enough to make a distinct determination. Weissman et al (1977) looked at symptom patterns in primary and secondary depressions and concluded that although the two groups had similar symptom patterns, they do differ in severity of symptoms with the secondary depressives reporting less severe symptoms. The major problem they cite in making this determination is the careful evaluation of the chronology that is required for the diagnosis of depression secondary to alcoholism.

Other studies have looked at the familial occurrence of alcoholism and affective illness. Winokur and Clayton (1968), in looking at this phenomenon, grouped alcoholism as either primary alcoholism with depression, or alcoholism with sociopathy. They found that the first degree relatives but not other relatives tended to have the same subtype of alcoholism as the proband, but the female relatives had more depression and the male relatives more alcoholism. Amark (1951), looking at these familial relationships, also found that there were more psychiatric problems in the relatives of alcoholics than would be expected in the general population and the majority of them carried the diagnosis of depression.

It would be tempting to divide people who suffer from both alcoholism and affective disorders into two groups—one in which the alcoholism predated and may have given rise to the depression and another in which the depression was primary and the alcoholism that developed was secondary. Unfortunately, the clinical picture is not always clear enough, at least initially while both processes are active. It therefore becomes essential that a period of alcohol-free time elapse before a definitive diagnosis is made and treatment for the depression is begun.

The majority of the work in this area has looked at unipolar depression. Less is understood in relationship to bipolar illness. Ascribing a causal relationship or even an association to binge drinking based on the cyclical nature of the condition is tenuous at best. Freed (1970) extensively reviewed the literature available at that time and felt that although manic depressives do use alcohol in excess, the nature of the relationship remained unclear.

Of interest in this regard is a recent double-blind, placebo-controlled study that found that when lithium was given to a group of alcoholic patients, there was significantly less relapse among the lithium-treated group than in the control group receiving a placebo (Fawcett et al, 1987).

ALCOHOLISM AND SUICIDE

Suicide is a cause of death that is far more common among alcoholics than in the general population and there have been many reports on the association between these two conditions. One perspective of these studies looks at a group of alcoholics and notes the incidence of suicide among them. In two groups of alcoholic patients, both Norvig and Nielsen (1956) and Kessel and Grossman (1961) found that 7% of those in whom follow-up could be ascertained had committed suicide — a number that is consistent among other authors as well

Another perspective looked at the alcohol consumption in groups of people who have successfully and unsuccessfully attempted suicide. East (1913) in one of the earliest papers on this subject, reviewed 1000 cases of attempted suicide and found alcoholism to be present in 39%. In other reports, both Moore (1939) and Dahlgren (1951) were able to establish a diagnosis of alcoholism in 30% of their suicidal patients.

A number of authors have attempted to determine the variables that would distinguish those alcoholics who have attempted suicide from those who have not. Koller and Castanos (1968) found that suicidal alcoholics tend to be male, to have experienced a higher incidence of parental loss, and to have been reared by relatives. Suicidal alcoholics also tend to come from smaller families and to have begun addictive drinking at an earlier age. Interpersonal loss six weeks prior to the suicide attempt also acted as a strong predictor (Murphy et al, 1979). In this same report, Murphy et al also found evidence for definite affective illness in 56% of the patients. Twenty-two of these patients were also found to have uncomplicated alcoholism. Noticeably absent in this study of suicides were patients diagnosed as antisocial personalities. Attkisson (1970), in looking at skid row alcoholics, found a higher incidence of suicide among younger alcoholics than among those in the later stage of the disease.

A recent prospective study of alcoholics who subsequently committed suicide found that although the presence of depression and dysphoria increased the risk of suicide, the predictive value of peptic ulcer as a risk factor of suicide in alcoholism was even greater (Berglund, 1984).

The strong association between suicide and alcoholism is obvious; however, the specific nature of this relationship is less clear. For example, alcoholics have very high rates of one-car traffic accidents. One hypothesis is that these accidents under the influence of alcohol are, in effect, covert suicide attempts. There is, in all likelihood, more than one relationship between these two conditions. A recent review of the literature regarding these relationships (Solomon, 1982) delineated three possible associations.

Alcoholism as a Form of Suicide

Suicide in some individuals is manifest by their overt and intentional attempts to take their lives. There are others, in whom this drive is present, and yet for some reason, they are unable to commit the final act of self-destruction in a consciously intentional manner and the act of suicide takes a more covert form such as frequent accidents, a particularly high-risk occupation, or more directly through the ingestion of a toxic substance and a life-style that is determined by the use of that substance. Alcoholism has been suggested to be such a case.

Menninger (1938), one of the foremost proponents of this position, described alcoholism as a form of "chronic suicide." Attempts have been made to subject this hypothesis to a scientific study and the results are mixed, both supporting (Palola et al, 1962) and refuting (Ross, 1973) this argument.

As a form of suicide, there appear to be two distinct methods by which alcohol may be used towards this end: the direct toxic effects of ethanol on the body and the indirect effects on the life-style of the abuser through an increased number of accidents, homicides, illness, and general social disruption. In both cases, alcohol becomes the form through which the suicide is carried out.

Alcoholism as a Cause of Suicide

The chronic use of alcohol can be deemed a cause of suicide from the medical, psychological, and social aspects of a person's life. Alcohol can exert a direct toxic effect on most organ systems of the body. In addition, it can also have a direct psychotoxic effect causing severe depression. In addition to these medical and psychological consequences of alcoholism, loss of family, friends, and employment are also common results of excessive drinking. These losses frequently exacerbate the depression that the alcoholic then attempts to medicate with further drinking. This pattern of increasing depression with alienation of emotional, psychological, and occupational support systems may frequently end in a suicide attempt (Rushing, 1969).

Alcoholism and Suicide as Manifestations of a Common Etiology

As previously described, the association between depression and alcoholism has been reported on by many authors. This relationship suggests the possibility that some alcoholics may be medicating themselves and both alcohol and suicide are both attempts to escape from painful, depressive affect. Rado (1933), in a psychoanalytic study of this phenomenon, coined the term "pharmacothymia" to describe a disorder in which drugs are used by certain people to find relief from intolerable psychic pain. The findings of Pitts and Winokur (1966) would lend support to this notion since, in their extensive study, they found suicide to be a frequent cause of death in only affective disorder and alcoholism. Additionally, they found that the relatives of patients who committed suicide had a high incidence of both alcoholism and affective disorders.

These three frameworks in which one might view the relationship between suicide and the abuse of alcohol are by no means mutually exclusive. For example, in some individuals, preexisting psychopathology may lend itself to the relief of anxiety and depression through the use of alcohol. The increased use of alcohol may further exacerbate the depression and subsequently destroy whatever relationships that may have existed, deepening the depression, and culminating in a suicide attempt with alcohol being used as the method.

ALCOHOLISM AND PERSONALITY DISORDERS

The relationship between alcoholism and sociopathy has probably presented more diagnostic confusion than any other psychiatric condition. Schuckit (1973), in particular, has emphasized the importance of carefully distinguishing between the alcoholic who, because of drinking becomes involved in events that could be labeled sociopathic from the true sociopath who is diagnosed by a wide range of behaviors, among which is excessive use of alcohol. Other distinguishing behaviors were noted by a number of authors. Rimmer et al (1972) found that sociopathic alcoholics tended to be younger and had become alcoholic at an earlier age. Other authors as well have confirmed this increased level of antisocial behavior in men who began drinking at an early age.

As might be expected, the familial concurrence of these two conditions is higher than might be expected by mere chance. This was confirmed in a report by Frances et al (1980), who found that alcoholics who reported at least one family member with a possible drinking problem also demonstrated more severe symptoms of alcoholism and more antisocial behavior. Winokur et al (1971) found a higher incidence of sociopathy in both the siblings and parents of their alcoholic patients.

A number of studies have indicated that alcoholics with the additional diagnosis of sociopathy carry a poorer prognosis than nonsociopathic alcoholics, suggesting that specific treatment approaches may be required for this patient population (Panepinto et al, 1970).

The borderline personality has been frequently linked with the abuse of alcohol, particularly in relationship to gratifying oral narcissistic needs and disinhibiting aggression. A recent study (Nace et al, 1983) looked at the prevalence of this diagnosis among alcoholics and found that 13% of alcoholic patients admitted to an inpatient alcoholism treatment ward were diagnosed as having a borderline disorder. These patients were also younger and had more suicide attempts and drug dependency.

Treatment of this patient group can prove particularly difficult and methods of treatment must address both conditions as described in a recent report by Hellman (1981).

SUMMARY

The relationship between psychiatric disorders and alcoholism has been the subject of many studies from a variety of perspectives. Much of the early literature in this area is descriptive and cannot be used for drawing any generalizations about these two conditions. Recently, this association has been put to more rigorous scientific scrutiny and certain relationships have begun to emerge.

The majority of alcoholics have alcoholism as their primary and, frequently, only problem. There are, however, alcoholics who manifest a wide range of psychiatric conditions that may interact with their alcoholism in several ways.

Alcohol abuse may contribute to the development of psychiatric problems based on its toxic effects on the physiological, psychological, and social functioning of the individual. Most often, there are elements of all three in the clinical presentations.

Suicide as a cause of death is far more common among alcoholics than in the general population. Although specific nature of this relationship is not yet fully clear, three possible associations have been proposed. Alcoholism as a form of suicide, alcoholism as a cause of suicide, and alcoholism and suicide as manifestation of a common etiology.

There are yet others who use alcohol in an attempt to medicate painful affects and disturbing psychiatric symptoms. These people are unlikely to seek help for their alcoholism until it becomes more of a problem than the primary psychiatric disorder.

Alcoholism can mask, mimic, precipitate, or independently coexist with the gamut of psychiatric disorders. Treatment for alcoholism is no longer only the treatment of the underlying preoedipal causes as described by Knight. Psychiatry and alcoholism have a long and confusing history. This history is replete with moral, religious, legal, and medical nuances that have made clarification of the relationship both ambiguous and frequently difficult. Consequently, the role of the psychiatrist has also been unclear. Better understanding of these relationships has begun to shed light on some of the more confusing yet potentially important aspects of both conditions.

REFERENCES

Alpert M, Silvers KN: Perceptual characteristics distinguishing auditory hallucinations in schizophrenia and acute alcoholic psychosis. *Am J Psychiatry* 1970; 123:298–302.

Amark CA: A study in alcoholism: Clinical, social, psychiatric and genetic investigations. *Acta Psychiatr Scand* 1951; 70:(suppl).

American Psychiatric Association: *Diagnostic and Statistical Manual of Mental Disorders*. (DSM III-R) Washington, DC, 1987. 3rd ed. 127–134, 165–174.

Attkisson CC: Suicide in San Francisco's skid row. *Arch Gen Psychiatry* 1970; 23:149–157.

Bach-y-Rita G, Lion JR, Erwin FR: Pathological intoxication: Clinical and electroencephalographic studies. *Am J Psychiatry* 1970; 127:698–703.

Bahn AK, Chandler CA: Alcoholism in psychiatric clinic patients. *Q J Stud Alcohol* 1961; 22(3):411–477.

Ban TA: Alcoholism and schizophrenia: Diagnostic and therapeutic considerations. *Alcoholism: Clin Exp Res* 1977; 1:113–117.

Banay RS: Pathological reaction to alcohol. I. Review of the literature and original case reports. *Q J Stud Alcohol* 1944; 4:580–605.

Berglund M: Suicide in alcoholism: A prospective study of 88 suicides. *Arch Gen Psychiatry* 1984; 41:888–891.

Bleuler E: *Dementia Praecox.* New York, International Universities Press, 1950.

Bowman KM, Jellinek EM: Alcoholic mental disorders *Q J Stud Alcohol* 1941; 2:312–390.

Coid J: Mania a potu: A critical review of pathological intoxication. *Psychol Med* 1979; 9:709–719.

Crowley TJ, Chesluck D, Dilts S, Hart R: Drug and alcohol abuse among psychiatric admissions. *Arch Gen Psychiatry* 1974; 30:13–20.

Dahlgren KG: On death-rates and causes of death in alcohol addicts. *Acta Psychiatr Neurol* 1951; 26:297–311.

East WN: On attempted suicide, with analysis of 1000 consecutive cases. *J Mental Sci* 1913; 59:428–478.

Fawcett J, Clark DC, Aagesen DO, Pisani VD, Tilkin JM, Sellers D, McGuire M, Gibbons RD. A double-blind, placebo-controlled trial of lithium carbonate therapy for alcoholism. *Arch Gen Psychiatry* 1987; 44:248–256.

Fenichel O: *The Psychoanalytic Theory of Neurosis.* New York, W W Norton, 1945. p 379.

Fowler RC, Liskow BL, Tanna VL, Van Valkenburg C: Psychiatric illness and alcoholism. *Alcoholism: Clin Exp Res* 1977; 1(2):125–128.

Frances R, Timms S, Buchy S: Studies of familial and nonfamilial alcoholism. I. Demographic studies. *Arch Gen Psychiatry* 1980; 37:564–566.

Freed EX: Alcoholism and manic-depressive disorders. *Q J Stud Alcohol* 1970; 31:62–69.

Freed EX: Alcoholism and schizophrenia: The search for perspectives. *Q J Stud Alcohol* 1975; 36:853–881.

Gibson S, Becker J: Alcoholism and depression: The factor structure of alcoholics responses to depressive inventories. *Q J Stud Alcohol* 1973; 34:400–408.

Gillis LS, Keet M: Prognostic factors and treatment results in hospitalized alcoholics. *Q J Stud Alcohol* 1969; 30:426–437.

Goodwin DW: Alcohol problems in adoptees raised apart from alcoholic biological parents. *Arch Gen Psychiatry* 1973; 28:238–243.

Goodwin DW, Alderson P, Rosenthal R: Clinical significance of hallucinations in psychiatric disorders. *Arch Gen Psychiatry* 1971; 24:76–80.

Gottheil E, McLellan AT, Druley KA (eds): *Substance Abuse and Psychiatric Illness.* Elmsford, NY Pergamon Press, 1980.

Gross MM, Lewis E, Hastey J: Acute alcoholic withdrawal syndrome, in Kissin B and Begleiter H (eds): *The Biology of Alcoholism Vol 3, Clinical Pathology.* New York, Plenum Press, 1963, 191–263.

Halley LI: Schizophrenia modified by alcohol. *Virg Med Mthly* 1940; 67:111–112.

Hamm JE, Major LF, Brown GL: The quantitative measurement of depression and anxiety in male alcoholics. *Am J Psychiatry* 1979; 136:580–582.

Hellman, JM: Alcohol abuse and the borderline patient. *Psychiatry* 1981; 44:307–317.

Hesselbrock MN, Meyer RE, Keener JJ: Psychopathology in hospitalized alcoholics. *Arch Gen Psychiatry* 1985; 42:1050–1055.

Idestrom CM: Psychiatric emergency service. *Acta Psychiatric Scand* 1974; 50:636–647.

Johanson E: A study of schizophrenia in the male: A psychiatric and social study based on 138 cases with follow-up. *Acta Psychiatry Neurol Scand (Suppl)* 1958; 33:125.

Keeler MH, Taylor CI, Miller W: Are all recently detoxified alcoholics depressed? *Am J Psychiatry* 1979; 136:586–588.

Kessel N, Grossman G: Suicide in alcoholics. *Brit J Med* 1961; 2:1671–1672.

Kesselman M, Solomon J, Beaudett M, Thornton B: Alcoholism and schizophrenia, in Solomon J: *Alcoholism and Clinical Psychiatry.* New York, Plenum Press, 1982, pp 69–80.

Kissin B: The bio-psycho-social perspective in alcoholism, in Solomon J (ed): *Alcoholism and Clinical Psychiatry.* New York, Plenum Press, 1982, pp 1–20.

Knight RP: The dynamics and treatment of chronic alcohol addiction. *Bull Menninger Clinic* 1937; 1:233–250.

Koller KM, Castanos JN: Attempted suicide and alcoholism. *Med J Aust* 1968; 13:835–837.

Levin HG: The discovery of addiction. *J Stud Alcohol* 1978; 39:143–174.

Maletsky BM: The alcohol provocation test. *J Clin Psychiatry* 1978; 39:407–411.

May PRA, Ebaugh PC: Pathological intoxication, alcoholic hallucinosis and other reactions in alcohol. *Q J Stud Alcohol* 1953; 14:200–227.

Mayfield DG, Montgomary D: Alcoholism, alcohol intoxication and suicide attempts. *Arch Gen Psychiatry* 1972; 27:349–353.

Menninger KA: *Man Against Himself*. New York, Harcourt Brace, 1938.

Moore, M: Alcoholism and attempted suicide. *New Engl J Med* 1939; 221:691–693.

Mott RH, Small IF, Anderson JM: Comparative study of hallucinations. *Arch Gen Psychiatry* 1965; 12:595–601.

Murphy GE, Armstrong JW, Hermele SL, Fisher JR, Clendenin WW: Suicide and alcoholism, interpersonal loss confirmed as a predictor. *Arch Gen Psychiatry* 1979; 36:650–669.

Nace EP, Saxon JJ, Shore N: A comparison of borderline and nonborderline alcoholic patients. *Arch Gen Psychiatry* 1983; 40:54–56.

Norvig J, Nielsen B: A follow-up study of 221 alcohol addicts in Denmark. *Q J Stud Alcohol* 1956; 17: 633–642.

Opler MK: Schizophrenia and culture. *Sci Amer* 1957; 197:103–110.

Palola EG, Dorpat TL, Larson WR: Alcoholism and suicidal behavior, in Pittman DJ, Snyder CR (eds): *Society, Culture and Drinking Patterns*. New York, Wiley, 1962; pp 511–534.

Panepinto WC, Higgins MJ, Keane-Dawes WY, Smith D: Underlying psychiatric diagnosis as an indicator of participation in alcoholism therapy. *Q J Stud Alcohol* 1970; 31:950–956.

Parker JB, Meiller RM, Andrews JW: Major psychiatric disorders masquerading as alcoholism. *5th Med J* 1960; 53:560–564.

Pitts FN, Winokur G: Affective disorders VII. Alcoholism and affective disorders. *J Psychiatr Res* 1966; 4:37–50.

Rado S: Psychoanalysis of pharmacothymia. *Psychoanal Quart* 1933; 2:1–23.

Rimmer J, Jacobsen B: Alcoholism in schizophrenics and their relatives. *J Stud Alcohol* 1977; 38:1781–1789.

Rimmer J, Reich T, Winokur G: Alcoholism V. Diagnosis and clinical variation among alcoholics. *Q J Stud Alcohol* 1972; 33:658–666.

Ross M: Suicide among physicians. *Dis Nerv Syst* 1973; 34:145–150.

Rounsaville BJ, Dolinsky ZS, Babor TF: Psychopathology as a predictor of treatment outcome in alcoholics. *Arch Gen Psychiatry* 1987; 44:505–513.

Rushing WA: Suicide as a possible consequence of alcoholism, in Rushing WA (ed): *Deviant Behavior and Social Process*. Chicago, Rand-McNally, 1969. pp 323–327.

Schuckit M: Alcoholism and sociopathy—Diagnostic confusion. *Q J Stud Alcohol* 1973; 34:157–164.

Schwarz L, Fjeld SP: The alcoholic patient in the psychiatric emergency room. *Q J Stud Alcohol* 1969; 30:104–111.

Shaw JA, Donley P, Morgan DW, Robinson JA: Treatment of depression in alcoholics. *Am J Psychiatry* 1975; 132:641–644.

Solomon J: Alcoholism and affective disorders: Methodological considerations, in Solomon J (ed): *Alcoholism and Clinical Psychiatry*. New York, Plenum Press, 1982, pp 81–86.

Solomon J: Alcoholism and suicide, in Solomon J (ed): *Alcoholism and Clinical Psychiatry*. New York, Plenum Press, 1982, pp 97–110.

Tamerin JS, Mendelson JH: The psychodynamics of chronic inebriation: Observations of alcoholics during the process of drinking in an experimental group setting. *Am J Psychiatry* 1969; 125:886–899.

Tarter R, McBride H, Buonpane N, Schneider DU: Differentiation of alcoholics, childhood history of minimal brain dysfunction, family history and drinking patterns. *Arch Gen Psychiatry* 1977; 34: 761–768.

Tomsovic M, Edwards RV: Treatment of schizophrenic and nonschizophrenic alcoholic: A controlled evaluation. *Q J Stud Alcohol* 1970; 31:932–949.

Tyndal M: Psychiatric study of one thousand alcoholic patients. *Can Psychiat Assoc J* 1974; 19:21–24.

Victor M, Adams RD, Collins GH: *The Wernicke-Korsakoff Syndrome*. Philadelphia, F. A. Davis, 1971.

Victor M, Hope JM: The phenomenon of auditory hallucinations in chronic alcoholism: A critical evaluation of the status of alcoholic hallucinosis. *J Nerv Ment Dis* 1958; 126:451–481.

Weissman MM, Pottenger M, Kleber H, Ruben HL, Williams D, Thompson WD: Symptom patterns in primary and secondary depression. *Arch Gen Psychiatry* 1977; 34:854–862.

Winokur G, Clayton PJ: Family history studies IV. Comparison of male and female alcoholics. *Q J Stud Alcohol* 1968; 29:885–891.

Winokur G, Rimmer J, Reich I: Alcoholism IV: Is there more than one type of alcoholism? *Brit J Psychiatry* 1971; 118:525–531.

CHAPTER 10

Alcohol Consumption During Pregnancy: The Dangers of Moderate Drinking

Ernest L. Abel, Ph.D.
Robert J. Sokol, M.D.

Fetal Alcohol Research Center
Department of Obstetrics and Gynecology
Wayne State University School of Medicine
Detroit, Michigan, USA

INTRODUCTION AND BACKGROUND

The effects of maternal alcohol consumption on the unborn child have been examined in thousands of clinical, epidemiological, and experimental studies published over the last 15 years. These studies clearly demonstrate an association between *heavy* drinking during pregnancy and adverse health effects on the unborn child. The spectrum of effects ranges from spontaneous abortion and infant mortality, through a cluster of abnormalities called "Fetal Alcohol Syndrome" (FAS), to individual "Fetal Alcohol Effects" (FAE), alternatively termed "Alcohol-Related Birth Defects" (ARBD). These include subtle behavioral disturbances such as hyperactivity, which occur in the absence of observable physical effects. Because none of these individual effects are exclusively associated with maternal drinking, demonstration of causation has been elusive. Diet, life-style, cigarette and drug use, as well as genetic factors may each be associated with expression of these adverse reproductive outcomes, with or without prenatal alcohol exposure. As a result, estimating the amount and frequency of alcohol consumption associated with fetal effects is still very conjectural. Furthermore, adverse effects in humans are seen only in a small percentage of children of even the heaviest alcohol users. This suggests that although prenatal alcohol exposure is a necessary condition for FAS, it is not sufficient—other risk factors may modify expression of FAS and other ARBDs. Thus, it is likely that a generic threshold equally applicable to all women will never be satisfactorily established. This has resulted in one of the more contentious public health issues in fetal alcohol research: Is there a threshold for alcohol-induced birth anomalies? Put another way: Is there any evidence that "occasional" drinking poses a danger for the unborn child?

More than 4000 relevant articles have been published on FAS/FAE in the last two decades (Abel, 1984). The present survey examines many of those articles that speak to the issues of threshold and reproductive risk in relation to "moderate" drinking. The need for better descriptions of patterns of drinking, and criteria for different levels of drinking, are also discussed. We conclude that, although the evidence to date suggests that chronic heavy drinking during pregnancy appears to be associated with certain risks to unborn children, there is

228

insufficient evidence to demonstrate any statistically significant or clinically substantial risk from an occasional drink during pregnancy.

EFFECTS OF ALCOHOL ON REPRODUCTION

Fetal Alcohol Syndrome

In 1973, Jones, Smith, and their colleagues described a pattern of birth defects occurring in children born to alcoholic women and labeled it Fetal Alcohol Syndrome (FAS). Since then, over 400 cases of FAS have been described in the world literature (Abel, 1984). However, no standardized criteria have been used in making the diagnoses in most of these cases. To bring greater standardization to this problem, the Fetal Alcohol Study Group of the Research Society on Alcoholism in 1980 formulated the criteria for diagnosis listed in Table 10.1. (These criteria are currently being reevaluated by this group.) Currently, to satisfy a diagnosis of FAS, an individual must exhibit an abnormality in each of the three general categories shown.

None of the features is singularly characteristic of fetal exposure to alcohol (and any may be seen individually even when there is no maternal drinking). Any of these individual abnormalities, as well as others associated with FAS, including low birthweight, eye and ear defects, heart murmurs, septal defects, genitourinary anomalies, mental retardation, hemangiomas, fingerprint and palmar crease abnormalities, etc., may also occur in isolation or in conjunction with other syndromes.

In our review of the world literature in this area (Abel and Sokol, 1987), we identified 20 relevant epidemiological papers in which a total of 88,236 births had been evaluated. Of these, 164 cases of FAS were documented. On the basis of these data, the worldwide incidence of the Fetal Alcohol Syndrome (FAS) is 1.9 per 1000 live births. Incidence rates varied considerably, however, depending on study site, ranging from 0.6 to 2.6 per 1000 (Abel and Sokol, 1987).

Estimates of the frequency of Fetal Alcohol Syndrome, based on data from women identified as "problem drinkers" or alcohol abusers, are considerably higher. Among alcoholic women in the United States, the incidence ranges from 24 to 42 per 1000 (Ouellette et al, 1977; Hanson et al, 1978; Sokol et al, 1980; Sokol et al, 1986). In Europe, the incidence ranges from 66 to 259 per 1000 live births (Siedenberg and Majewski, 1978; Halliday et al, 1982; Larsson et al, 1983; Aronson, 1984; Vitez et al, 1984).

Limitations of Human Studies

Alcohol does not have an all-or-none effect on the conceptus. Although dose-response effects have now been reported for craniofacial abnormalities and FAS, documentation of a spectrum of effects is not the same as documentation of a dose-response relationship in which the greater the dose, the more severe the damage. A case in point is alcohol-induced spontaneous abortion. Although spontaneous abortion is sometimes regarded as a different degree of response to the same agent that causes malformations, it may also represent a distinct man-

---

Table 10.1. Criteria for the diagnosis of fetal alcohol syndrome

1. Pre- and/or postnatal growth retardation (weight, length, and/or head circumference <10th percentile, when corrected for gestational or postnatal age)
2. Central nervous system (CNS) involvement (signs of neurologic abnormality, developmental delay, or intellectual impairment, e.g., mental retardation)
3. Characteristic facial dysmorphology (at least 2 of 3):

   a. Microcephaly (head circumference <3rd percentile)
   b. Microphthalmia and/or short palpebral fissures
   c. Poorly developed philtrum, thin upper lip, and flattening of the maxillary area

ifestation of exposure. For instance, recent studies in animals suggest that early embryonic death associated with in utero alcohol exposure is a consequence of alcohol-induced chromosomal damage (Kaufman, 1983; Kaufman and Bain, 1984). Since there is no evidence of chromosomal damage in patients with FAS or FAE (Obe and Majewski, 1978), mechanistically, FAS/FAE cannot be a similar, but graded, response to alcohol.

Three basic problems confront researchers evaluating alcohol-related birth defects in humans. The first is the issue of bias. In many published case reports and studies, the diagnosis and gathering of data for such birth defects have not been "blind" to the history of maternal alcohol abuse (Neugut, 1984). This leads to the possibility that some of the observed associations may be grossly inflated, that is, they are there solely because they were looked for. Nonetheless, when the effects are clearly identifiable (e.g., congenital anomalies or lowered birthweight), statistically significant relations between heavy maternal drinking and these anomalies occur even when evaluations are made blind to maternal history (e.g., Ouellette et al, 1977; Kuzma and Sokol, 1982; Ernhart et al, 1987).

A second problem facing researchers is accuracy of self-reported drinking. Misreporting of drinking levels by study participants can distort results, as discussed in detail later in this chapter. From the perspective of assessing the impact of "moderate" maternal drinking, underreporting would lead to Type I error, in this case identifying risk at a lower exposure than that at which it occurs.

The third major problem is "confounding." Alcohol is but one of many possible risk factors, such as social class, maternal illness, genetic susceptibility, smoking, diet, past health history, pregnancy complications, use of drugs, and exposure to environmental pollutants. In epidemiological studies, statistical techniques are used to try to control and adjust for as many of these cofactors as possible. The goal is to determine if any observable correlation between maternal alcohol consumption and pregnancy outcome is actually attributable to alcohol. But many pregnancy risks remain unknown and it is impossible to adjust for confounding completely.

It is probably misguided as well if the effort to eliminate or overadjust possible "confounding" factors actually eliminate or overemphasize cofactor(s) that act in concert with alcohol. These, or other risks, may in fact be important or even necessary cofactors for specific adverse alcohol effects on the conceptus. For example, Sokol et al (1980) found that of 204 women clinically identified as alcohol abusers, only 5 gave birth to children with FAS and considerably less than half of the offspring had any finding even potentially related to prenatal alcohol exposure. Since it is likely that many of these 204 were abusing alcohol throughout their pregnancies, it is reasonable to suspect that "host" and other factors modulated the risk for FAS and ARBD. In other words, it is likely that alcohol is a necessary, but not sufficient, risk factor for FAS. One or more cofactors were also present that either increased susceptibility or, conversely, protected individual fetuses. If this were not so, the number of FAS children born to these 204 alcoholic women ought to have been much higher. Indeed, in a subsequent analysis of an additional 8000 pregnancies, which included 25 cases of FAS, Sokol et al, (1986) reexamined this issue and found that two alcohol-related variables (positive Michigan Alcoholism Screening Test [MAST] and high percentage of drinking days) and two maternal characteristics (high parity, black race) contributed significantly — singly and jointly — as risks for FAS. In the absence of any of these four risks, the probability of being affected with FAS was 2%; if all four were present, the probability was 85%.

Thresholds

Several years ago, we examined the relation between level of alcohol consumption and Fetal Alcohol Syndrome in a retrospective evaluation of over 300 clinical reports (Abel, 1982). Based on the information contained in these reports, the estimated consumption by mothers of fetal alcohol children was an average of 14 drinks per day during gestation. As a daily average, this may represent both drinking and nondrinking days. If, instead of drinking every day, these women drank every other day, their average consumption per drinking day would have been about 28 drinks per drinking day!

Recent data from our ongoing epidemiological studies (Ernhart et al, 1987) now indicate that the threshold for FAS is 6 drinks per day. This threshold was determined by focussing on 25 cases of FAS out of 1290 prospectively studied pregnancies. To test the hypothesis that higher intake leads to FAS, the pregnancies were divided into five exposure groups consisting of 0, more than 0 but less than 2 drinks per day, etc., up to 6 or more drinks per day. There were no significant increments in risk up to 6 drinks per day. When these results were projected to the total study population, <1% of the women were drinking at or above this amount, but in this group, the risk for FAS was substantial.

Duration, as well as level of exposure, appears to be an important determinant of the occurrence of alcohol-related birth defects for both humans and animals. For example, in a prospective study, Jones et al (1984) divided pregnant women into three groups: (1) women who either binged one to three times during their first trimester (the time most likely to give rise to FAS), (2) those who drank heavily during this period, or (3) those who drank lightly. Children born to binge drinkers and light drinkers did not differ in birthweight, birth length, head circumference, prematurity, or spontaneous abortion rate and none of these children had FAS. Infants born to the heavy drinkers, however, had an increased incidence of spontaneous abortion, decreased birthweight, and FAS. This suggests that it is the chronic drinker, not the binge drinker, who is most at risk for FAS. Likewise, acute intragastric administration of alcohol to mice on individual days of pregnancy does not result in a significant increase in birth defects (Randall et al, 1981), but chronic alcohol consumption does (Randall et al, 1977).

Nonhuman primate models recently developed in Seattle (Clarren and Bowden, 1982; Inouye et al, 1985; Clarren et al, 1987) and Cincinnati (Scott and Fradkin, 1984), also suggest that adverse effects of alcohol do not occur except after relatively high exposure levels. In Seattle, Clarren et al (1987) administered alcohol in doses ranging from 0.3 to 4.1 g/kg once per week to pigtail macques. Animals were fasted for 24 h before each alcohol administration. Peak blood levels ranged from 24 to 549 mg%. Increased spontaneous abortion rates due to alcohol occurred only at blood alcohol levels of 205 mg% (1.8 g/kg) and above. At 549 mg% (4.1 g/kg), all animals aborted. In another study (Clarren and Bowden, 1982), two macque infants born to mothers given 2.5 g/kg of alcohol, producing blood alcohol levels (BAL) of 200 to 300 mg%, had normal facial morphology, no organ malformations, and no developmental brain anomalies. An infant whose mother was given the highest dose (BAL >300 mg%) had many of the facial features and cortical anomalies seen in FAS. If extrapolated to the human experience, these results support the contention that adverse effects of alcohol only occur with relatively heavy, persistent maternal drinking, producing high blood alcohol levels.

Scott and Fradkin (1984) used the same dosage range but divided the doses such that blood alcohol levels did not rise above 395 mg%. Facial features suggestive of FAS were not observed in any of their animals although they did find an increased rate of abortions. Birthweight was only reduced in animals exposed to the highest dose, but these animals caught up to controls by 23 days of age. These results also suggest a very high blood alcohol threshold for adverse effects.

Specific Fetal Alcohol Effects

Consumption of alcohol during pregnancy has been associated with a number of specific fetal effects at relatively low levels of exposure. However, on scrutiny, the reported relationships may not be as clearcut as they first appear.

Spontaneous Abortion

Spontaneous abortion rates were reported as being increased about twofold for women drinking one to two drinks per day or less during pregnancy (Harlap et al, 1980; Kline et al, 1980; Sokol et al, 1980). However, the increased risk in these studies actually may be due to the heaviest drinkers who only represent a small proportion of the study population (Sokol, 1980). The Harlap et al (1980) study was initially designed to examine the relation of birth control to pregnancy outcome and therefore was not specifically aimed at examining patterns of drinking. The number of "heavy" drinkers (more than two drinks/day) in the study was reported as only 0.5% of the study population, considerably below the national median and modal consumption of American women during pregnancy (Abel, 1984). It is more than likely that women in this study considerably underreported their alcohol consumption. A reasonable interpretation is that the risk for spontaneous abortion was detectable only among the 0.5% heaviest exposed pregnancies.

Kline et al (1980) retrospectively compared women who aborted spontaneously with a control group and concluded that as little as two drinks a week constituted a risk factor for spontaneous abortion. Although this study controlled for smoking, use of other drugs, and diet, it did not control for social class since all women in this study were on public assistance. When this study was repeated with private patients a similar relation between drinking and spontaneous abortion could not be found (Kolata, 1981).

In a recent study from our laboratory (Sokol et al, 1986), we further explored the relationship of maternal drinking pattern and risk for spontaneous abortion among women. A comprehensive inventory of variables reflecting embryonic–fetal exposure was calculated. The single variable found to be related significantly to spontaneous abortion was one reflecting an extremely heavy episode of drinking in the early first trimester.

As previously noted, studies in nonhuman primates are very consistent in reporting an increase in spontaneous abortion following alcohol exposure. However, the blood alcohol threshold level for this effect is around 205 mg% (Scott and Fradkin, 1984; Clarren et al, 1987). Altshuler and Shippenberg (1981) likewise reported the threshold for abortions in monkeys at BALs of 200 mg%, whereas at BALs of 150 mg%, pregnancies were not interrupted. In dogs, the BAL threshold was 205 mg% (Ellis and Pick, 1980). These studies in nonhuman primates and dogs are impressive in their consistency and in their support for suspicion of underreporting in human studies.

Lowered Birthweight

Lowered birthweight is one of the more reliably observed effects associated with in utero alcohol exposure in humans and animals. Based on a review of over 300 reported cases of FAS, the average birthweight of such children was 2000 grams (Abel, 1982). This may be compared with the median birthweight for all infants in the United States of over 3300 grams (U.S. Department of Health and Human Services, 1980).

In an often-cited report, Little (1977), found that consumption of two drinks per day produced a decrease in birthweight of 160 g. However, maternal drinking in this study ranged from zero to five drinks per day and three women in the study could have been classified as alcohol abusers. Only 7 of the 801 children in the study weighed under 2500 g. Little (1977) did not indicate the birthweights of the children born to the alcohol abusers or the drinking behavior of the mothers of the low-birthweight infants so that the alcohol abusers could have accounted for most of the relationship. Description of birthweights in relation to a range of alcohol exposures may have clarified this association. Again, major underreporting is also a concern.

Other studies, in fact, suggest a small proportion of alcohol abusers may be accounting for the bulk of reported effects concerning "occasional drinking." A prospective study in California, involving 5093 maternal–infant pairs (Kuzma and Sokol, 1982), found that average maternal alcohol intake was about 1.5 drinks per day and was not significantly related to birthweight. However, among a subset of the women, the authors were able to detect a 100-g decrease in birthweight with frequent drinking, a characteristic limited to only 3% of the total number of women. Sokol et al (1980) also found a decrease in birthweight associated with maternal drinking, but the decrease occurred only among pregnancies complicated by alcohol abuse and only amounted to 190 g below normal. In monkeys, Scott and Fradkin (1984) did not begin to observe a significant decrease in birthweight until blood alcohol levels were at least 167 mg%.

Craniofacial Abnormalities

The first report of a threshold for any fetal alcohol effect in humans was that of Ernhart et al (1987) of craniofacial anomalies. These researchers examined 1284 neonates from the Cleveland Prospective Study for 31 anatomic abnormalities. The exam was conducted without knowledge of alcohol exposure. Total number of anatomic abnormalities for each infant was related to embryonic alcohol exposure, expressed in ounces of absolute alcohol per day calculated from a two-week drinking history and Michigan Alcoholism Screening Test administered to the mother at her first prenatal visit.

The researchers were able to detect a threshold for craniofacial abnormalities at more than four drinks per day, with no effect attributable to alcohol below this level of embryonic exposure ("no effect zone"). Although there was a dose–response relationship above that level, only the heaviest drinking 2% experienced an increased risk for anatomic abnormalities.

A recent prospective study involving 32,870 pregnancies, however, did not find any evidence of an increase in head and neck anomalies associated with consumption of up to six or more drinks per day (Mills and Graubard, 1987). Typical craniofacial abnormalities associated with prenatal alcohol exposure in other studies were not examined, but for major and minor anomalies, particularly those of the genitourinary system, a relationship to heavy prenatal alcohol exposure was detected. The authors concluded that moderate exposure does not account for a substantive portion of congenital anomalies.

Abnormal Neurobehavioral and Neural Development

Newborns born to heavy drinkers or alcoholics have been found to experience many different neurobehavioral problems, including restlessness during sleep (Rosett et al, 1979), "hyperactivity" (Shaywitz et al, 1980) and lowered IQ scores (Streissguth et al, 1978).

Two studies of mental and motor development prospectively identified infants exposed in utero to alcohol and focused attention on infants who did not exhibit full FAS. Streissguth and her co-workers (1980) administered the Bayley Scales of Infant Development to a group of infants at age eight months. After statistical adjustment for a number of confounding variables, they were able to document significantly lower scores for children whose mothers drank moderately. However, infants born to women drinking more than eight drinks per day were included in categories of two or more drinks per day, as well as more than eight drinks per day. When these data were reanalyzed by specific dose and each infant was included only once, only the mental scores of the infants exposed to the higher amounts were different and their average score was still a normal 98 (Rosett and Weiner, 1984).

Golden and her colleagues (1982) also found lower Bayley scores associated with prenatal alcohol exposure. However, infants in this study had physical alcohol-related birth defects and their mothers had a history of maternal alcohol abuse, indicating a high probability of considerable alcohol exposure.

Studies in animals also suggest that, although the amount of actual exposure needed to produce behavioral deficits is lower than those producing other effects, actual levels are still high. For example, peak BALs are readily apparent within hours of administration and prenatal exposure to BALs above 100 mg%, but not below, impair learning in rats. Furthermore, learning ability "catches up" to control levels in animals exposed to peak BALs around 120 mg% but does not for animals exposed to peak BALs over 200 mg% (Abel, 1979). Studies using liquid alcohol diets are more difficult to evaluate in terms of BALs because blood is sampled usually only once and during times when animals may not be maximally ingesting alcohol. Nonetheless, blood alcohol levels for animals given maximal concentrations (e.g., 35% ethanol-derived calories) have BALs above 100 mg% and usually only animals with such high BALs differ significantly from controls (e.g., Riley et al, 1979).

In conclusion, although prenatal alcohol exposure is related to specific birth defects, it appears that the amount of exposure required to produce these effects may well be very high with only a limited proportion of pregnancies exposed heavily enough to document an effect. Since such studies rely for the most part on self report data much more attention needs to be paid to the accuracy of such reports.

ALCOHOL CONSUMPTION AND MEASUREMENT

Drinking Patterns in Pregnancy

Self-reports of alcohol consumption have inherent limitations and must be understood in gross terms, rather than in precise measurements. The amount of beverage actually imbibed in a "drink" can vary from 1 to 12 ounces. The validity of the response may depend on who is being questioned, who is doing the questioning, and the way the question is posed (Weiner et al, 1983). Heavy or dependent drinkers may be unable or unwilling to recall specifically what they drink. Self-reports of drinking during pregnancy are therefore of limited value in assessing adequately the dangers of a given number of "drinks" per day to a particular risk to the fetus. Because of denial, actual alcohol intake is likely to be underreported by the abusive drinker—the individual most likely to be at risk for giving birth to a child with alcohol-related birth defects (Sokol et al, 1981).

To examine this issue more closely, Ernhart et al (1988) selected 238 infants for infancy and early childhood followup. At the time of the first prenatal visit, the mothers of these infants were given the MAST. Mothers were also questioned about alcohol use during their subsequent prenatal visits. At four to five years after giving birth, these mothers were again asked about their drinking during the target pregnancy. Retrospective drinking reports were highly correlated with in-pregnancy reports, but for 41% of the women, drinking reports for the pregnancy period, but obtained retrospectively, were higher than those obtained during the pregnancy. Especially noteworthy was the fact that the retrospective report was a better predictor of alcohol-related birth defects than the in-pregnancy reports. This improved predictive validity suggests that the higher reports were more accurate. In addition, the only characteristic related to underreporting was the MAST score—the higher the MAST score the greater the underreporting. This suggests that previous self-reports of alcohol consumption by women most at risk for alcohol-related birth defects are those most likely to be gross underestimates—especially when women are considered to be problem drinkers by the MAST or by other screening methods. Consequently, the risk to the fetus of what might appear to be "two drinks a day" is likely the result of much higher intake.

Another case in point is a study using the "bogus pipeline." With this technique, the patient is told that her verbal or written response may be independently checked by laboratory tests of her blood or urine. In one study, 14% of pregnant patients said they drank when asked to complete a questionnaire only, whereas 27% said they drank if they were asked to complete a questionnaire and were told that lab tests would be also conducted to verify their responses (Lowe et al, 1986).

Not only have all investigators studying drinking during pregnancy been faced with the problem of obtaining reliable drinking histories, but a multitude of definitions of "problem drinking," "abusive drinking," "heavy drinking," and alcohol dependence have been used. These descriptions range from studies in Boston which defined heavy drinking as 45 drinks per month and at least 5 drinks on some occasions to 1 to 2 drinks per day in studies emanating from northern California (Harlap and Shiono, 1980). Such differences in definition make comparisons across studies difficult. It has been equally difficult to define such terms as "moderate," "social," and "light" drinking. Since there is no consensus in terminology, "moderate" drinking in one study can include women who are "heavy" drinkers in another. Even the same research group may use these terms inconsistently. For example, Streissguth defined women drinking 2 drinks per day as "heavy" drinkers in one study (Streissguth et al, 1980) and "moderate" drinkers in another (Landesman-Dwyer et al, 1980).

Although scientists sometimes express maternal drinking as so many ounces of absolute alcohol per day, calculated to decimal place precision, the difficulties in obtaining reliable drinking histories and the variability and complexity of human drinking behavior must be kept in mind in interpreting studies of drinking during pregnancy and especially the labels used to define such drinking. This is also true for studies in animals. For example, in their studies of alcohol's effects in nonhuman primates, Clarren and Bowden (1982) divided their dosage levels into "moderate" and "high" dosages. The moderate dosage produced a blood alcohol level of 200-300 mg%! Similarly, in their elegant study of alcohol's impact on craniofacial development in mice, Sulik et al (1981) administered dosages of alcohol producing peak BALs of 193 to 215 mg% and discussed these levels in terms of "social" drinking. Development of better measures of alcohol intake during pregnancy and better criteria for terms like "heavy," "moderate," "social" drinking, etc., would remove much of the uncertainty and controversy about the effects of different exposure levels.

CONCLUSION

Chronic abusive drinking during pregnancy is clearly a major risk to the conceptus. However, alcohol acts in concert with other environmental or genetic risks and is a necessary, but not always sufficient, casual agent. Adverse effects are seen even among chronic alcohol abusers only in a proportion of the offspring. Any one of the spectrum of fetal effects attributed to maternal alcohol exposure is known to occur in the absence of alcohol as well. Animal evidence supports an association of birth defects with alcohol exposure only at very high blood alcohol levels during pregnancy (e.g., legal intoxication). There is insufficient evidence to demonstrate risk to the unborn from occasional alcohol exposure during pregnancy.

REFERENCES

Abel EL: Prenatal effects of alcohol on adult learning in rats. *Pharmacol Biochem Behav* 1980; 10: 239-243.

Abel EL: *Marijuana, Tobacco and Alcohol Effects in Reproduction.* Boca Raton, FL, CRC Press, 1982.

Abel EL: *Fetal Alcohol Syndrome and Effects.* Westport, CT, Greenwood Press, 1984.

Abel EL, Sokol RJ: Incidence of fetal alcohol syndrome and economic impact of FAS-related anomalies. *Drug and Alcohol Dependence* 1987; 19:51-79.

Altshuler HL, Shippenberg TS: A subhuman primate model for fetal alcohol syndrome research. *Neurobehav Toxicol Teratol* 1981; 3:121-126.

Aronson M: *Children of Alcoholic Mothers.* Goteborg, Sweden, University of Goteborg, 1984, pp 1-36.

Clarren SK, Bowden DM: Fetal alcohol syndrome: A new primate model for binge drinking and its relevance to human ethanol teratogenesis. *J Pediatr* 1982; 101:819-824.

Clarren SK, Bowden DM, Astley SJ: Pregnancy outcomes after weekly oral administration of ethanol during gestation in the pig-tailed macaque (Macaca nmnistrina). *Teratol* 1987; 35:345-354.

Ellis FW, Pick JR: An animal model of the fetal alcohol syndrome in beagles. *Alcohol: Clin Exp Res* 1980; 4:123-134.

Ernhart CB, Morrow-Tlucak M, Sokol RJ, Martier S: Underreporting of alcohol abuse in pregnancy. *Alcohol: Clin Exp Res* 1988; 12:506-511.

Ernhart CB, Sokol RJ, Martier S, Moron P, Nadler D, Ager JW, Wolf A: Alcohol teratogenicity in the human: A detailed assessment of specificity, critical period, and threshold. *Am J Obstetr Gynecol* 1987; 156:33-39.

Golden NL, Sokol RJ, Kuhnert BR, Bottoms SF: Maternal alcohol use and infant development. *Pediatrics* 1982; 70:931–934.

Halliday JL, MacReid M, McClure G: Results of heavy drinking in pregnancy. *Brit J Obstetr Gynaecol* 1982; 89:892–895.

Hanson JW, Streissguth AP, Smith DW: The effects of moderate alcohol consumption during pregnancy on fetal growth and morphogenesis. *J Pediatr* 1978; 92:457–460.

Harlap S, Shiono PH: Alcohol, smoking and incidence of spontaneous abortions in the first and second trimester. *Lancet* 1980; 2:173–176.

Inouye RN, Kokich VG, Clarren SK, Bowden DM: Fetal alcohol syndrome: An examination of craniofacial dysmorphology in Macaca menstrina. *J Med Primatol* 1985; 14:35–48.

Jones KL, Chernoff FG, Kelley CD: Outcome of pregnancy in women who "binge" drink during the first trimester of pregnancy. *Clin Res* 1984; 32:114A.

Kaminski M, Rumeau-Rouquette C, Schwartz D: Alcohol consumption in pregnant women and the outcome of pregnancy. *Alcohol: Clin Exp Res* 1978; 2:155–163.

Kaufman MH: Ethanol induced chromosomal abnormalities at conception. *Nature* 1983; 302:258–160.

Kaufman MH, Bain IM: The development potential of ethanol-induced monosomic and trisomic conceptuses in the mouse. *J Exp Zool* 1984; 231:149–155.

Kline J, Shrout P, Stein Z, Susser M, Warburton D: Drinking during pregnancy and spontaneous abortion. *Lancet* 1980; 2:176–180.

Kolata GB: Fetal alcohol advisory debated. *Science* 1981; 214:642–645.

Kuzma JW, Sokol RJ: Maternal drinking behavior and decreased intrauterine growth. *Alcohol: Clin Exp Res* 1982; 6:396–402.

Landesman-Dwyer S, Ragozin AS, Little RE: Behavioral correlates of prenatal alcohol exposure: A four-year follow-up study. *Neurobehav Toxicol Teratol* 1980; 21:52A.

Larsson G: Prevention of Fetal Alcohol Effects: An antenatal program for early detection of pregnancies at risk. *Acta Obstet Gynecol Scand* 1983; 62:171–178.

Little RE: Moderate alcohol use during pregnancy and decreased infant birth weight. *Am J Public Health* 1977; 67:1154–1156.

Lowe JB, Windsor RA, Adams B, Morris J, Reese Y: Use of bogus pipeline method to increase accuracy of self-reported alcohol consumption among pregnant women. *J Stud Alcohol* 1986; 47:173–175.

Mills J, Graubared B: Is moderate drinking during pregnancy associated with an increased risk for malformation? *Pediatrics* 1987; 80:309–314.

Neugut RH: Epidemiological appraisal of the literature on the fetal alcohol syndrome in human. *Early Human Devel* 1981; 5:411–429.

Obe G, Majewski F: No elevation of exchange type—Aberrations in the lymphocytes of children with alcohol embryopathy. *Hum Genet* 1978; 43:31–36.

Ouellette EM, Rosett HL, Rosman NP, Weiner L: Adverse effects on offspring of maternal alcohol abuse during pregnancy. *New Engl J Med* 1977; 297:528–530.

Randall CL, Lochry EA, Hughes SS, Sutker PB: Dose-response effect of prenatal alcohol exposure on fetal growth and development in mice. *Subst Alcohol Actions-Misuse* 1981; 2:349–357.

Randall CL, Taylor WJ, Walker DW: Ethanol-induced malformations in mice. *Alcohol: Clin Exp Res* 1977; 1:219–223.

Riley EP, Lochry EA, Shapiro NR: Lack of response inhibition in rats prenatally exposed to alcohol. *Psychopharmacology* 1979; 62:47–52.

Rosett HL, Ouellette EM, Weiner L, Owens E: Therapy of heavy drinking during pregnancy. *Am J Obstet Gynecol* 1978; 51:41–46.

Rosett HL, Snyder P, Sander LW, Lee A, Cook P, Weiner L, Gould J: Effects of maternal drinking on neonate state regulations. *Dev Med Child Neurol* 1979; 21:464–473.

Rosett HL, Weiner L: *Alcohol and the Fetus.* New York, Oxford University Press, 1984.

Scott WJ Jr, Fradkin R: The effects of prenatal ethanol in cynomolgus monkeys Maca fascicularis. *Teratology* 1984; 29:49–56.

Shaywitz SE, Cohen DJ, Shaywitz BA: Behavior and learning deficits in children of normal intelligence born to alcoholic mothers. *J Pediatr* 1980; 96:978–982.

Sokol RJ: Alcohol and spontaneous abortion (letter to the editor). *Lancet* 1980; II:1079.

Sokol RJ: Alcohol and abnormal outcomes of pregnancy. *Can Med Assoc J* 1981; 125:143–148.

Sokol RJ, Ager J, Martier S, Debanne S, Ernhart C, Kuzma J, Miller SI: Significant determinants of susceptibility to alcohol teratogenicity. *NY Acad Sci* 1986; 477:87–100.

Sokol RJ, Martier S, Ager J, Abel EL: Human pregnancy loss and prenatal alcohol/marihuana exposure: No synergism detected. *Alcohol: Clin Exp Res* 1986; 10:56c.

Sokol RJ, Miller SI, Reed G: Alcohol abuse during pregnancy: An epidemiologic study. *Alcohol: Clin Exp Res* 1980; 4:135–145.

Streissguth AP, Barr HM, Martin DC, Herman CS: Effects of maternal alcohol, nicotine and caffeine use during pregnancy on infant mental and motor development at 8 months. *Alcohol: Clin Exp Res* 1980; 4:152–164.

Streissguth AP, Herman CS, Smith DW: Intelligence, behavior and dysmorphogenesis in the fetal alcohol syndrome: A report on 20 clinical cases. *J Pediatr* 1978; 92:363–367.

Sulik KK, Johnston MC, Webb MA: Fetal alcohol syndrome: Embryogenesis on a mouse model. *Science* 1981; 214:936–938.

U.S. Department of Health and Human Services: *Monthly Vital Statistics Report: Annual Summary for the United States, 1979.* Hyattsville, Maryland: National Center for Health Statistics, 1980.

Vitez M, Koranyi G, Gonczy E, Rudas T, Dzeizel E: A semiquantitative score system for epidemiologic studies of fetal alcohol syndrome. *Am J Epidemiol* 1984; 119:301–308.

Weiner L, Rosett HL, Edelin KC, Alpert JJ, Zuckerman B: Alcohol consumption by pregnant women. *Obstet Gynecol* 1983; 61:6–12.

CHAPTER 11

Biochemical and Hematological Markers of Alcoholism

Shoji Harada

Institute of Community Medicine
The University of Tsukuba, Japan

Dharam P. Agarwal and H. Werner Goedde

Institute of Human Genetics, University of Hamburg
Hamburg, F.R. Germany

INTRODUCTION

There has been a rapid increase in alcohol consumption and alcohol problems in many industrialized nations. In view of the limited therapeutic success normally achieved in the treatment of alcoholism and the constant risk of relapse during the course of treatment, all the measures that could help in the early detection and monitoring of alcohol abuse may be of great clinical significance. Moreover, the involvement of alcoholic genesis is increasingly taken into account in the differential diagnosis of many internal disorders. An early detection of excessive alcohol consumption as the possible primary cause of a disorder may be of high importance in developing the proper treatment strategies. Chronic alcohol abuse and heavy drinking leads to many cellular and tissue abnormalities as well as to numerous hematological and biochemical alterations (Holt et al, 1981; Whitfield, 1981; Seitz and Kommerell, 1985; Teschke, 1985; Salaspuro, 1986).

In the past, a number of tests, based on questionnaires and personality analysis (MAST = Michigan Alcoholism Screening Test, CAGE = Cut-down, Annoyed by criticism, Guilt feelings, Eye-opener) have been suggested (Mayfield et al, 1974; Selzer, 1981). Such tests are certainly appropriate to detect severe alcohol dependence associated with personal and social consequences (Bernadt et al, 1982). However, the usefulness of such tests in the early diagnosis of alcoholism and treatment monitoring is doubtful as the patients, particularly in the early stages of the disease, tend to hide their heavy alcohol consumption and the resulting family and social problems (Salaspuro, 1986).

Therefore, an objective clinical chemical measure of short-term and long-term alcohol consumption is an important factor in diagnosis and treatment monitoring of alcoholism. Such tests help in treatment outcome evaluation, in the epidemiology of alcohol use, in evaluation of the possible effects of drinking on the fetus and in the clinical decision when alcohol may be, but does not have to be, the source of a patient's symptoms. For practical reasons, only a peripheral source like blood could be used for routine analysis for the detection of excessive alcohol consumption.

This chapter focuses on the usefulness and shortcomings of some of the most commonly used biochemical and biological markers of alcohol abuse and alcoholism.

CLINICAL CHEMICAL CORRELATES OF ALCOHOL DRINKING

Among various biochemical and hematological state markers (e.g., GGT, AALT, ASAT, MCV, defined shortly) currently used for the routine detection of alcoholism and alcohol-related liver damage, none of them is specific if evaluated alone. Only after simultaneous measurement and combined evaluation of the different laboratory tests, a reliable detection and monitoring of alcohol abuse is possible. The lack of sensitivity and specificity of these tests indicates the fact that almost all the hitherto observed hematological and biochemical changes do not result from direct effects of alcohol or its metabolic products; rather the changes reflect only the consequences of cellular damage or metabolic disorder that are apparent only at advanced stages of the disease. Furthermore, the specificity of these tests is relatively low since most of the pathological findings have diverse origins and could also be caused by certain drugs. Thus, one is searching for a clinical chemical parameter resulting either from a direct consequence of drinking alcohol or due to its metabolites. Moreover, the alteration must be measurable in whole blood or blood fractions to allow an easy detection in early stages of the disease without the associated cellular and organ complications.

Gamma-Glutamyltransferase (GGT)

In the past several years, GGT determination has been the most widely used as well as the most disputed clinical chemical marker of alcohol abuse. The primary catalytic functions of gamma-glutamyltransferase (GGT, glutamine: D-glutamyl-peptide 5-glutamyltransferase, EC 2.3.2.2) are the transfer of gamma-glutamyl moiety to acceptor amino acids and cleavage of glutathione into glutamic acid and cysteinylglycine (Hanes and Hird, 1952). Cysteinylglycine is further cleaved by peptidase to free cysteine and glycine. The resulting amino acids are converted by the successive actions of gamma-glutamylcysteine synthetase and glutathione synthetase to glutathione (Meister, 1973).

GGT is widely distributed in various organs and is mainly localized in the membranes of cells such as epithelial cells lining the biliary tract, hepatic canaliculi, proximal renal tubules, pancreatic acinar tissue, pancreatic ductules, and intestinal brush border cells (Albert et al, 1964; Rutenburg et al, 1969; Kokot and Sledzinski, 1974). Most of the GGT activity is found in kidney, liver, prostate, pancreas, spleen, duodenum, and intestine. GGT is synthesized in the endoplasmic reticulum of the liver and transported to the plasma membranes through the Golgi apparatus before being excreted into blood or bile (Nishimura and Teschke, 1983). GGT is a glycoprotein with a molecular weight of 90,000 to 120,000 daltons depending on the isolation techniques. The isozymes of GGT show considerable heterogeneity regarding molecular weight and charge and in their tissue distribution.

The serum of healthy adults contains only trace amounts of GGT as compared with its high activity in the kidney. Most studies agree that liver is the source of most of the GGT activity in serum. Serum and liver GGT are identical in kinetic and physical characteristics. The electrophoretic heterogeneity of GGT isozymes in serum results from differences in sialic acid residues, carbohydrate content and hydrophobic domain of the enzyme (Teschke, 1985).

Various studies have emphasized the clinical significance of GGT determination in the screening of alcoholic liver damage and alcoholism (Orlowski and Szewczuk, 1961; Orlowski, 1963; Luchi and Cortis, 1978; Ishii et al, 1980; Sanchez-Craig and Annis, 1981; Shaw and Marsh, 1981; Seitz and Kommerell, 1985; Teschke, 1985). Although most of the reported studies clearly indicate that acute alcohol consumption has no effect on the serum GGT concentration in healthy subjects and in patients with alcohol liver injury (Nishimura and Teschke, 1980; Gill et al, 1982; Devgun et al, 1985), significant elevation in serum GGT has been reported in chronic alcoholics and heavy drinkers by a large number of investigators (Rosalki and Rau, 1972; Chalmers et al, 1981; Chick et al, 1981; Garvin et al, 1981; Gluud et al, 1981; Papoz et al, 1981; Orrego et al, 1985). Abnormally high serum GGT values have been observed in 50 to 90% of patients with a history of chronic alcohol consumption (Rollason et al, 1972; Rosalki and Rau, 1972; Wu et al, 1974; Kristenson et al, 1980; Penn et al, 1981; Nishimura and Teschke, 1983; Korri et al, 1985; Poikolinnen et al, 1985). However, serum GGT increase is independent of hepatic GGT activity (Selinger et al, 1982).

However, increased serum GGT activity in alcoholism lacks specificity (Salaspuro, 1987). Although serum GGT recovers to the normal level in four to five weeks after abstinence, it relapses to abnormal levels in two weeks with the beginning of heavy drinking (Wadstein and Skude, 1979a, 1979b). Nonalcoholic origins of elevated GGT were found to be quite prevalent among hospital admissions (Whitehead et al, 1981; Penn and Worthington, 1983). Only 50% of the elevated GGT values were due to alcohol in apparently healthy men (Penn et al, 1981). Drugs like phenobarbital or phenazone and many forms of nonalcoholic liver disease as well as smoking increase serum GGT levels (Rosalki and Rau, 1972; Okuno, 1973; Patel and O'Gorman, 1975; Chan-Yeung et al, 1981).

The mechanism of increased serum GGT activity following chronic alcohol consumption is not fully clear (Teschke, 1985; Salaspuro, 1986). It has been suggested that a rise in serum GGT following chronic alcohol consumption occurs as a result of hepatic induction of GGT at the site of the endoplasmic reticulum (Teschke et al, 1977).

Mean Corpuscular Volume (MCV)

A significantly high incidence of an increased MCV of red cells has been found to be an indicator of chronic heavy drinking and alcoholism (Unger and Johnson, 1974; Wu et al, 1974; Chalmers et al, 1978; Chick et al, 1981; Ryback et al, 1982; Weill et al, 1982). Although the mechanisms underlying alcohol-related alterations in MCV are still unclear, a direct effect of ethanol on the bone marrow or an underlying folate deficiency may be responsible for the observed increase in MCV in alcoholics (Sullivan and Herbert, 1964; Lindenbaum and Lieber, 1969; Wu et al, 1974).

Among various alcohol-related disorders, elevated MCV values were observed in 82% of patients with alcoholic hepatitis, 89% of alcoholic cirrhosis, and in 100% of alcoholics with normal livers (Buffet et al, 1975). Other studies showed higher MCV values in 30 to 95% of alcoholic patients (Carney and Sheffield, 1978; Morgan, 1980; Chalmers et al, 1981; Morgan et al, 1981a). MCV was found to correlate better with alcohol consumption than GGT in these studies. Abnormal MCV values have been found to be a better indicator of excessive alcohol consumption and in diagnosis of alcoholic liver disease in women than in men (Chalmers et al, 1978; Bhattacharyya and Rake, 1983).

However, elevated MCV values have also been observed in nonalcoholic liver diseases, reticulocytosis, vitamin B_{12} and folic acid deficiency, as well as being dependent on age, sex, and smoking status of the subjects (Okuno, 1973; Helman and Rubenstein, 1975; Whitfield et al, 1978; Chalmers et al, 1980; Eckardt et al, 1981; Papoz et al, 1981).

Aspartate Aminotransferase (ASAT)

Human ASAT (EC 2.6.1.1) enzyme exists in two forms, the soluble enzyme (s-ASAT) and the mitochondrial enzyme (m-ASAT), which differ from each other in their tissue distribution, kinetic, and immunological properties as well as in the amino acid sequence (Morino et al, 1964; Rej, 1978; Teranishi et al, 1978).

Elevated serum ASAT levels have been observed in chronic alcoholics or heavy drinkers (Ishii et al, 1979). Highest total ASAT (t-ASAT) values have been found in alcoholics with the history of alcoholism exceeding 10 years (Skude and Wadstein, 1977). However, there is neither a correlation between total serum ASAT and alcohol consumption nor a correlation with the duration of drinking (Teschke et al, 1980; Morgan et al, 1981b). Consequently, elevated ASAT is a general indicator of tissue and organ damage caused by either alcohol, viral infections, drugs, or toxins (Wroblewski, 1959; McIntyre and Heathcote, 1974).

During unspecific hepatic damage, serum levels of s-ASAT increase significantly, whereas m-ASAT level tends to increase to a greater extent in alcoholic liver disease. Thus, the determination of m-ASAT–t-ASAT ratio can be helpful in discriminating alcoholic hepatitis from other diseases (Panteghini et al, 1983). Indeed, mean m-ASAT–t-ASAT ratios were found to be similar in patients with chronic viral hepatitis and healthy controls, whereas the ratio in chronic alcoholics was found to be about four times higher (Nalpas et al, 1984). The sensitivity of the m-ASAT–s-ASAT ratio reached 93% in cases of alcoholic liver disease and 100% in alcoholics without liver disease (Nalpas et al, 1984). Immunochemical methods using a specific antibody against ASAT have been suggested to have advantages over the conventional spectrophotometeric methods (Salaspuro, 1987).

Alanine Aminotransferase (ALAT)

ALAT (EC 2.6.1.2) is present mainly in the liver and, to a lesser extent, in skeletal muscle, kidney, and heart. As a consequence of hepatocellular damage, ALAT is released into blood from the liver cytoplasm (Coodley, 1971). Serum ALAT levels are frequently elevated in patients with alcoholic liver disease (Matloff et al, 1980; Stamm et al, 1984a). In some cases of alcoholic liver disease, a lower-than-expected serum ALAT level reflected a lower hepatic ALAT activity due to a depletion of pyridoxal 5-phosphate in patients with alcoholic hepatitis. An inverted ALAT–ASAT ratio is the most characteristic indicator of alcoholic liver injury (Deritis et al, 1972; Cohen and Kaplan, 1979). An ALAT–ASAT ratio of more than 2 was found to be a reliable indicator of alcoholic liver disease (Correia et al, 1981; Salaspuro 1987).

Alkaline Phosphatase (AP)

Alkaline phosphatase (AP, EC 3.1.3.1) is located mainly in the bone, liver, placenta, and intestine. Acute alcohol drinking does not affect the serum AP concentrations, but elevated levels of this enzyme have been reported in alcoholics and heavy drinkers (Rosalki and Rau, 1972; Patel and O'Gorman, 1975; Lai et al, 1982). However, the overlap with levels obtained in nonalcoholic liver diseases is significant and renders it of limited value in the diagnosis of alcoholic liver disease.

Glutamate dehydrogenase (GDH)

GDH (EC 1.4.1.3) is a mitochondrial enzyme predominantly present in the liver (Schmidt and Schmidt, 1973). Abnormally high concentrations of serum GDH have been noted in patients with hepatic and biliary tract diseases (Ellis et al, 1978). Van Waes and Lieber (1977) found GDH to be a reliable marker of liver cell necrosis in the alcoholic. A subsequent study showed that severity of histologic lesions correlated positively with early GDH elevations (Worner and Lieber, 1980a, 1980b). In about 86% of the subjects with heavy alcohol consumption, elevated GDH values were recorded (Ghise-Beer and Grafe, 1986).

However, in other recent studies, GDH activity has not been found reliably to reflect the severity of hepatocyte necrosis and recent alcohol abuse (Worner and Lieber, 1980b; Mills et al, 1981; Jenkins et al, 1982; Teschke et al, 1983).

Alpha Amino-*n*-butyric acid (AANB)

A significant increase in plasma AANB was reported following chronic alcohol consumption in human and animal studies (Shaw and Lieber, 1977). The increased plasma AANB after chronic alcohol consumption may be due to its increased production as the result of severe disturbances in carbohydrate metabolism (Shaw and Lieber, 1978, 1980). Since dietary protein deficiency may even decrease the plasma AANB level (Lieber, 1980), nutritional factors have to be controlled in order to use the level of plasma AANB as a reflection of chronic alcohol consumption. The plasma ratio of AANB to leucine was found to be elevated in alcoholics (Shaw et al, 1976). There was a statistically significant positive correlation between this ratio and the degree of alcoholism (Shaw et al, 1978). The measurement of plasma AANB–leucine ratio has been suggested to be an empirical marker of alcohol-related liver disease (Ganju et al, 1979). However, a number of other studies demonstrated that the AANB–leucine ratio is increased nonspecifically by liver damage (Morgan et al, 1977; Dienstag et al, 1978; Ellingboe et al, 1978; Herrington et al, 1981; Jones et al, 1981; Chick et al, 1982).

High-Density Lipoprotein Cholesterol (HDL-C)

Increased levels of HDL-C associated with alcohol abuse have been reported (Danielsson et al, 1979; Williams et al, 1979; Ernst et al, 1980). Although HDL-C elevation may also result from microsomal system inducing drugs and physical exercise, it is considered a potential biochemical marker of chronic alcohol consumption (Barboriak et al, 1980; Devenyi et al, 1981; Sanchez-Craig and Annis, 1981; Barrett-Connor and Suarez, 1982). Alcohol consumption also increases HDL phospholipids and apolipoproteins A-I and A-II (Johansson and Medhus, 1974; Taskinen et al, 1982, 1985; Puchois et al, 1984).

Urinary Dolichols

Dolichols (poly-*cis* isoprenoid alcohols) containing an alpha-saturated isoprene unit act in the form of dolichyl phosphate as a glycosyl carrier lipid in the biosynthesis of *N*-linked glycoproteins (Parodi and Leloir, 1979; Hubbard and Ivatt, 1981; Hemming, 1983). High levels of dolichols are found mainly in the testes, thyroid, pancreas, pituitary gland, adrenals, and liver (Rupar and Carroll, 1978).

Increased urinary dolichol levels were found in chronic alcoholics and in newborns of alcoholic mothers (Wisniewski et al, 1983; Pullarkat and Raguthu, 1985). Urinary dolichol as related to urinary creatinine was found to be 2.5 to 4 times higher than that of nonalcoholic social drinkers (Roine et al, 1987). Increased dolichol was found in 68% of patients as compared to 44% patients with increased serum GGT. Since random urine samples are easier to obtain than blood samples, the determination of urinary dolichols as marker of alcoholism and alcohol abuse may be suitable for large-scale studies. However, further studies are required to establish specificity and sensitivity of this potential marker of alcoholism.

Carbohydrate Deficient Transferrin (CTD)

An abnormal molecular form of transferrin with altered isoelectric focusing properties was first detected in the serum of alcoholics (Stibler et al, 1979; Stibler and Borg, 1981). A more positively charged transferrin component with an isoelectric point between 5.7 to 5.9 was detected in higher frequency with increasing amounts of alcohol consumption. The presence of the abnormal transferrin component showing microheterogeneity was specifically related to high alcohol consumption and was observed in alcoholics consuming more than 60 g per day but normalized after about two weeks of abstinence (Stibler et al, 1980; Vesterberg et al, 1984; Storey et al, 1985; Schellenberg and Weill, 1986).

Subsequent studies showed a quantitative relationship between the abnormal transferrin content and reduced sialic acid of the whole transferrin (Stibler and Borg, 1981). Transferrin from alcoholic patients showed a 22% lower sialic acid concentration than control transferrin and at least two sialic acid residues were missing in a significant fraction of transferrin from alcoholics. It was later found that the apparent microheterogeneity of transferrin is due to reduced carbohydrates constituting the terminal trisaccharides of the glycans of transferrin—sialic acid, galactose, and N-acetylglucosamine (Stibler and Borg, 1986). This carbohydrate-deficient transferrin (CDT) showed about 91% sensitivity and 99% specificity for current alcohol abuse when evaluated in alcoholics, total abstainers, normal consumers, and patients with various diseases (Stibler et al, 1985). A recent study revealed normal CDT values in all of the 87 nonalcoholic patients irrespective of type or degree of liver pathology (Stibler and Hultcrantz, 1987). Eighty-seven percent of alcoholic patients with current alcohol abuse showed elevated levels of CDT whereas in abstaining alcoholics with persistent liver disease, the values were normal. A significant correlation was observed between CDT concentration and present level of daily alcohol consumption. Thus, CDT determination can be used also in patients with various liver diseases as a marker of current but not previous alcohol abuse.

Alcohol Dehydrogenase (ADH)

Elevated serum ADH levels have been reported in a number of alcohol-related and unrelated liver disorders (Mezey et al, 1968; Bogusz et al, 1969; Gromashevskaya et al, 1976; Wolf, 1979; Krivonos, 1980; Kato et al, 1984). However, plasma ADH activity in alcoholics and nonalcoholic psychiatric patients was found to be significantly raised only when higher AALT and GGT values were also observed (Meier-Tackmann et al, 1984). This increase in plasma ADH may be due to a generalized liver damage and therefore plasma ADH determination alone is not a useful diagnostic marker of alcoholism but could be of value when measured in combination with other biochemical parameters like GGT and MCV.

Aldehyde Dehydrogenase (ALDH)

A selective reduction in the activity of human liver cytosolic and erythrocyte ALDH has been reported (Jenkins and Peters, 1980; Goedde et al, 1983; Agarwal et al, 1983a). Significantly depleted erythrocyte ALDH activity in the blood of chronic alcoholics was noted as compared to healthy controls and nonalcoholic psychiatric and gastrointestinal patients (Agarwal et al, 1983a). Findings reported from other laboratories have further confirmed that erythrocyte ALDH is significantly reduced in alcoholics (Lin et al, 1984; Harada et al, 1985; Towell et al, 1985; Matthewson & Record, 1986; Towell et al, 1986). Moreover, the red cell ALDH activity was found to decrease progressively with increasing cell age. In alcoholics, even the younger cells showed significantly lower enzyme activity (Agarwal et al, 1985).

More recent studies show a lack of correlation between reduced erythrocyte ALDH activity and degree of alcohol-related liver damage (Matthewson & Record, 1986; Agarwal et al, 1987). Thus, erythrocytes may offer a suitable peripheral source for monitoring changes in ALDH activity in alcoholics during chronic alcohol abuse as well as in abstinence. Since the erythrocyte ALDH activity in alcoholics returns to normal values only after a prolonged abstinence (Agarwal et al, 1983a), the reduced red cell enzyme activity could be used as a potential biochemical parameter for monitoring of active alcohol abuse.

However, it remains unresolved whether reduced liver ALDH activity in alcoholics is a preexisting genetic trait representing a risk factor for alcoholism and alcohol-related liver disease or whether it is simply a consequence of excessive ethanol ingestion (Palmer and Jenkins, 1982; Thomas et al, 1982; Agarwal et al, 1983a; Jenkins et al, 1984; Matthewson and Record, 1986; Agarwal et al, 1987).

Acetaldehyde–Protein Adducts

Acetaldehyde forms more or less stable adducts with a number of proteins. The binding is dependent on acetaldehyde concentration, the duration of its reaction, and the presence of reducing agents (Tuma and Sorrell, 1985). Such acetaldehyde–protein adducts have been reported for hemoglobin (Stevens et al, 1981), actin, spectrin, and other erythrocyte membrane proteins (Gaines et al, 1977) as well as for enzymes like RNAase, lactate dehydrogenase, and glucose 6-phosphate dehydrogenase (Tuma and Sorrell, 1987). If acetaldehyde binds at functionally important positions of an enzyme, it may lead to loss in its catalytic properties (Tuma and Sorrell, 1985). According to recent investigations, acetaldehyde reversibly binds to erythrocyte proteins in the blood and is set free in the peripheral systems. Therefore, the concentration of acetaldehyde in red blood cells could be up to 10 times as high as in the plasma (Baraona et al, 1987). It is likely that erythrocyte proteins are particularly vulnerable to toxic effects of acetaldehyde during chronic alcohol consumption.

However, the use of acetaldehyde–protein adducts as laboratory markers of alcoholism is still theoretical and requires more studies.

CORRELATIONS BETWEEN DIFFERENT BIOCHEMICAL MARKERS

The observed biochemical changes taken as "markers" of alcohol abuse and alcoholism are not very specific and do not always correlate with each other. Hence, when evaluated singly, these markers show a poor diagnostic sensitivity and none of the laboratory tests alone is sensitive enough to discriminate between high and low alcohol consumption. Thus, a comparative assessment of diagnostic sensitivity of these clinical chemical markers may help in assessing a combination of diagnostic tests that might offer maximum discriminating capability.

In a study on population of men attending a multiphasic health-screening center, the pattern of correlation for GGT/TG (triglycerides), GGT/UA (uric acid), TG/ASAT, and TG/UA were all found unchanged with increase in alcohol consumption, whereas the pairs of variables GGT/MCV, UA/ASAT, ASAT/MCV, and GGT/ASAT all became more highly correlated as the level of alcohol consumption increased (Whitfield et al, 1981). GGT was found to be a better diagnostic marker for alcoholism compared with MCV (Papoz et al, 1981). In another study, although GGT was found to be the most sensitive single marker in patients of both sexes, its sensitivity was only 46% when considered alone (Cushman et al, 1984). A combination of GGT and MCV increased the sensitivity to 57%, and a combination of GGT, MCV, HDL, and ASAT further increased the diagnostic sensitivity up to 73%. Combining seven markers, 82% of males and 71% of females had at least one abnormally high value (Cushman et al, 1984). The data from these authors suggest that a combination of several tests may be useful in screening alcoholics; their sensitivity, however, seems low in ambulatory, relatively healthy, "middle-class" alcoholic populations.

In one study of 245 patients undergoing treatment for alcoholism, AANB and GGT but not MCV decreased following withdrawal and during abstinence. Among patients who relapsed, only AANB and GGT increased in the majority of subjects (Shaw et al, 1979). The combined use of AANB and GGT identified 28 out of 33 heavy drinkers, whereas 4 out of 33 patients in remission had positive tests. The sensitivity of MCV is generally enhanced by combining it with other parameters such as GGT, ASAT, GDH, and AP (Morgan et al, 1981b). Analysis of only GGT and MCV in 121 male alcoholics resulted in correct classification of 94% of nonalcoholics but only 36% of alcoholics. In contrast, analysis of 24 commonly used laboratory tests helped classification of 100% of nonalcoholics and 98% of alcoholics (Eckhardt et al, 1981).

A composite index of GGT and HDL-C in male alcoholics was found superior to GGT and HDL-C alone in discriminating abstinent/light, moderate, and heavy drinkers (Sanchez-Craig and Annis, 1981). Although there was a considerable overlap in the levels of GGT and AP in patients with different liver diseases, the ratio of GGT and AP was significantly higher in the group with alcoholic liver disease (Lai et al, 1982). When the ratio was higher than 1.4, the diagnostic efficiency for distinguishing the alcoholic group from the other groups was 78%.

In a recent study, about 93% of patients with liver disease showed elevated GGT and GDH values, whereas only about 40% and 44% of the patients had abnormal ASAT and AALT values, respectively (Ghise-Beer and Grafe, 1986). Generally, a combination of clinical laboratory findings helped in a better detection and exclusion of alcoholism in men (Stamm et al, 1984b). For the alcoholics, abnormal values for two or more of the five parameters, GGT, ASAT, ALAT, MCV, and creatinine, gave a diagnostic sensitivity of 85% and diagnostic specificity of 64%. For the nonalcoholics, the diagnostic specificity was 96% and diagnostic sensitivity 50%.

In a discriminant function analysis based on the values of GGT, HDL, MCV, cholesterol, urate, and lead in 7735 middle-aged men, a clear distinction could be achieved between heavy and occasional drinkers (Shaper et al, 1985). However, more than half of the heavy drinkers could not be detected by this combination of laboratory tests.

BIOLOGICAL MARKERS OF ALCOHOLISM

A number of studies have attempted to identify biological markers associated with alcoholism. An association with a known hereditary trait occurring in consistently higher frequency may help to identify a genetic predisposition to alcoholism. Studies linking alcoholism with color blindness, ABO blood groups, HLA antigens, C3, alpha$_1$-antitrypsin, alpha$_1$-acid glycoprotein (AAG), group specific component (Gc), glyoxalase I (GLO), platelet monoamine oxidase (MAO), and taste sensitivity to phenylthiocarbamide (PTC) have been reported (Cruz-Coke and Varela, 1966; Hill et al, 1975; Constans et al, 1983; Roberts et al, 1984; Harada et al, 1985; Ledig et al, 1986).

The fact that only a small percentage of alcohol abusers develop cirrhosis suggests that a possible predisposing factor is involved. However, the findings regarding an association of genetic markers and alcoholism are contradictory and nonreproducible (Failkow et al, 1966; Winokur et al, 1976). The hitherto reported possible associations between some common trait markers of biochemical nature and alcoholism are described in detail as follows.

ABO Blood Groups

Early studies concerning blood groups and alcoholism revealed an association of blood group A with alcoholism (Billington, 1956; Nordmo, 1959). Hill et al (1975) studied association and linkage of ABO, MNSs, Rh, Kell, Duffy, and Xg in alcoholics and their nonalcoholic first-degree relatives. Except for a higher frequency of homozygous recessive ss (MNSs system) in the nonalcoholic family members than in the alcoholics, no significant relationship between blood groups and alcoholism was noted. However, subsequent studies could not establish any significant link between the ABO system and alcoholism (Buckwalter et al, 1964; Reid et al, 1968; Camps et al, 1969; Swinson and Madden, 1973).

Human Leucocyte Antigens (HLA)

Significant associations between various human leucocyte antigens (HLA) such as HLA-B8, HLA-B13, HLA-B15, HLA-B40, HLA-DR3, and alcoholic hepatitis as well as alcoholic cirrhosis have been observed in several studies (Bailey et al, 1976; Bell and Nordhagen, 1978; Seignalet et al, 1980; Morgan et al, 1981a; Dick et al, 1982; Saunders et al, 1982; Robertson et al, 1984; Wilson et al, 1984; Doffoel et al, 1986). However, in other studies no such association could be established (Scott et al, 1977; Melendez et al, 1979; Gluud et al, 1981; Rada et al, 1981).

Platelet Monoamine Oxidase (MAO)

Monoamine oxidase (MAO, EC 1.4.3.4) catalyzes the oxidative deamination of catecholamines, indolamines, and other biogenic amines that possibly play an important role in the regulation of mood and behavior. Two forms of MAO, A and B, are known that are distributed mainly in the brain, liver, and blood platelets. In human platelets only the B form is detectable.

A number of studies have shown the occurrence of reduced brain and platelet MAO activity in alcoholics with a great deal of overlap in the values (Wiberg et al, 1977; Agarwal et al, 1979; Major and Murphy, 1979; Agarwal et al, 1983b; Major et al, 1985; Faraj et al, 1987). A temporary increase in the MAO activity has been noted during withdrawal and abstinence (Wiberg, 1979; Fowler et al, 1981; Agarwal et al, 1983c). In a recent study, in vitro inhibition of MAO activity by ethanol was found to be significantly higher in the platelets of alcoholics than in matched controls (Tabakoff et al, 1988).

Low platelet MAO activity associated with alcohol abuse has been thought to represent a genetic vulnerability factor for alcoholism (Alexopoulos et al, 1981). However, a link between MAO activity and genetic predisposition to alcoholism remains to be unequivocally established.

Glutathione S-Transferase (GST)

Human GST shows at least three sets of isozymes that differ in their tissue distribution, incidence of genetic variation, susceptibility to certain inhibitors, and in their electrophoretic mobilities (Strange et al, 1984). GST isozymes are assumed to play a protective role against various electrophilic carcinogens and toxic xenobiotics (Chasseaud, 1979; Sparnins et al, 1982). The null allele (GST1 0) may be responsible for various hepatic disease due to elevated exposure to certain carcinogenic compounds (Board, 1981).

The distribution of various GST isozymes in livers and lymphocytes of patients with alcoholic and nonalcoholic liver diseases showed that GST1 0 type is highly prevalent in livers of patients with acute hepatitis, alcoholic liver cirrhosis, and liver carcinoma as compared to apparently healthy livers (Harada et al, 1987). In livers from patients with chronic hepatitis, the GST1 2 phenotype was found in high incidence. The null allele was also found to be the most frequent type in the lymphocytes of alcoholics. Whether the presence of the 0 type among alcoholics indicates a genetic vulnerability has yet to be established.

Increased Alcohol Metabolism

A faster alcohol metabolism as a consequence of chronic alcohol abuse has been observed by a number of investigators (Salaspuro et al, 1978; Nuutinen et al, 1985). Any change in alcohol metabolism will affect steady-state blood ethanol, acetaldehyde, and acetate levels. Whether the altered levels of these products represent reliable trait or state biochemical markers remains undecided.

Blood Ethanol

The estimation of blood ethanol is the most direct test for initial diagnosis of alcohol abuse. Thirty-two percent of patients attending an emergency clinic had a blood alcohol concentration of 17.4 mmol/l (80 mg/dl) or more (Holt et al, 1980).

Enhanced ethanol elimination rates have been observed in alcoholics in a number of studies

(Kater et al, 1969; Mezey and Tobon, 1971; Misra et al, 1971; Salaspuro et al, 1978; Damgaard et al, 1982).

Blood Acetaldehyde

The direct toxic effects of alcohol and alcohol-related physical alterations have been attributed to acetaldehyde rather than to ethanol itself. Acetaldehyde is the first catabolic product of alcohol oxidation in human liver and is far more toxic than the parent compound.

Over the past few years, higher-than-normal blood acetaldehyde concentrations after drinking an acute dose of alcohol have been considered as an indicator of a possible risk factor associated with alcoholism (Schuckit, 1980). Alcoholics and their first-degree relatives have been found to show higher levels of steady-state blood acetaldehyde than matched healthy controls (Korsten et al, 1975; Schuckit and Rayses, 1979; Lindros et al, 1980; Nuutinen et al, 1983; Nuutinen et al, 1984). However, methodological pitfalls in the determination of blood and breath acetaldehyde have rendered these observations equivocal. Moreover, since the blood and breath acetaldehyde levels are also subject to alterations due to several factors like ethanol oxidation rate, genetically determined variations in alcohol dehydrogenase and aldehyde dehydrogenase isozymes, smoking, nutrition, and liver status, the determination of blood acetaldehyde may not be a reliable marker of alcohol abuse.

Blood Acetate

The level of blood acetate was found to be significantly higher in alcoholics than in healthy controls after chronic alcohol drinking (Nuutinen et al, 1985). In subsequent studies, mean blood acetate concentration of chronic alcoholics and heavy drinkers was found significantly higher than that of 53 nonalcoholics allowed to drink alcohol voluntarily as much as they tolerated (Salaspuro et al, 1987). The elevated blood acetate in alcoholics and heavy drinkers showed a sensitivity of 65%; the corresponding sensitivities for GGT, ASAT, and MCV were 64/35%, 31/21%, and 31/12%, respectively. The specificity of increased blood acetate was 92% (Korri et al, 1985).

Serum 2,3-Butanediol

Elevated amounts of 2,3-butanediol were detected in the serum of alcoholics drinking alcohol but not in the serum of nonalcoholics drinking distilled spirits (Rutstein et al, 1983). Subsequent studies confirmed this observation (Guze, 1984; Sisfontes et al, 1986). Moreover, about 30% of the alcoholic patients living in abstinence but who had drunk sufficient ethanol in the past as indicated by the presence of alcoholic cirrhosis had elevated blood 2,3-butanediol in their serum (Casazza et al, 1987). Whether elevated serum 2,3-butanediol is induced by chronic high ethanol ingestion or is a marker of predisposition to alcoholism has yet to be explored (Rutstein and Veech, 1987).

CONCLUDING REMARKS

A specific biochemical marker to detect chronic alcohol abuse is essential for the prevention, early diagnosis, and treatment monitoring of alcoholism. Ideally, such a marker should be easily measurable in the peripheral blood and should be able to detect alcohol abuse before the onset of alcohol-related organ and tissue damage. Although, no single biochemical marker has shown sufficient diagnostic efficiency, many currently used clinical chemical parameters have proven useful in the diagnosis of alcohol abuse and alcohol-related health problems. Use of screening questionnaires and clinical test combinations, together with sophisticated statistical analysis of groups of biochemical tests, can increase the diagnostic efficacy.

REFERENCES

Agarwal, DP, Goedde HW, Schrappe O: Blood platelet monoamine oxidase activity in schizophrenia, affective disorders and alcoholism, in Singer TP, von Kroff RW, Murphy DL (eds): *Monoamine Oxidase: Structure, Function and Altered Functions*. New York, Academic Press, 1979, pp 397-402.

Agarwal DP, Müller C, Korencke C, Mika U, Harada S, Goedde HW: Changes in erythrocyte and liver aldehyde dehydrogenase isozymes in alcoholics, in Flynn TG, Weiner H (eds): *Enzymology of Carbonyl Metabolism: Aldehyde Dehydrogenase, Aldehyde Reductase, and Alcohol Dehydrogenase*. New York, Alan R. Liss Inc., 1985, pp 113-127.

Agarwal DP, Philippu G, Milech U, Goedde HW, Schrappe O: Platelet monoamine oxidase activity in alcoholics. *Mod Probl Pharmacopsychiat* 1983b; 19:260-264.

Agarwal, DP, Philippu G, Milech U, Ziemsen B, Schrappe O, Goedde HW: Platelet monoamine oxidase and erythrocyte catechol-O-methyltransferase activity in alcoholism and controlled abstinence. *Drug Alcohol Dependence* 1983c; 12:85-91.

Agarwal DP, Tobar-Rojas L, Harada S, Goedde HW: Comparative study of erythrocyte aldehyde dehydrogenase in alcoholics and control subjects. *Pharmacol Biochem Behav* 1983a; 18:(Suppl.1) 89-95.

Agarwal DP, Volkens T, Hafer G, Goedde HW: Erythrocyte aldehyde dehydrogenase: Studies of properties and changes in acute and chronic alcohol intoxication, in Weiner H, Flynnn TG (eds): *Enzymology and Molecular Biology of Carbonyl Metabolism: Aldehyde Dehydrogenase, Aldo-Keto Reductase and Alcohol Dehydrogenase*. New York, Alan R. Liss Inc., 1987, pp 85-101.

Albert Z, Orlowski M, Szewczuk A: Histochemical and biochemical investigation of gamma-glutamyl transpeptidase in the tissue of man and laboratory rodents. *Acta Histochem* 1964 (Teria); 18:78-89.

Alexopoulos GS, Lieberman KW, Frances R, Stokes PE: Platelet MAO during the alcohol withdrawal syndrome. *Am J Psychiat* 1981; 138:1254-1255.

Bailey RJ, Krasner N, Eddeston ALFW: Histocompatibility antigens, autoantibodies and immunoglobulins in alcoholic liver disease. *Br Med J* 1976; 2:727-729.

Baraona E, DiPova C, Tabasco J, Lieber CS: Transport of acetaldehyde in red blood cells. *Alcohol Alcoholism* 1987; Suppl 1:203-206.

Barboriak JJ, Jacobson GR, Cushman P, Herrington RE, Lipo RF, Daley ME, Anderson AJ: Chronic alcohol abuse and high lipoprotein cholesterol. *Alcohol Clin Exp Res* 1980; 4:346-349.

Barrett-Connor E, Suarez L: A community study of alcohol and other factors associated with the distribution of high lipoprotein cholestrol in older vs. younger men. *Am J Epidemiol* 1982; 115:888-893.

Bell H, Nordhagen R: Association between HLA-BW40 and alcoholic liver disease with cirrhosis. *Br Med J* 1978; 1:822.

Bernadt MW, Mumford J, Taylor C, Smith B, Murray RM: Comparison of questionnaire and laboratory tests in the detection of excessive drinking and alcoholism. *Lancet* 1982; i:325-328.

Bhattacharyya DN, Rake MO: Correlations of alcohol consumption with liver damage in men and women. *Alcohol Alcoholism* 1983; 18:181-184.

Billington BF: Note on distribution of blood groups in bronchiectasis and portal cirrhosis. *Australas Ann Med* 1956; 5:20-22.

Board PG: Biochemical genetics of glutathione S-transferase in man. *Am J Hum Genet* 1981; 33:36-43.

Bogusz M, Gallus H, Chlipalski J: Serum enzymes and liver tests in chronic alcoholism. *Pol Tyg Lek* 1969; 24:1306-1308.

Buckwalter JA, Pollock CB, Hasleton G, Krohn JA, Nance MJ, Ferguson JL, Bondi RL, Jacobsen JJ, Lubin AH: The Iowa blood type disease research project. II. *J Iowa State Med Soc* 1964; 54:58-66.

Buffet C, Chaput J-C, Albuisson F, Subtil E, Etienne J-P: La microcytose dans l'hepatite chronic histologiquement prouvee. *Arch Fr Mal Appar Dig* 1975; 64:309-315.

Camps FE, Dodd BE, Lincoln PJ: Frequencies of secretors and nonsecretors of ABH groups substances among 1000 alcoholic patients. *Br Med J* 1969; 4:457-459.

Carney MWP, Sheffield B: Serum folate and B12 and haematological status of in-patient alcoholics. *Br J Addict* 1978; 73:3-7.

Casazza JP, Frietas J, Stambuk D, Morgan MY, Veech RL: The measurement of 1,2-propanediol, D,L-2,3-butanediol and meso-2,3-butanediol in controls and alcoholic cirrhotics. *Alcohol Alcoholism* 1987; Suppl 1:607-609.

Chalmers DM, Chanarin I, MacDermott S, Levi AJ: Sex-related differences in the haematological effects of excessive alcohol consumption. *J Clin Path* 1980; 33:3-7.

Chalmers DM, Levi AJ, Chanarin I, North WRS, Meade TW: Mean cell volume in a working population: Alcohol and oral contraception. *Br J Haematol* 1978; 43:631-636.

Chalmers DM, Rinsler MG, McDermott S, Spicet CC, Levi AJ: Biochemical and haematological indicators of excessive alcohol consumption. *Gut* 1981; 22:992-996.

Chan-Yeung M, Ferreira P, Frohlich J, Schulzer M, Tan F: The effect of age, smoking and alcohol on routine laboratory tests. *Am J Clin Pathol* 1981; 75:320-326.

Chasseaud LF: The role of glutathione and glutathione S-transferase in the metabolism of chemical carcinogenesis and other electrophilic agents. *Adv Cancer Res* 1979; 29:175–274.

Chick J, Kreitman N, Plant M: Mean cell volume and gamma-glutamyltranspeptidase as markers of drinking in working men. *Lancet* 1981; i:1249–1251.

Chick J, Longstaff M, Kreitman MP, Thacher D, Waite J: Plasma alpha-*n*-butyric acid leucine ratio and alcohol consumption in working men and in alcoholics. *J Stud Alcohol* 1982; 42:583–587.

Cohen JS, Kaplan MM: The SGOT/SGPT ratio—An indicator of alcoholic liver disease. *Am J Diag Dis* 1979; 24:835–838.

Constans J, Arlet P, Viau M, Bouissou C: Unusual sialilation of the serum DBP associated with Gc 1 allele in alcoholic cirrhosis of the liver. *Clin Chim Acta* 1983; 130:219–230.

Coodley EL: Enzyme diagnosis in hepatic disease. *Am J Gastroenetrol* 1971; 56:413–419.

Correia JP, Alves PS, Comilo EA: SGOT–SGPT ratios. *Dig Dis Sci* 1981; 26:284.

Cruz-Coke R, Varela A: Inheritance of alcoholism. *Lancet* 1966; ii:1282.

Cushman P, Jacobson G, Barboriak JJ, Anderson AJ: Biochemical markers for alcoholism: Sensitivity problems. *Alcohol Clin Exp Res* 1984; 8:253–257.

Damgaard SE, Deigaard A, Iversen H, Keiding S, Lundquist F, Ribenstein E, Winkler K: The rate of alcohol metabolism including measurements of acetaldehyde and acetate concentrations in alcoholics at low and high alcohol loads. *Alcohol Clin Exp Res* 1982; 6:436 (abstr.).

Danielsson B, Ekamn R, Fex G, Johansson BG, Kristenson H, Nilsson-Ehle P, Wadstein J. Changes in plasma high density lipoprotein in chronic male alcoholics during and after abuse. *Scand J Clin Lab Invest* 1979; 38:113–119.

Deritis F, Coltorti M, Guisti G: Serum transaminase activities in liver disease. *Lancet* 1972; i:685.

Devenyi P, Robinson GM, Kapur BM, Roncari DAK: High density lipoprotein cholesterol in male alcoholics with and without severe liver disease. *Am J Med* 1981; 71:589–594.

Devgun MS, Dunbar JA, Hagart J, Martin B, Ogston SA: Effect of acute and varying amounts of alcohol consumption on alkaline phosphatase, aspartate transferase and gamma-glutamyltransferase. *Alcohol Clin Exp Res* 1985; 9:235–237.

Dick HM, MacSween RNM, Hislop S, Mills P: HLA antigens and alcoholic liver disease. *Lancet* 1982; ii:325–326.

Dienstag JL, Carter EA, Wands JR, Isselbacher KJ, Fischer JE: Plasma alpha amino-*n*-butyric acid to leucine ratio. Nonspecificity as a marker for alcoholism. *Gastroenterology* 1978; 75:561–565.

Doffoel M, Tongio MM, Gut JP, Ventre G, Charrault A, Vetter D, Ledig M, North ML, Mayer S, Bockel R: Relationship between 34 HLA-A, HLA-B and HLA-DR antigens and three serological markers of viral infections in alcoholic cirrhosis. *Hepatology* 1986; 6:457–463.

Eckardt MJ, Ryback RS, Rawlings RR, Graubard BI: Biochemical diagnosis of alcoholism. A test of the discriminating capabilities of gamma–glutamyl transpeptidase and mean corpuscular volume. *J Am Med Assoc* 1981; 246:2707–2710.

Ellingboe J, Mendelson JH, Varanelli CC, Neuberger O, Borysow M: Plasma alpha amino-*n*-butyric acid:leucine ratio. Normal values in alcoholics. *J Stud Alcohol* 1978; 39:1467–1476.

Ellis G, Goldberg DM, Spooner RJ, Ward AM: Serum enzyme tests in diseases of the liver and biliary tree. *Am J Clin Pathol* 1978; 70:248–258.

Ernst N, Fisher M, Smith W: The association of plasma high-density lipoprotein with dietary intake and alcoholic consumption. The lipid research clinics program prevalence study. *Circulation* 1980; 62:41–48.

Failkow PJ, Thuline MC, Fenster RF: Lack of association between cirrhosis of the liver and common types of color blindness. *N Engl J Med* 1966; 275:584–587.

Faraj BA, Lenton JD, Kutner M, Vernon M Camp, Stammers TW, Lee SR, Lolies PA, Chandora D: Prevalence of low monoamine oxidase function in alcoholism. *Alcohol Clin Exp Res* 1987; 11:464–467.

Fowler CJ, Wiberg A, Oreland L, Danielsson A, Palm U, Winbald B: Monoamine oxidase activity and kinetic properties in platelet-rich plasma from controls, chronic alcoholics, and patients with nonalcoholic liver disease. *Biochem Med* 1981; 25:356–365.

Gaines KC, Salhany JM, Tuma DJ, Sorrell MF: Reactions of acetaldehyde with human erythrocyte membrane proteins. *FEBS Lett* 1977; 75:115–119.

Ganju S, Dubin A, Szanto PB, Steigmann F: Significance of plasma alpha-amino-*n*-butyric acid to leucine ratio in liver disease. *Gastroenterology* 1979; 76:1281.

Garvin RB, Foy DW, Alford GS: A critical examination of gamma-glutamyl transferase as a biochemical marker for alcohol abuse. *Addict Behav* 1981; 6:377–383.

Ghise-Beer E, Grafe G: Alkoholismus-Screening mit gamma-GT (GGTP) und GLDH. *Med Welt* 1986; 37:771–773.

Gill GV, Baylis PH, Flear CTG, Skillen AW, Diggle PH: Acute biochemical responses to moderate beer drinking. *Br Med J* 1982; 285:1770–1773.

Gluud C, Andersen I, Dietrichson O, Gluud B, Jacobsen A, Juhl E: Gamma-glutamyltransferase, aspartate aminotransferase and alkaline phosphatase as marker of alcohol consumption in outpatient alcoholics. *Eur J Clin Invest* 1981; 11:171–176.

Goedde HW, Agarwal DP, Harada S: The role of alcohol dehydrogenase and aldehyde dehydrogenase isozymes in alcohol metabolism, alcohol intolerance and alcoholism, in Rattazzi MC, Scandalios JG, Whitt GS (eds): *Isozymes: Curr Top Biol Med Res*, vol 8. New York, Alan R Liss., 1983, pp 175–193.

Gromashevskaya LL, Tatyanko NV, Kozlova VG: Blood serum alcohol dehydrogenase in diagonizing acute and chronic hepatic lesions. *Sov Med Moskva* 1976; 5:24–30.

Guze S: 2,3-Butanediol in the serum of alcoholics. *Psychiatr Cap Comm* 1984; April 4–5.

Hanes CS, Hird FJR: Enzyme transpeptidation reaction involving gamma-glutamyl transpeptidase. *Nature* 1952; 51:25–35.

Harada S, Agarwal DP, Goedde HW: Aldehyde dehydrogenase polymorphism and alcohol metabolism in alcoholics. *Alcohol* 1985; 2:391–392.

Harada S, Agarwal DP, Goedde HW: Aldehyde dehydrogenase and glutathione S-transferase polymorphism: Association between phenotype frequencies and alcoholism, in Goedde HW, Agarwal DP (ed): *Genetics and Alcoholism*. New York, Alan R. Liss Inc., 1987; pp 241–250.

Helman N, Rubenstein LS: The effects of age, sex and smoking on erythrocytes and leucocytes. *Am J Clin Pathol* 1975; 63:35–44.

Hemming FW: Biosynthesis of dolichols and related compounds, in Porter JW, Spurgeon SL (ed): *Biosynthesis of Isoprenoid Compounds*. New York, Wiley, 1983; vol 2, pp 305–354.

Herrington RE, Jacobsen GR, Daley ME, Lipo RF, Biller HB, Weissberger C: Use of plasma alpha-n-butyric acid leucine ratio to identify alcoholics. *J Stud Alcohol* 1981; 42:492–499.

Hill SY, Goodwin DW, Cadoret R, Osterland K, Doner SM: Association and linkage between alcoholism and eleven serological markers. *J Stud Alcohol* 1975; 36:981–982.

Holt S, Skinner HA, Israel Y: Early identification of alcohol abuse. 2. Clinical and laboratory indicators. *Can Med Ass J* 1981; 124:1279–1294.

Holt S, Stewart IC, Dixon JMJ, Elton RA, Taylor TV, Little K: Alcohol and the emergency service patient. *Br Med J* 1980; 281:638–640.

Hubbard SC, Ivatt RJ: Synthesis and processing of asparagine-linked oligosaccharides. *Ann Rev Biochem* 1981; 50:555–583.

Ishii H, Okuno F, Ebihara Y, Takagi T, Tsuchiya M: Hepatic and intestinal gamma glutamyl–transpeptidase activity. Its enhancement after chronic ethanol administration and significance as a marker of alcoholic liver injury. *Gastroenterology* 1980; 79:1132A.

Ishii H, Okuno F, Shigeta Y, Tsuchiya M: Enhanced serum glutamic oxalacetic transaminase activity of mitochondrial origin in chronic alcoholics, in Galanter M (ed): *Currents in Alcoholism*. New York, Grune and Stratton 1979, vol V, pp 101–108.

Jenkins WJ, Cakebread K, Palmer KR: Effect of alcohol consumption on hepatic aldehyde dehydrogenase activity in alcoholic patients. *Lancet* 1984; i:1048–1049.

Jenkins WJ, Peters TJ: Selectively reduced hepatic acetaldehyde dehydrogenase in alcoholics. *Lancet* 1980; i:628–629.

Jenkins WJ, Rosalki SB, Foo Y, Scheuer PJ, Nemesanszky E, Sherlock S: Serum glutamate dehydrogenase is not a reliable marker of liver cell necrosis in alcoholics. *J Clin Path* 1982; 35:207–210.

Johansson BG, Medhus A: Increase in plasma alpha-lipoproteins in chronic alcoholics after acute abuse. *Acta Med Scand* 1974; 195:273–276.

Jones JD, Morse RM, Furt RD: Plasma alpha n-butyric and leucine ratio in alcoholics. *Alcohol Clin Exp Res* 1981; 5:561–565.

Kater RMH, Carulli N, Iber FL: Deferences in the rate of ethanol metabolism in recently drinking alcoholic and non-drinking subjects. *Am J Clin Nutr* 1969; 22:1608–1617.

Kato S, Ishii H, Kano S, Hagihara S, Todoroki T, Nagata S, Takahashi H, Nagasaka M, Sato J, Tsuchiya M: Improved assay for alcohol dehydrogenase activity in serum by centrifugal analysis. *Clin Chem* 1984; 30:1817–1820.

Kokot F, Sledzinski S: Die gamma-glutamyltransferase. *Z klin Chem klin Biochem* 1974; 12:374–384.

Korri UM, Nuutinen H, Salaspuro M: Increased blood acetate: A new marker of alcoholism and heavy drinking. *Alcohol Clin Exp Res* 1985; 9:468–471.

Korsten MA, Matsuzaki S, Feinman L, Lieber CS: High blood acetaldehyde levels after ethanol administration. *N Engl J Med* 1975; 292:386–389.

Kristenson H, Trell E, Fex G, Hood B: Serum gamma-glutamyltransferase: Statistical distribution in a middle-aged male population and evaluation of alcohol habits in individuals with elevated levels. *Prev Med* 1980; 9:108–119.

Krivonos PS: Blood serum alcohol dehydrogenase in pulmonary tuberculosis patients suffering from chronic alcoholism. *Problemy Tuberkuleza* 1980; 6:27–30.

Lai CL, Ng RP, Lok ASF: The diagnostic value of the ratio of serum gamma-glutamyl transpeptidase to alkaline phosphatase in alcoholic liver disease. *Scand J Gastroent* 1982; 17:41–47.

Ledig M, Doffoel M, Ziessel M, Kopp P, Charrault A, Tongio MM, Mayer S, Bockel R, Mandel P: Frequencies of glyoxalase I phenotypes as biological markers in chronic alcoholism. *Alcohol* 1986; 3:11–14.

Lieber CS: Alcohol, protein metabolism and liver injury. *Gastroenterology* 1980; 79:373–390.

Lin CC, Potter JJ, Mezey E: Erythrocyte aldehyde dehydrogenase in alcoholism. *Alcohol Clin Exp Res* 1984; 8:539–542.

Lindenbaum J, Lieber CS: Haematologic effects of alcohol in man in the absence of nutritional deficiency. *N Eng J Med* 1969; 281:333–338.

Lindros KO, Stowell A, Pikkarainen P, Salaspuro M: Elevated blood acetaldehyde in alcoholics with accelerated ethanol elimination. *Pharmacol Biochem Behav* 1980; 13:Suppl. 1, 119–124.

Luchi P, Cortis G: Forensic considerations on the comparison of serum gamma-glutamytranspeptidase ("gamma-GT") activity in experimental acute alcoholic intoxication and in alcoholic car drivers who caused road accidents. *Forensic Sci* 1978; 11:33–39.

Major LF, Hawley RJ, Saini N, Garrick NA, Murphy DL: Brain and liver monoamine oxidase type A and type B activity in alcoholics and controls. *Alcohol Clin Exp Res* 1985; 9:6–9.

Major LF, Murphy DL: Platelet and plasma amine oxidase activity in alcoholic individuals. *Br J Psychiat* 1979; 132:548–554.

Matloff DS, Selinger MJ, Kaplan MM: Hepatic transaminase activity in alcoholic liver disease. *Gastroenterology* 1980; 1389–1392.

Matthewson K, Record CO: Erythrocyte aldehyde dehydrogenase activity in alcoholic subjects and its value as a marker for hepatic aldehyde dehydrogenase in subjects with and without liver disease. *Clin Sci* 1986; 70:295–299.

Mayfield D, McLeod G, Hall P: The CAGE questionnaire: validation of a new alcoholism screening instrument. *Am J Psychiat* 1974; 131:1121–1123.

McIntyre N, Heathcote J: The laboratory in the diagnosis and management of viral hepatitis. *Clin Gastroenterol* 1974; 3:317–336.

Meier-Tackmann D, Agarwal DP, Goedde HW: Plasma alcohol dehydrogenase in normal and alcoholic individuals. *Alcohol Alcoholism* 1984; 19:7–12.

Meister A: On the enzymology of amino acid transport. *Science* 1973; 180:33–39.

Melendez M, Vargas-Tank K, Fuentes C: Distribution of HLA histocompatibility antigens. ABO blood groups and Rh antigens in alcoholic liver disease. *Blut* 1979; 20:288–290.

Mezey E, Cherric GR, Holt PR: Serum alcohol dehydrogenase, an indicator of intrahepatic cholestasis. *N Engl J Med* 1968; 279:241–248.

Mezey E, Tobon F: Rate of ethanol clearance and activities of the ethanol oxidizing enzymes in chronic alcoholic patients. *Gastroenterol* 1971; 61:707–715.

Mills PR, Spooner RJ, Russell RI, Boyle B, MacSween RNM: Serum glutamate dehydrogenase as a marker of hepatocyte necrosis in alcoholic liver disease. *Br Med J* 1981; 23:754–755.

Misra PS, Lefevre A, Ishii H, Rubin E, Lieber CS: Increase of ethanol, meprobamate and pentobarbital metabolisms after chronic ethanol administration in man and in rat. *Am J Med* 1971; 51:346–351.

Morgan MY: Markers for detecting alcoholism and monitoring for continued abuse. *Pharmacol Biochem Behav* 1980; 13:1–8.

Morgan MY, Camilo ME, Luck W, Sherlock S, Hoffbrand AV: Macrocytosis in alcohol-related liver disease: Its value for screening. *Clin Lab Haematol* 1981a; 43:35–44.

Morgan MY, Colman JC, Sherlock S: The use of a combination of peripheral markers for diagonizing alcoholism and monitoring for continued abuse. *Br J Alcohol Alcoholism* 1981b; 16:167–177.

Morgan MY, Milsom JP, Sherlock S: Ratio of plasma alpha-amino-*n*-butyric acid to leucine as an empirical marker of alcoholism: Diagnostic value. *Science* 1977; 197:1183–1185.

Morino Y, Kagamiyama H, Wada H: Immunochemical distinction between glutamatic-oxaloacetic transaminase from the soluble and mitochondrial fractions of mammalian tissues. *J Biol Chem* 1964; 239: 943–944.

Nalpas B, Vassault A, Le Guillou A, Lesgourgues B, Ferry N, Lacour B, Berthelot P: Serum activity of mitochondrial asparate aminotransferase: A sensitive marker of alcoholism with or without alcoholic hepatitis. *Hepatology* 1984; 5:893–896.

Nishimura M, Teschke R: Effect of chronic alcohol consumption on the activities of liver plasma membrane enzymes: Gamma-glutamyltransferase, alkaline phosphatase and 5'-nucleotidase. *Biochem Pharmacol* 1980; 31:377–381.

Nishimura M, Teschke R: Alcohol and gamma-glutamyltransferase. *Klin Wschr* 1983; 61:265–275.

Nordmo SH: Blood groups in schizophrenia, alcoholism and mental deficiency. *Am J Psychiatry* 1959; 116:460–461.

Nuutinen H, Salaspuro M, Valle M, Lindros KO: Blood acetaldehyde concentration gradient between hepatic and antecubital venous blood in ethanol-intoxicated alcoholics and controls. *Eur J Clin Invest* 1984; 14:306–311.

Nuutinen H, Lindros KO, Hekali P, Salaspuro M: Elevated blood acetate as indicator of fast elimination in chronic alcoholics. *Alcohol* 1985; 2:623–626.

Nuutinen H, Lindros KO, Salaspuro M: Determinants of blood acetaldehyde level during ethanol oxidation in chronic alcoholics. *Eur J Clin Invest* 1983; 7:163–168.

Okuno T: Smoking and blood changes. *J Am Med Assoc* 1973; 225:1387–1388.

Orlowski M: The role of gamma-glutamyl transpeptidase in internal diseases. *Clin Arch Immun Therap Exp* 1963; 11:1–61.

Orlowski M, Szewczuk A: A note on the occurrence of gamma-glutamyltranspeptidase in human serum. *Clin Chim Acta* 1961; 6:430–432.

Orrego H, Blake JE, Israel Y: Relationship between gamma-glutamyltranspeptidase and mean urinary alcohol levels in alcoholics while drinking and after alcohol withdrawal. *Alcohol Clin Exp Res* 1985; 9:10–13.

Palmer KR, Jenkins WJ: Impaired acetaldehyde oxidation in alcoholics. *Gut* 1982; 23:729–733.

Panteghini M, Falsetti F, Chiari E, Malchiodi A: Determination of aspartate aminotransferase isozymes in hepatitic diseases — Preliminary findings. *Clin Chim Acta* 1983; 128:133–140.

Papoz L, Warnet JM, Pequignot G, Eschwege E, Claude JR, Schwarz D: Alcohol consumption in a healthy population. Relationship to gamma-glutamyltransferase activity and mean corpuscular volume. *J Am Med Ass* 1981; 245:1748–1751.

Parodi AJ, Leloir LF: The role of lipid intermediates in the glycosylation of proteins in the eukaryotic cell. *Biochem Biophys Acta* 1979; 559:1–37.

Patel S, O'Gorman P: Serum enzyme levels in alcoholism and drug dependency. *J Clin Path (Lond)* 1975; 28:414–417.

Penn R, Worthington LJ: Is serum gamma-glutamyltransferase a misleading test? *Br Med J* 1983; 286: 531–535.

Penn R, Worthington LJ, Clarke CA, Whitfield AGW: Gamma-glutamyltranspeptidase and alcohol intake. *Lancet* 1981; i:894.

Poikolinnen K, Kärkäinen P, Pikkarainen J: Correlations between biological markers and alcohol intake as measured daily by questionnaire in man. *J Stud Alcohol* 1985; 46:383–387.

Puchois P, Fontan M, Gentilini JL, Gelez P, Fruchart JC: Serum apoliprotein A-II, a biochemical indicator of alcohol abuse. *Clin Chem Acta* 1984; 185:185–189.

Pullarkat RK, Raguthu S: Elevated urinary dolichol levels in chronic alcoholics. *Alcohol Clin Exp Res* 1985; 9:28–30.

Rada RT, Knodell RG, Troup GM, Kellner R, Hermanson SM, Richards M: HLA antigen frequencies in cirrhotic and noncirrhotic male alcoholics: A controlled study. *Alcohol Clin Exp Res* 1981; 5: 188–191.

Reid NCRW, Brunt PW, Bias WB, Maddrey WC, Alonso BA, Iber FL: Genetic characteristic and cirrhosis: A control study of 200 patients. *Br Med J* 1968; 2:463–465.

Rej R: Aspartate aminotransferase activity and isoenzyme proportions in human liver tissues. *Clin Chem* 1978; 24:1971–1979.

Roberts EA, Cox DW, Medline A, Wanless IA: Occurrence of alpha-1-antitrypsin deficiency in 155 patients with alcoholic liver disease. *J Clin Pathol* 1984; 82:424–427.

Robertson DM, Morse RM, Moore SB, O'Fallon WM, Hurt RD: A study of HLA antigens in alcoholism. *Mayo Clin Proc* 1984; 59:243–246.

Roine RP, Turpeinen U, Ylikahri R, Salaspuro M: Urinary dolichol — A new marker of heavy alcohol consumption. *Alcohol Clin Exp Res* 1987; 11:525–527.

Rollason JG, Pincherle G, Robinson D: Serum gamma glutamyl transpeptidase in relation to alcohol consumption. *Clin Chim Acta* 1972; 39:75–80.

Rosalki SB, Rau D: Serum gamma-glutamyl transpeptidase activity in alcoholism. *Clin Chim Acta* 1972; 39:41–47.

Rupar CA, Carroll KK: Occurrence of dolichol in human tissues. *Lipid* 1978; 13:291–294.

Rutenburg AM, Kim H, Fishbein JW, Hanker JS, Wasserkrug HL, Schigman AM: Histochemical and ultrastructural demonstration of gamma-glutamyl transpeptidase activity. *Histochem Cytochem* 1969; 17:517–526.

Rutstein DD, Nickerson RJ, Vernon AA, Kishore P, Veech RL, Felver ME, Needham LL, Thacker SB: 2,3-Butanediol in serum of alcoholics. *Lancet* 1983; ii:1370.

Rutstein DD, Veech RL: Genetics and Alcoholism, epidemiological aspects, in Goedde HW, Agarwal DP (eds): *Genetics and Alcoholism.* New York, Alan R. Liss Inc., 1987, pp 33–44.

Ryback RS, Eckardt MJ, Felsher B, Rawlings RR: Biochemical and hematological correlates of alcoholism and liver disease. *J Am Med Ass* 1982; 248:2261–2265.

Salaspuro M: Conventional and coming laboratory markers of alcoholism and heavy drinking. *Alcohol Clin Exp Res* 1986; 6(suppl.):5–12.

Salaspuro M: Use of enzymes for the diagnosis of alcohol related organ damage. *Enzyme* 1987; 37: 87–107.

Salaspuro M, Korri UM, Nuutinen H, Roine R: Blood acetate and urinary dolichols – New markers of heavy drinking and alcoholism, in Goedde HW, Agarwal DP (ed): *Genetics and Alcoholism*. Alan R. Liss Inc., 1987; pp 231–240.

Salaspuro M, Lindros KQ, Pikkarainen J: Effect of 4-methylpyrazole on ethanol elimination rate and hepatic redox changes in alcoholics with adequate or inadequate nutrition and in alcoholic controls. *Metabolism* 1978; 27:631–639.

Sanchez-Craig M, Annis HM: Gamma-glutamyl transpeptidase and high density lipoproteins cholesterol in male problem drinkers: Advantages of a composite index for predicting alcohol consumption. *Alcohol Clin Exp Res* 1981; 5:540–544.

Saunders JB, Wodak AD, Haines A, Powell-Jackson PR, Portmans B, Davis M, Williams R: Accelerated development of alcoholic cirrhosis in patients with HLA-B8. *Lancet* 1982; i:1381–1384.

Schellenberg F, Weill J: Serum desialotransferrin in the detection of alcohol abuse. Definition of a Tf index. *Drug Alcohol Dep* 1987; 19:181–191.

Schmidt E, Schmidt FW: Gamma-glutamyl transpeptidase. *Dtsch Med Wochenschr* 1973; 98:1572–1578.

Schuckit MA: Biological markers: Metabolism and acute reactions to alcohol in sons of alcoholics. *Pharmacol Biochem Behav* 1980; 13:9–16.

Schuckit MA, Rayses V: Ethanol ingestion: Differences in blood acetaldehyde concentrations in relatives of alcoholics and controls. *Science* 1979; 203:54–55.

Scott BB, Rajah SM, Losowsky MS: Histocompatibility antigens in chronic liver disease. *Gastroenterology* 1977; 72:122–125.

Seignalet J, Blanc F, Lapinski H: Groupes HLA des cirrhoticques alcooliques. *Nouv Presse Med* 1980; 9:712.

Seitz H, Kommerell B: Laboratory markers for early detection of alcoholism. *Ärztl Lab* 1985; 31:109–115.

Selinger MJ, Matloff DS, Kaplan MM: Gamma-glutamyl transpeptidase activity in liver disease: Serum elevation is independent of hepatic GGTP activity. *Clin Chim Acta* 1982; 125:283–290.

Selzer ML: The Michigan Alcoholism Screening Test: The quest for a new diagnostic instrument. *Am J Psychiat* 1981; 127:89–94.

Shaper AG, Pocock SJ, Ashby D, Walker M: Biochemical and haematological response to alcohol intake. *Ann Clin Biochem* 1985; 22:50–61.

Shaw S, Lieber CS: Increased plasma amino n-butyric acid (AANB) due to excess hepatic production: A biochemical marker of alcholism. *Clin Res* 1977; 25:449A.

Shaw S, Lieber CS: Plasma amino acid abnormalities in the alcoholic. Respective role of alcohol, nutrition, and liver injury. *Gastroenterology* 1978; 74:677–682.

Shaw S, Lieber CS: Mechanism of increased gamma-glutamyl transpeptidase after chronic alcohol consumption: Hepatic microsomal induction rather than dietary imbalance. *Subst Alcohol Actions/Misuse* 1980; 1:423–428.

Shaw S, Lue S-L, Lieber CS: Biochemical tests for the detection of alcoholism: Comparison of Plasma alpha amino-n-butyric acid with other available tests. *Alcohol Clin Exp Res* 1978; 2:2–7.

Shaw S, Marsh E: The effect of one evening of social drinking on serum gamma-glutamyltransferase activity. *Clin Chem* 1981; 27:1036A.

Shaw S, Stimmel B, Lieber CS: Plasma alpha amino-n-butyric acid to leucine ratio: An empirical biochemical marker of alcoholism. Diagnostic value. *Science* 1976; 194:1057–1058.

Shaw S, Worner TM, Boryzow MF, Schmitz RE, Lieber CS: Detection of alcoholism relapse: Comparative diagnostic value of MCV, GGT and AANB. *Alcohol Clin Exp Res* 1979; 3:297–301.

Sisfontes L, Nyborg G, Jones AW, Blomstrand R: Occurrence of short chain aliphatic diols in human blood: Identification by gas chromatography-mass spectrometry. *Clin Chem Acta* 1986; 155:117–122.

Skude G, Wadstein J: Amylase, hepatic enzymes and bilirubin in serum of chronic alcoholics. *Acta Med Scand* 1977; 201:53–58.

Sparnins VL, Venegar PL, Wattenberg LW: Glutathione S-transferase activity. Enhancement by compounds inhibiting carcinogenesis and dietary constituents. *J Natl Cancer Inst* 1982; 68:493–496.

Stamm D, Hansert E, Feuerlein W: Excessive consumption of alcohol in men as biological influence factor in clinical laboratory investigations. *J Clin Chem Clin Biochem* 1984a; 22:65–77.

Stamm D, Hansert E, Feuerlein W: Detection and exclusion of alcoholism in men on the basis of clinical laboratory findings. *J Clin Chem Clin Biochem* 1984b; 22:79–96.

Stevens VJ, Fantl WJ, Newman CB, Sims RV, Cerami A, Peterson CM: Acetaldehyde adducts with hemoglobin. *J Clin Invest* 1981; 67:361–369.

Stibler H, Borg S: Evidence of a reduced sialic acid content in serum transferrin in male alcoholics. *Alcohol Clin Exp Res* 1981; 5:545–549.

Stibler H, Borg S: Carbohydrate composition of serum transferrin in alcoholic patients. *Alcohol Clin Exp Res* 1986; 10:61–64.

Stibler H, Borg S, Allgulander C: Clinical significance of abnormal heterogeneity of transferrin in relation to alcohol consumption. *Acta Med Scand* 1979; 206:275–281.

Stibler H, Borg S, Allgulander C: Abnormal microheterogeneity of transferrin—A new marker of alcoholism. *Subst Alcohol Actions Misuse* 1980; 1:247-252.

Stibler H, Borg S, Joustra M: Desialotransferrin—A new routine method for early detection of high alcohol consumption. *Alcohol Clin Exp Res* 1985; 9:210.

Stibler H, Hultcrantz R: Carbohydrate-deficient transferrin in serum in patients with liver diseases. *Alcohol Clin Exp Res* 1987; 11:468-473.

Storey E, Mack U, Powell L, Halliday J: Use of chromatofocusing to detect a transferrin variant in serum of alcoholic subjects. *Clin Chem* 1985; 31:1543-1545.

Strange RC, Faulder CG, Davis BA, Hume R, Brown JAH, Cotton W, Hopkinson DA: The human glutathione S-transferase: Studies on the tissue distribution and genetic variation of the GST1, GST2 and GST3 isozymes. *Ann Hum Genet* 1984; 48:11-20.

Sullivan LW, Herbert V: Mechanism of haematosuppression of ethanol. *J Clin Invest* 1964; 43:2048-2062.

Swinson RP, Madden JS: ABO blood groups and ABH substance secretion in alcoholics. *Q J Stud Alcohol* 1973; 34:64-70.

Tabakoff B, Hoffman P, Lee JM, Daito T, Willard B, De Leon-Jones F: Differences in platelet enzyme activity between alcoholics and nonalcoholics. *N Engl J Med* 1988; 318:134-139.

Taskinen M-R, Välimäki M, Nikkilä EA, Kuusi T, Ehnholm C, Ylikahri R: High density lipoprotein subfractions and postheparin plasma lipases in alcoholic men before and after ethanol withdrawal. *Metabolism* 1982; 31:1168-1173.

Taskinen MR, Välimäki M, Nikkilä EA, Kuusi T, Ylikahri R: Sequence of alcohol-induced initial changes in plasma lipoproteins (VDL and HDL) and lipolytic enzymes in man. *Metabolism* 1985; 34:112-119.

Teranishi H, Kagamiyama H, Teranishi K, Wada H, Yamano T, Morino Y: Cytosolic and mitochondrial isozymes of glutamate-oxaloacetic transaminase from human heart. *J Biol Chem* 1978; 253: 8842-8847.

Teschke R: Gamma-glutamyltransferase and other markers of alcoholism, in Seitz HK, Kommerell B (eds): *Alcohol Related Diseases in Gastroenterology*. Berlin, Springer Verlag, 1985, pp 48-64.

Teschke R, Brand A, Strohmeyer G: Induction of hepatic microsomal gamma-glutamyltransferase activity following chronic alcohol consumption. *Biochem Biophys Res Commun* 1977; 75:718-724.

Teschke R, Neuefeind M, Nishimura M, Strohmeyer G: Hepatic gamma-glutamyltransferase activity in alcoholic fatty liver: Comparison with other liver enzymes in man and rats. *Gut* 1983; 24:625-630.

Teschke R, Rauen J, Neuefeind M, Petrides AS, Strohmeyer G: Alcoholic liver disease associated with increased gamma-glutamyltransferase activity in serum and liver, in Thurman RG (ed): *Alcohol and Aldehyde Metabolizing Systems*. New York, Plenum, 1980, vol 4, pp 647-654.

Thomas M, Halsall S, Peters TJ: Role of hepatic aldehyde dehydrogenase in alcoholism: Demonstration of persistent reduction of cytosolic activity in abstaining patients. *Lancet* 1982; ii:1057-1059.

Towell JF, Barboriak JJ, Townsend WF, Kalbfleisch JH, Wang RIH: Erythrocyte aldehyde dehydrogenase: Assay of a potential biochemical marker of alcohol abuse. *Clin Chem* 1986; 32:734-738.

Towell JF, Townsend WF, Kalbfleisch JH, Wang RIH: Erythrocyte aldehyde dehydrogenase and clinical chemical markers of alcohol abuse and alcoholism. *Alcohol Drug Res* 1985; 6:15-21.

Tuma DJ, Sorrell MF: Hypothesis: Alcoholic liver injury and the covalent binding of acetaldehyde. *Alcohol Clin Exp Res* 1985; 9:306-309.

Tuma DJ, Sorrell MF: Functional consequences of acetaldehyde binding to proteins. *Alcohol Alcoholism* 1987; Suppl 1:61-66.

Unger KW, Johnson D Jr: Red blood cell mean corpuscular volumes: A potential indicator of alcohol usage in a working population. *Am J Med Sci* 1974; 267:281-289.

van Waes L, Lieber CS: Glutamate dehydrogenase: A reliable marker of liver cell necrosis in the alcoholic. *Br Med J* 1977; ii:1508-1510.

Vesterberg O, Petrén S, Schmidt D: Increased concentration of a transferrin variant after alcohol abuse. *Clin Chim Acta* 1984; 141:33-39.

Wadstein J, Skude G: Changes in amylase, hepatic enzymes and bilirubin in serum upon initiation of alcohol abstinance. *Acta Med Scand* 1979a; 205:313-316.

Wadstein J, Skude G: Serum ethanol, hepatic enzymes and length of debauch in chronic alcoholics. *Acta Med Scand* 1979b; 205:317-318.

Weill J, Schellenberg F, LeGoff A-M, Lamy J: The predictive value of gamma-glutamyltransferase and other peripheral markers in the screening of alcohol abuse, in Siest G, Heusghem C (eds): *Gammaglutamyltransferases: Advances in Biochemical Pharmacology*. Paris, Masson, 1982, 3rd series, pp 195-198.

Whitehead TP, Pandov H, Clark DM: Gamma-glutamyl transpeptidase and alcohol problems. *Lancet* 1981; i:663.

Whitfield JB: Alcohol related biochemical changes in heavy drinking. *Aust NZ J Med* 1981; 11:132-139.

Whitfield JB, Allen JK, Adena MA, Hensley WJ: Effect of drinking on correlations between biochemical variables. *Ann Clin Biochem* 1981; 18:143–145.

Whitfield JB, Hensley WJ, Bryden D, Gallagher H: Effect of age and sex on biochemical responses to drinking habits. *Med J Aust* 1978; ii:629–632.

Wiberg A: Increase in platelet monoamine oxidase activity during controlled abstinence after alcohol abuse. *Med Biol* 1979; 57:133–134.

Wiberg A, Gottfries CG, Oreland L: Low platelet monoamine oxidase activity in human alcoholics. *Med Biol* 1977; 55:181–186.

Williams P, Robinson D, Baily A: High density lipoprotein and coronary risk factors in normal men. *Lancet* 1979; i:72–75.

Wilson JS, Gossat D, Tait A, Rouse S, Juan XJ, Pirola RC: Evidence for an inherited predisposition to alcoholic pancreatitis. A controlled HLA typing study. *Dig Dis Sci* 1984; 29:727–730.

Winokur G, Tanna V, Elston R, Go R: Lack of association of genetic traits with alcoholism: C3, Ss, and ABO systems. *J Stud Alcohol* 1976; 37:1313–1315.

Wisniewski KE, Pullarkat RJ, Harin A, Vartalo M: Increased urinary dolichols in newborns whose mothers were heavy alcohol users. *Ann Neurol* 1983; 14:382.

Wolf C: Interés de la determinacion de enzimas plasmaticas en el curso de las hepatopatias. *La vie Medicale* 1979; 10:64–66.

Worner TM, Lieber CS: Plasma glutamate dehydrogenase: A marker of alcoholic liver injury. *Pharmacol Biochem Behav* 13 Suppl 1980a; 1:107–110.

Worner TM, Lieber CS: Plasma glutamate dehydrogenase: Clinical application in patients with alcoholic liver disease. *Alcohol Clin Exp Res* 1980b; 4:431–434.

Wroblewski F: The clinical significance of transaminase activities of serum. *Am J Med* 1959; 27:911–923.

Wu A, Chanarin I, Levi AJ: Macrocytosis of chronic alcoholism. *Lancet* 1974; i:829–830.

Section 4

Genetic Factors

CHAPTER 12

Family and Adoption Studies of Alcoholism*

Stephen H. Dinwiddie, M.D.

Department of Psychiatry, Washington University School of Medicine, St. Louis, USA

C. Robert Cloninger, M.D.

Departments of Psychiatry and Genetics and The Jewish Hospital, St. Louis, USA

The familial nature of alcoholism has been observed by writers since the time of Aristotle, an insight that has been repeatedly confirmed by systematic studies over the last century (Goodwin, 1987). Investigators such as Amark (1951) and Winokur et al (1970) have noted increased rates of alcoholism in first-degree relatives of alcoholics, and it has been estimated that about 40% of alcoholics have an alcoholic parent (Institute of Medicine, 1987). Cotton (1979) reviewed 39 family studies done over the preceding 40 years that involved a total of 6251 relatives of alcoholics and 4083 relatives of nonalcoholics. Since drinking patterns changed over the years and these studies differed considerably in the populations investigated, definitions used, and methodology chosen, it is no surprise that the precise numbers of affected family members differed from study to study; nevertheless, Cotton was able to conclude that ". . . regardless of the nature of the population of nonalcoholics studied, an alcoholic is more likely than a nonalcoholic to have a mother, father, or more distant relative who is an alcoholic" (p. 99).

More recent studies have continued to demonstrate familial aggregation in alcoholism. Guze and co-workers (1986) reported on a series of 500 psychiatric outpatients and 1249 of their first-degree relatives. Diagnoses were made on the basis of explicit, validated criteria, and the probands were followed up and reinterviewed 6 to 12 years later. After the second interview, further information was obtained from physicians, hospitals, and clinics, and based on all this information a second diagnosis was made by investigators blind to the original diagnosis.

Alcoholism diagnoses were subdivided into primary and secondary forms, based on the incidence of other psychiatric syndromes if any, and into definite and probable groups, based on number of symptoms (Table 12.1).

---

*This work was supported in part by National Institute of Mental Health grants MH-14677 and MH-31302, Research Scientist Award MH-00048, National Institute of Alcoholism and Alcohol Abuse, and a grant from the MacArthur Foundation Network on Risk and Protective Factors in Major Mental Disorders.

Table 12.1. Consistency of alcoholism diagnoses*

INITIAL DIAGNOSIS	N	FOLLOW-UP DIAGNOSIS	N	%	ALCOHOLISM DIAGNOSIS ON FOLLOW-UP
Primary alcoholism, definite	24	Primary alcoholism, definite,	9	37.5	
		Primary alcoholism, probable	3	12.5	
		Secondary alcoholism, definite	11	45.8	
		Secondary alcoholism, probable	0	0	96%
		No alcoholism	1	4.2	
Primary alcoholism, probable	4	Primary alcoholism, definite	3	75	
		Primary alcoholism, probable	0	0	100%
		Secondary alcoholism, definite	1	25	
		Secondary alcoholism, probable	0	0	
		No alcoholism	0	0	
Secondary alcoholism, definite	27	Primary alcoholism, definite	8	29.6	
		Primary alcoholism, probable	1	3.7	
		Secondary alcoholism, definite	15	55.6	89%
		Secondary alcoholism, probable	0	0	
		No alcoholism	3	11.1	
Secondary alcoholism, probable	15	Primary alcoholism, definite	1	6.7	
		Primary alcoholism, probable	0	0	
		Secondary alcoholism, definite	6	40	53%
		Secondary alcoholism, probable	1	6.7	
		No alcoholism	7	46.7	

*From Guze et al (1986).

At index, 70 cases of alcoholism were identified: 24 definite primary, 4 probable primary, 27 definite secondary, and 15 probable secondary. The diagnostic stability of the groups was satisfactory (intraclass correlation = .56) but shifting among the primary–secondary and definite–probable categories was evident. Primary and definite cases were more likely than secondary or probable cases to receive an alcoholism diagnosis at follow-up: 96% of the definite primary cases did so, versus 53.3% of the probable secondary ones. Unsurprisingly, diagnostic consistency improved with severity of affliction, as judged by number of symptoms recorded.

Consistent with earlier studies, familial aggregation of alcoholism was evident, with alcoholism rates significantly higher in relatives of alcoholics than in relatives of nonalcoholics, 15.3% versus 8.7% ($p < .001$). Male relatives of alcoholics had higher rates of alcoholism than did female relatives (27.2% versus 6.1%), and the proband's sex had little effect on the rate in relatives: 6.3% of the female relatives of female alcoholic probands had alcoholism versus 5.9% of female relatives of male alcoholic probands while corresponding figures for male relatives were 27.3% and 27.1% (Table 12.2).

Other studies (Penick et al, 1978; Frances et al, 1980, 1984; Penick et al, 1987) have reported that alcoholics with a family history of alcoholism tend to begin drinking earlier in life and to have more problems than those without a family history. This has sometimes been thought to be evidence of differences in the causes of the two forms, but the fact that those cases most reliably diagnosed are seen as aggregating within families while those not as reliably diagnosed are not might indicate that the difference between familial and nonfamilial alcoholism is an artifact of reliability, not necessarily indicative of fundamental genetic differences.

It has proven easier to establish the familial basis of alcoholism than it has been to determine its mode of inheritance. It has been long been recognized that the inheritance of alcoholism does not follow a classical Mendelian pattern. First- and second-degree relatives of alcoholics are about equally at risk for the illness (Kaij and Dock, 1975; Saunders and Wil-

Table 12.2. Alcoholism in first-degree relatives*

	PROBAND ALCOHOLIC (%)	PROBAND NONALCOHOLIC (%)	p
Alcoholism in all relatives of all probands	15.3	8.7	.001
Alcoholism in all relatives of male probands	15.2	6.1	.002
Alcoholism in all relatives of female probands	15.5	9.7	.054
Alcoholism in male relatives of all probands	27.2	16.8	.010
Alcoholism in female relatives of all probands	6.1	2.3	.013
Alcoholism in female relatives of male probands	6.3	0.73	.0145
Alcoholism in female relatives of female probands	5.9	2.8	.1812
Alcoholism in male relatives of male probands	27.1	12.6	.0137
Alcoholism in male relatives of female probands	27.3	18.3	.1218

*From Guze et al (1986).

liams, 1983), and, although men are more likely to develop alcoholism than women, the sex of the proband does not influence the degree of risk in relatives (Guze et al, 1986; Gilligan and Cloninger, 1987). Thus, the observed transmission of the liability for alcoholism does not fit the pattern expected if it were due to a single autosomal or sex-linked gene.

Considering a polygenic mode of transmission of the liability to development of alcoholism raises its own set of problems. Again, the lack of difference between first- and second-degree relatives in concordance for alcoholism does not fit with a simple polygenic pattern of inheritance, as pointed out by Cloninger et al (1979), since for first-degree relatives one-half their genes are identical by descent, versus one-quarter of the genes of second-degree relatives. The observed concordance rates in second-degree relatives are too high to fit that or any other simple genetic hypothesis.

Nonetheless, convincing evidence from studies of twins (Chapter 13; Kaprio et al, 1987), half-siblings (Schuckit et al, 1972), adoptees (discussed shortly) and many families shows that there is significant genetic contribution to the liability for and development of alcohol-related problems. How can these contributions be understood?

Environmental modification of the expression of alcoholism (Chapter 17; Goedde and Agarwal, 1987) must be considered in any developmental model. Alcoholism appears to be a complex phenotype, the end product of a long chain of development beginning with primary gene products and sequentially modified by interactions with multiple loci and many environmental factors (Cloninger et al, 1981, 1988). As such, depending on the relative contributions of different factors disposing to alcoholism, the manifestations of the phenotype in different individuals would be expected to differ on many dimensions. This would make more understandable the repeated observation that core symptoms of the disorder such as physical dependence, social problems, and depression correlate only weakly with one another (Park and Whitehead, 1973).

Giving more credence to this approach is the finding that, within the broad syndrome of alcoholism, certain complications appear to be under separate genetic control. It has been long recognized that there is great variation between individuals in their liability to develop specific complications of alcohol abuse (e.g., hepatic cirrhosis, pancreatitis, or alcoholic cardiomyopathy). This has raised the question of whether some alcoholics are constitutionally predisposed to developing certain types of end-organ damage, and, if so, whether this liability is under control independent of the predisposition for alcoholism. Hrubec and Omenn (1981) found significantly higher concordances for alcoholism in monozygotic twins than in dizygotes, and within these concordant twin pairs found significantly elevated concordance rates for hepatic cirrhosis and alcoholic psychosis among the monozygotes. They concluded that since the alcoholism alone did not sufficiently explain the different concordances for the end-organ damage, these liabilities were independently controlled.

Similarly, biochemical studies have found an abnormality in the activity of transketolase, a thiamine-dependent enzyme in the pentose phosphate pathway, in alcoholics with Wernicke–Korsakoff syndrome. Blass and Gibson (1977) cultured skin fibroblasts from four alcoholics who had developed this syndrome. The transketolase obtained from the cultured cells had a higher K_m (i.e., bound less strongly) to the cofactor thiamine pyrophosphate than did transketolase obtained from controls. This abnormality persisted for more than 20 generations even when the culture medium had an excess of thiamine and no ethanol, strongly suggesting that it was under genetic control, rather than being a consequence of nutrition or of Wernicke–Korsakoff syndrome. Later research (Kaczmarek and Nixon, 1983; Greenwood et al, 1984) showed that this abnormality was not restricted to alcoholics, but Mukherjee et al (1987) have recently shown that it appears to be more common in chronic alcoholics than in the general population.

Another example of end-organ damage that may be independent of the liability toward alcoholism is alcoholic cardiomyopathy. Lange and co-workers (1981) demonstrated a nonoxidative metabolic pathway for ethanol in heart muscle that involved the enzyme fatty acid ethyl ester synthase, which produced fatty acid ethyl esters potentially toxic to myocardium. Since myocardium does not contain alcohol dehydrogenase (Devor et al, 1987), prior to that finding the genesis of alcoholic cardiomyopathy was unclear.

The discovery of a transketolase isozyme and the elucidation of the nonoxidative pathway in myocardium both offer hope of establishing the existence of unique mechanisms that are under independent genetic control but associated with the heritable tendency toward alcoholism. These enzyme systems, like most enzyme systems generally—and in contrast to the diathesis toward alcoholism—may prove to be under relatively simple genetic control. This would explain the development of the specific pattern of end-organ damage seen in the individual with alcoholism.

The foregoing discussion serves to emphasize the point that alcoholism is best understood as a multidimensional phenotype, which can differ in clinical presentation, biochemical pathways, end-organ damage, neurophysiological parameters, neuropsychological performance, and other social and biological measures of alcohol abuse (Gilligan and Cloninger, 1987). Environmental influences can substantially modify outcomes on many dimensions, consequently altering the phenotypic expression of the disorder. The length and complexity of the pathway from genotype to phenotype is one cause of the significant clinical heterogeneity seen in alcoholism, a problem that has further hampered genetic analysis.

SECULAR TRENDS IN ALCOHOLISM

Recent epidemiologic studies show that purely genetic causes are insufficient to explain observed trends in alcohol abuse. Per-capita use of alcohol has been increasing worldwide, accompanied by increases in secondary indicators of alcoholism such as rates of death from alcoholic liver cirrhosis (Helzer, 1987). Data from the five sites of the Epidemiologic Catchment Area study in the United States (Robins et al, 1988) have shown that the alcohol disorders (Alcohol Abuse and Alcohol Dependence, based on the *DSM-III* criteria) are the most common of all psychiatric diagnoses ascertained in men and among the most common five diagnoses in women. Moreover, prevalence rates for these disorders are not much lower in younger than in middle-aged subjects, even though the latter have traveled further through the period of risk for development of the disorders (Robins et al, 1988). The implication of this finding is that not only is alcoholism an extremely common disorder, but that its lifetime prevalence is rising.

Under most circumstances, the population prevalence of heavy drinkers increases quadratically with increasing average consumption (Cloninger et al, 1986). If alcohol abuse could be differentiated into familial and nonfamilial forms, with the former presumably caused by specific biological–genetic factors and the latter by sporadic environmental factors, then increasing average consumption of alcohol should cause an increase (perhaps marked) in non-familial cases, while the prevalence of alcoholism in relatives of familial alcoholics should remain constant, adjusted for an increase of sporadic cases.

In contrast, if expression of a biological–genetic susceptibility to alcoholism were influenced by an interaction with sociocultural factors, relatives of alcoholics (who presumably would have a higher loading of genetic factors predisposing to alcoholism) would be expected to become alcoholic more often than relatives of nonalcoholics. In other words, those with a greater degree of biogenetic liability, when exposed to provocative environmental factors, would be at greatest risk (Cloninger, 1987).

In order to test these alternative hypotheses, Cloninger and co-workers in St. Louis (Cloninger et al, 1986) interviewed 286 hospitalized alcoholics, 157 convicted felons with a high frequency of alcohol abuse, and 60 controls with no psychiatric illness. In addition to the 503 probands, 1644 family members including 1141 first-degree relatives were interviewed. The cumulative risk of developing definite alcoholism by age 25 in men was found to increase by birth cohort, with the risk lowest in the older cohorts. In the oldest cohort, born before 1924, 26% had developed alcoholism by 25. The risk increased to 34% in the cohort born between 1925–34, and to 52% in those born between 1935–44, 63% in those born between 1945–54, and to 67% in those born after 1954 (see Fig. 12.1). This elevation of risk for alcoholism in the younger cohorts is especially impressive since they have yet to pass through

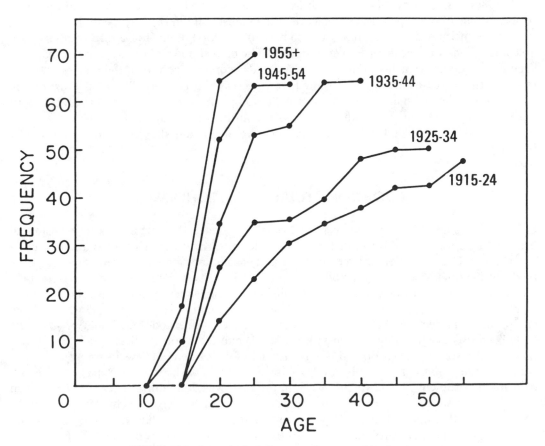

FIGURE 12.1. Rate of alcoholism as a function of birth cohort.

the entire period of risk. In those cohorts who have reached age 40, an additional 10 to 16% of the sample had developed alcoholism between the ages of 25 and 40. Similar findings, although smaller in magnitude, were found in the women in the sample.

These findings indicate that the increase in lifetime risk of alcoholism seen in the general population cannot be accounted for by an increase in the number of sporadic or nonfamilial cases. Instead, it appears that over time there has been an increase in the morbid risk of relatives of alcoholics. Since this change has occurred too rapidly to be accounted for by a change in gene frequency, it is apparent that the change in susceptibility of this population must be due to an interaction between genetic and environmental factors.

These findings cast doubt on the adequacy of dichotomizing alcoholism into familial and nonfamilial forms. Presumably the observed familial clustering of alcoholism is due to the fact that family members of alcoholics have, on average, a greater quantity of constitutional factors predisposing to alcoholism. Moreover, these susceptibility factors are the same as those active in nonfamilial or sporadic cases, which differ in degree, not kind, of predisposition.

In order to estimate changes in the transmissibility of alcoholism, Reich and co-workers (1988) applied mathematical modeling techniques to 60 female and 240 male alcoholics and their families from the same study. They also used interview data from a total of 831 first-degree relatives and 125 spouses of proband alcoholics in addition to the probands. Survival analysis was used to obtain estimates of the time to onset of alcoholism in this sample, and groups were subdivided by sex and age cohort.

The Multifactorial Model of Disease Transmission (Reich et al, 1975) was used to compute cohort and sex specific correlations between family members including parents, offspring, and spouses. These correlations were quantified by path analysis using the "Tau" model (Reich et al, 1980). The general Multifactorial Model was modified to include information about secular trends in the population prevalence of alcoholism and in the transmissibility (i.e., the proportion of variance in the liability due to heritable factors) of alcoholism. In addition, variable age-of-onset of the disorder was modeled. The data supported the hypothesis that children of alcoholics were differentially at risk for developing alcoholism themselves and that much of the increased prevalence resulted from increased transmissibility of the disorder in the younger cohorts. In men, the transmissibility ranged from 0.65 in the oldest cohort (born before 1929) to 0.98 in males born after 1962. Transmissibility in women was lower, ranging from 0.27 in the oldest cohort to 0.59 in the youngest, but showed a similar pattern of increase.

ADOPTION STUDIES IN ALCOHOLISM

Up to this point, discussion has centered on the evidence that alcoholism is transmitted between generations, and on models that are able to test and quantify types and degree of inheritance. The distinction between cultural and genetic inheritance has been ignored, since the Multifactorial Model cannot subdivide heritable elements, although the finding of marked secular changes in the inheritance of alcoholism is strong evidence that cultural or environmental factors have a profound effect on liability for the disorder. Separating genetic from environmental effects on the phenotype requires a different methodology, and two strategies have been used: twin studies (discussed in Ch. 13) and adoption studies.

Adoption studies of alcoholism began with a study by Roe (1944), who found no difference in alcohol abuse in a small sample of foster children with or without parental history of drinking problems. Little further work in the field was done until the early 1970s, when interest in the study of adopted-away children of alcoholics revived. Schuckit et al (1972), comparing half-siblings of alcoholics to other classes of relatives, had expected to find that full siblings of alcoholic probands were more often alcoholic than were half-sibs (Goodwin, 1987). Instead, they found no significant difference between the two groups. Alcoholic half-sibs were significantly more likely to have an alcoholic biological parent, however, again emphasizing the role of some heritable factor. Many of the subjects came from broken homes, which gave the investigators the chance to study what effect alcoholism in parent surrogates might have—in effect, transforming the project into an adoption study. As it turned out, alcoholism in the surrogates did not increase the risk of alcoholism in the children but having a biologic father with alcoholism significantly increased the risk of alcoholism in the sons.

The next study to appear, by Goodwin and colleagues (1973), began by identifying from an initial pool of 5483 adoptees 55 male Danish children who had at least one biologic parent with alcoholism and who had been adopted by six weeks of age by nonrelatives. These were matched by age and time of adoption with a control group of 78 male adoptees without a known history of alcoholism in their parents. At the time of the study, subjects and controls had a mean age of 30 years.

Participants in the study were assessed by a psychiatrist who used a semistructured interview schedule and who was not told to which group the interviewee belonged. Information about adoptees and biological parents was also obtained from law enforcement records. Comparisons between subjects and controls were made on a wide variety of demographic and diagnostic variables.

It was found that 10 of the 55 subjects met specified clinical criteria for alcoholism, versus 4 of the 78 controls. This difference was significant at the .02 level. The groups did not otherwise differ in amount of mental disturbance, other psychopathology, or percentage who were heavy drinkers but not alcoholic.

The second phase of the study (Goodwin et al, 1974) identified 20 adoptees from the first phase who had brothers who had not been adopted away and were raised by the biologic parents. A total of 35 such siblings were identified, of whom 6 were full sibs and 29 were half-sibs. Five of these were not included in the study because no information was available about the adopted siblings, leaving a total of 30 nonadopted brothers in the study. In addition, 50 nonadopted controls were identified from census records. As in the first phase, a psychiatrist blind to the status of the subjects conducted a structured interview of all participants.

A total of five men in both the adopted and nonadopted groups were diagnosed as alcoholic, giving the adoptees a slightly but nonsignificantly higher rate of alcoholism. Both groups had an elevated rate of alcoholism compared to the controls. Goodwin and his co-workers concluded that, if genetic factors were involved in the development of alcoholism, this risk was not increased by exposure to an alcoholic parent.

The last phase of the study (Goodwin et al, 1977) examined 49 women from the original pool of adoptees who had an alcoholic parent and compared them to 47 adopted women whose biologic parents had no record of psychiatric hospitalization. The groups did not differ on demographic characteristics including age, education, socioeconomic class, and marital history. The investigators used the same interview procedure as in the previous two phases.

Rates of alcoholism in the women were lower than in the men studied in the previous two projects. Two women in each group were considered either alcoholic or problem drinkers (i.e., had developed problems related to drinking but not numerous enough to meet the authors' criteria for alcoholism), giving a prevalence of 4% of each group. This was against a background of 0.1 to 1% of Danish women in the general population with alcoholism (Goodwin, 1986), implying that there was an elevated rate in the adoptees. However, the small numbers in the sample made it impossible to draw firm conclusions.

The groups were compared on 14 drinking problems, with only one area (alcoholic blackouts) being suggestive of a difference. Of the probands, 22% reported amnestic periods, compared to 6% of the controls. Although of marginal statistical significance ($p < .10$), this was intriguing in that the drinking habits of over 90% of each group were recorded as "moderate," defined as "neither a teetotaler nor heavy drinker." Later work has indicated that a positive family history for alcoholism may cause differences in subjective response to alcohol

(Schuckit, 1984) as well as in biological measures (Schuckit et al, 1987), even when the subject has no history of alcohol abuse.

Also of interest was the finding that both alcohol-abusing women in the control group had adoptive fathers described as alcoholic. This was in contrast to the study of adopted men, where none had a foster parent with known alcohol problems. Again, the numbers were too small to support firm conclusions, but the findings were consistent with a stronger environmental influence on the development of alcoholism in women as compared to men. Such influences could be protective (such as social pressures discouraging women to drink as heavily as men, thus not allowing the expression of a genetic loading for alcoholism) or provocative of alcoholism (such as the possible "alcoholicogenic" influence of living with a parent figure with the illness) or a combination of both.

Cadoret and Gath (1978) examined adoption records in Iowa for adult subjects who had one or more biologic parent with evidence of psychiatric illness, who were separated at birth from the parent(s) and who had no further contact with them, and who were eventually placed in a permanent adoptive home. From the 1646 records examined, 84 adoptive parents met criteria for inclusion in the study and agreed to be interviewed about the adoptee. Forty-five of the adoptees were also interviewed.

Two biologic parents were identified by adoption record review as alcoholic and an additional 4 as problem drinkers; of their children, 2 were diagnosed by explicit criteria (Feighner et al, 1972) as primary alcoholics. The parents of the only other primary alcoholic in the sample had no ascertained psychiatric illnesses. Thus, 2 children of 6 parents with alcohol problems were primary alcoholics, versus 1 child of 78 parents without ascertained alcohol problems, a difference that was statistically significant.

Six adoptees had definite secondary alcoholism (i.e., the onset of the alcoholism was later than another psychiatric illness) and one was regarded as having probable secondary alcoholism. None of their biologic parents had alcohol problems, though 3 had second-degree relatives with such problems. Combining definite and probable cases and primary and secondary alcoholism, it was found that there were 12 parents with alcohol problems themselves or who had relatives (other than the adoptee) with alcohol problems. Six children of these 12 themselves developed definite or probable alcoholism, either alone or in conjuction with other psychiatric illness. This was in comparison to 5 cases of alcohol problems in adoptees from the 72 families without ascertained alcoholism in the first- or second-degree relatives. The authors concluded that genetic factors were implicated in the development of alcoholism and found no effect of environmental factors including socioeconomic class of the adoptive parents, time spent in foster care prior to adoption, age of the adoptee, or presence of psychiatric problems in the adoptive family. Although alcohol problems in the adoptive family were not specifically reported, the authors noted that ". . . a lack of effect of the adoptive environment is suggested by the facts that no other alcoholism was reported in the families where adoptees became alcoholic, and that there were several families in the comparison group where alcoholism in the adoptive father was severe enough to lead to divorce but was not associated with alcoholism in the adoptee" (p. 257).

A second study by Cadoret et al (1980), using the same methodology, interviewed 55 adoptees and their adoptive parents. Also included in the study were 5 adoptees who agreed to be interviewed but whose adoptive parents did not and 32 whose parents were interviewed but who were themselves not interviewed, for a total of 92 cases. In addition to information about psychiatric diagnosis in the probands and in first- and second-degree biological relatives, the authors collected information about the presence of psychiatric disorders in the adoptive home and exposure to "discontinuous mothering" as a neonate prior to adoptive placement. Using the data gathered from this sample, the authors used a log-linear model to predict the development of alcoholism in adoptees, and found that the three factors most predictive were presence of biological first- and second-degree relatives with alcoholism and a history of childhood conduct disorder in the proband. Environmental variables were less predictive than the information about biological relatives, and prediction of alcoholism in the adoptees was not improved when the environmental factors were added to the model. In addition, the authors could not find evidence of any interaction between environmental and family-history variables.

In short, these three adoption studies confirmed earlier family studies implicating the involvement of genetic mechanisms in the genesis of alcoholism but, like the earlier studies, found no pattern of heritability consistent with any common genetic mechanism. Furthermore, the role of environmental influences remained undefined.

The Stockholm Adoption Study, originally reported by Bohman (1978), included a population of 2324 adoptees born between 1930 and 1949 in Stockholm and adopted by nonrelatives at an early age. The system of recordkeeping in Sweden ensured the availability of information about adoptees, their biological relatives, and their adoptive relatives. This information included registrations with community temperance boards for alcohol-related offenses and entries in the Criminal Register. In addition, registers of child welfare officers gave extensive information about occupation and social history, and health data were obtained from the National Health Insurance Board system.

Handicapped children or those thought to be at high risk for heritable disorders were less likely to be considered eligible for adoption, and adoptive homes were carefully scrutinized for stability. This had the effect of decreasing the range of environmental variability, which may in turn have emphasized the importance of genetic factors to some degree (Cloninger et al, 1985).

Early analysis of the data (Bohman, 1978) confirmed the importance of genetic predisposition to alcohol abuse, as in other studies. Cloninger et al (1981) extended the analysis, examining from the total sample the 862 men of known paternity who were placed with nonrelatives before the age of 3 years.

Of the 862 subjects, 151 (17.5%) had records of alcohol abuse, which could be classified as mild (one registration by the Temperance Board and no history of treatment, 7.4% of the sample), moderate (two or three registrations but no treatment, 4.2%), or severe (four or more registrations, compulsory treatment, or psychiatric hospitalization for alcoholism, 5.9%).

This yielded four groups of adoptees: three levels of severity of alcohol abuse and a group of nonabusers. These groups could be distinguished with a high degree of accuracy using information about alcohol abuse in both biological parents, their occupational status, and a history of criminality in the biological father (Table 12.3).

Also, discriminant functions were able to classify the biological parents of the abuser groups. Fathers of mild abusers were characterized by recurrent alcohol abuse without needing treatment, little criminality, and relatively higher occupational status than the fathers of the other abusers, whereas mothers of this group often were themselves mild alcohol abusers. Fathers of moderate alcoholics tended to have low occupational status, criminal convictions, and recurrent alcohol abuse. Their mothers resembled the mothers of nonalcoholics. Finally, the parents of severe abusers resembled those of the mild abusers, except that the fathers' occupational status was the lowest of the four groups.

The fact that these three functions were significant was evidence of genetic heterogeneity between the four groups. Using these discriminant functions, the groups could be classified as having low, mild, moderate, or severe genetic risk for abuse for cross-fostering analysis so that postnatal risk factors could be identified.

In fact, adoptees had a much lower incidence of alcohol abuse than their biological fathers, 18% versus 34%. It was found that those adoptees who stayed with their biological mothers for more than 6 months after birth had 1.5 times the risk of alcoholism as those who did not (23% vs. 16%, $p < .001$). Only one discriminant function involving environmental risk factors proved significant implying (in contrast to the genetic factors) less heterogeneity. Both mild and severe abusers tended to have high values on this function. Severe abusers had adoptive fathers with very low occupational status and extensive hospital care before placement. Mild abusers had similar characteristics, but these were less pronounced (Table 12.4).

Table 12.3. Biological parent variables found by discriminant analysis to distinguish four groups of adopted sons classified according to severity of alcohol abuse ($p < .0001$)*

BIOLOGICAL PARENT VARIABLE[‡]	VARIABLE MEANS OF EACH ADOPTEE GROUP[†]			
	NONE ($N = 711$)	MILD ($N = 64$)	MODERATE ($N = 36$)	SEVERE ($N = 51$)
Alcohol Abuse in Father				
Recurrent abuse (0,1)	.18↓	.31	.44↑	.22
Hospitalization or treatment (0,1)	.12	.03↓	.42↑	.14
Registrations (N)	1.86	1.28↓	5.03↑	1.57
Teenage onset (0,1)	.02	.02	.08↑	.00↓
Alcohol Abuse in Mother				
Registrations ($\sqrt{N}$)	.05	.09	.04↓	.10↑
Criminality in Father				
Convictions if recurrent abuse $(N) \cdot (0,1)$	.40	.55	2.03↑	.25↓
Property crimes (0,1)	.15	.14↓	.25↑	.20
Fraud (0,1)	.12	.17	.22↑	.06↓
Moderate jail terms (0,1)	.10	.08↓	.11	.16↑
Teenage onset (0,1)	.06	.05↓	.14↑	.10
Occupational Status				
Rating in father (1–5)	3.77↓	3.92	4.31	4.41↑
Rating in father if criminal $(1–5) \cdot (0,1)$	.92↓	1.02	2.42↑	1.06
Rating in mother if abuse $(1–5) \cdot (0,1)$	.13↓	.39↑	.14	.29

*From Cloninger et al (1981).

[†]The highest group mean is followed by ↑ and the lowest by ↓ to aid inspection.

[‡]Coding of variables is indicated in parentheses. Categorical (0,1) variable means are the proportion who have the factor. Interaction between two variables was coded as a conditional variable, like the number (N) of convictions if abuse was either absent (value 0) or present (value 1), and was scored as their product (N times 0 or 1).

Table 12.4. Variables about adoptive home environment and replacement experience found by discriminant analysis to distinguish four groups of adopted sons classified according to severity of alcohol abuse ($p < .025$)*

ADOPTIVE PLACEMENT VARIABLES[‡]	VARIABLE MEANS OF EACH ADOPTEE GROUP[†]			
	NONE ($N = 711$)	MILD ($N = 64$)	MODERATE ($N = 36$)	SEVERE ($N = 51$)
Reared by biological mother more than 6 months (0,1)	.26↓	.39↑	.31	.35
Age at final placement ($\sqrt{\text{days}}$)	15.46	15.13↓	18.01↑	16.65
Extent of hospital care ($\sqrt{\text{days}}$)	.71	.46	.33↓	1.39↑
Occupational status of adoptive father (1–5)	2.72↓	2.83	2.78	3.22↑

*From Cloninger et al (1981).

[†]The highest group mean is followed by ↑ and the lowest by ↓ to aid inspection.

[‡]Coding of variables is indicated in parentheses. Categorical (0,1) variable means are the proportion who have the factor.

Cross-fostering analysis showed that both genetic and environmental variables were significant factors in the development of mild alcohol abuse, and that the combination of both genetic and environmental predisposing factors increased the risk fourfold. For the moderate abusers, environmental factors played no significant role; having the genetic background increased the risk ninefold regardless of postnatal environment. The aspects of severe abuse that were different from other forms of alcohol abuse (e.g., low social status) were not significantly increased by either genetic or environmental factors alone. Instead, mild and severe abusers shared most genetic determinants, and the expression of mild or severe forms depended mostly on the postnatal factors such as social status.

Two subtypes of alcohol abuse emerged from this analysis. Type 1 ("milieu-limited") demonstrated significant gene–environment interaction; that is, given requisite genetic factors, postnatal environment influenced the degree of severity of the abuse. Biological parents tended to have repeated problems with alcohol abuse, but no associated criminality. In contrast, Type 2 ("male-limited") alcohol abuse tended to be highly heritable from father to son across different social backgrounds and was associated with earlier onset of alcohol problems and criminality in the biological fathers.

A similar analysis was performed to evaluate alcohol abuse in the 913 adopted women in the Stockholm Study (Gilligan et al, 1988b). Although having a biological parent with alcoholism increased the risk of alcohol abuse in the daughters, it was found that the alcoholic fathers who had an excess of alcohol-abusing daughters themselves had mild abuse and no property offenses, whereas alcoholic mothers of alcohol-abusing daughters tended to be of low occupational status and to have had minimal incarceration for criminality. Furthermore, the susceptibility to alcohol abuse was more often inherited from the mother, rather than from the father.

Alcohol abuse in the biologic fathers alone did not significantly increase alcohol abuse in the daughters, but maternal alcohol abuse by itself increased alcohol abuse in the daughters fourfold, as did the presence of alcoholism in both parents. Although this finding was statistically powerful, most of the adopted-away alcoholic women did not have alcoholic biological mothers. Discriminant analysis was then used to identify other predictive characteristics of the biological parents (Table 12.5), and this function was used in the cross-fostering analysis. Similarly, postnatal factors were used to classify environments into low- and high-risk

Table 12.5. Characteristics of the biological father (BF) and mother (BM) found by discriminant analysis to distinguish adopted-away daughters with alcohol abuse from others ($p < .005$)

BIOLOGICAL PARENT VARIABLES*	VALUE ON DISCRIMINANT FUNCTION[†]	VARIABLE MEANS OF EACH ADOPTEE GROUP	
		NO ABUSE ($N = 882$)	ANY ABUSE ($N = 31$)
Alcohol Abuse			
Registrations of father ($\sqrt{N}$)	+.32	.71	1.07
Any abuse by mother $(0,1)$[‡]	0	.03	.16
Criminality in Mothers			
Months in jail ($\sqrt{N}$)	−.67	.49	.13
Property crimes $(0,1)$	+.35	.05	.10
Fraud crimes $(0,1)$	+.26	.03	.06
Criminality in Fathers			
Months in jail per crime (N)	+.30	1.06	1.17
Property crime $(0,1)$	−.56	.18	.10
Occupational Status			
Fathers' rating $(1–5)$	+.29	3.85	4.23
Mothers' ratings $(1–5)$[‡]	0	4.27	4.51
Mothers' rating if abuse $(1–5)\cdot(0,1)$[‡]	+.69	.20	.74

*Coding of variables is indicated in parentheses. The means of variables that are either present (value 1) or absent (value 0) are the proportion who have that factor.

[†]High positive values on the discriminant function distinguish daughters with abuse from the others. The tabulated values are standardized discriminant coefficients which indicate the relative weight and direction of influence of each variable.

[‡]The interaction (product) of maternal occupational status and the presence or absence of alcohol abuse by her was more discriminating than either variable alone; only the interaction was included in the discriminant function. Occupational status was rated from 1 (professionals) to 5 (unskilled).

types. Alcohol-abusing daughters tended to have had more contact with their biological mothers before placement and less hospital care than the nonalcoholic adoptees. Placement in a rural adoptive home raised the risk of alcohol abuse from 3 to 8%, almost a threefold increase. The only factor identified in the adoptive parents was lower occupational status in the father. Exposure to alcohol abuse in the adoptive parents did not seem to increase the daughters' risk; out of the 27 such adoptive placements only one exposed daughter developed alcohol abuse.

Of the daughters with high congenital risk, 6.7% developed alcohol abuse, versus 2.3% of those of low risk ($p < .02$). High-risk postnatal environment only slightly increased the risk in genetically susceptible women, from 6.7 to 7.7%.

Only one subtype of alcohol abuse (Type 1 or "milieu-limited") was identified, characterized by generally mild abuse and little if any criminality. Postnatal environmental influences (such as having an adoptive father with a low-status occupation and living in a rural environment) appeared to be related to the development of alcohol abuse, but these influences accounted for only about 1% of the total variability in risk.

The characteristics of the two subforms of alcohol abuse identified by the Stockholm Study can be briefly summarized as follows: Type 1 or "milieu-limited" alcohol abuse was found to be transmissible to men and women and to be associated with repeated alcohol problems but no criminality in the biological parents. The genetic vulnerability to alcohol abuse could be extensively modified by environmental factors such that the manifestation of the disorder could be either mild or severe, depending on postnatal experience. In contrast, Type 2 or "male-limited" alcohol abuse, characterized by early onset and an association with criminality, appeared to be highly heritable from biological father to son and its expression was not significantly modified by environmental forces. This form was infrequent in women; in fact, no excess of criminality or alcohol abuse was seen in the daughters of Type 2 biological fathers (Cloninger et al, 1984).

Instead, daughters of Type 2 fathers tended to show an excess of somatoform disorders. These women were characterized by taking an average of two or more sick leaves per year from age 16 on and tended to have multiple unexplained somatic complaints (von Knorring et al, 1987). Among somatizers in general, an association with alcohol abuse and criminality was found (Cloninger, 1987b).

In sum, the Stockholm Study established the existence of distinct forms of alcohol abuse, and showed specific gene–environment interactions associated with its development. Subsequently, several lines of investigation have supported the validity of the distinction. Data from the St. Louis Family Study of Alcoholism reported by Gilligan et al (1988a) also showed heterogeneity in groups of families of alcoholics, and suggested that familial resemblance in "femalelike" (equivalent to Type 1) families could be attributed to multifactorial–polygenic and random environmental influences of roughly equal effect, while resemblance in "malelike" (Type 2) families could be accounted for by a large multifactorial–polygenic effect and a transmissible major effect. This was characterized as the effect of a semidominant gene with low frequency and high penetrance (von Knorring et al, 1987).

More support for the Type 1–Type 2 distinction came from a study that measured platelet monoamine oxidase (MAO) activity. Von Knorring and co-workers (1985) divided 31 male alcoholic subjects into two subgroups based on the findings from the Stockholm Study and found that, while platelet MAO activity of Type 1 subjects did not differ from control values (3.62 ± 0.25 nmol tryptamine/10^9 platelets/min vs. 4.17 ± 0.26), Type 2 values (2.93 ± 0.21 nmol tryptamine/10^9 platelets/min) were significantly lower than both Type 1 and control values. It was also found that the two groups differed on several personality traits as measured on subscales of the Zuckerman Sensation Seeking Scale and the Extraversion subscale from Eysenck's Personality Inventory (EPI). Type 2 alcoholics were found to score significantly higher on Boredom Susceptibility, Thrill and Adventure Seeking, and a modification of the Experience Seeking scale as well as the Extraversion scale from the EPI.

THE HERITABILITY OF ALCOHOLISM: NEW APPROACHES

Family and adoption studies have established that alcoholism is heritable. The pattern of inheritance is certainly not a simple one, and both the expression of the phenotype and the likelihood of its transmission between generations can be altered in specific ways through environmental influences, as shown by the Stockholm Study. Modeling techniques such as the Multifactorial Model can be used to estimate the transmissibility of disorders such as alcoholism and to quantify changes in heritability over time.

Although we can quantify and model the transmissible components of alcoholism, we have yet to answer the question of what precisely is transmitted between generations. A dimensional concept of alcoholism implies that answers are to be found at different levels.

One approach to understanding the developmental sequence leading to alcoholism is to identify the molecular genetic basis of alcoholism—the gene products that are later interactively modified by environmental factors. Molecular genetic studies of alcoholism, using restriction fragment length polymorphisms (RFLPs), hold promise of identifying the structure of genes predisposing to alcoholism. Linkage studies using candidate genes such as those for alcohol dehydrogenases, aldehyde dehydrogenases, or formaldehyde dehydrogenase may prove to be fruitful areas for research. In the absence of identified candidate genes, other techniques such as the use of "shotgun" probes (i.e., using large numbers of DNA probes to cover the entire human genome) or use of hypervariable DNA probes to look for close association with specified DNA sequences is unlikely to be as immediately useful (Devor et al, 1987).

Another complementary approach has already been discussed—subclassifying the alcoholism phenotype into groups that are more causally homogeneous, such as by the Type 1–Type 2 distinction. Specific environmental influences can then be identified and their relative contributions evaluated. Some of these will be found to be nontransmissible, but others, as has been demonstrated, are passed on between generations as part of the individual's cultural inheritance. Such classification should facilitate etiological studies.

Yet another approach focuses on the multifactorial background on which more specific molecular genetic factors are expressed. Cloninger (1987b) has recently proposed a general theory of personality that has specific implications for the understanding of the genesis of alcoholism.

PERSONALITY VARIABLES IN ALCOHOLISM

In order to place the development of alcoholism in perspective, it is first necessary to describe the role of underlying personality traits in the genesis of the illness. Factor analytic studies have repeatedly found that three major dimensions account for the majority of observed variability in personality assessment (Cloninger, 1987a, 1987b), but these cannot help determine the underlying causal structure. Cloninger has defined personality as "individual differences in the adaptive systems, involved in the reception, processing, and storing of information about the environment" (1987b) and has proposed an integrated biosocial theory of personality based on synthesis of data from neuropharmacologic studies on systems influencing learning and adaptation, ethologic studies of learning abilities in animals (where different behavioral systems can be studied in isolation), family studies of genetic and environmental determinants of personality, and psychophysiological and conditioning studies in humans. Based on this synthesis, Cloninger has hypothesized that there are three genetically independent dimensions of personality, each linked to a different brain system, which have predictable patterns of interaction with each other and with specific classes of environmental stimuli. Each brain system is complex, related to many different brain structures and neurotransmitters, but each is primarily influenced by a single monoamine neurotransmitter. These dimensions are outlined in Table 12.6 and are briefly described shortly. Further details are presented elsewhere (Cloninger, 1987b).

Table 12.6. Three major brain systems influencing stimulus–response characteristics*

BRAIN SYSTEM (Related Personality Dimension)	PRINCIPAL MONOAMINE NEUROMODULATOR	RELEVANT STIMULI	BEHAVIORAL RESPONSE
Behavioral activation (novelty seeking)	Dopamine	Novelty Potential reward Potential relief of monotony or punishment	Exploratory pursuit Appetitive approach Active avoidance, escape
Behavioral inhibition (harm avoidance)	Serotonin	Conditioned signals for punishment, novelty, or frustrative nonreward	Passive avoidance, extinction
Behavioral maintenance (reward dependence)	Norepinephrine	Conditioned signals for reward or relief of punishment	Resistance to extinction

*From Cloninger (1987b).

Novelty seeking, modulated primarily by the dopaminergic system, refers to a system of behavioral activation, a heritable tendency toward exploratory activity, pursuit of potential rewards, and avoidance of monotony or punishment. Individuals with higher-than-average scores in this dimension are described as fickle, impulsive, exploratory, and excitable. They are easily interested in new activities but tend to neglect details and easily become bored. In contrast, those lower in novelty seeking but average on the other two dimensions are said to be rigid, reflective, orderly, persistent, loyal, frugal, and slow tempered. They become interested in new activities only slowly, tend to become preoccupied with details, and have difficulty in making rapid decisions. Cloninger (1987a) has suggested that alcohol-seeking behavior may be considered a special kind of exploratory appetitive behavior, implying that at least a subgroup of alcoholics should be expected to be relatively high in novelty seeking.

Harm avoidance, reflecting behavioral inhibition and principally modulated by the serotonergic system, refers to the degree of response to aversive stimuli and their conditioned signals. Those individuals high on this dimension but average on the other two are described as cautious, tense, apprehensive, fearful, easily fatigued, and shy. Low-harm avoidance leads to expression of traits such as being confident, optimistic, relaxed, uninhibited, and energetic. Alcohol and benzodiazepines have been shown to block the expression of behavior learned through negative reinforcement and punishment, and development of tolerance to these agents can be hastened by procedures which increase serotonergic activity, or, conversely, delayed by lowered serotonergic activity (Cloninger, 1987a).

The third major dimension, reward dependence, is based on a system of behavioral maintenance, thought to be primarily related to noradrenergic pathways. Individuals with high values on this dimension coupled with average values on the other two leads are described as persistent, industrious, eager to please, sentimental, and empathic. Those lower than average are described as socially detached, practical, tough minded, and emotionally cool. High-reward dependence is associated with elevated response to social cues and praise, and persistence in previously rewarded behaviors, whereas those low in reward dependence tend not to be sensitive to social reinforcers and quickly terminate activities that are no longer rewarded. This system may be implicated in development of behavioral tolerance to alcohol and loss of control over alcohol intake.

Genetic variation in each brain system is hypothesized to be normally distributed throughout the population. Simultaneous deviations from mean values on more than one dimension lead to the generation of second- and third-order personality trait clusters, and extremes of these variants have been shown to correspond closely to clinically described personality disorders (Cloninger, 1987b). Specifically in regard to the development of alcoholism, two patterns on the triaxial personality model emerge. One group of alcoholics, corresponding to Type 1 and characterized by cognitive anxiety and loss of control over drinking, demonstrates traits of high reward dependence, high harm avoidance, and low novelty seeking. The other, corresponding to Type 2 and characterized by spontaneous alcohol seeking and inability to abstain from drinking, has the opposite personality profile, with high levels of novelty seeking, low harm avoidance, and low reward dependence (Cloninger, 1987a). It is important to note that these underlying personality traits are continuous variables, not discrete entities, and that many alcoholics have features of both. Thus, the Type 1–Type 2 distinction should be regarded as marking the extremes of a spectrum, rather than as manifestations of separate disease entities.

Further refinement of the clinical distinction between the two subforms of alcoholism was performed as part of the St. Louis Family Study of Alcoholism. Segregation analysis of pedigree data showed that different types of symptoms of alcoholism aggregated in separate families, and a discriminant function was generated that could classify alcoholics into their proper groups with a high degree of accuracy (Gilligan et al, 1988). Five Type 1 symptoms and four Type 2 symptoms were identified (Table 12.7).

Other studies have shown consistent differences between the two subtypes in personality traits (von Knorring et al, 1987) and platelet MAO activity (von Knorring et al, 1985) as predicted by Cloninger's hypothesis. Additional support has been given by a prospective longitudinal study of Swedish schoolchildren (Cloninger et al, 1988), which showed that personality traits of novelty seeking, reward dependence, and harm avoidance in 10 to 11 year olds as rated by teachers strongly predicted later risk of Type 2 alcoholism.

SUMMARY AND CONCLUSIONS

In tracing the complex and multiply determined path of alcoholism from genotype through environmental modification to final phenotype, it is apparent that several different levels of analysis are necessary. The transmissible component in alcoholism is not unitary; rather, it is in part composed of a number of specific genetic components. These may interact to influence the individual's vulnerability to developing alcoholism, whereas individual elements may be closely associated with specific manifestations of alcoholism such as particular end-organ diseases. Other genetic factors may be less specific, influencing the development of personality traits that may in turn predispose to alcoholism. Here as well, individual traits or com-

Table 12.7. Alcohol-related symptoms distinguishing
male relatives of female probands from male probands*

DISTINGUISHING CHARACTERISTICS OF MALE RELATIVES
Type 1 Features
Benders
Guilt
Onset after age 25
Loss of control
Cirrhosis/liver disease
Type 2 Features
Inability to abstain
Fights while drinking
Reckless driving while drinking
Treatment for alcohol abuse

*From Gilligan et al (1988).

binations of traits may influence the appearance of particular symptoms during the course of alcoholism, such as a propensity to binge drinking, loss of control, and so forth.

Any or all of these factors, in turn, may interact with environmental influences, with further modification of the phenotype being the ultimate result. Gene–environment interaction has been shown, for example, by the finding that in recent cohorts more genetically susceptible individuals have become alcoholic (i.e., the transmissibility of alcoholism has been increasing faster than can be accounted for by changes in gene frequency alone).

Within the ultimate phenotype of alcoholism, significant variability in the relative importance of many different causal factors remains. In order to best study heritable elements or risk factors for alcoholism, more homogeneous subtypes need to be distinguished. Such efforts in differentiation at the clinical level should be made in parallel with investigation of the molecular genetics of alcoholism, quantitative modeling of segregation patterns of symptoms within families, and assessment of underlying personality traits. By the use of such integrated strategies, many new hypotheses about the genesis of alcoholism can be tested, evaluating the role of specific environmental influences in the setting of more homogeneous genetic backgrounds.

REFERENCES

Amark C: A study in alcoholism. *Acta Neurol Psychiatr Scand* 1951; 26 (Suppl. 70):1–283.

Blass JD, Gibson GE: Abnormality of a thiamine-requiring enzyme in patients with Wernicke–Korsakoff syndrome. *NEJM* 1977; 297(25):1367–1370.

Bohman M: Some genetic aspects of alcoholism and criminality. *Arch Gen Psychiatry* 1978; 35:269–276.

Bohman M, Sigvardsson S, Cloninger CR: Maternal inheritance of alcohol abuse. *Arch Gen Psychiatry* 1981; 38:965–969.

Cadoret RJ, Cain CA, Grove WM: Development of alcoholism in adoptees raised apart from alcoholic biologic relatives. *Arch Gen Psychiatry* 1980; 37:561–563.

Cadoret RJ, Gath A: Inheritance of alcoholism in adoptees. *Brit J Psychiatry* 1978; 132:252–258.

Cloninger CR: Recent advances in family studies of alcoholism, in Goedde HW, Agarwal DP (eds) *Genetics and Alcoholism.* New York, Alan R. Liss, Inc., 1987; pp 47–60.

Cloninger CR: Neurogenetic adaptive mechanisms in alcoholism. *Science* 1987a; 236:410–416.

Cloninger CR: A systematic method for clinical description and classification of personality variants. *Arch Gen Psychiatry* 1987b; 44:573–588.

Cloninger CR, Bohman M, Sigvardsson S: Inheritance in alcohol abuse. *Arch Gen Psychiatry* 1981; 38:861–868.

Cloninger CR, Bohman M, Sigvardsson S, von Knorring A-L: Psychopathology in adopted-out children of alcoholics. *Recent Dev Alcohol* 1985; 3:37–51.

Cloninger CR, Lewis C, Rice J, Reich T: Strategies for resolution of biological and cultural inheritance, in Gershon ES, Mathysse S, Breakefield XO, Ciaranello RD (eds) *Genetic Research Strategies for Psychobiology and Psychiatry.* Pacific Grove, CA, Boxwood Press, 1981.

Cloninger CR, Reich T, Sigvardsson S, von Knorring A-L, Bohman M: Effects of changes in alcohol use between generations on the inheritance of alcohol abuse, in Rose RM, Barrett, JE (eds) *Alcoholism: Origins and Outcome.* New York, Raven Press, 1988; pp 49–74.

Cloninger CR, Reich T, Wetzel R: Alcoholism and affective disorders: Familial associations and genetic models, in Goodwin DW, Erickson C (eds) *Alcoholism and the Affective Disorders.* New York, Spectrum Publishing, 1988; 57–82.

Cloninger CR, Sigvardsson S, Bohman M: Childhood personality predicts alcohol abuse in young adults. *Alcohol Clin Exp Res* 1988; 12:494–505.

Cloninger CR, Sigvardsson S, Gilligan SB, von Knorring A-L, Reich T, Bohman M: Genetic heterogeneity and the classification of alcoholism. *Adv Alcohol & Subst Abuse,* in press, 1988.

Cloninger CR, Sigvardsson S, von Knorring A-L, Bohman M: An adoption study of somatoform disorders II. Identification of two discrete somatoform disorders. *Arch Gen Psychiatry* 1984; 41:863–871.

Cotton NS: The familial incidence of alcoholism. *J Stud Alcohol* 1979; 40(1):89–116.

Devor EJ, Reich T, Cloninger CR: Genetics of alcoholism and related end-organ damage. *Semin Liver Dis* 1987.

Feighner J, Robins E, Guze SB, Roodruff R, Winokur G, Munoz R: Diagnostic criteria for use in psychiatric research. *Arch Gen Psychiatry* 1972; 26:57–63.

Frances RJ, Bucky S, Alexopoulos GS: Outcome study of familial and nonfamilial alcoholism. *Am J Psychiatry* 1984; 141(11):1469–1471.

Frances RJ, Timm S, Bucky S: Studies of familial and nonfamilial alcoholism I. Demographic studies. *Arch Gen Psychiatry* 1980; 37:564–566.

Gilligan S, Cloninger CR: The genetics of alcoholism, in Crow K, Batt RD (eds): *Human Metabolism of Alcohol*. Boca Raton, FL, CRC Press, in press.

Gilligan SB, Reich T, Cloninger CR: Etiologic heterogeneity in alcoholism. *Genet Epidemiol* 1988a; 4: 394–414.

Gilligan SB, Reich T, Cloninger CR: Alcohol-related symptoms in heterogeneous families of hospitalized alcoholics. *Alcohol Clin Exp Res*, 1988b; 12:671–678.

Goedde HW, Agarwal DP (eds): *Genetics and Alcoholism*. New York, Alan R Liss, 1987.

Goodwin DW: Genetic factors in the development of alcoholism. *Psychiatr Clin NA* 1986; 9(33):427–433.

Goodwin DW: Adoption studies of alcoholism, in Goedde HW, Agarwal DP (eds): *Genetics and Alcoholism*. New York, Alan R. Liss, Inc., 1987; 61–70.

Goodwin DW: Genetic influences in alcoholism. *Adv Internal Med* 1987; 32:283–297.

Goodwin DW, Schulsinger F, Hermansen L, Guze SD, Winokur G: Alcohol problems in adoptees raised apart from alcoholic biological parents. *Arch Gen Psychiatry* 1973; 28:238–243.

Goodwin DW, Schulsinger F, Knop J, Mednick S, Guze SB: Alcoholism and depression in adopted-out daughters of alcoholics. *Arch Gen Psychiatry* 1977; 34:751–755.

Goodwin DW, Schulsinger F, Moller N, Hermansen L, Winokur G, Guze SB: Drinking problems in adopted and nonadopted sons of alcoholics. *Arch Gen Psychiatry* 1974; 31:164–169.

Greenwood J, Jeyasingham M, Pratt OE, Ryle PR, Shaw GK, Thomson AD: Heterogeneity of human erythrocyte transketolase: A preliminary report. *Alcohol Alcohol* 1984; 19(2):123–129.

Guze S, Cloninger CR, Martin R, Clayton PJ: Alcoholism as a medical disorder. *Compr Psychiatry* 1986; 27(6):501–510.

Helzer JE: Epidemiology of alcoholism. *J Consult Clin Psychol* 1987; 55(3):284–293.

Hrubec Z, Omenn GS: Evidence of genetic predisposition to alcoholic cirrhosis and psychosis: Twin concordances for alcoholism and its biological end points by zygosity among male veterans. *Alcohol Clin Exp Res* 1981; 5(2):207–215.

Institute of Medicine, Division of Health Sciences Policy: Heritable determinants of risk, in *Causes and Consequences of Alcohol Problems: An Agenda for Research*. Washington DC, National Academy Press, 1987.

Kaczmarek MJ, Nixon PF: Variants of transketolase from human erythrocytes. *Clin Chim Acta* 1983; 130:349–356.

Kaij L, Dock J: Grandsons of alcoholics. *Arch Gen Psychiatry* 1975; 32:1379–1381.

Lange LG, Bergmann SR, Sobel BE: Identification of fatty acid ethyl esters as products of rabbit myocardial ethanol metabolism. *J Biol Chem* 1981; 256(24):12,968–12,973.

Mukherjee AB, Svoronos S, Ghazanfari A, Martin PR, Fisher A, Roecklein B, Rodbard D, Staton R, Behar D, Berg CJ, Manjunath R: Transketolase abnormality in cultured fibroblasts from familial chronic alcoholic men and their male offspring. *J Clin Invest* 1987; 79:1039–1043.

Park, P, Whitehead PC: Developmental sequence and dimensions of alcoholism. *Q J Stud Alcohol* 1973; 34:887–904.

Penick EC, Powell BJ, Bingham SF, Liskow BI, Miller NS, Read MR: A comparative study of familial alcoholism. *J Stud Alcohol* 1987; 48(2):136–146.

Penick EC, Read MR, Crowley PA, Powell BJ: Differentiation of alcoholics by family history. *J Stud Alcohol* 1978; 39(11):1944–1948.

Reich T, Cloninger CR, van Eerdewegh P, Rice JP, Mullaney J: Secular trends in the familial transmission of alcoholism. *Alcohol Clin Exp Res* 1988; 12:458–464.

Reich T, Cloninger CR, Guze SB: The multifactorial model of disease transmission I. Description of the model and its use in psychiatry. *Brit J Psychiatry* 1975; 127:1–10.

Reich T, Rice J, Cloninger CR, Lewis C: The contribution of affected parents to the pool of affected individuals: Path analysis of the segregation distribution for alcoholism, in Robins LN, Clayton PJ, Wing J (eds): *The Social Consequences of Psychiatric Illness*. New York, Brunner/Mazel, 1980.

Robins LN, Helzer JE, Przybeck TR, Regier DA: Alcohol disorders in the community: A report from the Epidemiologic Catchment Area, in Rose RM, Barrett J (eds): *Alcoholism: Origins and Outcome*. New York, Raven Press, 1988.

Roe A: The adult adjustment of children of alcoholic parents raised in foster homes. *Q J Stud Alcohol* 1944; 5:378–393.

Saunders JB, Williams R: The genetics of alcoholism: Is there an inherited susceptibility to alcohol-related problems? *Alcohol Alcohol* 1983; 18(3):189–217.

Schuckit MA: Subjective responses to alcohol in sons of alcoholics and control subjects. *Arch Gen Psychiatry* 1984; 41:879–884.

Schuckit MA, Gold E, Risch C: Serum prolactin levels in sons of alcoholics and control subjects. *Am J Psychiatry* 1987; 144(7):854–859.

Schuckit MA, Goodwin DW, Winokur G: A study of alcoholism in half siblings. *Am J Psychiatry* 1972; 128(9):1132–1136.

Sigvardsson S, von Knorring A-L, Bohman M, Cloninger CR: An adoption study of somatoform disorders I. The relationship of somatization to psychiatric disability. *Arch Gen Psychiatry* 1984; 41:853–859.

von Knorring A-L, Bohman M, von Knorring L, Oreland L: Platelet MAO activity as a biological marker in subgroups of alcoholism. *Acta Psychiatr Scand* 1985; 72:51–58.

von Knorring L, von Knorring A-L, Smigan L, Lindberg U, Edholm M: Personality traits in subtypes of alcoholics. *J Stud Alcohol* 1987; 48(6):523–527.

Winokur G, Reich T, Rimmer J, Pitts FN: Alcoholism III. Diagnosis and familial psychiatric illness in 259 alcoholic probands. *Arch Gen Psychiatry* 1970; 23:104–111.

CHAPTER 13

The Contribution of Twin Studies to Alcoholism Research

E. Jane Marshall and Robin M. Murray

Institute of Psychiatry, De Crespigny Park
Denmark Hill, London, UK

About 1 birth in 100 produces twins; approximately one-third of these are monozygotic (MZ), some one-third are same sex dizygotic (DZ), and one-third opposite-sex DZ pairs. MZ twins result from the division of a single fertilized ovum and therefore share all their genes. On the other hand, DZ twins are produced by fertilization of two separate ova, and therefore share 50% of their genes, on average. Over 100 years ago Francis Galton pointed out that twins provide a natural experiment enabling a separation to be made between the effects of nature and nurture.

The twin strategy has been extensively applied to physical diseases, but the availability of genetic markers means that now there are many other ways of studying the genetics of medical disorders (Vogel and Motulsky, 1982; Weatherall, 1985). This has not been true for personality traits and behavior disorders where there remain few alternatives to the twin method — so much so that one of the hazards of being a twin is being pursued by psychiatric researchers!

Twins have been used to study alcohol-related problems in four main ways. First, investigators have compared similarity (or concordance) in MZ pairs with similarity in DZ pairs to ascertain whether there is a genetic contribution to etiology. Second, drinking behavior has been examined as a continuously variable characteristic, particularly in normal volunteer twins. Third, normal twins have been used to study genetic control over the metabolism of alcohol, and various responses to challenge doses of alcohol. Fourth, MZ pairs discordant for alcoholism have been used to ascertain whether certain characteristics of alcoholics are inherited or are a secondary consequence of the disorder.

THE CLASSICAL TWIN METHOD APPLIED TO ALCOHOLISM

The first twin study of alcoholism was reported in 1960 by the distinguished Swedish psychiatrist Lennart Kaij; only two other studies have examined concordance rates of alcoholism in twins, those of Hrubec and Omenn (1981) and Gurling et al (1981). These studies were carried out in Sweden, the United States, and England, respectively; span 20 years during which secular influences on alcoholism were changing; and employed different definitions of alcoholism and different sampling procedures.

Kaij's Study

Kaij's sample of 174 male twin pairs was derived from the registers of two county temperance boards that received all reports regarding alcohol abuse in southern Sweden. Kaij managed to interview 292 of the total of 348 male twins in their own homes, taking a medical, social, and drinking history. MZ twins were seen a second time for psychometric examination.

Drinking habits were classified according to two schemes, each comprising five categories. The first classification, based on official records, and independent of knowledge about zygosity, yielded an overall proband concordance rate of 25.4% for MZ twins and 15.8% for DZ twins. The second or "compound" classification, derived from both records and interview data, showed an MZ concordance rate of 53.5% and a DZ rate of 28.3%. With increasing alcohol abuse in the proband, the concordance among the MZ cotwins increased. Thus, for chronic alcoholism, 71.4% of MZ cotwins were also alcoholic compared with 32.3% of DZ cotwins.

Kaij assumed that the higher concordance rate in MZ than DZ twins was evidence of the operation of genetic factors. He does not appear to have known that both tuberculosis and leprosy show higher concordance rates in MZ than in DZ twins (Vogel and Motulsky, 1982). Indeed, he believed that since the MZ–DZ ratio was greatest for chronic alcoholism, heredity must be particularly important in the clinical condition. However, one must remember that the vast majority of Kaij's subjects were alcohol abusers, not chronic alcoholics — his 71.4% concordance rate for chronic alcoholism was based on the concordance of 10 out of 14 MZ cotwins. Furthermore, when Murray et al (1983) gave two eminent British clinicians case summaries of Kaij's 10 concordant monozygotic pairs, they concurred with his diagnoses but did not regard the majority of the alcoholic twins as severely dependent.

There are a number of problems with Kaij's study (Murray et al, 1983). Kaij accepted that his sample was likely to be biased toward "psychopaths" and that it was the antisocial behaviour of probands and not their alcohol abuse per se that often lead to their inclusion on the temperance board registers. Indeed, when Kaij (1970) reinvestigated men identified as alcohol abusers by Essen-Möller in an epidemiological survey, only 41 out of 153 alcohol abusers were registered with the temperance board. At the time of Kaij's study, work showing a genetic contribution to psychopathy and criminality had not yet been reported (Lancet, 1983). If his sample was indeed biased to the antisocial alcohol abuser, which then was the primary problem?

MZ concordance rates were higher when the compound classification was used. Kaij believed that this classification was objective because there was agreement between his two classification systems. But such agreement is not evidence that either system was valid. Indeed, the compound classification may have been biased by the extra information gained about the 32 MZ pairs who were interviewed a second time.

Zygosity was established by questioning about similarities and differences of complexion and anthropological traits. The twins were examined side by side as far as possible and only in doubtful cases were blood groups determined. However, alcoholism can drastically change an individual's appearance and Kaij did concede that a few discordant MZ twins might have been concealed in the supposedly DZ group. The relative paucity of MZ twins in his sample suggests that this may have happened.

Hrubec and Omenn's Study

Hrubec and Omenn (1981) examined the computerized medical records of 15,924 white, male twin pairs between the ages of 51 and 61 years who had served in the U.S. armed forces. Medical histories were compiled from military service records, Veteran's Administration records and from questionnaires to determine zygosity and eligibility for the study (returned by 87% of the sample). Zygosity was established by blood grouping in only about 5% of the sample.

Forty-one MZ twin pairs and 28 DZ twin pairs were concordant for alcoholism yielding casewise concordance rates of 26.3% and 11.9%, respectively. Concordance rates for liver cirrhosis were 14.6% and 5.4% for MZ and DZ twins, respectively, and for alcoholic psychosis 21.1% and 6.0%, respectively. These differences were all statistically significant.

When the interaction of concordance for alcoholism and its end points was evaluated, it was found that most of the observed twin concordance for alcoholic psychosis and liver cirrhosis was not a direct result of concordance for alcoholism. The higher MZ–DZ ratio for liver cirrhosis and alcoholic psychosis was considered evidence of a genetic predisposition to the organ specific complications of alcoholism. However, those veterans who fulfilled the criteria for alcoholism in this study had been ascertained through hospital admission records and were more likely to have had a severe alcohol problem with organ-specific complications.

Since none of the twins was interviewed, all information gathered was secondhand. Because of the low prevalence figures (2.6–3.1%), Hrubec and Omenn estimated that they had ascertained only 50% of cases of alcohol-related disorder. MZ twins are more likely to keep in touch with each other than DZ twins so there is likely to have been a bias to more complete information on the cotwins of MZ probands.

Gurling and Murray's Study

So far, only preliminary results from the third study have been published (Gurling et al, 1981; Gurling and Murray, 1987). The sample was derived from a register based at the Maudsley psychiatric hospital in London. Twins with an International Classification of Diseases (ICD) diagnosis of alcoholism or habitual excessive use of alcohol were traced using National Health Service, Department of Health and Social Security, and Home Office records.

This sample is therefore biased toward alcoholics with psychiatric problems and, unlike the other two studies, it includes women. Twenty-nine pairs of MZ twins and 40 pairs of same-sex DZ twins were investigated. Zygosity was determined by blood group in 54%, by resemblance questionnaire in 27%, and by fingerprints in 4%; case notes and reports were used in 12% of the sample. Thus, zygosity determination was more thorough in this study.

The prevalence of alcoholism in twins was similar to that for the hospital population as a whole, so twinning itself did not increase the risk of alcoholism. An adapted version of the Clinical Alcohol Interview Schedule (Caetano and Edwards, 1978) was used to generate a diagnosis of the World Health Organization (WHO) Alcohol Dependence Syndrome (Edwards et al, 1977). The Research Diagnostic Criteria (RDC) definition of alcoholism was determined from a SADS-L interview.

Preliminary pairwise concordance rates for alcoholism in MZ twins and DZ twins were 29% and 33%, respectively, using RDC criteria, and 21% and 25% using WHO criteria. Thus, no genetic predisposition could be detected. There was an excess of females in the MZ group and an excess of males in the DZ group.

In an effort to assess the effect of increasing consumption of alcohol in the British population, concordance rates were examined for twins born before and after 1930; rates in both MZ and DZ twins born after 1930 were greater, but there was no difference between MZ and DZ rates for either group. Thus, the greater availability of alcohol to the later-born twins increased their likelihood of becoming alcoholic, but there was still no evidence for a genetic effect.

Conclusions

The classical twin method has been applied to a variety of behavioral disorders. For example, the first twin study of schizophrenia (Luxenburger, 1928), has been followed by a dozen more, all of which have shown higher concordance rates in MZ than DZ twins (Gottesman and Shields, 1982). The success of such studies persuaded researchers to apply the same strategy to alcoholism.

However, the three reported studies on alcoholism are far from convincing. Indeed, that by Hrubec and Omenn is so lacking in firsthand information regarding the drinking habits of the majority of the sample that it is impossible to make any inferences from it about the genetics of alcoholism. Kaij's study is much more impressive, but even here there must be doubts about the ways in which twins were assigned to different zygosity and drinking categories. The small number of severe alcoholics means that it is best regarded as a study of alcohol abuse in an antisocial population. Once again, Gurling and Murray's study probably only refers to a particular type of alcoholic, in this case those with psychiatric problems.

Setting aside the questionable results of Hrubec and Omenn, we are faced with a situation in which two studies containing 45 and 69 pairs of twins, respectively, with an alcoholic proband, come to diametrically opposite conclusions concerning the operation of genetic factors on alcoholism. The lack of agreement may be a consequence of the different types of alcoholics studied, but a moment's thought produces another reason for the discrepancy—the samples of alcoholics are so small that the divergent results could have occurred by chance (Torgersen, 1987). A less palatable thought, but one that we discuss in the next section, is the possibility that the classical twin method cannot be applied to alcoholism without modification.

TWIN STUDIES OF NORMAL DRINKING

The influence of heredity on normal drinking habits has been investigated using "normal" (i.e., nonalcoholic) twin subjects. This has enabled researchers to study much larger samples and to employ sophisticated biometrical methods rather than rely solely on a comparison of MZ and DZ concordance rates. These studies often estimate such quantities as the proportion of the variance in liability to heavy drinking due to (1) additive gene effects, (2) common family environment (and therefore affecting both members of a twin pair), and (3) specific environmental factors unique to one twin. Thus, such studies can separate different sources of environmental variation.

A number of studies have either investigated only small numbers of twins or else only addressed a few questions about alcohol to their subjects in the course of larger enquiries. These studies are summarized in Table 13.1.

In the first major study Partanen et al (1966) interviewed 902 pairs of male twins from the Finnish Twin Register who were between 28 and 37 years old. Factor analysis of questions relating to alcohol consumption generated three main factors. "Density" was a measure of the frequency of the use of alcohol; "amount" referred to the volume consumed during a single drinking session, the duration of the session, and the degree of intoxication; and "lack of control" related mainly to dependency on alcohol.

Heritability* was estimated at .39 for density and .36 for amount, indicating the importance of genetic factors in normal drinking. However, the social consequences of drinking, namely drunkenness arrests, social complications, and addictive symptoms, did not show any significant genetic effect. Heritability for lack of control was higher in younger (.54) than older (−.07) twins. A second Finnish study (Kaprio et al, 1978) also noted that heritability for total alcohol consumption in males decreased with age and was close to zero in later life. In a study of 3810 male and female twin pairs, Jardine and Martin (1984) underscored the need to take age into account; 60% of the variation in alcohol consumption among younger

---

*Heritability estimates can range from zero to one; zero implies no genetic source of variation for an observed characteristic whereas a value of one implies that all the variation is genetic.

Table 13.1.

RATIO	SEX	NO. TWIN PAIRS	MZ	DZ	CHARACTERISTIC STUDIED	CONCORDANCE MZ	DZ	MZ/DZ RATIO
Conterio and Chiarelli (1962)	M	77	34	43	Drinking/nondrinking	100	86	1.4
					Quantity wine consumed	65	44	1.5
Jonsson and Nilsson (1968)	M	750			Nonconsumption	22	16	1.4
Cederlof et al (1977)*	M + F	12,898	5,025	7,873	Males ⎱ Normal	1.46	1.34	1.09
					Females ⎰ Drinking	1.44	1.34	1.07
					Males ⎱ Excessive	4.96	3.30	1.50
					Females ⎰ Drinking	13.12	6.12	2.14

						INTERCLASS CORRELATIONS		H?
Loehlin (1972)	M + F	850			Hangover	.55	.24	.620
					Never any heavy drinking	.46	.19	.540
					Excess alcohol use	.24	.06	.360
					Drink before breakfast	.15	−.03	.360
Perry (1972)	M + F	84	46	38	Amount alcohol consumed/week			.560
Pederson (1981)	M + F	137	75	62	Consumption of beer	.18	.43	—
					Consumption of wine	.08	.55	—
					Consumption of spirits	.44	.30	.280
					Heavy drinking	.68	.06[†]	
Kaprio et al (1981)	M	5,044	1,537	3,509	Alcohol use	.536	.279	.514

*Coincidence ratios and quotients between MZ and DZ ratios by sex and zygosity.
[†]Competition effect.

males was genetic whereas genetic factors did not appear to operate in older males. Taken together, these findings support the reasonable assumption that genetic factors do contribute to determining drinking habits, but environmental factors play an increasing role later in life.

Clifford et al (1981, 1984a) examined alcohol use in 494 twin pairs from the normal Volunteer Twin Register at the Institute of Psychiatry, London. A postal questionnaire assessed alcohol consumption in two ways, first with items from the Manitoba Health and Drinking Survey and second a weekly drinking diary. The questionnaire also included an assessment of the psychological and physical effects of alcohol and depression and anxiety. Zygosity was determined using the questionnaire of Kasriel and Eaves (1976) (reliability of 95%) and by blood grouping in a subsample.

A biometrical model (Fulker et al, 1980) was fitted to the alcohol consumption data, made up of the usual three parameters—additive genetic variance (VA), variance due to shared family environment of the twins (VCE), and specific environmental variance unique to each individual (VSE). For total weekly consumption in males, VA and VSE made up 40% and 32%, respectively, of the total variance with VCE accounting for the remaining 28%.

The results for females showed a more complex situation, with a negative correlation for alcohol consumption in DZ twins. The explanation seemed to be that the drinking habits of one member of a twin pair influenced the other in the opposite direction (i.e., a social modeling or "competition" effect). This effect is reminiscent of the fact that the families of alcoholics not only contain more alcoholics but also more teetotalers.

In a later paper, Clifford et al (1984b) noted that similarity in drinking habits depended on whether the twins were living together or not. Among MZ twins, the correlation in weekly alcohol consumption was .79 for those cohabiting and .50 for those living apart. The comparable correlations for DZ pairs were .60 and .33, respectively. Gedda and Brenci (1983) have also reported that living together increases the similarity in alcohol consumption among twin pairs. Since MZ pairs tend to live together until later into adult life than DZ pairs, this implies that MZ and DZ twins are subject to differential environmental effects.

These studies should also remind us that the concordance rates for chronic infectious diseases such as tuberculosis and leprosy are higher in MZ than DZ twins, and that one reason for this is likely to be the greater proximity of MZ over DZ pairs. The most satisfactory way of avoiding these possible biases is to study pairs of twins where each was reared in a different family. The disruption caused by World War II in Finland resulted in the breakup of many families. Kaprio et al (1984) therefore studied 30 MZ and 95 DZ pairs separated before age 11 and compared them with matched pairs reared together but living apart. The intrapair correlation in monthly alcohol use was greater for twins reared together than for those who spent their adolescence apart, thus confirming a common family effect. But among men, concordance rates for heavy alcohol use were higher in MZ than DZ pairs both among those reared together and among the separated pairs, thus implying a genetic effect. There were an insufficient number of heavy-drinking females available for analysis.

Conclusions

It has become increasingly evident that there are pitfalls in the interpretation of normal twin data on alcohol use. Twin studies relying on self-report invariably find MZ twin correlations that are approximately .20 greater than DZ twin correlations, no matter what behavior is being assessed (Loehlin and Nichols, 1976). Furthermore, many investigators provide little evidence that their zygosity determination and alcohol consumption histories are accurate. The study of Clifford et al (1981, 1984) was unusual in having a laboratory check on questionnaire determination of zygosity and also in comparing self-report data on drinking habits with levels of serum gamma glutamyl transpeptidase, if only in a small subsample.

Few studies take into account the effects of assortative mating (i.e., the fact that a barmaid who enjoys a drink is more likely to marry a heavy drinking customer than an abstemious clergyman). Several of the early studies examined only males. Indeed, not only are there fewer studies of female twins, but the results for female twins are more confusing, perhaps because of the operation of a within pair mutual effect in female DZ twins. In addition, MZ twins appear to share a more homogeneous drinking environment than DZ twins. It is clear that these two findings fly in the face of the most important assumptions that underpin the classical twin method.

In considering the extent to which we can generalize from the studies reported, we also must take into account the fact that normal volunteer twin registers contain an excess of MZ and female pairs. The Finnish studies are based on national registers and are not subject to this criticism, but nevertheless only cooperative twins could be examined. Estimates of the importance of genetic and environmental influences on the use and abuse of alcohol may therefore be specific to the samples studied. This is especially so because of the major changes in per capita consumption of alcohol, and attitudes toward it, which have occurred in many countries over the last 40 years. Thus, heritability values derived at different times and in different places can be expected to vary.

In view of all these caveats, it is perhaps surprising that so much agreement has emerged.

The major studies agree that there is a substantial genetic effect on many aspects of normal drinking and also that the environmental influence increases with age. This latter fact is consistent with the evidence that the environmental effects are predominantly nonfamilial (i.e., not due to shared upbringing) and that within families environmental effects give rise to differences as much as similarities in drinking behavior (Gabrielli and Plomin, 1985).

Finally, the finding of genetic factor(s) influencing drinking habits does not explain the mechanism of action or determine whether a putative genetic influence on alcohol consumption in normal drinkers will be of similar significance in abnormal drinkers.

ALCOHOL METABOLISM

Normal twins have also been used to examine genetic influences on the absorption, breakdown, and elimination of ethanol after a single challenge dose. Until recently, the sample sizes were small and only males had been studied. Table 13.2 shows that the heritability estimates for blood ethanol elimination ranged from .46 to an unlikely .98.

The small size of these samples fails to provide sufficient power to estimate genetic variance accurately. Martin et al (1985a), therefore, studied 206 pairs of Australian twins after a 0.75-g/kg dose of alcohol; the experiment was repeated four months later in 40 of the pairs. Not only did these investigators show an astonishing tenacity in examining 412 drunk twins, but they subjected their results to a rigorous biometrical analysis.

The heritabilities for peak blood alcohol concentration and rate of elimination of alcohol were .62 and .50, respectively. These figures are quite dissimilar to those of Vesell but are close to those reported by Kopun and Propping who had the next largest sample. In the 40 twin pairs who underwent repeat testing, the repeatability (test–retest reliability) results were .66 for peak blood alcohol concentration, and .39 for rate of elimination. Since the heritabilities did not differ significantly from the repeatability figures, this suggested that all the repeatable variation between people in the way that they metabolize alcohol is inherited.

A small portion (less than 12%) of the nonrepeatable variation could be attributed to differences in drinking experience. Correlations were found between blood alcohol levels and both the total number of years of drinking and the average weekly consumption of alcohol. However, some of the environmental effects were quite ephemeral. For example, the consumption of alcohol on the previous evening was associated with higher blood alcohol concentrations during absorption and lower readings during elimination.

An attempt was made to explain the heritable variation in terms of physical characteristics. The combined contribution of age, weight, adiposity, and lung volume to blood alcohol concentration was less than 10%. As the latter three variables are only partly inherited, the contribution of the four factors to the heritable portion was small.

Female blood alcohol concentrations were higher than those for males throughout. This

Table 13.2. Twin studies of alcohol elimination

	NUMBER OF PAIRS		DOSE OF ALCOHOL	HERITABILITY FOR BLOOD ALCOHOL ELIMINATION
	MZ	DZ		
Luth (1939)	10	10	0.5 g/kg	.63
Vesell et al (1971)	7	7	1 ml/kg 95% ethanol	.98
Kopun and Propping (1977)	19	21	1.2 ml/kg	.46
Martin et al (1985a)	85	121*	0.75 g/kg	.50

*Includes DZ opposite-sex pairs.

could not be explained by differences in skinfold thickness, weight, or lung volume. It might have been related to the difference in distribution of fatty tissue between the sexes.

Martin et al (1985a, 1985b) concluded that short-term environmental factors influence alcohol metabolism, particularly in the absorption phase, but that the repeatable variance in peak blood alcohol concentration and rate of elimination is due mainly to genetic factors.

BEHAVIORAL AND PHYSIOLOGICAL RESPONSES TO ALCOHOL

We all know that individuals differ in their response to alcohol—some become drunk and uncoordinated after a small amount, others appear relatively sober after consuming large quantities. Is this merely a consequence of repeated drinking causing tolerance, or are some people genetically less susceptible to intoxication?

Propping (1977a, 1977b) studied EEG patterns and psychomotor performance before and after alcohol ingestion in 52 pairs of male twins. The MZ twins who had nearly identical EEG patterns in the sober state showed identical EEG responses to alcohol. The EEGs of the DZ twins became more dissimilar as the experiment proceeded. However, there seemed to be little genetic influence on psychomotor responses.

In a preliminary study of 19 pairs of twins from the Institute of Psychiatry Register, Cobb et al (1984) examined physiological variables and psychomotor performance after ingestion of 0.8 mg/kg of alcohol. Genetic factors were found to contribute to the response of heart rate and body sway to the challenge dose. However, changes in blood alcohol, alertness, or craving for alcohol showed little genetic influence.

These studies are subject to the strictures of Martin et al (1978) that they are too small to detect genetic variance adequately. Martin and his colleagues (1985b) investigated psychomotor performance and physiological variables in their 206 normal twins after ingestion of 0.75 g/kg alcohol. As before, the tests were repeated in a proportion of the twins. Alcohol ingestion produced declines in psychomotor performance and increases in blood pressure, pulse rate, and skin temperature. There were sex differences for most measures, in particular for body sway; this was more marked in females than in males even after correction for sex differences in height, weight, drinking habits, and blood alcohol concentrations. Females also reported themselves more intoxicated.

The measures, of course, showed differences between subjects in the sober state. But for many of the tests, extra variation was exposed by alcohol ingestion. This was particularly true for motor coordination, body sway, and systolic blood pressure. An analysis of covariance showed that most of the additional variance exposed by alcohol was genetic in origin. Thus, there are genetic differences between individuals that determine how an individual will perform a given task under the influence of alcohol. The genes controlling these responses are quite independent of those that determine an individual's general level of performance when alcohol free.

Significant correlations were found between performance and blood alcohol concentrations, but this accounted for little of the genetic variance exposed by alcohol. Martin et al (1985a & b) concluded that since blood alcohol concentration seemed to exert such a minor influence on variation in psychomotor deficits, future studies should focus on stages of metabolism subsequent to the initial breakdown of alcohol for the source of this genetic variation.

COTWIN CONTROL STUDIES

The existence of MZ twins discordant for alcoholism provides a unique opportunity not only to detect abnormalities associated with alcoholism but also to determine whether these are inherited and therefore causal to alcoholism or whether they are consequent on it.

CT Scan Changes

Enlarged cerebral ventricles and widening of cortical sulci have been reported in a substantial proportion of alcoholics (Ron, 1983). Attributing these abnormalities to aspects of drinking history has been very difficult (Wilkinson and Carlen, 1980; Ron, 1983), partly because of the problems involved in obtaining an accurate drinking history but also because of the lack of well-matched control groups. Similar neuroradiological abnormalities reported in schizophrenia appear to stem from neurodevelopmental deviance early in life (Murray and Lewis, 1987). The lack of a correlation between computed tomography (CT) scan changes and drinking history has meant that it has been impossible to exclude the possibility that some of the abnormalities found in alcoholism also antedate the illness.

Since cerebral ventricular size is a highly heritable characteristic (Reveley et al, 1982), MZ cotwins discordant for alcoholism offer an almost perfect control group. Gurling et al (1984), therefore, examined ventricular volume in 11 MZ pairs discordant for the Alcohol Dependence Syndrome. The severely dependent twins had significant ventricular enlargement compared with their normal drinking cotwins. Furthermore, the ventricular changes correlated with the length of time the alcoholic cotwin had been drinking over 8 centiliters of pure alcohol per day (4 pints of beer per day or equivalent).

No significant differences were found in a second group of 10 pairs of MZ twins where the proband was a problem drinker but did not meet the criteria for alcohol dependence. However, Table 13.3 shows the intraclass correlations for several CT measures in normal MZ pairs and in the two groups of discordant MZ pairs. It can be seen that the highest correlations were in the normal pairs and the lowest in the pairs discordant for alcohol dependence; the pairs discordant for problem drinking were in an intermediate position. Thus, the use of twins can detect relatively small deleterious effects of problem drinking that would have gone unnoticed in a singleton study.

Brain density is particularly difficult to measure accurately and singleton studies of alcoholics have been very confusing. Gurling et al (1986) found increased density particularly in the frontal lobes in the 12 twins severely dependent on alcohol compared with their normal drinking cotwins. The increased frontal lobe density correlated with the number of years that alcohol consumption exceeded 8 centiliters per day (as had the ventricular volumes).

The finding of increased, rather than decreased, density in alcoholic twins was rather surprising. However, it did not appear to be an artefactual result, and now singleton studies have also noted this (Lishman-personal communication). It may be a consequence of loss of white rather than gray matter as suggested by Harper et al (1985).

Cognitive Deficits

Cognitive deficits have been frequently noted in alcoholics. Although the majority of authorities have considered these to be a secondary consequence of alcoholism, some workers believe they may be primary (Tarter, 1980). Kaij (1960) carried out an early cotwin control study

Table 13.3. Intraclass correlations in normal and discordant MZ twin pairs

| | | MZ PAIRS DISCORDANT FOR | |
| | | | |
CT SCAN VARIABLE	NORMAL MZ PAIRS	PROBLEM DRINKING ($n = 10$)	ALCOHOL DEPENDENCE SYNDROME ($n = 11$)
Ventricular volume	.84	.71	.50
Ventricle–brain ratio	.82	.69	.52
Largest ventricular area	.77	.68	.49

examining this question, but his results did not point to a firm conclusion. In a second co-twin study, Bergman et al (1975) found an association between alcohol consumption and field-dependent cognitive style. Gurling and Murray (1987) administered the Bexley Maudsley Automated Psychological Screening Tests to the same 23 pairs of discordant MZ twins described earlier.

Compared with their more sober cotwins, the 12 severely dependent alcoholics showed significant deficits on visual spatial ability, visual spatial recognition memory, the category sorting test, and the memory and location tasks of the tactual performance test. The 11 problem drinkers did not have significantly inferior performances on specific tests, but when all the tests were combined their overall scores were lower than those of their cotwins. The study provided no support for the idea that psychological deficits predate alcoholism. They indicate that not only does alcoholism have an adverse effect on performance measures of cognition but that detectable cognitive decline occurs even in nondependent drinkers.

Psychiatric Disorder

Many psychiatrists believe that alcoholism is frequently secondary to neurosis and on this basis energetically treat what they believe is the primary neurotic disorder. However, it is equally possible that the neurotic symptoms are consequent upon the alcoholism. Mullan et al (1986) therefore, used the cotwin control method to examine the relationship between alcoholism and neurosis. They assumed that MZ, and to some extent DZ, pairs discordant for alcoholism have similar personality traits and liability to neurosis before one becomes alcoholic.

In both the MZ and DZ pairs, an RDC diagnosis of neurosis (phobia, generalized anxiety disorder, panic disorder, or obsessive compulsive disorder) was more common in the alcoholic probands than in their nonalcoholic cotwins. The latter group had a lifetime rate of neurosis at 19% whereas the overall rates in alcoholic probands (32%) and alcoholic cotwins (38%) were much higher. The excess of neurosis in the alcoholics over the nonalcoholic cotwins suggests that much of the neurosis is a consequence rather than a cause of the alcoholism.

The twins also completed the Eysenck Personality Questionnaire (Eysenck and Eysenck, 1975) and the Severity of Alcohol Dependence Questionnaire (or SADQ) (Stockwell et al, 1983). Among the nonalcoholic cotwins, the mean neuroticism scores for both males and females were within normal limits, but the alcoholics showed significantly increased neuroticism scores. The difference between two members of a twin pair on SADQ scores correlated with the difference between the two members in neuroticism. Thus, the more dependent the alcoholic twin, the more his or her neuroticism score rose, suggesting that the increased neuroticism was a function of the severity of dependence.

Depression: Alcoholics have an increased rate of depression, as do their first-degree relatives. Murray et al (1984) examined the prevalence of RDC-defined depression in the Maudsley twin sample. Eighty-three percent of the alcoholic probands received a lifetime diagnosis of depression, compared with 65% of the alcoholic cotwins and 51% of the nonalcoholic cotwins. These findings imply that depression was secondary to the alcoholism only in a minority of cases. Further analysis suggested that both heredity and some common family environmental factors contributed to the high rates of depression in nonalcoholic cotwins.

Criminality: Alcoholics often have criminal records. Indeed, in the twin study of Kaij (1960), which we discussed earlier, 44 of the 45 probands described in detail had such a record. The frequency of criminal convictions in alcoholic probands and their sober cotwins was studied in the Maudsley sample. Although 20 (41%) of the probands had been convicted of an offense not directly involving alcohol (and many more had alcohol-related convictions), only one DZ cotwin had such a conviction and not a single MZ cotwin did. This strongly suggests that in this particular sample of alcoholics, criminal behavior follows alcoholism rather than the reverse.

Schizophrenia: Kendler (1986) used the same twin register as Hrubec and Omenn (1981) to investigate twins with both schizophrenia and alcoholism. Thirty-four MZ and 47 DZ male twin probands from the overall sample had both diagnoses. Schizophrenia and alcoholism occurring separately were significantly more common in the MZ than in the DZ cotwins, as were cases of schizophrenia and alcoholism occurring together. These results indicate that the genetic factors that predispose to the development of alcoholism and schizophrenia together in the same individual are the same as those predisposing to their occurrence alone.

SUMMARY

Of the three reported twin studies of alcoholism, one suggests a modest genetic influence, one finds no such evidence, and one is methodologically inadequate. Not only are these studies too small to come to any firm conclusions, but it seems that the assumptions of the classical twin method may be violated in alcoholism. The normal twin studies show that the drinking environment may be more similar for MZ than DZ pairs and that heavy drinking by one twin may have a paradoxical effect on the consumption of the second twin. Furthermore, not only do specific environmental effects play an increasing role with age but differences in the cultural influences operating on drinking mean that the contribution of such nonfamilial effects can be expected to vary in time and place.

The work of Martin and his colleagues has begun to elucidate the role of transmissible factors in the kinetics of alcohol metabolism and in the psychomotor and physiological response to alcohol. This type of study, using challenge doses of alcohol, is extremely labor intensive, but in the future it may well be usefully combined with more sophisticated biochemical and molecular genetic approaches.

Finally, it appears that twin studies in alcoholism are more useful in identifying environmental rather than genetic effects. The cotwin control method has already proved its value in examining the effects of alcohol abuse on brain structure and function. It could be applied with benefit to the study of many other aspects of alcoholism.

REFERENCES

Bergman H, Norlin B, Borg S, Fyro B: Field Dependence in relation to alcohol consumption. A co-twin control study. *Percept Mot Skills* 1975; 41:855–859.

Caetano R, Edwards G, Oppenheim AN, Taylor C: Building a standardised alcoholism interview schedule. *Drug Alcohol Depend* 1978; 3:189–197.

Cederlof R, Friberg L, Lundman T: The interactions of smoking, environment and heredity and their implications for a disease aetiology. *Acta Med Scand (Suppl)* 1977; 612:1–128.

Clifford CA, Fulker DW, Gurling HMD, Murray RM: Preliminary findings from a twin study of alcohol use, In Gedda L, Parisi P, Nance WE (eds): *Twin Research 3 Part C. Epidemiological and Clinical Studies.* New York, Alan R. Liss, Inc., 1981, pp 47–52.

Clifford CA, Fulker DW, Murray RM: Genetic and environmental influences on drinking patterns in normal twins. In Krasner N, Madden JS, Walker RJ (eds): *Alcohol Related Problems.* New York, Wiley, 1984a, pp 115–126.

Clifford CA, Hopper JL, Fulker DW, Murray RM: A genetic and environmental analysis of a twin family study of alcohol use, anxiety and depression. *Genet Epidemiol* 1984b; 1:63–79.

Cobb MJ, Blizard RA, Fulker DW, Murray RM: Preliminary findings from a study of the effects of a challenge dose of alcohol in male twins. *Acta Genet Med Gemellol* 1984; 33:451–456.

Conterio F, Chiarelli B: Study of the inheritance of some daily life habits. *Heredity* 1962; 17:347–359.

Edwards G, Gross MM, Keller M, Moser J, Room R: *Alcohol-Related Disabilities.* Geneva, World Health Organisation, 1977.

Eysenck HJ, Eysenck SBG: *Manual of the Eysenck Personality Questionnaire.* London, Hodder and Stoughton, 1975.

Fulker DW, Eysenck SBG, Zuckerman M: A genetic and environmental analysis of sensation seeking. *J Res Personality* 1980; 14:261–281.

Gabrielli WF, Plomin R: Drinking behaviour in the Colorado adoptee and twin sample. *J Stud Alcohol* 1985; 46:24–31.

Gedda L, Brenci G: Twins living apart test: Progress report. *Acta Genet Med Gemellol* 1983; 32:17–22.

Gottesman II, Shields J: *Schizophrenia: the epigenetic puzzle.* Cambridge, England, Cambridge University Press, 1982.

Gurling HMD, Murray RM: Genetic influence, brain morphology and cognitive deficits in alcoholic twins, In Goedde HW, Agarwal DP (eds): *Genetics and Alcoholism.* New York, Alan R. Liss Inc., 1987, pp 71–82.

Gurling HMD, Murray RM, Clifford CA: Investigations into the genetics of alcohol dependence and into its effect on brain function, In Gedda L, Parisi P, Nance WE (eds): *Twin Research 3 Part C. Epidemiological and Clinical Studies.* New York, Alan R. Liss, Inc. 1981, pp 77–87.

Gurling HMD, Murray RM, Ron MA: Increased brain radiodensity in alcoholism. A co-twin control study. *Arch Gen Psychiatry* 1986; 43:764–767.

Gurling HMD, Reveley MA, Murray RM: Increased cerebral ventricular volume in monozygotic twins discordant for alcoholism. *Lancet* 1984, 1:986–988.

Harper CG, Kril JJ, Holloway RL: Brain shrinkage in chronic alcoholics: A pathological study. *Brit Med J* 1985; 290:501–504.

Hrubec Z, Omenn GS: Evidence of genetic predisposition to alcoholic cirrhosis and psychosis. *Alcohol Clin Exp Res* 1981; 5:207–215.

Jardine R, Martin NG: Causes of variation in drinking habits in a large twin sample. *Acta Genet Med Gemellol* 1984; 33:435–450.

Jonsson E, Nilsson T: Alkoholkonsumtion hos monozygota och dizygota tvillingpar. *Nord Hyg Tidskr* 1968; 49:21–25.

Kaij L: *Alcoholism in Twins.* Stockholm, Sweden, Almquist and Wiksell, 1960.

Kaij L: Biases in a Swedish social register of alcoholics. *Soc Psychiat* 1970; 5:216–218.

Kaprio J, Koskenvuo M, Langinvainio H: Finnish twins reared apart IV: smoking and drinking habits. A preliminary analysis of the effects of heredity and environment. *Acta Genet Med Gemellol* 1984; 33:425–433.

Kaprio J, Koskenvuo M, Sarna S: Cigarette smoking, use of alcohol and leisure-time physical activity among same-sexed adult male twins, In Gedda L, Parisi P, Nance WE (eds): *Twin Research 3 Part C. Epidemiological and Clinical Studies.* New York, Alan R. Liss Inc., 1981, pp 37–46.

Kaprio J, Sarna S, Koskenvuo M, Rantasalo I: *Baseline characteristics of the Finnish Twin Registry:* Section II: History of symptoms and illnesses, use of drugs, physical characteristics, smoking, alcohol and physical activity. Helsinki, Finland, Department of Public Health Science M37, 1978.

Kasriel J, Eaves LJ: The zygosity of twins: Further evidence on the agreement between diagnosis by blood group and written questionnaires. *J Biosoc Sci* 1976; 8:263–266.

Kendler KS: A twin study of individuals with both schizophrenia and alcoholism. *Br J Psychiat* 1986; 147:48–53.

Kopun M, Propping P: The kinetics of ethanol absorption and elimination in twins and supplementary repetitive experiments in singleton subjects. *Eur J Clin Pharmacol* 1977; 11:337–344.

Anonymous. Crime as destiny? *Lancet*: 983; 1:35–36.

Loehlin JC: An analysis of alcohol-related questionnaire items from the National Merit Twin Study. *Ann NY Acad Sci* 1972; 197:110–113.

Loehlin JC, Nichols RC: *Heredity, Environment and Personality.* Austin: University of Texas Press, 1976.

Luth KF: Untersuchungen uber die Alkohol blut konzentration nach Alkoholgabe bei 10 eineiigen und 10 zweieiigen Zwillingspaaren. *Dtsch Z Gerichtl Med* 1939; 32:145–164.

Luxenburger H: Vorlaufiger Bericht über psychiatrische serienuntersuchungen an Zwilingen. *Zeitschrift für die gesamte Neurologie und Psychiatrie*, 1928; 116:297–326.

Lykken DT, Tellegen A, DeRubens R: Volunteer bias in twin research; the rule of two thirds. *Soc Biol* 1978; 25:1–9.

Martin NG, Eaves LJ, Kearsey MJ, Davies P: The power of the classical twin study. *Heredity* 1978; 40:97–116.

Martin NG, Perl J, Oakeshott JG, Gibson JB, Starmer GA, Wilks AV: A twin study of ethanol metabolism. *Behav Genet* 1985a; 15:93–109.

Martin NG, Oakeshott JG, Gibson JB, Starmer GA, Perl J, Wilks AV: A twin study of psychomotor and physiological responses to an acute dose of alcohol. *Behav Genet* 1985b; 15:305–347.

Mullan MJ, Gurling HMD, Oppenheimer BE, Murray RM: The relationship between alcoholism and neurosis: Evidence from a twin study. *Br J Psychiat* 1986; 148:435–441.

Murray RM, Clifford CA, Gurling HMD: Twin and adoption studies. How good is the evidence for a genetic role?, in Galanter M (ed): *Recent Developments in Alcoholism.* New York, Plenum Press, 1983, pp 25–48.

Murray RM, Gurling HMD, Bernadt M, Ewusi-Mensah I, Saunders J, Clifford CA in Edwards G, Littleton J (eds): *Pharmacological Treatments for Alcoholism*. London, Croom Helm 1984.

Murray RM, Lewis SW: Is schizophrenia a neurodevelopmental disorder? *Brit Med J* 1987; 295:681–682.

Partanen J, Bruun K, Markkanen T: *Inheritance of Drinking Behaviour*. Helsinki, Finland, Finnish Foundation for Alcohol Studies, 1966; 14–159.

Pederson N: Twin similarity for usage of common drugs, In Gedda L, Parisi P, Nance WE (eds): *Twin Research 3 Part C Epidemiological and Clinical Studies*. New York, Alan R. Liss, Inc., 1981, pp 53–59.

Perry A: The effect of heredity on attitudes towards alcohol, cigarettes and coffee. *J Appl Psychol* 1973; 58:275–277.

Propping P: Genetic control of ethanol action on central nervous system. *Hum Genet* 1977a; 35:309–334.

Propping P: Psychophysiologic test performance in normal twins and in a pair of identical twins with essential tremor that is suppressed by alcohol. *Hum Genet* 1977b; 36:321–325.

Reveley AM, Reveley MA, Clifford CA, Murray RM: Cerebral ventricular size in twins discordant for schizophrenia. *Lancet* 1982; 1:540–541.

Ron MA: The alcoholic brain. *Psychol Med Monograph Supplement 3* 1983.

Shields J: *Monozygotic Twins Brought up Apart and Brought up Together*. London, Oxford University Press, 1962.

Stockwell T, Murphy D, Hodgson R: The severity of alcohol dependence questionnaire: Its uses, reliability and validity *Br J Addiction* 1983; 78:145–155.

Tarter RE: Brain damage in chronic alcoholics, in Richter D: *Addiction and Brain Damage*. London, Croom Helm, 1980, pp 267–297.

Torgersen S: Sampling problems in twin research. *J Psychiat Res* 1987; 21; 385–390.

Vesell ES, Page JG, Passananti GT: Genetic and environmental factors affecting ethanol metabolism in man. *Clin Pharmacol Ther* 1971; 12:192–201.

Vogel F, Motulsky AG: *Human Genetics*. Heidelberg: Springer-Verlag, 1986.

Weatherall DJ: *The New Genetics of Clinical Practice*. London, Oxford University Press, 1985.

Wilkinson DA, Carlen PL: Relationship of neuropsychological test performance to brain morphology in amnesic and nonamnesic chronic alcoholics. *Acata Psychiatr Scand* 1980; 62 (Suppl 286):89–101.

CHAPTER 14

Biomedical and Genetic Markers
of Alcoholism

Marc A. Schuckit, M.D.

University of California, San Diego,
School of Medicine, Alcohol Research Center,
Veterans Administration Medical Center
San Diego, California, USA

INTRODUCTION

There is ample evidence from family, twin, and adoption studies that alcoholism is a genetically influenced disorder (Goodwin, 1985). Although all studies agree (Roe 1944; Murray, 1981), the relative uniformity of results from the adoption work makes it likely that important genetic factors come to play in this disorder.

Even when one assumes the importance of genetic influences, a number of issues remain and impact on the study of biomedical and genetic aspects of this disorder. First, despite the availability of state markers of heavy drinking (Skinner and Holt, 1983; Irwin et al, 1988; Schuckit and Irwin, 1988), the diagnosis of actual alcoholism still rests with a careful clinical history usually obtained from the patient *and* a resource person. This lack of diagnostic precision adds to a probable heterogeneity within samples of alcoholics, a factor that can complicate any genetic study.

An important issue related to the use of historical data for diagnosis is the observation that the same symptoms are likely to be seen in a variety of problems (Goodwin and Guze, 1984). Thus, patients can present with syndromes that meet diagnostic criteria for alcoholism when their primary or first appearing disorder is a major depressive episode, the antisocial personality disorder, or an anxiety syndrome. In these instances, genetic factors involved in the primary or first appearing illness could, at least theoretically, obscure our ability to evaluate the importance of genetic influences in alcoholism. A case in point involves the "dual diagnosis" patients who fulfill criteria for both alcoholism and depressive disorder (Schuckit, 1985b). Severe sadness is relatively common among alcoholics, probably because alcohol can cause serious, although temporary, episodes of depression (Schuckit, 1986b). When the depressive symptomatology developed in the context of problematic drinking (i.e., primary alcoholism with secondary depressive disorder), the sadness is likely to disappear on its own. However, at least 5% of alcoholic males and up to 15% of alcoholic females may have an independent affective disorder (i.e., primary depressive disease with secondary alcoholism). These depressions are likely to appear during abstinence as well as in the context of heavy drinking. Affective disorder is itself genetically influenced (Schuckit, 1985a) and evaluations of populations with primary alcoholism combined with patients who have primary depressive disorder and secondary alcoholism could make it difficult to disentangle data related to the alcoholism risk itself. This is important because alcoholism and depressive disorder congregate in different families and show little evidence of genetic linkage (Angst, 1966; Cloninger et al, 1983).

A similar problem occurs regarding the relationship between alcoholism and the antisocial personality disorder (ASPD) (Schuckit, 1973). In the context of heavy drinking, violent behavior and criminal acts can appear and, while individuals with primary ASPD (with an onset of antisocial behavior prior to the age of 16) are highly likely to develop severe secondary alcohol-related problems (Schuckit 1983b), the ASPD appears to be genetically influenced (Crowe, 1972; Cloninger et al, 1975). Although there is some symptom overlap, the two disorders appear to be separate illnesses. This conclusion is supported by the lack of evidence of an increase in primary alcoholism in the families of men with ASPD (Vaillant, 1982; Hesselbrock et al, 1985), as well as the absence of an increase of ASPD in adopted-out children of alcoholics (Goodwin et al, 1974; Cadoret et al, 1985). Finally, men fulfilling criteria for primary ASPD who develop secondary alcoholism appear to have a clinical course distinct from that observed among primary alcoholics (Stabenau, 1984; Vaillant, 1984; Hesselbrock et al, 1986). It is possible to conclude that "family and adoption data indicate a surprising degree of independence between genetic factors that predispose to alcoholism and those that predispose to ASPD" (Cloninger and Reich, 1981; Cloninger et al, 1983). Based on this information, studies of genetic factors in alcoholism should probably focus on primary alcoholics and exclude patients with primary ASPD and secondary alcoholism.

Another important methodological issue in studies of genetic factors in alcoholism is the need to recognize the possible importance of subtypes of alcoholics. For example, Cloninger et al (1984) have hypothesized at least two types of alcoholism. The first has a later onset, a more benign course, is likely to be seen equally in men and women, and appears to respond to early life environmental events. The second subtype, seen mostly in men, has an earlier onset, a more severe course, and the father is more likely to have committed serious crimes — here, genetic factors appear to be of greater importance (Cloninger et al, 1984; Cloninger 1987). Other potentially important subdivisions of alcoholics could include those with and without close family members with this disorder, subtypes related to age of onset, characteristics related to misuse of other substances, and so on. Thus, the presence of subtypes needs to be considered in any studies of genetic factors in alcoholism.

A third methodologic issue, one underscored by the hypothesized subtype proposed by Cloninger et al (1984) is the need to remember the potential importance of environmental events. Many of the original adoption studies of alcoholics reported that once the impact of a biological alcoholic parent was considered, there was little evidence that being raised by an alcoholic further increased the risk. In fact, in several studies there was a trend for those men who had an alcoholic rearing parent to show a *decreased* risk for the expression of alcoholism in adulthood (Schuckit et al, 1972; Goodwin et al, 1974). However, recent studies have suggested that if one broadens the concept of alcoholism in the rearing family to include more distant relatives, it is possible that this factor might indeed add to the risk (Beardslee et al, 1986; Cadoret et al, 1987). In a similar light, elsewhere in this text we are reminded that peer pressures, the availability of alcohol, and attitudes to drinking and drunkenness seem, by common sense, to all combine to influence the alcoholism risk. These could occur either directly or indirectly through influences on the decision to drink or to occasionally imbibe to excess.

This introduction, therefore, reminds us that biomedical and genetic aspects of alcoholism are complex. The optimal research is interdisciplinary and many of the attributes of children of alcoholics outlined shortly come from collaborative studies using methods described in more detail in other sections of this text. While we consider the results of studies of populations at high risk for alcoholism, it is also important to remember that heterogeneity remains within the studied samples and that any specific investigation can only focus on a limited part of the picture.

METHODS FOR STUDY OF MEN AT HIGH RISK FOR ALCOHOLISM

The studies described in the next section are searching for trait markers of an alcoholism vulnerability, observable either before the illness develops or while problems are in remission. Unfortunately, heavy drinking and the associated life-style with the increased risk for trauma and nutritional deficiencies are capable of producing in some people biological, physiological, and emotional or cognitive changes that might remain for extended periods after abstinence (Schuckit, 1985a). Thus, characterizing alcoholics after even 20 years of abstinence could reveal cirrhosis, brain damage, evidence of a peripheral neuropathy, or problems that did not predate the alcoholism and are not appropriate trait markers of a vulnerability toward this disorder. As a result, most investigators have chosen to attempt to identify trait markers by observing individuals at high risk for the future development of alcoholism but who have not yet experienced major alcohol-related life problems.

There are at least three possible approaches for studies of populations at high risk for alcoholism. The first, and most potentially potent, is evaluating children of alcoholics adopted out and reared by nonalcoholic parents. These cohort investigations of offspring of alcoholics are time consuming and expensive and few examples can yet be cited. The second approach is to intensively study a limited number of families of alcoholics, searching for markers that are present in alcoholic relatives, but absent in nonaffected family members. Although such studies can give useful information about the probable pattern of inheritance of alcoholism, these approaches require personal interviews and testing of multiple generations of single families, making them time consuming and expensive, and laboratories are rarely able to gather data from more than a limited number of cases. Most studies of populations at high risk for alcoholism have utilized cohorts or groups of normal individuals chosen because of their date of birth, their educational institution, or through their use of public resources or contact with police agencies. It is this approach that is emphasized here.

One large cohort of 9000 complication-free, full-term births (some of whom have an alcoholic biological parent) born in Copenhagen between 1951 and 1961 is presently being evaluated and has produced some of the results discussed below (Schulsinger et al, 1986). Other investigations have focused on biological sons of alcoholics who are identified at various ages, evaluated, and in some instances challenged with ethanol. This approach has included evaluations of male cohorts in their late teens to early twenties, children in their prepubertal to early adolescent years, as well as a group of women (Schuckit, 1984a; Begleiter, 1987; Lex and Mendelson, 1987).

As an example, our laboratory has focused on drinking, but not yet alcoholic, sons of alcoholics who were selected through a mailed questionnaire sent to students and staff at the University. Other studies of high risk populations have used slightly different methods. For example, Tarter et al (1984) have evaluated cognitive and psychomotor test performance without ethanol challenges in a series of men whose fathers were receiving care in an alcohol treatment program. The same investigators and others have also selected males in their mid-teens who were in trouble with the law (Schaeffer et al, 1984) or utilized labor unions, social organizations, and churches to identify both male and female children of alcoholics. In another series of studies, Begleiter et al (1984) focused on community volunteers in their preteen years to study electrophysiological attributes of young sons of alcoholic fathers, and a similar approach was used by Behar and colleagues (1983).

In summary, based on the hypothesis that alcoholism is likely to be a polygenic multifactorial disorder, a number of laboratories have turned toward the search for trait markers of a vulnerability to this disorder. Most investigations are presently focusing on evaluations of young men and women at high risk for the future development of alcoholism who are family history positive (FHP), usually defined through primary alcoholism in a biological father. These subjects are compared to family history negative (FHN) controls who were selected because of an absence of alcoholism in any close biological relative. All studies measure baseline attributes of FHP and FHN individuals, and some laboratories, our own included, go on to observe possible FHP–FHN differences after a beverage challenge. The next section reviews some results from these studies of populations at high risk for alcoholism.

RECENT RESULTS FROM EVALUATIONS OF POPULATIONS AT RISK FOR ALCOHOLISM

This section presents findings relating to several potential trait markers of a vulnerability toward alcoholism. It is assumed that the reader will turn to some recently published reviews as well as some of the original papers for a more detailed description of research methodology and results (Schuckit, 1985a, 1986a). Whenever possible, emphasis is placed on findings that have been published or presented within the last two years.

In reviewing this section, it is important to keep the findings in perspective. Even after a potential marker has been identified and replicated in other laboratories, there are important research steps that must still be taken. First, the association between the marker that has been identified in children of alcoholics and the future development of alcoholism must be established through follow up studies. Second, the genetic basis of the biological marker must be determined. Third, the actual mechanisms responsible for the expression of the vulnerability need to be studied.

The investigations outlined below are divided into possible differences between FHPs and FHNs at baseline (without challenges), and results observed after drinking alcohol.

Some Baseline Differences

A promising lead for baseline differences between FHPs and FHNs comes from evaluations of *event-related potentials* (ERPs). These are computer-averaged brain waves measuring electrophysiological brain reactions to stimuli (Porjesz and Begleiter, 1983). One form of the ERP, a positive wave observed approximately 300 ms after a stimulus, the P300 or P3, occurs in normal individuals after they experience an anticipated, but rare, event. Following up on observations of a nonreversible flattened amplitude of P3 in alcoholics, Begleiter et al (1984) documented a similar small P3 wave in the preadolescent sons of alcoholics using a rather complex visual paradigm. These basic findings have been replicated by Begleiter's group (Begleiter, 1987), and a similar result has been reported in a late teen to early twenties sample of men in Connecticut (O'Connor, 1985). This latter finding is important because the original reports focused on inner-city black children of hospitalized alcoholics, while the Connecticut investigation studied Caucasian men with relatively high levels of functioning. However, also utilizing Caucasian students at a university, Polich and Bloom (1988) and Polich et al (1988) were unable to replicate these findings using a less difficult auditory event-related task. These findings raise a question about the generalizability of the P3 findings to more highly functioning groups and/or to a less complex behavioral task but do not undercut the probable importance of the P3 as the potential marker within at least some populations.

A second potentially important baseline correlate of the family history of alcoholism might involve *neuropsychological deficits*. Some differences in cognitive test results have been observed between healthy FHP and FHN men selected from the cohort of children born in a Copenhagen hospital between 1959 and 1961 (Drejer et al, 1985). Pregnant women were generally referred to this facility because of expected difficulties in delivery, and these children became part of a neonatal project evaluating possible problems at birth and at one year. From that original cohort of 9125 children, 488 offspring with alcoholic fathers were identified, including 255 men, 32 of whom had died or who had immigrated by the time of the study. This left 223 sons of alcoholic fathers plus a selected group of 107 control sons of nonalcoholics for evaluation. Of these, only 134 FHPs and 70 FHNs (approximately 60% of the original sample) were successfully followed up at a mean age of 19, when they were given a series of 12 neuropsychological tests generating 17 scores. Out of the 17 values the two family history groups were similar on 14 (82%). The three tests on which the FHPs performed significantly more poorly included the vocabulary subtest of the Wechsler Adult Intelligence Scale, errors on the Halstead–Reitan Category Test, and errors on the Porteus Maze. Using the same sample, Knop and colleagues (1985) reported data on childhood behavior for 95 of the 223 FHPs (43%) and 49 of the original 107 controls (46%). Information on this subset of men revealed that more of the FHPs had to repeat a grade (20% versus 6%), had been placed in a special class (20% versus 11%), or had been referred to a school psychologist (51% versus 34%). However, the teacher's questionnaire revealed that the FHPs and FHNs were similar on signs of nervousness, violence, levels of demonstrated independence, mathematical proficiency, and evidence of withdrawn behavior.

Another approach to studying possible neuropsychological deficits in sons of alcoholics utilized a subgroup of boys referred for evaluation from the juvenile court to a psychiatric facility (Tarter et al, 1984). Of these 101 referrals, 41 delinquent, Caucasian males with a mean age of 16 years and 9 years of schooling were selected for evaluation, including 16 who had an alcoholic biological father and 25 who had no known close alcoholic relative. Overall, the two groups were similar on the Wechsler Intelligence Scale, and the Childhood History Checklist revealed no significant differences on most items. However, the FHPs had lower scores for reading comprehension and poorer performance on the auditory attention span for words and for objects. FHPs also performed more poorly on verbal intelligence, several memory tests, and on the Trail Making Test. On the other hand, Workman-Daniels and Hesselbrock (1987) evaluated 21 young adult offspring of alcoholic parents and 21 controls with a battery of neuropsychological test measures including the Category Test, Trail Making Test, the Wechsler Memory Test, and the Wechsler Adult Intelligence Scale, among others. Their findings did not suggest that cognitive deficits distinguish persons with a family history of alcoholism. Consistent with those negative results is our analysis of 24 matched FHP–FHN pairs (48 men) in our laboratory (Schuckit et al, 1987). At baseline (before beverage challenge), the FHPs and FHNs demonstrated no significant difference on the total nor component test scores of the Halstead Category Test, showed no differential on the Trail Making Test, and had similar scores on our measures of motor and cognitive performance. Also, an ongoing study of 50 children of alcoholics and 50 controls in their mid-teens found no significant differences on verbal, performance, or total IQ scores (Johnson, 1987). These findings as well as those of Workman-Daniels and Hesselbrock raise the possibility that FHPs and FHNs who are carefully matched on the usual drinking and drug use histories and who are selected from relatively functional groups (such as students or employed individuals) demonstrate little consistent evidence of neurocognitive test performance impairment. Although these groups certainly represent the majority of individuals in the United States, this does not negate the possibility that other samples of children of alcoholics, especially those focusing on individuals already in trouble with the law or those residing in inner city areas, might demonstrate neurocognitive deficits as part of their clinical picture. However, it still needs to be demonstrated that these latter consequences did not mostly reflect the results of trauma and nutritional deficiencies.

A third type of baseline measure used for comparing FHPs and FHNs involves patterns of *enzymes* or *biochemical markers*. Two relevant enzymes, discussed in detail earlier, are the patterns of alcohol and acetaldehyde metabolizing proteins. At least within Oriental groups, the genetically controlled absence of the low K_m aldehyde dehydrogenase (ALDH) isoenzyme results in significantly elevated levels of acetaldehyde and subsequent physiological discomfort after drinking (Goedde et al, 1979, 1983; Harada et al, 1983). The one-third to one-half of Orientals missing the low K_m form may be less likely to drink or drink heavily, and there is evidence that they have a significantly lower alcoholism risk than the remaining Orientals (Suwaki and Ohara, 1985). Thus, at least within one population group there is a genetically controlled isoenzyme pattern that appears to have a significant correlation with the alcoholism risk.

An additional example of a protein marker that might associate with the alcoholism risk is monoamine oxidase (MAO), an enzyme important in the degradation of brain neurotransmitters. This has been reported to have abnormally low activity levels in alcoholics, although it is not clear whether this activity returns to normal after an extended period of abstinence (Sullivan et al, 1979). There is preliminary evidence that sons of alcoholics may also demonstrate lower levels of MAO activity, although most studies have demonstrated only a trend and not significant differences from control populations (Schuckit et al, 1982). To echo some of the comments made in the introductory section to this chapter, Oreland and colleagues (1985) suggest that the MAO activity levels may be especially low in children of alcoholics demonstrating the type 2 subgroup described by Cloninger et al (1984) — men with an earlier onset and more severe course for their alcohol-related problems.

Another type of baseline measure used to potentially differentiate FHPs from FHNs focuses on *personality*. This approach relates to the observation that, at least among the general population, those who seek to drink and those who drink more heavily may be more susceptible to boredom or more likely to be sensation seekers (MacAndrew 1979; de Wit et al, 1987), and observations that alcoholics compared to controls can demonstrate relatively unique patterns on a variety of personality tests. The latter includes subtests of the Minnesota Multiphasic Personality Inventory (MMPI), (MacAndrew, 1979; Saunders and Schuckit, 1981; MacAndrew, 1986), feelings of control over one's destiny, levels of anxiety, and so on. However, once the focus is placed on primary alcoholics rather than on individuals with primary ASPD or primary drug abuse, it is difficult to document whether these personality attributes continue after years of abstinence. The test results might relate to life stresses as well as effects of ethanol on brain functioning and not be observable before the alcoholism developed (Kammeier et al, 1973; Vaillant, 1983). Depending on the population studied, various subgroups of FHPs have been shown to differ from FHNs on a number of possible tests, including a potential association between the alcoholism risk, the Tridimensional Personality Questionnaire (TPQ), and Cloninger's type 2 alcoholics (Schulsinger et al, 1986; Cloninger, 1987). On the other hand, in a 33-year follow-up of a cohort originally studied at age 14, Drake (1987) found no association between earlier personality attributes and later alcoholism. Also, tests of functional sons of alcoholics in their teens to early twenties carried out in our laboratory have revealed no personality differences on the Locus of Control Scale, the Eysenck Personality Inventory, various subtests of the MMPI, measures of trait anxiety, nor on an indirect measure of personality, the Rod and Frame Test. Corroborating evidence has come from findings generated in additional laboratories (Saunders and Schuckit, 1981; Schuckit 1982; Schuckit 1983a; Schuckit and Penn, 1985; Manning 1986; Tarter et al, 1986).

The diversity of test methods, the span of populations studied, and different approaches to data analyses make it difficult to draw many definitive conclusions from this review of baseline comparisons of FHPs and FHNs. Both the quality of the data and the relative consistency of results make it likely that P3 amplitude is a potentially important marker of an alcoholism vulnerability, at least within some populations of children of alcoholics. Measures of blood enzymes, especially ALDH patterns and MAO, are also intriguing and may add a useful dimension in this area of research, especially relating to alcoholic subtypes. However, it is impossible to draw valid conclusions regarding other potential baseline measures including impairment on cognitive functioning and personality profiles.

Results from Ethanol Challenges

These studies are a logical progression of the baseline evaluations. Here, not only are subjects evaluated when they enter the laboratory, but they also receive an ethanol challenge. Possibly reflecting the need to use clinically relevant doses of beverage alcohol, most of these studies are limited to individuals age 18 or over.

Subjects for the challenge investigations are tested in laboratory conditions over between

1 and 3 sessions. Using our work as an example, men selected for study are subsequently tested individually on three occasions, where they receive placebo, 0.75 mL/kg of ethanol, or 1.1 mL/kg of beverage alcohol. Subjects are unaware of the hypotheses being tested, and the two family-history groups are similar on scores of the effects they expect to feel from three drinks (Schuckit, 1984a). The ethanol is given as a 20% by volume solution (for active beverage) in a sugar-free, noncaffeinated beverage drunk over a 10-minute period. The carbonation, room temperature, and percentage of ethanol per volume were chosen to maximize absorption of ethanol in the small intestine. Before the challenge, laboratory personnel determine the subject's baseline level of functioning on a variety of cognitive and psychomotor tests, mood and anxiety scales, and personality measures and draw blood for a variety of tests including hormonal levels. After drinking the beverage, individuals are observed for 3 to 4 hours during which their reactions to the two doses of ethanol and placebo are established. A number of findings have been generated from these investigations.

A Decreased Reaction to Ethanol

A consistent result from the challenge studies in various laboratories is documentation of a *decreased intensity of reaction to ethanol in sons of alcoholics.* Differences between the two family history groups after ethanol were observed despite identical blood alcohol concentrations (BACs), similar histories on the usual quantity and frequency of drinking, and similar reactions to placebo. The first area of FHP–FHN differences involved subjective feelings of intoxication measured on an analogue scale at baseline and again at regular intervals after drinking. Subjects were required to rate the intensity of different aspects of intoxication including overall drug effect, dizziness, nausea, feelings of discomfort, levels of high, and so on. Despite all the similarities between the FHP and FHN groups outlined above, the FHP men rated themselves significantly less intoxicated than did the FHNs. Overall, FHN subjects scored approximately 40% higher on the "drug effect" item over the 4 hours after the lower ethanol dose challenge, and scored almost 25% higher after the high dose (Schuckit, 1984a). In both settings, the maximum group differences were observed 60 to 120 minutes after the drink had been consumed. Similar findings have been replicated on several occasions in our own laboratory and have been reported by Pollock et al (1986), Erwin (1987), Wilson (1987), and by O'Malley and Maisto (1985).

In our own laboratory, as well as in several others, FHP subjects also demonstrated a smaller decrement in psychomotor performance after drinking. For example, to measure the level of sway in the upper body we asked subjects to stand still with hands at their sides and feet together. Although there were no group differences at baseline or after consuming placebo, the FHN subjects showed significantly greater increases in body sway after drinking an active dose of ethanol (Schuckit, 1985c). A similar trend for group differences was reported by Lex and Mendelson (1987) using a sample of young adult women in Boston, and a trend in the same direction was noted for men by Erwin (1987) and by Wilson (1987).

The third domain of reaction to ethanol in FHPs and FHNs has involved an evaluation of hormonal responses to a beverage challenge. Our laboratory has focused on two hormones released in different parts of the body but known to change with appropriate doses of ethanol. Thus, prolactin and cortisol were selected as potential objective measures of the intensity of reaction to alcohol. Preliminary analyses of changes in these hormones initially revealed less intense responses in FHP subjects for cortisol and prolactin after drinking, although those observations were carried out without placebo controls (Schuckit et al, 1983; Schuckit, 1984b). Subsequently, both hormones have been reevaluated in a new sample of 30 FHP–FHN pairs (60 men), each of whom were exposed to the full three-dose paradigm. Results for prolactin demonstrated that even after controlling for hormonal changes following placebo, the sons of alcoholics demonstrated significantly lower prolactin levels after the high-dose ethanol challenge, with a trend in the same direction after the low-dose alcohol (Schuckit et al, 1987a). The cortisol results following the three-dose challenge also corroborated the earlier findings, demonstrating that the FHPs developed lower cortisol levels after drinking the higher-dose ethanol, although no significant changes in cortisol were observed in either group after the low-dose challenge (Schuckit et al, 1987b; Schuckit and Gold, 1988).

Several other interesting hormonal differences between FHPs and FHNs have also been noted. Erwin (1987) has evaluated 20 FHP–FHN pairs after alcohol, reporting that the FHNs demonstrated a greater decrease in beta endorphin after drinking. In addition, following up on earlier observations in alcoholics, Moss (1986), Linnoila (1985), and George et al (1986) carried out an ethanol challenge in a series of 9 FHPs and 9 controls aged 18 to 25 years. Infusion of thyrotropin-releasing hormone (TRH) resulted in a greater level of increase in thyroid-stimulating hormone (TSH) in the sons of alcoholics than in controls (George et al, 1986; Moss, 1986). Each of these findings requires further corroboration before they can be properly placed in perspective.

Physiological Responses to Ethanol

Ethanol challenge tests have also been carried out in the context of several physiological measures. For example, background electroencephalograms (EEGs) have demonstrated an apparent lower level of alpha power in alcoholics compared to controls, findings that tend to remain even after protracted periods of abstinence. Recognizing the importance of genetic regulation of EEG patterns, several investigators have been able to demonstrate similar potential differences between sons of alcoholics and controls. Thus, before an ethanol challenge the FHPs were more likely to demonstrate lower amounts of alpha power and also showed greater increases in this frequency band following a modest ethanol challenge (Volavka et al, 1982; Pollock et al, 1983). Several additional physiological evaluations of relatively small samples include the documentation by Linnoila (1985) of less intense changes in saccadic eye movement in FHPs following a challenge with a benzodiazepine, and the evaluation of nine FHP/FHN pairs of Newlin and Aldrich (1986) showing possible differences on intensity of autonomic response to an ethanol challenge.

In summary, there is relatively consistent evidence that sons and daughters of alcoholics in their late teens to early twenties differ from appropriate controls when challenged with modest doses of ethanol. Much work remains to be done in order to demonstrate whether the decreased intensity of reaction correlates with the actual future development of alcoholism. Even if this were true, the intensity of behavioral or biological response to ethanol is an imperfect marker at best, because subjects and controls must be matched as carefully as possible on demographic characteristics and substance intake histories as these could impact changes observed after an ethanol challenge. These factors make it difficult to apply this specific series of measures to multiple members of multiple generations of families. It is hoped, however, that the present studies will lead to greater understanding of the actual biological mechanisms contributing to the decreased intensity of response to alcohol challenges. This in turn might help identify a more appropriate protein marker by quantity and frequency of alcohol intake.

CONCLUSIONS AND IMPLICATIONS

The purpose of this chapter is, in part, to give a reference for individuals interested in understanding more about recent findings on biomedical and genetic aspects of alcoholism by presenting some of the most promising and interesting results from studies of populations at high risk, and, whenever possible, placing these into clinical and research perspectives.

It is unlikely that anyone is predestined to alcoholism or that all those predisposed exhibit the same mechanism of risk. Rather, there are probably multiple biological and genetically influenced factors that increase or decrease an individual's future risk for developing serious and pervasive alcohol-related life problems. For example, it is possible that in a heavy-drinking society that pushes both drinking and drunkenness, an impaired ability to use internal feeling states to monitor modest levels of intoxication could put some individuals at a handicap in their ability to learn when to stop drinking during an evening. Thus, people more sensitive to the effects of alcohol can learn by trial and error what happens when they pass beyond modest feelings of intoxication, while those less sensitive may have more trouble using internal cues to tell them when to stop drinking. If such a high risk individual had opted to become a nondrinker or if he or she followed an absolute rule of never imbibing more than two or three drinks during an evening, then the theoretical biological factors would have no influence on the final alcoholism risk. On the other hand, if the person tries to drink the way other people do in society, he or she is more likely than his coeval to develop more persistent and pervasive alcohol-related life problems. Once the heavy intake is established, a different set of factors relating to psychological and physical dependence as well as acute and protracted abstinence symptoms could then perpetuate the disorder and increase the chance for exacerbations.

It would seem likely that even if the above scenario is valid, there are probably multiple biological factors that could impact on the sensitivity to ethanol. One could relate to a general body or central nervous system (CNS) ability to adapt quickly to external stimuli, including alcohol effects. Another series of possible influences could involve specific neurochemical systems as, for example, dopamine tone and serotonin activities have been shown to possibly influence reactions to ethanol and/or the desire to imbibe fluids (Naranjo et al, 1985). It might also be feasible that mechanisms impacting on cellular tolerance, such as changes in cell membrane fluidity, could influence the alcohol sensitivity (Goldstein, 1983). These examples are listed to demonstrate the diversity of biological factors that might be genetically influenced and that might in turn impact on the alcohol sensitivity. In each of these instances, one would expect an interaction between biology and the environment to give the final alcoholism risk. Equally compelling and complex postulations could be formed regarding the potential importance of the P3, baseline neurocognitive deficits, or background cortical EEGs as they relate to the alcoholism risk.

At this point in the research on biological mediators of a genetic influence, the methodologies being used are of as much interest as the results themselves. In general, researchers have taken advantage of persistent differences between alcoholics and control subjects to identify foci for studies of populations at high risk for the future development of alcoholism. Potential trait markers of greatest interest are those that not only differentiate alcoholic from control subjects but also retain their efficacy with extended periods of abstinence. It is these measures that are generally used to compare the children of alcoholics and children of controls.

The results of the studies of populations at high risk for alcoholism are affected by the research approaches. Different markers might be identified in young prepubertal children than in older or highly functional children of alcoholics. Data might also be affected by the definition of alcoholism used and by whether children of primary or secondary alcoholics were evaluated.

This review has focused on only one aspect of investigations of genetic factors as they might relate to the alcoholism risk. Important animal studies are also helping to elucidate the biological and genetically controlled factors that can impact on the choice of an organism to drink or continue drinking, susceptibility to the development of tolerance and physical dependence, and levels of brain sensitivity to the effects of alcohol (Deitrich and Spuhler, 1984; Li, 1984). Aspects of these studies are presented elsewhere in the text. A decision was also made to emphasize studies on Occidental groups, although additional important factors have been demonstrated to be of specific importance in Orientals, and one might hypothesize the possibility that yet other factors might impact on the rate of alcoholism among Jews and Native Americans.

The findings presented in this chapter contain a number of clinical and research implications. First, the studies outlined underscore the possibility that both biological and genetic factors are important in the vulnerability toward alcoholism. Taken together with family, twin, and adoption studies, the results can be used to highlight the importance of biological factors and to emphasize the probability that alcoholism is not just a moral weakness.

Second, the series of studies contains implications for the prevention of alcoholism. The fourfold increased risk for alcoholism in children of alcoholics emphasizes how vulnerable this particular group is to the development of alcohol-related life problems. These individuals might be chosen as a focus for intensive prevention efforts in the future. Hopefully, some of the differences between children of alcoholics and controls might also indicate areas of research that might identify those factors associated with the highest risk. This in turn could help markedly improved prevention efforts.

Third, identification of the biological factors associated with a vulnerability toward alcoholism could help clinicians develop more specific and effective treatments. Further progress will also help to identify those sons and daughters of alcoholics who have inherited the traits that increase the vulnerability. These individuals can then be followed over time in order to identify the social and cultural factors that maximize the chances for expression of the vulnerability as well as the factors that might provide some protective action. It is possible that manipulation of environmental influences might prove to be as effective as possible changes in biological attributes.

REFERENCES

Angst J: *Zur Aetiologie und Nosologie endogener depressiver.* Psychosen. Berlin, Springer-Verlag, 1966, pp 182–186.

Beardslee WR, Son L, Vaillant GE: Exposure to parental alcoholism during childhood and outcome in adulthood: A prospective longitudinal study. *Brit J Psychiatry* 1986; 149:584–591.

Begleiter H: Neurophysiology in boys at risk of alcoholism. Presented at the Conference The Genetics of Alcoholism: A Family Legacy? New York, April 2–3, 1987.

Begleiter H, Porjesz B, Bihari B, Kissin B: Event-related brain potentials in boys at risk for alcoholism. *Science* 1984; 227:1493–1496.

Behar D, Berg CJ, Rapoport JL, Nelson W, Linnoila M, Cohen M, Bozevich C, Marshall T: Behavioral and physiological effects of ethanol in high risk and control children: A pilot study. *Alcohol Clin Exp Res* 1983; 7:404–410.

Cadoret RJ, O'Gorman TW, Troughton E, Haywood E: Alcoholism and antisocial personality. *Arch Gen Psychiatry* 1985; 42:181–187.

Cadoret RJ, Troughton E, O'Gorman TW: Genetic and environmental factors in alcohol abuse and antisocial personality. *J Stud Alcohol* 1987; 48:1–8.

Cloninger CR: A neurobiological learning model of personality. *Science* 1987; 75:411–416.

Cloninger CR, Bohman M, Sigvardsson S, von Knorring AL: Psychopathology in adopted-out children of alcoholics, in Galanter M (ed): *Recent Developments in Alcoholism.* New York, Plenum Press, 1984, pp 37–51.

Cloninger CR, Reich T: Genetic heterogeneity in alcoholism and sociopathy, in Ketty SS (ed): *Genetics of Neurological and Psychiatric Disorders.* New York, Raven Press, 1981, pp 127–141.

Cloninger CR, Reich T, Guze SB: The multifactorial model of disease transmission: II. Sex differences in the familial transmission of sociopathy (Antisocial Personality). *Brit J Psychiatry* 1975; 7:11–22.

Cloninger CR, Reich T, Yokoyama S: Genetic diversity, genome organization, and investigation of the etiology of psychiatry diseases. *Psychiatr Devel* 1983; 3:225–246.

Crowe RR: The adopted offspring of women criminal offenders. *Arch Gen Psychiatry* 1972; 27:600–603.

Deitrich RA, Spuhler K: Genetics of alcoholism and alcohol actions, in Smart R, Sellers EM (eds): *Research Advances in Alcohol and Drug Problems.* New York, Plenum Publishing Co., 1984, vol 8, pp 47–98.

de Wit H, Uhlenhuth EH, Pierri J, Johanson CE: Individual differences in behavioral and subjective responses to alcohol. *Alcohol Clin Exp Res* 1987; 11:52–59.

Drake R: Predicting alcoholism in a 33 year follow-up of adolescent children of alcoholism. Presented at the Joint Meeting of the Research Society on Alcoholism and the Committee on Problems of Drug Dependence. Philadelphia, June 19, 1987.

Drejer K, Theilgaard A, Teasdale TW, Schulsinger F, Goodwin DW: A prospective study of young men at high risk for alcoholism: Neuropsychological assessment. *Alcohol Clin Exp Res* 1985; 9:498–502.

Erwin GV: Markers of a genetic susceptibility toward alcoholism. Presented at the Genetics of Alcoholism: A National Conference, New York, April 3, 1987.

George DT, Moss, HB, Guthrie S, Johnson J, Linnoila M: Enhanced TSH response to TRH in sons of alcoholics. Presented at the American Psychiatric Association Annual Meeting, Washington, DC, May 12, 1986.

Goedde HW, Harada S, Agarwal DP: Racial differences in alcohol sensitivity: A new hypothesis. *Hum Genet* 1979; 51:331–334.

Goedde HW, Agarwal DP, Harada S: The role of alcohol dehydrogenase and aldehyde dehydrogenase isozymes in alcohol metabolism, and alcohol sensitivity and alcoholism, in Rattazzi MC, Scandalios JG, Whitt GS (eds): *Isozymes: Curr Top Biol Med Res.* New York, Alan R Liss Inc, vol 8, 1983, pp 175–193.

Goldstein D: *Pharmacology of Alcohol.* New York, Oxford University Press, 1983, pp 48–64.

Goodwin DW: Alcoholism and genetics. *Arch Gen Psychiatry* 1985; 42:171–174.

Goodwin DW, Guze SB: *Psychiatric Diagnosis.* New York, Oxford University Press, 3rd ed, 1984, p 240.

Goodwin DW, Schulsinger F, Moller N, Hermansen L, Winokur G, Guze SB: Drinking problems in adopted and nonadopted sons of alcoholism. *Arch Gen Psychiatry* 1974; 31:164–169.

Harada S, Agarwal DP, Goedde HW, Ishikawa B: Aldehyde dehydrogenase isozyme variation and alcoholism in Japan. *Pharmacol Biochem Behav* 1983; 18:151–153.

Hesselbrock VM, Hesselbrock MN, Stabenau JR: Alcoholism in men patients subtyped by family history and antisocial personality. *J Stud Alcohol* 1985; 46:59–64.

Hesselbrock VM, Hesselbrock MN, Workman-Daniels KL: Effect of major depression and antisocial personality on alcoholism: Course and motivational patterns. *J Stud Alcohol* 1986; 47:207–212.

Irwin M, Baird S, Smith TL, Schuckit MA: Monitoring heavy drinking in recovering alcoholic men. *Am J Psychiatry* 1988; 595–599.

Johnson J: Cognitive performance patterns in school aged children from alcoholic and nonalcoholic families. Presented at the Joint Meeting of the Research Society on Alcoholism and the Committee on the Problems of Drug Dependence, Philadelphia, June 19, 1987.

Kammeier M, Hoffman H, Lopes R: Personality characteristics of alcoholics as college freshman and at the time of treatment. *Quart J Stud Alcohol* 1973; 34:390–399.

Knop J, Teasdale TW, Schulsinger F: A prospective study of young men at high risk for alcoholism: School behavior and achievement. *J Stud Alcohol* 1985; 46:273–278.

Lex BW, Mendelson JH: Alcoholism and family history in women. Presented at the Genetics of Alcoholism: A National Conference, New York, April 2, 1987.

Li TK: An animal model of alcoholism. Presented at the American College of Neuropsychopharmacology, San Juan, Puerto Rico, 1984.

Linnoila M: Biological markers in alcoholism. Presented at the World Congress of Psychiatry, Philadelphia, September 13, 1985.

MacAndrew C: On the possibility of the psychometric detection of persons who are prone to the abuse of alcohol and other substances. *Addict Behav* 1979; 4:11–20.

MacAndrew C: Toward the psychometric detection of substance misuse in young men: The SAP scale. *J Stud Alcohol* 1986; 47:161–166.

Manning DT: The prevalence of type A personality in the children of alcoholics. *Alcohol Clin Exp Res* 1986; 10:184–189.

Moss HB: Enhanced thyrotropin response to tyrotropin releasing hormone in boys at risk for development of alcoholism. *Arch Gen Psychiatry* 1986; 43:1137–1142.

Murray RM: Twin and adoption studies—How good is the evidence for a genetic role? in Galanter M (ed): *Recent Developments in Alcoholism,* New York, Plenum Press, 1981, pp 25–48.

Naranjo C, Sellers EM, Wu P, Lawrin M: Moderation of ethanol drinking, in Naranjo C and Sellers EM (eds): *Research Advances in New Psychopharmacological Treatments for Alcoholism.* New York, Excerpta Medica Co., 1985, pp 171–188.

Newlin DB and Aldrich K: Reverse tolerance to alcohol in sons of alcoholics. Presented at the Research Society on Alcoholism Annual Meeting, San Francisco, April 18–22, 1986.

O'Connor S: Correlates of increased risk for alcoholism in young men. Presented at the World Congress on Biological Psychiatry, Philadelphia, September 12, 1985.

O'Malley SS, Maisto SA: The effects of family drinking history on responses to alcohol: Expectancies and reactions to intoxication. *J Stud Alcohol* 1985; 46:289–297.

Oreland L, von Knorring L, von Knorring AL, Bohman M: Studies on the connection between alcoholism and low platelet monoamine oxidase activity. *Prog Alcohol Res* 1985; 1:83–117.

Polich J, Bloom F: Event-related brain potentials in individuals at high and low risk for developing alcoholism: Failure to replicate. *Alcohol Clin Exp Res* 1988; 12:368–373.

Polich, J, Haier RJ, Buchsbaum M, Bloom FS: Assessment of young men at risk for alcoholism with P300 from a visual discrimination task. *J Stud Alcohol* 1988; 49:186–190.

Pollock VE, Teasdale TW, Gabrielli W, Knop J: Subjective and objective measures of response to alcohol among young men at risk for alcoholism. *J Stud Alcohol* 1986; 47:297–304.

Pollock VE, Volavka J, Goodwin DW, Mednick SA, Gabrielli WF, Knop J, Schulsinger F: The EEG after alcohol administration in men at risk for alcoholism. *Arch Gen Psychiatry* 1983; 40:857–881.

Porjesz B, Begleiter H: Brain dysfunction and alcohol, in Kissin B, Begleiter H (eds): *The Pathogenesis of Alcoholism*. New York, Plenum Press, 1983, pp 415–483.

Roe A: The adult adjustment of children of alcoholic parents raised in foster-homes. *Q J Stud Alcohol* 1944; 5:378–393.

Saunders GR, Schuckit MA: Brief communication: MMPI scores in young men with alcoholic relatives and controls. *J Nerv Ment Dis* 1981; 169:456–458.

Schaeffer KW, Parsons OA, Yohman JR: Neuropsychological differences between male familial and nonfamilial alcoholics and nonalcoholics. *Alcohol Clin Exp Res* 1984; 8:347–358.

Schuckit MA: Alcoholism and sociopathy—Diagnostic confusion. *Q J Stud Alcohol* 1973; 34:157–164.

Schuckit MA: Anxiety and assertiveness in sons of alcoholics and controls. *J Clin Psychiatry* 1982; 43: 238–239.

Schuckit MA: Extroversion and neuroticism in young men. *Am J Psychiatry* 1983a; 140:1223–1224.

Schuckit MA: Alcoholism and psychiatric disorders. *Hosp Community Psychiatry* 1983b; 34:1022–1027.

Schuckit MA: Subjective responses to alcohol in sons of alcoholics and controls. *Arch Gen Psychiatry* 1984a; 41:879–884.

Schuckit MA: Differences in plasma cortisol after ethanol in relatives of alcoholics and controls. *J Clin Psychiatry* 1984b; 45:374–379.

Schuckit MA: Trait (and state) markers of a predisposition to psychopathology, in Michael R (ed): *Psychiatry*. New York, Basic Books, 1985a, vol. 3, pp 1–19.

Schuckit MA: The clinical implications of primary diagnostic groups among alcoholics. *Arch Gen Psychiatry* 1985b; 42:1043–1049.

Schuckit MA: Ethanol-induced changes in body sway in men at high alcoholism risk. *Arch Gen Psychiatry* 1985c; 42:375–379

Schuckit MA: Biological markers in alcoholism. *Prog Neuro-Psycho-Pharmacol Biol Psychiatry* 1986a; 10:191–199.

Schuckit MA: Genetic and clinical implications of alcoholism and affective disorder. *Am J Psychiatry* 1986b; 143:140–147.

Schuckit MA, Butters N, Lyn L, Gold EO, Irwin M: Neuropsychological deficits and the risk for alcoholism. *Neuropsychopharmacol*, 1987; 1:45–53.

Schuckit MA, Gold EO: A simultaneous evaluation of multiple markers of ethanol/placebo challenges in sons of alcoholics and controls. *Arch Gen Psychiatry* 1988; 45:211–216.

Schuckit MA, Gold EO, Risch SC: Changes in blood prolactin levels in sons of alcoholics and controls. *Am J Psychiatry* 1987a; 144:854–859.

Schuckit MA, Gold EO, Risch SC: Plasma cortisol levels following ethanol in sons of alcoholics and controls. *Arch Gen Psychiatry* 1987b; 144:942–945.

Schuckit MA, Goodwin DA, and Winokur GA: A study of alcoholism in half-siblings. *Am J Psychiatry* 1972; 128:1132.

Schuckit MA, Irwin M: The diagnoses of alcoholism, in Geokas M (ed): *Medical Clinics of North America*, 1988; 72:1133–1153.

Schuckit MA, Parker DC, Rossman LR: Prolactin responses to ethanol in men at elevated risk for alcoholism and controls. *Biol Psychiatry* 1983; 18:1153–1159.

Schuckit MA, Penn NE: Performance on the rod and frame for men at elevated risk for alcoholism and controls. *Am J Drug Alcohol Abuse* 1985; 111:113–118.

Schuckit MA, Shaskan E, Duby J, Vega R, Moss R: Platelet MAO activities in the relatives of alcoholics and controls: A prospective study. *Arch Gen Psychiatry* 1982; 39:137–140.

Schulsinger F, Knop J, Goodwin DW, Teasdale TW, Mikkelson U: A prospective study of young men at high risk for alcoholism. *Arch Gen Psychiatry* 1986; 43:755–760.

Skinner HA, Holt S: Early intervention for alcohol problems. *J Royal College Gen Practitioners* 1983; 33:787–794.

Stabenau JR: Implications of family history of alcoholism, antisocial personality, and sex differences in alcohol dependence. *Am J Psychiatry* 1984; 141:1178–1182.

Sullivan JL, Cavenar JO, Maltbie AA, Lister P, Zung WWK: Familial biochemical and clinical correlates of alcoholics with low platelet monoamine oxidase activity. *Biol Psychiatry* 1979; 14:385.

Suwaki J, Ohara H: Alcohol-induced facial flushing and drinking behavior in Japanese men. *J Stud Alcohol* 1985; 461:196–198.

Tarter RE, Hegedus AM, Goldstein G, Shelly C, Alterman AI: Adolescent sons of alcoholics: Neuropsychological personality characteristics. *Alcohol Clin Exp Res* 1984; 8:216–222.

Tarter RE, Jacob T, Hill S, Hegedus AM, Carra J: Perceptual field dependency: Predisposing trait or consequence of alcoholism. *J Stud Alcohol* 1986; 47:498–499.

Tasman A, O'Connor SJ, Hesselbrock V: Neuroelectric correlates of risk for alcoholism. Presented at the American Psychiatric Association Annual Meeting, Washington, DC, May 12, 1986.

Vaillant GE: Natural history of male alcoholism: Is alcoholism the cart to sociopathy? Presented at the American Psychiatric Association Annual Meeting, Toronto, Ontario, May 5, 1982.

Vaillant GE: *The Natural History of Alcoholism*. Cambridge, MA, Harvard University Press, 1983.

Vaillant GE: The course of alcoholism and lessons for treatment, in Grinspoon L (ed): *Psychiatric Update III*. American Psychiatric Press, Washington DC, 1984, pp 311–319.

Volavka J, Pollock V, Gabrielli WF, Mednick SA: The EEG in persons at risk for alcoholism, in Galanter M (ed): *Currents in Alcoholism*. New York, Grune and Stratton, Inc., 1982, vol VIII, pp 116–123.

Wilson J: Adult children of alcoholics: Cognitive and psychomotor characteristics. Presented at the Joint Meeting of the Research Society on Alcoholism and the Committee on the Problems of Drug Dependence, Philadelphia, June 19, 1987.

Workman-Daniels KL, Hesselbrock VM: Childhood problem behavior and neuropsychological functioning in persons at risk for alcoholism. *J Stud Alcohol* 1987; 48:187–193.

Section 5

Sociocultural and Environmental Determinants

CHAPTER 15

Cross-Cultural Studies
on Alcoholism

J. Westermeyer

Department of Psychiatry, University Hospital,
Mayo Memorial Building, Minneapolis, USA

PREHISTORIC ERA

Two methods are available to study alcohol (and other psychoactive substances) in the prehistoric era. One approach is to examine the archeological record. For example, wine containers have been dredged from shipwrecks in the Mediterranean Sea. Another approach consists of studying alcohol use in preliterate societies existent in historical and contemporary times. Descriptions of drinking practices in preliterate societies go back centuries (Daily, 1968), and still continue today. These studies may be broadly referred to as anthropological studies, although the data have been collected not only by anthropologists, but also by physicians, other social scientists, missionaries and various sojourners, including physicians (Westermeyer, 1971, 1972a).

Both the archeological and anthropological record indicate great inventiveness and ingenuity regarding alcohol production. By the dawn of history (which began at different times in different areas, and is still occurring in some places today), it was evident that the human family had found many carbohydrate sources for alcohol. Rice, wheat, rye, and other grains were employed by Asians and later by Northern Europeans. Para-Mediterranean, African, and Asian peoples utilized fruits, including cherries and grapes (Europe), bananas (Africa), and plums (Asia). Northern Europeans used honey along with grains to produce mead. Mammalian milk from cows, horses, and camels was fermented into alcohol over a large area from the high steppes of Asia through the Middle East to Africa. Europeans utilized several vegetable tubers, such as potatoes. In the New World, several societies obtained alcohol from cactus to produce a drink called pulque today (Waddell, 1976).

Two methods of alcohol production were known from earliest historical times. The most widely used method was the short-term production of beer, pulque, or mead containing 3 to 6% alcohol. Longer-term wine production, technically a more complex process heir to many potential problems, was a more specialized skill. The resulting more potent drink, 6 to 12% alcohol, was obtained largely from rice and grapes. The archeological record demonstrates that trade, oftentimes a vigorous one, focused on the exchange of alcohol for other materials of the era.

Written reports on preliterate societies mostly describe highly ritualized or ceremonial use of alcohol (Horton, 1943; Smith, 1968). Occasions for drinking include harvest time, the new year, marriage, birth, death, welcoming guests, and establishing fictive kinship. Amounts of alcohol consumed were prescribed. Just as refusal to drink was not socially acceptable—the so-called "drinking imperative"—choosing to drink at one's own volition was also taboo (Westermeyer, 1971). Intoxication on alcohol, as well as on other psychoactive substances, sometimes had religious symbolism, including communion with the spirit world (Carpenter, 1959). Drinking events have often marked a "time out" period, during which individuals were temporarily relieved of obligatory social behaviors. Many ancient traditions continue to this day, such as wine in the Catholic mass and at Jewish high holiday feasts, the pre-Lenten festivals (e.g., Mardi Gras) and harvest festivals (e.g., Oktoberfest), and "zu bruderschaft trinken" of Europe (Bacon, 1951, MacAndrew and Edgerton, 1969).

Drinking practices typically had symbolic and ritual functions that were highly culture bound. Even contiguous groups might have drinking practices that were remarkably different in structure and function (Horton, 1943; Carstairs, 1954; Hes, 1970). Thus, drinking practices could serve as a means of determining ethnic identity and separating cultural groups from each other. Conversely, overlapping, supracommunal drinking practices did serve and have continued to serve as a means for uniting disparate groups, reducing intergroup tensions, settling disputes, and facilitating cooperation (Heath, 1971; Reddy, 1971; Wolcott, 1974).

Alcohol drinking, when long present and stabilized in preliterate tribal and peasant society, appears to produce few problems for the individual, family, or society (Bacon, 1951, Westermeyer, 1971). However, the occasional exception from folklore reports shows that acute intoxication could be problematic. For example, the violent Nordic "berserker" was apt to become violent after overimbibing on mead. Several Biblical myths demonstrate problems associated with drunkenness, including Lot's incest and other immoralities.

Introduction of alcoholic beverages into preliterate societies, exemplified by Australian aborigines, Eskimos, American Indians, and Oceanic peoples, has produced problems that have persisted over decades and even centuries of exposure to alcohol (Honigmann and Honigmann, 1945; Ogan, 1966; Chegwidden and Flaherty, 1977). Thus, preliterate societies do not have innate societal defenses against new drinking patterns or new forms of alcohol but must develop alcohol-related practices, strictures, and taboos over time. The record suggests that these taboos and controls over drinking practices develop as a response to problems that societies encounter as a result of increasing alcohol abuse (MacAndrews and Edgerton, 1969; Marshall, 1975; Paredes, 1975).

During this early prehistorical era there were some natural limitations to the amount of alcohol consumption that a society could tolerate and still survive. Carbohydrate stores were limited, so that any one individual or family could devote only a small portion of their grain, vegetable, fruit, honey, or milk to alcohol. Survival of the family would be endangered, and starvation would ensue if excess calories were converted to alcohol. Another limiting factor was the need to work at physical labor (hunting, gathering, gardening) in order to survive—activities at odds with frequent intoxication or chronic alcoholism. Consequently, chronic alcohol abuse and dependence has rarely been observed in self-sustaining preliterate societies. Episodic alcohol intoxication (with and without untoward consequences) did occur in preliterate societies (Bunzel, 1940; MacAndrew and Edgerton, 1969).

THE AGRICULTURAL REVOLUTION TO THE COLUMBIAN ERA

Writing developed in most areas following the move from hunting–gathering societies to gardening–farming societies. This dawn of the agricultural era was fostered by domestication of plants and animals, in association with more efficient stone tools (called neoliths or "new stones") and later iron tools. History records that the development of population centers, complex government, technological and artistic development, and monotheism was fostered by excess carbohydrate production per farmer. This excess carbohydrate made it feasible to support nonagricultural workers as artisans, rulers, merchants, and soldiers. Excess carbohydrate also permitted greater devotion of societal carbohydrate reserves to alcohol production. It thus became possible for some people to abuse alcohol at frequent episodes, or even daily. By the Galenic period, well into the Iron Age, medical and psychiatric complications of chronic alcoholism were well described.

Further technological advances in alcohol production occurred during this era. One of these, ascribed to the Arabs, was distillation to increase alcohol content. Distillation was applied to grain mashes (e.g., whiskeys, scotch), tuber mashes (e.g., vodka), cane mashes (e.g., rum), and fruit mashes (e.g., cognac, brandies, kirschwasser). Another advance was the natural carbonization of wines. This was accomplished in Southeast Asia by burying large pottery casks of rice wine underground for several months—a method used to produce *lao hai* in Laos (Westermeyer, 1983). Processing carbonated grape wine in thick bottles with special corks later resulted in the production of champagne in France.

Wines and distilled beverages became increasingly important commercial products during this era. Alcohol in the form of wine or distilled beverage composed a method of storing calories over periods of months and years. Sea trade in wines had occurred in the Mediterranean region for some time, but distillation and the enrichment of wines with distilled alcohol resulted in some land trade. Mixing of beverage alcohol with herbal remedies became well established by this time, although it was probably known earlier. For example, wine and opium were mixed to produce laudanum. This was a step towards establishing alcohol as a medicament to be taken for pain or insomnia or other malady. This removed decision making regarding drinking practices outside of group or societal control. Individuals might then decide whether to use alcohol for relief of their own individual discomfiture.

During this era acute alcohol abuse began to produce not only individual damage but societal damage. For example, an Islamic fortress was overrun because a night guard was drunk. Subsequently, the Islamic religion forbade the use of alcohol. The Aztecs also had stringent class-related laws for drinking at times that were not legally prescribed, or in excessive amounts (Paredes, 1975).

THE POST-COLUMBIAN ERA TO THE MODERN ERA

Rapid, efficient, and relatively safe sea travel brought about some significant changes in alcohol economics and use. One result was the spread of alcohol technologies, so that wines and distilled beverages were added to local beers. Alcohol imports became status symbols in some areas. Traditional rituals, ceremonies, and taboos for local beverages did not typically extend to imported alcohol beverages. Improved farming tools and methods, the use of new farm products to produce alcohol (especially sugar cane for rum and gin), and slave labor resulted in greater availability of lower cost alcohol in many regions. Groups without excess carbohydrates, especially hunting–gathering groups often supported by affluent societies that had occupied their lands, gained access to affordable alcohol but without social controls to guide and govern drinking (Levy, 1966; Chegwidden and Flaherty, 1977). Emergence of widespread alcohol problems in certain ethnic groups began for the first time during this era. A distinct deviant social role, the public inebriate, appeared on most continents and continues as a social dilemma in many countries today (Gallant et al, 1973; Dennis, 1975).

A prototype of alcoholism as a widespread social problem was the Gin Epidemic in England during the late seventeenth and early eighteenth centuries. This epidemic had its origins in such diverse elements as cultural diffusion of technologies and customs, the Industrial Revolution, efficient transoceanic transportation, colonial trade, and agroeconomics. Corn, a new grain from the Americas, often available in excess in England, was being distilled there. Manufactured goods from England were shipped directly to the Canadian–American colonies and then to the Caribbean colonies. These ships picked up furs and other local products as they unloaded cargo in the New World. By the time they reached the Caribbean, the ships had discharged their cargo and needed ballast or heavy cargo for the return trip to England. Gin was taken on board for this purpose. Due to the low cost of slave labor in the Caribbean and the absence of an import tax, a calorie of gin could be purchased in England at less cost than a calorie of bread. Cheap calories, absence of social traditions for gin, and harsh social conditions contributed to heavy, daily drinking among many English men, women, and children, especially, but not exclusively, among the poorer unskilled laboring classes. Fetal alcohol syndrome was first described during this epidemic. Abstinence-oriented Christian religions appeared for the first time in England, later spreading to mainland Europe. Artists and pamphleteers of the time identified and opposed these heavy drinking practices. A heavy tariff was imposed on imported alcohol to make imported alcohol more expensive than other foodstuffs. The Gin Epidemic gradually declined under the influence of these antialcohol religious, mass media, and legal efforts (Coffey, 1966; Thurn, 1978; Rodin, 1981).

THE MODERN ERA

During the twentieth century, other sociocultural changes in alcohol related problems have occurred. Especially in the last few decades, these changes have accelerated greatly. Further technological development in the agricultural field has resulted in even greater availability of low-cost carbohydrate for potential fermentation to alcohol. Some of these changes are historically novel; others are reappearances or exacerbations of older problems. Societies with little or no previous alcoholism now experience notable drinking problems (Sargent, 1967; MacAndrew and Edgerton, 1969; Hocking, 1970).

One new problem has been widespread alcoholism among teenagers and young adults, especially in the last two or three decades. The decreasing relative cost of alcohol, along with access of adolescents to money, has made it possible for young people in many lands to abuse alcohol. This adolescent problem has been associated with increasing youthful suicide, crime, runaways, school dropouts, venereal disease, teenage pregnancy, and unwed motherhood in many countries. Fetal alcohol syndrome, lost to medical awareness for about two centuries, has reappeared as a public health problem (Cameron, 1968; Westermeyer, 1986).

Acute and chronic intoxication have presented new risks to the individual and the group in societies using advanced technologies. The intoxicated worker driving an ox team or hoeing a garden might be underproductive, but not a risk. Today the heavy machine operator, truck driver, or airline pilot, if intoxicated, puts self, others, and large capital sums at great and imminent risk. The high prevalence of alcoholism across all classes has also led to impaired decision making by business and financial experts, political leaders, and professionals, with resultant damage to individuals, families, corporations and social institutions. Parent-related characteristics favoring adolescent-onset substance abuse include increasing solo parent families, child neglect, child abuse, and incest. Public immorality has occurred in association with alcoholism in all sectors of society, including educators, clergy, physicians, and elected officials (Stull, 1972; Westermeyer, 1986).

Alcohol abuse has increased in many countries that had centuries of controlled, moderate use as well as in those with episodic, excessive use. For example, recent decades have seen an increase in hepatic cirrhosis and other medical problems in the para-Mediterranean countries where alcoholism was rare a few decades ago (Karayannis and Kelepouris, 1967; Fernandez, 1976; Bonfiglio et al, 1977). Violence, psychiatric disorders, and behavioral problems associated with acute intoxication have increased in Northern Europeans (Walsh and Walsh, 1973; Keleher, 1976). These same differences have been observed among American Indian tribes, with more controlled, chronic abuse among Pueblos and more acute binge abuse among Navahos (Kunitz et al, 1971) and Chippewa (Westermeyer and Brantner, 1972). Changing concepts and symbols among Indians regarding drinking have also ensued in association with changing patterns and laws (Kunitz and Levy, 1974). Untoward changes in drinking practices have also occurred in Asia over the last few decades (Sargent, 1967).

Rapid sociocultural change has accompanied increasing alcohol abuse and dependence in numerous regions (Westermeyer, 1972b; Caetano et al, 1983; Nason, 1974). This phenomenon has typically occurred in a context of rural-to-urban migration, salaried work replacing farm work, increased disposable income, and admixing of ethnic groups (Lemert, 1964; Gillis et al, 1973; Gluckman, 1974). Increased alcohol abuse has been ascribed to such instrumental factors as religiosity giving way to secularism, and impersonal, impotent rather than self-governed neighborhoods, and extended family control giving way to nuclear family control — all of which have undermined informal social controls.

Loss of traditional controls has resulted in the evolution of numerous strategies to control excessive drinking, whether acute or chronic. These have included formal and informal, legal, and volunteer methods. Some of these simply replicate the measures devised during the Gin Epidemic. For example, abstinence-oriented fundamentalist Christianity has had numerous converts in Latin America and North America, and alcohol abuse has stimulated abstinence-oriented fundamentalist Islam in the Middle East and South Asia (Hippler, 1973). Mass media campaigns, some sponsored by governments and some voluntary, have been initiated to bolster abstinence or moderation over excess. Increased alcohol taxation has been implemented in many areas to reduce the level of drinking. Newer methods of legal control have also appeared in recent decades. Total prohibition against commercial alcohol production was attempted in some non-Islamic countries in the first half of the twentieth century, including Denmark, parts of Oceania, and the United States. Prohibition was later abandoned when the public failed to support it. Special interest groups have organized to oppose abusive drinking. One such organization is Mothers Against Drunken Driving (MADD), a group composed of women whose children have been killed as a result of intoxicated drivers. They monitor legislators' records, attend legal proceedings and observe judges' decisions in drunken-driving cases, and speak at various public and treatment settings. Occupational groups have also mobilized to limit excessive drinking to confront peers on their abusive use of alcohol and to support peers recovering from alcoholism. Perhaps the earliest groups were those fostered in Yugoslavia. Other recent examples have included Attorneys Concerned for Attorneys, Physicians Serving Physicians, airline pilots' associations, and other occupational groups in the United States. Recently high school, undergraduate, graduate, and professional students have formed such groups, usually with an older advisor participating in the group. Parent, school, and neighborhood organizations have evolved to deal with the ready availability of alcohol to youth, with peer pressures to drink excessively, and with the isolation and frustration of the nuclear family attempting to cope with an alcoholic adolescent (Swed, 1966; Brunne, 1975). New treatment modalities, such as disulfiram, have proven effective in overcoming culturally sanctioned drinking pressures (Savard, 1968).

Legislation to deal with public alcohol abuse has become more sophisticated in many areas (Marshall, 1975). Rather than totally forbid all alcohol sales, limits have been placed on the hours and location of sale, on the age of the purchaser, and on the amount sold per individual per unit time. While effective up to a point, restriction — when excessive — has resulted in illegal production of "bootleg" alcohol and wasteful hours spent queuing up for alcohol purchases (Connell, 1961).

Culture-bound healing techniques have been applied in the treatment of alcoholism. Examples include the Native American Church, with its peyote ritual, among American Indians (Bergman, 1971; Albaugh and Anderson, 1974). The role of ethnicity in treatment seeking has been well described (Kane, 1981). Ethnically influenced social variables such as residence, marital status, and employment when entering treatment remain important determinants of outcome (Westermeyer and Peake, 1983).

Epidemiological studies have long indicated that rates of alcoholism vary widely among cultures (Bales, 1946). Even within samples of identified alcoholic patients, the rate of amnesic episodes (i.e., "blackout") and alcoholic psychosis can differ significantly (Rimmer et al, 1971; Negrete, 1973). The relationship of alcoholic pathology to sociocultural factors is a complex matter (Westermeyer, 1982, 1985) but one that we must understand more fully if we are to reduce the high rates of alcoholism in many countries.

REFERENCES

Albaugh BJ, Anderson PO: Peyote in the treatment of alcoholism among American Indians. *Am J Psychiatry* 1974; 131:1247–1250.

Bacon SD: Studies of drinking in Jewish culture, 1. General introduction. *Q J Stud Alcohol* 1951; 12:444–450.

Bales RF: Cultural differences in rates of alcoholism. *Q J Stud Alcohol* 1946; 6:480–499.

Bergman RL: Navaho peyote use: Its apparent safety. *Am J Psychiatry* 1971; 128:695–699.

Bonfiglio G, Falli S, Pacini A: Alcoholism in Italy: An outline highlighting some special features. *Brit J Addiction* 1977; 72:3–12.

Brunne K: *Alcohol Control Policies in Public Health Perspective.* Helsinki, Finnish Foundation of Alcohol Studies, 1975.

Bunzel R: Role of alcoholism in two Central American cultures. *Psychiatry* 1940; 3:361–387.

Caetano R, Suzman RM, Rosen DH, Vorhees-Rosen DJ: The Shetland Islands: Longitudinal changes in alcohol consumption in a changing environment. *Brit J Addiction* 1983; 78:21–36.

Cameron DC: Youth and drugs. *JAMA* 1968; 206:1267–1271.

Carpenter ES: Alcohol in the Iroquois dream quest. *Am J Psychiatry* 1959; 116:148–151.

Carstairs GM: Daru and Bhang: Cultural factors in the choice of intoxicants. *Q J Stud Alcohol* 1954; 15:220–237.

Chegwidden M, Flaherty BJ: Aboriginal versus non-Aboriginal alcoholics in an alcohol withdrawal unit. *Med J Australia* 1977; 1:699–703.

Coffey TG: Beer street: Gin lane, Some views of 18th-century drinking. *Q J Stud Alcohol* 1966; 27:669–692.

Connell KH: Illicit distillation: An Irish peasant industry. *Historical Studies of Ireland* 1961; 3:58–91.

Daily RC: The role of alcohol among North American Indian tribes as reported in the Jesuit Relations. *Anthropologica* 1968; 10:45–47.

Dennis PA: The role of the drunk in a Oaxacan village. *A Anthropologist* 1975; 77(4):856–863.

Fernandez FA: The state of alcoholism in Spain covering its epidemiological and aetiological aspects. *Brit J Addiction* 1976; 71:235–242.

Gallant DM, Bishop MP, Mouledoux A, Faulkner MA, Brisola RA, Swanson, WA: The revolving door alcoholic. *Arch Gen Psychiatry* 1973; 28:633–635.

Gillis JS, Lewis J, Slabbert M: Alcoholism among the Cape Coloureds. *So Afr Med J* 1973; 47:1374–1382.

Gluckman LK: Alcohol and the Maori in historical perspective. *N Z Med J* 1974; 79:553–555.

Heath D: Peasants, revolution, and drinking: Interethnic drinking patterns in two Bolivian communities. *Human Organization* 1971; 30:179–186.

Hes JP: Drinking in a Yeminite rural settlement in Israel. *Brit J Addiction* 1970; 65:293–296.

Hippler AE: Fundamentalist Christianity: An Alaskan Athabascan technique for overcoming alcohol abuse. *Transcult Psychiatr Res Rev* 1973; 10:173–179.

Hocking RB: Problems arising from alcohol in the New Hebrides. *Med J Aust* 1970; 2:908–910.

Honigmann J, Honigmann I: Drinking in an Indian–white community. *Q J Stud Alcohol* 1945; 5:575–619.

Horton D: The function of alcohol in primitive societies; a cross-cultural study. *Q J Stud Alcohol* 1943; 4:199–320.

Kane G: *Inner City Alcoholism: An Ecological and Cross Cultural Study*, New York, Human Sciences Press, 1981.

Karayannis AD, Kelepouris MB: Impressions of the drinking habits and alcohol problem in modern Greece. *Brit J Addiction* 1967; 62:71–73.

Keleher MJ: Alcohol and affective disorder in Irish mental hospital admissions. *J Irish Med Assoc* 1976; 69:140–143.

Kunitz SJ, Levy JE: Changing ideas of alcohol use among Navaho Indians. *Q J Stud Alcohol* 1974; 25:243–259.

Kunitz SJ, Levy JE, Odoroff CL, Bollinger J: The epidemiology of alcoholism in two southwestern Indian tribes. *Q J Stud Alcohol* 1971; 32:706–720.

Lemert EM: Drinking in Hawaiian plantation society. *Q J Stud Alcohol* 1964; 25:689–713.

Levy RI: Ma'ohi drinking patterns in the Society Islands. *J Polynes Soc* 1966; 75:304–320.

MacAndrew C, Edgerton RB: *Drunken Comportment: A Social Explanation.* Chicago, Aldine, 1969.

Marshall M: The politics of prohibition on Namoluk Atoll. *J Stud Alcohol* 1975; 36:597–610.

Nason JD: Sardines and other fried fish; The consumption of alcoholic beverages on a Micronesian island. *J Stud Alcohol* 1974; 36:611–625.

Negrete JC: Cultural influences on performance of alcoholics: A comparative study. *Q J Stud Alcohol* 1973; 34:905–916.

Ogan E: Drinking behavior and race relations. *Am Anthropologist* 1966; 68:181–188.

Paredes A: Social control of drinking among the Aztec Indians of Mesoamerica. *J Stud Alcohol* 1975; 36:1139–1153.

Reddy GP: Where liquor decides everything: Drinking subculture among tribes of Andhra. *Social Welfare* 1971; 7:4–5.

Rimmer J, Pitts FN, Reich T, Winokur G: Alcoholism: II. Sex, socioeconomic status and race in two hospitalized samples. *Q J Stud Alcohol* 1971; 32:942–952.

Rodin AE: Infants and gin mania in 18th-century London. *JAMA* 1981; 245:1237–1239.

Sargent MJ: Changes in Japanese drinking patterns. *Q J Stud Alcohol* 1967; 28:709–722.

Savard RJ: Effects of disulfiram therapy on relationships within the Navajo drinking group. *Q J Stud Alcohol* 1968; 29:909–916.

Smith WR: Sacrifice among the Semnites, in Lessa, WA, and Vogt EZ (eds): *Reader in Comparative Religion*. New York, Harper & Row, 1965, pp 39–48.

Stull DD: Victims of modernization: Accident rates and Papago Indian adjustment. *Human Organization* 1972; 31:227–240.

Swed JF: Gossip, drinking and social control: Consensus and communication in a Newfoundland parish. *Ethnology* 1966; 5:434–441.

Thurn RJ: The gin plague. *Minn Med* 1978; 61:241–243.

Waddell JO: The place of the cactus wine ritual in the Papago Indian ecosystem, in Bharati A (ed). *Realm of the Extra Human: Ideas and Actions*. The Hague, Mouton, 1976, pp. 213–218.

Walsh BM, Walsh D: Validity of indices of alcoholism: A comment from the Irish experience. *Brit J Prev Soc Med* 1973; 27:18–26.

Westermeyer J: Use of alcohol and opium by the Meo of Laos. *Am J Psychiatry* 1971; 127:1019–1023.

Westermeyer J: Options regarding alcohol use among the Chippewa. *Am J Orthopsychiatry* 1972a; 42:398–403.

Westermeyer J: Chippewa and majority alcoholism in the Twin Cities: A comparison. *J Nerv Ment Dis* 1972b; 155:322–327.

Westermeyer J: Alcoholism and psychiatry: A cross-cultural perspective, in Solomon J (ed): *Alcoholism and Clinical Psychiatry*. New York, Plenum Press, 1982, pp 35–48.

Westermeyer J: *Poppies, Pipes and People*. Berkeley, Univ. of California Press, 1983.

Westermeyer J: Substance abuse and psychopathology: Sociocultural factors, in Alterman AI (ed): *Substance Abuse and Psychopathology*. New York, Plenum Press, 1985, pp 45–68.

Westermeyer J: *A Clinical Guide to Alcohol and Drug Problems*. New York, Praeger, 1986.

Westermeyer J, Brantner J: Violent death and alcohol use among the Chippewa in Minnesota. *Minn Med* 1972; 55:749–752.

Westermeyer J, Peake E: A ten year follow up of alcoholic Native Americans in Minnesota. *Am J Psychiatry* 1983; 140:189–194.

Wolcott HF: *African Beer Garden of Bulawayo: Integrated Drinking in a Segregated Society*. New Brunswick, N.J.: Rutgers Center of Alcohol Studies, 1974.

CHAPTER 16

Environmental Factors in
Alcohol Use and Its Outcomes

Dwight B. Heath

Department of Anthropology
Brown University
Providence, Rhode Island, USA

THE IMPORTANCE OF ENVIRONMENTAL FACTORS

There is probably no scientist in the field of alcohol studies today who would deny that "the environment" (or "environmental factors") must be taken into consideration if we are to understand alcohol use and its outcomes in any human population. Even those who have been most articulate in conducting and fostering research on genetic and other biochemical aspects of alcoholism have been consistent in their insistence that little can be accomplished if one fails to attend adequately to both heredity and environment, nature and nurture, or biological inheritance *and* the setting in which the organism must operate. In that sense, we have come a long way since a few decades ago when there was still some serious debate about which category was crucial, as if they were contrastive and competitive rather than being complementary and interactive.

To illustrate, in introducing the first major international and multidisciplinary conference on genetics and alcoholism, the editors of this volume were careful to list as one of their key questions at the very outset: "Can one separate genetic contributions from the environmental influences?" (Goedde and Agarwal, 1987). They also emphasized early that: "complex genetic-environmental interactions must be taken into account . . ." (Goedde and Agarwal, 1987). Although the participants at that conference provided important data and interpretations that updated our understanding of many aspects of the interrelations between genetics and alcoholism, there was general agreement that, whatever genetic predisposing factor(s) may sometime be found, a simple Mendelian model of inheritance will not be adequate. The need for combining (rather than contrasting) nature and nurture and for analyzing the roles of relevant environmental factors was stressed independently by several of those genetically oriented scientists.

The theme was succinctly reiterated in a recent publication of the U.S. National Academy of Sciences: "A substantial percentage of alcoholics have at least one parent who is alcoholic. The percentage varies from study to study, but tends to range around 40 percent. . . . However, a purely genetic explanation of risk is not sufficient. Not all alcoholics have a traceable family risk and even in cases with familial risk, alcohol-related behavior appears to depend upon an 'appropriate' environment for expression in many cases" (Institute of Medicine, 1987).

Although the present volume is focused on genetic and biomedical factors, this seems an appropriate context in which to explore some of the meanings of "an 'appropriate' environment." This chapter describes in simple terms the broad range of environmental variables that have already been discussed in the literature as being relevant to alcoholism and suggests some of the many kinds of data, methods, and concepts that seem potentially useful in striving toward an integration of genetic, biomedical, and environmental factors.

THE RISK OF A "SCIENCE OF LEFTOVERS"

Clyde Kluckhohn (1949) once referred to anthropology as "the science of leftovers," in which archeologists dig remains that are of no interest to classicists or art historians, linguists analyze hundreds of tongues that are scorned by grammarians and philologists, ethnographers study populations that are ignored by sociologists, and others in the small cadre of anthropologists pay attention to much of the overall human heritage that other scholars dismiss as "tribal" or "primitive," whether in religion, law, art, or other fields. In the ensuing years, anthropology as an academic discipline has undergone significant fractionation, and the centrifugal effect of increasing specialization sometimes obscures linkages among parts of a culture that are crucial.

In a similar manner, there may be a risk if "the environment" be construed as little more than a residual category — a label for leftovers — the ignominious "black box" to which anything except genetic and other clearly biological factors will be relegated. If that were the case, giving lip service to the relevance of environmental factors would do little to enhance or advance our understanding. On the contrary, it might well be an obstacle inasmuch as a wide range of variables that are already identified and that have already been studied in some detail might be ignored.

This discussion can also be construed as, in many respects, dealing with the category labeled "setting," in what has come to be called the "public health model of addiction," in which etiological factors are conceived as comprising the drug (the agent, in largely chemical and pharmacological terms), the set (the host, in both physiological and psychological terms), and the setting (analogous to "the environment," in its broadly unspecified scope). By attempting to explicate some of the diverse ways in which researchers have analyzed "environmental factors," we will also be signaling several potentially important components of "the setting."

KEY DIMENSIONS OF THE ENVIRONMENT

Science is not well served if we continue to use the term "environment" in a vague, almost residual sense, with reference to any *or* all factors other than genetics. Such a label becomes another mysterious "black box," something that can be pointed to, and left without further consideration.

One of the best ways to demystify a "black box" is to describe several of its key dimensions. In the hope of stimulating more pointed and thoughtful consideration of environmental factors as they relate to drinking and its outcomes, therefore, this chapter briefly reviews several meanings that have been given to the concept of "the environment" as it relates to alcohol and several factors that have been subsumed under that broad rubric.

The problem is not that we are ignorant about environmental factors and how they affect individuals. A number of relevant environmental factors have been identified over the years, and we well understand how some of them interact with the biological organism to result in particular outcomes, which are often expressed in different rates and types of alcohol-related activities and problems. Far from being at a loss to identify relevant aspects of the environment, we have the opposite problem — the embarrassment of riches, in which we cannot yet isolate which among the many relate to a particular case or how they interact with each other to result in a given expression of biological potential.

It is clear that there is little unanimity among researchers about the relative importance among several kinds of environmental factors and even less about how they affect an individual's choices and behavior. At this stage, there is not even agreement on whether the environment should most fruitfully be viewed as an entity or a context. In most of the usages discussed below, "the environment" that seems like an entity from the point of view of a given population, seems like a context or setting from the point of view of an individual, or another population. This confusion does not mean that the referents are abstract and abstruse, with only vague and indirect effects on the human organism. On the contrary, many are very real, concrete, and active. For convenience, I have selected nine major dimensions of the environment — which might be considered "types" of environmental factors — the natural environment, social settings, availability and legal constraints, media and "the intellectual climate," social structure and organization, religious systems, the city, other cultures, and cultural systems.

In this context, it is not feasible to review the literature in detail with respect to any of these topics, but a brief note about some of the ways in which people have construed these as environmental factors relevant to alcohol use and its outcomes should be helpful in highlighting the complexity and the promise of closer investigation into environmental factors as they interact with genetic and biomedical ones. Further details on most of these categories can be found in two articles in which the diverse and scattered anthropological literature on alcohol — from the beginning to 1970 (Heath, 1975) and 1970 to 1980 (Heath, 1987a) — are reviewed.

The Natural Environment as Setting: Geography and Ecology

There is an important sense in which the global or natural environment interacts significantly with genetic and other biological factors in shaping all kinds of behavior. Much that is written about ecological determinants has to do with limits that constrain human activity, such as extreme aridity disallowing agriculture, extreme cold requiring special clothing, high altitudes interfering with activity, and so forth. Except among specialists, there is much less attention paid to geography and ecology as enabling and facilitating, rather than limiting, the human experience. The presence of certain flora favors the discovery and refinement of fermentation; various raw materials lend themselves to use in tools and utensils, and so forth.

Geographical and ecological factors in this gross sense have been invoked to account for the absence of alcoholic beverages in aboriginal times throughout the arctic regions of the world, where cold limits both plant life and the microorganisms that effect fermentation. However, the similar absence of alcohol throughout most of North America and the islands of the Pacific prior to European contact cannot be attributed to such environmental limitations. Another aspect of the arctic that has attracted attention is the relationship of time and light; from the vantage point of median latitudes, the "six-month night" is interpreted as perhaps a rationale for heavy drinking as an escape from gloom, although recent examination of police records in some Eskimo communities does not reveal such seasonality. The simple and repetitive diet of carbohydrates, olive oil, wine, and cheese that has long predominated throughout much of the Mediterranean basin is being studied anew for clues to health. Industrialization and international commerce have tended to blur what used to be fairly distinctive regions where specific beverages predominated, with "wine cultures" differing from both "beer cultures" and "spirits cultures." A given dose of ethanol clearly has a greater impact on the human brain at higher elevations, but customary drunkenness and binge drinking are by no means limited to relatively anoxic areas.

Some generalizations that might be viewed as cultural–ecological are similarly interesting, but the fact that exceptions come readily to mind makes them less than compelling. For example, should we try to make anything of the widespread cooccurrence of dairying and drinking patterns that tend to be physically harmful? Since France's infamously high rate of cirrhosis is not shared by many similarly viticultural nations, is it perhaps more a reflection of diet (or other factors) than an index of alcoholism or *alcoolisation*? Social survey researchers tend to emphasize religious factors to account for marked regional differences in drinking patterns among the people of the United States.

In sum, environment in the sense of geology, climate, and similar geographical and ecological factors provides a stage on which certain kinds of behavior are possible or not, with varying degrees of ease or difficulty and with differing effects on the human organism. But the variation that occurs among human populations within a given ecological niche, or even during the history of a given population in the same niche, demonstrate clearly that the natural environment is by no means crucial in shaping drinking patterns or their outcomes (cf. Smith and Hanham, 1982).

Social Settings: Space, Materiel, and Mood

Far more rigorous attention has been paid to the local environments that people create for themselves, the settings in which they choose to drink. When these are cotidian places where people also eat their meals or otherwise interact with their families, relatively high annual per capita consumption can occur without associated problems. Some settings for drinking that are set apart also combine a variety of functions: one U.S. bar may be well known as a venue for homosexual encounters and another as a hangout for college students; some English pubs act as neighborhood social clubs for a permanent clientele while others cater to transients and tourists; a Mexican *pulquería* and a Peruvian *chichería* not only look very different but are used very differently, although they serve similar homebrews to peasants. In various U.S. cities, social scientists have described several types of public drinking establishments, without even mentioning "Indian bars," which also serve as employment or rental agencies, and strategic places for Native Americans newly arrived from the reservations to learn how to adjust to urban life. It has even been suggested that "national character" is vividly implied in the differing spatial layout, furnishings, lighting, and other characteristics of the German beer garden, French sidewalk café, and American cocktail lounge (Csikszentmihalyi, 1968).

It has been demonstrated that low lighting increases the amount people drink, and even that the tempo of background music is in inverse relationship to the speed of drinking. Social stratification is reinforced (rather than ignored) in some pubs, and sexual advances, encouraged in some, are taboo in others. Even within a given place as an overall setting, the social environment at a given table impinges on drinkers: long-term detailed quantitative observations show that the amount one drinks in some taverns correlates closely with the size of the immediate group but correlates very little with the amount of time spent drinking.

Mexican-American women drink more in the company of each other than they do in the company of men, and mixed couples often select beverages that are ignored by either sex alone. The differential impact of attitudes and examples set by age-peers on the one hand, and by parents on the other, have been shown to be significant in shaping adolescent drinking patterns in many Western cultures. Although a single container could, in a physical sense, serve for virtually any beverage, most cultures have some differentiation in terms of forms and functions of drinking vessels, and the extreme complexity of such variation in some cultures is accompanied by strongly held attitudes about the propriety of their use in given times and places.

The idea that drinking should be a focal activity in itself is relatively rare around the world, and tends to be associated with relatively high rates of physiological and other drinking problems. When drinking is a routine adjunct to meals, there tend to be fewer problems, and when it is imbedded in a ritual context (religious or secular), it tends similarly to be innocuous. Heavy reliance on laws setting a minimum purchase age for alcoholic beverages is sometimes counterproductive, just as overall prohibition has failed except where embedded in a religious context; some suggest that the special appeal of a "forbidden fruit" is important, while others point to ambivalence or hypocrisy.

MacAndrew and Edgerton's (1969) suggestion that drunkenness serves as a "timeout," during which some general restrictive rules of behavior are lifted — but only partially — was an important early demonstration, on the basis of historical and ethnographic documents, that drunken comportment is shaped by learning as well as by the interplay of pharmacochemical effects on neurophysiology. More recently, a number of psychologists working under controlled laboratory conditions are offering a richly detailed corpus on expectancies (or expectations) as they affect drunkenness, moods, attitudes, and behavior (Marlatt and Nathan, 1978). Differing markedly in methodology and scale, these two types of research have yielded nicely complementary findings.

The importance of social contexts is reflected in the fact that a couple of international and multidisciplinary symposia yielded diverse and interesting volumes (Harford and Gaines, 1981; Single and Storm, 1985).

Availability and Legal Constraints: Access and Control

Although ethanol is a natural product, cheap and fairly easy to produce from a wide variety of raw materials in most parts of the world, alcoholic beverages have often been subject to unusual taxation and legal controls throughout history. It is a truism that an individual, even with a strong genetic predisposition, would not develop alcoholism in the absence of alcoholic beverages. It is not so clear, however, that limiting access to alcohol is a universally effective and efficient way to lessen drinking problems. On the contrary, there is abundant evidence that problems and consumption are not significantly correlated (except at the highest levels) in individuals (Sadava, 1985) or in groups (Cahalan and Room, 1974).

A very different view has attracted considerable attention in recent years as "the single distribution model" or "control of availability model" in the name of preventive public health (Moore and Gerstein, 1987). Departing from a statistical model based on the premise that per capita consumption in any population follows a lognormal curve, they hold that reducing overall consumption is the best way to lessen alcoholism. Statistical data from many countries do fit this pattern, but some striking exceptions are ignored (Giesbrecht et al, 1983; Grant, 1985). For example, the French high consumption and high cirrhosis rate are well known, but Italy and many non-Western cultures have the former without the latter; Ireland and Finland are exceptionally low in terms of per capita consumption but exceptionally high in terms of drinking problems (Davies and Walsh, 1983).

Among the constraints on availability that have been widely used is taxation — to the point where it comprises more than half of the price of alcoholic beverages in many countries. Licensing of public outlets and restriction of hours of sales are also common; the minimum purchase age has recently been raised to 21 in all of the United States. State monopolies are often justified as less likely to promote consumption than private enterprise, and restrictions on advertising are being widely fostered in the name of public health. A requirement that containers carry labels warning of various health risks has already been enacted in Mexico, and other countries are considering it. Indexing prices of alcoholic beverages so that they maintain a steady relationship to prices of other goods during inflation assumes price elasticity that has been disproven among heavy drinkers in many societies.

India, Russia, Sweden, and the United States have all had fruitless experiments with total prohibition at the national level, although political entities at lower levels (such as towns, counties, and Indian reservations in the United States, states in India, and others elsewhere) still sometimes choose local prohibition or other varying degrees of optional control. In such instances, illicit production and distribution appear almost invariably to have rapidly provided an alternate source, except among those few populations for whom prohibition was imbedded in a context of religious faith.

In recent years, a self-styled "neotemperance movement" has become vocal and politically influential in the United States, where a variety of constraints on availability, legal liabilities on those who serve drinks, punishments for drunk driving, and so forth, are being implemented (Moore and Gerstein, 1981; West, 1984). The World Health Organization and others have fostered such controls as the most appropriate alcohol policies for all countries (Grant, 1985), sometimes in the face of considerable contradictory evidence (Heath, 1988).

The literature is too vast to summarize in this context, but a few examples illustrate that this dimension of the environment is not so crucial or easy a way to diminish alcohol-related problems as the theorists would have us believe. Many cross-national studies show that pricing affects consumption among moderate drinkers, but heavy drinkers tend to sacrifice other expenditures. Regular patrons at many public drinking establishments have been seen to adjust the pace of their drinking so that they consume the same amount regardless of closing hours. The pressures on a beverage industry to promote its products are similar whether it is privately or publicly owned.

Insofar as the term "addiction" continues to enjoy currency within the scientific community, it tends to be with behavioral rather than biological referents. Although there is less reference to "physiological dependence," many scholars are still concerned with what appear to be excessive or inappropriate risk-taking behaviors on the part of a few individuals who act as if they were preoccupied with something to the point where it interferes with other important aspects of their living. Insofar as "alcoholism" or the "alcohol dependence syndrome" fits this model, it is little wonder that control of availability is unlikely to significantly diminish drinking among those for whom it already is problematic.

Media and "the Intellectual Climate"

Throughout much of the world in recent decades, media of mass communication, both electronic and print, are playing a large and increasing role in entertainment, education, and other representations, often including advertising as a significant portion of the content. Because of their ubiquity, popularity, and presumed impact on norms and behavior of the audiences, the media have come under close scrutiny as environmental factors that may significantly shape alcohol use and its outcomes.

For example, dogged analysis of large samples of fictional television shows in the United States revealed a number of patterns that the investigators consider problematic (DeFoe et al, 1983). Among all scenes that depict drinking, alcoholic beverages predominate overwhelmingly, although the populace customarily drinks nonalcoholic beverages much more often. Positive affective associations with drinking predominate, with virtually no negative consequences portrayed. Contexts often suggest that taking a drink is a normal immediate response to bad news or other stress, a pattern that also occurs regularly in novels, short stories, plays, and films. Some interpret such findings as an indictment of the media and call for more realistic depiction of drinking; others have taken the initiative as consultants and are actively cooperating with writers and producers toward achieving such change. The logic behind such concern is sometimes that members of the audience wish to emulate media representations, and sometimes a very different view—that media representations are not so much of ideals to be copied, but rather of prevailing norms that reflect "the intellectual climate" of the times. In short, the indictment of permissiveness toward alcohol in media representations is similar whether those representations are construed as realistic or as distinctly unrealistic.

Somewhat similar as an occasion for confusion are historical and thematic analyses of depictions of drinking and drunkenness in the films of various countries. Behaviors and attitudes portrayed in earlier films tend often to be interpreted as reflecting how people felt about alcohol then, whereas contemporary depictions tend often to be interpreted as inappropriately favorable to alcohol.

With respect to newspapers and magazines, some critics hold that the significant portion of their budget that is derived from advertisements for alcoholic beverages must influence their editorial policies. Superficial psychological interpretations of visual advertisements have enjoyed some popularity among lay readers, although there is little methodology behind their highlighting of sex, death, and other titillating themes. For that matter, even in the many systematic attempts that have been made to analyze the impact that advertising has on drinking, results are inconsistent, with recent exposure sometimes increasing, sometimes decreasing, and sometimes having no perceptible effect on ad lib drinking. Calls for a ban, or various restrictions, on advertising are common, and industry organizations in some countries voluntarily adhere to their own code of ethics (e.g., against portraying youthful drinkers, against fostering drunkenness, and so forth).

Although mass communications both shape and are shaped by popular opinions, no one has yet been able convincingly to segregate—much less, to measure—those influences. For those reasons, among others, they deserve consideration as a relevant dimension of the environment, although we cannot yet offer meaningful estimates of how they interact with genetic, biomedical, and other environmental factors with respect to drinking and its outcomes.

Social Structure and Organization: Systems of Status

In sociological and anthropological terms, patterns of social relationships among groups and individuals are dimensions of the environment that impinge significantly in many ways and at almost all times. In this context, brief mention of a few distinctive systems of status will illustrate the relevance of this as a category that deserves analysis, even though exhaustive treatment of the subject would require a monograph.

In many societies, the way in which one drinks signals social status in important ways. There are instances in which men in India have been expelled from their caste (and, thereby, effectively rendered social nonentities) when found guilty of violating the taboo on drinking. In many Western countries, survey data show that consumption tends to be higher among those of higher socioeconomic class, although a wide range of alcohol-related problems (such as spouse abuse, child abuse and neglect, job loss, arrest for drunkenness, and others) are more common in lower classes. Insofar as sex is a socially significant category as well as a biological one, it is noteworthy that women almost everywhere drink differently from men, in both qualitative and quantitative terms. Certain beverages, as well as certain drinking vessels, have special meanings and are restricted to special categories of individuals.

Apart from such relatively enduring aspects of social organization as those noted above, there are ephemeral statuses that affect both one's drinking behavior and the view that others take of it. Age is one of the most nearly universal, although many societies that permit limited drinking by young people have relatively few problem drinkers as they mature. In industrial countries, it is often thought that adult males drink more heavily while temporarily unemployed, but some recent studies show that specific workplaces tend to favor drinking. A few occupations appear to put individuals at high risk for drinking problems: sailors, police, firefighters, publicans, and bartenders are among those. In cross-cultural perspective, it has been noted that societies with corporate kin groups, bride price, and a concentrated village form of settlement tend to be relatively free of drunkenness (Field, 1962).

Broad social categories that are sometimes labeled "ethnic groups," "subcultures," "minorities," or similar have often been cited as crucial demonstrations that beliefs, attitudes, and values are more important than per capita consumption in determining what portion of a population will experience drinking problems and what kinds of problems (if any) will occur. Probably the best-known illustrative contrast is that between Jews and Irish immigrants in the United States, but Mormons, blacks, and many other "ethnic groups" have also been analyzed in similar terms. The image of "the drunken Indian," especially vulnerable to alcohol, long served as a rationale for disallowing the sale of liquor to Native Americans and Canadian Natives. For reasons that will be explained more fully below, it seems appropriate to discuss them under the rubric "Cultural Systems."

There can be no doubt that certain features of social structure and organization constitute environmental factors that interact with genetic and biomedical factors in shaping how, when, with whom, and for what reasons people drink, as well as how they behave in other respects. This brief listing is meant to direct the attention of researchers who are not familiar with this literature to some of the many linkages that have been noted. As is the case with respect to many of the other types of environmental factors, studies have not always been rigorous or comparable, and data and interpretations are often inconsistent or even contradictory. These shortcomings do not imply that systems of status are irrelevant to alcoholism, but that each distinctive context deserves special attention to its own terms.

Religious Systems: Beliefs and the Supernatural

Every population has some beliefs about the supernatural, even in the absence of a formal church, liturgy, and clergy, and many of those beliefs impinge strongly on codes of workaday behavior, including drinking. There are many tribes in sub-Saharan Africa and other groups in Latin America for whom drunkenness is not only allowed but positively valued and actively sought as a means of achieving religious experience. By contrast, many Protestant sects abhor alcohol and forbid its use; those few members of such groups who experiment with drinking tend often to become problem drinkers. A remarkable historical process, which remains to be well described, was the broad and rapid spread of an ethic of abstinence among most of the early converts to Islam, many of whom had grown up in contexts where drinking and even drunkenness were openly enjoyed. Orthodox Jews around the world are interesting, and some would say anomalous, inasmuch as both sexes and all ages drink wine in ritual contexts, but problem drinkers are rare among them.

Orgiastic rites in honor of Bacchus and Dionysus, both gods of wine in classic Greece and Rome, are well known in the mainstream of Western culture history. Wine continues to be a central symbol in Christian communion, and Jellinek (1976) among others, suggested that wine, like water and blood, often represents the primal life force. As such, like various homebrewed beers, it is often viewed as the ideal offering for various deities.

It is evident from even such cursory notes (which are developed in much greater detail in Heath, 1975, 1987a) that religions, like other systems of belief, constitute environmental factors that influence individuals and groups in various ways. Whether a given religious system favors drinking or not, and how drunken comportment relates to other imperatives, is an empirical question that can only be answered within a cultural context. But the fact that many problem drinkers who convert to Protestantism remain abstinent for the rest of their lives is only one among many lines of evidence that this is yet another dimension of the environment that interacts with genetic and biomedical factors to shape drinking and its outcomes.

The City as a Special Kind of Place: Two Kinds of Urbanization

Although it should be construed as more a long-term process than a brief event, "the urban revolution" is broadly viewed as constituting a major change wrought by human beings in terms of reshaping their environment. When viewed as an historical process within a societal frame of reference, urbanization usually refers to a combination of relatively dense population, usually linked with markedly increased occupational specialization, sharper delineation of social classes and other categories, permanent architecture and improved modes of transportation, and even greater centralization of political power. When the term is used with reference to an individual or a household, by contrast, urbanization usually refers to the adaptations and adjustments that newcomers have to make after moving from a rural or village context to that of a city. The change in scale almost invariably implies changes in how one finds housing, how one earns a living, bases and expectations of social relationships, and a wide range of other aspects of workaday life.

Sociologists and anthropologists who have studied peasant and tribal populations around the world find that both kinds of urbanization are often accompanied by the substitution (rapid or gradual) of new sets of values and attitudes for traditional ones. This never occurs in any complete sense, and the persistence of selected nonurban patterns of belief and behavior is often vigorous and long lived. A general pattern, however, is for some newcomers to feel adrift in the city, cut off from a world that was well known and predictable on the one hand, and not yet comfortable (or accepted) in a new world which may seem cool, confusing, and capricious. Easy access to alcoholic beverages may combine with disorientation and disillusionment to favor heavier than usual drinking in the city. Or drinking may have very different meanings from what it had elsewhere. Not all urban drinking is deleterious, any more than all urbanization erodes values; sharing drinks often serves as a means by which individuals with limited resources build up "social credit" among colleagues who can be expected to help them in time of need (e.g., Waddell, 1975; Collmann, 1979). It also deserves mention that there are a few cultures in which the rural folk drink more, and more often, than their urban relatives.

The commoditization of labor and the segregation between "work" and other aspects of life characterize some, but not all, cities. The anonymity that some people find attractive in the city others find stressful. Not all who live in a "Skid Row," as concentrations of indigent homeless persons are often called, drink, although that in the stereotype, nor is rural-to-urban migration necessarily irreversible, although we read little about the return flow. Many of the assumptions that scientists as well as laypersons hold with respect to the influence of the city on drinking and drinking problems are far from universally accurate. Urbanization, like so many other dimensions of the environment, is a variable that must be evaluated in specific cases if one is to discern how it affects what people do with alcohol.

Other Cultures as Environmental Forces: Acculturation and Anomie

In assessing the impact of environmental factors on minority or subjugated populations, it is easy to point to other cultures as the sources of harmful new habits or of psychic and social stress that prompts drinking as a form of escape. North American Indians and Eskimos, Australian Aborigines, the San or "Bushmen" of Africa, and many other populations have been described in those terms by many different observers who voice alarm at the rapid loss of traditional lifeways and the substitution of pervasive and often harmful drinking when they come into close and sustained contact with people of European descent.

The negative impact need not be malevolently motivated, as when increasing drinking problems among Jews are said to result from their increasing acceptance and incorporation into the dominant patterns of Gentile culture in the United States. For that matter, a theoretical and methodological shortcoming of the large literature that discusses alcohol in relation to acculturation is that some authors emphasize the negative aspects and others the positive. For some, acculturation has to do primarily with the discrediting of traditional values that were cherished, the repudiation of old gods, confrontation with "racial" prejudice, devaluation of old skills and a demand for new kinds of competence; for others, acculturation refers more to one's having achieved those new kinds of competence, learning the other language, embracing new values, and generally achieving a different kind of integration, oriented to a different cultural system. This problem is especially acute in comparing studies that rely on social surveys in which one or a few key questions serve as an index of "degree of acculturation." Studies that link high rates of drinking and drinking problems with high rates of acculturation may not necessarily contradict others that show similarly high correlations with low rates of acculturation. This important source of confusion remains to be systematically addressed, although there is much rhetoric and there are many public health policy decisions that are made on the basis of confused or inconsistent usages of acculturation as a process.

Closely related to the anthropological concept of acculturation is the sociological concept of anomie, which is marred by different dual meaning. Some authors use it to refer to a loss of values, the disoriented sense some people have when they have rejected old ways but have not yet accepted new ones. Others use it to refer to the plight of someone who has chosen to embrace a new set of values, but who finds that access is blocked or that they fail to yield the rewards that had been expected. Anomic individuals, of whichever sort, seem often to drink excessively and to incur a variety of other problems.

What is not widely recognized is that some North American Indian populations are virtually abstinent, and many are temperate. Within each community, of course, there is significant individual variation in terms of drinking and problems. Several Eskimo communities in both Canada and the United States have elected to have local prohibition, demonstrating that native populations are by no means passive objects in relation to intrusive forces. Recent fears about the homogenization of drinking cultures around the world attribute enormous attractiveness to Western products, and imply that traditional customs are easily overcome; four centuries and more of historical experience do not strongly support such assumptions.

Acculturation certainly is a reality and often one that hurts people who often respond by drinking too much. The same can be said of anomie, whether in the sense of normlessness or in the sense of inability to achieve new goals. They are aspects of the environment that affect large segments of the world's population, especially those who are subordinate in multiethnic or multicultural nations. There have been few attempts to relate such studies to research on genetic and biomedical factors, but, with sharper operational definitions and criteria for measurement, they might be revealing, especially in relation to the epidemiology of various problems that are often linked with drinking.

Cultural Systems: Norms, Attitudes, and Values

The anthropological usage of the term "culture" has already been introduced in this chapter and has been more thoroughly explored with relation to alcohol use and its outcomes elsewhere (Heath, 1975, 1982, 1987a, 1987b). It is the basis of "the sociocultural model" for preventive public health, which emphasizes education as the best means of influencing norms, attitudes, and values which, in turn, seem to be major determinants of what and how one drinks, as well as one's behavior in connection with drinking.

A familiar example is Irish culture, in which the overall rate of abstention is exceptionally high, and neither women nor children are supposed to drink. Unmarried men who habitually spend the evening with their mates at the pub, striving to "drink like a man," and keeping up with "rounds" purchased by each member of the group, often suffer severe psychological and physical damage which is commonly attributed to alcohol. In striking contrast is Orthodox Jewish or Armenian culture, where liquor is savored as a good thing for all to enjoy in small quantities; it is shared with both sexes and all ages, within a warm family context, and appreciative drinking (without drunkenness or associated problems) is typical for all.

The Nature of Culture

In one sense, culture refers to virtually all aspects of the ways in which human beings rely on learned rather than instinctive behavior, including all except the first among the dimensions of the environment that have been discussed here. But usage has focused in recent years much more on the normative and evaluative aspects which so drastically shape the choices that individuals make in their daily lives. Culture is an abstraction in the sense that it includes generalizations *from* behavior (such as rules), but it is also very real in the sense that it includes generalizations *of* behavior (such as patterns). Every layperson becomes acutely aware of culture, less in terms of his or her own workaday experience, than when confronted with some contrasting cultural element, whether it be body painting instead of clothing, polygyny instead of monogamy, a category of people who "laugh at inappropriate times," alien foods, a frustratingly different attitude toward punctuality, or difficulty in judging how friendly a stranger means to be. In simplest terms, one's own culture is often mistaken for "human nature," while other cultures are often mistaken for "curious customs."

In some respects, each human being is like *all* other human beings (needing air, being a vertebrate, unable to eat iron ore, and so forth); in some respects, each human being is like *no* other human beings (in terms of memories, details of knowledge, DNA sequencing, and so forth), and in some respects, each human being is like *some* others (this is the realm of culture, including dress, language, range of diet, and so forth).

The Individual and the Group

To acknowledge that culture plays a major role in shaping most of what most people do most of the time is not to say that culture determines behavior. It does set some limits, but it also is an enabling force, providing a vast set of ready-made answers to questions and solutions to problems. The fact that the range of culturally appropriate responses in one group may differ markedly from those in another does not mean that people are automatons uniformly conditioned and uniformly responding. Ample evidence of this is readily at hand in the range of individual variation in dressing, speaking, walking, or sitting in any given population — even though the dominant or modal pattern is clearly *more* different from the ways of dressing, speaking, walking, or sitting that occur in another population.

The human neonate has few of the skills and little of the knowledge that become the basis of almost every deliberate action. A long process of learning (called enculturation or socialization) communicates information, motor habits, ways of thinking, and even ways of perceiving the world. In part this occurs through exhortation, but much more by example and by sometimes subtle ongoing processes of reward and punishment that continues throughout one's lifetime.

In this connection, it is also important to note that the individual holds a variety of social statuses within a cultural system so that different sets of expectations may be brought into play for different roles. The fact that an individual is an adult, by the criteria of the culture, may be important for some things and not for others; similarly one's gender, occupation, social class, level of schooling, color of skin, height, weight, physical condition, kinship, and a host of other variables may each offer certain opportunities and pose certain obstacles. The marvel is that a well-socialized individual is able to recognize which of many potential roles is pertinent in a given context and to adopt the appropriate repertorie of attitudes and activities.

With specific reference to drinking, the widespread ban on drinking by children illustrates this well, inasmuch as most people are able easily to adjust as they mature and begin drinking. Similarly, the double standard that often obtains between men's and women's drinking and associated behavior is undoubtedly resented by many but it is adhered to by more.

Types of Norms and of Deviance

In another context (Harford et al, 1980), we have already described various kinds of norms: the normal norm (a general or typical formulation of what people say they do); the normative norm (prescriptions and proscriptions about what people say people ought to do); and the modal norm (an empirical statement of what people actually do). Although they may occasionally be congruent, it seems more common that those norms differ from each other with respect to a given situation.

When one violates a normative norm, there may be trouble — unless "everyone is doing it" (modal norm). Someone who deviates too far from either of those norms may be labeled deviant, and such labeling can lead to ostracism or other sanctions. This appears to be how the alcoholic, who may start as "the life of the party," gradually loses the goodwill of those in his or her social network and becomes increasingly isolated. It can also, of course, be how a counterculture can be formed among like-minded deviants from one system who may gravitate together to form a new system with its own very different norms (as on "Skid Row"). But it would be misleading to think of any culture's norms as being immutable.

Persistence and Change

Norms, like other aspects of culture, have a tendency to persist inasmuch as they are shared and valued by many people, but they are also liable to change for various reasons. If significant alterations in some other aspect of the environment cause a cultural trait to be no longer appropriate, adaptive change may well take place gradually as individuals alter their own actions. If what people actually do becomes too markedly discrepant with what they ought to do, even normative norms can be reshaped to conform with reality. The acceptability of a woman's drinking in public is recent in some cultures, and the idea that an intoxicated person is funny has disappeared from many of the same cultures. These examples show that it is misleading to speak in a gross way of a trend toward greater or lesser permissiveness.

How the Parts Fit Together

Italian drinking patterns nicely illustrate the integration of culture, as well as some practical implications of "the sociocultural model" as a policy for prevention of alcoholism. In reconciling an exceptionally high rate of per capita consumption and an exceptionally low rate of alcohol-related problems, one notes that children are introduced early to drinking small quantities of watered wine. This occurs as a normal part of eating, with the enthusiastic support of the family, at home as well as in restaurants. Drinking thus becomes an integral part of daily life, not a special way of achieving relaxation, relieving psychic stress, gaining delusions of power, or escaping reality. The Italian association of drink with food has physiological as well as psychological advantages over some cultural patterns that divorce alcohol from food and make quick drunkenness a goal. The psychoactive effect of alcoholic beverages is little sought or appreciated, with less than intoxicating amounts typical on most occasions when Italians drink. Obviously, there are individual Italians whose behavior differs from these normative statements, and there are festive occasions when some variant norms apply. But the general pattern of drinking as a normal, wholesome, enjoyable aspect of everyday life—not an unwholesome, risky, and mysterious activity to be undertaken in peculiar contexts that are set apart from family and the normal routines of living—undoubtedly constitutes a strong environmental factor (or complex of environmental factors) that must affect one's predilection to heavy drinking and one's susceptibility to many kinds of problems.

The integration of diverse aspects of culture also serves as the logical basis for "the sociocultural model" (which is often directly contrasted with "the control of availability model") of prevention. We have already discussed (under the section "Availability and Legal Constraints" previously) how ease of access does not imply abuse, and the proliferation of controls does not prevent it. If people can be taught to view drinking in different ways, they can also be taught to drink in different ways and to have different expectations of what drinking can do. In a sense, this tends to happen in the normal course of the life cycle for many people, but particular norms and goals may be more appropriate for a given community.

Some critics who dismiss education as ineffective as a means of, in effect, innoculating someone against alcoholism, are premature in their criticism. When they assert that education doesn't work, they are invariably referring to some limited experiment within the context of formal schooling, in which whatever information may have been communicated by a teacher, was woefully out of context. Education (in the sense of enculturation or socialization) is an ongoing process that involves people of all ages, in a wide range of normal workaday situations, learning by doing as well as by being told.

It is not that education doesn't work; the sad fact is that it hasn't been tried in a sufficiently ambitious, long-term, communitywide way. A program like the Framingham study (or similar projects in Finland, Japan, and elsewhere) that set out to educate entire communities about the heart, its functioning, its susceptibilities, relations with diet, exercise, and so forth, could probably have an epidemiologically significant impact on drinking and its outcomes.

However important the cultural system may be as a mediator between the original genetic material and the way in which a mature adult functions, it must be viewed as only one among many dimensions of the environment. In weighing the potential role of culturally relevant education as a means of minimizing the potentially deleterious consequences of alcohol consumption, we have come full circle, to the fundamental question introduced at the beginning of this chapter. It is not yet possible to separate genetic contributions from the environmental influences, and much more must be done by all concerned if we are seriously to undertake an accounting of the complex genetic–environmental interactions that remain only vaguely recognized and even less understood.

REFERENCES

Cahalan D, Room R: *Problem Drinking among American Men*. New Brunswick, NJ, Rutgers Center of Alcohol Studies, 1974.

Collmann J: Social order and the exchange of liquor: A theory of drinking among Australian Aborigines. *J Anthrop Res* 1979; 35:208–224.

Csikszentmihalyi M: A cross-cultural comparison of some structural characteristics of group drinking. *Human Dev* (Basel) 1968; 11:201–216.

Davies P, Walsh D: *Alcohol Problems and Alcohol in Europe*. London, Croom Holm, 1983.

DeFoe JR, Breed W, Breed LA: Drinking on television: a five-year study. *J Drug Educ* 1983; 13:25–38.

Field PB: A new cross-cultural study of drunkenness, in Pittman DJ, Snyder CR (eds): *Society, Culture and Drinking Patterns*. New York, Wiley, 1962, pp 48–74.

Giesbrecht N, Cahannes N, Moskalewics J, Osterberg E, Room R (eds): *Consequences of Drinking: Trends in Alcohol Problem Statistics in Seven Countries*. Toronto, Addiction Research Foundation, 1983.

Goedde HW, Agarwal DP (eds): *Genetics and Alcoholism*. New York, Alan R. Liss, 1987; pp 3–20.

Grant M (ed): *Alcohol Policies*. Copenhagen, World Health Organization Regional Office for Europe, 1985.

Harford TC, Gaines LS: *Social Drinking Contexts*. Rockville, MD, National Institute on Alcohol Abuse and Alcoholism, 1981.

Harford TC, Parker DA, Light L (eds): *Normative Approaches to the Prevention of Alcohol Abuse and Alcoholism*. Rockville, MD, National Institute on Alcohol Abuse and Alcoholism, 1980.

Heath DB: A critical review of ethnographic studies of alcohol use, in Gibbins R, Israel Y, Kalant H, Popham R, Schmidt W, Smart R (eds): *Research Advances in Alcohol and Drug Problems*. New York, Wiley, 1975, vol 2, pp 1–92.

Heath DB: Sociocultural variants in alcoholism, in Pattison EM, Kaufman E (eds): *Encyclopedic Handbook of Alcoholism*. New York, Gardner Press, 1982, pp 426–440.

Heath DB: A decade of development in the anthropological study of alcohol use: 1970–1980, in Douglas M (ed): *Constructive Drinking: Perspectives on Drink from Anthropology*. Cambridge and Paris, Cambridge University Press and Editions de la Maison des Sciences de l'Homme, 1987a, pp 16–69.

Heath DB: Anthropology and alcohol studies: Current issues. *Ann Rev Anthropol* 1987b; 16:99–120.

Heath DB: Alcohol control policies and drinking patterns: An international game of politics against science. *J Substance Abuse*, 1988; 1:109–115.

Institute of Medicine: *Causes and Consequences of Alcohol Problems: An Agenda for Research*. Washington, National Academy Press, 1987, pp 93.

Jellinek EM: The symbolism of drinking: A cultural–historical approach. *J Stud Alcohol* 1976; 38:849–866.

Kluckhohn C: *Mirror for Man: Anthropology in Action*. New York, Whittlesey House, 1949.

MacAndrew C, Edgerton RB: *Drunken Comportment: a Social Explanation*. Chicago, Aldine, 1969.

Marlatt GA, Nathan PE (eds): *Behavioral Approaches to Alcoholism*. New Brunswick, NJ, Rutgers Center of Alcohol Studies, 1978.

Moore MH, Gerstein DR (eds): *Alcohol and Public Policy: Beyond the Shadow of Prohibition*. Washington, National Academy Press, 1981.

Sadava SW: Problem behavior theory and consumption and consequences of alcohol use. *J Stud Alcohol* 1985; 46:392–397.

Single E, Storm T (eds): *Public Drinking and Public Policy*. Toronto, Addiction Research Foundation, 1985.

Smith CJ, Hanham RQ: *Alcohol Abuse: Geographical Perspectives*. Washington, Association of American Geographers, 1982.

Waddell JO: For individual power and social credit: The use of alcohol among Tucson Papagos. *Hum Org* 1975; 34:9–15.

West LJ (ed): *Alcoholism and Related Problems: Issues for the American Public*. Englewood Cliffs, NJ, Prentice-Hall, 1984.

CHAPTER 17

Gene–Environment Interactions in Alcoholism

Elliot S. Vesell, M.D.

Department of Pharmacology
The Pennsylvania State University College of Medicine
The Milton S. Hershey Medical Center
Hershey, Pennsylvania, USA

CONTROVERSIAL NATURE OF THE SUBJECT

Numerous reasons can be offered for the intense, often acrimonious controversies that surround the subjects of the causes of alcoholism and the relative roles of genes and environment in its etiology. Who bears responsibility for this tragic disease: prevailing societal conditions and mores that tacitly condone, and thereby encourage, inebriation or the families of patients, through possible transmission of causative genes and too permissive an attitude toward alcohol consumption? Disagreement over these issues is understandable in light of present uncertainty concerning the precise underlying nature of this dread, commonly occurring disease.

By contrast to the discouraging situation with respect to understanding causes of alcoholism, biochemical defects have been identified that are responsible for several hundred inborn errors of metabolism. For these disorders a specific reaction catalyzed by a specific mutant enzyme is blocked, thereby causing accumulation of the substrate in the body to toxic concentrations. Again, unlike the situation in alcoholism, a simple monogenic pattern of mendelian transmission of these aberrant genes has been elucidated (generally autosomal recessive).

Clinically, these accomplishments for many inborn errors of metabolism have had profound significance: an accurate diagnosis can often be made before symptoms manifest themselves and before tissue damage occurs. Such early diagnosis, through measurement of an abnormally elevated substance in body fluids, often allows dietary alterations to be instituted that either minimize or avoid entirely tissue damage, thereby significantly improving the patient's prognosis. Ultimately, gene therapy may provide a source of the normal enzyme to produce a definitive cure in some of these patients.

If in alcoholism similar progress could be achieved in elucidating etiology, the clinical and therapeutic benefits might likewise be enormous. Despite the problems and obstacles enumerated at the outset, excellent research in this area has been performed, and a diverse array of genetic factors has been implicated in the causation of alcoholism. Nevertheless, at present neither the precise mode of transmission of these genetic factors nor the precise function of the genes implicated is clear. Possibly their penetrance or expressivity is incomplete. Much of the following discussion must of necessity be speculative, because, unfortunately, that is the present state of our knowledge on causes of alcoholism. One optimistic corollary is that there is a critical need for future research to clarify this nebulous subject.

Given the probable clinical heterogeneity of the disease referred to as alcoholism, it seems likely that several different genetic factors may participate. If different types of alcoholism exist, each caused by different genes, then it is also reasonable to anticipate that a slightly different set of environmental factors modulates these distinct genes and hence the clinical course and severity of each form of the disease.

From these considerations, it is understandable how research in different laboratories that focuses on different aspects of the problem of alcoholism would be expected to yield different results with respect to the relative contributions of genetic and environmental factors. Answers would differ depending on the particular step or level under investigation. Although results of research focused at one level would be expected to differ from the results of research directed at another level, the critical, but as yet unanswered, question arises of the relevance of each experimental model or paradigm to the human disease alcoholism. Due to present incomplete knowledge of the nature of alcoholism, we cannot agree on how close each experimental model comes to the human disease. The excellent research by the groups of C. R. Cloninger et al (1986) and M. A. Schuckit (1986), who have established a role for genetic factors in human alcoholism, is particularly noteworthy. Since they themselves describe their studies in preceding chapters of this volume, only the following conclusions from their work are summarized briefly here: (1) alcoholism in humans is a complex, heterogeneous disease; (2) each of at least three clinically distinct forms of alcoholism shows different patterns of genetic transmission and of influence by environmental factors; (3) complex interactions occur between genes and environment to influence the clinical expression and severity of the disease.

STUDIES INDICATING GENETIC DETERMINANTS OF ALCOHOLISM

Even though the search for specific biochemical and genetic markers of alcoholism has proved disappointing in that a specific biochemical and genetic lesion common to a large proportion of alcoholic subjects has yet to be identified, nevertheless, numerous studies in man (see the preceding chapters by Cloninger and Schuckit) and laboratory animals (Li et al, 1986) reveal that genetic factors control many behavioral, physiological, and biochemical responses to alcohol. For example, one such response is alcohol drinking behavior in rats (Ericksson, 1968; Li et al, 1979) and in mice (McClearn and Rodgers, 1959). Other examples of genetic regulation of variations in behavioral and biochemical responses to alcohol include sensitivity to alcohol of the central nervous system (McClearn and Kakihana, 1973; Riley et al, 1977) and whole body (Mizoi et al, 1979). In addition, genetic factors have been implicated in causing interindividual variations in alcohol metabolism (Vesell et al, 1971; Kopun and Propping, 1977; Thurman, 1980; Martin et al, 1985), as well as in the development of CNS diseases secondary to alcoholism (Propping et al, 1987), and also tolerance to ethanol (Grieve et al, 1979; Meisch, 1982) and physical dependence upon ethanol (Goldstein, 1973).

Genetic variations among Orientals and Caucasians in sensitivity to ethanol and in the capacity to consume ethanol without flushing have been reported (Wolff, 1972). Flushing among Orientals on drinking ethanol has been shown to be due to the absence of a low K_m acetaldehyde dehydrogenase isozyme that is present in virtually all Caucasians (Goedde et al, 1979, 1983; Harada et al, 1983; Yoshihara et al, 1983). Absence of this isozyme in tissues of Orientals exhibiting the inherited trait of flushing after ethanol ingestion renders affected subjects intolerant to the consumption of even small amounts of ethanol. Such small amounts of ethanol produce in affected subjects very high blood acetaldehyde concentrations. This dysphoric response to ingestion of even small amounts of ethanol may protect affected subjects from developing alcoholism. Although this specific genetic protective mechanism cannot be invoked in Caucasian subjects to explain differences among them in risk of developing alcoholism, another genetic polymorphism might exist in the latter group to produce markedly different susceptibilities to ethanol.

GENE–ENVIRONMENT INTERACTIONS IN POLYGENIC TRAITS

Critical factors determining the phenotype of most inborn errors of metabolism are the character of the mutant allele and its presence in single or double dose in the affected subject. This principle applies to most *monogenically* transmitted traits: genotype determines phenotype with a relatively small role played by environmental factors. By contrast, in *polygenically* controlled traits, such as in primary hypertension and probably some forms of alcoholism, the reverse applies. Environmental factors play a proportionately larger role in determining phenotype because they modulate to different extents the multiple genetic loci involved. By definition, in *polygenically* controlled traits, two or more genetic loci contribute to the phenotype, whereas for *monogenically* controlled traits only a single genetic locus participates.

Alcoholism is considered by many to be a complex behavioral trait, and the current, genetic conception of how genes control such traits is that they are polygenically regulated. The extent to which these multiple genetic loci are expressed depends on many diverse, but as yet incompletely identified, environmental and developmental factors. Thus, in polygenic traits separation of phenotypic expression into neat compartments designated "genes" or "environment" is conceptually erroneous and misleading. Rather, both genes and environment participate intimately, dynamically interacting to influence the phenotype. Neither could work independently of the other. Thus, in a polygenic model assessment of the influence of heredity is impossible out of the context of environmental influence, and vice versa. One frequently used, convenient notion of "heritability" for polygenically controlled traits is that of a ratio or fraction in which the numerator is the variance due to genetic factors and the denominator is the total variance due to genetic plus environmental factors. Clearly, the numerator cannot exist alone, but only in relation to the denominator, which includes environmental contributions to variance. Furthermore, this fraction continuously fluctuates as the prevailing environmental conditions change. To cite an often misunderstood example, the value of "heritability" for variations in rates of ethanol elimination should not be expected to be constant for all groups examined, but rather will differ considerably in proportion to the environmental diversity that exists among groups. Thus, the value for "heritability" of 98% obtained by Vesell et al (1971) for twins who were selected to be environmentally homogeneous with respect to prior abstinence from ethanol is understandably much higher than the value of 46% reported by Kopun and Propping (1977) for twins who differed with respect to ethanol consumption. Rather than being contradictory, these results should be considered confirmatory since they show that in a polygenically controlled trait as the extent of environmental diversity among subjects increases, the value of "heritability" declines.

In light of these differences in design of twin studies, it cannot be overemphasized that to apply the twin technique to study variations in rates of drug elimination, critical environmental factors affecting drug disposition must be kept balanced and equal among all twins in order to reveal a significant genetic contribution to phenotypic variation. It may be argued that the purpose of the twin study is not to disclose genetic, but environmental, contributions to phenotypic variation. However, for such a purpose twin studies are inefficient and inappropriate, since the twins still differ genetically among themselves, and it is possible to eliminate entirely genetic variation as a contribution to phenotypic variation by adopting another experimental design. That design involves the use of each volunteer as his or her own control, as described in the next section.

GENE–ENVIRONMENT INTERACTIONS THAT AFFECT DRUG METABOLISM AS MODELS OF GENE–ENVIRONMENT INTERACTIONS IN ALCOHOLISM

Human models of alcoholism have not been sufficiently developed and refined to allow experiments to be performed that isolate and identify in a precise manner the role of different environmental factors on the expression of the phenotype. However, in clinical pharmacology, the use of the antipyrine test in carefully selected normal volunteers permits investigation of a single host factor, such as one of those in the outer circle of Fig 17.1, with minimum interference from the others that are held constant. Differences in antipyrine clearance, measured both before and after experimental imposition of this single host factor, serve to indicate the role that each factor can play in influencing the normal subject's hepatic drug-metabolizing capacity. Using this approach, dose-response curves of a particular host factor's effects on drug metabolism can be generated. Also, the influence of several host factors can be either investigated in combination or compared when studied individually.

Unlike the numerous problems that beset studies to identify host factors that cause alcoholism, much progress has been achieved in investigating host factors that influence the disposition of drugs eliminated primarily through hepatic metabolism. This progress has occurred largely through availability of normal human subjects who can safely ingest single doses of various model drugs, such as antipyrine, aminopyrine, amobarbital, debrisoquine, sparteine, mephenytoin, acetaminophen, theophylline, etc. Antipyrine has proven particularly fruitful

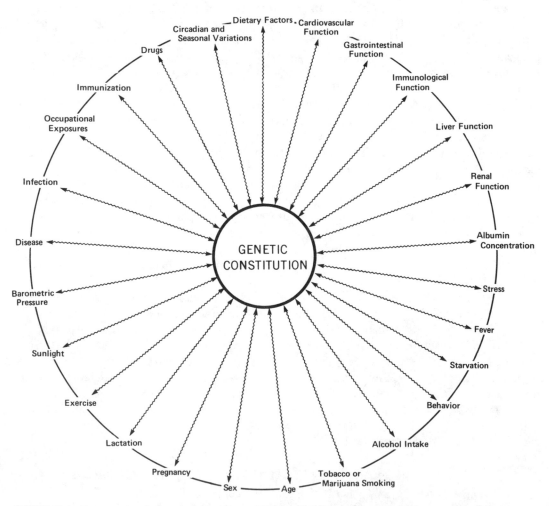

FIGURE 17.1. This circular design suggests the multiplicity of either well-established or suspected host factors that may influence drug response in man. A line joins all such factors in the outer circle to indicate their close interrelationship. Arrows from each factor in the outer circle are wavy to indicate that effects of each host factor on drug response may occur at multiple sites and through different processes that include drug absorption, distribution, metabolism, excretion, receptor action, and combinations thereof.

in disclosing numerous environmental factors that can interact with each other as well as with genetic factors to determine antipyrine elimination rates and plasma antipyrine concentrations.

The design of Figure 17.1 suggests dynamic interaction of such host factors. In contrast to alcoholics, the subjects used to identify the factors shown in Figure 17.1 were all carefully selected and uniform with respect to almost every factor in the outer circle. This standardization of prevailing environmental conditions among the subjects permitted each variable to be investigated independently of all others. Dose-response curves could be generated, relating increments of a specific factor to subsequent changes in antipyrine disposition. This model drug approach is exceedingly sensitive in detecting factors that can affect drug disposition, mainly because each subject serves as his or her own control (Vesell, 1979). Use of subjects as their own control eliminates extraneous contributions from many genetic factors and environmental perturbations that occur in the alternative experimental design where the control and experimental subjects differ, forming two separate groups that are compared. Nevertheless, like all laboratory tests, the model drug approach has limitations. Occasionally, it has disappointed some investigators whose expectations from it were unrealistic or unwarranted (Vesell, 1979).

The main limitation as well as advantage of the model drug approach depends directly on the pharmacologic characteristics of the drug selected for administration. With respect to antipyrine, the principal advantage is that antipyrine decay in saliva and plasma reflects directly antipyrine metabolism in the liver by three biochemically distinguishable cytochrome P-450 isozymes. Since antipyrine given orally in aqueous solution is absorbed completely from the gastrointestinal tract, distributes in "total body water," is not bound significantly to tissue or plasma proteins, and is not eliminated to an appreciable extent by renal mechanisms, antipyrine decay in plasma and in saliva sensitivity reflects its rate of hepatic biotransformation. Furthermore, since antipyrine is a drug with low hepatic extraction, its elimination is independent of hepatic blood flow. No other model drug yet proposed enjoys so many advantages as an indicator of hepatic drug-metabolizing capacity. Nevertheless, antipyrine elimination can only reflect the activities of a few of the many hepatic drug-metabolizing enzymes. Other such enzymes, not directly involved in antipyrine biotransformation, may be influenced to a greater or lesser extent than the antipyrine-metabolizing enzymes by a particular genetic or environmental factor. Hence, these effects may not be accurately disclosed with antipyrine. For example, the metabolism of debrisoquine and sparteine occurs through a different isozyme of cytochrome P-450. For this reason, if many hepatic drug-metabolizing enzymes are to be investigated simultaneously, several model drugs in addition to antipyrine need to be used in combination.

Pharmacogenetics, the study of genetically determined variations in drug response, focuses on interindividual variations in response to drugs because they are frequently encountered and often present clinical problems. For example, the extent of these intersubject variations in response can reach fortyfold, depending on the particular drug and population. For drugs with low therapeutic indices, each patient's dosage regimen needs to be carefully adjusted to avoid drug toxicity or undertreatment.

Since many drugs are plant alkaloids, it is not surprising that genetic variations also exist in response to some dietary constituents and that some inborn errors of metabolism are worsened by dietary constituents. For example, galactosemia, phenylketonuria, Wilson's disease, celiac disease, and lactose intolerance due to lactase deficiency are exacerbated by foods containing galactose, phenylalanine, copper, gluten, and milk, respectively. Also, in several other inborn errors of intermediary metabolism, crises can be precipitated by certain drugs. For example, in diabetes mellitus, gout, and several forms of porphyria, administration of adrenal glucocorticoids, thiazide diuretics, and barbiturates, respectively, should be avoided.

Another group of inborn errors of metabolism exists in which the aberrant (mutant) protein participates directly, rather than indirectly, in drug disposition or action. These entities, the main focus in the past of the field of pharmacogenetics, include several rare monogeni-

cally transmitted conditions (acatalasia, atypical plasma cholinesterase, phenytoin sensitivity, and warfarin resistance) as well as more commonly occurring monogenically transmitted
conditions (slow acetylation of isoniazid and other drugs, glucose-6-phosphate dehydrogenase
deficiency, sensitivity to debrisoquine and sensitivity to mephenytoin). Abundantly reviewed
in the past (Kalow, 1962; Motulsky, 1964; La Du, 1972; Vesell, 1973; Vessell and Penno,
1983; Weinshilboum and Vesell, 1984), these pharmacogenetic conditions will not be described
in detail here. Each exemplifies how genetic constitution can determine drug toxicity. In general, toxicity arises in a genetically susceptible individual from accumulation of parent drug
due to a block in its biotransformation to inactive metabolites, as mentioned above for other
inborn errors of metabolism. Transmitted in classical mendelian fashion by alleles at a single but different locus, each of these metabolic blocks is described as monogenic. In most
cases, a double dose of a mutant gene is required to produce the defect (recessive phenotype),
but rarely, as in phenytoin toxicity, a single gene seems to suffice (dominant phenotype).

In 1968, the influence of genetic factors on drug response and toxicity was extended well
beyond the aforementioned monogenic conditions to other entities encompassing different
drugs (Vesell and Page, 1968a, 1968b, 1968c; Penno et al, 1981). These new pharmacogenetic
conditions involved drugs characterized by: (1) extensive hepatic metabolism through cytochrome–P-450-dependent monooxygenases and (2) large interindividual variations in rates of
elimination. Almost a dozen different drugs were given to normal uninduced twins who were
nonsmokers, otherwise unmedicated, and not chronic consumers of ethanol. These drugs
included antipyrine (Vesell and Page, 1968a; Penno et al, 1981), phenylbutazone (Vesell and
Page, 1968b), bishydroxycoumarin (Vesell and Page, 1968c), ethanol (Vesell et al, 1971), halothane (Cascorbi et al, 1971), nortriptyline (Alexanderson et al, 1969), amobarbital (Endrenyi
et al, 1976), phenytoin (Andreasen et al, 1973), salicylate (Furst et al, 1977), and tolbutamide
(Scott and Poffenbarger, 1979).

Genetic control over extensive interindividual variations in rates of elimination of these
drugs was indicated by larger pharmacokinetic differences within dizygotic than within
monozygotic twins (Vesell and Page, 1968a, 1968b, 1968c; Alexanderson et al, 1969; Cascorbi
et al, 1971; Vesell et al, 1971; Andreasen et al, 1973; Endrenyi et al, 1976; Furst et al, 1977;
Scott and Poffenbarger, 1979; Penno et al, 1981). Intraindividual variations were small compared to interindividual variations in these carefully selected, uninduced twins living under
uniform environmental conditions. Although such observations supported a genetic basis for
the large interindividual variations in the disposition of these drugs, the precise mendelian
mode of transmission of these factors could not be elucidated just from the twin studies on
parent drugs. Thus, when pedigree analysis was attempted solely on the basis of kinetic studies
performed on the parent drug, rather than on principal metabolites, the mode of transmission of interindividual variations for bishydroxycoumarin (Motulsky, 1964), phenylbutazone
(Whittaker and Price Evans, 1970), and nortriptyline (Asberg et al, 1971) was either unclear
or else more compatible with a polygenic than a monogenic mechanism. In light of current
information, a polygenic attribution is misleading because more recent examinations of individual metabolic pathways have disclosed monogenic transmission (Vesell and Penno, 1983).

Since some twins participated in several of these studies, it was possible to determine
whether their rates of biotransformation of different drugs were closely correlated. Although
some correlations occurred, rates of clearance of most drugs investigated were independent
of one another (Vesell and Page, 1968c). This result was notable for several reasons. It suggested that the twin studies had disclosed several discrete genetic entities, rather than one or
two, that determined large variations in the metabolism of numerous drugs. Furthermore, the
existence of separate genetic entities, each involving a different isozyme of hepatic cytochrome
P-450, agreed with simultaneously emerging evidence for extensive heterogeneity of this hepatic hemoprotein (Alvares et al, 1969; Lu and Levin, 1974; Ryan et al, 1975; Wang et al,
1980; Nebert et al, 1982). Thus correlations between drugs, each biotransformed by multiple pathways, needed to be established not simply by following the kinetics of their parent
forms but rather by measuring and comparing rates of formation of individual metabolites.

FUTURE GENETIC APPROACHES TO ALCOHOLISM

Among Caucasians alcoholism is probably not caused by a simple monogenic polymorphism, such as the pharmacogenetic polymorphisms described above. Involvement of only a single enzyme, such as an isozyme of liver alcohol or acetaldehyde dehydrogenase, seems unlikely; but even the genetic control of these enzymes is highly complex and many different genetic loci participate (Smith et al, 1986; Li and Bosron, 1987). Rather, the brain and the brain nuclei involved with the development of addiction seem to be the sites that need to be investigated to establish a firmer foothold on the causes of alcoholism.

Pharmacogenetic polymorphisms involving the metabolism of the drugs described above may serve as useful paradigms in that even though monogenically transmitted they show how environmental host factors can under some circumstances modify phenotype. The same principle may apply in alcoholism. This possibility suggests why studies of genetic causes of alcoholism should progress beyond reliance on clinical signs and symptoms of the full-blown disease to more sensitive methods of phenotyping subjects and of tracing patterns of genetic transmission. One promising new method, exemplified by recent breakthroughs in the genetics of Huntington's disease, Duchenne muscular dystrophy and cystic fibrosis, consists of focusing on DNA itself, searching for restriction fragment length polymorphisms (RFLPs) closely linked to the particular genetic locus of interest. This approach, although difficult, offers great promise in that its application to other genetically transmitted human diseases has been dramatically successful. By analogy, use of RFLPs in families with several alcoholic members may permit us to come closer to, and ultimately identify, the causative gene(s).

REFERENCES

Alexanderson B, Price Evans DA, Sjoqvist F: Steady-state plasma levels of nortriptyline in twins. Influence of genetic factors and drug therapy. *Br Med J* 1969; 4:764–768.

Alvares AP, Schilling G, Levin W, Kuntzman R, Brand L, Mark LC: Cytochromes P-450 and b_5 in human liver microsomes. *Clin Pharmacol Ther* 1969; 10:655–659.

Andreasen PB, Froland A, Skovsted L, Andersen SA, Hauge M: Diphenylhydantoin half-life in man and its inhibition by phenylbutazone: The role of genetic factors. *Acta Med Scand* 1973; 193:561–564.

Asberg M, Price Evans DA, Sjoqvist F: Genetic control of nortriptyline kinetics in man: A study of relative of propositus with high plasma concentrations. *J Med Genet* 1971; 8:129–135.

Cascorbi HF, Vesell ES, Blake DA, Helrich M: Genetic and environmental influence on halothane metabolism in twins. *Clin Pharmacol Ther* 1971; 12:50–55.

Cloninger CR, Sigvardsson S, Reich T, Bohman M: Inheritance of risk to develop alcoholism, in Braude MC, Chao HM (eds): *Genetic and Biological Markers in Drug Abuse and Alcoholism*. Rockville, Maryland, NIDA Research Monograph 66, 1986, pp 86–96.

Endrenyi L, Inaba T, Kalow W: Genetic study of amobarbital elimination based on its kinetics in twins. *Clin Pharmacol Ther* 1976; 20:701–714.

Eriksson K: Genetic selection for voluntary alcohol consumption in the albino rat. *Science* 1968; 159: 739–741.

Furst DE, Gupta N, Paulus HE: Salicylate metabolism in twins: Evidence suggesting a genetic influence and induction of salicylurate formation. *J Clin Invest* 1977; 60:32–42.

Goedde HW, Harada S, Agarwal DP: Racial differences in alcohol sensitivity: A new hypothesis. *Hum Genet* 1979; 51:331–334.

Goedde HW, Agarwal DP, Harada S: The role of alcohol dehydrogenase and aldehyde dehydrogenase isozymes in alcohol metabolism, alcohol sensitivity and alcoholism, in Rattazzi MC, Scandalios JG, Whitt GS (eds): *Isozymes: Curr Top Biol Med Res*. New York, Alan R Liss Inc, vol 8, 1983, pp 175–193.

Goldstein DB: Inherited differences in intensity of alcohol withdrawal reactions in mice. *Nature* 1973; 245:154–156.

Grieve SJ, Griffiths PJ, Littleton JM: Genetic influences on the rate of development of ethanol tolerance and the ethanol dependence withdrawal syndrome in mice. *Drug Alcohol Depend* 1979; 4:77–86.

Harada S, Agarwal DP, Goedde HW, Ishikawa B: Aldehyde dehydrogenase isozyme variation and alcoholism in Japan. *Pharmacol Biochem Behav* 1983; 18(Supp. 1):151–153.

Kalow W: *Pharmacogenetics: Heredity and the Response to Drugs*. Philadelphia, Saunders, 1962.

Kopun M, Propping P: The kinetics of ethanol absorption and elimination in twins and supplementary repetitive experiments in singleton subjects. *Eur J Clin Pharmacol* 1977; 11:337–344.

La Du BN: Pharmacogenetics: Defective enzymes in relation to reactions to drugs. *Annu Rev Med* 1972; 23:453–468.

Li T-K, Bosron WF: Distribution and properties of human alcohol dehydrogenase isoenzymes, in Rubin E (ed): *Alcohol and the Cell*. New York, The New York Academy of Sciences, Annals of the New York Academy of Sciences, 1987, vol 492, pp 1–10.

Li T-K, Lumeng L, McBride WJ, Waller MB: Progress toward a voluntary oral consumption model of alcoholism. *Drug Alcohol Depend* 1979; 4:45–60.

Li T-K, Lumeng L, McBride WJ, Waller MB, Murphy JM: Studies on an animal model of alcoholism, in Braude MC, Chao HM (eds): *Genetic and Biological Markers in Drug Abuse and Alcoholism*, Rockville, Maryland, NIDA Research Monograph 66, 1986, pp 41–49.

Lu AYH, Levin W: The resolution and reconstitution of the liver microsomal hydroxylation system. *Biochim Biophys Acta* 1974; 344:205–240.

Martin NG, Perl J, Oakeshott JG, Gibson JB, Starmer GA, Wilks AV: A twin study of ethanol metabolism. *Behav Genet* 1985; 15:93–109.

McClearn GE, Kakihana R: Selective breeding for ethanol sensitivity in mice. *Behav Genet* 1973; 3:409–410.

McClearn GE, Rodgers DA: Differences in alcohol preference among inbred strains of mice. *J Stud Alcohol* 1959; 20:691–695.

Meisch R: Animal studies of alcohol intake. *Br J Psychiatry* 1982; 141:113–120.

Mizoi Y, Ijiri J, Tatsuno Y, Kijima T, Fujiwara S, Adachi J: Relationship between facial flushing and blood acetaldehyde levels after ethanol intake. *Pharmacol Biochem Behav* 1979; 10:303–311.

Motulsky A: Pharmacogenetics. *Prog Med Genet* 1964; 3:49–74.

Nebert DW, Negishi M, Lang MA, Hjelmeland LM, Eisen HJ: The Ah locus of multigene family necessary for survival in a chemically adverse environment: Comparison with the immune system. *Adv Genet* 1982; 21:1–52.

Penno MB, Dvorchik BH, Vesell ES: Genetic variations in rates of antipyrine metabolite formation: A study in uninduced twins. *Proc Natl Acad Sci USA* 1981; 78:5193–5196.

Propping P, Friedl W, Uhlhaas S, Kaufmann A: Genetic influences on CNS diseases secondary to alcoholism, in Goedde HW, Agarwal DP (eds): *Genetics and Alcoholism*. Progress in Clinical and Biological Research, vol 241. New York, Alan R Liss, 1987, pp 97–105.

Riley EP, Worsham ED, Lester D, Freed EX: Selective breeding of rats for differences in reactivity to alcohol. *J Stud Alcohol* 1977; 38:1705–1717.

Ryan D, Lu AYH, Kawalek J, West SB, Levin W: Highly purified cytochrome P-448 and P-450 from rat liver microsomes. *Biochem Biophys Res Commun* 1975; 64:1134–1141.

Schuckit MA: Genetic and biological markers in alcoholism and drug abuse, in Braude MC, Chao HM (eds): *Genetic and Biological Markers in Drug Abuse and Alcoholism*. Rockville, Maryland, NIDA Research Monograph 66, 1986, pp 97–108.

Scott J, Poffenbarger PL: Pharmacogenetics of tolbutamide metabolism in humans. *Diabetes* 1979; 28:41–51.

Smith M, Duester G, Hatfield GW: Development of DNA probes to investigate genetic variation of alcohol metabolizing enzymes, in Braude MC, Chao HM (eds): *Genetic and Biological Markers in Drug Abuse and Alcoholism*. Rockville, Maryland, NIDA Research Monograph 66, 1986, pp 50–56.

Thurman RG: Ethanol elimination rate is inherited in the rat. *Adv Exp Med Biol* 1980; 132:655–662.

Vesell ES: Advances in pharmacogenetics. *Prog Med Genet* 1973; 9:291–367.

Vesell ES: The antipyrine test in clinical pharmacology: Conceptions and misconceptions. *Clin Pharmacol Ther* 1979; 26:275–286.

Vesell ES, Page JG: Genetic control of drug levels in man: Antipyrine. *Science* 1968a; 161:72–73.

Vesell ES, Page JG: Genetic control of drug levels in man: Phenylbutazone. *Science* 1968b; 159:1479–1480.

Vesell ES, Page JG: Genetic control of dicoumarol levels in man. *J Clin Invest* 1968c; 47:2657–2663.

Vesell ES, Page JG, Passananti GT: Genetic and environmental factors affecting ethanol metabolism in man. *Clin Pharmacol Ther* 1971; 12:192–201.

Vesell ES, Penno MB: Assessment of methods to identify sources of interindividual pharmacokinetic variations. *Clin Pharmacokinet* 1983; 8:378–409.

Wang P, Mason PS, Guengerich FP: Purification of human liver cytochrome P-450 and comparison to the enzyme isolated from rat liver. *Arch Biochem Biophys* 1980; 199:206–219.

Weinshilboum RM, Vesell ES: Human pharmacogenetics and new directions in pharmacogenetics. *Fed Proc Symposiums* 1984; 43:2295–2342.

Whittaker JA, Price Evans DA: Genetic control of phenylbutazone metabolism in man. *Br Med J* 1970; 4:323–328.

Wolff PH: Ethnic differences in alcohol sensitivity. *Science* 1972; 175:449–450.

Yoshihara H, Sato N, Kamada T, Low H: Low K_m ALDH isozyme and alcoholic liver injury. *Pharmacol Biochem Behav* 1983; 18(Supp. 1):425–428.

CHAPTER 18

Economic Aspects of
Alcohol Control Policies

Alan Maynard and Andrew Jones

Center for Health Economics at York
York, United Kingdom

INTRODUCTION

This chapter provides an economic framework for the discussion of alcohol policy objectives and the efficiency of alternative alcohol policy instruments. The contribution of economic analysis to the alcohol policy debate takes a variety of forms. First, economics provides a conceptual framework that can be used to organize the abundance of material that is generated by the use and abuse of alcohol. The main organizing principle in this chapter is the distinction between the supply and demand for alcohol products.

Second, economics can provide information and evidence to improve the quality of decision making. To take the example of tax policy, before advocating the use of taxation as an alcohol control policy it is clearly important to have a reliable indication of how consumption will respond to a change in price, what proportion of a tax change will be borne by consumers and what by producers or their suppliers and employees, how employment and exports will be affected, and what effect the tax will have on the distribution of income. The discipline of economics can be used to investigate all of these questions.

The chapter is divided into three main sections. In section 1 the supply of alcohol products is analyzed and the structure–conduct–performance approach is adopted to describe the market for these goods. Section 2 presents recent trends in consumption and provides a survey of econometric studies of the demand for alcohol products, paying particular attention to estimates of price and income elasticities. Section 3 reviews the extent of public sector involvement with alcohol products and shows how economic analysis may be applied to the question of taxation. The research that has been carried out to investigate the social costs of alcohol is presented and the section concludes with a discussion of the objectives and evaluations of alcohol control policies.

THE SUPPLY OF ADDICTIVE GOODS

Introduction

The standard approach to the economics of industries and firms is the structure–conduct–performance paradigm. This approach can be applied to all countries to elicit the nature of the suppliers of alcohol products. Broadly speaking, "structure" refers to the environment in

The Centre for Health Economics at York (in conjunction with the Institute of Health Studies, University of Hull and the Department of Health Education at Leeds Polytechnic) is a WHO Collaborating Centre in Psychosocial and Economic Aspects of Health.

which production takes place, but within that definition it is useful to distinguish three levels of structure:

1. The economic system which usually corresponds to geopolitical boundaries. For instance, we might contrast a Western, industrialized economy with a sophisticated financial sector, advanced media of mass communication, and a general "consumer culture" with a Third World economy, perhaps dominated by cash crops, with low per capita purchasing power, poor communications, and a large informal sector.

2. The industry which will cross geopolitical boundaries and is conventionally defined by the products it produces.

3. The firm which is the basic unit of production that, in the case of the alcohol, is likely to cross geopolitical and industrial boundaries. The firm is conventionally defined by its ownership.

"Conduct" refers to the strategies and rules of behavior adopted by firms. The standard assumption in much economic analysis is that the sole objective of capitalist enterprises is the maximization of their profits. However, this need not always be the case and many models exist that suggest additional or alternative objectives (e.g., sales maximization).

The term "performance" relates to how firms perform in terms of selected indicators such as profitability, employment, and survival. The latter raises the question of entry and exit to and from the industry and mergers and takeovers within the industry. This introduces a feedback from firms' performance to the structure of the industry.

The structure–conduct–performance paradigm used in industrial economics is based on the premise that there is a two-way link between structure and performance via conduct. The use of this paradigm for developing and analyzing policies that may mitigate the costs arising from the use of addictive goods has not been developed extensively or systematically. However, with such data it would be possible to model the impact of given prevention policies on profits, employment, conduct, and the structure of the alcohol industry. Thus a question such as what would be the effects of a 10% reduction in consumption could be investigated to determine which owners and employees would lose what profits and employment and to predict how these decisions makers might behave, both economically and politically, as a result of these changes. Although such analysis is not presented, some indications of the structure, conduct, and performance of the UK alcohol industry is given.

Structure

Substantial data exist about the structure of the alcohol and tobacco industry and they show that it is highly concentrated. An imperfect, but useful, description, using largely secondary sources, of the international alcohol trade is provided by the controversial World Health Organization (WHO) report (WHO (1982)) written by Cavanagh and Clairmonte and later published independently (Cavanagh and Clairmonte, 1985). This study, together with Booth and Hartley (1987b) which concentrates on the UK, highlights both the oligopolistic (few sellers) nature of the market in alcohol and its integration and diversification.

In the UK six firms dominate the brewing sector: Bass Charrington, Allied Lyon, Scottish and Newcastle, Grand Metropolitan through their brewing subsidiary Watney Mann and Truman, Whitbreads, and Courage, which is now owned by Hanson Trust having previously belonged to the Imperial Group. Booth and Hartley (1987b) show that in 1982 Bass Charrington had the largest market share, as a percentage of volume sales, of 20%, while Courage (then owned by Imperial) was lowest with 9%. Together the six firms had 78.5% of the market, indicating a highly concentrated industry.

However, the high concentration of the brewing industry is a relatively modern phenomenon. Concentration did not increase markedly until the late 1950s. This absence of concentration was primarily due to problems in handling and distribution in the era before keg beer was widely available. In the 1950s and 1960s, the industry experienced a merger boom the main motives of which were the establishment of retail network of tied houses and the exploitation of technological change which eased the distribution problems of the product.

The concentration of the brewing sector is also reflected in employment. In 1980 the five firm concentration ratio was 54 per cent (i.e., the proportion of total employment attributable to the top five employers). Census of production data from 1983 shows that the seven largest establishments in the sector, with an average employment of 1657, employed 29% of the total, and the 25 establishments that employed more than 500 workers accounted for 61% of total employment.

By far the least concentrated section of the alcohol industry is wine manufacture. However, the five major suppliers of wine to the UK, who account for around for 30% of the off-trade sales, are all owned by the major brewers. This reflects the widespread horizontal integration of the market. Bass Charrington is a major wine importer (Hedges and Baker) and, together with Whitbreads, own a soft-drink firm, Canada Dry. Allied Lyon owns various wine interests (Grants of St James, Victoria Wines, Harvey's Sherries), have major cider interests (Whiteways), and have interests in the spirits market (Teachers and Stewart and Sons). Whitbreads owns Long John distilleries and have substantive interests in the small independent brewers. Watney Mann is owned by Grand Metropolitan, which earns a high proportion of its profit from wine sales, a leisure industries operation with substantial interests in hotels. Grand Metropolitan owns International Distillers and Croft (sherry), Morgan (rum), and J & B (whisky). Scottish and Newcastle owns Mackinlay and McPherson (spirits). Courage breweries owns a spirits firm (Saccone and Speed) and Guinness, through a now-notorious takeover, owns the Distillers company.

The retailing of wine is dominated by the brewers (Allied Lyon, Grand Metropolitan, Whitbreads, and Bass Charrington) and by general retailers such as Sainsburys, Marks and Spencers, and Associated Dairies (which owns the supermarket chain ASDA). The spirits market is well penetrated by the brewers in addition to multinationals such as Seagram's, Hiram Walker, and Lonro.

Thus, the market for alcohol in the UK is characterized by a few firms who dominate the market for beer (the market leader) and who have substantive interests in wine and spirits. Furthermore, these firms tend not only to produce and distribute their products but also to own outlets such as public houses and off-license shops. The international links of the industry are also considerable. These characteristics are indicative of the substantial market power of these producers that enables them to affect public policy substantially.

As to the firms themselves, there is considerable evidence of economies of scale in the brewing industry (e.g., see Booth and Hartley, 1987b). A number of studies have been carried out to try and identify the "minimum efficient scale" (MES) for plants in the industry. This provides an indication of the extent of economies of scale. Pratten (1971) estimated the MES for the UK beer industry to be 3% of the total UK market. Cockerill (1977) suggests that the MES takes a range of values and gives a figure of 5% for 1982–83. The highest estimate comes from Scherer (1980) who suggests 9.2% of the UK market.

Conduct and Performance

The conduct of firms involves a variety of decisions including their choice of location, how many people to employ, how much to spend on advertising and so on. Once a firm's objectives and the structure of its industry have been specified, economic modeling can lead to the specification of a number of important concepts. These include the aggregate supply function, the profit function, and factor demands such as the labor demand function. In principle, all of these could be estimated, however, the paucity of data means that few, if any, reliable econometric studies have been published.

However, data do exist to describe trends in the alcohol and tobacco industries' performance, in particular their records on employment and profitability. These are shown in Table 18.1. Data from the UK Census of Production shows that the number employed in alcohol

Table 18.1. Employment, profitability, and exports in the UK alcohol industry (selected years)

YEAR	NUMBERS EMPLOYED (thousands) ALCOHOL	RATE OF RETURN ON ASSETS (%) BREWING	U.K. EXPORTS (£ 1000)			
			BEER	SPIRITS	WINE	CIDER
1960	—	16.8	—	—	—	—
1963	107.8	—	—	—	—	—
1965	—	14.9	3,091	116,864	478	—
1970	101.9	14.9	5,251	210,752	6,027	906
1975	97.3	16.8	11,538	404,755	14,038	2,152
1976	92.5	18.8	13,665	482,268	17,680	2,973
1977	92.9	21.1	17,106	568,000	23,060	4,047
1978	93.5	22.7	17,440	729,997	27,058	3,921
1979	88.3	21.3	18,165	784,085	26,087	3,485
1980	84.7	18.2	19,000	833,906	24,597	3,307
1981	76.6	17.6	21,468	880,397	25,814	3,723
1982	69.3	17.8	23,129	981,430	29,176	2,810
1983	63.6	17.5	28,168	970,081	33,269	3,621
1984	60.0	—	35,605	1,060,673	38,423	4,827
1985	56.3	—	42,490	1,143,207	41,415	5,054

Sources: Godfrey (1986a), Booth and Hartley (1987a); Profitability and exports: Booth and Hartley (1987a).

manufacturing (brewing and malting, spirits distilling and compounding, and the manufacture of British wines, cider, and perry) almost halved between 1963 and 1983 (falling by 41%). This fall was concentrated in the brewing sector where numbers fell by 54%. In 1985 the Department of Employment's figure for employment in alcohol manufacture was 76,000, 1.4% of total manufacturing employment while the census of production figure was 60,000. However the UK Brewers' Society have estimated a total employment in drink-related jobs of 750,000 (Thurman, 1983), but this figure includes related sectors such as clubs and restaurants as well as manufacturing.

Table 18.1 illustrates the trends in the overall profitability of the industry. Such data are notoriously difficult to interpret, but the rate of return on assets in the brewing industry has remained fairly stable over the period starting at 16.8% in 1960 rising to a peak of 22.7% in 1978, and falling back to 17.5% by 1983.

Conclusion

This section has described the production of alcohol products in the UK. The structure–conduct–performance paradigm illuminates the structure of these industries nicely. There is considerable concentration of ownership, employment is declining in brewing (due in part to capital substitution), and profits are not inconsiderable. The adoption of new control policies would threaten the economic welfare of these producers and, as a consequence, they are a powerful lobby in the political market place.

THE DEMAND FOR ALCOHOL PRODUCTS

Consumption Trends

The data in Table 18.2 show the expenditure series for the UK consumption of alcoholic drinks over the period 1960–86. Total consumer expenditure measured at constant prices for alcoholic drink as a whole peaked in 1979 then declined until 1982 before it resumed its upward trend between 1983 and 1986. Within this overall pattern the time trends of beer and spirits are similar, but that of wine shows a continuous proportionate growth over the whole

Table 18.2. Consumer expenditure on alcohol drinks at constant 1980 prices (£ million)

YEAR	ALCOHOLIC DRINK	BEER	SPIRITS	WINE, CIDER, AND PERRY	
1960	4,750	3,409		1,479*	
1961	5,103	3,601		1,640*	
1962	5,210	3,672		1,679*	
1963	5,388	3,705	1,192		632
1964	5,738	3,876	1,287		712
1965	5,686	3,907	1,236		695
1966	5,911	4,032	1,282		749
1967	6,154	4,165	1,304		841
1968	6,483	4,301	1,396		933
1969	6,609	4,558	1,330		913
1970	7,073	4,718	1,559		956
1971	7,544	4,941	1,654		1,105
1972	8,122	5,098	1,883		1,258
1973	9,211	5,394	2,334		1,522
1974	9,435	5,396	2,495		1,564
1975	9,350	5,567	2,378		1,459
1976	9,448	5,623	2,325		1,554
1977	9,487	5,467	2,428		1,618
1978	9,930	5,548	2,616		1,766
1979	10,382	5,588	2,890		1,904
1980	9,954	5,320	2,720		1,914
1981	9,612	5,000	2,561		2,051
1982	9,370	4,825	2,427		2,118
1983	9,730	4,914	2,494		2,322
1984	9,983	4,943	2,525		2,515
1985	10,224	4,934	2,658		2,632
1986	10,297	4,935	2,646		2,716

Source: Central Statistical Office—national income and expenditure accounts.
*Sum of the cost of spirits, wine, cider and perry for the years 1960–1962.

period. The market shares of the three product groups have exhibited significant changes. Beer remains the dominant product, holding just less than 50% of the market in 1985, but along with the spirits market it has exhibited a declining market share against wine and other alcohol products.

From an economic point of view, an important indicator of consumers' behaviour is the share of alcohol in total expenditure. Using aggregate expenditure to calculate the overall expenditure share shows that alcoholic drinks have risen from 5.5% in 1960 to 7.4% in 1984. The disaggregated pattern is similar to that for market shares. Although it has shown considerable variation around the trend, particularly a marked decline between the late 1950s and 1965, the share of beer in total expenditure has remained relatively stable; in 1984 it was 4.0%. Spirits have shown even greater stability, in 1960 their share was 1.6% while in 1984 it was 1.8%. These trends for beer and spirits are in dramatic contrast to the growth of wine consumption in the consumer's budget. In 1960 wine formed only 0.6% of total expenditure, by 1984 it had risen to 1.6%. It is this rise in the importance of wine consumption that explains most of the increased share of alcohol in consumer's expenditure.

Expenditure and budget shares are the most obvious way of examining trends in consumption from the economist's perspective. However, another way of describing market trends, of particular relevance to public health, is to translate the data into a series showing consumption in liters of pure alcohol per head of population (aged 15 or over). This series is shown in Table 18.3 and it can be seen that over the period per capita alcohol consumption increased by 60%, peaking in 1980, declining until 1982, and rising since then. In terms of pure alcohol the market share of beer declined from 73% in 1960 to 57% in 1985, that of spirits rose from 17 to 22%, that of wine from 7 to 17% and cider from 3 to 5%.

Table 18.3. Consumption per capita of pure alcohol (in liters per head of population aged 15 and over)—calendar year date

YEAR	BEER	SPIRITS	WINE	CIDER	TOTAL
1960	4.4	1.0	0.4	0.17	6.0
1961	4.6	1.0	0.4	0.18	6.2
1962	4.6	1.0	0.4	0.16	6.3
1964	4.8	1.2	0.5	0.17	6.7
1965	4.8	1.1	0.5	0.17	6.6
1966	4.8	1.1	0.5	0.19	6.6
1967	4.9	1.1	0.5	0.22	6.7
1968	5.0	1.2	0.6	0.22	7.0
1969	5.2	1.1	0.6	0.25	7.1
1970	5.4	1.2	0.6	0.27	7.5
1971	5.6	1.3	0.7	0.27	7.9
1972	5.7	1.5	0.8	0.27	8.3
1973	5.9	1.8	1.0	0.29	9.0
1974	6.0	2.0	1.1	0.30	9.4
1975	6.1	1.9	1.0	0.34	9.3
1976	6.1	2.1	1.0	0.40	9.6
1977	6.0	1.8	1.0	0.37	9.2
1978	6.2	2.2	1.1	0.38	9.9
1979	6.2	2.4	1.2	0.39	10.2
1980	5.9	2.2	1.2	0.38	9.7
1981	5.6	2.1	1.3	0.41	9.4
1982	5.5	2.0	1.3	0.48	9.3
1983	5.5	2.0	1.4	0.54	9.4
1984	5.5	2.0	1.6	0.53	9.6
1985	5.4	2.1	1.6	0.51	9.6
1986	5.3	2.1	1.7	0.52	9.6

Notes: These estimates assume average alcohol content as follows:

Beer—4% alcohol
Wine—12% alcohol
Spirits—40% alcohol
Cider—8% alcohol

Source: *Annual Abstract of Statistics*, The Brewers Society, UK Statistical Handbook (1961-1968).

Thus the alcohol market in the UK has exhibited considerable growth and significant shifts in market shares during the period since the early 1960s. One factor contributing to these trends has been the movement of alcohol prices in relation to the price of other goods. Over the period 1963–1984 the retail price index (RPI) rose from 100 to 631.6 (Table 18.4). For the same period the beer index rose to 808.5, that for wine and cider to 501.5 and that for spirits to 465.0. A central argument of the economic theory of consumer behavior is that consumption will be inversely related to the real price of the good in question. From these figures it is clear that the real price of beer in terms of the RPI has risen markedly over the period while the real prices of wine and cider, and spirits have fallen. These variations in the movements between the RPI and the products' prices are explained largely by tax changes, an issue that is explored below.

Empirical Studies of the Demand for Alcohol Products

Applied Demand Analysis

The theoretical foundations of demand analysis are rooted in individual behavior. The basic approach is to specify the individual's preferences and to argue that they will select a bundle of consumption goods according to those preferences subject to the financial constraint of their income and the prices of the goods. The specification of preferences can be given an explicit mathematical form and a number of attempts have been made to incorporate char-

Table 18.4. Current price indices (1963 = 100)

YEAR	BEER	SPIRITS	WINE AND CIDER	TOBACCO	ALL ITEMS
1963	100.0	100.0	100.0	100.0	100.0
1964	105.6	106.5	105.9	105.9	103.6
1965	116.6	114.3	111.9	116.8	108.7
1966	121.8	119.0	116.7	119.3	113.1
1967	126.7	121.5	116.0	119.3	116.0
1968	128.2	125.1	120.1	125.0	121.6
1969	136.2	131.3	133.2	135.8	128.3
1970	148.3	131.9	137.5	138.1	135.8
1971	159.5	136.3	141.7	140.8	147.5
1972	168.4	138.9	147.8	142.8	157.1
1973	173.1	144.6	158.7	144.6	170.1
1974	198.4	151.7	181.5	168.3	199.0
1975	248.0	189.8	225.7	216.9	246.3
1976	297.4	215.6	250.5	154.1	284.9
1977	344.5	241.4	272.0	312.3	327.3
1978	370.0	252.8	288.2	309.0	356.7
1979	423.3	279.8	330.2	338.1	404.7
1980	515.6	328.2	378.0	396.2	471.1
1981	615.0	373.0	419.1	488.8	525.3
1982	684.5	406.4	456.8	564.5	570.2
1983	746.5	431.4	473.2	602.5	600.9
1984	808.5	465.0	501.5	665.4	631.6
1985	881.4	488.4	525.4	723.4	659.1
1986	925.5	505.4	529.9	793.2	682.9

Source: Central Statistical Office—national income and expenditure accounts.

acteristics which are particularly relevant to addictive goods. These include the influence of addiction on behavior and the interaction between hazardous consumption and health.

The main outcome of modeling consumer behavior is a set of demand functions which relate consumption to prices, income, and other factors such as advertising and health education. In practice, most of the econometric studies of the demand for alcohol and tobacco have used aggregate expenditure data. This implies that the theoretical demand functions are aggregated over individuals or alternatively are treated as a representative individual. However, there has recently been increasing use of individual and household survey data from sources such as the UK Family Expenditure Survey (see Atkinson et al, 1984).

Econometric models of demand consist of two components: the functional form of the equations (the deterministic component) and the assumptions made about the equation errors (the stochastic component). These components, and hence the appropriate estimation procedure, are determined normally by the type of data in use and by the underlying economic model. For instance, the use of cross-section survey data that identifies smokers and non-smokers and their sociodemographic characteristics allows the analyst to use models of discrete choice (e.g., probit and logit). Although time-series data on aggregate expenditure can be used to estimate single-demand equations or alternatively systems of equations, exploiting the cross-equation restrictions implied by economic theory to improve the statistical efficiency of the estimation.

It should be emphasized that the assumptions made about functional form and stochastic structure of the model ought both to be tested using techniques that are commonly available in the econometrics literature. It is often assumed that the demand equation is linear in its parameters allowing the use of ordinary least squares estimation, this assumption can and should be tested. The majority of applied studies also assume that the error term on the estimating equation has a normal distribution with zero mean and a constant variance and is uncorrelated across observations. This assumption should also be tested as violations can bias or affect the efficiency of the estimated parameters.

Having specified, estimated, and tested a demand function that relates consumption to prices, income, and other relevant factors some guidance is needed to interpret the results. A central concept in the interpretation of demand equations is the elasticity of demand. This measures the proportional response of consumption to a proportional change in a determinant of demand. For example, the price elasticity of demand for beer is defined as,

$$\text{Own-price elasticity of beer} = \frac{\%\text{ change in consumption of beer}}{\%\text{ change in price of beer}}$$

Similar definitions would apply for the income elasticity, the advertising elasticity, and the cross-price elasticity of demand (the latter relates the consumption of one good, say beer, to the price of another, say wine). A beer price elasticity of -0.5 implies that a 10% increase in the price of beer will reduce the consumption of beer by 5%. The attraction of this concept is that the elasticity is independent of the units in which consumption, price, income, and so on are measured.

Two notes of caution should be sounded for the interpretation of elasticities:

1. In general, elasticities will vary according to the point on the demand function at which they are measured. Only under very special restrictions will demand functions lead to elasticities that are fixed numbers. However, for convenience many of the empirical studies described as follows have adopted these restrictions, which imply that the demand function is linear in the logarithms of the relevant variables. This point is of particular importance in cross-sectional studies of income elasticities which in general should be allowed to vary across the income distribution (see Atkinson et al, 1984).
2. Elasticities are defined in terms of infinitesimal changes and must therefore be used with care when dealing with proportionately large changes in the variables. If the price of cigarettes rises by 10% econometric estimates of the price elasticity are likely to provide a reliable prediction of the effect on consumption. But if the price of cigarettes trebles overnight, the elasticity estimates will be a weak basis for forecasting effects on consumption.

The Demand for Alcohol Products

Table 18.5 shows the results of four different UK studies of the demand for alcoholic drinks. The data for price elasticities show considerable variation, except in the case of beer where the estimates are small in all of the models. For example, the Central Statistical Office (CSO)

Table 18.5. Estimates of elasticities in alcohol

STUDY AUTHORS	TIME PERIOD		ELASTICITY ESTIMATES		
			BEER	SPIRITS	WINE
(a) Price Elasticities					
Walsh (1982)	1955–1975		−0.13	−0.47	−0.28
			−0.26	−0.45	−0.38
McGuinness (1980)	1956–1979		−0.30	−0.38	−0.17
Duffy (1982)	1963–1978		N.A.	−0.8 to	−0.7 to
				−1.0	−1.0
H.M. Treasury (1980)	N.A.		−0.2	−1.3	−1.1
(b) Income Elasticities					
Walsh (1982)		Exp.	0.13	1.20	0.51
		Vol.	0.12	0.99	0.49
McGuinness (1980)			0.13	1.54	1.11
Duffy (1982)			0.8 to	1.6	2.2 to
			1.1		2.5
H.M. Treasury (1980)			0.7	2.5	1.8

Source: Godfrey (1986b), Table 2, text, and Table 3.

estimates (H.M. Treasury 1980, and private communication) indicate that a 1% change in the price of beer will lead to a 0.2% change in the quantity consumed. The Walsh (1982) and McGuinness (1980) results for spirits and wine are lower than those of Duffy and the CSO. The latter forecast changes in spirits and wine consumption following a 1% increase in their prices of 1.3 and 1.1%. The price elasticity of a good clearly has a central role to play when it comes to changes in the tax rate. The use of alcohol appears to be significantly responsive to tax changes.

The data in Table 18.5 also give estimates of income elasticities (i.e., the responsiveness of demand to small changes in income). Again, the Duffy and CSO estimates are higher. The CSO figures indicate that a 1% increase in income will lead to increases in beer, spirits, and wine consumption of 0.7, 2.5, and 1.8%, respectively. The dispersion of these estimates and of the price elasticities is a cause for some concern, as is the fact that the estimates are derived from data that are at least seven years old. Work underway at York using more recent data is seeking to explore the causes of the variations in the estimates and their stability over time (see Godfrey, 1986b).

There has been considerable debate about the size and statistical significance of the advertising elasticity. The managers of both the alcohol and tobacco industries have argued that advertising does not increase the overall size of the market but merely affects the market share of their brands. Duffy (1982) found a significant but low advertising elasticity for beer consumption of 0.07. In his wine equation there was no evidence that advertising affected demand and the results for spirits were mixed and insignificant. Walsh's (1982) estimate of the beer advertising elasticity was also low (0.1) and his other results, together with those of McGuinness (1980), do not suggest that advertising has much effect on the level of alcohol consumption.

However, there are at least two reasons why further research work on the effects of advertising is needed. First, the results mentioned above are aggregated and little is known about the effects of advertising on particular social class, age, and gender groups. For example, it is possible that the advertising industry targets its efforts on the young so as to influence life cycle preferences. Second, the definition of advertising used in the studies is narrow, including only expenditure in the media. Both alcohol and tobacco companies sponsor art and sports events and this enables them to deliver certain "messages" about their products to consumers. Indeed, advertising in its widest sense might include "role models" provided by celebrities and other public figures. Although the former could be incorporated into econometric models if data were made available by the industries, the latter is more difficult to model.

Another possible influence on the consumption of alcohol is ease of access. The number of licenses, used as a proxy for access, was found to be significant in the works of McGuinness and Walsh. The latter also found significant effects in the spirits and wine equations. Work is underway to extend these results in a variety of ways (Godfrey, 1986b).

To stabilize consumption it is necessary that Treasury Ministers adjust tax rates to take account of price and income changes. The effect of price and income on alcohol use are significant and the scope for using such control methods are considerable.

PUBLIC POLICY AND ADDICTIVE GOODS

The Role of the Public Sector

The markets for alcohol and tobacco are tightly regulated by governments who tend to exhibit some schizophrenia in their attitudes towards addiction policies. This stems from the products' capacity to damage the health and welfare of their citizens while generating significant tax revenues, employment, and exports—a trade-off between health and wealth. In the case of alcohol consumption, the CPRS (Central Policy Review Staff (1979)) noted that, in the UK, "The Government has a vested interest in this consumption. It annually yields revenu of some £2,000m. The exports and jobs that the industry provides are important to the economy" (p22).

In 1985, the tax yield from alcohol had grown to £5,972m forming 13.9% of total taxes on expenditure and 4.6% of total government current account receipts (see e.g., Godfrey and Powell, 1987). The ratio of alcohol exports to imports in 1985 was 1.5:1 (although this balance of trade has declined over recent years with the growth of wine imports and the decline of whisky exports). Total direct employment in the alcohol manufacturing industries in 1985 was 60,000 (compared with 88,300 in 1979).

There are inevitable trade-offs to be made between the wealth of the community and its health. Nowhere is this more evident than with regard to alcohol products whose consumption results in the premature death and increased morbidity for thousands of people each year. The nature of the constraints and relationships in tax revenue policy are outlined here as are the attempts to determine the costs associated with the use of alcohol. The use of econometric techniques outlined earlier in relation to price and income effects are more likely to be useful in the formulation of trade and tax revenue policies than prevention policy. As indicated towards the end of the section, the application of such techniques to analyze the use–policy–harm links is perhaps more productive in terms of investigating whether consumption (use) can be influenced by policy (e.g., a tax hike) to reduce harm (e.g., mortality from liver cirrhosis). The range of policies that can be manipulated to affect harm is wide (e.g., licensing, education, advertising, road traffic laws, and risk assessment) and the relative influences of these factors requires careful investigation if cost effective prevention policies are to be identified.

Social Costs

An important factor which may influence public policy towards addictive goods is health status of citizens. Alcohol causes numerous premature deaths in the UK and much avoidable morbidity. The social costs of alcohol are not inconsiderable.

However, the epidemiological knowledge that forms the basis of any attempt to quantify the costs to society associated with the use of alcohol is inadequate (McDonnell and Maynard, 1985a). As a consequence, any estimates of the total social costs associated with the use of alcohol are incomplete and qualitatively poor. A "guestimate" of the UK social costs of alcohol use is given in Table 18.6. The social cost of alcohol in 1983–84 was approximately £1600 million and approximately £2 billion in 1985 (Maynard, et al, 1987).

Not only are these data poor, even "simple" indicators like alcohol related mortality are difficult to establish. Using published data McDonnell and Maynard (1985c) estimated that the number of alcohol related deaths in 1983 was between 5000 and 7800. The range of these estimates illustrates the poor quality of the basic epidemiological data. It was also calculated that these deaths generated between 115,980 and 185,384 premature life years lost.

However, these data are believed to be serious underestimates of mortality in the UK associated with alcohol use. This belief is based partly on the findings of the Malmo study, which involved the reanalysis of mortality among middle-aged men, using longitudinal survey techniques. This work indicated that official Swedish mortality data under-estimated true alcohol related mortality by a factor of between 6 and 8 (see e.g., Petersson et al, 1982).

Using such findings it has been argued (*British Medical Journal*, 1986 and Royal College of Psychiatrists, 1986) that the likely annual alcohol associated mortality level in the UK may be as high as 25,000. A report of the Royal College of General Practitioners even suggests that alcohol related premature mortality may be as high as 40,000 per year. These and other estimates (see e.g., Maynard, 1986) cannot be substantiated by scientific fact at present because the requisite scientific research has not been carried out in Britain or elsewhere (with

Table 18.6. Total resource costs of alcohol misuse in England and Wales (1983 prices)

	£ mn*
(1) The Social Cost to Industry	
a. Sickness absence	748.09
b. Housework services	50.25
c. Unemployment	172.39
d. Premature death	675.47
(2) The Social Cost to the National Health Service	
a. Psychiatric hospitals, in-patient costs (alcoholic psychosis, alcohol dependence syndrome, nondependent abuse of alcohol)	20.56
b. Nonpsychiatric hospitals, in-patient costs (alcoholic psychosis, alcohol dependence syndrome, alcoholic cirrhosis, and liver disease)	8.31
c. Other alcohol-related diseases, in-patient costs	84.87
d. GP visits	2.17
(3) Society's Response to Alcohol-related Problems	
a. Expenditure by national alcohol bodies	0.34
b. Research	0.62
(4) The Social Cost of Material Damage	
a. Road traffic accidents (damage)	107.53
(5) The Social Cost of Criminal Activities	
a. Police involvement in traffic offenses (excluding road traffic accidents)	5.07
b. Police involvement in road traffic accidents (includes judiciary and insurance administration)	15.02
c. Drink-related court cases	18.76
Total (including unemployment and premature death)	1909.48
Total (excluding unemployment and premature death)	1061.48

Source: McDonnell and Maynard (1985b).
*Million pounds.

the exception of Sweden). So, although it is known that existing data may underestimate alcohol-related mortality, it is not known by how much these data are inadequate measures of this aspect of "damage."

A note of caution should be sounded. If public policy is to be influenced by a concern for social costs, care should be taken to clarify the nature of those costs. From an economic perspective the individual is sovereign and, to put it crudely, should be free to decide how to depreciate his/her human capital stock and when to die (Littlechild and Wiseman, 1986). The liberal neoclassical economist would argue that, provided the use of alcohol generates only private costs, only a paternalist can advocate the infringement of individual liberty by additional control policies.

This rather "fundamentalist" viewpoint needs to be qualified in a number of ways. First, it is based on the individual having access to the same information as policymakers on the effects of their behavior. Second, it ignores the influence of addiction and the diminished responsibility that it can entail. Related to this is the fact that in the majority of cases these habits are acquired during adolescence, a period when individuals are open to particularly powerful peer group pressures. The sovereignty of the adult drinker, for instance, may be severely curtailed by the burden of an addiction inherited from their earlier years. Many adult drinkers express a desire to quit the habit, and this may bring into question the normative significance of the economists' dictum that true preferences are only revealed in observed behavior (Wright, 1987).

These issues aside, it is clear that alcohol impose costs on third party or externalities, ranging from injuries and deaths in motor accidents caused by drunken driving to alcohol-related theft and violent crime. However, care should be taken to distinguish policies aimed at reducing costs from those based on paternalism.

The Appropriate Policy Mix

What are the objectives of addiction policy? Some health promotion–education agencies seem to advocate the removal of all the social costs associated with these consumption activities. However, efficient policy formation must look at the costs and benefits at the margin, emphasizing changes in the costs of policy formation and execution and the resulting change in benefits.

Considerable research is going into the measurement of these benefits in terms of the generation of additional years of life and the quality of those years (quality adjusted life years or QALYs). One priority for research is to identify the costs of alternative ways of producing desired outcomes (QALYs). The pursuit of efficiency is not concerned with minimizing the costs of policy formation and execution, if it was the "efficient" policy would be to do nothing. Neither is efficienct policy formation concerned with maximizing benefits (e.g., QALYs, reduced mortality, or social costs) regardless of the costs in terms of designing and implementing policies and their consequences for the "losing" industries (i.e., reduced employment and incomes). Given the existence of scarcity, it is essential to identify the cheapest way of generating QALYs (health improvements) and spending limited budgets on the best QALY-acquiring activities. Benefits and costs have to be traded off at the margin and the efficient policy is unlikely to lead to the removal of all the costs associated with the use of addictive substances.

This emphasis on selectivity and the benefits of policies, measured in terms of life years saved, highlights the importance of targeting policies at certain groups who are particularly "at risk." The potential gain, in terms of QALYs, will be particularly large if addiction-related deaths can be prevented among young people. In this context it is relevant to look at recent work in the United States that has carried out an econometric analysis of youth alcohol abuse and motor accident mortality (Grossman and Coate, 1985 and Saffer and Grossman, 1986). These authors evaluate an increase in the legal minimum drinking age and increased alcohol taxation as means of reducing accident mortality. They conclude that a uniform drinking age of 21 in all U.S. states would reduce deaths among 18-to-20-year-olds by 7%. More strikingly, they predict that a policy that offset the erosion in the real federal beer tax that has occurred since the 1950s and that taxed the alcohol in beer at the same rate as spirits would reduce deaths among 18-to-20-year-olds by 34% and among 21-to-24-year-olds by 52% (Grossman and Coate, 1985).

To summarize, efficient policy formation should be informed by cost and benefit information. It is commonplace for the costs of efficient addiction policies to be underplayed and for policy to be formulated largely in terms of benefits (reduced mortality, lower social costs, and increased QALYs). Furthermore, these benefit estimates tend to be crude, emphasizing totals rather than margins. Thus, the economic basis of policy formation is incomplete and inadequate. Social cost estimates, such as those in Table 18.6, although illuminating some aspects of the policy problems, are largely irrelevant for the purposes of formulating efficient prevention policies. Such policies need to be informed by data about the costs and benefits at the margin. The next section introduces a call for improved and internationally comparable data sets to help satisfy this need.

DATA REQUIREMENTS AND THE "RESEARCH BOX"

In order to assist the development of reliable economic studies of the demand and supply of alcohol products, it would be useful to compare methods and results across countries. In particular the collection and analysis of the data set out in Table 18.7 would enable policy makers and economists to identify the strengths and weaknesses of existing estimates and to set about improving any deficiencies. For those intending to carry out their own empirical analysis of the demand for addictive goods Table 18.8 sets out an agenda for the research methodology

Table 18.7. Data requirements for international comparison

All data to be generated on a quarterly basis	
Alcohol: a data series from 1960 to 1986 for all alcohol in total and beer, wine, spirits, and other alcoholic products separately	
Expenditure at current and constant prices	Estimate of social costs, emphasizing gaps
Litres of pure alcohol, per capita aged 15 years and over	Mortality associated with alcohol use
Price indices	
Factor price indices (e.g., labor and raw materials)	

Table 18.8. The "research box": an outline for applied demand analysis

(1) For each study the following information would be set down:
    (a) Methods
        (i) functional form of equation estimates (e.g., log-log)
        (ii) time period (indicate whether quarterly or yearly data used)
        (iii) estimation technique (ordinary least square, two-stage least squares, etc.)
    (b) Results
        (i) which estimates were statistically valid?
        (ii) what elasticity estimates were generated (giving their standard errors if possible)?

(2) These data would be collected for all demand equations in which any or all of the following variables were included:
        (i) price
        (ii) income
        (iii) advertising
        (iv) access (e.g., number of outlets, number of licenses, and hours)
        (v) health education
(These data might be for aggregate markets (e.g., beer, spirits, and wine) or for subsets thereof (e.g., teenage beer consumption))

For guidance on the statistical testing of demand models, see Godfrey (1986b).

and the presentation of results. It is hoped that these will consist of data sets and econometric approaches and will allow reliable international comparisons to be made.

At present, the extent of economic analysis in the markets for addictive substances is limited, but it is beginning to develop in a substantive fashion. The scope for "gains from trade" across international boundaries seem potentially large in terms of developing methods of analysis and providing inputs into the process of policy formation. However, progress of this type will not take place unless basic data sources (economic and epidemiological) are improved. (A succinct and insightful review of some European data is provided by Powell, 1988.)

An essential ingredient into the process of improving data and using it to inform policy decision making is the generation of information such as that outlined in Tables 18.7 and 18.8. If such basic and essential facets of policy formation are not addressed systematically, it is likely that the present increase in analysis of the markets for alcohol products will develop less efficiently than it otherwise might. At worst, the current stirring of policy reform could come to nought.

EXECUTIVE SUMMARY

This chapter provided an economic framework for the discussion of policy objectives and for the analysis of the efficiency of alternative policy instruments used to regulate the market for alcohol.

The first section of the chapter analyzed the supply of alcohol and examined the structure, conduct and performance of the three industries. Using UK evidence, it showed that patterns of ownership, employment, trade (imports and exports), and integration continually change and are amenable to economic analysis.

In Section 2 the recent trends in the consumption of alcohol products were described prior to a survey of econometric techniques and results about the demand for alcohol. Particular attention was paid to price and income elasticities of demand (i.e., the estimation of the effects of small changes in price on the consumption of alcohol). The potential of fiscal measures to control consumption is shown to be considerable.

The nature and extent of Government regulation of the alcohol market was the subject of Section 3. The objectives of taxation policy and the relation of estimates of social cost to policy formation are discussed. It is shown that the evolution of consumption (e.g., of alcohol) — harm (e.g. road traffic accident deaths) and the appraisal of alternative policy instruments (e.g., minimum drinking ages and alcohol taxation policies) in terms of their effects on use and harm is an area in which econometric techniques can be used productively to illustrate the nature of policy options, although much work is still needed to investigate the links between use and harm. The conclusion of this section is that efficient policy formation should be informed by cost and benefit (improvements in health) information.

These three sections are drawn together in Section 4, which sets out a detailed proposal for the collection of data and the conduct of economic research on an international level. Such data collection and its analysis enables policy makers to learn more about the costs and benefits of their own domestic policies as well as those of foreign neighbors rather than live in virtual ignorance of costs and outcomes domestically and internationally as they do now.

The scope for the use of economic analysis to investigate the supply and demand for alcohol is considerable. Such analysis can illuminate the policy debate with estimates of the costs and benefits (outcomes) of competing policies that can be used to regulate a product which causes much ill health. This approach will generate considerable benefits to users and producers alike.

REFERENCES

Atkinson AB, Gomulka J, Stern N: Expenditure on alcohol by households: Evidence from the family expenditure survey 1970–1980, ESRC programme on taxation, incentives and the distribution of income, working paper No. 60; 1984.

Bain JS: *Barriers to New Competition*. Cambridge, England, Cambridge University Press, 1956.

Booth M, Hartley K: Profitability in the UK Brewing and Tobacco industries. Unpublished draft, University of York, England; 1987a.

Booth M, Hartley K: Structure, concentration and scale economies. Unpublished draft, University of York, England; 1987b.

Government hypocrisy on drugs. *British Medical Journal*: 1986; 292:712–73.

Cavanagh LJ, Clairmonte FF: *Alcohol Beverages: Dimensions of Corporate Power*, London, Croom Helm, 1985.

Central Policy Review Staff: Alcohol policies, unpublished; 1979.

Cockerill, A: Economies of scale, industrial structure and efficiency: The brewing industry in nine nations, in Jacqvemin A and de Jong HW (eds), Welfare Aspects of Industrial Markets, The Hague, Martinus Nijhoff.

Cropper J: Health, investment in health and occupational choice. *J Political Economy* 1977; 85:1273–1294.

Duffy M: The effect of advertising on the total consumption of alcoholic drinks in the United Kingdom: Some econometric evidence. *J Advertising* 1982; 1:105–117.

Finsberg G: Hansard (House of Commons) 43rd series, column 337, January 26th, 1982.

Godfrey C: Employment in the alcohol and tobacco industries and its relationship to prevention policies. Addiction Research Centre, University of York (mimeograph), England, 1986a.

Godfrey C: Factors influencing the consumption of tobacco and alcohol: A review of demand models. Discussion Paper 17, Centre for Health Economics, University of York, England, 1986b.

Godfrey C, Hardman G, Maynard A: Measuring UK tobacco and alcohol consumption, Data note 2. *Br J Addiction* 1986; 81(2):287–293.

Godfrey C, Maynard A: An economic theory of alcohol consumption and abuse, in Choudron D. (ed), *Alcohol Control Policies*. Toronto, Addiction Research Centre, 1989.

Godfrey C, Powell M: Alcohol and tobacco taxation: Barriers to a public health perspective. *Q J Social Affairs* 1985; 1(4):329-353.

Godfrey C, Powell M: Budget strategies for alcohol and tobacco tax in 1987 and beyond, Discussion Paper 22, Centre for Health Economics, University of York, England, 1987.

Grossman M, Coate D: Youth alcohol use and motor vehicle mortality. National Bureau of Economic Research, working paper; 1985.

H.M. Treasury: The change in revenue from an indirect tax change. *Economic Trends*, 1980; 97-107.

Holtermann S, Burchall A: The costs of alcohol misuse, Government Economic Service working paper No. 37, London, England, 1981.

International Order of Good Templars: Alcoholic beverages: Dimensions of corporate power, *The Globe*, No. 4, Oslo, Norway, December 1983.

Ippolito PH: Information and the life cycle consumption of hazardous goods. *Economic Inquiry*, 1981; XIX:529-568.

Jones AM: The role of social interaction and addiction in a double hurdle model of cigarette consumption. Unpublished draft, University of York, England, 1987.

Kendall RE, de Roumanie M, Ritson EB: The effect of economic changes on Scottish drinking habits, 1972-82. *Br J Addiction*, 1983; 78:365.

Littlechild SC, Wiseman J: Principles on public policy relevant to smoking. *Policy Studies*, January 1986.

Maynard A, Kennan P: The economics of addiction: A survey of the literature and a proposed research strategy prepared for the SSRC Research Panel on Addiction, unpublished, London, 1981.

Maynard A: Economic aspects of addiction policy. *Health Promotion* 1986; 2:2.

Maynard A, Hardman G, & Whelan A: Measuring the social costs of addictive substances, *Br J Addiction*, 1987; 82, 701-6.

McDonnell R, Maynard A: Counting the cost of alcohol: Gaps in epidemiological knowledge. *Community Medicine*, 1985a; 7(1):4-17.

McDonnell R, Maynard A: The costs of alcohol misuse. *Br J Addiction* 1985b; 80:27-35.

McDonnell R, Maynard A: Estimation of life years lost from alcohol related premature death. *Alcohol Alcoholism* 1985c; 20(4):435-443.

McGuinness AT: An econometric analysis of total demand for alcoholic beverages in the UK, 1956-1975. *J Industrial Economics* 1980; 85-109.

Moore MH, Gerstein DR (eds): Alcohol and public policy: *Beyond the shadow of prohibition*. Washington DC, National Academy Press, 1981, 463 pp..

Petersson B, Kristensson H, Krantz P, Trell E, Starnby NM: Alcohol related death: A major contributor to mortality in urban middle aged men. *Lancet* 1982 (ii):1088-1090.

Pratten C: Economies of scale in manufacturing industry, occasional paper No. 28, Dept. of Applied Economics, University of Cambridge, England, 1971.

Powell, M., Alcohol and tobacco tax in the European Community, *Br J Addiction*, data note 15, 1988, 83:971-78.

Royal College of General Practitioners. Alcohol: A balanced view, Report from general practice, No. 24, London, 1986.

Royal College of Psychiatrists: Alcohol: *Our Favourite Drug: New Report on Alcohol and Alcohol-related Problems*. London, Tavistock, 1986; pp 128.

Saffer H, Grossman M: Endogenous drinking age laws and highway mortality rates of young drivers, working paper No. 1982; National Bureau for Economic Research, 1986.

Scherer FM: *Industrial market structure and economic performance*. Chicago, Rand McNally, 1980.

Smith RT: The legal and illegal markets for taxed goods: Pure theory and application to State Government taxation of distilled spirits. *Law and Economics*, 1976; 19:393, 429.

Thurman C: The structure and role of the British alcoholic drinks industry, in, Grant M, Plant M, Williams A (eds), *Economies and Alcohol*. London, Croom Helm, 1983.

Walsh BM: The demand for alcohol in the UK: A comment. *J Industrial Economics* 1982. 30:439-446.

Wright SJ: Self-ratings of health: The influence of age and smoking status and the role of different explanatory models. *Psychology and Health*, 1987.

CHAPTER 19

Editorial Remarks:
Biomedical and Genetic Aspects
of Alcoholism: Current Issues
and Future Directions

H. Werner Goedde and Dharam P. Agarwal

Institute of Human Genetics
University of Hamburg
Hamburg, F.R. Germany

BIOMEDICAL ASPECTS OF ALCOHOLISM
Problems and Research Strategies

Alcoholism is one of the most challenging current health problems in the Western countries with far-reaching medical, social, and economic consequences. Since the recognition of alcoholism as a disease, the government expenditure is growing everywhere to provide adequate facilities for treatment and rehabilitation. Thus, each year hundreds of billions of dollars are spent on health care costs related to alcoholism in the developed countries.

It is now well accepted that chronic alcohol drinking produces a variety of physiological and physical changes in humans. The severity of alcohol effects depends on factors like the dosage of ethanol, total period of heavy drinking, an individual's genetic background, specific environmental makeup, as well as behavioral circumstances. Thus, there are a series of factors that are all interacting in predisposing or protecting an individual against alcoholism and alcohol-related disorders: the availability of alcohol and the price, an individual's socio-cultural, psychological, physiological, and genetic makeup.

Epidemiological studies have revealed that the incidence of alcoholism in a community is influenced by per capita alcohol consumption and covariates with the relative price and availability of alcoholic drinks (Chick, 1982). The prevalence and incidence of heavy alcohol consumption has been constantly increasing in recent years and present estimates show that alcohol consumption will continue to increase in the coming years. A general population survey made in 1984 in the United States concerning drinking patterns and drinking problems revealed that 18% of all men and 5% of all women were frequent heavy drinkers (Hilton, 1987). Striking sex-related and age-related differences were noted in this survey, with greater proportions of men than women and greater proportion of younger than older drinkers reporting heavy drinking, intoxication, and drinking problems.

Racial patterns of alcoholic beverage use also indicate certain differences. In a large survey comprising about 60,000 persons living in the United States, self-reported alcohol consumption was found to be quite similar in whites and blacks, while Asians consumed significantly lower amounts (Klatsky et al, 1983). Men of all races reported more drinking than women.

Comparison with earlier data showed a significant decline in reported proportions of abstainers and heavy drinkers as well as apparent narrowing of race–sex differences. Studies in the general population of the United States indicate that there are more heavy drinking and alcohol-related problems among Hispanic population than among other ethnic groups (Caetano, 1983). A comparative survey of alcohol consumption patterns among American Indian and white college students also indicated that a significantly higher proportion of Indians were heavy drinkers and had more problems associated with drinking (Hughes and Dodder, 1984). Additional research is needed to explain some of these differences in the drinking behavior. An assessment of drinking norms and beliefs in relation to drinking practices may help in defining problems with drinking in a particular ethnic or racial group.

The effects of alcohol on liver, brain, and other vital organs (heart, skeletal muscle, pancreas, etc.) have been the subject of intensive research in the early 1960s and the following years. The liver is one of the organs most significantly damaged and physiologically altered as a result of chronic alcohol intake. The two most common alcohol-related hepatic complications are cirrhosis and hepatitis. Alcoholic brain damage is another most important pathological outcome of chronic alcohol abuse. Although significant advances in our understanding of the biomedical basis of alcoholism have emerged in the past years, a number of issues remain unsettled. Although substantial progress has been made in understanding the basic mechanisms that underlie the development of tolerance and physical dependence using animal models, most of the proposed mechanisms have still to be validated in humans. Besides the study of the basis and mechanism of the disease, the major areas of current biomedical research in alcoholism include diagnosis, treatment, management, and prevention of alcoholism.

Diagnosis of alcohol-related physicochemical alterations is one of the main ways of early detection of alcoholism. A number of biochemical and clinical chemical markers of alcohol abuse are being widely used for the diagnosis as well as for monitoring the treatment of alcoholism. However, none of the markers, single or in combination with other parameters, is specific and sensitive enough to allow a reliable identification of alcohol abuse. The inherent weakness of some commonly used markers such as gamma-glutamyl transferase, mean corpuscular volume and aspartate aminotransferase as indicators of heavy alcohol intake is apparent. Several less known biochemical correlates of alcohol abuse like erythrocyte aldehyde dehyrogenase, serum dolichol, carbohydrate deficient transferrin, and blood acetate merit further study regarding their diagnostic efficiency.

One of the primary goals of alcoholism research is to understand the basis of various clinical phenomena like loss of control, craving, tolerance, and physical dependence in order to devise effective treatment programs. Besides various treatment strategies, the recognition and management of different gastrointestinal and other medical complications as the consequence of alcoholism is certainly important. Short-term and long-term treatment of alcoholism involves recognition of alcoholism, modification of the alcohol-seeking and alcohol-abusing behavior, as well as management of the withdrawal and abstinent state. However, progress made in the recent years in the actual treatment of alcoholism has been rather disappointing. The contemporary medical treatment programs of alcoholism and its secondary consequences are limited in scope and expensive.

Prevention of alcoholism and related disorders consists of early detection and intervention. The mass prevention strategy is based on reduction of alcohol consumption and changing the public and private environment; the selective prevention focuses on early detection of high-risk groups and heavy drinkers in their initial stages of the disease (Raduco-Thomas et al, 1980). However, the current public health prevention strategies mainly concentrate on disease treatment and management programs. Biomedical research dealing with early identification of target groups as a tool of primary prevention via effective intervention needs a high priority. Availability of suitable biomedical indicators of alcohol abuse and potential risk groups is essential and more intense search for such markers is necessary to achieve the goals leading to effective prevention.

GENETIC ASPECTS OF ALCOHOLISM

Current Issues

In recent years, great progress has been made in biomedical and psychiatric research supporting the important contribution of genetic factors in alcoholism. It is now well accepted that the most important determinant of an individuals drinking problems is a positive family history of alcoholism. A particular profession or occupation may also be determinantal in an individual's liability to alcoholism. In order to examine the evidence for the inheritance of alcoholism, one may ask the following questions: Is alcoholism really hereditary? Are there genetically distinct forms of alcoholism? What are the predisposing factors? Is alcoholism a monogenic or a polygenic disorder? Can one separate genetic contributions from the environmental influences? What is the mode of transmission of the biological risk factors? Is it possible to modulate genetic influences through prevention and intervention strategies (e.g., making alcohol nonavailable, effective treatment)?

The current evidence strongly suggests that alcoholism may be a genetically influenced complex multifactorial disorder. However, no single gene defect with Mendelian pattern of inheritance is expected to explain the heredity mode of the disease. Very few studies give specific findings indicating a basic genetic contribution in alcoholism. A phenotypic characteristic, even if it is evidently hereditary, may occur due to different mechanisms. If alcoholism is genetically influenced, possible biological mediators of this tendency could involve differences between groups at high and at low risk for the future development of alcoholism: in the way they metabolize ethanol, how they react to acute doses of the drug, and whether they show differences in the development of levels of tolerance and in the vulnerability to chronic consequences of alcohol intake (Schuckit, 1985). Genetically transmitted factors predisposing to alcoholism may be broadly divided into three categories: (1) depression or personality disorders, (2) central nervous system (CNS) responses to alcohol, and (3) metabolic variations.

Family Studies

Recent family studies emphasize fundamental differences in the concept of the two major research paradigms currently used in genetic studies in alcoholism. One model views alcoholism as a discrete disease entity with a unitary cause, whereas the other paradigm considers alcoholism as a multilevel disorder with many steps between the genotype and the phenotype (Cloninger, 1987). Among the most common strategies employed thus far to identify hereditary factors in alcoholism are (1) family studies (family system variables, drinking behavior, drinking history), (2) twin studies (alcohol metabolism, pattern of alcohol use and abuse), (3) adoption studies (biological parents vs foster parents), and (4) high-risk groups (identification of biological markers of vulnerability to alcoholism).

For many years, alcoholism was regarded as a distinct disease that may be transmitted from generation to generation (Goodwin, 1981). A familial association could result from cultural factors tending to favor heavy drinking in family members. Drinking may be discouraged in some families for religious, cultural, or climatic grounds whereas in other families, constraints on heavy drinking may be virtually nonexistent. Interfamily and interclass differences in alcohol use may also account for part of the variation in alcoholism rates among families. Heritable familial attributes as well as similarities in the social environment of family members may also play a role in familial transmission of alcoholism (Kaufmann, 1984). Higher family incidence of alcohol use and abuse does not necessarily reflect genetic determination of alcoholism. Besides family traditions and cultural habits, there are within-family environmental effects like parental loss, birth order, and the sex of the immediately elder siblings that may influence an individual's drinking behavior.

To investigate the relationship between alcoholism-associated psychopathology and genetic types and subtypes, longitudinal family studies are essential. Indeed, studies for the past many years have shown a higher frequency of alcoholism and related disorders among the relatives of alcoholics. Family investigations of alcoholic probands have yielded consistently higher rates of alcoholism than would be expected in the general population (Goodwin, 1976). When lifetime prevalence of alcoholism in relatives of alcoholics were compared to that in the general population, a fourfold increased risk in first-degree relatives and a twofold increased risk in second-degree relatives was observed (Cloninger and Reich, 1983).

The mechanism mediating between alcoholism and family history of alcoholism remains obscure, however. Moreover, family history alone does not allow identification of the mechanisms mediating alcoholism as well as to judge whether alcoholism is genetically determined or transmitted in families due to social reasons. As pointed out by Cotton (1979) in her extensive review on the familial incidence of alcoholism, the observed findings are subject to a number of methodological considerations like the source of the information, the nature of the samples analyzed, family history, failure to include underaged relatives in the studies, and lack of comparable control groups. The hitherto reported studies identify neither particular genes for predisposition nor prove any typical pattern of inheritance.

Future research should devote more attention to differentiate between alcoholics with and alcoholics without a family history of alcoholism. This may help recognize high-risk individuals who become alcoholics despite the absence of a positive family history of alcoholism.

Twin and Adoption Studies

Since both genetic and environmental influences are shared by family members in an intact family, twin and adoption studies may help in separating genetic factors from the environmental factors in the etiology of alcoholism. Most twin studies applied so far to the problem of alcoholism indicate a modest genetic predisposition (Partanen et al, 1966; Kaprio et al, 1979; Hrubec and Omenn, 1981). However, the recently available data on twin studies do not provide a conclusive evidence for a genetic role in alcoholism (Murray et al, 1983; Clifford et al, 1981; 1984; Gurling and Murray, 1987).

Adoption studies conducted in Denmark and Sweden have provided substantial evidence that alcoholism is genetically influenced and that there are distinct patterns of alcoholism with different genetic and environmental causes (Goodwin, 1976; Bohman, 1978; Cadoret and Gath, 1978; Bohman et al, 1981; Cloninger et al, 1981). These studies led to the tentative identification of at least three distinct genetic types of alcohol abusers with characteristic clinical features and heterogeneous genetic and environmental backgrounds (Bohman et al, 1984). However, further work is needed to identify various subtypes on the basis of biological and genetic markers that may differentiate these disease subtypes.

Gene-Environment Interactions

While discussing the role of genetic factors in alcoholism, complex genetic–environmental interactions must also be taken into account. Multiple genetic factors exert a modest but significant effect at several levels. Environmental influences such as moral and religious instructions, exposure to alcoholic beverages, drinking patterns of the family and peer groups, and the degree of anxiety and stress in an individual's life have to be considered while investigating the role of hereditary factors in alcoholism. For recognition and separation of genetic and environmental factors, the age, diet, health, life-style, behavior, culture, and social traditions have to be taken into consideration regarding their contribution towards increased risk against alcoholism.

Although the family studies demonstrate that alcoholism runs in families, it is difficult to say whether this propensity is entirely genetic or environmental or more likely a combination of the two. Adoption and twin studies have indeed proven useful in partly answering the question of "nature versus nurture" as well as "nature and nurture" interactions; however, the precise mode of inheritance of these factors in alcoholism is still an unresolved matter.

A key role of environmental factors is evident in some heritable forms of alcoholism associated with antisocial personality, impulsiveness, sensation-seeking behavior, and extreme emotional volatility (Hesselbrock and Hesselbrock 1984; Tarter et al, 1985; Cloninger et al, 1988). However, the putative environmental factors remain obscure in their nature and there is a strong need for a specific definition of factors which interact with specific genes that predispose to alcoholism. In future prospective studies, a distinction between congenital predisposition and postnatal environmental effects in the development of alcoholism should be made.

Biological Markers of Alcoholism

A number of biological markers or mediators interacting with environmental factors might predispose individuals towards development of alcoholism. Usually, such trait markers are observable either before the onset of alcoholism or even after a prolonged abstinence. A number of investigators have tried to identify trait markers by studying young men and women at high risk for the development of alcoholism in prospective studies. Many studies have attempted to identify biological markers of a genetic propensity. One approach is to establish a link between alcoholism and a trait already known to be genetic. For identification and evaluation of risk factors for alcoholism, one often looks for environmental factors related to life-style, geography, diet, occupation, and the like.

A risk factor or predictor for future alcoholism must fulfill the following criteria: (1) there is an increased likelihood of developing the disorder; (2) it has to be heritable and not a secondary effect of the disorder; (3) it must be observable in the well state and the ill state; (4) some relatives must have the factor independent of the disease; (5) the factor has to be genetically transmitted in families. An association with a known hereditary trait occurring in consistently higher frequency may help to identify a genetic predisposition to alcoholism. However, the reported association of certain genetic markers and alcoholism are contradictory and nonreproducible. More research is thus needed to establish any link between a potential genetic marker and alcoholism.

Behavioral Markers

Genetic differences at the CNS level of alcohol effects may also contribute to the etiology of alcoholism. The differential reaction may be an indicator for genetic vulnerability to alcoholism. Hyperactivity may be one aspect of the genetically mediated predisposition to alcoholism. Recent findings show that sons of alcoholics are distinguishable from controls in their pattern of cortical evoked responses and EEGs, as well as by greater static ataxia and poorer perceptual motor capacity (Schuckit, 1985). When adolescent sons of alcoholics and nonalcoholics were compared on a battery of intellectual, neuropsychological, personality, and behavioral parameters, the former group demonstrated certain deficits in perceptual motor ability, memory, and language processing (Tarter et al, 1984). They also had auditory and visual attentional impairment regarding reading comprehension. In addition, the sons of alcoholics presented a more neurotic personality profile than sons of nonalcoholics.

Changes in the electroencephalogram (EEG) and cortical evoked potentials have been noted in acute alcohol intoxications and development of tolerance. It has been shown that alcoholics on the average have poorly synchronized EEG patterns when compared to controls (Propping et al, 1981). The EEG with a poor alpha wave activity may be regarded as a trait that increases the disposition for alcoholism, at least in females. Gabrielli et al (1982) compared male children at high risk and low risk for alcoholism; they found a faster EEG activity in the former group and concluded that this may be a potential biological marker for a predisposition to alcoholism in sons of alcoholics.

Metabolic Factors

Factors determining alcohol elimination rate and metabolism in an individual may have pronounced effect on the etiology and pathophysiology of alcoholism. Twin studies have indicated that interindividual variability in the rate of ethanol metabolism is under genetic control. Also, ethnic differences in the metabolism of alcohol have been known for years. A higher rate of alcohol metabolism in Chinese, native Americans, and Japanese as compared to Caucasians has been reported.

Genetically determined variations in alcohol and acetaldehyde metabolism via genetic variations in the enzymes involved in alcohol metabolism (alcohol dehydrogenase and aldehyde dehydrogenase) seem to be responsible for individual and racial differences in alcohol drinking habits, acute and chronic reactions to alcohol, as well as vulnerability to organ damage after chronic alcohol abuse (Agarwal and Goedde, 1986; Goedde and Agarwal, 1906). Alcohol sensitivity and associated discomfort symptoms accompanying alcohol ingestion may be determinantal for the significantly low incidence of alcoholism in Orientals. Significantly lower incidence of mitochondrial aldehyde dehydrogenase (ALDH I) isozyme deficiency has been observed in alcoholics as compared to psychiatric patients, drug dependents and healthy controls in Japan. Individuals sensitive to alcohol by virtue of their genetically controlled deficiency of a key enzyme of alcohol metabolism (in this case, the mitochondrial aldehyde dehydrogenase) may be discouraged from abuse of alcohol due to initial aversive reaction to alcohol drinking (Goedde et al, 1983; 1986). The high prevalence of alcoholism among native Americans despite their inherent intolerance to alcohol may be due to their altered social structure (Goedde et al, 1986; Agarwal and Goedde, 1987).

A possible mediator role of acetaldehyde in psychopharmacological effects of alcohol drinking including reinforcement, tolerance, and physical dependence is both controversial and even contradictory. However, persistently higher blood acetaldehyde level in alcoholics and high-risk individuals after alcohol drinking may serve as an important biological marker concerning a genetic propensity towards alcoholism (Schuckit and Rayses, 1979; Lindros et al, 1980; Salaspuro and Lindros, 1985). Elevated acetaldehyde levels could enhance the risk for organ damage and could also lead to the production of higher amounts of biogenic amine–aldehyde condensation products like tetrahydropapaveroline (THP) and tetrahydroisoquinoline (TIQ). Genetic differences in the metabolism of ethanol and acetaldehyde involving synthesis and degradation of different condensation products may be responsible for variation in tolerance and addiction to alcohol in humans.

FUTURE DIRECTIONS

The studies bearing on possible genetic modes of transmission are inconclusive, although the genetic influence on several determinants of normal and abnormal drinking, on the metabolism of alcohol and on some of the physiological effects including those in the CNS is evident. Moreover, none of the evidence hitherto reviewed suggests that susceptibility to alcoholism is inherited via a simple Mendelian dominant, recessive, or X-linked transmission. Behaviors influencing the development of alcoholism may have multiple etiological paths. The resolution of heterogeneous etiologies of alcoholism is crucial for understanding its genetic basis. Moreover, it is important to identify and distinguish between personality attributes that might be predictive of alcohol use and abuse and those that indicate changes secondary to alcohol drinking.

Future research on biomedical and genetic aspects of alcoholism should be concerned with the above mentioned problems and in addition take into account the following aspects: (1)

extension of knowledge on the genetic components of alcoholism in prospective studies, (2) recognition of genetic predisposition and gene–environment interactions leading to effective prevention and treatment strategies, (3) the functional connection between neuronal processes and the addictive behavior has to be further elucidated, (4) animal models of human alcoholism need more attention, (5) the effect of maternal drinking on the fetus, and (6) molecular genetic approaches that may offer better biological markers of alcoholism.

Different Forms of Alcoholism

The three alcoholic phenotypes described by Bohman et al (1984) may represent a cluster of different metabolic and mental disorders and behavioral traits grouped together artificially by a "clinical model" of alcoholism. Many genes may operate to produce a single phenotype predisposed to alcoholism. More research is urgently needed to allow a better differentiation of the various disease forms with changing environmental backgrounds.

Animal Models

Numerous animal studies have been reported on the possible mechanisms responsible for the production of tolerance and dependence to alcohol. However, the criteria for tolerance and dependence are many and varied. Generally, to assess the genetic influence on the development of tolerance, investigations in inbred strains and selected lines of mice and rats have been carried out. Since one cannot duplicate in animals the complex social conditions which may have important contributions in human alcoholism, only biological effects of alcohol can be studied using a particular animal model. Although alcohol-accepting animal strains have been developed, yet no pharmacologically motivated drinking could be demonstrated under experimental conditions. Thus, relevance of animal studies for the human situation remains limited. In future studies, as suggested by Dole (1986), conditions have to be searched in which the specific pharmacological drive dominates over the nutritional appeal.

Maternal Drinking

Maternal chronic alcohol consumption during pregnancy may lead to an impaired growth and disturbed central nervous system disorders in the offsprings, commonly known as fetal alcohol syndrome (FAS). The genetic contribution to the alcohol-related birth defects is still unclear and the effects of moderate drinking during pregnancy has not been established unequivocally due to the well-known confounding environmental and genetic risk factors in alcoholism. Moreover, the role of variations in ethanol and acetaldehyde metabolism in fetal alcohol effects is still obscure and more research is required in this direction.

Molecular Biological Approaches

Besides the advances made in the field of alcoholism at the social, psychological, and biochemical levels, molecular biological approaches may further help in the identification and characterization of specific genes involved in alcoholism. In particular, searching for restriction fragment length polymorphisms (RFLPs) closely linked to a possible causative gene and cloning of the specific genes will help to identify people at high risk for alcoholism.

REFERENCES

Agarwal DP, Goedde HW: Ethanol oxidation: Ethnic variation in metabolism and response, in Kalow W, Goedde HW, Agarwal DP (eds): *Ethnic Differences in Reactions to Drugs and Xenobiotics*, New York, Alan R Liss, Inc, 1986, pp 99–111.

Agarwal DP, Goedde HW: Genetic variation in alcohol metabolizing enzymes: Implications in alcohol use and abuse, in Goedde HW, Agarwal DP (eds): *Genetics and Alcoholism*, New York, Alan R Liss, Inc, 1987, pp 121–140.

Bohman M: Some genetic aspects of alcoholism and criminality. *Arch Gen Psychiatry* 1978; 35:269–276.

Bohman M, Cloninger CR, von Knorring A-L, Sigvardsson S: An adoption study of somatoform disorders. III. Cross-fostering analysis and genetic relationship to alcoholism and criminality. *Arch Gen Psychiatry* 1984; 41:872–878.

Bohman M, Sigvardsson S, Cloninger CR: Maternal inheritance of alcohol abuse. Cross-fostering analysis of adopted women. *Arch Gen Psychiatry* 1981; 38:965–969.

Cadoret RJ, Gath A: Inheritance of alcoholism in adoptees. *Br J Psychiatry* 1978; 132:252–258.

Caetano R: Drinking patterns and alcohol problems among Hispanics in the U.S.: A review. *Drug Alcohol Depend* 1983; 12:37–59.

Chick J: Epidemiology of alcohol use and its hazards. *Brit Med Bull* 1982: 38:3–8.

Clifford CA, Fulker DW, Gurling HMD, Murray RM: Preliminary findings from a twin study of alcohol use, in Gedda L, Parisi P, Nance WA *(eds): Twin Research*, vol 3, New York, Alan R Liss, Inc, 1981, pp 47.

Clifford CA, Hopper JL, Fulker DW, Murray RM: A genetic and environmental analysis of a twin family study of alcohol use, anxiety and depression. *Genet Epidemiol* 1984; 1:63–79.

Cloninger CR: Recent advances in family studies of alcoholism, in Goedde HW, Agarwal DP (eds): *Genetics and Alcoholism*, New York, Alan R Liss, Inc, 1987, pp 47–60.

Cloninger CR, Bohman M, Sigvardsson S: Inheritance of alcohol abuse. Cross-fostering analysis of adopted men. *Arch Gen Psychiatry* 1981; 38:861–868.

Cloninger CR, Reich T: Genetic heterogeneity in alcoholism and sociopathy, in Kety SS, Rowland LP, Sidman RL, Mathysse SW (eds): *Genetics of Neurological and Psychiatric Disorders*, New York, Raven Press, 1983, pp 145–166.

Cloninger CR, Sigvardsson S, Bohmann M: Childhood personality predicts alcohol abuse in young adults. *Alcohol Clin Exp Res* 1988; 12:494–505.

Cotton NS: The familial incidence of alcoholism. A review. *Q J Stud Alcohol* 1979; 40:89–116.

Dole VP: On the relevance of animal models to alcoholism in humans. *Alcohol Clin Exp Res* 1986; 10: 361–363.

Gabrielli WF, Mednick SA, Volavka J, Pollock VE, Schulsinger F, Itil TM: Electroencephalograms in children of alcoholic fathers. *Psychophysiology* 1982; 19:404–407.

Goedde HW, Agarwal DP: Aldehyde oxidation: Ethnic variation in metabolism and response, in Kalow W, Goedde HW, Agarwal DP (eds): *Ethnic Differences in Reactions to Drugs and Xenobiotics*. New York, Alan R Liss, Inc, 1986, pp 113–138.

Goedde HW, Agarwal DP, Harada S: The role of alcohol dehydrogenase and aldehyde dehydrogenase isozymes in alcohol metabolism, alcohol sensitivity and alcoholism, in Rattazzi MC, Scandalios JG, Whitt GS (eds): *Isozymes: Curr Top Biol Med Res*. New York, Alan R Liss Inc, vol 8, 1983, pp 175–193.

Goedde HW, Agarwal DP, Harada S, Whittaker JO, Rothhammer F, Lisker R: Aldehyde dehydrogenase polymorphism in North American, South American and Mexican Indians. *Am J Hum Genet* 1986; 38:70–74.

Goodwin DW: *Is Alcoholism Hereditary?* New York, Oxford University Press, 1976.

Goodwin DW: Genetic component of alcoholism. *Ann Rev Med* 1981; 32:93–99.

Gurling HMD, Murray RM: Genetic influence, brain morphology, and cognitive deficits in alcoholic twins, in Goedde HW, Agarwal DP (eds): *Genetics and Alcoholism*. New York, Alan R Liss Inc, 1987, pp 71–82.

Hesselbrock M, Hesselbrock V: Alcoholism and the antisocial personality. *Amer Psychiat Assoc Meeting*, 1984, Los Angeles, May 5–11.

Hilton ME: Drinking patterns and drinking problems in 1984: Results from a general population survey. *Alcohol Clin Exp Res* 1987; 11:167–175.

Hrubec Z, Omenn GS: Evidence of genetic predisposition to alcoholic cirrhosis and psychosis: Twin concordance for alcoholism and its biological end points by zygosity among male veterans. *Alcohol Clin Exp Res* 1981; 5:207–215.

Hughes SP, Dodder RA: Alcohol consumption patterns among American Indian and White college students. *J Stud Alcohol* 1984; 45:433–439.

Kaprio J, Sarna S, Koskenvuo M, Rantasalo I: *Finnish Twin Registry Baseline Characteristics*, Helsinki, University of Helsinki Press, 1979, Section 2.

Kaufmann E: Family system variables in alcoholism. *Alcohol Clin Exp Res* 1984; 8:4–8.

Klatsky AL, Siegelaub AB, Landy C, Friedman GD: Racial patterns of alcohol beverage use. *Alcohol Clin Exp Res* 1983; 7:372–377.

Lindros DO, Stowell A, Pikkarainen P, Salaspuro M: Elevated blood acetaldehyde in alcoholics with accelerated ethanol elimination. *Pharmacol Biochem Behav* 1980; 13 (suppl 1):119–124.

Murray RM, Clifford CA, Gurling HMD: Twin and adoption studies: How good is the evidence for a genetic role? in Gallanter M (ed): *Recent Developments in Alcoholism*, vol 1, New York Plenum Press, 1983, pp 25–47.

Partanen J, Bruun, K, Markkanen T: Inheritance of drinking behavior. A study on intelligence, personality and use of alcohol of adult twins. *The Finnish Foundation for Alcohol Studies* 1966; 14: 1–159.

Propping P, Krüger J, Mark N: Genetic predisposition to alcoholism. An EEG study in alcoholics and their relatives. *Hum Genet* 1981; 59:51–59.

Raduco-Thomas S, Garcin F, Raduco-Thomas C, Marquis PA, Lambert J, Laforge H, Denver D, Laperriere A, Laacroix D, Gaudreault V: Primary and secondary prevention of alcoholism: Emerging trends and research strategy. *Prog Neuro-Psychopharmacol* 1980; 3:579–600.

Salaspuro MK, Lindros KO: Metabolism and toxicity of acetaldehyde, in Seitz HK, Kommerell B (eds): *Alcohol Related Diseases in Gastroenterology*. Berlin, Springer Verlag, 1985, pp 106–123.

Schuckit MA: Genetics and the risk for alcoholism. *JAMA.* 1985; 254:2614–2617.

Schuckit MA, Rayses V: Ethanol ingestion: Differences in blood acetaldehyde concentrations in relatives of alcoholics and controls. *Science* 1979; 203:54–55.

Tarter RE, Alterman AI, Edwards KL: Vulnerability to alcoholism in men: A behavior-genetic perspective. *J Stud Alcohol* 1985; 46:329–356.

Tarter RE, Hegedus AM, Goldstein G, Shelly C, Alterman A: Adolescent sons of alcoholics: Neurophysiological and personality characteristics. *Alcohol Clin Exp Res* 1984; 8:216–222.

Index